Knowing Fear

No passion so effectually robs the mind of all its powers of acting and reasoning as *fear*.

— Edmund Burke, "On the Sublime and Beautiful,"
in *The Works of the Right Hon. Edmund Burke*,
vol. 1 (London: Holdsworth and Ball, 1834), 38.

Where there is no imagination, there is no horror.

— Sherlock Holmes, *A Study in Scarlet*,
in Sir Arthur Conan Doyle, *The Complete Sherlock Holmes*,
vol. 1 (New York: Barnes & Noble, 2003), 34.

Knowing Fear

Science, Knowledge and the Development of the Horror Genre

JASON COLAVITO

McFarland & Company, Inc., Publishers

Jefferson, North Carolina, and London

LIBRARY OF CONGRESS CATALOGUING-IN-PUBLICATION DATA

Colavito, Jason.
    Knowing fear : science, knowledge and the development of the
horror genre / Jason Colavito.
       p.   cm.
    Includes bibliographical references and index.

    ISBN-13: 978-0-7864-3273-8
    softcover : 50# alkaline paper ∞

    1. Horror in literature.   2. Horror tales—History and
criticism.   3. Horror films—History and criticism.   4. Horror
in art.   I. Title.
PN56.H6C65   2008
809'.9164 — dc22   2007036507

British Library cataloguing data are available

On the cover: Lithograph of Thurston the Great Magician, 1915
(McManus-Young Collection, Library of Congress)

Manufactured in the United States of America

McFarland & Company, Inc., Publishers
  Box 611, Jefferson, North Carolina 28640
   www.mcfarlandpub.com

TABLE OF CONTENTS

PREFACE

One by one the crows came to roost in the empty trees of my boyhood hometown. It was a ritual repeated each night from autumn until spring, a vast mass of feathers and claws. The black birds landed on dead branches and stared with their unblinking eyes at those who trod the ground beneath. By dusk the trees became so full of crows that, in the dimming light of dying day, they appeared to have grown black, nocturnal leaves. At times it seemed as though the crows would overrun the city and drive away any semblance of humanity. It was, as many said, like a scene from Alfred Hitchcock's *The Birds*, except that these birds were real, and there were many, many more of them.

It is different now; the birds are gone, frightened away by scientific devices meant to disperse them. Scientists estimated that Auburn, New York, a city of fewer than thirty thousand souls, played host to seventy thousand crows during those winters, making it home to one of the world's largest populations of crows, still officially called a "murder" in the old-fashioned terminology for animal groupings. A legend had begun to grow up about the crows, a legend that said the great murder embodied the spirits of the dead buried in the city's historic and ornate Fort Hill Cemetery, but the dead have lain there for more than two centuries, and the crows held sway for less than a decade. Perhaps the dead were restless, or perhaps the myth-mongers found a good hook for a made-up ancient mystery.

There are other horrors to be had in the town where I grew up. In 1805, in a fit of Romantic pique, the city fathers named the town for the "loveliest village of the plain" in Oliver Goldsmith's ominously named poem "The Deserted Village" (1770), oblivious to the poem's tale of an idyll reduced to "shapeless ruin."[1] Auburn was at the center of the "Burned Over District," the Victorian realm of religious fervor and fire-and-brimstone preaching. It was also one of the founding centers of Spiritualism, that odd nineteenth century belief that gifted mediums could communicate with the dead through table-rapping séances and automatic writing. The movement's annual publication, *The Spiritualist Register, with a Counting House & Speaker's Almanac; Containing Facts and Statistics of Spiritualism*, called the city home. In 1857, within its

1

limits lived a Mr. and Mrs. U. Clark, trance speakers and publishers of the *Register* and its weekly publication, *Clarion*.

Ghosts, too, were said to haunt Auburn's vast expanses of decaying Victorian mansions—in better repair now than they were in my youth—and in truth the ghosts of the nineteenth century figuratively colored what remained of a city that in the 1860s was one of America's largest but had become a post-industrial backwater. In 1959 the author H. Beam Piper imagined in "The Answer" a nuclear war beginning in Auburn when American and Soviet forces mistake a meteor's destruction of my hometown for the start of atomic Armageddon.

It was hardly any wonder, then, that I began to read Poe and Stoker at a young age, or that horror stories of ghosts and monsters never seemed anything but normal. Well, at least to me anyway. Of course, there were others who held different views on my literary tastes...

About This Book

Under the influence of Freudian psychoanalysis, horror is traditionally seen as primarily sexual in nature; and most criticism of the genre proceeds from psychoanalytical frameworks emphasizing castration anxieties, phallic symbols, fanged vaginas, and other Freudian baggage. Noël Carroll, the noted film philosopher, first tried to understand horror through psychoanalysis:

> [W]ithin our culture the horror genre is explicitly acknowledged as a vehicle for expressing psychoanalytically significant themes such as repressed sexuality, oral sadism, necrophilia, etc.... As a matter of social tradition, psychoanalysis is more or less the *lingua franca* of the horror film and thus the privileged critical tool for discussing the genre. In fact, horror films often seem to be little more than bowdlerized, pop psychoanalysis, so enmeshed is Freudian psychology with the genre.[2]

However, by the time he wrote *The Philosophy of Horror* (1990), Carroll had come to view the horror genre as an art form best explained by cognitive psychology and analytical philosophy. He was primarily concerned with the emotional and aesthetic effects of horror and the psychological and philosophical reasons people might want to experience what in real life would be damaging situations—the way "fictional monsters can excite real emotions in readers and spectators."[3] Since we will be exploring the *content* of horror rather than its effects, we can for now simply take as a given that audiences enjoy horror on some mental level.

I agree that critical obsession with psychoanalysis often obscures other facets of horror, especially those that are not directly linked to emotions or the libido. Since our minds are what make us human, it is only natural that our greatest fears should stem from the source of what sets us apart from animals.

This book tells the story of horror through the prism of what I believe is the genre's overarching concern: the role of knowledge, often manifested as "science," "technology," or "wisdom." It is my contention that horror records humanity's uneasy relationship with its own ability to reason, to understand, and to know; and that horror stories are a way of understanding and ultimately transcending the limits of mind, knowledge, and science through fear. Horror stories may deal directly with knowledge within their plots, through characters engaged in science, the occult, or skepticism, or indirectly by reflecting external, real-life developments in the scientific understanding of the human body, the human mind, or the cosmos at large. Each section of this book will explore successive periods of horror through chapters outlining selected cultural developments, literary developments, and developments in the visual and performing arts.

I should also state what this book is not. This book is not a comprehensive history of horror; there is simply too much horror to do so, though I have made every effort to include as many works as discussion will allow. Given the problems of simply *defining* horror, trying to catalogue everything that falls within that definition is an impossible task. Instead, I have tried to choose representative horrors, some famous and some obscure. So, if your favorite horror isn't in here, don't fear. I have to save something for another book. Since there is a wealth of studies of individual horror works, I have chosen to survey a greater number of works in this book rather than focus on any one to the exclusion of others.

Nor is this book a comprehensive criticism of specific horror works, or even horror as a genre. Currently, the vogue in literary criticism is a form of historicism that places the primary importance on a literary work's relationship to the time and place of its creation. The author's biography, cultural assumptions, and influences are held as the most important facet of understanding a work. The New Criticism, or formalism — the study of the work itself outside the context in which it was created — is out of fashion, a product of an earlier age that could still believe a particular literary product was both self-contained and universal and not a reflection of race, class, and gender issues.

Though I will analyze and discuss horror works, some closely, I will be applying literary and film criticism's methods and techniques in a way that will examine the texts themselves in the context of a specific cultural dimension that I believe influenced the development of horror more than any other: The rise of science. In so doing, I will emphasize the content of the works rather than the biographies of their authors to link the stories to specific trends in intellectual history which they clearly reflect. I will also occasionally spotlight the way many academic critics of horror have applied psychoanalytic frameworks to produce highly sexualized readings that contrast (but do not necessarily contradict) the more intellectual themes we will discuss.

We will see that the story of science and the story of horror are conjoined twins, one full of humanity's highest aspirations and the other its darkest nightmares. Though science may survive without horror, horror cannot survive without the anxieties created by the changing role of human knowledge and science in our society.

INTRODUCTION:
FROM PROMETHEUS TO FAUST

> The oldest and strongest emotion of mankind is fear, and the oldest and strongest kind of fear is fear of the unknown.
> — H. P. Lovecraft,
> *Supernatural Horror in Literature* (1927)[1]

"How can you read *that*?"

I can remember nearly every time someone has asked me that question when I've been caught with a collection of horror stories, a vampire novel, or any book with a vaguely sinister cover. Substitute "watch" for read and the same question can be heard whenever a new slasher movie, ghost movie, or monster movie opens; for even though horror movies are immensely profitable, they are still not quite respectable. Fear, it seems, is not among the refined emotions critics look for in high art.

But horror is always with us. It lurks in the dark recesses of the soul and the shadows that cut across even the brightest of lights. It is the gnawing fear that the placid surface of our world can and will be shattered by forces beyond our control. For this reason humanity tries, with varying degrees of success, to illuminate the dark places in the world and in our minds, hoping that the light of knowledge can break the power of the unknown evils lying in wait and restore our lives to the imagined happiness of some forgotten past or fantasy future. We study the sciences, psychology, and other fields to make sense of the world and our place in it. And we tell ourselves stories about the horrors that our knowledge helps convince us we have banished. But those things that fade before the light do not stay dead, and knowledge itself is often a source of its own, more exacting terrors. This is the nature of the horror story.

When we think of horror, we often think of monsters: vampires, ghosts, werewolves, witches, and the things that go bump in the night. This is part of horror to be sure, but horror goes beyond simple myths about things that should not be. It is an active essence that captures our fears and crystallizes them into a shape we can understand and set down on paper, on film, or in memory — virtual as well as mental. The monsters of horror can take many shapes, and they can symbolize many things, but one constant remains across time, from the earliest horror stories to the most recent: Knowledge, whether forbidden or achieved, is a primal source of horror.

This goes against most of our instincts, especially for those living in what we call "Western civilization," where knowledge is not just the lifeblood of the economy but the way we understand out world: science. For twenty-first century individuals, it is sometimes difficult to imagine a way in which knowledge could be bad, or in fact the source of horror. Instead, when we think about horror at all, we think about it in the terms of Freudian psychoanalysis, positing a range of explanations for the "true" meaning of horror stories, especially psycho-sexual explanations. This is the most popular school of thought about horror, producing works with titles like Walter Evans's "Monster Movies: A Sexual Theory" (Monsters reflect "two central features of adolescent sexuality, masturbation and menstruation"), Richard K. Sanderson's "Glutting the Maw of Death: Suicide and Procreation in *Frankenstein*" ("Victor reveals his fear of female sexual autonomy and his own ambivalent femininity"), and Joan Copjec's "Vampires, Breast Feeding, and Anxiety" ("I will argue that the political advocacy of breast-feeding cannot be properly understood unless one sees it for what it is: the precise equivalent of vampire fiction").[2] There are many, many more that follow such Freudian views of horror.

Thus do scholars come to interpret Dracula's fangs as "oral displacement of genital sex, steeped and transformed in nineteenth-century Romanticism."[3] Or, to a greater extreme, begin to see sexual interpretations that aren't really there, like this one by the horror critic David J. Skal, who felt a little funny when he saw an advertisement for Aurora's 1960s build-your-own monster models of Dracula, Frankenstein's Monster, and the Wolf Man:

> Most of the pubescent boys for whom the monster models were intended were no doubt conducting private, one-fisted physical experiments, and, while the official Scout's handbook frowned upon masturbation, the *Boy's Life* ad presented a subliminal tease: Dracula, in his typical mesmeric stance, strokes and pulls at the air; the Frankenstein monster is caught in a startled, "hands-off" pose, and the Wolf Man's hair-spouting palms hardly require comment.[4]

Or maybe they just strike their iconic poses from the famed 1930s and 1940s movies whose scenes the models capture. Somehow, Boris Karloff's stiff-armed Frankenstein walk never struck me as interrupted masturbation. But while it is beyond dispute that many horror stories deal at some level with sexuality, which after all is one of the basic drives of human life, what Skal and many of the other critics miss is that illicit sexuality is but a subset of a larger horror, one that views knowledge — sexual knowledge included — as the deepest and most profound source of horror a human can know. This horror extends to both forbidden knowledge, which causes horror, and protective knowledge, whose loss or corruption creates chaos and pain.

The Mythic Origins of Knowledge-Horror

The tradition of horror stories has deep roots, which stretch back to the earliest human stories and fables. These roots reach directly to the mind itself, for what is horror if not the experience of terror, dread, fear, and unease? These are biological responses to works of art — the horror stories — and they arise from our deepest, most primal reactions. In fact, of all the literary and film genres, perhaps only horror and romance trigger instinctive and physical responses. There is nothing natural or biological about the western, the family comedy, or police procedural. But almost every animal experiences fear since it is a useful instinct for avoiding predators and keeping out of danger, and humans have the imagination to visualize fears yet to come or fears that they may never encounter but dread anyway. That is horror, and it is intrinsic to human nature.

Anatomically modern humans arose sometime around 100,000 to 200,000 years ago, evolving from earlier species like *Homo erectus*; but only during the upper Paleolithic period (35,000–10,000 BCE) do we see archaeological evidence for language, art, and religion — the precursors of modern humanity and therefore modern horror. These first humans are believed to have lived in small family groups, sustaining themselves by foraging and hunting. During this age, the wandering bands of hunter-gatherers viewed the world through a prism of supernaturalism, wonder, and awe — a situation that hardly changed when they settled down to farm. Nevertheless, the wild was a terrifying place, full of powerful animals, violent weather, and irrational happenings of all kinds. The early humans who painted animals on the walls of caves, like those at Lascaux, and their successors who set up stones, like those at Stonehenge, all across the Neolithic (8,000 BCE to 3,000 BCE) landscape, did so to cast in a permanent way the mythologies that sustained them. They wanted to give form to the shadows in their minds. Scholars like Dolf Zillmann and Rhonda Gibson see in these ancient people the origins of horror fiction, people who told stories about gods, demons, and wild animals — the source of fear. But they dismiss the potent horror of the ancient world as something less than real — as deliberate lies that were "products of the human imagination, driven by fear and narcissism." Our ancestors, they speculate, "exaggerated" the world's horrors because tales of monsters and demons were useful for "controlling believers," a process of manipulation and control that continues to this very day.[5] This is, however, a cynical and reductive approach.

According to David Lewis-Williams and David Pearce, the neurological structure of our brains leads us to understand the cosmos as a set of stacked layers, roughly equivalent to the Christian view of Hell, Earth, and Heaven. Humans live somewhere in the middle of this great stack of planes of existence, with the levels of heaven, light, and the gods usually located above the plane of the earth; and the levels of the underworld, darkness, and demons usually located in the planes below earth. For our purposes, we are most concerned with the malevolent hell dimensions envisioned as existing beneath our very feet.

This multi-level depiction of the universe is consistent across the world and through the ages, from our Paleolithic ancestors to today. It derived from the essential characteristics of the evolving human mind. Lewis-Williams and Pearce further argue that our biochemistry induces us to experience "neuro-logically generated mystical states"[6] as a realm of the supernatural, whose basic manifestations—vast caverns of geometric shapes, vortices, animals, and mon-sters—remain consistent across space and time, though the way they are expe-rienced is governed by cultural expectations. This, they argue, is most apparent during altered states of consciousness brought about by sensory deprivation, trances, hallucinogenic drugs, or a number of other causes. It is during these conditions that humans experience the supernatural, the infernal, and the divine. But when in this state, what one culture may experience as a benign animal guide or an angel may be viewed by another as a hideous chimera grotesquely mingling human and animal, or even demon or devil. The same process occurs during periods of transition between wake and sleep, periods when the ancients saw incubi and succubae and very modern people experi-ence the supernatural in the form of alien abductions; that is, space monsters in an intergalactic spirit realm.

In ancient cultures, and in some traditional cultures today, there was a guide to the strange and frightening realm of the supernatural—the shaman, popularly known as the witch-doctor or medicine man. Shamanism was humanity's first religious belief system, and it involved the understanding that chosen individuals could transcend this world to interact with the spirit world on behalf of others. To become a shaman, an individual had to be equipped with knowledge, sanctified and handed down from time immemorial, that allowed him to enter the world of the supernatural, interact with the beings found therein, and therefore influence the course of events on earth. The shaman had the power to venture from plane to plane—between Heaven, Earth, and Hell. He also had the power to change shapes and to take on animal form. But the transition from this world to the netherworld was not without its cost, and the shaman experienced great pain and stress in his travels. Further, there was always the chance that the shaman would not return to this world: "The danger is present, too, in the malevolence of certain spirits, and the shaman may have to do battle with inimical forces which have stolen the souls of the sick."[7]

Here, then, in the first spiritual system devised by humankind do we see the same dark forces that would haunt our dreams for millennia to come. The shaman alone could stand against the horror because of the special knowledge he and his ancestors had gathered, and it was this sacred knowledge that was his protector against the darkness and against the monsters.

But not all monsters existed in the human mind. Early humans encountered gigantic animals, such as the woolly mammoth or *Gigantopithecus,* the ten-foot-tall gorilla-like creature, both of which died out at the end of the last Ice Age, around ten thousand years ago. Memories of these monsters filtered down through the ages, and the bones of these beasts, and even the long-extinct dinosaurs, may well have given rise to mythology's early monsters.[8] Dragons, for example, bear an uncanny resemblance to the skeletons of dinosaurs; and woolly mammoth bones resemble human bones enough to be confused for the remains of giants—so much so that the Romans used to set them up in their temples as relics of the lost race of giants. In a world before science, there was no way to know whether the skeletons of "dragons" and "giants" were not indicative of still greater horrors lurking in the forests beyond civilization, and knowledge of these creatures—however mythological or spurious—was a precious and protective commodity. This extended to the monsters presumed to live in the diabolical realms beyond the earth.

As Lewis-Williams and Pearce discuss, early mythologies show how the knowledge of the spirit realm, and how to win its rewards and avoid its terrors, became the possession of a sacred priesthood who monopolized this valuable wisdom. In the ancient Sumerian *Epic of Gilgamesh*, the title hero Gilgamesh, for instance, was said to have journeyed across the known world for knowledge of how to live forever, though he failed in his quest. In the world of Gilgamesh, religion, "founded on access to other realms," had already become institutionalized, the sacred knowledge of light and dark already restricted to an elite who alone could mediate between humanity and the Others.[9]

The ancient Greeks, too, knew all about this mixture of darkness and light, the way knowledge can hold back the shadows but ultimately destroys the very souls who wield its power. They expressed this eloquently in the myth of Prometheus, the Titan who in Greek cosmology created humanity in the earliest days of the earth. Prometheus—whose name itself means "foresight"—endowed his creation with the ability to think, to reason, and to know. He went still further and taught the first men the arts of civilization, imparting to them the wisdom of the gods themselves. Impudently, Prometheus carried himself to the heights of Mount Olympus, the home of the gods, and seized fire from the divine sanctuary, bringing the precious flame of life and light, forevermore a symbol of knowledge, to the cold and hungry humans cowering in the darkness below.

Prometheus gave humanity knowledge, but in so doing he trespassed on the will of Zeus, king of all the gods, who undertook to punish the Titan for his sins. Worst of all, Prometheus had still more knowledge, the possession of which would destroy the very fabric of the universal order, for Prometheus knew which of Zeus's paramours would bear him a son powerful enough to overthrow his father and establish a new cosmological order. But Prometheus refused to tell, and Zeus had Prometheus chained to a rock on Mount Caucasus, where each day a vulture (some say an eagle) swept down from the sky to eat his liver. As a god, Prometheus could not die, and his liver grew back as soon as the bird finished its unwholesome meal. Nevertheless, Prometheus was made to suffer endlessly until such a day as a descendent of Io would free him from his torments. Thus was knowledge the cause of pain, but its endurance made Prometheus a hero, as the poet Aeschylus made the god say in *Prometheus Bound*:

> Known to me, known was the message that he
> Hath proclaimed, and for none is it shameful to bear
> At the hands of his enemies evil and wrong.
> So now let him cast, if it please him, the two–
> Edged curl of his lightning, and shatter the sky
> With his thundering frenzy of furious winds;
> Let the earth be uptorn from her roots by the storm
> Of his anger, and Ocean with turbulent tides
> Pile up, till engulfed are the paths of the stars;
> Down to the bottomless blackness of Tartarus
> Let my body be cast, caught in the whirling
> Waters of Destiny:
> For with death *I* shall not be stricken!¹⁰

Such is the essence of the Greek tragic hero, for whom the depths of misery is the possession of unsanctioned knowledge. Prometheus was not alone in the tragedy of knowing too much. The Greeks told also of Tereisias, the blind prophet who prophesied too well, revealing what the gods wished to remain hidden. For this he was tormented by Harpies, who fouled his food and menaced him until Jason and the Argonauts rescued him from his fate. Oedipus had the opposite problem, for his lack of knowledge led him to fulfill a prophecy that he would kill his father and take his mother for a wife. When he learned the truth, the knowledge was too much for him, and he blinded himself.

The Judeo-Christian tale of Adam and Eve is another example of the dangerous consequences of knowing too much. In Eden God set up trees to provide the first humans with food, but God also created a serpent who tempted Eve with the fruit of the Tree of Knowledge:

Now the serpent was more subtil than any beast of the field which the LORD God had made. And he said unto the woman, Yea, hath God said, Ye shall not eat of every tree of the garden? And the woman said unto the serpent, We may eat of the fruit of the trees of the garden: But of the fruit of the tree which is in the midst of the garden, God hath said, Ye shall not eat of it, neither shall ye touch it, lest ye die. And the serpent said unto the woman, Ye shall not surely die: For God doth know that in the day ye eat thereof, then your eyes shall be opened, and ye shall be as gods, knowing good and evil. And when the woman saw that the tree was good

The Tree of Knowledge. In this 1590 illustration by Theodor de Bry, Adam and Eve eat from the Tree of Knowledge on the advice of the serpent, leading to their expulsion from paradise and a life of hardship and toil. This foundational myth helped cement the links between forbidden knowledge, sin, and punishment found in horror fiction (Library of Congress, LC-USZC4-5347).

for food, and that it was pleasant to the eyes, and a tree to be desired to make one wise, she took of the fruit thereof, and did eat, and gave also unto her husband with her; and he did eat. And the eyes of them both were opened, and they knew that they were naked; and they sewed fig leaves together, and made themselves aprons [Genesis 3:1–6].

This forbidden fruit of the Tree of Knowledge — the act of knowing — caused the Fall of Man, and God was none too happy with his creation's discovery of knowledge that God had intended to let rot on the vine:

Unto the woman he said, I will greatly multiply thy sorrow and thy conception; in sorrow thou shalt bring forth children; and thy desire shall be to thy husband, and he shall rule over thee. And unto Adam he said, Because thou hast hearkened unto the voice of thy wife, and hast eaten of the tree, of which I commanded thee, saying, Thou shalt not eat of it: cursed is the ground for thy sake; in sorrow shalt thou eat of it all the days of thy life; Thorns also and thistles shall it bring forth to thee; and thou shalt eat the herb of the field; In the sweat of thy face shalt thou eat bread, till thou return unto the ground; for out of it wast thou taken: for dust thou art, and unto dust shalt thou return.... And the LORD God said, Behold, the man is become as one of us, to know good and evil: and now, lest he put forth his hand, and take also of the tree of life, and eat, and live for ever: Therefore the LORD God sent him forth from the garden of Eden, to till the ground from whence he was taken. So he drove out the man; and he placed at the east of the garden of Eden Cherubims, and a flaming sword which turned every way, to keep the way of the tree of life [Genesis 3: 16–24].

For the Exiles from Eden, the price of knowledge was eternal toil and the sorrow and tragedy — yes, the horror — that darkens human life. Surely there is a poignancy in God's lament that Adam has "become as one of us," a recognition that the burden of knowledge is not one to be lightly shared. However, this tale is not a true horror story in our sense of the word, since this passage evokes only feelings of sadness, loss, and despair. It is closer to what we mean by horror than Prometheus was, but its purpose was not to frighten or terrify.

Nevertheless, the two tales of Prometheus and Eden laid the mythological foundation for what would become the Western tradition of the horror story, our modern mythology and a genre tied uniquely to a single source of ultimate horror, the very act of knowing, itself the defining characteristic of being human. However, the ancient world never developed horror tales in our sense of them; that had to wait for another, more modern time. But before we explore this, we must first ask what we mean when we talk about "horror stories."

What Is Horror?

The horror story as we know it today is a unique product of Western culture and a sort of ersatz mythology, one whose rise came in tandem with the development of the West's major contribution to world culture: modern science. Every society has its tales of supernatural menace, but it was in the West at the end of the eighteenth century that the horror story found its voice and flourished as a unique metaphor for the displacement from the past, from tradition, and from culture that modern science ushered in with its rapid development and promotion of change. Though this particular mood would spread outside the West, perhaps most prominently in Japan, it was Western civilization that gave birth to the horror genre in its modern form.

Literature responded to scientific progress in two ways: Science fiction represented our hopes and aspirations, the Golden Age that Progress was to bring. But if science fiction represented our dreams, horror art in all its myriad forms crystallized our nightmares, the dark fears that fester beneath the surface. Even science fiction concealed a quiet undercurrent of horror, often disguised under the name "fantastic literature," or later, "the weird tale." It was the soot on the shining citadel of Progress. Many science fiction scholars claim that sci-fi is a cognitive and philosophical genre while horror is purely emotional, with the implication that this is a lesser state.[11] This view is only half true, for it is the feeling of fear that most clearly defines what we mean when we talk of "horror" stories. But horror has its own philosophy and cognitive pleasures, as we shall see.

The emotion of horror is a combination of fear and revulsion, and it is related closely to terror, a feeling of fear and anxiety. When we speak of "horror" as a genre, we are often referring to the whole range of feelings connected to the emotion of horror, as well as dread, discomfort, revulsion, fear, and terror. Of course this is not the same fear one feels when faced with a real-life fright, but the same emotional working we feel when we cry at a tragedy or laugh at a comedy. In the case of horror, that artistic emotion is fear.

Many scholars do not recognize horror as a distinct genre but prefer to see it as a subset of the fantasy and science fiction genres (though, in its Gothic form, it predates and inspired both), or to call all three areas "speculative fiction." Others, like Noël Carroll, define the horror genre as a body of stories that revolve around a "monster" that must be evaluated and which does not conform to current scientific beliefs. Carroll, for example, rejects stories of psychological horror, creepiness, or cruelty as falling outside horror's true intent: monsters that challenge scientific understanding.[12] On the other hand, the noted critic Edmund Wilson believed that only psychological horror represented truly worthy horror fiction, while horror focused on the existence of monsters and ghosts was merely childish.

I believe that the horror genre can reasonably be expanded to include the entirety—from the unknown to monsters to well-known terrors like serial killers or mental illness—and that all are related to the knowledge and science.* While it is true that horror does not have a more or less uniform set of

---

Carroll divides psycho killers into supernatural monsters like Freddy Krueger of A Nightmare on Elm Street *and human, if pathological, individuals like Hannibal Lecter of* Red Dragon. *Only*

trappings like sci-fi or westerns do, I believe it is a genre unto itself, one whose animating feature is neither setting nor plot nor even the presence of an indescribable monster but instead the feeling of fear.

Stephen King proposed that "horror" exists on three levels: terror, a purely mental state of anticipatory fear at an unknown or unseen evil; lower down falls "horror," a combination of mental fear and physical revulsion at a known evil; and at the bottom of the heap is pure revulsion at a disgusting or otherwise distasteful occurrence.[13] Horror fiction — in whatever medium — explores these feelings of fear, revulsion, and dread. But delineating exactly where the boundaries for horror fiction fall is a notoriously tricky business, and one that requires a little bit of explanation and discussion. Let us begin with an outline for some of the major categories of horror:

Supernatural Horror

The most common type of traditional horror story (and the one Noël Carroll had in mind) involves a supernatural menace, such as a ghost, a vampire, or a monster. The horror of the story derives from the fear and revulsion the protagonist feels upon encountering the supernatural. This is the realm of the witch, the werewolf, the ghost, and the vampire. Celebrated works in this arena include Bram Stoker's *Dracula* (vampire) and Shirley Jackson's *The Haunting of Hill House* (ghost).

Weird Tale

The weird tale is a particular subset of horror fiction that draws from supernatural horror and dark fantasy (see below) but hints at greater terrors. The horror of the story derives from the realization by the protagonist or the reader that natural law has been violated and that powers beyond our comprehension are at work. As the celebrated writer of weird tales, H. P. Lovecraft, explained: "A certain atmosphere of breathless and unexplainable dread of outer, unknown forces must be present; and there must be a hint, expressed with a seriousness and portentousness becoming its subject, of that most terrible conception of the human brain — a malign and particular suspension or defeat of those fixed laws of Nature which are our only safeguard against the assaults of chaos and the daemons of unplumbed space."[14] Other writers of weird tales include Algernon Blackwood, Arthur Machen, and Ramsey Campbell.

[continued] *the former category are "horrors" in his reading, though he concedes that one might classify serial killers as "science fictions of the mind" and thus make them monsters, too. (Noël Carroll, "Humor and Horror,"* The Journal of Aesthetics and Art Criticism, *57, no. 2 [Spring 1999]: 148.)*

Contes Cruelles

Contes cruelles are straightforward tales of suffering, cruelty, and physical pain, fear and torture. They do not include supernatural elements but instead derive their horrors from the gruesomeness of the punishments visited on their characters, often at the hands of serial killers or psychopaths, and the psychological impact on both victim and audience. Edgar Allan Poe's "The Pit and the Pendulum" is an example of this, as are the various iterations of the *Saw* and *Hostel* movie franchises.

Psychological Horror

Similar to the *contes cruelles*, psychological horror frequently dispenses with supernaturalism to concentrate on horrors grounded in the real world. Unlike the *contes cruelles*, however, psychological horror locates the source of horror in the mind of the psychopath, serial killer, or other villain. It is the villain's motivation for causing suffering that provokes the fear response. The prototype of this school of horror was Robert Bloch's *Psycho* and its Hitchcock film counterpart.

Dark Fantasy

The term "dark fantasy" is sometimes used as a synonym for supernatural horror and at other times refers to horror stories set in sword-and-sorcery realms usually associated with *Lord of the Rings*–style fantasy literature. Dark fantasy is a nebulous term that currently describes works straddling the border between supernatural horror, science fiction, and high fantasy. It draws elements from all these genres and can include mythological landscapes and creatures. H. P. Lovecraft is often included in this genre, as is *The Vampire Chronicles'* Anne Rice and Poppy Z. Brite.

Science Fiction

Horror is often found in dark works of science fiction, and science fiction trappings are often used in horror stories. As a result, the line dividing sci-fi from horror is a blurry one, and works like John Campbell's "Who Goes There?" (made into the films *The Thing from Another World* and *The Thing*) or Philip K. Dick's darker writings could sit in either category. The film *Alien* is a horror story even though it is set in outer space.

Other Genres

Other genres not normally associated with the supernatural or science fiction can include elements of horror as well; in fact, horror can occur in almost any type of art. The *Lifetime* network, for example, has developed an entire category of women-in-peril television movies that draw on elements of horror even as they cleave to the structures of the domestic drama. Harlequin Books has a line of horror-romances in which one or both partners in a relationship is a supernatural creature. Even *Scooby-Doo* manages to include horror elements while taking the form of a Saturday morning cartoon comedy.

Of course, these categories overlap with each other and cross-fertilize at will. It is often difficult to assign a work to one category or another, and some cut across all of them. For example, where should *Frankenstein* fall? Is it supernatural because it features a monster, a weird tale because it violates natural law, or science fiction due to its medical trappings? Perhaps it is dark fantasy or even primarily psychological, since both book and film attempt to rationalize the monster and make him a sympathetic figure. I have chosen to view "horror" broadly rather than categorize too carefully, and I will view all of the above as aspects of "horror."

For our purposes, I use the term "horror" to cover stories in a variety of media and genres whose primary aim is to elicit feelings of fear, terror, revulsion, or dread. Although I focus primarily on supernatural horror, the weird tale, and psychological horror, I will discuss fantasy, science fiction, and other genres when they stray into the territory of horror. I also focus primarily on Anglo-American horror fiction, with occasional examples from other cultural horror traditions, mostly because this is the story of horror in the Western tradition and partially because the majority of horror can be found in English-speaking countries. Lastly, to keep things simple, I use the term "horror" to refer to horror tales in a variety of media, rather than the more pretentious term "horror art" which is often used to discuss horror fiction, cinema, comics, television, gaming, etc., all together. I think that "horror" is a more effective term, and when clarification is needed we always have the medium-specific names (e.g. "horror comics") to fall back on.

I also propose a loose framework for understanding the phases of horror as the genre grew and developed over time, beginning with the creation of the horror genre with the Gothic writers of the late eighteenth century. (Prior to this date, while there were scary stories, there was no genre of horror.) These periods are dominated by themes reflecting the concerns of the eras of their creation, and these themes are related to the intellectual developments of the age. The periods are not discrete, however, so while one theme may dominate in a certain time period, it often emerges before its period of dominance and fades away while another theme rises in its place. For example, by my count, in the 1890s one could find examples of evolutionary, spiritualist, and cosmic horror all at the same time. Therefore, the dates I propose here are overlapping and only approximations. Gothic fiction, for example, still has its advocates even two centuries after its dominance of the horror genre faded.

Gothic Horror (c. 1750–c. 1845)

This period covers the early history of horror at the end of the eighteenth century and the beginning of the nineteenth, a time when horror looked back to an imagined past of castles and monsters. Including landmarks of the genre ranging from the Gothic masters (Walpole, Radcliffe, etc.) to Edgar Allan Poe, this period was dominated by the Romantic reaction to Enlightenment materialism and rationalism, as horror literature attempted to explore the negative consequences of Enlightenment values.

Biological Horror (c. 1815–c. 1900)

Nineteenth century "biological" horror begins with Shelley's *Frankenstein* and includes horror classics like Stoker's *Dracula*, Stevenson's *Dr. Jekyll and Mr. Hyde*, and Wells' *The Island of Dr. Moreau*. Nineteenth century horror reacted to the development of the life sciences, especially the theory of evolution and the invention of psychoanalysis. The period's horror literature presaged, digested, and metamorphosed scientific developments to produce the most important period in horror.

Spiritualist Horror (c. 1865–c. 1920)

The rapid technological development and concurrent development of pseudoscience before the First World War was reflected in horror's preoccupation with ghosts and hauntings—a particular theme reflecting a discontent with scientific progress and the negative consequences of uncovering "forbidden" and "unnatural" knowledge. Photography and spiritualism contributed to the development of horror in this era as the genre incorporated and colonized the new sciences to produce its unique art.

Cosmic Horror (c. 1895–c. 1945)

The development of "cosmic horror" occurred in reaction to the changing scientific understanding of the universe in the wake of Einstein's theory of relativity, as exemplified in H. P. Lovecraft's Cthulhu Mythos and H. G. Wells' *The War of the Worlds*. Victorian supernatural horror transformed into extraterrestrial and transdimensional cosmic horror, positing alien invasions and powers outside material space, which helped to create a nightmare vocabulary with which to explore the results of a relativistic and atheistic cosmos.

Psycho-Atomic Horror (c. 1940–c. 1975)

Following World War II, science became institutionalized and gradually infiltrated most aspects of life, and horror—now represented by cinema and television as well as the written word and comic books—reflected the increasingly science-based society in which it thrived. This resulted in a rash of 1950s mutant monster movies, the invasion of extraterrestrials into the public consciousness, and the psychologizing tendency of horror like Robert Bloch's (and Hitchcock's) *Psycho* that sought to explain horror through the tools of modern science. It was, in short, the application of reason to rationalize irrational horror.

Body Horror (c. 1965–c. 2000)

The period following the 1960s was an era defined by increasing reproductive freedom, biotechnological advances, and an increased turn toward "body horror"—the ritual mutilation of the human body (e.g. "slasher" films, vampires, splatterpunk). This development correlated with scientific discoveries in contraception, infertility treatments, medicine, and biotechnology in which the body became the source of horror. Highlights of the era include *The Omen*, *The Exorcist*, *Alien*, the 1980s slasher films, and the emergence of horror online and in the gaming world.

Horror of Helplessness (c. 1990–present)

As the twentieth century Cold War order broke down into a postmodern, fractured, and violent aftermath, horror's focus shifted away from institutional science toward a different form of knowledge, the revelation of hidden truths and the breakdown of absolute truth. Horror also reflected the uncertain fate of free will in a time when science reduced the human mind and soul to a series of genetic and neurological imperatives over which humans had little control. In works like *Buffy the Vampire Slayer* or Elizabeth Kostova's *The Historian*, knowledge has become a weapon wielded in defense of one's beliefs. In *Saw* and its ilk, fatalism turned to graphic and extreme violence.

This book examines each of these periods sequentially by looking at the scientific and cultural background of the period, its expression in literature, and its expression in the visual and performing arts. Doing so will allow us to trace the impact of developments in science and philosophy on the horror genre and demonstrate the way horror uniquely reflected the role of knowledge in a changing Western world.

Entering the World of Horror

Let us take for our guide in our exploration of horror and knowledge a man for whom knowing became the last and greatest horror, a certain Dr. Faust, late of Germany and Hell, a man whose intertwining themes of knowledge and damnation shall follow us through our journey into the heart of horror. An early sixteenth century vagabond necromancer, magician, and juggler going by Dr. Johann Faust of Heidelberg provided the outline for the legendary character that would bear his name, an amalgamation of a number of medieval necromancers remade into a new character, a man who sold his soul to the Devil for the price of knowledge.[15] The original Faust was more charlatan than sorcerer, an accomplished liar and trickster who claimed communion with demons as a way of making a living. As the English playwright Christopher Marlowe (1564–1593) put it in his *Tragical History of Doctor Faustus** (1604):

> falling to a devilish exercise,
> And glutted now with learning's golden gifts,
> He surfeits upon cursed necromancy[16]

The Faust (or the Latinate Faustus) legend originates at the end of the sixteenth century with a 1587 "biography" (the *Faustbuch*) published in Frankfurt which combines a number of medieval folk tales about wizards and Satan worshippers retold as Faust tales. Translated into English in 1592, it was read by Marlowe, who based his famous play on it. In the play Marlowe invests Faust with the trappings of classical tragedy, giving shape and form to the legends that circulated throughout the Continent, some of which are still told today. He also includes a great deal of religious imagery and appeals to Christ and to God, typical of the piety of Elizabethan England, and a fair amount of blood, typical of the violent and graphic Elizabethan and Jacobean stages. In Marlowe's telling, full of hubris, John Faustus exhausts his studies of earthly knowledge, mastering medicine, philosophy, and astrology. A keen intellect, he wishes for more. He wants the very power of the gods, accessible through the forbidden knowledge of the necromancers:

> These metaphysics of magicians
> And necromantic books are heavenly;
> Lines, circles, scenes, letters, and characters,
> Ay, these are those that Faustus most desires.
> O what a world of profit and delight,
> Of power, of honour, of omnipotence
> Is promis'd to the studious artisan![17]

For Faustus, knowledge is power, and he is willing to do anything to obtain this knowledge. He summons a demon from hell to do his bidding. This is Mephistopheles, servant to Lucifer himself. Faustus and Mephistopheles make a deal whereby the demon agrees to serve Faustus for twenty-four years and provide him with all the knowledge he could desire in exchange for Faustus' eternal soul. Faustus forces the demon to tell him the secrets of astronomy and astrology, and he learns the dark arts of calling up the shades of the dead to

---

The quoted material from Doctor Faustus *is from the First Folio 1604 "A" text of the play, which differs slightly from the 1616 "B" text, with modernized spelling.*

The Tragicall Historie of the Life and Death of Doctor Fauſtus.

With new Additions.

Written by CH. MAR.

Printed at London for *Iohn Wright*, and are to be ſold at his ſhop without Newgate. 1631.

seize their lost secrets. Even Lucifer himself arrives to present Faustus with a book of demoniac knowledge.

After many adventures, Faustus' hour comes, and the Devil and his minions arrive to take Faustus down to Hell:

> My God! My God! look not so fierce on me!
> Adders and serpents, let me breathe awhile!
> Ugly hell, gape not! come not, Lucifer!
> I'll burn my books!— Ah, Mephistophilis![18]

Faustus, though, cannot bring himself to renounce his learning in favor of complete submission to God and his revealed truths, so Hell swallows him after a number of soliloquies in which Faustus wrestles with himself over his inability to forgo science in favor of faith. The Chorus sums up the lesson we are meant to take from the over-learned Faustus' damnation:

> Cut is the branch that might have grown full straight,
> And burned is Apollo's laurel bough,
> That sometimes grew within this learned man.
> Faustus is gone; regard his hellish fall,
> Whose fiendful fortune may exhort the wise,
> Only to wonder at unlawful things,
> Whose deepness doth entice such forward wits
> To practice more than heavenly power permits.[19]

Or, in other words, knowing too much is deadly; and like God exiling Adam and Eve or Zeus smiting Prometheus, there are things the divine does not wish for humanity to know.

Keeping mindful of Faustus' fate, let us venture forth and explore the world that followed Faustus, a world whose deep superstitions and emerging scientific worldview created the conditions that yielded the first true works of what we would consider pure horror. It was the era of Renaissance and Reformation, giving way to Enlightenment, to reason, and (of course), to horror: A world where witches lived side by side with scientists, and superstition and science were not yet separate.

Opposite: Doctor Faustus conjuring Mephistopheles. In this illustration from the 1620 edition of Marlowe's *Doctor Faustus* we see Dr. Faustus using a book of occult lore to call the demon Mephistopheles from Hell, thus joining the pursuit of knowledge to the experience of horror. Faustus provided the prototype for the mad scientist, a stock character in the horror genre (Beinecke Rare Book and Manuscript Library, Yale University).

PART I

Darkness and Enlightenment
*The Gothic and Its Aftermath
(c. 1750–c. 1845)*

1

SCIENCE AND SOCIETY

For more than two centuries, the horror genre has served as a medium through which its creators and its audience could explore their anxieties and fears, and over this time it has been the only fiction genre to offer a sustained and detailed critique of the defining characteristic of Western civilization: its pursuit of science and reason. It did so because horror developed in a particular time and place, and it assumed many of the attitudes and the conflicts that characterized the Enlightenment and subsequent reactions to it. Though the horror produced today derives most directly from the forms and themes invented in the nineteenth century, the Victorians themselves drew on a still older source to create their terrors. Therefore, to understand the whole story of modern horror, the first of the seven major thematic trends this book considers is the Gothic, which grew out of a particular cultural milieu that emerged as the eighteenth century gave way to the nineteenth.

Though all of the trends discussed in this book overlap to some degree with one another, the Gothic was identifiably the first and earliest school of horror. Before it, there were works of fiction and art that were morbid (like the medieval allegory of the *danse macabre* in which skeletons mimed the roles of living people) or bloody (like Elizabethan and Jacobean theater in works like Shakespeare's gory cannibal drama *Titus Andronicus*). But only with the Gothic do we find gruesomeness and morbidity combined with the particular element of fear that together gave rise to a genre we now know as horror. However, there has been some debate about what period the Gothic covers, with some scholars limiting it to the eighteenth century and others extending it through the nineteenth,[1] going so far as to include even Oscar Wilde's *Picture of Dorian Gray* (1891) as the "last" Gothic novel. For our purposes, we will take a limited view of the Gothic and discuss it as a reaction to and processing of eighteenth century developments in science.

The period immediately before the advent of the first wave of horror fiction at the end of the eighteenth century was a study in contrasts, a period of darkness and light, both intertwined and inseparable. It was a time of witch-burnings and *philosophes*, of vampire hunting and rationalism. Like Faustus at his studies, the scholars of the eighteenth century turned to the occult as a source of hidden knowledge, knowledge that would bring both boons and terrors and paved the way for horror literature's eventual emergence. Even the great scientist Isaac Newton, after all, did more than record the laws of physics and invent calculus; he also attempted alchemy, the medieval "science" of turning base metals to gold, and he firmly believed in astrology.[2]

It is hard for us in the twenty-first century to understand just how little was known in the eighteenth, and consequently how important any scrap of knowledge must have been. At that time an entire continent, Antarctica, was still unknown, and the outline of a second, Australia, was uncharted. The interior of all but Europe was still a blank on the map. Even knowing the time of day was difficult, since an accurate clock did not emerge until 1764 — the same year Gothic fiction was born. While science paused to wonder at all there was to know, the unknown was frightening and disturbing for the vast majority of the population still unschooled in the age before universal public education. As a result, the human mind struggled to fill in the blanks, and too often this took the form of imaginary knowledge, myths and legends about magical creatures and beings, many of whom, following religious beliefs, were believed to be evil.

It was from this mixture of medieval superstition and modern, secular reason that horror fiction took its inspiration and its first form. In so doing, horror would draw on both aspects of eighteenth century society.

Witches

Since the Middle Ages, the Catholic Church had trafficked in visions of hellfire damnation and the reality of evil spirits as a way of convincing the laity of the Church's utility, and therefore the necessity of the tithes and taxes paid to support its priests. The Protestant Reformation changed nothing in this regard, for many of the reform churches were even more convinced of diabolical operations on earth (often in the form of the Pope); and they considered the old faith insufficiently interested in all things diabolical. John Calvin, for example, believed God had already decided who was condemned to Hell. The Puritans followed this line and used the cudgel of damnation to convince their people to exercise earthly virtue to "prove" they were destined for Heaven. Life was a constant struggle between the forces of God and the myriad temptations and deceptions of the Devil. If the Pope and Martin Luther agreed on nothing else, they agreed that demons walked the earth and tempted mortal men into sin.

The Puritans brought the European concept of sin and guilt to the United States with the founding of the Massachusetts Bay Colony. Their English predecessors have often been credited with spurring the scientific revolution overtaking Europe (of which, more below), though this influence is now seen as overstated.[3] God, they thought, was to be known through Nature, whose laws embodied reason.[4] Therefore, in line with this the Puritans created the idea that nature was to some degree a mechanical construction that could be explored through scientific inquiry and could be controlled by appropriate knowledge. The Puritans, however, also had a "strong antirational streak" and a deep conviction that they possessed the one and only truth.[5] They also believed that ideas had a dangerous power, and for that reason the English Puritans supported legislation requiring authors' names on every publication to better track who made use of this intellectual magic.[6] This zeal spread to the supernatural, which American Puritans, more extreme and hidebound than their European cousins, in particular were eager to explore, and which they held to be as real as the scientific phenomena their English brethren studied.

The Rev. Cotton Mather (1663–1729), spiritual guardian of the virtue of the Puritan colonies clinging to the coast of colonial America, was convinced that the supernatural was always lurking just outside the boundaries of civilization. In this, he echoed the sentiments of most of his fellows, the founders of the early European villages that gave birth to the United States. Writing in the *Magnalia Christi Americana*, Mather explained that the devil was not just real but manifest: "Molestations from *evil spirits*, in more sensible and surprising operations than those *finer methods*, wherein they commonly work upon the minds of men, but especially *ill* men, have so abounded in this country that I question whether any one town has been free from *sad examples* of them."[7] The supernatural, and more specifically the work of the Devil, was an everyday occurrence in the lives of the profoundly religious early Americans, for the same belief in Divine Providence that had guided the Puritans across the ocean to the shores of America could and did easily slide into a conviction that demonic forces opposed to God were just as real.

Examples were not hard to come by, and Mather and other religious figures spread and shared knowledge of them to serve as protection against diabolical influence and to reinforce the power of their faith to tame and control the forces of darkness. Both Cotton Mather and his father, Increase Mather, ministers both, were convinced of witchcraft's diabolical influence on human beings. In the typical scenario, a woman was believed to be led astray by the Devil, who sexually molested the woman and imbued her with magical powers that she would use to harm her community. The Devil would leave his mark on her body, often in the form of an oddly shaped mole. Though it could appear anywhere, it was frequently hidden on or near the woman's genitals or anus. Such women were believed to gather in the woods for orgiastic rites at which they worshipped the Devil and cast spells. Mather wrote, for example, of a woman who was possessed by the Devil:

> She said that she had not yet made a *formal covenant* with her devil, but only promised that she would go with him when he called her, which she had sundry

A Woman Torn in Pieces by the Devil. Seventeenth and eighteenth century people strongly believed in the power of the devil. This illustration from Robert Burton's *Wonderful Prodigies of Divine Judgement and Mercy* (1685) shows a devil claiming and tearing apart a woman from the German village of Oster as punishment for the sins of cursing and giving herself over to the devil. The belief that such supernatural events were really occurring helped fuel the witch hysteria and vampire plagues of the era.

times done accordingly; and that he told her that at Christmas they would have a *merry meeting* and then the agreement between them should be subscribed. ... She declared that her devil appear'd unto her first in the shape of a deer, skipping about her, and at last proceeded so far in that shape to talk with her; and that the devil had frequently carnal knowledge of her. Upon this confession, with other concurrent evidence, the woman was executed....[8]

Other examples of the supernatural which Mather recorded involved stones thrown by invisible hands, children taken with fits caused by an Irish witch, and diabolical waves carrying away passengers on a ship after the sound of turkeys filled the air. Mather, and many of his readers, undoubtedly believed in the literal truth of the supernatural occurrences he recorded, and the belief in witchcraft was widespread throughout the Massachusetts colonies. Between the founding of the New England colonies in the 1620s and the beginning of the eighteenth century, more than three hundred were accused of being "witches," and between thirty and one hundred were executed.

This manifested most famously at the Salem Witch Trials of 1692–1693, in which twenty-four persons, mostly young girls, died after being accused of engaging in witchcraft. Nineteen were hanged, and the others died in prison or by torture. In one particularly brutal case, Giles Corey was pressed to death under the weight of stones for refusing to stand trial on witchcraft charges. More typical was the case of Bridget Bishop, indicted for witchcraft on several counts. The first indictment, in the name of King William and Queen Mary, charged her with practicing sorcery on Mercy Davis, who on "the s'd Nyneteenth Day of April in the fourth Year aboves'd and divers other Dayes and times as well before as after, was & is hurt Tortured Afflicted Pined, Consumed, wasted: & tormented ag't the Peace of our said Sovereigne Lord And Lady the King & Queen and ag't the forme of the Statute in that Case made & provided."[9] These pains and punishments were assumed to be the result of Bishop's malfeasance, and the evidence appeared to lead back to Bishop.

After two more indictments, a trial, and two physical examinations (which found a "preternathurall Excresence of flesh"[10] near her anus—the witch's mark), she was executed June 10, 1692. The witch craze had begun when eight Salem girls, including a minister's daughter, began to act strangely and have odd mood swings, and the town elders suspected the work of the supernatural. A doctor suggested the girls were bewitched, and a witch hunt ensued when the girls began to accuse adult women of being witches. Something close to collective hysteria ensued, dozens died, and in the aftermath even some of the judges who sat at the witch trials came to believe that a grave injustice had been perpetrated. But during the trials, the town and its magistrates believed that witches were real, that they knew their powers and limits, and that their reign of terror needed to be stopped.

Many explanations have been proposed for the witch craze in eighteenth century New England, including the hallucinogenic fungus ergot (which may have caused the accusers' physical symptoms) and adolescent practical jokes gone too far.[11] As John Putnam Demos demonstrated in *Entertaining Satan*, his account of witchcraft's cultural role in New England, accusations of witchery were not confined to Salem but extended as far as Puritan culture. According to Demos, a belief in witchcraft served a number of social functions; prominent among them was the utilization of accusations of witchcraft as a way for "upright" citizens to seek revenge on or punish those who defied cultural boundaries.[12] For example, unmarried girls and widows were frequent targets, as were (perceived) homosexual men. Accusations abounded when disease or famine struck and a scapegoat was needed, as also happened in England a century earlier.[13] The absence of knowledge or understanding of the cause of such catastrophes led to the creation of false knowledge — of witchcraft — and the consequences were deadly. But what is beyond dispute is that for the individuals involved, witchcraft, diabolism, and the manifest presence of the Devil on earth were givens, accepted as facts of existence.

However, witchcraft panics were not confined to the future United States; Europe, too, had seen a wave of witch burnings during the Reformation and the Counter-Reformation. By some estimates, Europeans killed up to half a million persons, mostly women, during the witch hysteria of the fifteenth to seventeenth centuries. In fact, it was during this period that two churchmen commissioned by Pope Innocent VIII, Heinrich Kramer and James Sprenger, wrote the famous *Malleus Maleficarum* (*The Hammer of Witches*) (1486), a credulous guide to hunting sorcerers. It was apparently effective, since Europe's witch craze died out several decades before Salem started hanging its witches.

In 1735 Britain finally outlawed the hanging of witches and subjected those who claimed magic powers to a fine and imprisonment instead. The Witchcraft Act was last used in 1944 against Helen Duncan, an alleged witch and psychic medium who authorities feared would reveal D-Day preparations. The Witchcraft Act was finally repealed in 1951. But by the dawn of the eighteenth century, witches were mostly passé, and Europe faced a different supernatural menace: the vampire.

The Vampire

The term vampire is variously said to derive from Hungarian, the Slavic languages, Greek, or Turkish but usually refers to a life-draining member of the reanimated dead.[14] The belief originated in the mists of the past, perhaps with the Assyrians, and continued through classical antiquity and the medieval period, though not always by the name vampire and not always with the same symptoms. Vampires were an ancient curse, one whose form changed through time but revolved around the idea that the dead returned from their graves to draw energy, vitality, or blood from the living, usually their relatives. In Eastern Europe, the belief was reinforced by medieval Orthodox Christian teachings that the bodies of sinners would remain uncorrupted until absolution was granted, leaving them free to walk among the living at night.[15] Western Europe encountered the vampire sometime in the seventeenth century, when the word first entered the French language, and through it, other languages. The French university, the Sorbonne, received requests from Polish clergy for instructions on how to dispense with vampire corpses as early as 1693.[16] The word is believed to have entered the English language sometime in the seventeenth century, and the phenomenon of vampirism became universally known not long after.[17]

Vampires = dead came to draw life from the living — energy/vitality — creeping horror

Around the same time, vampirism began to affect the populations of Europe. In the 1920s, the credulous churchman Montague Summers (incidentally, editor of the first modern, scholarly edition of the *Malleus Maleficarum*) quoted a certain John Heinrich Zopfius, who in 1733 wrote a *Dissertatio de Uampyris Seruiensibus* (*Dissertation on Serbian Vampires*), as saying that those afflicted by the vampire suffer "suffocation and a total deficiency of spirits," followed by death. When asked the cause of their suffering, they blame a recently deceased personage.[18] The creatures were believed to be destroyable by pinning the vampire to its grave or mutilating the blood-gorged corpse. Such was the traditional folk "knowledge" used to combat the creeping horror.

The vampire craze that swept seventeenth century Europe reached its peak in the early eighteenth century when a wave of vampirism seemed to affect all of Europe, especially the British Isles, Germany, Hungary, the Balkans, and Eastern Europe, and even spread into parts of Africa. Dom Augustin Calmet, a French clergyman, recorded what he knew of the outbreak, and incidentally the first use of the word vampire in French:

> In this present age and for about sixty years past, we have been the hearers and the witnesses of a new series of extraordinary incidents and occurrences. Hungary, Moravia, Silesia, Poland, are the principal theatre of these happenings. For here we are told that dead men, men who have been dead for several months, I say, return from the tomb, are heard to speak, walk about, infest hamlets and villages, injure both men and animals, whose blood they drain thereby making them sick and ill, and at length actually causing death. Nor can men deliver themselves from these terrible visitations, nor secure themselves from these horrid attacks, unless they dig the corpses up from the graves, drive a sharp stake through these bodies, cut off the heads, tear out the hearts; or else they burn the bodies to ashes. The name given to these ghosts is Oupires, or Vampires, that is to say, blood-suckers, and the particulars which are related of them are so singular, so detailed, accompanied with circumstances so probable and so likely, as well as with the most weighty and well-attested legal deposition that it seems impossible not to subscribe to the belief which prevails in these countries that these Apparitions do actually come forth from their graves and that they are able to produce the terrible effects which are so widely and so positively attributed to them.[19]

The stories from this period are remarkable in their geographic distribution and their similarities. In 1727 a Serbian soldier returned to life to drain his beloved; his corpse was destroyed. In 1732, seventeen people in a Hungarian village died of vampirism; a corpse was found and destroyed. In 1738 another Serbian man returned from the dead to attack his son and five others. The representatives in Belgrade opened the graves of the deceased to find the fiend:

> When they came to that of the old man, they found him with his eyes open, having a fine colour, with natural respiration, nevertheless motionless as the dead: whence they concluded that he was most undoubtedly a vampire. The executioner drove a stake into his heart; they then raised a pile and reduced the corpse to ashes.[20]

In fact, so bad had the vampire situation become that the Sorbonne was said to have passed two resolutions in 1700 and 1710 prohibiting the beheading

medieval beliefs → dead walked until absolution

and mutilation of suspected vampire corpses.[21] One does not pass such restrictions (two, no less) unless there is a widespread practice of desecrating corpses in such a way. However, Pope Benedict XIV recognized the superstitious nature of the vampire threat and in 1749 spoke out against mutilating corpses.[22] Only as late as 1823 did the United Kingdom pass a law mandating that suicide victims should be buried "without any stake being driven through the body," as was customary to prevent the corpse from rising again.[23]

Scholars religious and secular turned their attention to vampires and produced a series of works on the subject. Besides Zopfius's *Dissertatio*, a Prof. Philip Rohr wrote *De Masticatione Mortuorum* (1679), Heineccius wrote *De absolutione mortuorum excommunicatorum* (1709), Michael Ranft wrote *De Masticatione Mortuorum in Tumulis Liber* (1728), and John Christian Stock gave us a *Dissertation de Cadaueribus Sanguisugis* (1732). All these volumes dealt with the hungry dead, and in 1740 we find a French volume by the aforementioned Dom Augustin Calmet doing the same. In 1774 Gioseppe Davanzati, Archbishop of Trani, wrote a *Dissertazione sopra I Vampire*. Such output continued into the beginning of the nineteenth century, with a number of French publications on the history, habits, and appearances of vampires.[24] Like Faust, academics plumbed the occult for hidden truths, and for a certain type of scholar the horror of the vampire was a subject of serious academic study.

Today it is obvious that the vampire panic was the result of individuals looking to affix blame for deaths they could not understand. Vampirism's suffocation and wasting away closely paralleled the symptoms of tuberculosis and other diseases, but in an era before germ theory, when there was no way to understand what caused the illness, victims' families sought a reason. In this, vampirism and witchcraft shared a similar explanatory utility. Thus the vampire hunts became a way to do *something* about a disease they could not stop or control, a way of attaining "knowledge" about horrors they could not understand. The "vampire" corpses uncovered in such hunts were merely the result of a poor understanding of bodily decomposition, which bloats corpses and fills their mouths with putrid blood, mimicking the supposed fattening of a gorging vampire. Nevertheless, many believed in the reality of the vampire and believed they had found evidence of its existence, and not just in Europe. Vampire beliefs persisted in New England as late as 1854, when corpses were still ritually exhumed and mutilated during tuberculosis ("consumption") outbreaks, the bones disarticulated and placed in a "skull and crossbones" formation.[25] In the twentieth century, vampires were said to still be staked in parts of Romania.[26]

Only two decades after the peak of the vampire panic, on Christmas Eve 1764, Horace Walpole published *The Castle of Otranto*, the first horror novel. It would have been a nice symmetry had he made use of the vampire motif, but instead he turned toward a different horror, the ghost, whose existence was in serious doubt even as the vampire and the witch were still thought real.

The Age of Reason

It may be difficult to believe that the same period that saw witch burnings and vampire hunts was also the celebrated Age of Reason, and yet it was. While their countrymen were tramping through graveyards to exhume the predatory dead, Europe's leading philosophers were pioneering a radical new form of thought, one that dispensed with the superstitions left over from the medieval period and that was dedicated to enshrining reason as the living embodiment of all that is good and noble in the human mind.

Traditionally, the Enlightenment is thought to begin with Newton's description of the physical world in purely material terms. Newtonian physics (and Copernicus's heliocentric universe before it) replaced the traditional view of God as arbiter of the world's every action with a rational understanding of the material processes involved. Newton, though, was not entirely a creature of pure Reason, believing, as we have seen, that astrology and alchemy were also valid paths to truth.

In truth, though, the Enlightenment was part of a larger Age of Reason that grew out of the Renaissance. Renaissance scholars rejected the received wisdom of the Church and its dogmas and instead tried to uncover lost truths hidden in Greek and Roman manuscripts. Based on the perceived superiority of imperial Rome to their own world, they believed that since Adam and Eve, the world had only degenerated, and a long line of philosophers (from at least Lucretius on[27]) had looked back to a lost golden age. The Renaissance scholars looked to the past as inspiration and aimed to restore the classical world's glories. After a while, of course, they ran out of classical past to mine, and the later Enlightenment scholars (to simplify a bit too much) instead projected their thoughts forward to a glorious future in which humans would cast aside irrationality and become perfect creatures of pure reason. They were looking, so they said, for a "science of man" that would lead to an understanding of humanity and the world.[28]

The Enlightenment should not, however, be thought of as a single project since it had no unified direction. It would be more accurate to think instead of multiple strands that coalesced in the late eighteenth century into a philosophy we think of today as the Enlightenment, including rationalism, progress, and scientific inquiry.[29] The accumulation of knowledge was a goal of the Enlightenment, and reason, experiment, and science were held to be the guide to permanent and absolute truths about nature.[30] This strongly contrasted with the received wisdom of the Church and the recovered ancient knowledge of the Renaissance. For the first time, society would be its own authority, constructing its own knowledge based on reason and inquiry rather than faith and dogma.

Typical of the new style of thought, Voltaire reversed the Renaissance worship of ancient models in discussing the then-current dispute over the rel-

Chained library at Wimborne Minster. In the seventeenth and eighteenth centuries, knowledge was so valuable a commodity that some libraries would chain their books to the wall to prevent patrons from absconding with them. The dark, cramped, and restricted conditions of the era's libraries helped turn the scholar into the pale, dour figure of horror literature and popular stereotypes.

ative superiority of Greco-Roman Antiquity. Voltaire came down squarely on the side of the modern: "Molière, in his good pieces, is as superior to the pure but cold Terence, and to the droll Aristophanes, as to Dancourt the buffoon. There are therefore spheres in which the moderns are far superior to the ancients, and others, very few in number, in which we are their inferiors. It is to this that the whole dispute is reduced."[31] In many ways the past was seen as a storehouse of outmoded superstitions— religion included — which needed to give way before the power of reason. Or, again quoting Voltaire on the Middle Ages, "It is necessary to know the history of that age only in order to scorn it."[32] Humanity would progress, but progress meant inevitably that the biblical view of Adam created perfect in Eden could no longer be true. The idea of progress meant things were getting better, and so they must have been worse the further back one looked.

The champions of this line of thought are still household names today — Voltaire, Hume, Rousseau, Kant, Descartes, Spinoza, etc.— and the Enlightenment thinkers did more than any generation before them to define how the modern, Western world thinks. John Locke, Thomas Hobbes, Jean-Jacques Rousseau, and Thomas Jefferson differed on the details, but they all agreed that society involved a compact or contract between the governed and the government, inspiring the American Constitution and its imitators. Voltaire, Hume, and Descartes advocated a skeptical position regarding human knowledge in general and religion in particular. Hume, for example, published a devastating critique of the traditional arguments for the existence of God; Jefferson's Declaration of Independence left room only for a vaguely theistic "creator," with which the later Constitution entirely dispensed. Adam Smith advocated capitalist economics.

All of this was consistent with the Enlightenment's supreme contribution to thought, the idea of "natural law." This concept held that moral and ethical considerations derived from inherent truths about the world, human nature, and their workings. Thus the laws of men are governed by their relationship to the objective nature of things. In other words, natural law tells us that we are endowed with "unalienable rights" imposed by the universe, nature, a pantheistic creator or God. Simultaneously, Enlightenment philosophers sought to find the laws of nature and to understand how the world worked. Presumably, scientific laws and natural law were expected to someday merge when the true order of things was worked out to its ultimate completion.

For our purposes, the "take home message" of the Enlightenment was an understanding that the world worked by rational principles which could be discovered through reason and through scientific investigation. In other words, the mysteries of time and space could be reduced to scientific or philosophical postulates that could produce definite answers based on investigation and logic. This ran counter to the prevailing folk-belief in God's (and the Devil's) direct intervention in the universe. But within a few decades the intelligentsia, who made up the audience for literature in an age of illiteracy, were largely converted to some form of Enlightenment reason. This intelligentsia was primed to be amused by supernaturalism in literature, and thus horror literature, much the way they were amused by the claims of Franz Mesmer.

In 1779, Franz Anton Mesmer, an expatriate Viennese doctor then living in Paris, became famous for his claims of "animal magnetism," which postulated that mechanical laws of nature could be applied to humans. The same forces that held the planets in their orbits could be used to control the behavior of individuals.[33] Mesmer believed his techniques could be used to cure illness, and his "mesmerized" patients could be sent into trances or convulsions, and became responsive to suggestion. Mesmerism developed into something of a fad and swept Europe, attracting a large number of followers. In popular imaginings, mesmerism implied the doctor's complete control over his patients, and it supplied a plot point for D. H. Lawrence, Balzac, Poe, Hawthorne and others.

Mesmerism was the first of many pseudosciences and fads to find their way into horror, a genre that fed on such claims as fuel for its ongoing critique of science and reason.

The End of the Age of Reason

The Enlightenment (or, if you subscribe to Gertrude Himmelfarb's ideas, the three Enlightenments—British, French, and American[34]) is often said to have led to the American Revolution and the French Revolution, though it would probably be more accurate to say that Enlightenment ideas were used to justify these complex events. The Americans used Enlightenment principles to underscore their claims to representative self-government, and in France the divine right of the French kings increasingly came to seem anachronistic in an age that viewed government as a (mostly) secular compact between subject and ruler. Though the French Revolution had many causes, Enlightenment philosophy was used to justify it and to sketch out the path toward the glorious future of human perfectibility. Robespierre summed it up in his speech on the "Republic of Virtue": "In one word, we want to fulfill the wishes of nature, accomplish the destiny of humanity, keep the promises of philosophy, absolve Providence from the long reign of crime and tyranny."[35] This eventually took the form of the Terror in which ideological nonconformists were guillotined in numbers that shocked the Euro-American world, perhaps twenty thousand citizens.[36] Citizens were stripped of their rights, and the government implemented strict controls on the economy and on political activities, which foreshadowed later and more gruesome dictatorships.[37] The Terror aimed to return France to the state of nature, where natural law and secular reason could reign. The Revolutionaries also overran Notre Dame Cathedral in Paris and rechristened it the Temple of Reason in honor of their new universal faith.

In the aftermath of the Revolution's excesses, and its failure, artists, poets, writers, and thinkers rejected the Enlightenment's reduction of human endeavor to materialistic pure reason in favor of a new, more emotional philosophy later called Romanticism. By its very definition, Romanticism was hardly consistent, and its practitioners— ranging from Goethe to Poe to Byron — all held different views that revolved around a few ideas. These new Romantic thinkers celebrated individualism, irrationality, and all things medieval and oriental, in direct contrast to the Enlightenment's love of rationalism and the classical past. They appealed not to reason alone but to reason guided by emotion, and held that feelings were the route to truth. Foremost among these new feelings was the idea of nationalism, which held that humans were part of natural, organic ethnic groupings that by right ought to have an independent homeland.[38] The Romantics probed many a dark path, and as we shall see, they were responsible for much of what would become modern horror.

An early proponent of Romanticism was Horace Walpole, who in his life and works put Romanticism into practice and thus gave birth to the horror genre, a genre tied inexorably to Romanticism, irrationalism, and the horror of knowledge — and its absence.

2

LITERARY DEVELOPMENTS

Horror fiction has its origins in the Romantic period's reaction against the Enlightenment-era worship of science and reason, though it is not entirely synonymous with the Romantic Movement. The Romantics believed that Enlightenment thinkers were cold and mechanical, and that they had sacrificed emotion and soul in favor of pure reason. The fantastic literature that emerged from this period, whether it be horror, romance, historical fiction, or science fiction, was rooted in the idea that emotional truths can supersede or contradict nonfiction facts. This related closely to what Nietzsche would later describe as the dichotomy of the Apollonian and Dionysian elements inherent in tragedy, and ultimately all literature. In *Birth of Tragedy*, Nietzsche described the way the primal darkness underpinned tragedy, the first form of stagecraft.[1] Apollo may have been the god of reason and the father of the Enlightenment, but in the Romantic period his rational influence came to be seen as a mere curb or guide for the true, violent, and emotional passion of Dionysus, whose orgies reflected the subconscious, the primitive, and the sublime. The sublime, in particular, was an important if vague concept that sought the feeling one achieved when confronted with an overwhelming force that takes control of one's soul and fills one with intense and all-consuming feelings.[2] Sunsets, landscapes, and beauty were traditional ways to seek the sublime.

Horror took its inspiration from the "sublime" pleasure that could be found in unreason, emotion, and dreams. Terror, in particular, was the most important tool for creating feelings of awe, wonder, and even reverence.[3] Fear, as the philosopher Edmund Burke claimed in *A Philosophic Enquiry into the Origins of Our Ideas of the Sublime and Beautiful* (1757), was the chief and most potent emotion, producing the strongest emotional response which blocks out any other feeling, bringing us to the sublime in a way even beauty could not. Therefore a literature that could induce fear could use it to focus the mind on Romantic notions. Burke's essay marked perhaps the first time a literary genre emerged from a philosophy or had a treatise as its birth certificate, reinforcing the intimate relationship between horror and knowledge.

Burke's influential essay argued that dark nights, loud sounds, spookiness, imposing architecture, and death could cause fear and thus an experience of the sublime.[4] These were the same aspects that took written form in Gothic literature. In this, the origins of horror make clear the relationship the genre had to the intellectual developments that preceded it. Horror sought to find emotional release in a retreat from reason and an artistic rejection of the emerging scientific world-view that the Age of Reason inaugurated. Within the horror story, therefore, it is unsurprising that there are two sources of terror: the unknown, and the forbidden knowledge that should not be known. This reflects the inherent duality of the emotional world the Romantics sought to give parity with the intellectual: The emotions that give us joy also produce fear.

From this understanding of the dual nature of emotion and its tortured relationship to reason came the earliest true horror fiction, the Gothic, and the genre grew exponentially from this root. This early horror fiction presents us with numerous examples of what Noël Carroll called the "Discovery Plot" wherein the protagonists stumble across, discover, or unearth something that defies the rational, normal pattern of existence and must devote their resources to both suppressing the horrific discovery and proving to a skeptical world (the reader included) that the horror exists. "Such a plot," said Carroll, "celebrates the existence of things beyond the common knowledge," thus reinforcing the role of knowledge in producing the frightening effect. In fact, Carroll argues that horror stories "are predominantly concerned with knowledge as a theme,"[5] and the role of knowledge in the horror is multifaceted, as we shall see. Though Carroll limits his analysis to the role of knowledge within the horror story (that is, the way the characters perceive it), knowledge is further reflected in the relationship of horror stories and themes to the role of science and knowledge in the culture at large.

However, as Carroll noted, Romanticism and the horror genre are not completely at one, and Romantics like Walt Whitman disapproved of "frantic novels" like those of the Gothic writers.[6] But this is to be expected because horror inherited the ambiguous duality of science — birthed both by the Enlightenment's worship of it and Romanticism's critique. Horror was dark, while both the Enlightenment and the Romantics strove for the light. Therefore, the genre cannot fit easily with either system but instead drew from both to dramatize the West's uneasy relationship with knowledge and science, and its opposite, emotion. In other words, horror stories can serve two purposes: To reinforce the role of science in understanding the seemingly inexplicable, or to undermine confidence in science's understanding of the world. The former represents an affinity with the Enlightenment; the latter with Romanticism. Both themes recurred in horror down through the ages, playing out the Enlightenment and Romantic dichotomy down to today.

Literary critics typically group Gothic stories according to their writing style, leitmotifs, and time period, bringing in most of the horror written between Horace Walpole in 1764 and Mary Shelley in 1818. Instead, I would like to explore horror thematically, and in so doing look at a particular type of horror prevalent in the Gothic period and its aftermath: A horror rooted in the past. The stories we will examine in this chapter are largely united by their setting: taking place in the Middle Ages, the remote past, or a mythic time outside of history. In later chapters we will explore horror more clearly linked to the present and its concerns. But for now we shall look at Gothic fiction and the practitioners influenced by the particularly historical horror the period created.

Gothic Fiction

The Enlightenment of the mid–eighteenth century had a madness for classical architecture based on Greco-Roman models, so it must have seemed a bit odd that Horace Walpole (1717–1797), a former member of Parliament, began reconstructing his home at Twickenham, Strawberry Hill, with medieval details drawn from the out-of-fashion Gothic school (Gothic then being an adjective to describe anything from the fall of Rome to the Renaissance, rather than the more restricted twelfth to fifteenth century meaning used today). He pasted wallpaper filled with Gothic architectural elements on the ceilings, and he nailed cardboard crenellations to the home to mimic the look of medieval fortifications. He built towers and added pointed arches and stained glass. Between 1750 and 1770, Walpole transformed his modest cottage into an ersatz Gothic castle. During this time, Horace Walpole, forerunner of the Romantics, had a dream:

> I waked one morning, in the beginning of last June [1764], from a dream, from which, all I could recover, was, that I thought myself in an ancient castle (a very natural dream for a head like mine filled with Gothic story), and that on the uppermost banister of a great staircase I saw a gigantic hand in armour. In the evening I sat down, and began to write....[7]

Two months later, Walpole finished his work, *The Castle of Otranto*, the first representative of what would become the Gothic school of horror fiction. The story itself is melodramatic and convoluted; a certain Prince Manfred schemes to marry the bride intended for his late son, Conrad, in order to found a dynasty in the Italian duchy of Otranto. Isabella, the bride, escapes Manfred's clutches with the help of Theodore, a peasant lad who in reality is the son of the late Prince Alfonso, whose land Manfred usurped. Theodore and Isabella marry and reclaim his birthright while Manfred retreats to a monastery to seek God's forgiveness for his many sins. As David B. Morris points out, many of the pairings in *Castle of Otranto* are vaguely (legally or symbolically) incestuous, adding a further sexual dimension to the story's terrors.[8]

That much was the barest skeleton of the plot; what set *Otranto* apart from the other novels, legends, and ballads of the day was Walpole's use of the supernatural to add coloring to his story, and the medieval (by way of the Italian Renaissance) setting of castles and crypts which produced a jarring, dark, and sepulchral air. At the time, the medieval period was considered a "dark age" of decay, in contrast to the bright lights of classical antiquity and the Renaissance bordering it on either side. *Otranto* did much to reverse this judgment, and its employment of medieval coloring helped restore the Middle Ages as a worthy period of study and emulation, partially because Walpole presented the novel as a hoax, a "genuine" manuscript of the Middle Ages, which fooled even some at Cambridge University for a time[9], thus beginning horror's fascination with blurring the lines between fact and fiction and challenging our knowledge of and confidence in what is real.* To this end, the book's medieval setting reflects the power of the rediscovered-yet-unknown past.

The story of *Otranto* begins with a prophecy: *"the castle and lordship of Otranto should pass from the present family, whenever the real owner should be grown too large to inhabit it."*[10] The resolution of this prophecy was a matter of speculation for the Otrantonians, for it seemed to make no sense at all, at least not until the end of the book. Meanwhile, all is not well inside Manfred's castle. Conrad, of course, did not simply die; no, a tremendous, monstrously large helmet, materializing from supernatural domain, crushed the unfortunate lad to death:

> The horror of the spectacle, the ignorance of all around how this misfortune had happened, and, above all, the tremendous phenomenon before him, took away the prince's speech. Yet his silence lasted longer than even grief could occasion. He fixed his eyes on what he wished in vain to believe a vision; and seemed less attentive to his loss, than buried in meditation on the stupendous object that had occasioned it. He touched, he examined, the fatal casque; nor could even the bleeding, mangled remains of the young prince divert the eyes of Manfred from the portent before him. All who had known his partial fondness for young Conrad were as much surprised at their prince's insensibility, as thunderstruck themselves at the miracle of the helmet.[11]

Thereafter, additional pieces of the giant's armor begin to materialize, seeming to come from a statue of Prince Alfonso; and the castle of Otranto is besieged by supernatural manifestations. Paintings came to life, lightning destroys the castle, and visions of Alfonso appear on the horizon when his son comes to reclaim his throne: "The moment Theodore appeared, the walls of the castle behind Manfred were thrown down with a mighty force, and the form of Alfonso, dilated to an immense magnitude, appeared in the centre of the ruins."[12] The giant proclaimed Theodore his heir, and the people accepted the spectral verdict. Thus was the ambiguous and odd prophecy fulfilled.

Compare, for example, with the opening narration of The Texas Chain Saw Massacre *(1973), which claims that the film is based on actual events, or* The Blair Witch Project *(1999), which masqueraded as a documentary, complete with website and back story, fooling many until the hoax was revealed.*

The Castle of Otranto. This illustration from a 1791 edition of *The Castle of Otranto* shows the Italian castle on which the story was supposedly based. In fact "Otranto" is a French transliteration of the area's original Italian name, Taranto. This castle was rebuilt by Alfonso I of Aragon between 1485 and 1489, but Horace Walpole actually modeled the castle in his novel on his own home of Strawberry Hill (Beinecke Rare Book and Manuscript Library, Yale University).

Otranto was not the first work to make use of spectral themes; Daniel Defoe's "A Relation of the Apparition of Mrs. Veal" (1706) had featured a ghostly visitation, though a kindly one, which the author presents as true, based as it was on an allegedly real haunting of people who actually existed. And even Shakespeare had made use of the knowledgeable ghost in both *Macbeth* (Banquo) and *Hamlet* (Hamlet's father) a century before. Nevertheless, *Otranto* was the first novel to combine all of the elements later associated with the Gothic in one place, and to place them in the service of horror.

Gothic horror became defined by a certain set of characteristics tied closely to themes from the emerging Romantic Movement. Following Walpole's (and Burke's) formula, the typical Gothic novel featured an ancient and mysterious castle, well stocked with dungeons, crypts, and secret passages. It featured a villainous nobleman, and a pair of virtuous lovers. It also featured at least one, but preferably multiple, spectral, ghostly, or otherworldly entities, replete with a wide range of supernatural special effects. Too, the Gothic novel usually featured an ancient secret, prophesy, or manuscript whose arcane and forbidden knowledge was the source of or illuminated the horror. In *Otranto*, an ancient prophecy fills this role, and this preternatural knowledge sets the plot in motion. The ghost, too, is possessed of secret knowledge — Theodore's true identity — and he uses it to seek his vengeance. Though Theodore knows his own identity, it is only the ghost's concurrence that proves it to the peasantry and thus demonstrates the "truth."

However, Walpole wanted to make one more point about the role of knowledge in his Gothic tale. He purposely left the source of the spectral emanations unexplained. They simply *happen*—irrationally, perhaps; supernaturally, definitely. There is no earthly explanation for them, and the only comfort the reader is allowed is a vision of a saint accepting Alfonso into Heaven at the end, though even that is cold comfort when the unhappy dead can rise at any time to reveal hidden truths and upset the *status quo*. In this sense, Walpole views knowledge as a double-edged sword; as (dis)embodied in Alfonso's ghost, it is symbolically its own actor, revealing that which is hidden. It both restores the previous order and destroys the current one. Most importantly, the secrets that overturn Manfred's rule act independently of either Manfred or Theodore, neither of whom is in control of the knowledge they seek to conceal or reveal. The horror, at one level, is that secrets have a power all their own.

Walpole's novel today reads as both overwrought and undercooked, but it was highly influential among the literary elite, despite selling only a few hundred copies at first. And it is important to remember that Walpole *was* writing for an elite audience, those who could afford books that often cost more than an average laborer earned in two weeks of work.[13] Walpole, the son of a British prime minister and himself a member of Parliament, was a well-placed member of society writing for similarly placed friends. Only at the end of the eighteenth century would Gothicism become fuel for a mass readership, after the stories had been turned into popular plays and chapbooks.

After Otranto

Otranto was followed by a plethora of imitators, whose work was mostly set in medieval European castles, and featuring ghosts, demons, ancient curses, and the other stock-in-trade items that were forever after associated with the stereotypes of horror, seemingly utilizing Edmund Burke's entire list of terror-inducing horrors that could lead to an experience of the sublime.[14] Anna Lititia Barbauld published in 1773 the three-paragraph "Sir Bertrand: A Fragment" which built on Otranto's Gothic trappings, if three paragraphs can be said to build much on top of a hundred-page book. Clara Reeve followed in 1777 with *The Old English Baron*, its plot largely recycled from Walpole, as the author herself admitted in the preface, where she explains that the novel was "the literary offspring of *The Castle of Otranto*, written upon the same plan."[15] She does, however, complain that Walpole's ghost and bloody set pieces are much too strong and too outrageous for a literary audience. Instead, her ghost would be sober and confined to "certain limits of credibility."[16] Some later authors would go a step further and dispense with the ghost altogether and complete the transition from supernatural revel to dark melodrama.

Ann Radcliffe (1764–1823), born in the year of *Otranto*, became the most famous of the Gothic authors; and in her six novels she made strong use of the trappings of the Gothic to weave tales of supernatural dread, and — more importantly — make reading horror both fashionable and acceptable for the elite and middle class in a world where novels were still considered the inferior cousins to histories, fit only for women and children. In Radcliffe's novels, bloody or spectral details are used to suggest worlds of horror, and the atmosphere of fear and dread they evoke is among the greatest in all horror. This is perhaps exemplified best in her most famous novel, *The Mysteries of Udolpho* (1797).

Set in 1584, the plot of *Udolpho* revolves around the orphaned Emily St. Aubert's struggle to escape the clutches of a European nobleman and join her lover. After her father's death, Emily is left in the charge of her aunt, Madame Cheron, who has little sympathy for her sensitive niece. The aunt marries the villainous Montoni, who uses the threat of violence to force Cheron to disinherit Emily in favor of himself. Montoni attempts to maneuver the vulnerable Emily into marriage with Count Morano, but Emily refuses. In order to escape the fate Montoni has arranged for her, Emily must uncover the hidden truth behind long-buried secrets, including her true identity. Again it is forbidden knowledge that moves the plot and inspires the horrors Emily encounters.

But it is the atmosphere that is most effective in a Radcliffe novel. Take, for example, this prototypical scene of horror in which the beleaguered Emily encounters one of the milder horrors, a veiled painting, in Montoni's ancient and massive castle in Udolpho:

> Emily passed on with faltering steps, and having paused a moment at the door, before she attempted to open it, she then hastily entered the chamber, and went towards the picture, which appeared to be enclosed in a frame of uncommon size, that hung in a dark part of the room. She paused again, and then, with a timid hand, lifted the veil; but instantly let it fall — perceiving that what it had concealed was no picture, and, before she could leave the chamber, she dropped senseless on the floor.[17]

It is the details that make the scene: the *size* of the frame, the not-quite revelation of what it contains. The only fault in this is that the atmospheric details in Radcliffe's works generally have little or nothing to do with the human dramas that are her novels' true plots.

Radcliffe, however, adds another layer to the tangled web of knowledge and horror. In her novels, she explains away the supernatural horrors with naturalistic or mechanistic explanations, such as optical illusions, hallucinations, and dreams. Often the explanations failed to do justice to the power of the earlier horror. In *Supernatural Horror in Literature*, the later horror writer H. P. Lovecraft derided these rationalizations as "laboured," and Jane Austen made fun of them in *Northanger Abbey*; nevertheless, Radcliffe attempted to firmly link horror with a rational-scientific world-view, wherein the supernatural could be explained and its effects understood as the product of human or natural events. E. J. Clery, however, takes a counterintuitive view and argues that Radcliffe's naturalistic explanations actually reinforce supernaturalism by creating a world where coincidence serves the purposes of Divine Justice, the highest power.[18] In other words, the machinations of the mechanical plot in their elaborate complexity are to be taken as evidence of God's plan, without which the coincidences necessary for a happy resolution could not occur, though this explanation is not entirely convincing and is a bit "labored."

Walpole and Radcliffe had, however, created two opposing schools of supernatural horror, both of which continue down to this day. Walpole favored the irrational horror in which otherworldly intervention was real, while Radcliffe favored a scientific horror whereby human agency is the cause of the true horrors, no matter what form they appeared to take. Radcliffe added the further introduction of rationalism — what would later become science — into the world of horror. But despite melodramatic plots that revolve around love matches, generalized villainy, and other staples of the domestic drama, in both Walpole and Radcliffe it is knowledge that drives the horror: knowledge of the supernatural imparted to or hidden from the reader, and knowledge of the supernatural known to or hidden from the characters in the novels. In both cases, the horror derives from what is known, and what is unknown.

Also of note is Matthew Gregory Lewis' (1775–1818) gory novel *The Monk* (1796). The story concerns Ambrosius, a Spanish monk whose undoing comes when he deflowers Matilda, his pupil. Unsated by this violation of chastity, Ambrosius rapes and murders the virgin Antonia. Several lengthy digressions into other melodramatic or spooky stories (some taken almost verbatim from German tales) ensue. When we return to Ambrosius, the monk has fallen into the hands of the Inquisition, from which he escapes only by selling his soul to the Devil. Ambrosius tries to repent his sins and escape Satan's clutches, but the arch-fiend prevents this, and Ambrosius undergoes a long and painful death. Many have noted the explicitly sexualized content of the story, and it is erotic excess that leads to the monk's destruction[19]; however, the crowning horror of the story comes when the demon tells the monk what would have happened had the monk refused the bargain. Knowledge of what might have been makes his torture in Hell's fires all the worse.

Charles Robert Maturin's (1782–1824) *Melmoth the Wanderer* (1820) featured another victim of a devil's bargain, condemned to prolonged life unless he can find another willing to take his place. A scholar named John Melmoth sells his soul to the Devil in exchange for one hundred and fifty years of life and the chance to obtain the knowledge he could never have learned in one mortal lifetime, but he repents his hubris, and the core of the book concerns his many and varied adventures trying to undo the curse. He searches death chambers, madhouses, and other Burkean set-pieces of Gothic terror to find someone desperate enough to take on his burden, but no one will. As his story unfolds through the framework of old manuscripts and books, we are meant to feel his existential sadness and misery.

As should be obvious, Gothic novels had a strong sexual component, not least of all because the scheming villain was frequently attempting to violate the chastity of the story's fair maiden. However, to say that the "cultural work of the gothic was to testify to the terrific power of sex," as Ruth Perry did in 2004,[20] or that the Gothic is a genre with a pronounced "sadomasochistic element," as Martin Rubio did a few years earlier,[21] is to overstate the case, since sex was never the exclusive property of the Gothic, as the Marquis de Sade or Jane Austen could testify. Instead, the Gothic's special province was the nightmare — of which sex was but one facet, used to highlight the physical, emotional, and intellectual vulnerability of the heroine — and thus the reader — before the horror of the irrational and the experience of the sublime.

The devil's bargains of the British Gothic echoed the Continental reemergence of old Dr. Faustus, the prototypical mad scientist, this time as Faust, the eponymous hero of Johann Wolfgang von Goethe's (1749–1832) two-part epic play (1808–1832) in which the good doctor sells his soul, experiences pleasure and pain, and is saved through love. In Goethe's version, Faust's trouble is that he seeks to transcend the metaphysical limits of human capacity by applying his knowledge to experiences that take him above the human level, courting destruction. The play is not horror, but it is both cosmic and tragic. Also not quite horror but still grotesque was the French writer Victor Hugo's *Notre-Dame de Paris* (1831), better known in English as *The Hunchback of Notre Dame*. The story features a deformed bell-ringing hunchback, Quasimodo, and a cast of characters who play out the dramas of their lives before the medieval Notre Dame Cathedral (the recent Revolution's Temple of Reason), the focal point of the book. We are meant to sympathize with Quasimodo as he loves and loses the beautiful Gypsy girl Esmeralda and his own life in a series of coincidences and tragedies. The Gothic of the cathedral's ancient architecture is meant to mirror the Gothic trappings of the novel.

In the Gothic, the supernatural plays an ambiguous role. On the one hand, ghosts and demons are "real," and the reader, remembering the world of vampires and witches outside their doors, is expected to believe in their power; but they are also "unreal" in the sense that they are literary creations that are both good and evil, active agents and passive symbols. Fortunately most Gothic novels (dozens of which were published between 1790 and 1840) essentially used the supernatural and the horrible as window dressing to color an otherwise standard issue plot; i.e., lovers wrongfully parted reunite to defeat a (usually) aristocratic villain's evil plans. This plot continued on through the publication of Emily Brontë's *Wuthering Heights* in 1847 and beyond. In fact, the plot of many Gothic novels can be described without reference to most of the supernatural events, with obvious exceptions like *The Monk* and *Melmoth*, whose very difference makes them still worth reading. It was up to the successors of the Gothic writers to reverse the equation.

Short Stories

The Gothic novel, however, was a rarified beast marketed to the wealthy few in search of the sublime. In the realm of shorter fiction, small, cheaply printed paperbound chapbooks—some known as bluebooks for the color of their covers—brought Gothic stories to a large audience. Typically, these works featured a lurid engraving to set the stage for a sensational story of thirty-six or seventy-two pages, often derived, condensed, or copied directly from Gothic novels or plays. Original works utilizing Gothic themes appeared frequently as well. All of the bluebooks were aimed at a mass audience, rather than the elite readership, reducing in the way of short stories the complexities of the Gothic novel to brief and formulaic "tales of terror" and dispensing largely with the sublime in favor of shocks, frights, and chills. This was an important transition from Gothic romance to modern horror.

Bluebooks were widely circulated and shared in lending libraries or from booksellers offering them for less than a shilling, providing everyone from sailors to chimneysweeps to servants with a taste of the Gothic that the elite enjoyed in leather-bound volumes. Radcliffe's *Mysteries of Udolpho*, by contrast, was unaffordable at a full pound plus five shillings.*[22] Notable among the bluebooks was Sara Wilkinson's *The Castle Spectre, an Ancient Romance* (1829), a twenty-four–page prose rendering of a popular Gothic play by *The Monk*'s Matthew Lewis (see chapter 3). The anonymous *The Mysterious Spaniard; or, The Ruins of St. Luke's Abbey: A Romance* (1807) utilized Gothic trappings in a story of intrigue and an evil cult of Illuminati. Chapbook stories like these were often collected into anthologies with titles like *Endless Entertainment; or Comic, Terrific, and Legendary Tales* (1826).

Some of the material in bluebooks had previously appeared in popular magazines like *Tell-Tale* or *Endless Entertainment* (as in the aforementioned anthology), which published Gothic stories. A great deal of Gothic horror appeared in *Blackwood's Edinburgh Magazine*, a Scottish publication of miscellany founded in 1817 as the *Edinburgh Monthly*. Horror stories from the likes of Sir Walter Scott, James Hogg, and John Galt appeared in its pages along with countless tales from authors now unknown. *Blackwood's* was one of the most influential arbiters of horror fiction in the Victorian period, and later in the

---

There were twenty shillings to the pound until Britain decimalized its coinage in 1971. Therefore, the four volumes of Udolpho *were twenty-five times more expensive than a chapbook, which told the same story with an economy of words and therefore an economy of expense. The chapbook* The Veiled Picture *(1802) actually condensed* Udolpho *itself into a few pages.*

century it would serialize Conrad's *Heart of Darkness*. Many of *Blackwood's* early stories utilized a number of Gothic elements, usually mental illness, violence, and other macabre fare (being buried alive was a favorite topic), but usually relied less on the supernatural than their chapbook or novelistic counterparts. Samuel Warren contributed several entries in a series, *Passages from the Diary of a Late Physician* (1830–1837), which featured a doctor as narrator. The reader was made to experience the doctor's struggle for scientific objectivity as he confronted graphic acts of unspeakable violence, the supernatural, and bizarre mental and medical aberrations. *Blackwood's* was published under various titles until 1980, when it finally folded.

Blackwood's fiction was a strong influence on the American author Edgar Allan Poe, who satirized the more formulaic aspects of the magazine's horror in "How to Write a *Blackwood* Article" (1838). Poe understood the conventions of Gothic horror, and he drew from them to craft his own unique brand of fiction. Instead of horror supplementing a melodramatic plot, in the new fiction of Poe as in the chapbook horrors the horror *was* the plot, and the purpose of his work. But unlike the chapbook writers, Poe's work transcended mere sensation to turn the short horror story into literature.

Edgar Allan Poe and American Horror

Though the Gothic had begun in England, its influence spread slowly across the Atlantic in the decades after *Otranto*. The beginning of the nineteenth century saw Gothic atmosphere tinge the emerging American literature, about a generation later than in Europe.[23] Washington Irving's stories, such as "The Legend of Sleepy Hollow" with its Headless Horseman, are colored by Gothic touches, even if their horrors are tinged with good cheer; and Nathaniel Hawthorne's works, like *The Scarlet Letter* and *The House of the Seven Gables*, show the same influence. Dark and saturated with the horrors of the Puritan religion that had initiated America's witch trials, Hawthorne's books cut to the heart of America's religious hypocrisy and dealt with issues of innocence and guilt through the prism of knowledge and morality. In *The Scarlet Letter* (1850), for example, Hester Prynn commits adultery, but the tragedy is the pain her trysts with the Reverend Dimmesdale cause, and the way exposure of the secret knowledge of the affair destroys lives. Guilty knowledge destroys Dimmesdale from the inside out, as his health fails and he tortures himself in punishment. As in the British Gothic, allegations of witchcraft and hints of a demonic "Black Man" of the woods are mere coloring to the story. Of note, however, is the depiction of Hester's husband, Roger Chillingworth, as a demented and evil doctor ("leech"), one of many such mad scientists in Hawthorne's fiction.

Edgar Allan Poe (1809–1849), on the other hand, made horror the primary focus of his short stories and his only novel, *The Narrative of A. Gordon*

Pym (1837). An orphan never formally adopted by the Virginia merchant, John Allan, who took him in, Poe attended school in England and Virginia until his gambling debts caused his premature withdrawal from college. Nevertheless, the young Poe demonstrated significant literary gifts and published his first volume of poetry at the age of eighteen. After six months in the army, he began writing short fiction, producing by his death seventy-two short stories, fifty poems, and one novel. These were published in newspapers and magazines as well as collected between hard covers. The cousin he married when she was fourteen died in 1847, and Poe succumbed to drink and grief, dying on the streets of Baltimore in October of 1849.

Most Poe stories, in imitation of the Gothic, are set in an imaginary and vaguely defined European location of uncertain time. Many are meant to be medieval in nature; even those stories putatively set in the present (usually represented as 18–, with the final years left off, as per convention) are not well linked to real times or real places but instead to a parallel world that is in many ways outside of time. In Poe's best stories, the plot is itself an elaborate combination of atmosphere, morbidity, and terror; and he located the source of his horrors in the human mind. In "The Black Cat" (1842/3) for example, the narrator murders his wife and his black cat, but he becomes convinced — obsessed — with the idea that the cat is haunting him. He sees it everywhere, and he hears its plaintive mewing, so much so that he is compelled to reveal his grisly crime when he comes to believe he has sealed up the *living* cat in his basement wall.

Similarly, in "The Tell-Tale Heart" (1843) a man kills another and becomes convinced that the victim's heart is beating beneath the floorboards of his room, driving him to madness. In the story, we feel the narrator come unhinged as he and the police sit in the room discussing the murder. The imagined beating of the heart compels the narrator to come clean and reveal his crime because he, like the narrator of "The Black Cat," can no longer live with his guilty knowledge of his secret sin.

Both tales are narrated by the murderers, who initially present themselves as normal, rational creatures. They speak plainly and are at pains to convince us that they are reliable narrators. It is only later that we see how disturbed they are, and the horror the reader experiences derives directly from our understanding of the narrators' unreliability and the creeping disquiet their abnormal psychology produces in the audience. It is this dual knowledge — the reader's knowledge of the "truth" and our discovery of the narrators' madness (which is to say irrationality) — that produces the stories' strange effects.

From a slightly different point of view, the narrator in "The Fall of the House of Usher" (1839) observes the disturbed workings of Roderick Usher's mind and is horrified at what he finds. The story tells of a man who travels to the House of Usher, an old Gothic-style pile in which Roderick and his twin sister Madeline are the last of the Ushers, a family tainted by incest. Roderick has asked his friend to come and cheer him because both he and Madeline are sick. However, during the narrator's stay Madeline dies. Roderick, deprived of the sister who was his soul, goes mad and becomes convinced that she was in fact buried alive. During a great storm he and his friend think they see the bloodied and emaciated form of Madeline standing before them. She clasps Roderick, and both fall dead to the floor as the narrator flees, neither able to live independently of one another.

In a supreme example of Gothic style employed in service of horror, Poe describes the destruction of Usher's house:

> The storm was still abroad in all its wrath as I found myself crossing the old causeway. Suddenly there shot along the path a wild light, and I turned to see whence a gleam so unusual could have issued; for the vast house and its shadows were alone behind me. The radiance was that of the full, setting, and blood-red moon which now shone vividly through that once barely-discernible fissure, of which I have before spoken as extending from the roof of the building, in a zigzag direction, to the base. While I gazed, this fissure rapidly widened — there came a fierce breath of the whirlwind — the entire orb of the satellite burst at once upon my sight — my brain reeled as I saw the mighty walls rushing asunder — there was a long tumultuous shouting sound like the voice of a thousand waters— and the deep and dank tarn at my feet closed sullenly and silently over the fragments of the *"House of Usher."*[24]

There are clear echoes of Manfred's fallen castle here, and the Gothic detail is superb, with the obvious parallel between the broken house and Usher's broken mind. But, of course, Poe's stories covered more than just disturbed minds. Several dealt outright with the supernatural, though usually at an angle, and almost always mitigated by an understanding of the psychology of the characters or narrator. In Poe's first horror tale, "MS Found in a Bottle" (1833), the narrator, professing his strong skepticism of the supernatural, writes of the doomed voyage of his ship, beginning with a premonition that all is not well. The ship encounters all manner of foul weather and ends up lost in unknown waters. The skeptical narrator tries to make the best of things and paints a new name for the battered ship as he comes to view his adventure as a scientific exploration: "the thoughtless touches of the brush are spread out into the word DISCOVERY."[25] It is part of the narrator's slowly developing rejection of his knee-jerk skepticism as he comes to embrace, hesitantly but inevitably, a truly scientific, sublime wonder even in the face of terrible despair:

> To conceive the horror of my sensations is, I presume, utterly impossible; yet a curiosity to penetrate the mysteries of these awful regions, predominates even over my despair, and will reconcile me to the most hideous aspect of death. It is evident that we are hurrying onward to some exciting knowledge — some never-to-be-imparted secret, whose attainment is destruction.[26]

The narrator is then consumed by the horrible, fabulous, supernatural abyss into which the earth's oceans were once rumored to flow. The lesson about the dangers of forbidden knowledge is obvious.

Poe returned to this theme in *The Narrative of A. Gordon Pym*, a novel in which the title hero travels to the Antarctic on a voyage of horrific discovery. At the pole, Pym and his companions find indentures—chasms—whose shape "bore also some little resemblance to alphabetical characters," though Pym is convinced to the last that were "the work of nature."[27] They also come across a race of degenerate cannibals (who cry "Tekeli-li") and only narrowly escape in a canoe, to die on the ocean. Again, the price of discovery is death; and Pym is denied the ultimate revelation, supplied only in a note from a fictional "editor" that the great fissures resembling letters were in fact notations in Egyptian, Ethiopian, and Arabic. As the editor slyly notes, this revelation "open[s] a wide field for speculation and exciting conjecture."[28] Thus is the reader provided knowledge that contextualizes Pym's horror and produces a different shudder of understanding than the characters themselves experience. By contrast, in "The Facts in the Case of M. Valdemar" (1845), Poe made use of the craze for mesmerism as a way to turn scientific wonder into horror. In the story, mesmeric power is used to keep M. Valdemar suspended in a trance state even past death, and when the mesmeric spell is released, Valdemar collapses into a sticky, putrescent ooze. So powerful was mesmerism's hold that many readers thought the story true, which quite amused Poe, who toyed with his readers' confusion.[29]

Even in Poe's most purely fear-driven tales, the theme of knowledge and understanding is evident. In the famous "Pit and the Pendulum" (1842), the narrator endures a series of horrific tortures, like Melmoth, at the hands of the medieval Inquisition: placed at the edge of an abyss to fall and die, strapped to a table where a descending pendulum threatens to slice him to death; and chased with hot irons. Nevertheless, the narrator does not physically suffer any of these harms but instead *anticipates* them with "shuddering reason."[30] It is the *expectation* of torture, the working of the human mind and its reason, that produces all of the narrator's terror, and indeed is the same sort of vicarious horror the reader experiences in reading of them. Similarly, in "The Masque of the Red Death" (1842), Prince Prospero seals himself and his courtiers in his castle to ignore and forget of the Red Death killing his people. Inside "it was folly to grieve, or to think."[31] But the Red Death arrives after all, symbolizing the truth the prince and his minions tried to will themselves to forget. The knowledge, and the horror, could not be suppressed.

The link between horror and suppressed or hidden knowledge led Poe toward a new genre, the detective story. In "The Murders in the Rue Morgue" (1841), Poe created the first modern detective story, in which the hero, C. Auguste Dupin, solves a ghastly and horrific crime (the murder of two women, by an escaped orangutan) by ferreting out the hidden truth through clues and "ratiocination," which Arthur Conan Doyle would later have Sherlock Holmes call "deduction." In this tale, as in "The Purloined Letter" (1844), "The Mystery of Marie Rogêt" (1842/3), and "The Gold Bug" (1843), horrific elements are mixed with deduction and logic, spilling out of the horror genre and moving decisively toward detection, the latter genre a clear outgrowth of horror, whose heritage it would continue to mine into the twenty-first century.

Last in our tour of Poe, we must say a word about his poetry, which celebrated the emotions of horror and thus in a way rebuked the emerging rational, scientific worldview his tales of ratiocination and detection celebrated. This ambivalent attitude toward science was very Romantic, and it was best summed up in his "Sonnet — To Science" (1829), in which Poe asked, has not Science "dragged [the goddess] Diana from her car," taken away the deities of nature,

> ... and from me:
> The summer dream beneath the tamarind tree?[32]

Best known of Poe's poems, "The Raven" (1845) is a meditation on madness, in which the narrator becomes taken with a talking raven perched above his chamber door. The raven can only say "nevermore," which the grief-stricken narrator takes for oracular answers to his questions on life, on death, and on his lost love, Lenore. Equally effective is "Ulalume" (1847), in which the narrator wanders through a nightmare scene only to chance upon the tomb of his lost love. He had tried to suppress and forget about her, but Psyche, his unconscious and irrational mind, drove him forward into a world of pain and suffering. In Poe's poems, the scientific worldview does not hold the answers, and the irrational and unconscious continue to make their will felt despite reason's best efforts.

Impact of the Gothic

Such questions about the role of an all-explaining scientific-materialist philosophy would become increasingly prominent as the horror genre developed. After Poe, the Gothic school of horror faded from prominence during the nineteenth century, and "pure" Gothic novels and stories became increasingly rare. Nevertheless, they had made a major contribution to the development of horror literature, and for the first time fear became a legitimate aim for writers to strive toward.

The Gothic gave us some of the most beloved (and overused) conventions in all horror. Windswept moors, atmospheric weather, and damsels in distress were all Gothic conventions. So too was the dissolute hero who stands ineffective before the evil before him, saved only by outside agencies beyond his control. Like *Otranto*'s Theodore, the heroes of horror were rarely active agents in their own salvation but merely beneficiaries of the villain's fatal weakness. Above all, the dark and spooky castle is the greatest of the Gothic's contributions to horror, found later in such works as *Dracula* and the Universal horror films, and

Illustration of "The Raven." Edgar Allan Poe's poem "The Raven" was a best-seller in its day and one of the few memorable horror poems. This illustration from a 1903 edition of "The Raven" depicts the narrator confronted with the horror of the raven in a scene often alluded to in literature, film, and art (Library of Congress, LC-USZ62-108225).

in a different sense in the haunted house stories of later centuries. It is impossible to imagine the bleakness of Stephen King's Marsden House from *'Salem's Lot* or the *Psycho* house without recognizing in them a reflection of the Gothic gloom of *Otranto*'s castle.

Gothic elements continued to lend color and flavor to new types of horror literature which reflected the changing relationship between scientific advances and society's nightmares. This relationship between horror and science, of horror mitigating between humanity's dreams of technological progress and nightmares of atavistic revenge, emerged from the unique environment of the Romantic period and continued to grow and develop as science advanced and horror continued to play out fears about where the path of discovery might lead. But before we explore this theme further, we should briefly examine some of the aesthetic developments the Gothic school originated and influenced, as well as the role of the Gothic in the performing arts.

3

HORROR IN THE ARTS

Because of its dramatic portrayal of monsters, madness, and the supernatural, the horror genre was practically made for the visual and performing arts where the sense of fear could be heightened by *seeing* and thus *experiencing* horror at a deeper, sensory level. In fact, some of the most popular entries in the early history of each new art form —from dime novels to movies to television to video games to the Internet— were horror. However, in the era before projected or electronic entertainment, there were considerably fewer avenues for the portrayal of horror; consequently, it would not be until the twentieth century that the visual and performing arts fully developed their own language of horror and a unique interpretation of the themes with which literature had been wrestling since the beginning of the genre. Nevertheless, even from the beginning horror had its share of influence on the aesthetics of modern life.

Beauty in Ruins

Horror was present in art from the earliest, and as we approach the modern, period we find works that produce a shudder of horror. In the fifteenth century woodcuts depicted the grisly executions carried out by Vlad the Impaler, whose other name, Dracula, would inspire the famous vampire. Christian churches were replete with scenes depicting the tortures of Hell, such as Hieronymus Bosch's *Garden of Earthly Delights* (c. 1500), whose right-hand panel depicts the damned. In it we see in the background a ruined city emanating spectral light. In the foreground demons and devils play among a surreal landscape of body parts, musical instruments, and the tortured damned. In the lower right corner, a pig wearing a wimple appears to kiss one poor soul. Similarly, Pieter Brugel's *The Triumph of Death* (c. 1562) is a masterpiece of horror. In it, a plague is given literal form as a marauding army of skeletons marching through a village, massacring what few living remain. In especially creepy scenes reminiscent of the *danse macabre*, skeletons play the role of priests in a ruined church, while on the other side of the picture a skeleton wields a sword to execute a blindfolded man. Even the king is not immune; a skeleton robs him as he lies dying. In the background, volcanoes explode against a stark beach. It is, in short, the most expressive and terrifying horror painting ever made.

In the seventeenth century, *memento mori* pictures helped viewers "remember you are mortal" through their depiction of skulls and other funereal themes. Philippe de Champaigne's painting *Memento mori* (c. 1655) is typical of the genre, depicting a skull situated on a table between a flower and an hourglass. Also popular were the Renaissance era "grotesques" which featured studies of deformity and ugliness, as depicted by the era's master artists, including Leonardo da Vinci. In the eighteenth century, the Spanish artist Goya depicted a range of witches, satyrs, and other grotesque supernatural creatures. In *Pretty Teacher!* (1799), an old crone has a naked beauty on her broomstick, indoctrinating the younger woman into a life of witchcraft and sexual abandon. Henry Fuseli's *The Nightmare* (1781) depicted a woman swooning while an imp or monster representing the weight of a nightmare squats on her chest. The Romantic poet William Blake created a series of powerful watercolor illustrations to Dante's *Divine Comedy* (1824–1827) which depicted a range of monsters and demons.

Later, the Romantic spirit, however, manifested itself in art in two ways that pertain directly to our inquiry. First, it made medieval themes popular again for perhaps the first time since the emperor Charles V was painted as a knight during the waning of the Middle Ages. In the interval, it had been customary to paint either modern clothing or the togas of classical antiquity when creating a historical painting, but that changed with the American Benjamin West, who created a stir by using historically accurate clothes in his paintings. He made some of the first modern paintings depicting medieval scenes in the 1760s, including *The Death of Chevalier Bayard* and a cycle of eight paintings depicting the life of King Edward III for Windsor Castle.[1] Though Voltaire had found the Middle Ages fit only for scorn, paintings on medieval themes would grow increasingly popular through the nineteenth century, producing highly polished and romantic (in the later sense of the word) visions of an imagined past. But the Romantics (in the old sense) also depicted something different in their art.

The Romantics were among the first to seek out beauty in decay and ruin, and they especially enjoyed creating dramatic and sensual paintings depicting collapsing remnants of the ancient and medieval past. Giovanni Paolo Pannini depicted Roman ruins from his perch in Italy,[2] and Hugh Robert became famous for his depiction of Roman ruins, the first of which was displayed at the Paris Salon of 1767. As Diderot said after viewing Robert's paintings, "There is more poetry, more that is accidental, not merely in a thatched cottage, but in a single tree which has endured the years and the seasons, than in the entire façade of a palace. One must ruin a palace to make it an object of interest."[3] Such paintings typically featured crumbling obelisks, arches, and columns set amidst weeds and overgrowth; and they evoked a sense of peace and awe in the face of the inevitable passage of time. Thomas Cole, for example, in his monumental series *The Course of Empire* (1834–1836) depicted the rise of a classical civilization and its collapse, finishing the series with *Destruction*, depicting the violent end of an empire, and *Desolation*, which lingers quietly over the serene ruins of a once-great society; in the foreground a single composite column covered in overgrowth speaks to what was lost.

Such poetic evocations of despair and ruin were preceded by an architectural fetish for the same. At manors across England, architects constructed artificial ruins where real ones did not exist to construct a Romantic landscape to frame formal gardens. At Stowe, ruins were added as early as 1738. A certain Antonio Chichi even became famous creating cork models of ruins to adorn Continental drawing rooms in the 1780s.[4]

But the people of this era enjoyed ruins as a *beautiful* experience, not a horrific one; and they further pursued Classical or pagan ruins for their aesthetic enjoyment. It would not be until the publication of *The Castle of Otranto* that medieval ruins came into vogue, or that the Romantic "beauty in ruins" could be transfigured into its opposite: horror.

Ragland Castle. Artists in the Romantic period found beauty in ruins, and the ruins of Romanesque and Gothic structures, like Ragland Castle, provided suitably moody and atmospheric backdrops for the contemplation of horror and the sublime.

Gothic Gloom

This was largely because the English (and, to a lesser extent, the Continentals) of the eighteenth century viewed the medieval period as a time of superstition and misery. It was an age of barbarism and best left forgotten as that dark "middle time" between the glorious achievements of Greco-Roman antiquity and the even more glorious achievements of the modern age. In the architecture of the period, classic forms were all the rage, and Greco-Roman columns sprouted wherever a builder's trowel plowed. England was, of course, sprinkled with the ruins of Gothic abbeys and monasteries razed by Henry VIII, but these reminders of the past simply served as justification for the current celebration of classical forms. Pointed arches and flying buttresses were out; round arches and ionic columns were in.

This was not the case for Horace Walpole, who, as we have seen, did more than merely write *The Castle of Otranto*; he set off a mania for all things medieval that would touch most aspects of nineteenth century aesthetics. Walpole liked the medieval glamour of the Gothic school, and he sought out its remains wherever he could. As we saw, Walpole's home of Strawberry Hill was the first in what might be termed the "Gothic revival" style of architecture. He filled the rooms of his home with pointed arches and elaborately carved fireplaces, vaulted ceilings and stained glass windows. He even constructed towers with crenellation of the kind a medieval archer might have used to shoot at some approaching enemy. The moody, atmospheric look and feel of battlements and vaulting was a marked contrast to the Greco-Roman forms then en vogue. So impressed was Walpole with his handiwork, that he set *Otranto* in a fantasy realm modeled closely on Strawberry Hill. The architectural details referenced throughout the story were to be found in Walpole's own home. Therefore, in the public mind it was little stretch to casually link the Gothic in literature with the Gothic in architecture, and to see romantic-horror — that combination of romance and fear unique to the Gothic and those inspired by it — in a landscape of medieval architecture.

From Strawberry Hill, the rage for all things Gothic spread like wildfire. Churches, homes, and government buildings all adorned themselves with the characteristics of medieval grace. Some estimated that the Gothic revival produced more Gothic architecture than the original Gothic period. By 1830, the style (actually several different variations on the theme over the course of a century and a half, including the Queen Anne and the Romanesque Revival) was exported to the United States, and a plethora of Victorian homes sprang up with towers, pointed arches, and medieval details, until the style faded from prominence near the end of the nineteenth century.[5] The neo–Gothic probably reached its apex when the British government commissioned Sir Charles Berry to build a new Parliament building after the original burned to the ground in 1834. Completed over the next thirty years, the Palace of Westminster (home to the famous clock tower and Big Ben, its bell) was a masterpiece of Gothic revival architecture.

Queen Anne Gothic revival mansion. Gothic revival and Queen Anne architecture used medieval motifs to literally make a home into a miniature castle. However, Victorian mansions were expensive to keep up, and many were turned into apartments or left to decay, becoming neighborhood "haunted houses" due to their spooky appearance. This house, located in Houston, had already become rundown, subdivided, and used for a fruit stand by 1943, when John Vachon took this picture (Library of Congress, Prints & Photographs Division, FSA-OWI Collection, LC-DIG-fsac-1a35441).

But despite this, it is Walpole's version of the Gothic that we remember today: A gloomy, mystic style associated with his version of horror. Perhaps it is for this reason that today American haunted houses are almost invariably portrayed as neo–Gothic Victorians (or, in Europe, actual Gothic castles), complete with the signs of decay completing the illusion of age. Whether the house is Hill House from Shirley Jackson's novel, the Overlook Hotel in Stephen King's *The Shining*, or the Addams Family's turreted abode, the haunted house remembers fearfully the nineteenth century's infatuation with medieval architecture and that architecture's link with ghosts, goblins, and other assorted horrors. Walpole's twin births of Gothic architecture and Gothic fiction sealed the aesthetic link between the two once and for all.

Horrors in Wax

During the French Revolution, Marie Tussaud searched through the piles of corpses left by the guillotine to pull out the severed heads of prominent indi-

Wax museum. Waxworks were popular amusements from the eighteenth century onward, inspired by Madame Tussauds in London. The Acorn Wax Museum in New York was one of many such attractions that sprang up in the nineteenth and twentieth centuries (Library of Congress, Prints and Photographs Division, LC-B22-349-12).

viduals whose death masks she wanted to make for her museum. Tussaud had inherited a wax museum in 1794 from Dr. Phillipe Curtius, who had a reputation in Paris as a great modeler in wax, and she wanted to expand on Curtius' Caverne des Grands Voleurs (Chamber of Great Criminals) with additional morbid and/or grisly images. She took her show on the road in 1802, traveling to the United Kingdom where she would put down permanent roots after the outbreak of the Napoleonic Wars made a return to France impossible. The museum traveled around the United Kingdom until 1835, when it found a permanent home in London. From her new base on Baker Street (later home to Sherlock Holmes), Tussaud displayed, among the prosaic sculptures of famous and historical figures, the horrors of the Revolution in wax, to which she and her successors added the portraits of notorious murderers. Also on display was the original guillotine used to create the originals of the severed heads she presented in facsimile.

Tussaud called her display the "Chamber of Comparative Physiognomy" to give it an air of scientific utility (because it was believed criminals possessed criminal features that could be identified), and the morbid room quickly became the star attraction of Madame Tussauds Wax Museum. The magazine *Punch* named it the "Chamber of Horrors" in 1846, and it has gone by that name ever since. A wax figure of Dr. William Palmer, a multiple murderer who poisoned his patients and his family in the 1850s, became its top draw in that decade. The *Spectator* said that the Chamber was a disgrace to civilization, but Charles Dickens thought it educational.[6] The museum moved to Marylebone Road in 1884, where it still operates today, depicting contemporary killers and villains along with a few of the original lot. The Tussauds Group now runs branches in New York, Las Vegas, Hong Kong, and Amsterdam, each complete with its own "Chamber of Horrors."

Stage Adaptations

As noted earlier, Gothic novels' use of supernatural events wedded to some form of a love story made them inherently dramatic and ripe for dramatization. In the era before the motion picture, and in an era still characterized by widespread illiteracy, the stage served as the vehicle for adapting Gothic horrors for a larger audience. Unfortunately, the era's stagecraft was less than clear in how and what it adapted from literature. Bertrand Evans noted that in the late eighteenth century, plays were produced out of a common stock of Gothic elements borrowed haphazardly from any number of sources, sometimes whole and sometimes in part. Further, "we cannot always guess what has been adapted; sometimes even an explicit acknowledgement of source proves false."[7] Fortunately, the first Gothic novel's path to the stage is fairly easy to trace.

We find Walpole's *Otranto* dramatized, though surprisingly, this did not occur until 1781, thirty-five years after its publication, when a Robert Jephson created the first Gothic play out of the parts of *Otranto*. Jephson, however, did not adapt the book literally for the stage, and he dispensed with a great number of the supernatural events Walpole had taken such pains to establish. For example, the large helmet that crushes Conrad at the opening of the novel is absent in the play; and even the climactic scene in which the enormous ghost of Alfred confirms his son's birthright vanishes from this early treatment.[8] This was necessary because supposedly genteel eighteenth century play-goers were unused to blatant depictions of the supernatural and the unwholesome, which were affronts to both taste and reason. It was quite a change from the time when Shakespeare could depict cannibalism onstage in *Titus Andronicus*.

Instead, what Jephson retains is the skeleton of the plot and some of the medieval atmosphere with which Walpole imbued his tale. The stage version retains the castle and its medieval trappings, the robed figures, and the raving Gothic villain, here transformed from Manfred the usurper to Raymond, count of Narbonne, also the title of the play. This is also the most significant of the plot changes: In this version, Raymond/Manfred is not the author of the previous dynasty's demise, but merely inheritor of an ancestral curse due to a forgotten ancestor's usurpation. Thus Raymond, unlike Manfred, is innocent (literally, "not knowing" in Latin) of the crime of his forebear, making his eventual self-destruction all the more tragic. While Manfred falls due to guilty knowledge, Raymond is destroyed by what he does not know. In both cases, the hero (Theodore) is an afterthought, powerless until an outside force defeats the villain.

Gothic drama had hit its stride, and the late eighteenth through the early nineteenth centuries delivered scores of plays whose villains grew more villainous and whose plots grew darker and more explicit in their depiction of the stock elements of Gothic fiction: Dorothea Celesia's *Almida*; Colman's *The Iron Chest*; C.R. Maturin's *Bentram; or, The Castle of St. Aldobrand*; and Sophia Lee's *Almeyda, Queen of Grenada*, to name a few. Matthew G. Lewis, author of *The Monk*, offered in *The Castle Spectre* (1797) one of the first Gothic plays to dramatize the supernatural as a real and active force in life. The usurping Earl Osmond has murdered Angela's mother and separated Angela from her lover, the rightful Earl Percy. He sealed Angela up in his castle, where, taken by her beauty, Osmond wants to force Angela into marriage. He is prevented from doing so by the ghost of Angela's mother, who provides a distraction, allowing Angela to grab a knife and stab Osmond to death. The resemblance to *Otranto* is obvious, but the play went on to become one of the most successful on the eighteenth century.

But critics decried the use of a ghost — the supernatural — in the theater, as they had with all depictions of the supernatural in the 1790s. *The Analytical Review* argued in 1798 that *The Castle Spectre* was "truly humiliating to the pride of national taste," replacing the high art of theater with mere "stage-trick and scenery."[9] The popularity of on-stage ghosts prompted *The Monthly Review* to complain in 1800 that sensational "spectres" had nearly driven high art like Shakespeare from the stage. Ghosts were irrational, but the worse sin was that Gothic plays were popular — and therefore to be opposed by supporters of high culture and refinement.

Because of the controversy over Lewis's depiction of the ghost in *Spectre*, he published a special note for readers in its printed edition in which he defended his supernatural entity with a wholly typical eighteenth century explanation:

> Against my Spectre many objections have been urged: one of them I think rather curious. She ought not to appear, because the belief in Ghosts no longer exists! In my opinion, that is the very reason why she may be produced without danger; for there is now no fear of increasing the influence of superstition, or strengthening the prejudices of the weak-minded.[10]

However, ghosts were becoming popular entertainment elsewhere, as in the "phantasmagoria" shows. These involved a type of magic lantern used to project ghostly images before stunned audiences both in special shows devoted to the machine and as a special effect in Gothic plays. We shall say more about the phantasmagoria in Chapter 9. Ghosts would also invade the nineteenth century as mediums and photographers raced to contact the dead, as we shall see in Part III.

Jeffrey N. Cox argued that Gothic plays clearly reflected the attitudes of the day, the liberation and the horror of the French Revolution, and the Romantic urge toward the irrational.[11] In the case of *The Castle Spectre*, the play also clearly took its place in the ongoing development of a rational and scientific world-view in the face of continuing superstitious belief. (And it might be noted that Shakespeare never needed to apologize for Banquo's ghost!*) Gothic villains usually represent the forces of chaos and unreason, and though the villain is always defeated, the viewer is meant to focus on him and, to a degree, identify with his Luciferian challenge to the laws of time, space, and reason. He is, to some extent, Napoleon and also Satan.

With this we can take flight from Walpole, the early Gothic masters, and their assorted works. Because the Gothic set the stage for the horrors that were to come, they are owed our respect; however, the veritable explosion of superior horror over the course of the nineteenth and twentieth centuries has left many of their Gothic forebears wanting, with the notable exception of Poe. Again excepting Poe, few early Gothic writers are still read with frequency, and fewer still of their works shock or bring forth feelings of terror. This is not their fault; time and culture change and what was shocking once is commonplace today.

In the Gothic we have seen the way authors, artists, and architects embraced a particular view of the past, one that celebrated periods of history formerly disparaged. In literature and in plays we have seen the way the Gothic writers made use of medieval accoutrements to create a moody and atmospheric landscape against which tales of terror could profitably perform. Further, we have seen the way the Gothic embraced Romanticism and worked diligently against the cool classicism of the rational Enlightenment. More than anything else, it was this marriage of the irrational and the horrible, of the knowledge of fear with the fear of knowledge, that helped define the parameters in which modern horror would grow.

Shakespeare's use of the supernatural caused headaches for critics who opposed the supernatural in Gothic drama but extolled the Bard. To get around the contradiction, they came up with three justifications: 1. Shakespeare lived in earlier times when belief in ghosts was still reasonable; 2. Shakespeare had to use ghosts because Elizabethan audiences had debased tastes; and 3. Shakespeare was a genius of such caliber that he could break the rules of taste and use the supernatural without besmirching his brilliance. These explanations obviously had the whiff of elitism (Michael Gamer, Romanticism and the Gothic: Genre, Reception, and Canon Formation [Cambridge: Cambridge University Press, 2000], 130).

PART II

Between God and Beast
*Biological Horror
(c. 1815–c. 1900)*

4

SCIENCE AND SOCIETY

The Gothic writers were fond of employing ghosts as their supernatural envoys, symbolically using the disembodied spirits as representations of mental conditions, whether they be rational or irrational. But as we explore our second theme, biological horror, we will see writers move away from immaterial entities toward a more physical form of the supernatural: the monster. The monster make take many forms—a reanimated corpse, a vampire, a bizarre vivisectionist experiment—but he is invariably a corporeal being, a bizarre, liminal creature poised somewhere on the continuum between man and beast. Dracula, Frankenstein's Monster, and Mr. Hyde are but three of the most famous of these beast-men, and their struggles to navigate the uncharted space between the world of humankind and the mythically charged realm of the animal reflected the period's emerging discomfort with advances in the life sciences and the subsequent displacement of older world-views of divine protection and human exceptionalism.

Traditional Views

Ancient shamans once viewed humans and animals as inherently linked, and as we have seen, the shaman believed himself capable of transforming into an animal when navigating the spirit realm. This close association with the animal world did not long last into the Christian era, when Biblical accounts of creation appeared to justify the belief that humanity was distinct from the animal world and was indeed God's special creation. In Genesis we read that God merely willed the birds and beasts and plants into existence, but he took great care with humanity: "And the LORD God formed man of the dust of the ground, and breathed into his nostrils the breath of life; and man became a living soul" (2:7). Biblically, the human was distinct from the rest of creation, and God gave him not just dominion over the animals but even the image of the deity himself: "Let us make man in our image, after our likeness: and let them have dominion over the fish of the sea, and over the fowl of the air, and

over the cattle, and over all the earth, and over every creeping thing that creep-
eth upon the earth" (Genesis 1:26). This verse would be used into the twenty-
first century to justify both environmental exploitation and the need to protect
and preserve creation.

In the life sciences, this belief manifested itself as the continuation into
the nineteenth century of the ancient Greek idea of the Great Chain of Being.[1]
This concept, originating in Plato and Aristotle, imagined the biological world
as a ladder on whose rungs rested the various classes of plant and animal, each
step more complex than the rung beneath it. At the bottom were amoebas,
bugs, and so on. Higher up we find the reptiles and birds, then mammals, until
at the apex of earthly creation we find the human being. The Chain was viewed
as a fixed hierarchy on which stood unchanging species on a young and
unchanging earth, just as God had made them in the six days of creation back
on October 23–29, 4004 BCE, as famously calculated by the learned Bishop
James Ussher in 1658. (Sir John Lightfoot, in 1644, had reached the same conclusion but added that creation occurred at nine in the morning.) Any fossils
in the ground were simply the unfortunate victims of Noah's flood.

In the traditional view, Man, the Master of Creation, governed the earth,
around which moved the heavenly bodies, beyond whose farthest reach sat the
throne of God. These were the realms of the blessed and the angels, moving
ever upward toward more blissful heavens until one reached the Godhead — or
at least that's how Dante and Milton imagined it. Thus was all creation bound
together in a single system, stretching from the lowest amoeba straight to the
highest power, God himself. This traditional belief, with variations based on
geography and religion, governed much of Western thought from Plato through
the Enlightenment.

The early researchers into the ways of the world traditionally believed
themselves working within the tradition of philosophy, following Aristotle,
who conducted early investigations into the natural world. They were known
as natural philosophers until 1833, when at the request of the Romantic poet
Samuel Taylor Coleridge, the philosopher of science William Whewell coined
the term "scientist," which symbolically announced that the field of science
had moved out of philosophy and into its own professional domain.

Falling to Earth

Beginning with the Enlightenment and continuing through the nineteenth
century, Western philosophy and science undertook a dramatic reappraisal of
the place of humanity in the cosmic scheme. As we have already seen, Enlightenment skeptics like David Hume and Voltaire assailed religious belief and
challenged church dogmas. Hume famously sought to refute the Argument
from Design, which religious believers held (and still hold) proves the existence

of God through evidence of his design. The complexity and beauty of the earthly world was, they said, like finding a watch in a field. It simply implied the idea of a divine watchmaker. Hume said that this was not so, and even if there were design it implies nothing about the designer, let alone that he is the Christian God. But it was advances on the scientific front that posed the greatest challenge to the traditional view of humanity's place in the universe.

The first scientific attack on the traditional world-view came from the discovery that the Earth was much older than 4004 BCE. Geologists in the eighteenth century gradually came to understand that the layers of rock buried in the ground represented a record of the conditions on Earth in ages past, and they soon uncovered curious fossils within the layers they unearthed. If Noah's flood had deposited them all, surely the animals should be all mixed up and jumbled. But this was not so; there were different species in different layers, and the largest animals did not sink to the bottom as the flood theory predicted. The first response to this shocking news was to postulate multiple creations, of which humanity was the last and most perfect.[2] The discovery of dinosaurs in the early nineteenth century (formally so named by Richard Owen in 1841) posed another problem, since the great "lizards" were clearly no longer living, challenging the supposition that Earth's species were fixed and unchanging.

Another view of the natural history of the Earth was obviously needed to account for the evidence each turn of the spade uncovered, and some of the period's best minds went to work developing a new theory. Between 1740 and 1820, Maupertuis, de Maillet, Buffon, Diderot, Erasmus Darwin, Lamark, and E. Geoffrey St. Hilaire, among others, all proposed variations on the idea that life had *evolved* rather than been created instantly in its present form.[3] The gist of these thinkers' theories was that animal types could be classified by their similarity to one another, and the degree of shared traits clearly implied that the species had a biological relationship to one another. These ideas, unfortunately, were not accepted in their own time both because of the strength of traditional views and because of the lack of a workable mechanism to account for the method by which one species could give rise to another. Lamark famously argued that parents could pass acquired traits on to their children, so that a giraffe straining to reach higher leaves would pass on its neck strain to its children, who would have longer necks. The theory failed when such changes could not be observed in experiments. Erasmus Darwin, Charles' grandfather, understood that species were not fixed and intuited from his study of animals that similar species likely emerged from a common ancestor, and from this he proposed the basic outline of what would become the theory of evolution, including for the first time a role for sexual selection. He believed species progressed from simple organisms like microscopic sea shells to complex, and he added the Latin inscription *e conchis omnia* (everything from shells) to his coat of arms in honor of this idea. His massive work, *Zoonomia* (1794), outlined his belief in evolution, a belief he passed on to his grandson, who would provide the scientific basis for the current evolutionary theory.[4] He was viciously attacked by the Anglican Church, which considered the idea heretical.

The story of Charles Darwin is by now familiar. When sailing on board the *Beagle*, Darwin had occasion to view the diversity of life on Earth, recognized how animals were well adapted to their ecological niches, and came to understand how evolution via natural selection could best explain the patterns he found in nature. Darwin's key insight was the role of natural selection, which produced differential reproduction; that is, individuals exhibiting traits that better adapted them to the environment were more likely to reproduce, so over time their offspring would outnumber those less adapted, thus yielding changes in the overall makeup of the species.

With the publication of Darwin's *The Origin of Species* in 1859, the emerging scientific establishment was confronted with a theory of evolution that both accounted for observations and proposed a workable mechanism to explain changes, something other evolutionary theories lacked. More importantly, and more devastatingly, Darwin for the first time divorced evolution from the old idea of progress, breaking the Great Chain of Being. In the new evolution there was no "higher" or "lower" or inexorable progress toward divine "perfection." Instead, there was only "change." This disturbed nineteenth century minds more than any other aspect of evolutionary theory, for at a stroke it divorced humanity from God's special creation and it reduced, if only by implication, humans to merely one among many animals, not even worthy of the title of the highest being. As Darwin summed it up in the famous conclusion to his great work,

> Thus, from the war of nature, from famine and death, the most exalted object which we are capable of conceiving, namely, the production of the higher animals, directly follows. There is grandeur in this view of life, with its several powers, having been originally breathed into a few forms or into one; and that, whilst this planet has gone cycling on according to the fixed law of gravity, from so simple a beginning endless forms most beautiful and most wonderful have been, and are being, evolved.[5]

Over the next twenty years, leading scientists came to adopt the theory of evolution, swayed by the mass of evidence and the broad explanatory power of the theory. More traditional forces, such as organized religion, denounced the theory and spent a great deal of time and energy attempting to refute it. The battle between "Darwinism" and "creationism" raged throughout the closing decades of the nineteenth century, and indeed it continues under other names ("Intelligent Design" most recently) down to this very day. Critics contended, not without reason, that evolution removed God from the equation and promoted atheism. Was man to be merely one of the beasts, a talking animal and nothing more? Even Darwin ducked the question at first, leaving humans out of *The Origin of Species* and turning to them only later in *Descent of Man* (1871).

It would be almost a century until believers in evolution outnumbered creationists world-wide,[6] though never in the United States.

For the Victorians coming to terms with Darwin's theories, the broad explanatory power of the concept of evolution was a major sea change in thought. Over time, evolution would become the most important theory in science and give rise to the rapid and dramatic advances of twentieth- and twenty-first–century biological and medical science. But for early evolutionary thinkers, Darwin's idea that competition for reproductive advantage was the primary drive pushing species toward change led to the conclusion that nature was inevitably hostile and adversarial, that Darwinian survival of the fittest implied that aggression and violence were the hallmark of the natural state (what Alfred, Lord Tennyson had called nature "red in tooth and claw"[7]). This endless competition for survival implied that humans, as one of the animals, were also driven inexorably to seek bloody and violent advantage unless civilization could somehow restrain them. It was, to many, a horrific idea.

Support for the theory came in the form of fossils that seemed to show transitional forms between monkey and man: Neanderthals, discovered in 1856; Java Man (*Homo erectus*) in 1891; and Piltdown Man in 1912. The last in this list was widely accepted as a human ancestor "still ascending only very gradually from the subhuman," as H. G. Wells put it in his *Outline of History* (1920),[8] until 1953, when investigations revealed that the Piltdown fossil was a hoax made up of a human skull and a chimpanzee jaw, and not very old ones or a very good hoax at that.[9] Opponents of evolution hailed the hoax as proof that scientists manufactured evidence and ignored frauds to support their theories, while scientists pointed out that science itself detected and publicized the hoax. Nevertheless, the hoaxer — never conclusively identified* — sidetracked evolutionary theory for decades.

Evolution had gained widespread scientific acceptance by the turn of the twentieth century, but religious conservatives lobbied for laws forbidding the teaching of anything other than Biblical creation in public schools. In 1925 John Scopes was put on trial for teaching evolution in a Tennessee classroom in violation of one such law. He was found guilty in the famous "Monkey Trial," and although the religious viewpoint was made to look ridiculous, bans on evolution would remain in place until 1968.

Groping Toward Heaven

If evolutionary theory seemed to drive humanity back down into the dirt, advances in medicine and technology prodded humans upward to seize the

---

Those suspected of planting the fake fossils include Charles Dawson, the discoverer of the fossils; Arthur Smith Woodward, the geologist who named Piltdown Man; Martin Hinton, a British Museum clerk who kept stained bones in a box; and even Arthur Conan Doyle, the creator of Sherlock Holmes.

trappings of divinity. Benjamin Franklin may have been the first to harness the power of lightning, but electricity quite literally electrified the scientific establishment. Michael Faraday made important discoveries about electric properties. In Italy, Luigi Galvani began experimenting with the application of electricity to frogs' legs, learning that in doing so he could make their muscles contract. In fact, sufficiently large doses of electricity could even stimulate the muscles of the recently deceased to exhibit lifelike contractions. In theory, at least, it seemed as though the newfound power of electricity might hold the key to the resurrection of the dead. The idea, of course, is not so far-fetched, since modern defibrillators essentially revive the dead by jolting their hearts with electricity. In other words, it became theoretically possible to bridge the gap between living and dead tissue and thus to break the veil between life and death.

The medical profession became increasingly professionalized, moving away from superstitions, blood-letting, leeches, and herbs toward a more sophisticated and experiment-based form of inquiry, producing remarkable advances. Doctors were increasingly able to save lives rather than merely mitigate the conditions of death. The discovery of ether made surgery less risky, as did the late nineteenth century discovery of hygiene's positive effects retarding the spread of illness. Louis Pasteur found a way to make liquids safe by boiling them, and the inklings of germ theory gradually coalesced. Humans would become masters over the power of life and death, or so it seemed.

Elsewhere, scientific progress made great strides through the nineteenth century. The invention of the telegraph and the rapid development of the world's railroad networks tied together people as never before. Industrialization had made manufacturing more efficient and brought more consumer products to market. Explorers charted the farthest reaches of the globe, from Captain Cook's voyages through the Pacific to Stanley's treks through darkest Africa. These adventurers came, they saw, and they conquered, adding vast tracts of the Earth's surface to the European empires and to the United States. Between 1750 and 1900, the states of Europe and the United States gobbled up around two-thirds of all land. America doubled in size, and doubled again. The Russian Empire spread from St. Petersburg straight to the Pacific and into Alaska. The British and French empires competed to dominate Africa and Asia, and Britain eventually became the single largest empire in world history, controlling at its height nearly fourteen million square miles—twenty-five percent of the Earth's land surface—and almost a quarter of the world's population, 444 million people.[10]

Freedom, too, appeared to blossom. Revolutions yielded concessions to democracy in Europe, and by century's end most European states had some form of representative government, if only in name. Slavery was banished— in the British Empire in 1833, in the Russian Empire (under the name serfdom) in 1861, and in the United States in 1867. Women generally gained new rights to hold and inherit property, and agitation for women's suffrage even made it seem possible that women would get the vote, as they did after World War I. Literacy blossomed, and a mass media began to form. For the first time, the majority of people had a literature to call their own, albeit in the form of penny newspapers, "penny-dreadfuls" and dime novels. They were cheap, they were sensational, and they were effective. With an audience beyond the educated elite, the writing profession flourished.

The optimism of the era was perhaps best exemplified by the great Exhibitions of progress held throughout the century — in Victoria's London, in Napoleon III's Paris, in Franz Joseph's Vienna, and finally in the United States: the World's Columbian Exposition of 1893. Famed as the "White City," the Chicago exposition summed up the best in science, industry, and architecture. It was here that Henry Ford demonstrated the first automobile, and its tremendous neo–Gothic exhibition halls were aglow with the blazing light of the first large-scale application of electrification, exemplified in the Palace of Electricity. The experience, said one observer, was overwhelming: "I saw so many wonderful things I hardly know what I liked most, and everything is so confused in my mind I hardly know now what I did see."[11]

A shining citadel of progress, the White City was built at the Columbian Exposition of 1893 to showcase the emerging world of science and technology thought to usher in a century of peace, prosperity, and technological progress. For many, it was their first experience of electricity, which lit the city brilliantly into the night (Library of Congress, Prints and Photographs Division, LC-USZ62-104795).

This great landscape of Progress signaled that the world was headed for a utopia of perfection and glory. Yet this was also the period that gave us the defining classics of the horror genre: *Frankenstein, Dracula, Dr. Jekyll* and *Mr. Hyde,* and more. One might pause to wonder why this golden era produced so much horror literature, but beneath the shiny veneer of the Gilded Age and the *Belle Époque,* darkness was beginning to gather. It manifested itself in bizarre and increasingly brutal violence both in the real world and in horror fiction as villains both fictional and real attempted to deal with the rapidly changing world emerging from the shadows of the Enlightenment.

Horrors of the Real World

Medical knowledge, for one thing, did not come free. Prior to the eighteenth century, British medicine was largely confined to external treatments and anatomy was thought superfluous to such work. From the eighteenth century on, however, doctors in training needed cadavers for their work, since anatomy lessons required anatomy on which to practice. As the ranks of doctors grew with advances in medicine, the number of bodies needed for dissection quickly outstripped the available supply. The British government turned over the bodies of hanged criminals for public dissection so "further terror and peculiar infamy" would accompany a death sentence.[12] However, this was not enough, leading to one of the period's most morbid scandals, the "resurrection men," whose grisly crimes inspired Robert Louis Stevenson when he turned his pen to horror.

It may seem odd to us that many people, in an era when executions were still conducted in public, were dreadfully afraid of dissections. But so it was. The resurrection men (also known as body snatchers or ghouls) operated in the mid–eighteenth century and into the nineteenth. Often they were medical students, but some were mere profiteers. They patrolled the graveyards at night and dug up freshly buried corpses, selling the bodies to unscrupulous doctors for dissection. By the nineteenth century, rival gangs were competing for the job.[13] Aggrieved relatives guarded their beloved dead, and cemeteries became like fortresses, complete with iron gates and even "primitive land mines."[14] In response, the body snatchers began to steal corpses from undertakers or to pose as relatives to claim bodies for their own purposes. When the supply of corpses ran low, the resurrection men occasionally made their own corpses through homicidal means. The confession of two body snatchers, William Burke and William Hare, that they had murdered seventeen people to sell for dissection, a process called "burking" in Burke's honor, prompted the government to act in 1832, granting physicians the right to any corpse unclaimed 48 hours after death. In the United States, body snatching continued apace until the early twentieth century, despite legislation to stop it and a scandal when

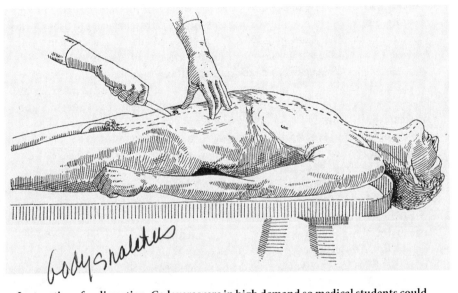

Instructions for dissection. Cadavers were in high demand so medical students could learn the art of dissection, as illustrated in this engraving from an early medical textbook. The need for human bodies led to a lucrative trade in grave-robbing and an ongoing scandal for the medical profession (National Library of Medicine).

the body of President Benjamin Harrison's father was snatched and sold for dissection.

The public was horrified by the whole morbid business, and undoubtedly it contributed to the era's fascination with graves and graveyards. Tombstones of this period are among the largest and most complex carved, and cemeteries became closer to parks where relatives of the deceased could go for a quiet afternoon stroll. Yet as Edgar Allan Poe's story "The Premature Burial" (1844) attests, peace was not the only thing on the minds of cemetery visitors. The nineteenth century also had a mortal fear of being buried alive, and popular literature made frequent report of people so entombed. Inventors developed devices those buried alive could use to signal above ground their living condition, and many made provisions for their bodies to sit out for some days before burial in case the doctors were wrong and they were not dead. The London Association for the Prevention of Premature Burial formed in 1896, and it issued tips on avoiding such an unwholesome end, "the most horrible fate that could possibly befall a human creature," in the words of one Association member.[15] Remember, this was the era that followed the vampire craze, and the reports of undead corpses sitting sentient in their graves may well have brought even sober minds to the conclusion that all who rest in the tomb need not necessarily be dead. Mistakes happen.

The era also saw a sharp rise in the number of sensational murders perpetrated, and many of the new wave of prominent murderers seemed to be playing out frustrations and anxieties about the changing role of women in Victorian society. Beginning in 1837, a number of women (and a few men) were attacked by a cloaked figure said to resemble a giant bat, and in 1845 the agile figure, known as Spring-Heeled Jack for his preternatural jumping ability, murdered a thirteen-year-old prostitute. He was said to shoot blue flame from his mouth, and he became the subject of cheap, sensational paperback novels. Sightings continued until 1904.[16] On the more mundane end of the spectrum, a number of female murderesses did away with husbands, lovers, and rivals; and their dirty laundry aired in court, where rapt audiences sat spellbound at revelations about the manner by which the victims were dispatched and the sexual oddities that prompted the alleged crimes. Marie Lafarge, Madeleine Smith, and Florence Maybrick became virtual household names thanks to the rise of the popular press, when for the first time the great unwashed masses had access to cheap and sensational journalism. As one Victorian era critic put it, "nothing is permitted to screen corpse and coffin."[17] In France, in particular, the crime of *vitriolage* came into vogue, the crime being the throwing of sulfuric acid at a victim. One French town saw sixteen women hurl acid in just a single year. Crime, contemporary observers feared, had become a "contagion" spreading through the female population.[18] Such gruesome but fascinating crimes became the bread and butter of Victorian newspapers, stories known as "sensation-horror."

The newspapers also brought word of a far more disturbing trend, one unique to the industrial, urbanizing world coming into being in the nineteenth century: the serial killer. Famously, in 1888 Jack the Ripper terrorized London and set the pattern for the methodical and violent predators of the next century. Beginning August 31, 1888, a series of mutilated corpses were discovered in London's East End. The killer had violently dispatched his victims, attempting (but failing) to remove their heads and stabbing wildly at their abdomens. The first victim was merely mutilated; the third only killed, as though the killer were interrupted before completing his planned murder. The second and fourth victims, Annie Chapman and Catherine Eddowes, were disemboweled and their uteruses and other organs removed. The fifth and final victim, Mary Jane Kelly, was completely eviscerated on November 9, 1888, her body torn to shreds and barely recognizable as human, her heart stolen.[19]

Police received communications allegedly from the killer signed by a "Jack the Ripper," and newspaper accounts of this forever linked the name to the series of crimes. Later, a box containing a kidney (the organ was alleged to have come from one of the victims) was sent to the police. Though now thought to be hoaxes, such missives lent a gruesome color to the story, which was reported in detail exceeding the most graphic of the penny-dreadful novels. The *Penny Illustrated*, for example, described Kelly's murder this way:

The spectacle that was presented on the door being thrown open was ghastly in the extreme. The body of Mary Kelly was so horribly hacked and gashed that, but for the long hair, it was scarcely possible to say with any certainty that it was the body of a woman lying entirely naked on the wretched bed, with legs outspread and drawn up to the trunk. The ears and nose had been slashed off, the flesh cut from one cheek, and the throat cut through to the bone. In addition to this, one breast had been removed, the flesh roughly torn from the thigh, and the abdomen ripped as in previous cases, several of the organs having been removed from the trunk and laid on the table beside the bed. In addition to the various mutilations thus described there were miscellaneous cuts and slashed [*sic*] about the person of the unfortunate young woman, as though her fiendish assailant, having exhausted his ingenuity in systematic destruction, had given a few random parting strokes before pocketing his weapon and going out into the night.[20]

Papers featuring "Ripper news," unsurprisingly, sold extraordinarily well as even respectable denizens of London indulged in the vicarious thrills of a real-life horror show. Fictional horror would have to compete with reality, and not for the last time. The murders stopped with Kelly, and although the investigation continued, the killer was never caught, and his (or her) identity remains a mystery to this day, despite a vast number of suspects put forward by amateur sleuths.

Only a few years later and on the other side of the world, another serial killer filled newspapers with accounts of his horrific crimes, greater in number and perhaps more heinous than those of the famous Ripper. Dr. Henry Howard Holmes, born Herman Webster Mudgett, considered himself born evil, and his childhood enjoyments include dissecting and cutting up animals he killed himself. When he grew older, he and a medical school friend stole a corpse from the dissecting room to fool an insurance company into paying out for the friend's untimely "death." After medical school, Mudgett, now known by the more refined name of Holmes, became a pharmacist and channeled his profits into a more fully developed mission of evil. At 63rd and Wallace in Chicago, home to the great World's Columbian Exposition of 1893, he constructed a four-story neo–Gothic pharmacy-cum-palace known popularly as Holmes Castle. He turned over the construction staff several times on claims that their work was not to his standards, but in reality he wanted to hide from them the secret rooms and gas jets he was installing throughout the building. When another of Holmes' corpse-switching insurance frauds went wrong, authorities became suspicious and in 1895 began to investigate Holmes further, this time on suspicion of murder.

Inside the Castle, investigators found evidence of torture: a dissecting table, a rack, and worse. Parts of bodies and other evidence was found in lime pits, stuffed in chimneys, and buried under the floor. Holmes, like the resurrection men of old, had sold some of the remains of his victims to medical schools, and he destroyed the rest, so the true number was impossible to tell. Worse, he had apparently brought a number of people in to view the partially

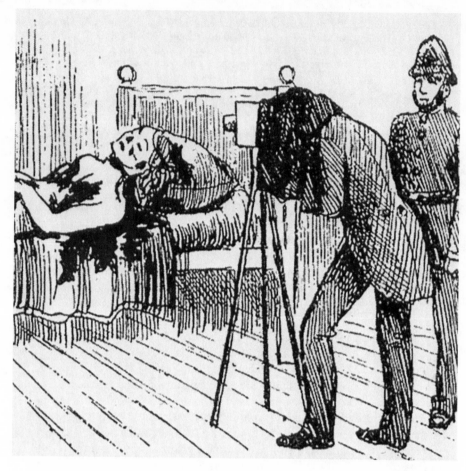

Illustrated Police News. Jack the Ripper murdered his last victim, Mary Jane Kelly, in a particularly gruesome manner. Newspapers, like the ***Illustrated Police News,*** rushed to create gruesome and graphic illustrations to attract readers to their publications with the promise of the horrible.

dissected remains under the pretense that they were corpses from a medical college, but none who saw questioned the pharmacist's actions or informed the police. He had reduced his victims to meat and stripped away any semblance of their humanity, and he did it with an audience. Holmes confessed to twenty-seven murders, but only nine could be confirmed. Just before his hanging in 1896, he retracted his confession and said instead that he had killed only twice, during botched operations.[21] The story was a sensation, and Holmes was dubbed the "Criminal of the Century."[22] He, like Jack the Ripper eight years earlier, had become a criminal celebrity. He is now believed to have killed anywhere up to two hundred people.

The murders in the *fin de siècle* seemed tailor-made to confirm Darwin's theory that humans were merely animals, beholden only to the natural instinct to kill or be killed. A popular misunderstanding of evolution, Social Darwinism, was especially pernicious and held that individuals are in constant competition, and only the best will survive. This was thought to apply on a larger scale to national and racial groups as well. Partially under this influence, colonialism wrought its own horrors on the vulnerable populations the European governments brought under their yoke. Americans and Australians pursued policies designed to reduce or eliminate their native populations, seen now as "unfit." Darwinian theories further reinforced these racist notions, as early supporters of evolution attempted to classify human beings by race, assigning each a slot on the developmental scale. Whole cultures, too, were assigned a place on an evolutionary continuum from savagery through barbarism to civilization, at whose apex stood the white man. Africans, in particular, were seen as the least evolved, closest to the apes, and therefore worthy of exploitation.

No one exploited Africa more heinously that King Leopold II of Belgium, who ruled the Congo Free State, that broad swath of central Africa now known as the Democratic Republic of Congo, as his personal possession and treated the native African population as his personal chattel. To outside appearances, Leopold's Congo was a model of benevolence, with "progress" arriving from Europe in the form of "railroads, steamboats, schools, missions, hospitals, orphan asylums, and trade schools."[23] In fact, Leopold's Congo was a charnel house of murder, slavery, abuse, and atrocities. Soldiers were required to cut off the hands of their victims as proof they completed their missions, and the population was brutally repressed as the organs of state were subverted for the sole purpose of extracting wealth to send back to His Majesty's coffers.[24] Leopold's agents, in the words of the king's official report on the atrocities, "convert themselves into despots, claiming the women and the food; they kill without pity all those who attempt to resist their whims."[25] Joseph Conrad would later immortalize the Congo tragedy as the "heart of darkness."

Across the nineteenth century landscape, the paradox of progress led to a schizophrenic century, one simultaneously defined by progress and by brutality, by science and by savagery. It is therefore unsurprising that this period created the horror fiction icons that ever after defined the genre: Frankenstein's Monster, Dracula, and Jekyll and Hyde. These horror figures attempted to bridge the contradictory impulses of the society in which they were formed, and they attempted to navigate the shifting boundaries between humanity's traditional role as separate from and ruling over nature with its new position as merely one part of a bloody, violent world of competition, exploitation, and fear. No other genre would come closer to providing a modern mythology by which these anxieties could be so fruitfully explored.

5

LITERARY DEVELOPMENTS

Against the backdrop of official progress and secret sins, horror fiction came to play a major role in providing a way to think about and process the vast changes taking place in nineteenth century society, and indeed the changes still occurring today. It was, in a sense, a cleansing nightmare that embodied a culture's fears in order to exorcise them, or at least tuck them safely away between dusty covers. And everywhere in the expanding field of horror fiction, we find the theme of dangerous knowledge.

We have already examined the Discovery Plot, popular in Gothic fiction, wherein the protagonist encounters an unimaginable evil or a supernatural entity and works to persuade others of its existence and to stop it. But in this period we find another plot line achieving prominence. This is Noël Carroll's Overreacher Plot. In many ways the opposite of the Discovery Plot, the Overreacher "embark[s] on the pursuit of hidden, unholy, or forbidden knowledge" which in turn causes evil to be unleashed, "and the consequent destruction is the stuff of the story."[1] The Overreacher is typically a mad scientist, hell-bent (literally, often enough) on transgressing the accepted boundaries of human knowledge to pursue that which ought not to be known. He is Frankenstein seeking artificial life; he is Dr. Jekyll seeking to exorcise evil; he is Dr. Moreau seeking to craft beings in his own image. He is in every case a demigod brought low by hubris and the unquenchable urge to *know*. He is, in essence, science unchained, and he symbolizes fears about the destruction that untethered knowing can bring.

It is important to understand, though, that both plots are concerned with knowledge as a source of horror. The period under discussion here finds both the discovery and overreacher plots in evidence as the heroes (and villains) of popular horror attempt to deal with the unsettling changes new scientific knowledge brought about. In this period we also find a preoccupation with "body-horror," that is, with horror directed toward the physical beings of the protagonist and the supernatural entity: Vampires, walking corpses, evil twins. These are physical terrors which embody in their beings the struggle of humanity to re-imagine its relationship with the animal kingdom and the natural

78

world. These entities are the horrors of evolution, beasts in the literal and metaphorical senses. As we shall see, a parallel development of spiritualist horror would do the same for the human soul. But that would come later.

Our discussion should start with the epitome of the mad scientist novel, *Frankenstein*, which many critics place in the category of Gothic horrors. While the book shares many characteristics with the Gothic writers, and indeed is a Gothic novel, its focus on science and the role of the scientist set it apart from that school. Further, the novel's clear preoccupation with the physical nature of life and death and mankind's place in creation link it to the school of biological horror that emerged in the nineteenth century. Therefore, I have placed *Frankenstein* here as spiritual godfather to the overreaching scientist plot. So we turn now to Mary Shelley's book and the odd dream that started it all.

The Modern Prometheus

As is well known now, Mary Shelley, the author of *Frankenstein; or, the Modern Prometheus*, spent the summer of 1816 in Geneva with her husband, Percy Bysshe Shelley, the famous Lord Byron, and John Polidori, all Romantic poets. The four of them enjoyed hearing German ghost stories while on their tour, and they contrived a contest whereby each would compose a suitably Gothic tale of the supernatural for the others' amusement. Mary Shelley recounted that the three poets' efforts were dreadful, though Polidori's would eventually yield a horror story famous in its own right, as we will discuss later. Shelley herself retired to her rooms on the night of a great thunderstorm and had a most remarkable dream. It was based, as she confessed, on discussions with her friends of bizarre medical experiments and the life-mimicking properties of galvanism which, they mused, might have the power to animate dead tissue and so produce artificial life. In the dream,

> I saw the pale student of unhallowed arts kneeling beside the thing he had put together. I saw the hideous phantasm of a man stretched out, and then, on the working of some powerful engine, show signs of life, and stir with an uneasy, half-vital motion ... looking on him with yellow, watery, but speculative eyes. I opened mine in terror.... On the morrow I announced that I *had thought of a story*.[2]

That story, of course, was *Frankenstein*. Shelley's husband encouraged her in her efforts and at his urging it was expanded from a short story into a full-length novel, published as three volumes in 1818 and again as two volumes some years later, ending in a single-volume revised edition in 1831. As the subtitle clearly implies, the student in question is to be imagined as the modern counterpart to Prometheus, the Titan who gave life and knowledge to humanity at the expense of his own suffering. Unlike the Titan, the student who seized the fire of the gods would see no eventual redemption.

The novel opens in the cold wastes of the Arctic, a land of ice and snow, which symbolically is as far as the Earth can remove one from the warmth we (as warm-blooded mammals, anyway) associate with life. It is a land of death, a place where life seems entirely absent. Here Captain Walton encounters the Creature, whose accented English was remarkable. The Creature has come to seek out its maker, Victor Frankenstein, who is traveling on board Walton's ship. "You seek for knowledge and wisdom, as I once did," Frankenstein says in agreeing to tell Walton the narrative of his woes, and he wishes the knowledge he imparts to Walton will not be the same bane it was to him.[3] With that warning, Victor Frankenstein relates his story.

"Natural Philosophy," Victor says, "is the genius that has regulated my fate," and as such formed the basis of his studies from the earliest days through university. But it is not the "modern system of science" that captures young Victor's fancy but the alchemical investigations of Albertus Magnus, the discoverer of arsenic. Victor, a denizen of Switzerland, becomes obsessed with alchemy and its practitioners and reads deeply of their "secret store of knowledge."[4] He abandons this line for more legitimate science as he matures to adulthood, but the pernicious suggestion of occult lore forever lurks in the back of his mind, coming to the fore when he realizes that modern science appears to conclude prematurely that the miraculous and the occult are *prima facie* impossible. Victor instead focuses his energies on discovering the animating principle by which the mass of muscle and bone that is the body quivers with life. This becomes the purpose of his research, and his downfall.

Through a process that Victor declaims is too dangerous to reveal, he discovers the secret of life and is able to bestow life on dead tissue. Working with corpses culled from dissecting rooms and charnel houses, much as real medical students and resurrection men were then doing, Victor constructs in his "workshop of filthy creation"[5] a patched-together body made of many parts. Though Victor shudders to relate the story, it is not the electric, orgasmic creation of the movies we see here but a quiet and subdued moment when the Creature comes slowly to life. It was the proverbial dark and stormy night, and "by the glimmer of the half-extinguished light, I saw the dull yellow eye of the creature open; it breathed hard, and a convulsive motion agitated its limbs ... breathless horror and disgust filled my heart."[6] He recoiled in instant revulsion at the thing he had made. The creature was misshapen, ugly, horrid, a thing out of Dante or worse. Victor had reached too far, he had dared to seize the power that rightfully belonged to the gods alone; and because he was not himself divine, his creation was but a mockery of God's creation. Victor flees, abandoning his work. The Creature is possessed of superhuman power and speed, despite his inhuman appearance.

As is well known, Victor's rejection impresses on the Creature the accumulated pain of his unnatural parent's hatred. Alone and unloved, the Creature turns his wrath on his creator, destroying those he loves. When Victor encounters the escaped Creature while on a hike in the mountains, the Creature

N.º 37.

Sibly Del.   Ames, Sculp

EDWᴰ KELLY, A MAGICIAN.
in the act of invoking the Spirit of a Desceased Person.
Dʳ Dee's Works.

"Edward Kelly, a Magician." Occult knowledge is often considered a gateway to invoking spirits and resurrecting the dead in horror literature. This illustration shows the Elizabethan sorcerer-alchemist Edward Kelly (1555–1597) calling forth the dead into a semblance of life. Victor Frankenstein studied such alchemists in order to accomplish his own version of resurrecting the dead: the creation of his Monster.

speaks to Victor in carefully modulated and perfectly correct language. He tells Victor of his existential loneliness, of the horror of being alone in the world, isolated from society, driven to the glaciers and mountaintops where he might be alone. He relates his tragic history, how he had to learn to speak and to feed himself and even to refrain from touching fire. He tells, too, of how all but a select few ran in terror from him, and how even those encounters ended in tragedy. Those who did care—a blind man and a child—had a defect that allowed them compassion. The blind man could not see, and the child was too young to fear; in other words, they lacked the knowledge they would need to fear the Creature's image or a lesson on why ugly is evil.

The reader understands and sympathizes with the bastard Creature. His pain is all the worse because we see that his mind is sharp, and indeed every bit the equal to or better than that of his creator. He can learn with remarkable speed, but he is doomed by his appearance to be shunned despite possessing the mental indications of a human soul:

> Was I then a monster, a blot upon the earth, from which all men fled, and whom all men disowned? I cannot describe to you the agony that these reflections inflicted upon me; I tried to dispel them, but sorrow only increased with knowledge…. Of what a strange nature is knowledge! It clings to the mind, when one has once seized on it, like a lichen on the rock…. What was I?[7]

The Creature says that he wished he could have remained ignorant and blissful, but despaired that he could not. Instead, he read books, including *Paradise Lost*, and absorbed their lessons. An Adam raised from the offal, the Creature demands a mate, which Victor agrees to create on the promise the pair will quit Europe. Victor begins work in a remote hut on a Scottish island, far from civilization. Only now does Victor begin to feel ethical qualms about the Bride he is fashioning from dead tissue, for she "in all probability was to become a thinking and reasoning animal [who] might refuse to comply with a compact made before her creation."[8] He wondered, only now, too late, whether he had the right to condemn a fellow being to a life of misery. He leaves his work unfinished, and the original Creature devotes himself to revenge, killing Victor's wife on their wedding night. The subsequent chase finds the Creature and Victor in the Arctic where the story began, and results in the (putative) death of both creator and created. The moral of the story comes from Victor's own lips:

> "Man," I cried, "how ignorant art thou in thy pride of Wisdom! Cease; you know not what it is you say."[9]

Obviously, in *Frankenstein* we can see the working-out of the knowledge theme both within the story and in relation to the developments in science then occurring. We have first Victor's overreaching, and his subsequent punishment for attaining forbidden knowledge. And, externally, we have the novel in relationship to the achievements of nineteenth century science, and the uneasy moral implications of each "advance" in science's understanding of humanity's relationship to nature.

The success of *Frankenstein* spawned a number of adaptations. We will discuss theatrical versions in the next chapter, but here we should mention a Gothic bluebook featuring an anonymous story called "The Monster Made by Man" (1825), which jettisons most of the novel's framework to focus closely on Ernest Wallberg, the Frankenstein character, who dared to play God. Instead of seeking "useful knowledge," Ernest pursues astrology and alchemy, which the author calls "ignorant knowledge." This he uses to make a man from clay, to provide "living proofs of his superior knowledge and power."[10] The story dwells longer on the creation scene than does the novel, and it hammers home the terror of the scientist's search for Faustian knowledge. It was derivative, but effective.

Academics mined Shelley's novel for a great deal of additional subjects for analysis, including, but not limited to, "the spectacle of masculinity," "androgyny," "feminine subversion," and "racism."[11] But, as Victor himself makes clear, the great theme of the novel is knowledge, of reaching beyond what it is acceptable to know. Of course, there are lesser themes in the book; the creation of the monster is a scene of birth, a birth in which the Creature emerges with reason, strength and cunning—traditionally masculine traits—but without the compassion, beauty and grace that are traditionally seen as the woman's contribution to each birth. And of course there are aspects of gender and class, as there are in all books featuring human characters for whom such things are part of their lived experience.

But in the final analysis, what is scary about *Frankenstein* is not gender issues. We do not tremble in fear from its depiction of the role of women or male insecurities. Instead we tremble at the Creature, the physical embodiment of the consequences of exceeding the limits of what is wholesome and good to know. Victor Frankenstein as mad scientist is torn apart by the moral failings of his mission and his uneasy relationship with his Creature. But as Christopher P. Toumey notes, and as we shall see, the mad scientists that followed Frankenstein were increasingly amoral and almost free of any introspection about the results of their experiments.[12] These scientists would only emerge at century's end, however. Before them came a different sort of horror, also rooted in Mary Shelley's 1816 vacation in Switzerland: the vampire.

Enter the Vampire

Though Shelley had dismissed John Polidori's contribution to their ghostly amusements during the summer of 1816, she was being slightly dishonest. Based on the story he told the gathering, Polidori composed a novella which he titled *The Vampyre,* and when it saw publication in *The New Monthly Magazine* in

1819, it immediately caused a stir for it was attributed to Lord Byron's pen. Because of its clever use of Gothic trappings, a present-day setting, and exotic locations across Europe, *The Vampyre* became highly influential and a model for all subsequent vampire fiction. Based on this model, future vampires would not be the ghastly beings of folklore, the pestilence-driven creatures returning to suck the life from their relatives and friends. Instead, they would be aristocratic outsiders closely associated with seduction rather than disease.

The story follows the Discovery Plot, wherein our hero, young Aubrey, slowly comes to realize that the glamorous Lord Ruthven, a European nobleman, is not all that he seems to be. Lord Ruthven is deathly pale and apparently immune to the attentions of London's society ladies. As Aubrey embarks on the Grand Tour of Europe with the mysterious stranger, disconcerting letters arrive informing Aubrey that the ladies back in London have become debauched. Aubrey further notices that beggars who were the recipients of his lordship's charity have also fallen into vice and shame. Upon catching Lord Ruthven with an adulteress, Aubrey takes leave of the lord and proceeds to Greece on his own. There a young Greek girl, Ianthe, relates the tradition of the vampire; but Aubrey is skeptical: "when she found him so incredulous, she begged of him to believe her, for it had been, remarked, that those who had dared to question their existence, always had some proof given, which obliged them, with grief and heartbreaking, to confess it was true."[13] Upon hearing of the fiend's appearance, Aubrey recognizes Lord Ruthven's actual nature. Aubrey falls in love with Ianthe, but alas, she succumbs to the vampire's dread attentions and is left a corpse.

Despite witnessing Lord Ruthven's apparent death, Aubrey comes to realize that the vampire is not dead and is in fact after his sister, whom the monster intends to marry. Aubrey tries to warn her, but she and his family believe him insane. Aubrey dies a shaken man, but his deathbed confession of all he had seen finally convinces his sister's guardians that the threat was real. "The guardians hastened to protect Miss Aubrey; but when they arrived, it was too late. Lord Ruthven had disappeared, and Aubrey's sister had glutted the thirst of a VAMPYRE!"[14]

As too often happens in horror, the authorities understand only too late that their cherished dogmas about how the world works are terribly wrong, and the raving lunatic is the only one who knows the truth. James Malcolm Rhymer adapted the idea of the aristocrat as literal parasite on society for his popular serial *Varney the Vampire; or, The Feast of Blood: A Romance* (1845–1847), which was released in pamphlet installments decorated with dramatic line drawings, costing a penny per copy. (Thomas Preskett Prest was once thought the author, but most now ascribe *Varney* to Rhymer based on his journals.) For that and their gory content, such works became known as the "penny dreadfuls," and *Varney* was the most famous example. It ran around a thousand pages in 237 chapters.

Varney tells the story of Sir Francis Varney, late an aristocrat but more recently a vampire, who during the reign of George II wreaks a terrible vengeance on the members of the Bannerworth family. He cycles through a number of melodramatic adventures that result in death and destruction, and his own near annihilation several times, before he tires of his predatory lifestyle and hurls himself bodily into Mt. Vesuvius to put an end to himself and to his unholy existence. Gothic in its style, sensational in its content, *Varney*'s most important contributions are twofold: First, the vampire is himself a sentient, feeling character driven by his unnatural desires. It is his mental anguish and his inability to rectify his morality with his base, animal hungers that define him, and destroy him. He is a beast, suspended between the animal world and the human. This leads directly to his second contribution; Varney is the first vampire to have fangs, as we see in the story's first suspenseful attack scene:

> The eyes look like polished tin; the lips are drawn back, and the principal feature next to those dreadful eyes is the teeth — the fearful looking teeth — projecting like those of some wild animal, hideously, glaringly white, and fang-like. It approaches the bed with a strange, gliding movement. It clashes together the long nails that literally appear to hang from the finger ends. No sound comes from its lips. Is she going mad — that young and beautiful girl exposed to so much terror?[15]

Note the specifically "animal" nature of the teeth, clearly linking Varney with the atavistic horrors lower down the Great Chain of Being. Also of note is the author's insistence in the 1847 preface to the bound copy that Varney was "real" and that his death was attested in the "public prints for the year 1713."[16] This harks back to the Gothic fetish for historicizing their horrors.

A tighter and more focused story was J. Sheridan LeFanu's novella *Carmilla* (1872), which offered an interesting twist on the emerging vampire myth. This time the aristocratic parasite was a woman. Set in a quiet region of Austria-Hungary, the province of Styria, the story follows the Discovery Plot with strong echoes of Polidori's *The Vampyre* crossed with *Varney*. Published in three issues of *The Dark Blue*, the story tells of a young, half–English girl name Laura, who lives in a great rural *schloss*, or castle, near the ruined village of Karnstein, and who had a dream at age six of being bitten by a beautiful girl. That girl, Carmilla, turns up twelve years later, and both recognize the other from their preternatural experience. Laura's family takes her in and the two girls become close friends until Carmilla begins making odd sexual advances on Laura. When Carmilla's things arrive at the *schloss*, Laura discovers a painting of Mircalla, Countess Karnstein, dated A.D. 1698. The painting is identical in every detail to Carmilla, who claims Mircalla was an ancestor.

Laura begins to have bad dreams about a "sooty-black animal that resembled a monstrous cat" biting her on the chest and her health goes into decline.[17] The situation does not improve until General Spielsdorf arrives at the *schloss* and explains how his niece had died of the same symptoms after meeting a young heiress named Millarca. The general aims to "relieve our earth of certain monsters, and enable honest people to sleep in their beds without being assailed by murderers."[18] The general alone is possessed of the truth about Millarca, Mircalla, and Carmilla. He sets out with Laura to put a stop to the whole business, which the modern reader will have guessed before the end. All three women are the same, the preternaturally preserved vampire countess, using anagrams of her own name as she lures new victims to their doom. LeFanu takes pains to point out the Gothic architecture of Carmilla's ruined village as the general and Laura's father open Mircalla's tomb, decapitate her and burn the body to ashes. Suitably chastened, the formerly innocent Laura admits that "it is difficult to deny, or even to doubt the existence of such a phenomenon as the Vampire."[19] The final chapter of the story relates many of the supposed laws of the vampire, as derived from the non-fiction works of the previous century (see Chapter 1). The rather silly and arbitrary rules (such as limiting vampires to anagrams of their own names) provide a slim hope that knowledge of these quirks can offer some protection against an otherwise unstoppable menace.

A summary does not do justice to the atmosphere of the story, or its subtle psychosexual undercurrents of lesbianism, then known as the "German vice" (Styria was a German-speaking part of Austria-Hungary). In the story, Laura's innocence (= not knowing) of vampirism is equivalent to her innocence of lesbianism, and her gradual education in both schools produces the horror of the story, as she becomes corrupted by unwholesome knowledge no girl should possess. The message of the story, like most discovery plots, is that what you don't know can and will hurt you.

Polidori's *Vampyre*, *Varney*, and *Carmilla* all contributed important aspects to the vampire mythos. Two decades after LeFanu's lesbian blood-suckers, the last and greatest of the nineteenth century beast-men, Count Dracula, would weave together their precedents into the acme of vampire fiction.

Dracula

The first American edition of Bram Stoker's *Dracula* includes a preface that clearly places the work in the hallowed tradition of Gothic declarations that the following story is completely true; it also gives a good indication that the novel makes ample use of the classic Discovery Plot. Stoker says the book is "a history almost at variance with the possibilities of latter-day belief."[20] Of course, such declarations prepare the reader to suspend disbelief (in Byron's phrase) and to accept the reality of the monster about to be revealed. The tone is set by an illustration of Castle Dracula drawn in high Gothic style, complete with pointed arches, set against the moon. However, what follows goes beyond the horrors of Gothic castles, and indeed beyond the earlier examples of vampire stories. *Dracula* gave us perhaps the most complete myth of beast-man ever written.

The outline of Stoker's novel is a familiar one, even to those who have never read it. A British agent by the name of Jonathan Harker travels from England to Austria-Hungary, where he intends to go to the Transylvanian estate of the mysterious Count Dracula in order to facilitate the purchase of several London properties on the nobleman's behalf. The journey from the relative light of civilization — that is, Vienna and Budapest — to the darkness of the farthest recesses of the empire ("one of the wildest and least known portions of Europe"[21]) is a harrowing one, and Harker's trip is plagued by intimations of a looming evil: bad dreams, peasant superstitions, and the like. An old woman gives Harker a crucifix to protect him, and other peasants warn him about the *vrolok*, or vampire. Despite this, Harker travels to Dracula's castle on board the count's spectral carriage, unwilling to believe anything is wrong. Events at the castle gradually impress upon Harker the conviction that Dracula is not wholly

Budapest. The Austro-Hungarian Empire is the setting for a number of horror tales, like *Dracula* and Algernon Blackwood's "The Willows." The empire straddled the divide between Europe and the uncivilized world outside civilization's sway. The Hungarian capital was the last stop on the journey from the sophistication of the modern world toward the untrammeled horrors of the primitive, atavistic areas beyond. In *Dracula,* Jonathan Harker writes that on quitting Budapest, "we were leaving the West and entering the East" (Library of Congress, Prints and Photographs Division, Photochrom Collection, LC-DIG-ppmsc-09476).

a benevolent aristocrat. When Harker realizes he is a prisoner of Dracula, it is too late; the count has left for England where he will soon encounter Harker's fiancée, Mina Murray.

Sinister tidings herald the count's arrival in England, where the ship carrying him arrives at Whitby with all aboard dead. Shortly after, Mina's best friend, Lucy Westenra, begins to succumb to a mysterious wasting illness which her friends are unable to arrest. Her doctor, John Seward, sends to Amsterdam for an expert opinion, and Dr. Abraham Van Helsing arrives with grave suspicions. He is not just a scientist but immensely learned in the ways of the occult, and he immediately understands the gravity of the situation. His heroic attempts to stave off the vampire are in vain, and Lucy succumbs only to rise again as the undead. Van Helsing leads a party including Lucy's fiancé, Arthur Holmwood, to destroy the vampire she has become. Only now do the others believe Van Helsing when they see with their own eyes the truth that should have been before them: Vampires are real. The search is then on for Dracula, who is busy sucking Mina dry even as her now-husband Jonathan, recently escaped from Castle Dracula, is powerless to stop him. Only by working together and utilizing Van Helsing's esoteric knowledge, Mina's psychic link to her corrupter, and the Victorian era's technology can they destroy the count's hiding places in London and drive him back to his native Transylvania. They beat the count's slow passage by ship and by horse-cart by taking a train, and they put an end to his menace where it began, at his dilapidated castle.

The mechanics of the plot do not begin to touch on the rich tapestry of color, imagery, and event that make reading *Dracula* such an engaging experience. Nor does it but hint at the role knowledge plays in driving the book's horror. But before we can look at this knowledge-horror, we must address the most talked-about aspect of *Dracula*: sex. Probably in all horror literature, no other book has garnered such a volume of psychosexual interpretation. For example, John Allen Stevenson viewed *Dracula* as a story of sexual competition between the count and the novel's other men for their women. Stephanie Demetrakopoulos imagined the novel as reflecting a secret desire for sex-role exchange and an uncomfortable feminism. Talia Schaffer, on the other hand, viewed the novel as a chronicle of suppressed homoerotic longing, with Dracula as a nightmare version of Oscar Wilde.[22] Most critics, though, agreed that the vampire's fangs represent the penis, that his bite is an oral regression of normal genital sex, and that the novel deals primarily with the Victorian anxiety about changing sex roles and the repression of sexual desire. This is fine as far as it goes—and there is undoubted sexual energy in the vampire's embrace—but to reduce the whole of *Dracula* (or indeed all vampire fiction) to mere Freudian allegories of forbidden sex is simplistic and misses the themes of horror that permeate and underlie the book's terrors.

It is my contention that knowledge-horror is a significant factor in the horror of *Dracula*, and for a number of reasons. First, there are the dual Discovery Plots that find first Jonathan and then Lucy's companions gradually awakening the horrible revelation of the thing that should not be. We also have the contrast between Dr. Seward and Dr. Van Helsing as both men attempt to use their view of science to understand the horrible events transpiring before them. Lastly, we have the description of Dracula's own mental state, the figure of the monster himself, to contemplate. Of the Discovery Plots, enough has been said in the outline to make them sufficiently transparent. However, to thoroughly understand the differences between Drs. Seward and Van Helsing we must digress for a moment on the meaning of science.

As formally construed, science is a method of inquiry rather than a defined body of knowledge, a way of learning through hypothesizing and testing rather than a set of facts to be learned. However, during the nineteenth century many real-life scientists came to embrace "scientism," the belief that science, as an institution, possessed the answers to all mysteries, or at least the only method whereby such answers could be found. In practice, scientism led to a dogmatic assumption that what is known is all that can be known and further discoveries merely supplement existing knowledge. In *Dracula*, Dr. Seward plays that role.

Seward runs a sanitarium, an asylum for the criminally insane, where he devotes his energies to classifying the various forms of madness that have seized his irrational inmates. To do this, he dictates his notes, especially those regarding a certain Renfield, who is obsessed with eating living beings, into a Dictaphone, a hallmark of Victorian high technology and a precursor to the tape recorder. Seward attempts to be objective in his studies, up-to-date in his technology and methodology, and thoroughly scientific in his experiments, which he conducts on Renfield to see how far he will go to satisfy his blood-lust: flies, spiders, birds, cats, and so on. This almost single-minded devotion to scientific inquiry blinds Dr. Seward to the irrational and atavistic horror gradually overtaking his world, so much so that he does not realize that Renfield has come under Dracula's power, and he cannot believe that Lucy is the vampire's dinner. In fact, before the mystery unfolding around him, Seward confesses to his diary that "I am beginning to wonder if my long habit of life amongst the insane is beginning to tell upon my own brain."[23]

Van Helsing, on the other hand, is the consummate scientist unconstrained by scientism; he is the epitome of pre–Enlightenment science. Van Helsing's chief attribute is his store of occult and esoteric knowledge which he can correlate and put together to understand the patterns around him. When Lucy dies, he tells Seward that if Seward could read Van Helsing's heart at the development, he would pity Van Helsing more than any other soul. Why? Seward asks. "Because I know!" Van Helsing replies.[24] That, in the end, is the crux of the horror. To know is to fear; Dr. Seward does not yet know the threat before him, and so he cannot yet fear.

That Van Helsing is Dutch is no coincidence, since Dutch scientists were leaders in the first wave of science in the sixteenth and seventeenth centuries. Van Helsing's titles, as given in his letter-head, confirm his place in the pantheon of knowledge: "Abraham Van Helsing, M. D., D. Ph., D. Lit., etc., etc.," yet he is a profound believer in the supernatural.[25] These two attributes are not wholly opposed, as modern scientists would have it, for science in the old sense saw the whole world as its field of inquiry (Newton, we remember, was an alchemist), and the supernatural was part of that world. Van Helsing alone can follow the evidence to its logical conclusion and see the truth, for he is science (the method) rather than scientism (the belief). In this, he follows Victor Frankenstein, who is also a scientist in the spirit of pre–Enlightenment experimentation, though with better results.

As Dr. Van Helsing explains, the undead Dracula was himself a scientist during his life as a medieval prince, and it is his pursuit of forbidden knowledge that gave him an unholy immortality, and his great learning has made him a most formidable vampire, one capable of growth, intellectual development, and change:

> I have studied, over and over again since they came into my hands, all the papers relating to this monster, and the more I have studied, the greater seems the necessity to utterly stamp him out. All through there are signs of his advance. Not only of his power, but of his knowledge of it. As I learned from the researches of my friend Arminius of Buda-Pesth, he was in life a most wonderful man. Soldier, statesman, and alchemist—which latter was the highest development of the science knowledge of his time. He had a mighty brain, a learning beyond compare, and a heart that knew no fear and no remorse. He dared even to attend the Scholomance, and there was no branch of knowledge of his time that he did not essay.[26]

As though to drive home the point about the connection between Dracula and unholy knowledge, the Scholomance was, in Transylvanian legend, a school run by the Devil who taught scholars the secrets of nature; that is, they learned a type of science, but the wrong type—one given (erroneously) from authority on high (well, down low) rather than up from the evidence below.[27] And so Dracula is also a product of the superstitious-religious world in which he lived. When he comes to Renfield in the night, he speaks in the words of the New Testament Devil: "All these lives will I give you, ay, and many more and greater, through countless ages, if you will fall down and worship me!"[28] These are the words of the Devil in Matthew 4:9,* and they clearly show Dracula's handicap, for he is tied to the old world of faith, can be wounded by crucifixes, and is subject to their power in a way modern men, who loosed the bonds of religion, are not.

To stop the fiend, Jonathan Harker demands more information from the Dutch professor: "The knowledge may help us to defeat him!"[29] Right he is. Van

---

*"And [the Devil] saith unto him [Jesus], All these things will I give thee, if thou wilt fall down and worship me" (King James Version).

Helsing makes clear that Dracula's powers are great, but his knowledge of them is as yet incomplete, even after centuries, and so he can still be beaten. But, Van Helsing maintains, this is only because Dracula does not yet know his full strength. He is, in many ways, still a "child-brain" unsure of himself. Worse, his knowledge is in many ways frozen in its medieval, superstitious state. This weakness—the imperfection of Dracula's own self-knowledge—is their only chance.

Thus, we have here three types of science: Dracula's science-as-magic, Seward's science-as-dogma, and Van Helsing's science-as-method-of-inquiry. Only one of these three can succeed, and in the end it is Van Helsing's version that proves its worth, for it is the only one large enough to encompass the whole range of learning: historical, empirical, logistical, and even esoteric. Dracula cannot adjust to the modern, and Seward (not to mention the other men) only reluctantly comes to embrace the truth when it is undeniable. Van Helsing alone follows the evidence and draws conclusions based on that evidence.

Other Monsters

In his rather catholic empiricism Van Helsing is not unlike Sherlock Holmes, Arthur Conan Doyle's famous detective, who famously said that "when you have eliminated the impossible, whatever remains, *however improbable, must be the truth.*"[30] For Van Helsing that includes vampires; and Holmes would entertain such a possibility if ever he had reason to suspect it. In a late story, "The Adventure of the Sussex Vampire" (1924), Holmes found a natural and all-too-human explanation for a vampire visitation in an English country home. Doyle, however, was a devout believer in the supernatural, as we shall see in Chapter 7, though he nonetheless perpetuated the Radcliffe tradition of naturalistic explanations for supernatural horrors when he sent his detective out to battle monsters. Holmes's investigation of the spectral Hound of the Baskervilles in the novel of the same name (1901–1902) is probably Holmes's most famous such encounter between rationality and the supernatural. There, a glowing demonic dog haunts Henry Baskerville, and Holmes and Watson manage to track down its earthly origins, including the phosphorus-based paint that gave the dog its glow and the naturalist who employed the hound to eliminate his rival for the Baskerville inheritance.

But these rationalizing tendencies fell at the end of the long tradition of monstrous horrors in the burgeoning horror field. In the last half of the nineteenth century the proliferation of literary magazines and newspapers featuring sensational stories offered increasing space—and increasing demand—for content (often at Christmastime, as per British tradition). This is where Sherlock Holmes found his audience, and as the number of publications increased, a fluorescence of horror fiction resulted. Many of these stories reflected the idea of evolutionary horror in the form of monsters, which sell well in any medium.

Bram Stoker himself contributed several stories to the genre, including *The Lair of the White Worm* (1911) with its title beast, an ancient survival which must be discovered, and then destroyed. In "The Squaw" (1893), tourists shudder at the instruments of torture ancient Germans once used, and an American asks to test out the iron maiden, because "nothin's too terrible to the explorin' mind."[31] Unfortunately a demented cat attacks the German running the mechanism (who "had in him the blood of his predecessors"[32]), inadvertently causing the American's death. A story of Barry Pain's, "The End of a Show" (1901), dealt with a quack who offered "POPULAR SCIENCE LECTURES"[33] helping a monster, presumably a deformed circus freak, escape the pain of living with a non-standard, inhuman body. As we will see in the next chapter, such circus freaks were taken as living proof of evolution's horrors.

Fitz-James O'Brien, once hailed as the successor to Poe, offered an interesting take on the supernatural monster in "What Was It?" (1859). In the story, the narrator questions his ideas about reality when he is confronted with a paranormal creature invisible to the naked eye. The creature is attacking residents in his boarding house, and they fear for their lives. Nevertheless, the judicious application of science allowed the protagonist a measure of control over the unworldly creature. While the other inhabitants of the haunted house panic at the creature's attacks, the narrator understands that the creature has mass and weight, and so cannot be a ghost. He reasons that invisibility is "not *theoretically impossible*" since glass is clear and we can feel the invisible air. Therefore, after incapacitating the creature, the boarders make a cast of it in plaster of Paris, and discover the creature to be a "distorted, uncouth, and horrible" human.[34] O'Brien died in the Civil War, leaving behind only one volume of his collected horror.

The theme of invisibility was picked up by Ambrose Bierce in "The Damned Thing" (1893) in which a spectral animal is found to be very real, but of a color lying outside the spectrum of visible light. Bierce was a witty and crisp writer of horror, and, as we shall see in our discussion of spiritualist horrors, a master of the ghost story.

Monsters of Their Own Making

Not all the monstrous horrors were natural; some found their origins at the hands of mankind itself, which sought to force evolutionary forces forward. In so doing, these tales engage questions about the origins and fate of the human soul, and indeed what makes us human, which is also a major theme of spiritualist horror. Such was the tale of a certain Dr. Jekyll, from the pen of Robert Louis Stevenson, otherwise known for his tales of adventure for boys. Often sick with consumption (tuberculosis), Stevenson devoted much of his energy to creating fantasies like *Treasure Island* and *Kidnapped*. But Stevenson also had a morbid streak, as exemplified by "The Body-Snatcher" (1884), a rather vicious little tale based on the scandal of the resurrection men and what could happen when the body to be dissected is no longer an anonymous commodity. Two years later, Stevenson produced *The Strange Case of Dr. Jekyll and Mr. Hyde*, apparently after experiencing, like Mary Shelley, a deeply impressive nightmare. The novella explored the dark side of human nature, the atavistic, animal self that lies buried within each individual. As an early reviewer put it, "What is worth mentioning, because otherwise a good many people will miss it, is that a noble moral underlies the marvelous tale."[35] That moral, apparently, is that true self-knowledge will lead inexorably to death.

The story of *Dr. Jekyll and Mr. Hyde* (meant, Stevenson said, to be pronounced "Jee-kill") is a tale of an overreaching scientist who begins his quest for knowledge with the best of intentions, only to release forces that eventually fall far beyond his control and destroy him. In this he is like Victor Frankenstein, but the object of his experiments is not an external projection but an internal demon. As is well known, the kindly Dr. Henry Jekyll wants to purge the human mind of evil, and to do so he works on a potion that will separate what is good in a man from what is bad, with the understanding that the bad could be suppressed or eliminated. In Jekyll's view, evil is synonymous with passion, desire, violence, and license. Instead, his potion releases his darker side, giving it physical form as Jekyll transforms into Edward Hyde with each dose. This dark self is dwarfish, misshapen, and ugly. He is also unruly and violent, committing murder and engaging in other criminal acts. "That child of Hell," Jekyll writes before his death, "had nothing human."[36] As the story progresses, Dr. Jekyll loses control over Hyde, who begins to emerge at will. Using the last of his self-control, Jekyll realizes that Hyde must be destroyed, and so both men, who are one, lose their lives to the passions they could not master.

Not surprisingly, the academy has proposed a number of readings for the novella that focus on sexuality. Janice Doanne and Devon Hodges, for example, proposed that the book was a working-out of anxiety about blurring gender roles.[37] A number of scholars are similarly interested in the novel's homosexual implications.[38] However, *Jekyll and Hyde* is often read as a discourse on the Freudian subconscious mind, as represented by Hyde, struggling against its repression by the superego, represented by Jekyll. However, since the unconscious was not proposed by Freud himself until 1900, and not available in English until later, it is not precisely accurate to speak of the novella that way. Instead, I think there is a more subtle reading that incorporates the subconscious explanation into the framework of biological horror.

Today we think of the unconscious mind (seat of the passions and drives) as a "primitive" part of the brain, which evolved earlier than our forebrains (the seat of reason) and thus connects us with our ancestral species. In *Jekyll and Hyde* the violent passions of Mr. Hyde and his "evil" nature represent humanity in the state of nature, as depicted by Victorian evolutionary thinkers who followed Hobbes' dictum that primitive life was "nasty, brutish, and short." In his diminutive size, his brute ugliness, and even his hairiness, Edward Hyde is a caveman dragged into the nineteenth century, a throwback to the earliest humans, before civilization had neutered them and tamed their violent urges. He is free, as the cavemen were, but he is also incapable of civilized self-control for his animal nature prevents higher considerations. Though Mr. Hyde is clearly a part of Dr. Jekyll, and a part of all of us, he is also the dormant ancestral form evolution built our civilized selves atop. This is why Jekyll is horrified of Hyde, and also why he can recognize him as an inseparable part of his being, though he needed to think of him as "hellish but inorganic"[39] even unto the last. However, Jekyll must have recognized that civilization is what is inorganic; therefore, it is Jekyll's repression and restraint that is false, not Hyde's animal depravity. The question therefore is, what is the true face of humanity? Are we animals, or self-denying angels, or something in between?

This question is also evident in Oscar Wilde's *The Picture of Dorian Gray* (1891), in which a young man is able to indulge in secret sins by means of a magical painting of himself which displays the signs of his misdeeds and ages in his stead. Dorian can keep his public face flawless and his sins hidden. Exposure would destroy him, and the weight of his burden destroys Dorian's mind, for the burden of maintaining a double life and knowing that which is hidden (including, for Wilde, homosexuality) leads to "the living death of his own soul": mental illness and annihilation.[40] In the end, the painting is restored to "exquisite youth and beauty" while Dorian Gray falls to dust.[41] Once more, the false front of civilization masks deeper passions derived from our human, natural, and animal nature, which the Victorians assumed was evil since it stood against the values of traditional civilization.

These animalistic drives lurking beneath the thin veneer of civilization also animate Joseph Conrad's *Heart of Darkness* (serialized in 1899, in book form in 1902), which takes for its inspiration the savagery King Leopold's agents unleashed on the natives of the Congo, a formerly pristine country whose inhabitants were believed to live in the state of nature before the Belgians came. In Conrad's tale, Marlow, the narrator, travels through the Congo (though it is never specifically named) in search of Kurtz, a white government agent (representing in his ethnic composition "all Europe") responsible for horrific atrocities. Kurtz believed that whites appeared "like supernatural beings" to the natives, and that power could be used for immense good.[42] But acting in the name of civilization, the colonizers have become evil; no one is entirely blameless, and the whole enterprise of imperialism and colonialism is seen to destroy the souls of those involved. Chinua Achebe famously criticized the novel as representing Africa as a place of darkness where civilized white men revert to ancient barbarism, where Africans are mere animals, part and parcel of the primal jungle.[43] Both readings share a similar undercurrent: The primitive within humanity is a threat to the higher developments of so-called civilization, and the natural world, subject to evolutionary forces and red in tooth and claw, is to be avoided for the sake of our souls.

To Become a Man

But what of those souls? In *The Time Machine* (1895), science fiction writer H.G. Wells (1866–1946) imagined a future in which humanity had evolved into two separate species, a civilized, effete race and a brute, animalistic one. The two forces at play in Stevenson's, Conrad's, and Wilde's works here take definite form, with Darwinism providing a sobering explanation for one way the duality within the human soul (and between bourgeoisie and proletariat) could be resolved. Tellingly, the civilized and beautiful race is not the master of this future Earth but is instead food for the bestial race living below the surface. *The Time Machine* was metaphor that applied equally to the dual nature of the human mind and the problems of social class in late–Victorian England. In *The Invisible Man* (1897), Wells told of an overreaching scientist who turns himself invisible, with tragic consequences. As we shall see in Chapter 11, *The War of the Worlds* speculated on an alien invasion and the horrors that come from beyond.

However interesting, much of Wells' work is beyond our horror scope; but among his darker works, Wells contributed one novel that crosses the bright fields of scientific romance, as the genre was then known, to the dark moors of horror: *The Island of Dr. Moreau* (1896).

In the story, Edward Prendick finds himself shipwrecked in the Pacific Ocean somewhere west of the South American coast. He is apparently the sole survivor when he is rescued by a passing ship. Prendick tells his rescuer, Montgomery, that he studied natural history, which his rescuer is pleased to hear, as he too studied biology at college. After the captain tosses them overboard, Montgomery and his oddly bestial assistant bring Prendick to a small island where they are employed, and to which they were bringing a large stock of animals. The master of this island is Dr. Moreau, whom Prendick eventually remembers was once a notorious vivisectionist, cutting and mutilating animals in the name of science until public protest forced him into exile.

On the island, Prendick is haunted by the screams of animals coming from Moreau's labs, and he is increasingly uncertain about the strange, bestial servants employed in Moreau's compound and animalistic creatures wandering the forest, human in shape but "the unmistakable mark of the beast" giving them a pig-like air.[44] The unnatural combination of man and beast perplexes and then frightens Prendick. He meets some of these Beast People and (eventually) figures out that Moreau has made himself a god among them, and enforces a code of humanity upon pain of return to his compound, the House of Pain, for a second dose of vivisection: "Not to go on all Fours; *that* is the

Law. Are we not Men? Not to suck up the Drink; *that* is the Law. Are we not Men?"[45] Moreau adapted the visage and manner of the Old Testament god in his hubris.

Moreau makes Prendick understand that the beasts are the results of Moreau's experiments, creatures molded into the shape of man from the flesh of beasts. They are not the result of the gentle process of natural evolution but the violent seizure of evolution's power (this was before the modern understanding of genetics) by Dr. Moreau, who gave them form and voice, and the Law. Moreau succinctly describes the Overreacher Plot in his explanation:

> I have studied [molding animals into men] for years, gaining knowledge as I go....
> And yet this extraordinary branch of knowledge has never been sought as an end,
> and systematically, by modern investigators, until I took it up...! I was the first man
> to take up this question armed with antiseptic surgery, and with a really scientific
> knowledge of the laws of growth.[46]

Moreau justifies his tortures by appealing to the higher mission of science, and the transient nature of pain and suffering in the face of what can be gained: "A mind truly open to what science has to teach must see that it is a little thing."[47] According to Moreau, both pain and pleasure are leftover sensations from mankind's animal nature, and the evolution he aims to force will take humanity beyond pleasure and pain, and thus beyond good and evil into a pure world of reason and science. He can do this without guilt because the study of Nature "makes a man at last as remorseless as Nature."[48] But it is not to last, for the animal nature cannot be suppressed, and all Moreau's efforts slowly but inexorably revert back to their original natures, the humanity and the reason he bestowed on them sloughed like a snake shedding an unwanted skin.

Moreau's island world begins to unravel when a beast-person kills a rabbit and tastes blood. The reawakened carnivorous instincts cannot be suppressed, and the remainder of the novel is a chronicle of the disintegration of Moreau's dream, beginning with Moreau's own death by one of his creatures and proceeding through the destruction of his labs to the devolution of his creatures back toward the animal forms from which they were made. The veneer of civilization Moreau gave them vanished, their language reverted to grunts, and their bodies fell back to the animal. Prendick, too, feels himself having gone wild, and he comes to understand how transient and fragile our humanity is against the great weight of the animal that lives inside and on whose billion-year-old instincts our brief reign was built.

Therefore the horror is multifaceted and open to many interpretations. Moreau was the overreaching scientists whose pursuit of forbidden knowledge condemns him to oblivion. But the novel is also the story of how the animal, inhuman creatures from which we evolved live on within us. Moreau-as-god dies, just as our knowledge of evolution led many to believe, in Nietzsche's phrase, that "God is dead," and the consequences may well be similar. Without the higher aspirations of religion (or Moreau's hand and Law) giving humanity a certain dignity, we are but animals whose baser instincts have free rein in the absence of divinely sanctioned morality. Yet this is not entirely bad, for while it means the end of the old order, it also frees each creature to find its true nature and escape the pain that repression, conformity, and fear forced on it. It is the ambiguity of *The Island of Dr. Moreau* that makes it so disquieting.

A late echo of this evolutionary horror can be found in Richard Connell's "The Most Dangerous Game" (1924). Here a man finds himself marooned on a desert island where the sadistic big game hunter Gen. Zaroff rules. Zaroff is bored by hunting and feels only humans are worthy prey. The narrative explores how Rainsford, the castaway, deals with being hunted like an animal. Rainsford eventually proves to Zaroff that he is no beast and outwits the general at his own game. But in the process, both men lose a bit of their humanity.

The Horror of Science

Susan J. Navarette argued in *The Shape of Fear* that Victorian horror fiction paralleled the development of Victorian science. Just as the highest form of science sought a pure and impersonal objectivity that removes the scientist from emotional involvement, death and self-negation are the inevitable result of scientific hubris in the Victorian horror story.[49] In both, the scientist or seeker of knowledge loses himself, a sacrifice on the altar of wisdom. We see this in *Frankenstein*, *Jekyll and Hyde*, and *Moreau* wherein the scientists meet their ends at the hands of the monsters they raised up but could not control. We see it, too, in *Dracula* where the vampire-alchemist's reward for his demonic knowledge is undeath, and eventually destruction; and also in the loss of identity experienced by those seeking to destroy Dracula. As the book's final note makes clear, the child whom Mina finally gave birth to subsumes the identities of the men who fought to save Mina and avenge Lucy. In each case, the price of knowledge is self-destruction, a Faustian resonance of that archetypical overreacher's damnation.

Victorian evolutionary horror tried to explore the issues raised by Victorian evolutionary science, and it attempted to find a path back toward a more comfortable world order where man and beast were more distinct. However, such a world could no longer exist, for even the destruction of liminal figures as Dracula or Hyde, or Dr. Moreau, who bridge that man-beast divide, cannot put right what science has undone. Clearly, in this school of horror the seeker of knowledge encounters only terror and pain, the sole reward for probing nature's secrets. The message seems clear: Do not trespass on those realms of knowledge forbidden to you.

As we shall see, that message did not quite carry over into the era's horror arts.

6

HORROR IN THE ARTS

While the late Victorian period spawned what were arguably the most important and best-loved horror novels, the period's performing and visual arts had plenty of catching up to do before they would reach the same level of depth and sophistication as their literary cousins. The period's arts were still based primarily on the written word, and it would only be with the coming of film in the succeeding periods that horror arts would truly come into their own. For now, horror art was usually produced to supplement existing literary works or to adapt them for new audiences. However, since biological horror and its concomitant physical terrors were inherently dramatic, and ripe for depiction in the arts, this generally took the form of illustrations for horror stories and novels or dramatizations thereof. Both were popular throughout the nineteenth century, and the most popular works received multiple stage treatments.

The performing arts, though, sometimes featured some original horrors, including that marvel of marvels, the traveling circus freak show, whose mentally and physically disabled inhabitants were put on display for the astonishment and horror of those who came to see them.

Monsters of the Midway

Frankenstein had spoken of a man-made monster, whose shattered visage and misshapen features were repulsive and shocking. *Dr. Moreau* tells us of the disgust its narrator felt before the scientist's beast-men. Stories of such creatures, though, were not only exciting; they were also pleasurable to read. Public infatuation with the deformed had a long pedigree in the western imagination. Dwarves and midgets, for example, were frequent entertainers at royal courts throughout the Middle Ages. Edgar Allan Poe wrote a horror story about one such dwarf's horrible revenge in his tale "Hop-Frog" (1849). Extremely tall people, too, were objects of wonder, as were three-legged people, conjoined twins, hydrocephalic individuals, the limbless, and other congenitally abnormal persons. In the sixteenth century such people were considered signs of God's will, which in the academic Latin of the age was rendered as *monstrum*, for sign, yielding the word monster. By the seventeenth century, these monsters were exhibited at fairs, and in the eighteenth they were objects of scientific interest as well as public amusement.[1] During the nineteenth century, as evolutionary theory gained ground, human oddities became living proof of the changes that Darwin proposed were responsible for the evolution of new species. Queen Victoria's accession was marked with a Hyde Park Fair freak show, and the shows continued through the century with increasing popularity. And unlike the royal entertainers, anyone could go and see these horrors at the traveling circus.

The freak show was easy to find, advertised with large banners promising extreme bizarreness that waits within. The show in P. T. Barnum's traveling circus was the archetype. Under its tents, the American viewer could view animal acts, jugglers, clowns, and so on. But the audience also saw non–Western peoples displayed as ethnological specimens, on par with the caged animals on exhibit. Barnum's intention was to display a "Congress of Nations" wherein the most outrageous and grotesque specimen of each non–Western people ("Cannibals, Nubians, Zulus, Mohammedans, Pagans, Indians, Wild Men," etc.) would be displayed for the amusement of his Anglo-American audiences.[2] This spilled over and eventually became part of the infamous freak show, featuring such wonders as Jo-Jo the Dog-Faced Russian Boy, the Hairy Family of Burma, Tom Thumb (actually Charles Stratton) the midget, and others. They were displayed alongside artificial oddities like a patched-together Fejee Mermaid, made of spare animal parts sewn together and displayed since 1843 as the real deal.

As Matthew Sweet pointed out, Victorian freak shows were careful to frame their exhibits in terms of science and education. Advertisements pointed to the benefits of the exhibitions for "All who desire Amusement with Instruction" and "All who wish to know and understand Nature."[3] (This was for a talking fish.) With the coming of evolutionary theory, the freak show took on an air of scientific rationality as all walks of Victorian life were encouraged to come and see the bizarre and outrageous specimens that confirmed the veracity of *The Origin of Species*, for did not these oddities prove that animals and humans developed by chance and natural selection? The audience was also encouraged to poke them with sticks, for an added fee.

Beginning in 1880, a Southeast Asian woman named Krao Farini was displayed as the Missing Link between man and ape, flesh-and-blood confirmation of the truth of Darwin's evolutionary speculations. The publicity materials for an 1887 showing of Farini claimed that "The usual argument against the Darwinian theory that man and monkey had a common ancestor has always been that no animal has hitherto been discovered in the transmission state between monkey and man."[4] Farini, with a hairy body and cheek pouches for carrying food, was "living proof" of this sought-after connection.[5] Similarly,

Freak show. Rare conditions and birth defects provided entertainment for generations of sideshow patrons, some of whom would pay extra to poke them with sticks. This poster shows a number of freaks on exhibit in one of the shows descended from P.T. Barnum's: An armless man, a dwarf, a bearded lady, and so on (Library of Congress, LC-USZC4-3333).

Julia Pastrana, known as the Nondescript, was also displayed as the Baboon Lady, large as a gorilla and just as hairy. It was implied that she was the sad result of a coupling between a human and a monkey in Mexico. So popular was the Baboon Lady that after her death in 1860, her body was continuously displayed at freak shows and fairs until 1973, when it entered the vaults of Oslo's Institute of Forensic Medicine.[6]

The greatest of the Victorian freaks was probably Joseph Merrick, better known as the Elephant Man, who likely suffered from neurofibromatosis (formerly thought to be elephantiasis), a disease that caused abnormal bone growth, giving him a hideously deformed appearance. His head was a mass of bone and protuberances, and the right side of his body was significantly impacted by his greatly enlarged bones. The British showman Tom Norman put him on display, and he earned a good living from exhibiting his deformities to politely aghast audiences. He later ended up in Dr. Frederick Treves'

Whitechapel Hospital (in the neighborhood Jack the Ripper terrorized) where he was subject to display and examination by eager medical students. He died in 1890.

But the display of human oddities was not confined to those that confirmed evolution; those who rejected Darwin's views found plenty to support their position as well. Biblical artifacts were in great demand, and in 1840 an alleged fossilized human skeleton was held up as proof of the Holy Bible's account of Noah's Flood destroying the wicked.[7] More famous was the strange case of the Cardiff Giant, alleged to be the fossilized remains of a Biblical giant killed off by the Flood. The Giant was dug out of the ground near Cardiff, New York, in 1869, and a great debate arose on whether the artifact was a petrified giant or a statue recently carved. Many learned men lined up on either side of the debate, until it was finally discovered that a local atheist named George Hull carved and buried the statue to demonstrate that the Bible should not be taken literally. Even after a Yale paleontologist declared it fake and Hull confessed his hoax, the public still came to see it. P. T. Barnum tried to lease it, and when the deal failed, he had a replica made and displayed it as the genuine fake instead. A number of other fake giants continued to plague the late nineteenth century in imitation of the first. The original fake is still an attraction at the Farmer's Museum in Cooperstown, New York.[8]

Horrors in Art

The freak show's advertisements often featured lurid and misleading pictures of the horrors awaiting visitors within. These paintings drew on an emerging and burgeoning artistic trade in horror images, one driven in large part by the development of illustrations added to printed text. Of immediate note are the black-and-white illustrations that accompanied the lengthy horror serial *Varney the Vampire*. The illustration on the front page depicts a caped skeleton figure with arms outstretched leering over the supine body of a young girl. Both appear to rise from a tomb, and the whole scene is surrounded by bat-winged demons. The illustration accompanying the first page of the story shows a bearded, emaciated vampire violently pulling a supine young woman from a bed, his hand on her breast and his mouth lurching for her throat. The scene occurs against a black backdrop with the woman bright white and the vampire only slightly less so. Other drawings are equally atmospheric and make good use of shadows and contrast to heighten the suspense and excitement of their subjects. However, in many places the images appear rushed, and they lack the polish of fine art. They were meant as disposable art for a penny publication, to be put down as quickly as it was picked up.

Many other novels and stories carried Gothic illustrations of this style, but no illustrator was more famous or more justly heralded for his exquisitely

Doré illustration of the *Brazen Serpent*. Gustave Doré's illustrations utilized Gothic and Romantic motifs to give form to demons, ghosts and other things that go bump in the night. Here we see Doré's painting (engraved by Alphonse François) of Moses placing a bronze serpent on a pole to heal those bitten in the attack of serpents sent by God in Numbers 21:6 (Library of Congress, Prints and Photographs Division, LC-USZ62-106980).

wrought images of the horrific and the bizarre than the French engraver Gustave Doré (1832–1883), best known for his illustrations of Dante's *Divine Comedy* and Milton's *Paradise Lost*. After modest success in Paris, Doré moved to London where his illustrations won popular acclaim but poor critical reception. He prepared illustrations for more than two hundred books, and most of these illustrations were wholesome, and even holy. However, a good number explored the dark and the horrific in great detail, and these are the best-remembered. He also illustrated Poe's most famous poem, "The Raven." In one particularly striking image, Doré depicted the figure of the Grim Reaper, a shroud-clad skeleton with a scythe, sitting atop the Moon while the raven flies in front. In the final images, we see ghostly figures hovering before a darkened mansion while the raven flies (again) before the Moon. In the last image, the poem's narrator lies crumpled on the floor while the raven's shadow envelops him.

Better known are Doré's depictions of scenes from *Inferno* and *Paradise Lost*. Here Doré makes ample use of Gothic conventions in depicting great towering landscapes of jagged rocks and deep shadows. His demons are monstrous

The Vampire by Philip Burne-Jones. The painting *The Vampire* was one of the earliest to feature a blood-sucking creature of the night, and one of the first to make the monster a woman. The painting influenced Rudyard Kipling to write a poem on the subject, which in turn inspired a number of plays and early movies about "vamps," non-supernatural women who used men for sex and money.

beings, complete with horns and great bat-wings. The icy pit in which Satan is held fast is depicted with cold precision, and the expert use of light and reflection makes the viewer feel a chill. The icicles are so convincingly depicted that in places it feels as though one could reach into the picture and snap one off.

The monochromatic etchings of Max Klinger, a German Symbolist, explored the subjectivity of experience. In *Abduction* (1881), Klinger depicted a pterodactyl breaking out of a man's bedroom and stealing a woman's glove, which is said to represent the man's sexual longings and desires. It was part of a series called *The Glove* which dealt with dreams and sexual frustration. Klinger believed that the stark black-and-white of his etchings was the perfect medium for exploring dark and repressed impulses.[9]

Philip Burne-Jones, the son of the Pre-Raphaelite painter Edward Burne-Jones (1861–1926), brought the era's horror fiction to the realm of painting. *The Vampire* (1897) depicts an unconscious or sleeping man draped across a lush bed. His arm dangles limply off the bed's edge, indicating his helplessness. A white-clad woman is leaning into the vulnerable man, and she wears an expression of lust and desire. Her shadow fills the back wall. No fangs or bloodsucking is shown, but the image neatly reverses the classic image of the male vampire violating a supine female (as in the *Varney* illustrations), and there is little doubt as to the female figure's purpose. Obviously, there is a whole world of psychosexual interpretation open in the painting. *The Vampire* was displayed at the New Gallery in London, and it is unusual both for the female vampire, a rarity since *Carmilla*, and for the depiction of a vampire, since creatures of horror were rare in serious Victorian art, though mythological monsters and historical violence were quite common. (An Edvard Munch painting known as *Vampire* [1893] is actually a dark and atmospheric take on "love and pain," in which a woman is embracing a man, not sucking his blood.) Another vampire image from the period was Estienne Csok's *The Vampires* (1907), which depicts ravenous naked women.

Burne-Jones's *The Vampire* inspired a rather dull poem by Rudyard Kipling, also called "The Vampire" but which lacks any direct otherworldly menace implied by the painting. That, in turn, bequeathed a play by Porter Emerson Browne, *A Fool There Was*, which premiered in 1909. That play followed Kipling in replacing the supernatural vampire with a sexually voracious woman, producing suitably tragic results for the husband she leads astray. The big sensation of the production was the graphic depiction of the husband's suicide.[10] The story was filmed in 1915 during the wave of "vamp" films, named for the life-draining women in them, and yielding the immortal line, "Kiss me, my fool."

Horror on the Stage

Plays like *A Fool There Was* were a dime a dozen in the late Victorian world, but true horror was harder to come by. Five years after the publication of *Frankenstein*, it was adapted for the stage in the notable R. B. Peake play, *Presumption; or, the Fate of Frankenstein*, the first of many such interpretations. The play specifically links Frankenstein to Faust in its first act when Frankenstein's assistant Fritz (made famous as the hunchback of the movie versions) makes the comparison: "[L]ike Doctor Faustus, my master is raising the Devil."[11] The action took place on a stage set featuring a staircase leading up to Victor Frankenstein's workshop, from which the audience heard — but did not see — the moment when the Creature comes to life. The Creature follows Victor out of the room, and the audience is meant to gasp. Much melodramatic mayhem and several romantic pairings ensue, interrupted by the vengeful monster. In this version an avalanche does in the monster and his maker, though in H. H. Milner's *The Man and the Monster; or, The Fate of Frankenstein* (1826), after the Creature and Victor chase each other, the monster is finally destroyed when he plunges into Mt. Etna, much as Varney the vampire would do two decades later. Shelley's narrative had been reduced to a simple story of creation, rampage, and destruction, losing something of its depth and complexity, but thereby reemphasizing the negative role of science by removing any ambiguity.

In *Presumption* the monster was memorably played by Thomas Potter Cooke, who was said to have performed the part more than 350 times (the play ran a then-impressive thirty-seven performances in its first run), and for which he was forever remembered. A brawny former sailor, he wore yellow and green greasepaint lines to imitate the sutures of Frankenstein's labors. He was dressed in tight-fitting, yellow-brown leggings, a brown shirt, and a black belt in order to emphasize his musculature. Mary Shelley heard about an early performance at "the Lyceum [where they] vivified the monster in such a Manner as caused the ladies to faint away & a hubbub to ensue — however, they diminished the horrors in the sequel, & it is having a run."[12] However, she soon learned that this did not happen as told, and the audience emerged unscathed. Shelley caught a performance at the English Royal Opera House on August 29, 1823, and she greatly enjoyed Cooke's acting, though not the play's handling of her story. She later inserted some ideas from the play into her 1831 revision of the novel, notably the word "presumption."

The success of *Presumption* spawned a host of imitators, and the stage came alive with monsters. *The Demon of Switzerland* premiered in 1823, and *The Man and the Monster; or, the Fate of Frankenstein* arrived in 1826 (both by Milner), as did the French *Le Monstre et le magicien*. Comedies like *Frankenstein; or, The Model Man* bowed in 1849, *The Man and the Monster* played through the 1850s, and the musical comedy *Frankenstein, or, The Vampire's Victim* debuted in 1887. Counting dramas, burlesques, and musicals, the story was dramatized at least thirteen times before being committed to film for the first time in 1910 and then dozens more times thereafter.[13]

John Polidori's *The Vampyre* found its voice on stage in the 1820s in Charles Nodier's *Le Vampire* and James Robinson Planché's *The Vampire; or, The Bride of the Isles*. Several additional adaptations were produced in the following years, launching a "craze" for vampire plays.

Bram Stoker produced a stage version of *Dracula* as *Dracula: The Undead* in 1897, the same year as his book's publication, in order to keep at bay the "play pirates" who produced unauthorized adaptations of popular works without compensating their authors. Four hours long, it was performed just once, May 17, 1897, at the Lyceum in London, where *Presumption* had once played.[14] However, the story only became a stage success with a new adaptation in 1927, as we shall see.

Stevenson's *Dr. Jekyll and Mr. Hyde* became a stage production in 1887, which followed the novella's storyline with one major alteration. This Dr. Jekyll was possessed of a girlfriend with whom he engaged in a chaste courtship, all the better to emphasize Mr. Hyde's animalistic, bestial lust. Though Stevenson

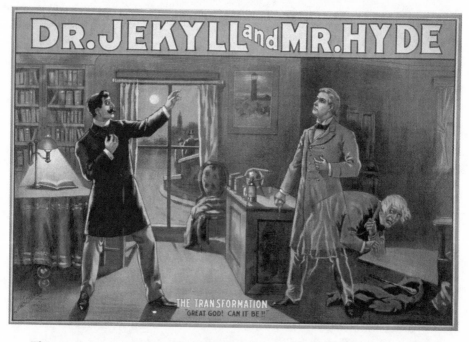

The transformation of Dr. Jekyll. This poster for a theatrical production of *Jekyll and Hyde* about a year after Stevenson published the book superimposes Dr. Jekyll and Mr. Hyde (right) to indicate that they are one and the same. The astonished onlooker can only gasp in horror that an upright Victorian gentleman can hide an atavistic secret beneath the veneer of propriety (Library of Congress, LC-USZC4-8267).

himself disliked this sexual interpretation of his book, Hyde's beast-man libido became the defining element of the story when it came to film.[15] Audiences reportedly enjoyed attending productions of *Jekyll and Hyde* to see how skillfully various actors could affect the transformation from Jekyll to Hyde without the benefit of makeup.[16] Versions of the story remained popular on stage even after the release of several film versions in the first decades of the twentieth century.

Across the English Channel, France made a major contribution to the development of horror theater when in that fateful year of 1897 Oscar Méténier opened a small, three hundred–seat theater at the impasse Chaptal in the Pigalle district of Paris, the city's red-light district, to promote naturalist drama. It was called *Le Théâtre du Grand-Guignol* (literally, "theater of the big puppet"), and it specialized in the most horrific theatrical experiences money could buy. The director of the theater after its first year, Max Maurey, liked to say that his theater's success was measured by the number of audience members who fainted during performances. To achieve the desired effect, the Grand Guignol made ample use of leftover organs from area butcher shops to give an air of sickening realism to their gory dramas. This contrasted strongly with the prevailing restraint of late Belle Époque theater. Playwright Andre de Lorde's one- and two-act plays of insanity and violence transgressed every standard of decency and taste, though more often than not the worst of the horrors occurred offstage, where their anticipation, and the viewer's imagination, terrified more than stage blood ever could.[17]

Little of the experience of the early Grand Guignol survives today, but we know from the printed texts of the plays that many dealt with the same themes as the biological horror of the era. Plays with titles (in translation) like *The Tell-Tale Heart* (1900, after Poe's story), *The Haunted House* (1902), *The Final Torture* (1904) and almost a thousand others told stories of atavistic, animalistic forces hidden within seemingly civilized humans, waiting for the right time to emerge. They also deal with physical deformities and the uneasy relationship between mind and body. Those who violate ethical norms, and those who overreach in their quest for knowledge, are especially punished. However, the theater suffered its own punishment in the 1960s when it could no longer compete with film horror and was forced to shut down.

Horror Cinema Begins

The era of film began at the end of the Victorian age, in 1896, and it is often claimed that viewers of an early French film depicting an oncoming train were so frightened by the reality of the moving image that they ran away in terror. However, no evidence for this event exists outside of second-hand sources. What we do know is that early filmmakers drew a great deal of inspiration from the novels they had read and the plays they watched. Inevitably, this included some of the classics of the horror genre. In 1896 the French director Georges Méliès filmed *Le Manoir du Diable* (known in America as *The Haunted Castle*). The two-minute film made heavy use of Gothic imagery and showed a devil transforming into a bat and being dispatched via a crucifix. By 1915, there were at least seventeen films with "vampire" in the title, though many of these were actually films about sexually adventurous women ("vamps") or criminals. *In the Grip of the Vampire* (1913) was about a master criminal named "The Vampire" who used drugs to incapacitate a woman until a hypnotist restored her. Similarly, *A Magnetic Influence* (1912), *In the Grip of a Charlatan* (1913), *The Invisible Power* (1914), *The Innocent Sinner* (1915), and dozens more pre–1920 films all told stories of doctors and hypnotists abusing their mind-altering powers to control the innocent, usually young girls, often with horrific results.

In the first two decades of film, *Jekyll and Hyde* was filmed nine times, and no less a luminary than Thomas Edison committed *Frankenstein* to film for the first time. In this 1910 version, which ran only sixteen minutes, the mad scientist brews up his monster in a vat; the creature vanishes on Frankenstein's wedding night when the scientist and his bride display true love, causing the being of hate to disappear, and yielding a happy ending.

But lest we think Edison's films full of sweetness and light, the inventor had first adapted his camera to a real-life horror. Edison traveled to Auburn, New York, in 1901 to film the operation of an invention from his labs, the electric chair (developed by Edison employee Harold P. Brown), in its first important employment, executing President William McKinley's assassin, Leon Czolgosz. The chair was developed as a "humane" alternative to hanging or firing squad, since it was believed to be a relatively painless way to kill. The three-and-a-half minute film was called *Execution of Czolgosz with Panorama of Auburn Prison*, and it begins logically enough with a panorama of the famed Auburn Prison. We then see a stiffly reenacted scene in which guards remove Czolgosz from his cell and strap him into the chair. The switch is thrown, and after three jolts the convict apparently expires painlessly and cleanly. Of course, real electrocutions were not so clean or so quick, and some required several administrations before the burning body would die. Edison went on to demonstrate the wonders of electrocution with a 1903 film in which he shot the electrocution of an elephant named Topsy, which had killed three men, including her trainer. Rapt audiences flocked to see the film, as well as Edison's live demonstrations on smaller animals. It was another form of a freak show.

The electric executioner was the epitome of Victorian science. In it we see the triumph of progress and technology, the highest aspirations of science, and we see it lashed to the very bestial animal-men who reminded Victorians of their evolutionary heritage. Victorian scientists had created a perfect solution. In the name of humanity, they strapped those who transgressed against civilization into the electric embrace of the very empire of reason their irrational and atavistic actions denied. Here we see come together all the strands of biological horror. We have the criminal who bridges the divide between rational man and violent beast, the scientist who masters the forces of nature to create a new world order of science and reason, and the inevitable result: death. Here Edison was a Frankenstein or a Moreau, and the result was the same. Others would leave the body and its horror to the scientists and turn instead toward the human soul to find their salvation. They, too, would find horror within.

PART III

The Ghost in the Machine
Spiritualist Horror
(c. 1865–c. 1920)

7

SCIENCE AND SOCIETY

If biological horror dealt with uneasy feelings related to the physical body and its relationship with the natural world, spiritualist horror did the opposite. This strand of horror concerned itself with the incorporeal: the human soul and its survival in a material — and materialist — world. In supernatural fiction, the soul often takes the form of a ghost or spirit, whose unearthly and immaterial nature provides eloquent and terrifying rebuttal to those who claim that all that exists is what can be seen, heard, or felt. This ghost exists in a liminal space, poised somewhere between the physical world of flesh and blood and the (presumed) afterlife of pure spirit. Thus, like the beast-men of biological horror, the spiritualist horrors are also mediators between two worlds. They symbolically link humankind with the higher realms of pure form, and they speak to the survival of the spark of genius within the flesh that is the defining essence of our humanity. These ghosts and other spiritualist horrors represent the era's anxiety about the spirit and the soul in an age of mechanization and materialism, an anxiety that expressed itself as "profound depressions, self-hatred and melancholy," in the words of A. N. Wilson.[1]

Traditional Views

The nineteenth century, as we have seen, was a time of rapid change on a number of fronts. Spiritual values and beliefs were one of those frontiers of change as the Victorians continued to deal with the fallout from the Enlightenment's critique of faith and celebration of science. This impacted beliefs about the fate of the human soul, which had a long and mostly unchallenged history before this time. As we have seen, ancient shamans believed themselves capable of entering the realm of the spirits, and their acceptance of the reality of otherworldly and immaterial entities was the very backbone of their faith. The shaman could project his consciousness onto other planes, and if his soul could enter and leave his body at will, then it stood to reason that body and soul were not synonymous but were instead separate, and that the soul might live on after death. Plato famously described his realm of pure forms where immaterial perfection resided and held that the soul could exist freely outside the corporeal form. This is the view that entered Christian belief, following the Biblical idea that God had breathed life into Adam, and thus imbued him with a soul. Christians then argued that each individual had a soul that after death lived on, receiving divine punishment or reward for the individual's behavior on earth. René Descartes defended the separation of soul and flesh with his famous mind-body dualism.

Aristotle, on the other hand, believed the soul to be part and parcel of the material being, nothing more than the animating spirit, the spark of life. This was the view that gradually influenced and then became the guiding principle of scientific inquiry into the spirit as science came to reject traditional beliefs when evidence for them could not be found. As we have seen, the Enlightenment further damaged traditional views through the development of science and reason, which attacked and deconstructed the religious and spiritual worldview. In our last section we explored the ways this manifested itself in the natural sciences. Now we must turn to faith and the social sciences to explore a different set of reactions to the Enlightenment and the different horrors it produced.

Faith and Doubt

The Enlightenment had profoundly affected the intellectual class, and in the nineteenth century, the learned elite came largely to embrace the rational-scientific paradigm the Enlightenment had established. This entailed a belief in the scientific method as the most valuable tool for understanding the world and an assumption that the phenomena of the natural world were susceptible to scientific inquiry. Though many scientists remained Christians (and many still are today), Western science developed its theories and knowledge base independent of religion, faith, and the supernatural. This occurred because science is a process of building up from observations of the natural world to more generalized explanations of its workings. Since our observations derive, by definition, from that which can be observed, the material world is the natural subject for scientific inquiry (thus science's methodological naturalism). The spiritual realm was not, and indeed produced no evidence for its existence. Anyone who claimed to know what lay beyond the material world was lying or deluded. Without evidence, to a certain type of skeptical scientific mind, the reality of the supernatural or the divine was unknowable and therefore not just beyond our knowledge but not worth thinking about. To a degree, this led to a burgeoning of the ranks of atheists and agnostics, of whom the nineteenth century produced a great number, including Karl Marx, George Bernard Shaw, and Charles Bradlaugh.

With the coming of evolutionary theory, it became possible to hold a complete world-view without reference to God, by understanding the world through the physics of Newton and the biology of Darwin. As a result, many in the Victorian era simply dispensed with the divine altogether. Nietzsche famously declared that "God is dead," and Thomas Hardy attended services for him in his poem "God's Funeral" (1908–1910). As the old century gave way to the new, twentieth century thinkers could look forward to a world of science and reason and predict, as the Marxists did, the end of religion.

These beliefs did not filter down below the educated classes until the widespread implementation of secular schooling in the twentieth century, and there was always an alternative elite of religious and faith-based intellectuals and educators who stood opposed to materialistic science. For example, when Erasmus Darwin was developing his early theory of evolution, Canon Seward of Lichfield Cathedral vehemently opposed Darwin's implication that species were not fixed in their form by a divine creator, and he used his influence to force Darwin into twenty years of silence on pain of economic ruin.[2] However, the forces the Enlightenment unleashed could not be stopped, and for those who drew their morality from traditional culture and their Christian faith, this was a horrible notion. Many feared that humanity would become wild and immoral, filled with license and debauchery if the fear of God and the authority of faith waned.

The art and social critic John Ruskin, writing at the end of the nineteenth century, summed up this view when he described how the decline of faith would hollow out the great rituals of society and undo the civilizing influence of God's word. Specifically, he blamed the evolutionary theories of Charles Darwin and T. H. Huxley for letting loose the flood:

> [E]xcept in eggs of vermin, embryos of apes and other idols of genesis enthroned in Mr Darwin's and Mr Huxley's shrines, or in such extinction as may be proper for lice, or double-ends as may be discoverable in amphisbaenas, there is henceforward for man, neither alpha nor omega — neither beginning nor end, neither nativity nor judgement; no Christmas Day except for pudding; no Michaelmas except for goose; no Dies Irae, or day of final capital punishment, for anything.[3]

In other words, the Enlightenment and evolution had unmoored man from traditional morals, and his soul was adrift in a world of atheism and immorality. Though the power of the traditional churches had waned by the end of the century, alternative forms of spirituality competed to take up the slack and provide a supernatural counterbalance to the Darwinian and Newtonian view.

Utopia and Armageddon

One manifestation of this was a strong belief in utopianism and the establishment of many ideal communities where every member would live in peace and harmony in a genuine community of the spirit. Beginning in 1817, the British socialist Richard Owen spent his fortune building such model communities, including Indiana's famous New Harmony, which lasted until 1828. French rebels tried to turn Paris into a commune in 1871, but it ended two months later in blood, death, and one of the most frightening and horrific internal battles in French history. An estimated ten thousand to fifty thousand died. More peaceful communities, like the Shakers, adapted utopian ideals to a religious framework and found more success.

In England, a wave of prophets proclaiming the end of days attracted a large following (both in Britain and the United States). John Nelson Darby, a former Church of England priest, was the most influential of these prophets, founding a school of Biblical literalism that carried over into modern American fundamentalist beliefs. He invented the belief in the Rapture, when God's chosen would fly into the sky to meet Christ before Satan was loosed again on the earth, as the book of Revelation predicted.[4] As we shall see, Darby's literalism would influence American reactions to evolution and even more liberal forms of faith into the twenty-first century. Nineteenth century America, in particular, saw an explosion of religious fervor in the decades after the Enlightenment. Just as the Romantic Movement had caught the fancy of artists and writers, the religiously minded turned toward a revival of their faith to provide a reaction to the trend toward cold reason.

The Second Great Awakening was the result of this fervor, and it found its center in central and western New York State. There the fervor burned with a fire so intense the region became known as the Burned-Over District.[5] The Awakening referred to the opened eyes of the thousands who rediscovered Christ through an intense and passionate new faith, a faith outside the mainstream and established churches. This was an early version of the personal Jesus sought in many of today's Evangelical faiths. In upstate New York, Mormonism was founded in Fayette in the 1820s when Joseph Smith, its prophet, claimed an angel had shown him golden tablets on which was written a new testament of Jesus Christ. The Oneida Community, founded in the 1830s, advocated spouse-swapping free love as a glorious celebration of God. The community collapsed in the 1880s when jealousy among the mutual spouses and a teen sex scandal undercut its utopian message. It did, however, produce fine flatware that is still manufactured today.[6]

Most famously, Vermont farmer William Miller preached the coming of the End Times, scheduled for October 22, 1844, a date Miller settled on after determining that the learned Bishop Ussher (who, we recall, placed creation in 4004 BCE) was wrong about the End, which the bishop had thought would happen in 1996. So-called Millerites believed in the preacher's prophecy and gathered in fields on the appointed day to await Christ's return. When it failed to occur, the incident became known as "The Great Disappointment." Nevertheless, Millerite groups continued with revised dates through the century, becoming eventually the Seventh-Day Adventists, from which the Jehovah's Witnesses would later emerge.

In addition to evangelicalism and Mormonism, another notable religion founded in the Victorian era was Mary Baker Eddy's Christian Science, founded in 1875, which contrary to its name actually shuns modern science in favor of prayer and meditation, the only medicine the faith allows. Christian Scientists rejected the Darwinists' materialism and instead believe that all is spirit, a belief known in philosophy as idealism. For them, evolution, physics, etc., are merely illusions that are true only insofar as they describe the unreal realm we see rather than the spiritual realm we do not. Today the faith is best known for its newspaper, *The Christian-Science Monitor*.

Spiritualism

Christian sects may have been longing for the End of Days and busy embracing the spirit realm to find their faith in opposition to the physical world of the new science, but those not affiliated with these groups had their own version of a spiritual awakening. This was the secular faith that came in many forms but went by the collective name of Spiritualism. Not coincidentally, the spiritualist era began in upstate New York, the site of the Burned-Over District, not long after the first flames died to dull embers.

In Hydesville, New York, in 1848, Margaret and Catherine Fox, two school-girls, made a miraculous claim. They told their parents that they could talk with the dead. This was accomplished, they said, by making rapping noises on wood surfaces in response to mysterious rapping from ghostly visitors. By this method the girls learned that their home sheltered the shade of a thirty-one-year-old murdered man whose body lay buried in the cellar. The local media, and then the national newspapers, celebrated the sisters, and they developed a stage show, first performed in Rochester and Auburn, in which they claimed to communicate with a variety of spirits. During these shows, the sisters report-edly displayed telekinetic powers, inducing the spirits to move objects and even the table at which they sat. P. T. Barnum displayed the girls as the world's great-est mediums, and thus was born Spiritualism.[7] Late in life Margaret confessed that it was all a hoax, but by then it was too late.

Others had taken up the spiritualist banner. The Davenport brothers of Buffalo, New York, launched their career as mediums in 1854 at the tender ages of eleven and fifteen. They held séances in darkened rooms where for the benefit of their paying audience they entreated the dead to speak. The dead obliged by at first rapping on the table and later by taking possession of one or the other boy and using him to write messages or to speak. It was reported that during the séances the boys would fly through the room, and the ghostly hands of the spirits were sometimes glimpsed. Until 1877, when one brother died, the

Davenport Brothers toured the United States, the capitals of Europe, and Australia. They reportedly earned $600,000. Though the British magician John Nevil Maskelyne created a magic show that duplicated the Davenports' feats, the brothers maintained that they were in genuine contact with the dead, until the famed magician Harry Houdini extracted a confession in the 1920s that the séances were nothing but theatrical effects.[8] Houdini was a debunker of fake mediums, and he spent a great deal of time uncovering the methods by which they fooled their audiences. However, condemnations of spiritualist mediums by newspapers, clergy, and scientists only reinforced the public image of Spiritualism as a powerful alternative to "official" ways of knowing since otherwise the powerful would have no reason to condemn them so viciously or so often.

On the other side of the Atlantic, Caroline Crowe's book *The Night Side of Nature* (1848) was the first to treat ghost stories as legitimate objects for scientific scrutiny, and its collection of supposedly real-life hauntings became highly influential and helped support the claims of the American mediums.[9] The time was right, though, for a belief in the supernatural, and the emerging doctrine of Spiritualism seemed to provide one acceptable way to do so. Spiritualists believed that the soul survived death, that certain individuals were capable of communicating with the spirits, and that the dead could provide religious and moral guidance to the living. Coming as it did at a time when fundamentalist preachers and a Mormon prophet claimed direct communication with God and His angels, and at a time when New Englanders were still staking vampires, the idea that humans could commune with the souls of the departed was less outrageous than it might seem today. In an age of rapid technological and scientific change, it must have seemed comforting to find a sense of timelessness, history, and continuity by speaking to one's dead relatives.

In a typical spiritualist séance, a group would gather in a darkened room and sit around a large table. At the head of the table sat the medium, usually but not always a woman, who was believed to possess a link to the realm of the spirits (like the shamans before them) and through whom the spirits would act or speak. For only $1 an hour, or $5 per evening (low by nineteenth century standards),[10] the medium would frequently enter a trance state in which she became the passive and unconscious vehicle for one or more "spirit guides" with whom she was especially familiar, historical figures (Ben Franklin was a favorite for his "scientific" credibility[11]), or deceased relatives of those in attendance at the séance. The spirits thus conjured would communicate in a variety of ways. They would rap on the table in answer to questions; they would possess the passive medium and write with her hand; they would talk through the medium's mouth; they would levitate the table or cause objects or the medium to fly about the room; and they would occasionally materialize, frequently out of a special cabinet located behind the medium. Most of these effects were accomplished by trickery.[12] The great scientist Michael Faraday exposed the unconscious muscular tics that caused tables to shake, Harvard sent

Houdini poster. Harry Houdini was an ardent opponent of psychics, and his stage show sought to discredit mediums and Spiritualists by exposing their tricks. Despite Houdini's popularity, Spiritualism still attracted a large following in the years after his death, and mediums continue to this day to use the same "talk-to-the-dead" techniques that Houdini once exposed (Library of Congress, LC-USZC4-709).

Photograph from a séance. Spiritualist mediums claimed to be a bridge between two worlds. Allegedly taken at a 1901 séance, this photograph was believed to show the faces of departed souls who hovered in spectral form around the sitter. In reality, photographers used double exposures to produce the ghostly effects (Library of Congress, LC-USZC4-1845).

a team to debunk the Davenports' rope tricks, and S. J. Davey and Richard Hodgson recreated séances using standard stage illusions and tricks. However, séances were often so skillful and convincing that hardened skeptics, who could not believe they were capable of being fooled, came to believe in Spiritualism. The evidence was before them, and it seemed foolhardy to do otherwise.

Whereas Matthew Lewis, the author of the Gothic play *The Castle Spectre*, could claim in the eighteenth century that no one believed in ghosts any more, large numbers of nineteenth century Americans and Europeans became devotees of the supernatural, as did luminaries like the abolitionist William Lloyd Garrison, the newspaper editor Horace Greeley, and author James Fenimore Cooper.[13] Mediums levitated tables for Napoleon III, Czar Alexander II, and other crowned heads of Europe.[14] Mary Todd Lincoln held séances in the White House despite her presidential husband's misgivings. Sir Arthur Conan Doyle, creator of the arch-rationalist character Sherlock Holmes, came to embrace Spiritualism after his son's death, and he devoted much of the rest of his life to defending the faith. Even Alfred Russell Wallace, who developed a theory of evolution at the same time as Darwin, was reported to attend séances and believe in Spiritualism. There were, by 1860, an estimated one to three million spiritualist believers and 231 professional mediums in a country of only around thirty million.[15] The abolitionist and Unitarian minister Theodore Parker confessed that despite repeated debunking, "in 1856, it seems more likely that Spiritualism would become the religion of America than in 156 that Christianity would be the religion of the Roman Empire, or in 756 that Mohammedanism would be that of the Arabian population."[16] Of course, there were contrary opinions. In England, George Eliot declared that "so far as 'spiritualism' (by which I mean, of course, spirit-communications by rapping, guidance of the pencil, etc.) has come within reach of my judgment on our side of the water, it has appeared to me either as degrading folly, imbecile in the estimate of evidence, or else as impudent imposture."[17]

Spiritualism was, above all else, a powerful reaction to the materialism of the educated elite.[18] It was at heart the very antithesis of science, positing a spiritual basis for the phenomena of the world rather than the material one explored by science and reason, though in time they came to view the spirit realm as merely a higher form of matter. Yet at the same time Spiritualism sought to make use of modern science, explaining its phenomena with pseudoscientific terms; and many leading scientists investigated Spiritualism in the hopes of offering scientific proof of life after death. Spiritualists were fond of likening mediums to telegraphs, the exciting new communication technology that also made use of invisible forces (electricity) to communicate across distance.[19]

The spiritualists came to believe that the phenomena they uncovered were natural, rather than supernatural, and an extension of the observable world on another plane of existence, one susceptible to scientific scrutiny: "Let us ever bear in mind," wrote a skeptic-turned-believer named John Edmonds, "that spiritual intercourse is not supernatural, but in compliance with fixed laws affecting the whole human family."[20] Organizations like the Society for Psychical Research, founded by Cambridge scholars in 1882, and the American Society for Psychical Research, founded in 1885 by Harvard scholars, and both still extant today, attempted to use the methods of science to prove these spiritualist claims. They tested a number of mediums and sought to probe the causes of the manifestations and spirit messages they brought about. Though the scientists appeared to have some success, their results were in fact the result of deceptive mediums and wishful thinking.

Spiritualism had its last hurrah after World War I, when many grieving individuals came to embrace it in the hope of speaking with the war's dead. However, the faith gradually died away during the Great Depression, and today the last of the old-school spiritualists live on in Lily Dale, New York, at their famous compound, though their latter-day descendants, the TV and hotline psychics, still use the same tricks developed in an earlier era.

Because of Spiritualism's popularity, it was unsurprising that ghosts and spiritualist phenomena should find their way into horror literature.

Ghosts and Hauntings

The Victorian and Edwardian eras were also a time of ghosts and hauntings, when those who believed in the spiritualist message came to embrace the idea that the souls of the departed walked the earth and could break through the veil separating earth from the spirit realms, and not always via séance and medium. The Society for Psychical Research in Britain and the American Society for Psychical Research in the United States devoted resources to studying ghosts and hauntings and came to the conclusion that when ghosts made their appearance they were not the ancient and deranged midnight specters in death shrouds of Gothic fiction but instead were largely silent, appearing even in broad daylight, and were usually clear and distinct depictions of recently deceased murders and suicides wearing modern clothing.[21]

Technology facilitated and enabled this process. The telephone, for example, brought disembodied human voices across great distances in a way almost akin to magic, and the twin discoveries of photography and x-rays played a significant role in promoting belief in the supernatural. After the invention of photography in 1826 and their subsequent popularity after the American Civil War, it was believed that cameras could capture aspects of nature invisible to the naked eye, including the incorporeal form of spirits. The evidence for this was blurry double-exposures that seemed to show pale, unearthly ghosts floating idly in otherwise unremarkable images. As we shall see in Chapter 9, the ghost photograph became something an art form in the late nineteenth century as professional photographers sought to create an array of bizarre and frightening images of the invisible dead. In 1895, Conrad Röntgen's discovery of X-rays added a new dimension to the spirit photograph.

X-rays had the capability of seeing straight through individuals, revealing their bones and apparently presenting an almost supernatural power. X-rays appeared to fulfill the Spiritualists' claims that there were areas beyond the visible in which spirits and ghosts could live, for what were X-rays but invisible beams that could see the unseeable and reveal realms beyond the ability of our senses to detect. As Alan Grove points out, "Because of Röntgen's discovery, medicine has become gothic — not, like Victor Frankenstein, because the doctor creates a monster by abusing his powers, but because the doctor *is* a supernatural creature who now wields the power of ghosts."[22] The X-ray had revealed within the living flesh the visage of the person after death, when the stuff of life had rotted away and only the bones remained. As we shall see, the ghostly power of photography and X-rays became a part of the period's supernatural horror when advancing technology made "gothicism, science fiction, and scientific reality appear one and the same."[23] Science, rather than dispers-

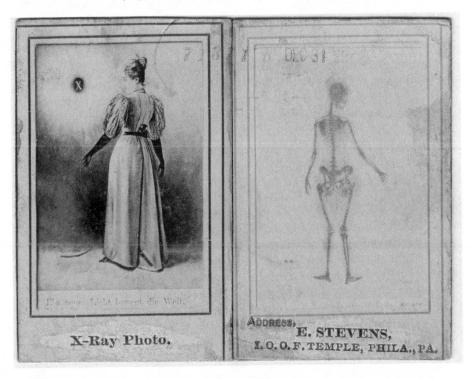

Early X-ray. The X-ray from 1896 at right shows the skeleton of the woman at left. The ghostly images created by X-rays prompted many to wonder whether other types of rays might be found that could illuminate the spirit world as easily as X-rays laid bare hidden parts of the physical world (Library of Congress, LC-DIG-ppmsca-12628).

ing old superstitions and fears, instead fed them and provided apparent evidence to further supernatural claims.

Science of the Soul

Victorian and Edwardian scientists turned their attention to the human soul with the same enthusiasm with which they pursued their investigation of the human body. In 1907, Dr. Duncan MacDougall contemplated how to prove the existence of the soul. He reasoned that if it existed, the soul would escape the body at death, as the spiritualists and religions claimed. Therefore, it should be subject to scientific measurement if it had true form or mass. He therefore gathered six terminally ill individuals and placed their sick beds atop a scale. He monitored their weights at the moment of death and concluded that each dying person lost approximately twenty-one grams, which he believed was the weight of the soul. Though his research was inconsistent and had significant flaws, the idea that the soul weighs twenty-one grams lives on a century later.[24]

But Victorian science was not solely, or even predominantly, interested in explaining the religious concept of the soul, which many came to believe did not have an independent existence as the spiritualists claimed. In fact, most scientists opposed spiritualist claims, but agreed that the scientific method could be equally well adapted to studying minds as well as bodies. These scientists sought to investigate the animating force of the human by studying the brain and how its characteristics impacted human behavior. One school of thought, that of phrenology, claimed to deduce mental traits by reading the bumps on a person's head, which corresponded to the development of brain areas inside the skull. The belief originated in Vienna in the eighteenth century and enjoyed a vogue in the United States at the same time as Spiritualism, from the 1830s through the end of the century. It was, in some ways, the first scientific study of the mind. However, a more important study occurred, also in Vienna, when Sigmund Freud (1856–1939) began to probe the mysteries of the mind from a novel direction.

Freud had worked in biology and neurophysiology before he turned his attention to the mind, which famously happened while exploring the concept of hysteria, the disease characterized by muscle complaints, nervousness, moodiness, and other symptoms. In the most frequently given version, Freud began to wonder whether women with hysteria were suffering from a mental rather than physical condition, and if so whether it would be possible to explore their unconscious desires to find the root cause. He came to believe that examining the psychological causes of hysteria was a more effective treatment than the then-standard practice of having a doctor rub the patient's genitals to induce an "hysterical paroxysm," what is now known to be an orgasm, to relieve stress. From this sexual origin there proceeded psychoanalysis.

Freud built on nineteenth century theories of the unconscious mind to explore the ways in which suppressed, repressed, and poorly understood drives and desires affected conscious behavior and defined human personalities. He sought to explore this area of the mind through dreams, which he believed contained coded symbols for unconscious activities. As Freud explored the unconscious of his patients, he found that many described scenes of childhood sexual abuse, which he later realized were largely imaginary constructions. From these, however, he developed the idea that the libido was the ruling passion of the unconscious and that the human mind was driven by sexuality and especially its repression.[25] This manifested in the notorious Oedipus complex, named after the Greek tragic hero, in which each (male) individual was believed to play out a nursery drama in which he sees the mother as the first object of his love, wishes to commit incest with her, and therefore resents his father, who is his rival for his mother's love. In girls, the Electra complex, focusing on the father, served the same purpose, though with the added complication of penis envy, in which girls secretly long for the power and freedom a phallus provides. Freud further argued in *Totem and Taboo* (1913) that primitive human societies were built around the Oedipal longings of a tribe's young men, who sought to kill their chief in order to seize the tribe's women. Therefore, substitution rituals, like animal sacrifice, were instituted among men to quell this homicidal urge.

Freud viewed himself as an iconoclast and often compared himself to figures who brought destruction: Hannibal, the conquistadores, and Cromwell.[26] He self-consciously tried to provoke society and outrage the complacent. Freud's frank discussions of sexuality were said to be shocking in their time, as was his suggestion that all humans possess a death instinct by which they seek to return to a state of equilibrium through non-existence. In an age when the Victorians put children on a pedestal as embodiments of virtue and innocence, Freud was claiming that even infants were driven by sexuality, seeking pleasure in oral, anal, and genital phases of development. For our purposes it is sufficient to understand that Freudian psychology popularized the idea of the unconscious and brought sexuality into the forefront of thought, a position it never again wholly surrendered.[27]

Freud's work was first published in English by the Society for Psychical Research, which hoped to use his theories of the unconscious to bolster the case for Spiritualism by showing that the mind had hidden dimensions that might include the telepathic.[28]

While many of Freud's ideas fell out of favor through the twentieth century, they became highly influential, especially in later horror fiction. Freudian psychology posed a powerful challenge to the supremacy of reason, for it argued that the unconscious and the libido were the guiding lights of the human mind, and that people behaved in certain ways without being aware of exactly why this was so. As a result, they could not be said to function as rational agents, since they were guided by irrational, unconscious desires. Future horror authors would employ many of these ideas in the development of psychological horror during the twentieth century, when many horror works became explicitly sexual and rooted in explicitly Freudian theories. By the 1970s, body horror had become a playground for warmed-over Freudian sexual situations.

Freud also turned his attention to horror fiction in 1919, when he wrote an essay called "The Uncanny." Using examples from German literature, he described the sensation one experiences when a familiar object becomes suddenly strange, or when the strange takes on aspects of the familiar. This entails moving beyond merely frightening toward a complex combination of terror, wonder, and awe, not unlike Burke's concept of terror and the sublime. Earlier ideas of the uncanny equated it with fear of the unknown; for example, automata (robots) are said to produce feelings of the uncanny because they are almost but not quite like human beings; the unnaturally reanimated dead (or parts thereof) can be uncanny because they are almost but not quite like the living. But Freud instead argued that horror fiction produces feelings of the uncanny by taking repressed and unconscious desires and rendering them in the dream-images derived from repressed fears. By causing repressed desires to return to the conscious, we experience the uncanny. In this way, superficially "frightening" objects, like haunted houses or ghosts, become "uncanny" objects when coupled with a returning repression. Of course, Freud would not be Freud without recourse to sexual explanations, so it is no coincidence that he sees dismembered hands and heads and gouged-out eyes in horror stories as displaced anxiety about castration. It is this anxiety that produces the uncanny.[29]

As the nineteenth century gave way to the twentieth, a world of wonder and horror had opened up, when the walls between science and superstition seemed to fall apart, and when progress paradoxically seemed to reinforce ancient beliefs. From this mixture of rapid technological development and the renewal of faith in things unseen, late Victorian horror fiction developed a fascination with the ghost story, a trend that would continue for as long as Spiritualism itself. These ghost stories attempted to make sense of science's discoveries and Spiritualism's claims, depicting a middle ground in which science served as mediator between faith and doubt. This essential tension between skeptic and believer came to define Spiritualist horror, when the doubter was inexorably and inevitably converted to believer through exposure to unmentionable horror.

8

LITERARY DEVELOPMENTS

Ghost stories have always been with us. Odysseus encountered ghostly shades in *The Odyssey*, and tales of haunted places grace both myth and history. As we have seen, Gothic fiction made use of specters as largely extraneous coloring for its crumbling castles, and to an extent the ghost story never died. However, there was something of a lull between 1820 and 1850, after which the ghost story began to come back into vogue. After the American Civil War, ghost fiction reached new heights and by 1920 thousands of ghost stories and novels of all levels of quality had been published in a bewildering array of magazines, newspapers, books, and pamphlets. The Victorians produced ghost stories meant to scare, ghost stories meant to disturb, and an entire body of ghost stories designed for humor or to parody other stories. However, there has been a lack of scholarship into the ghost story of this age, and the true number may never be known.[1] What scholarship there is tends to focus on gender issues, such as Vanessa Dickerson's suggestion that ghost stories written by men were scientific, clinical, and diagnostic, whereas those written by women contained "eruptions of female libidinal energy" because women felt like ghosts in their own society.[2] Ghost stories, of course, were much more than displaced libidos.

The technological progress of the Victorian era was among the most dramatic in human history, and it is therefore logical that Victorian literature tried to grapple with the developments shaking the foundation of society. In an age that forecast progress and imagined that technology would lead to continued improvements, ghost stories functioned as a medium through which the past could directly affect the present. In the Gothic period we saw stories of ghosts and hauntings that were set in an imaginary version of the medieval past, but with the classic Victorian and Edwardian ghost story we instead find the past impinging on the present, the ghost serving as the symbolic link between the unfinished business of previous ages and the unyielding modernity of the present. At the same time, the stories also retold in fictional form the spiritualist version of human destiny, taking for its art claims about the survival of the human soul. In a way, this too was a remnant of the past surviving into the present, for the soul was a relic of religion, and religion appeared to be losing ground to materialist science.

Most ghost tales take the form of a Discovery Plot. In them, the protagonist comes into contact with an otherworldly spirit entity, strives to understand what he has seen, and then spends the remainder of the story attempting to prove to himself or to others that the entity in question is real. However, in the best of these stories the real heart of the tale is a battle between a believer and a skeptic wherein the tension between science and superstition is made palpable. In these stories, one character comes to represent the position of faith and tradition, and the other represents the Western tradition of rationalism and science. As we shall see, in stories like "How Love Came to Professor Guildea," that one character is a scientist does not necessarily make him the bearer of the skeptical viewpoint. Nevertheless, because these stories are ghost stories, more often than not the skeptic must end as a believer, converted to a new way of thinking and an understanding that dogmatic scientism is a poor substitute for a wider understanding of the true reality of the world. In other words, the ghost in a Victorian ghost story makes the spiritual realm real by submitting the spiritual to the first test of Victorian science, "seeing is believing," even if the evidence cannot always be trusted.[3]

Given the vast number of ghost stories coming down to us, it is impossible to adequately survey all of them. Therefore, I would like to present a discussion of a few of the most significant along with some obscure but interesting gems that help put the masterpieces into focus and demonstrate how these ghost stories deal with the changing role of science and knowledge directly, in a way other genres pointedly did not. To begin, we should examine a pre–Victorian story that served as the model for what was to come.

Haunted Chambers, Haunted Minds

The great Romantic, Sir Walter Scott, author of *Ivanhoe*, also produced the archetype for the ghost story as it developed in the Victorian period. His "The Tapestried Chamber" (1829) served as a template for the ghost story as a confrontation between skepticism and belief. In the story, General Browne returns to Britain from the American Revolution and passes by an old castle in a quaint English village. Its owner, Lord Woodville, an old friend, invites him to stay at the castle. However, the general passes a poor night, his sleep interrupted by the appearance of a woman in high heels. "Upon a face which wore the fixed features of a corpse were imprinted the traces of the vilest and most hideous passions which had animated her while she lived."[4] Worse, she lay on the bed beside him! The general worries that his friend will doubt him and consider him superstitious and deluded by his own imagination, but Lord Woodville dispenses with "the possibilities by which it is fashionable to explain

"The Vigil of Arms." Typical nineteenth-century illustrations of ghosts drew on Gothic imagery, as did many of the stories with which they were paired. This illustration of a medieval knight menaced by a skeletal specter combines a number of horror clichés often found in the era's ghost stories: the ghost, the terrified hero, a dark night, and bats.

supernatural appearances."[5] He tells Browne that the Tapestried Chamber, in which he slept, was rumored to be haunted and had in fact been shut up before Browne's arrival for fear of the ghost. Woodville, a "complete sceptic" when it came to ghosts, put the courageous Browne in the chamber purposely as an experiment to disprove the reality of the ghost, an experiment that failed.[6] Before leaving, Browne sees a portrait hanging in the gallery wall of the woman from the chamber, whom Woodville says was involved in incest and murder. Woodville blocks up the chamber and thus contains the supernatural menace, having converted to the belief that the supernatural is in fact real.

Here we have in short and embryonic form the major characteristics of ghost fiction: a skeptic (Woodville), a believer (Browne), and an entity (ghost) that defies the skeptical world-view. However, since the reader is unaware that Woodville is a skeptic until the end of the story, this angle does not produce the same tension and drama that it would in later stories. Nevertheless, the basic scenario of the ghost tale is obvious, and the great question of the *subjectivity* versus *objectivity* of ghostly visions would continue through the Victorian ghost tales.

The prolific Victorian novelist Charles Dickens made use of ghosts in his fiction, including the specters in *A Christmas Carol* (1843) and *The Haunted Man* (1848), and the short stories "The Story of Bagman's Uncle" (1837), "To

Be Taken with a Grain of Salt" (1865; one of the only ghost stories about jury duty), and "No. 1 Branch Line: The Signalman" (1866), in which a ghostly vision serves as a premonition of doom. These little tales, some humorous and some chilling, reinforced the idea that the supernatural was part and parcel of everyday experience, and in them the rational narrators come to embrace the irrational. The novelist Wilkie Collins, best known for his detective novels like *The Moonstone* (1869), also wrote a number of ghost stories, such as "The Dream-Woman" (1855), who is a grisly succubus out to kill, and "Mrs. Zant and the Ghost" (1887), in which Collins claims neutrality in the battle between faith and doubt, for the "facts" of the case should be sufficient to prove whether Mrs. Zant died of her own fear and illness or was the victim of a ghostly vengeance. Similarly, Mrs. Henry Wood's story "Reality or Delusion?" (1874) presents the "facts" of its case and asks the reader to decide whether the events had a supernatural origin. In the story, Daniel killed himself on All Hallows Eve unbeknownst to Maria, who thought she saw him alive when in reality he was already dead. The narrator is left to wonder whether this was a true ghostly vision or "some imagination of the brain."[7] However the closing lines leave little doubt as to the ghost's reality.

J. Sheridan Le Fanu, whom we last encountered with his lesbian vampire novella *Carmilla*, was also a prolific producer of ghost stories. His "Strange Event in the Life of Schalken the Painter" (1839) told of a man returned from the dead to claim a bride. In "An Account of Some Strange Disturbances in Aungier Street" (1853), a young medical student and his cousin take up residence in a house dating back to the remote past, at least as long ago as James II (d. 1701), and which had never been brought up to date. It was reported to be haunted by a "hanging judge" who hanged himself. The narrator, Dick, is superstitious and believes in the supernatural; his cousin Tom is a skeptic who ridicules Dick's beliefs but is "destined to receive a lesson."[8] When Dick becomes disturbed by ghostly visions of the judge in his dreams, he and his cousin "true to the imputed materialism of medicine" try to cure him "not by exorcism" but by drugs.[9] The narrator gives a most extraordinary justification for his continued belief in the objective reality of the supernatural, in a speech that clearly shows the relationship between the story and developments in Spiritualism and science. Here Dick contemplates whether what he has seen was his own mind playing tricks on him:

> Was it, in short, *subjective* (to borrow the technical slang of the day) and not the palpable aggression and intrusion of an external agent? That, good friend, as we will both admit, by no means follows. The evil spirit, who enthralled my senses in the shape of that portrait, may have been just as near me, just as energetic, just as malignant, though I saw him not. What means the whole moral code of revealed religion regarding the due keeping of our own bodies, soberness, temperance, etc.? here is an obvious connection between the material and the invisible; the healthy tone of the system, and its unimpaired energy, may, for aught we can tell, guard us against influences which would otherwise render life itself terrific. The mesmerist

and the electro-biologist will fail upon an average with nine patients out of ten — so may the evil spirit. Special conditions of the corporeal system are indispensable to the production of certain spiritual phenomena. The operation succeeds sometimes — sometimes fails — that is all.[10]

The men contemplate a number of explanations — optical illusions, a rat — but the ghostly phenomena multiply to the point that even the skeptical Tom begins to believe, especially when the judge from Dick's dream stands before him in the night. Tom admits that he kept the visions quiet for fear that Dick would turn on him as he did on Dick's own visions. They commiserate and move out of the house, both convinced by personal experience with forces beyond those of this earth, and materialist science, that the supernatural is not only real but manifest in this world.

The theme of the subjective experience of the supernatural continues in Le Fanu's "Green Tea" (1872), a novella that tells the story of the Reverend Jennings, who is pursued by a macabre vision after consuming the title beverage. He begins to see a spectral monkey, which he believes is an evil spirit harassing him without apparent reason. The story is told by the skeptical Dr. Martin Hesselius, who is not a materialist scientist but instead some form of spiritualist, for he believes that "the natural world is but the ultimate expression of that spiritual world from which, and in which alone, it has life." Thus a human being is but a spirit, "different in point of material form from what we ordinarily understand by matter."[11] Rejecting materialist explanations, Mr. Jennings has come to believe that humans have evil spirits within them, and these spirits can appear when a person is sufficiently primed to see beyond the illusion of the material world. This, Jennings thinks, is the origin of his evil monkey, who has taken to squatting on his Bible and calling out blasphemies while he tries to preach. The monkey threw fits whenever Jennings tried to pray until he gave up his prayers, and it eventually began imploring Jennings to kill himself. This he eventually does, and Dr. Hesselius provides a conclusion explaining why this occurred. It is his idea that "spiritual, though not immaterial" fluid around the brain can be affected by strong stimulants like green tea, which open the inner eye and produce spirit visions in the "nervous tissue." This can be easily cured with the right medicines, and the only reason Dr. Hesselius failed in the case of Mr. Jennings, he says, is because Jennings suffered from "hereditary suicidal mania."[12] Absent that, and his cure was assured.

In this story, we see a number of themes, but prominent among them is the spiritualist idea that supernatural occurrences are real but have a naturalistic explanation. In this story, Dr. Hesselius posits that the spectral monkey has its origins in the brain, but he also believes that the brain fluid at fault is shared with the spirit world, a sort of scientific version of the human soul. Therefore, the supernatural events of the story are grounded in a form of science, though not the form of science represented by the materialist mainstream. Thus in this story we see Le Fanu working through the spiritualist beliefs about life, death, and science through the guise of a doctor and a minister, both of whom should be opposed to Spiritualism by their professional positions but nevertheless embrace it as a self-evident truth on the basis of experience. Here the subjective experience of the supernatural leads the men to the conviction of its objective truth, though in vastly different ways.

The French writer Guy de Maupassant (1850–1893) was obsessed with insanity and devoted a great number of his late tales to the horrors of diseased minds before he went mad himself from syphilis and died in an asylum after a suicide attempt. All told, Maupassant wrote three hundred short stories, of which just thirty-nine are typically classified as horror. In "Diary of a Mad Man" (1885) Maupassant tells of a judge who kills for the thrill of it and then purposely condemns an innocent man for the crime. In "The Horla" (1887) a man feels himself losing his vital essence, and he becomes convinced that a ghostly entity is sucking away his life-force. He starts off as a skeptic but transforms his opinion as liquids begin to disappear from their glasses and he catches sight of one glass being drunk by an invisible entity. When he sees a cloud pass between him and his mirror, he finally snaps, and in his madness burns down his house to escape the ghost, promising to commit suicide if the job remained undone.

However, Maupassant's horror is probably best remembered* for a pair of short stories about severed hands that kill. In "The Flayed Hand" (1875), a severed hand bought at auction kills its owner, and the narrator is driven to madness by visions of ghostly hands. In "The Hand" (1883), Judge Bermutier pronounces a verdict on the death of Sir John Rowell, who was strangled in Corsica. Sir John keeps a large severed hand tied up in his room and believes it is possessed of its own free will. After Sir John's death, the hand vanishes but reappears on Sir John's grave. The skeptical judge offers a materialist explanation, that the hand's original owner returned to reclaim his member and put an end to the man who had separated it from him, but the tale implies that neither the judge, nor his audience, nor we readers are meant to believe this "official" version of the story.

Also from France, Gaston Leroux's *The Phantom of the Opera* (1909–1910; in English, 1911) made use of the forms of a ghost story to tell of a more human horror. The Paris Opera House is haunted by a specter known as the Phantom, who threatens retribution if the managers do not pay him ransom and reserve box five for his use. The Phantom is in fact Erik, a physically and emotionally scarred genius who uses the ghostly disguise to get what he wants. After new managers refuse his demand, he takes vengeance on Christine Daaé, to whom he has appeared as the Angel of Music, sent, he says, from her dead father. He

---

*Maupassant's most famous story is probably "The Necklace" (1884), which is sometimes anthologized as a horror story, though its clever plot and twist ending are more social drama than tale of terror.

teaches her to sing like an angel, and then he kidnaps her when he becomes jealous of her relationship with her fiancé, a viscount named Raoul. Erik tries to make Christine marry him, holds Raoul in a torture chamber, and threatens to blow up the Opera House. Though frightened by Erik's facial deformities, Christine pities him and kisses him, pleasing him enough to release Raoul and give his blessing to their union. Especially effective in the novel is the hall of mirrors into which Raoul is plunged, a hexagon of reflecting surfaces that together give the illusion of infinity in a very small space.

Uncertain Horrors

We met the cynical Ambrose Bierce (1842–1914?), Civil War soldier turned journalist and author, a little while back with his tale of an invisible monster; "Bitter Bierce," as he was known, was also a master of the ghost story and spiritualist horror, as well of realistic tales of the brutality of war. His supernatural fiction was somewhat of an anomaly since Bierce himself was a skeptic in the matter and defined a ghost, in his incomparably witty *Devil's Dictionary* (1911; 1906 as *The Cynic's Wordbook*), as "The outward and visible sign of an inward fear." He further described the silliness associated with ghostly visitations:

> There is one insuperable obstacle to a belief in ghosts. A ghost never comes naked: he appears either in a winding-sheet or "in his habit as he lived." To believe in him, then, is to believe that not only have the dead the power to make themselves visible after there is nothing left of them, but that the same power inheres in textile fabrics. Supposing the products of the loom to have this ability, what object would they have in exercising it? And why does not the apparition of a suit of clothes sometimes walk abroad without a ghost in it? These be riddles of significance. They reach away down and get a convulsive grip on the very tap-root of this flourishing faith.[13]

Nevertheless, Bierce's short fiction is a model of clarity and spine-tingling fear, mixed with his trademark wit and satire. Seldom running more than a few pages, each tale of terror crisply states its subject and cuts to the climax, which parsimony Bierce believed distinguished the short form, deriding the novel as a "short story padded."[14] In "A Diagnosis of Death" (1901) a doctor and a patient discuss the validity of ghosts; the patient believes and the doctor doubts. The patient claimed to have seen the ghost of a Dr. Mannering, but disclaims that he saw the living man on the street, so he knows it was a hallucination. The doctor, however, attended Mannering's deathbed, and knew he was three years gone. He urges the patient to go play the violin to ward off the impending diagnosis of death, but the next day the patient is found dead, Chopin's death march on the music stand before him. In "The Boarded Window" (1889), a panther steals a corpse, but it turns out the corpse wasn't quite dead.

The tale "Moxon's Master" (1899) is a bit more ambitious and posits whether machines are capable of thought; if so, the idea of the soul is a false illusion and merely another example of the force that animates the machine.

Taking a spiritualist idea that all matter has a form of life and "vibrations" make that so, the scientist Moxon believes wood can be conscious and devises a thinking automaton that can play chess. Upon understanding this, the narrator "exulted in a new sense of knowledge, a new pride of reason," for he is privy to great revelations at the hands of Moxon, his mentor.[15] But Moxon has overreached and his thinking machine decides it has had enough of Moxon and murders him. However, the ending of the story strongly implies the automaton is a fake, and the reader is left to decide what or who was inside. In analyzing the story, scholars wonder whether it "really" describes a homosexual love triangle between Moxon, his assistant and the narrator or a heterosexual one with an imaginary girlfriend never mentioned in the story, with the girlfriend and the assistant both assumed to hide in the automaton to seek vengeance on Moxon for favoring the narrator.[16] The overreaching scientist plot is apparently too obvious and common to command attention when there are hidden sexual meanings to ferret out. A more interesting interpretation was put forward by Daniel Canty, who thought the lightning bolt that burns down Moxon's lab after the murder is a symbol for God, who punishes Moxon for creating a soulless thinking machine.[17]

Bierce also produced a number of atmospheric tales that became influential for other authors. "Haïta the Shepherd" (1891) is a gentle fable about the impossibility of happiness, and "An Inhabitant of Carcosa" (1886) tells a spectral story of a man who discovers himself to be a ghost inhabiting a ruined city. The story concludes with the disclaimer that it was transmitted from the spirit of Hoseib Alar Robardin to the psychic medium Bayrolles, who reoccurs in "The Moonlit Road" (1907) to provide another vehicle for the dead to explain the supernatural occurrences in the plot. However, Bierce's most famous story is one that is not quite supernatural and more tragic than horrific. "An Occurrence at Owl Creek Bridge" (1890) tells of Peyton Farquhar, who is hanged on Owl Creek Bridge. Miraculously, the rope snaps and he is able to escape. He makes his way home and is about to embrace his wife when he feels pain, his neck snaps, and he dangles off Owl Creek Bridge. The story eloquently presents the last moments of the man's life and the power the mind possesses to conjure realities it wishes were true.

Ambrose Bierce, soldier, warrior, and author, the man who kept a skull on his desk and told visitors it belonged to his editor, traveled to Mexico in 1913 to observe Pancho Villa and the Mexican Revolution. He was never seen again, and it is assumed that he died in that country.

The Spirit of Madness

In the last three years of the nineteenth century, three extraordinary ghost stories brought the genre to its zenith with tales of uncertain hauntings whose subjectivity provided wildly different but equally enlightening perspectives on tension between skeptic and believer in the *fin de siècle*. The president of the Society of Psychical Research and scholar of religion William James (served 1894–1896) was the brother of novelist Henry James, whose ghost novel *The Turn of the Screw* (1898) was published after his brother's presidency. The author drew on some of his brother's society's findings as he developed his novel, but he took pains to explain that he did not feel compelled to follow the Society's "scientific" understanding of ghosts because he wanted to tell a good story, not merely reproduce the Society's findings. However, as Francis X. Roellinger pointed out, James's ghosts fit quite well with the "scientific" ghost and the case studies from his brother's Society.[18]

The Turn of the Screw is another entry in that British genre, the Christmas ghost story, and in this one the framing devise of a group gathered around the Christmas hearth serves as our entryway into the story. A man hires a governess to care for a young niece and nephew with whom he has been saddled after the children's parents' deaths in far-off India and for whom he cares nothing. The governess is lured with the promise of a hefty paycheck, and she takes up residence in the man's country estate while he remains in London. Here the narrative picks up in the governess's own words, in the form of a manuscript she left behind. The niece was in residence, and the nephew was away at boarding school, so the governess's burden seemed light. She at first enjoyed living in the country house, Bly, which was an architectural shambles of various periods and styles, though looking back on it she now saw the house as a monstrosity.

The nephew, Miles, is kicked out of school for being dangerous, and the governess sees this as an ill omen since by reputation he is a gentle child. Now she has two children to watch over, Miles and his sister Flora. The governess also learns that her predecessor, Miss Jessel, died mysteriously. The governess begins to experience preternatural strangeness, which she likens at one point to a "mystery of Udolpho," after Ann Radcliffe, though she is thinking, like Radcliffe, of a naturalistic explanation rather than a supernatural one.[19] She sees a man, and she comes to realize he is after someone other than her: "The flash of this knowledge—for it was knowledge in the midst of dread—produced in me the most extraordinary effect, started, as I stood there, a sudden vibration of duty and courage."[20] Only gradually does the truth come out, that this man is the ghost of Peter Quint, a former servant at Bly and lover of the late Miss Jessel, and the governess believes Quint is after young Miles. Quint was "clever" and "so deep," but also abusive, and his evil genius appeared to survive even death.[21]

The governess becomes quite protective of Miles and Flora, convinced that her intuition is correct and the spirit of Quint and that of Jessel are conspiring to corrupt the children and make use of them for their inexplicable purposes. The governess realizes that Miles and Flora are aware of the ghosts

("They know!"[22]) and in communion with them, though the children disclaim any knowledge when asked directly. "The more I go over it, the more I see in it, and the more I see in it, the more I fear. I don't know what I *don't* see — what I *don't* fear!"[23] In other words, the governess believes her fear derives as much from her knowledge of the horror surrounding her as the horror itself and she worries for what she is yet too ignorant to fear. Miss Jessel seems to have power over Flora, who sickens and is sent away. Quint holds sway over Miles, and when the governess confronts Miles about his dismissal from school, she also screams bloody murder at the ghost of Quint, proclaiming her triumph over the ghost. Miles, screaming once, dies of heart failure.

Scholars are divided in their opinion of what "really" happened in *The Turn of the Screw*, falling into two camps. One holds that the story is a tale of a ghostly haunting, taking at face value the governess's story. The other camp believes the governess insane and that the story is the record of her hallucinations and madness. Edmund Wilson, the eminent twentieth century critic, inaugurated this school of thought in a 1938 essay calling for an explicitly Freudian reading of the novel in which the governess is treated as a "neurotic case of sex repression."[24] By this reading, the towers of Bly House are phallic symbols, and the governess is acting out repressed sexual rage at the patriarchy, as represented by Miles and his (absent) uncle. As Willie van Peer and Ewout van der Camp noted, however, these two interpretations are not mutually exclusive and can both be true.[25] In fact, the Freudian interpretation is quite clever but forgets that fiction is, well, fictional, and therefore while a case can be made for the governess's insanity, the ghosts need not be false since fiction is free to play by its own rules. In the world within *The Turn of the Screw* it may just be possible that Freudian interpretations are the false reality and ghosts are the truth that Freudian theories unfairly obscure. Since it is a novel, and not an autobiography, we can never know.

Charlotte Perkins Gilman's "The Yellow Wallpaper" (1892) is another extraordinary tale of a woman who believes she is being haunted, though in this story the madness is more readily apparent. The husband of the unnamed female narrator believes her depressed and hysterical, and when they take an ancient summer house — the kind that should be haunted — he assigns her a room and schedules each moment of her day, supposedly for her rest. She believes her assigned room was once a boys' gymnasium or nursery, with bars on the windows ("for little children"[26]), rings in the walls, a bed nailed to the floor, and the decayed remains of splotchy yellow wallpaper. A gate guards the stairs. She is not supposed to write, but she sets down her story. The narrator's "nervous weakness like mine is sure to lead to all manner of excited fancies," and sure enough she begins to see things in the pattern of the wallpaper.[27] She sees the shape of a woman moving behind the pattern, and she believes the woman is shaking the shapes on the wall and even escaping the room during the day. The narrator begins to peel off the wallpaper, believing it her means of escape, and in the end she locks herself in her room while her husband tries to break in. The narrator leaves the room by crawling over the prostrate body of her fainting husband.

Nineteenth century readers understood the story as an Edgar Allan Poe–style tale of a disturbed mind, or even a warning about the dangers of bad decorating (said one Victorian reviewer: "[T]he model husband will be inclined seriously to consider the subject of repapering his wife's bed chamber according to the ethics of [designer] William Morris"[28]). In the twentieth century, feminist critics instead interpreted it as an eloquent testimony of the way men (represented by the husband) ignore, control, and repress women (represented by the narrator), who consequently go mad. Gilman herself hoped the story would show doctors, specifically the one who treated her for nervous ailments, the importance of engaging women's minds intellectually (the narrator wasn't supposed to write for fear of stimulation) rather than letting them go mad from inactivity and calling it a "rest" cure.[29] There is some indication that doctors did take the lesson.

The third entry in our unholy triptych is also a tale of madness and features an insane, or at least mindless, figure and an ambiguous haunting; but here the themes of spiritualist horror are brought to their apex.

Love, Faith, and Doubt

Robert S. Hichens's (1864–1950) "How Love Came to Professor Guildea" (1900) is one of the greatest ghost stories in the English language, and happily for us, it also exemplifies the themes Victorian spiritualist horror sought to explore: faith versus doubt, and objectivity versus subjectivity. As such, it is disheartening that scholars have all but ignored the story even while calling it a "classic" (which as Mark Twain said is a book praised but unread), though it remains a favorite of anthologists and was dramatized for the *Escape* radio show in February 1948. One of the few scholarly references to it occurred in 1912, when the American writer and editor Frederic Taber Cooper referred to the story as "a hideous bit of morbidity," whose very flaw was that it was a ghost story, preferring instead the author's more naturalistic (non-horror) tales of disturbed individuals.[30] Edmund Wilson simply called it trash.[31]

We begin by meeting Father Murchison and the eminent scientist Professor Frederic Guildea, who are the best of friends even though "the one was all faith, the other all scepticism."[32] The Father lives through love, but Guildea is so consumed with investigation and fruitful inquiry that he lacks even a moment for love. The Father by faith and Guildea by temperament are both celibate, and they enjoy each other's fierce intelligence. Over dinner at the professor's house, Guildea argues that the results of his experiments speak for themselves as pure and objective research, lacking as they do any sentimental reason for their undertaking; however, the Father believes that if animated by love (soul), objective science could achieve still grander benefits. Guildea introduces Murchison to his parrot, Napoleon, whom he purchased for an experiment and failed to discard. He avers that the animal has no mind, but merely imitates slavishly whatever he hears. He is inhuman and indifferent to affection, as is the professor himself, who wanted nothing in life but to be alone with his research and his learning. The priest pities him for this.

A year and a half after this dinner, Guildea tells the Father that he has the uncomfortable sensation that someone or something is attracted to him. He believes a black figure he had seen on a bench in the park has gotten into his house, though he could find no trace of the person. Guildea is sure, due to "mental sensation," that the entity is still inside and in fact falling in love with him.[33] He says he is not frightened, but scientifically curious about and a bit irritated by this thing that he hesitates to call a ghost. The priest realizes he is protesting too much. Nevertheless, the Father thinks Guildea is mentally unhinged, a point to which the professor objects. "But," says the priest, following the skeptic David Hume's line,* "which is more natural—for me to believe in your hysteria or in the truth of such a story as you told me?"[34] The professor vows to prove the existence of the ghostly entity within three days' time.

Two days after he has his proof. But the proof is not in the form of a "conventional, white-robed, cloud-like figure. Bless my soul, no! I haven't fallen so low as that."[35] Instead, the professor believes Napoleon, the parrot, is aware of the ghost and is imitating its movements. The priest thinks the professor has gone mad until the parrot begins to react to an unseen presence, appearing to enjoy a good pat on the head and a scratch under the chin. Watching further, the priest realizes the bird is imitating a mentally feeble individual, the kind that develops unreasonable attachments to people and objects. The bird speaks with a dangerous and amorous voice, but in words that are too unclear to make out. The professor is afraid of the irrational entity, saying that "I could fight against brain—but this!"[36]

Naturalistic explanations are ruled out one by one. There have been no strange visitors to influence the bird, and parrots only imitate familiar voices. Guildea declaims a belief in hauntings, but says that "I simply state a fact, which I cannot understand, and which is beginning to be very painful to me."[37] It is unclear whether his pain is solely from the ghost or from the challenge the ghost presents to his skeptical world-view. In a neat reversal, the priest plays the part of the skeptic here:

*"No testimony is sufficient to establish a miracle, unless the testimony be of such a kind, that its falsehood would be more miraculous, than the fact, which it endeavors to establish." (David Hume, Enquiry Concerning Human Understanding, in John Locke, George Berkeley, and David Hume, English Philosophers of the Seventeenth and Eighteenth Centuries, vol. 37 (New York: P. F. Collier and Son, 1910), 401.)

Woman with parrot. In "How Love Came to Professor Guildea," the professor's parrot reacts to the unseen presence of a ghostly woman. Because of animals' liminal state as creatures less than human but more than mere objects, they have been frequently associated with the supernatural, as in the witch's familiar or the dog that senses an invisible menace. For this reason, animals like "Guildea's" parrot and the monkey from "Green Tea" appear frequently in horror literature as agents of fear (Library of Congress, Prints and Photographs Division, LC-DIG-ggbain-02490).

"Are you convinced?" said Guildea, rather irritably.

"No. The whole matter is very strange. But till I hear, see or feel — as you do — the presence of something, I cannot believe."

"You mean that you will not?"

"Perhaps."[38]

Father Murchison, a man whose profession requires him to believe in messages and signs from God's supernatural kingdom, cannot accept Guildea's haunting; and he spends an evening probing his inner torment as he wrestles with faith and doubt. The next night Napoleon is gone, sold to stop its lovesick imitation; and Guildea claims that the ghost has become tactile, touched him, and would not leave his side, even when he traveled to France for a lecture. Guildea's health declines and he begs the Father for help, but the Father can sense no ghost. The priest suggests that Guildea try to put aside his indifference to feeling and use his emotions to give the ghost the love it craves. Instead, Guildea suddenly feels the ghost wants to leave. Throwing open the door, the priest tries to humor his friend and speed its passage out. In the climax of the story, he sees on the park bench outside the house the huddled black figure that Guildea saw at the beginning of the affair, but it vanishes as he tries to approach. Inside the house, Guildea has died with an expression of terror on his face. A medical examiner declares it heart failure from overwork. He and the priest agree that Guildea should have "lived very differently," though for different reasons.[39]

The story is superficially a morality tale in which a man who lacks love has it visited on him involuntarily. However, even the characters within the story dismiss this idea, and there are deeper themes at work. It is important to note that Guildea is a scientist, committed to reason, objectivity, and dispassionate inquiry. His is the world of logic and the mind. The ghost, however, is the ghost of an idiot, which at the time and under the Binet-Simon scale (see Chapter 10) was someone of significant mental retardation. In other words, the ghost is irrational and the opposite of Guildea's cold reason. The idiot ghost symbolically (dis)embodies the emotions that the scientist cannot experience, the very human feelings of love, need, and desire that science, in its form as Victorian scientism, simply cannot tolerate. In science, emotion corrupts the data, distorts the evidence, and produces false results. The ghostly emotions that haunt Professor Guildea similarly corrupt his research and destroy the veneer of objectivity he sought to make the purpose of his life. He is reduced to pleading special cases and trying to convince Father Murchison, who represents both traditional faith and, paradoxically, skepticism, that his experience is real. "How Love Came to Professor Guildea" has a clear similarity to Le Fanu's "Green Tea," the story that inspired it, but with a role reversal that makes this the superior story. The reversal of the typical roles, with the scientist as believer and the man of faith as skeptic, add an extra layer of meaning to this meditation on the complementary and contradictory aspects of the various meanings of faith and doubt.

Hichens was a prolific writer of tales, many of which featured horror or the supernatural. He returned to the themes of "Guildea" in *Dweller at the Threshold* (1911), which also involved men of the cloth and a man of science probing a spiritualist mystery, this time involving mesmerism and an invasion of personality.

Psychic Detectives

As a counterpoint to the scientists of horror literature struggling to understand supernatural stories, a number of tales featured detectives engaged in the same activity. Detective fiction became extremely popular following the debut of Sherlock Holmes, and it is little wonder that there would be some spillover between these two popular genres, horror and detection, especially since many writers like Edgar Allan Poe, Wilkie Collins, and Sir Arthur Conan Doyle wrote in both. We saw a bit of this overlap when Holmes himself looked into the mystery of the Hound of the Baskervilles, but the cases other detectives faced did not always end in neatly rational conclusions.

Two that did include Catherine L. Pirkis's "The Ghost of Fountain Lane" (1894), which featured a female detective investigating a ghost that turned out to be less than ghostly; and Ernest Bramah's "The Ghost at Massingham Mansions" (1924), in which the detective Louis Carlyle investigates ghostly happenings at an apartment complex. Following the dictum that material explanations take precedence over spiritualist ones, Carlyle uncovers the earthly causes of the spectral manifestations.

On the other hand, E. and H. Heron (pen names of Kate and Hesketh Prichard) produced a series of detective tales in which Flaxman Low used scientific methodology to investigate supernatural mysteries. In "The Story of Baelbrow" (1898), Low has to tease out the truth from a haunting in which a formerly benevolent ghost suddenly seems to launch violent attacks on a professor and his daughter. The house is built on an old Neolithic burial ground, and Low reasons that a spirit from the barrow has entered the body of a mummy the professor has recently purchased. As Low explains, "The invisible is real; the material only subserves its manifestation. The impalpable reality already existed, when you provided for it a physical medium for action by unwrapping the mummy's form."[40] A quick investigation proves this is so, and the mummy is destroyed to end the haunting.

Later Hauntings

It remains for us to survey a few of the spiritualist horrors that followed the turn of the twentieth century, a time when the horror story was not just popular but ubiquitous, and a time when the volume of ghost tales produced far outstripped the available quality. Many of the later ghost stories are variations on their predecessors, but among them are a few notable stories of exceeding quality and some that have unique takes on common subjects. Ralph A. Cram's "In Krofsberg Keep" (1895), for example, provides an interesting variation on "The Tapestried Chamber Room" with a much more active and malevolent ghost, a Count Albert, who has a homicidal bent.

However, the master of the early twentieth century ghost story was undoubtedly the Cambridge scholar of medieval history Montague Rhodes James (1862–1936). His finely wrought and very English ghost stories were collected in four anthologies, *Ghost Stories of an Antiquary* (1904), *More Ghost Stories of an Antiquary* (1911), *A Thin Ghost and Others* (1919), and *A Warning to the Curious and Other Ghost Stories* (1925). Framed largely as Christmas ghost stories, most told of a scholar whose single-minded pursuit of knowledge leads him to ancient artifacts that unlock spiritualist forces, which return from beyond the grave to seek their revenge.

In "Count Magnus" (1904), a Mr. Wraxall is an intelligent and cultured scholar-traveler possessed of "over-inquisitiveness," for which he suffered a horrible fate.[41] He travels to Sweden to pursue an ancient trove of manuscripts concerning the De la Gardie family for a forthcoming book. At their ancient mansion, he becomes interested in the mansion's builder, a Count Magnus, an ugly man of whom much evil was spoken. It was said that Magnus terrorized the tenants of his lands, killing those who trespassed against him even after his death; and it was rumored that he went on a "Black Pilgrimage," which excites Wraxall's curiosity.

In the old books, Wraxall discovers alchemical treatises and hints of Magnus's dark arts written in his own hand. He also finds on Magnus's ornate Gothic tomb a depiction of some kind of misshapen cloaked figure. So engrossed is Wraxall in study that he fails to notice a chanting that seems to call Count Magnus back from the grave. The great locks holding fast his sarcophagus are torn asunder, and Wraxall flees in panic when the lid appears to rise. He feels himself pursued by Magnus and the cloaked figure from the tomb, and he feels isolated because no one will believe he had an encounter with the unexplained. He is found dead; the condition of the body makes viewers faint, and the house where he died is abandoned forever.

In "Oh, Whistle, and I'll Come to You, My Lad" (1904), Prof. Parkins discovers in the ruins of an old Templar church a strange little whistle inscribed with Latin. He blows it out of fancy, and that foolish act calls up a ghostly adversary. As a "convinced disbeliever in what is called 'the supernatural,'" Parkins refuses to accept that the whistle possesses strange powers.[42] The ghost comes at night, rising up from the bed, cloaked in the linens (the very stereotype of the sheeted ghost!). Parkins avoids death only by the timely intervention of a friend, who having seen similar events in India, rescues him. "The

Treasure of Abbot Thomas" (1904) has yet another antiquary, this one discovering the treasure of a sixteenth century abbot after uncovering clues left on Renaissance stained glass windows. Removing the treasure, however, unleashed the gold's supernatural guardian. The antiquary is forced to accept the reality of the supernatural after his struggle to escape the guardian's terrific clutches.

The effectiveness of M. R. James's stories derives from his use of the everyday details of scholarly life — reading books, searching records, collecting evidence — to provide a quotidian baseline against which the supernatural stands in stark and dramatic relief.

Sir Arthur Conan Doyle, a medical doctor and the author of the rationalist Sherlock Holmes stories, converted to spiritualism shortly after the death of his son, and his non–Holmes fiction displayed a marked tendency toward the supernatural and the romantic, much as did his life. He wrote several nonfiction books on Spiritualism, including *The Coming of the Fairies* (1922) and *The Edge of the Unknown* (1930), and incorporated his beliefs into his horror tales. "The Captain of the Pole-Star" (1883) involves a ghost haunting a ship sailing in the Arctic. The narrator, the ship's doctor, believes the captain has gone mad when he tells of the ghost, and the captain eventually flees into the snows in search of the ghost of his beloved. The narrator does not believe in ghosts, but a final note by his father is meant to assure us that the ghost must be real. In "Lot No. 249" (1892), some Oxford College students live in a large, Gothic dormitory. The Egyptologist in the room below has a mummy, and only gradually do the students discover that the sounds coming from the room are those of the resurrected corpse, which the Egyptologist can bring to life by temporarily imparting vital power into it. As the boys turn from skeptics to believers, they come to realize that the Egyptologist is using the mummy to commit murder. Eventually Abercrombie Smith, one of the students, destroys the mummy and the Egyptologist's secret spell-book of "wisdom which is nowhere else to be found" to end the reign of terror.[43]

In Doyle's "Playing with Fire" (1900) a medium makes use of Mesmer's animal magnetism to contact the spirit world. A rationalist from Scotland, who — critically — lacks a materialist prejudice, represents science; and the narrator is a disinterested third party. At a séance, a spirit (speaking through the medium) tells the audience it has come to teach and enlighten. A Frenchman attending the séance asks for his thoughts to materialize. The spirit obliges, and a horse condenses out of spiritual substance and tramples through the hall. Everyone is frightened, but unhurt, and the story ends with the narrator telling the readers that it is possible he was the victim of a hoax, but if any reader with occult knowledge can shed light on what has happened, he may write to a given address.

W. W. Jacobs's "The Monkey's Paw" (1902) is justly famous. A dried and mummified paw of a monkey serves as a magic talisman to grant its owner three wishes. It does so because an Indian fakir put a spell on it to prove that man is ruled by fate, and that tampering with fate leads only to tears. Herbert

White and his wife come into possession of it, and Mrs. White finds it hard to believe in magic in this day and age. Herbert wishes for two hundred pounds, and gets it as compensation when his son is killed. He ascribes it to coincidence, but Mrs. White wants to use the paw to bring back her beloved boy. They wish for it, and a knock at the door makes it seem that the wish had been granted, but at the last moment Herbert's fear overcomes him and he expends his last wish putting down that which he called up, to his wife's dismay, and leaving the reader to wonder whether it was real.

The English poet and writer Walter de la Mare's novel *The Return* (1910) tells of the spirit of an eighteenth century pirate who reaches out of the past to possess the body of the modern Arthur Lawford. So strong becomes the pirate's possession that the living man's features contort into the face of the long-dead man. The conceit of the story is that the death of the body does not imply the death of the mind, and the possession of a body belongs only to whichever mind most strongly fights for it. The novel makes excellent use of spiritualist themes, as it probes the mysteries of the spirit realm adjacent to but beyond the material world of everyday life. De la Mare's shorter fiction also explored horrific themes, including vampirism, evil trees, ghosts, demons, and so on.

Oliver Onions's novella "The Beckoning Fair One" (1911) is frequently acclaimed as one of the best ghost stories in English. It is the story of an author named Paul Oleron who moves into a London house where at first he conducts his daily life as he always had, encountering a number of individuals and dealing with the problems facing the impending publication of the novel on which he is working. He waxes philosophical on how charming it would be if the noises in the old house were evidence of ghosts and if he might himself be creating a future ghost through his expended energy: "[A]s his own body stood in friendly relation to his soul, so, by an extension and an attenuation, his habitation might fantastically be supposed to stand in some relation to himself ... It would be rather a joke if he ... should turn out to be laying the foundation of a future ghost!"[44] Unfortunately, just such an event occurred in the past, and a ghostly entity haunts the house. Oleron, like Guildea before him, becomes aware of the ghost through mental sensations, and Oleron determines to remain in his haunted house to find out *what* haunted it:

> And he was conscious of nothing so much as a voracious inquisitiveness. He wanted to *know*. He was resolved to know. Nothing but the knowledge would satisfy him; and craftily he cast about for means whereby he might attain it.[45]

As Oleron becomes obsessed with discovering more about the ghost, his outside life falls away and he becomes an agoraphobic recluse. He favors darkness to the light, and he ceases work on his novel and even destroys it in the fire, an offering to his obsession, the ghost. His girlfriend tries to save him from his deepening madness, but her failure leads to a climax of horror.

Another rental property of horror is found in Bram Stoker's "The Judge's

House" (1891). This time the offending real estate, like that of Le Fanu's "An Account of Some Strange Disturbances in Aungier Street," belonged to a cruel hanging judge. The landlady avers that the supernatural rumors are simply a misunderstanding of ordinary things like rats and bugs, as though they were better company for the renter, a student named Malcolmson. He is terrorized by giant rats, though they do not prevent him from getting plenty of sleep. Unfortunately, the ghost of the judge crawls out of a portrait of him on the wall and it hangs the student using the rope from the house's alarm bell. The judge returns to his painting with an evil grin on his face, or so thought the crowd that entered the house at the sound of the alarm.

Based on Jewish legends, Bavarian Gustav Meyrink's German-language novel *Der Golem* (1913; book form in 1915) tells of a sixteenth century rabbi who creates an artificial man from clay and breathes life into him to create a monster that will protect the Jewish community. Here inanimate matter is given a spirit, and the echoes with Mary Shelley's *Frankenstein* are unmistakable.

In H. F. Arnold's "The Night Wire" (1926), it is modern technology rather than moldy old houses and ancient curses that serve to transmit horror across time and space. The story concerns two journalists who work the overnight shift at a newspaper, monitoring the news wires for developments. The telegraph seems almost ghostly itself since it can carry thoughts across the ether, and their job is to translate the Morse code into usable text. As the narrator looks over his companion Morgan's copy he finds several stories datelined Xebico. They tell of a weird fog that settled over the city, the uncertainty of the town's scientists about its cause, and the ghosts that seem to inhabit the fog. The town panics, and the reporter on the wire expresses fear until the revelation that the fog brings peace and joy. The reports cut off abruptly, and when the narrator goes to Morgan to discuss what he thinks is a hoax, he finds Morgan dead. He wonders if Morgan did not accurately relay to his cooling body the facts of what happened to his soul after death.

The indication of larger truths shared by vast numbers in a world outside our own in "The Night Wire" provides us with a bridge to the next phase of horror, the cosmic, which we will explore in Part IV. The ghost story, however, did not simply vanish. It continued on in different forms and for different purposes, and it is still very much alive today. However, the spiritualist underpinning of the ghost tale faded away with the 1920s, as spiritualism itself succumbed to both the rise of industrial science and the revitalization of evangelical religion, neither of which left much room for a pseudoscience of ectoplasm and spirit realms. The ghost story would henceforth adopt the tone and tenor of the new age, and as we shall see, tales like Shirley Jackson's *The Haunting of Hill House* (1959) and movies like *The Others* (2001) would rework classic spiritualist forms and imbue them with the essence of the eras in which these new works were created. Of course, spiritualist horror was not confined to literature but left an indelible impact on the visual and performing arts as well, which is quite a feat for a belief founded in the unseen.

9

HORROR IN THE ARTS

Spiritualist horror was ubiquitous in late Victorian and early twentieth century prose, but the haunted world they depicted extended too to the visual and performing arts, where morbidity, ghosts, and existential dread made their presence felt. Unlike biological horror, whose terrors were those of the visible world, the spiritualist horrors dealt with the mind and the soul, whose invisible nature made them more difficult to transform into art. However, the Victorians found a number of clever ways to make the unseen seen, and their successors in the early twentieth century made good use of the new medium of film to construct cinematic visions of the invisible world within the human mind. Ghosts, too, continued to appear on stage, and mediumistic séances were themselves often a piece of performance art. This was par for the course, since the Victorians had a deep fascination with death that penetrated everyday life.

Part of this was due to high mortality rates, but part was also due to the era's loss of faith in the comforting nostrums of religion and the subsequent need to find rituals to help ease the pain and grief felt at the passing of a loved one. These rituals became something of a public performance. It was expected that widows would remain in mourning for twenty-eight months after their spouse's death, with their dress and actions reflecting a gradual lessening of the mourning. For the first year of "deep mourning," they dressed only in black and left home only to go to church. Thereafter they could wear gray or purple and leave home more frequently during "half-mourning." A year was standard mourning for other relations; for men a black armband signified mourning, with no restriction on activities. Britain's Queen Victoria famously remained in mourning for the four decades of her life remaining after the death of her husband, Prince-Consort Albert, in 1861, wearing black every day and ordering the servants to set places for Albert and tend to his things as though he were still living. In Austria-Hungary, funerals were great public events, and visitors to Vienna would line the streets to watch the great parades held in honor of the dead. Funerals for the imperial family were the best entertainment, but all the empire's rich and powerful strived to emulate their showiness.

However, no piece of Victorian morbidity produces today quite the same reaction as the *memento mori* photograph, those strange pictures of loved ones reclining in their caskets or propped up on chairs in the hours and days after their deaths, the last reminder of someone who had been and gone. Though beloved in their own time, they have come down to us as creepy reminders of the triumph of death.

Photographing the Dead

The introduction of photography in 1839 changed the way Victorians related to their world, for it made it possible to create what were believed to be exact reproductions of reality, something painting and engraving had only approximated heretofore, and only for the very rich. In a way, each photograph was a reminder of the past, for it captured an image of something that once was but would be no more. The person or scene before the camera's lens would change after the shutter snapped, but the memory of it would linger on in the photograph for all time. Therefore, when the subject of a photographic portrait had died, his image could continue as a ghostly echo of a living soul that once breathed and walked the earth. For the Victorians, the idea that the deceased should be remembered with a portrait was traditional, and photography was a way to bring that tradition to the masses who could not afford an artist's painted portrait.

With the invention of ever cheaper and more efficient photographic techniques through the century (early cameras required fifteen minutes or more of motionless exposure, accounting for the stiff look of early portraits), photographs of the dead became more popular. Parents would have photographs of their deceased infants taken with the baby propped in a lifelike position and surrounded by toys. Older individuals were depicted in a reposed position, as though they were sleeping. Occasionally, the deceased was propped up in a chair or against a wall, dressed in his or her finery, for a final portrait. Mostly, the dead were made to look as though they were living, but this illusion did not always hold. Pictures of the assassinated Abraham Lincoln were published in newspapers across the United States in 1865 (the body went on a cross-country viewing tour), and in Europe the dramatic 1889 suicide of Crown Prince Rudolph of Austria was commemorated with a photograph of the prince in his casket, a white bandage masking the hole he blew in his head.

Matthew Brady introduced photography to war, and his images of what Lincoln called the Civil War's "honored dead" have become justly famous. Brady recorded battle scenes after the action ended because cameras were too slow to capture motion, and he also posed some of the corpses to heighten the dramatic effect. Nevertheless, he and other war photographers captured the horror of war with their eloquent and frightening vistas of devastation and carnage. The less honored dead found their place in the canon of photography, as

Harvest of death. The Civil War was the bloodiest fought on American soil, and it was the first American war captured on film. Mathew Brady's photographs, like this one of dead soldiers at the 1863 battle of Gettysburg, brought the horror of war into America's drawing rooms with a realism that words and engravings could not match (Library of Congress, Prints and Photographs Division, Civil War Photographs, LC-B8184-7964-A).

crime scenes too became subjects for the photographer's art. The Jack the Ripper killings were commemorated with photographs of the victims' bodies, their battered and ruined corpses laid out or propped up for the camera to record the evidence of the Ripper's crimes. The pictures taken of Jack the Ripper's final victim, her limbs unrecognizable in an explosion of blood, are still shocking even by today's standards.

As attitudes toward death changed in the twentieth century and became more clinical, sequestering the dying in hospitals rather than homes, *memento mori* photography died out. However, crime scene photography and war photography continued the camera's fascination with the dead, even if these images were seen more rarely and often censored to avoid giving shock or offense.

Early photographers tried to give their audiences a shock by photographing not just the bodies of the dead but also their souls. The long exposure time required for early cameras to produce a photograph meant that subjects sitting for a portrait had to remain very still, but when someone did not, the image became a translucent blur through which the background was often visible. As a result, many Victorian daguerreotypes, ambrotypes, and other photographic techniques produced a ghostly image that some spiritualists took for the real thing. The camera, it was thought, could not lie, but savvy photographers learned to exploit the camera's reputation for capturing reality and its ability to manipulate it to produce false ghost photographs that could be marketed as legitimate images of spirits from another plane of existence.

To accomplish this, the spirit photographer would take a partial exposure of a given subject against a plain background and then finish the exposure in another location. The resulting "double exposure" produced images of transparent or translucent "ghosts" hovering or manifesting, and because the first exposure could be done ahead, such images could be produced on demand.[1] The results look false to today's eyes, but many are quite effective as early examples of special effects, and it is not impossible to understand how some people could have been fooled by the cleverest of these. In 1885, Dick Willoughby, a prospector from Alaska, produced a photograph of a ghost city he said appeared over Muir Glacier. It sold thousands of copies before an astute viewer recognized the ghost city as a superimposing of Bristol, England, onto the glacier.[2]

The Society for Psychical Research investigated a number of such ghost photographs, including one sent to them in 1891 from a Miss Sybell Corbet who believed she had captured the image of an elderly man's ghost partially visible in a chair she was photographing with a one-hour exposure. A skeptical Dr. Barrett, of the Society, dismissed the "ghost" as a photographic accident:

> I believe that one of the servants came into the room, sat down in the chair, crossed his legs and then uncrossed them, looked down for a moment and then at the camera, saw he was being taken, so got up and went away, having been in the chair about 20 to 30 seconds. This will give the ghost of an apparently older man from a young man, *with no legs,* and a semi transparent face....[3]

He even reproduced the photograph in an experiment; however, the Society did not deem it impossible that a ghost could be captured on film. That belief continued into the twenty-first century when amateur and professional "ghost hunters" used more sophisticated cameras, both still and video, to track down "ghosts," which more often than not were artifacts of the photographic process or dust in the air or on lenses. David Starr Jordan, the famed Victorian ichthyologist, satirized the ghost photographs in 1896 with "sympsychography," which he humorously claimed in *Popular Science Monthly* was a new technique for imprinting mental images onto photographic plates via invisible brain waves, just as invisible X-rays could make an image of the inside of the body. He illustrated this with an "impression of ultimate feline reality," a blurry image of a cat. Unfortunately, his hoax was too good, and many readers believed he had discovered a new method to commune with the spirit world.[4]

Horror on Canvas

Though photography may have changed the way artists depicted reality, painting still had much to say about human life, and horror. The Swiss-German artist Arnold Böcklin painted five versions of *Isle of the Dead* (so named later by an art dealer) between 1880 and 1886, in which a white-clad oarsman ferries a coffin toward a large island, a rocky expanse with buildings seemingly carved into the living rock, several tall pine trees jutting up from the center. Rachmaninoff was so inspired by its eeriness that he composed a symphonic poem about it in 1907. Adolf Hitler was said to be obsessed by the image, and he owned one of the originals. The painting inspired a movie of the same name in 1945.

During the late nineteenth century in Berlin, the painter's art was frequently compared to the ability of psychic mediums or mesmerists to channel thoughts and emotions, a comparison that influenced the work of Edvard Munch, who believed in psychic phenomena and Spiritualist "vibrations" and "waves."[5] Munch's work reflected his own sense of horror and doom. His family life was a nightmare of suffering and pain: "I inherited two of mankind's most frightful enemies—the heritage of consumption and insanity—illness and madness and death were the black angels that stood at my cradle."[6] This carried over into his paintings, especially the one for which he is best known.

A subtle type of horror infuses Munch's most famous painting, *The Scream* (1893). Actually, *The Scream* is a series of images: two in oil, two in pastels, and a series of prints, each of which depicts essentially the same iconic image. In it a human figure of indeterminate age or gender is standing on a bridge, which spans a river. The background is a wild, swirling red sunset which is reflected in the water. The human figure has its hands raised to the sides of its head, its body curving in an uncomfortable posture and its mouth is open in a sharp O-shape, frozen in a full-on scream. Though highly stylized and expressionistic, *The Scream* nevertheless captures its subject so vividly that the agonized shriek is almost audible. However, an alternate interpretation, drawing on Munch's writings, holds that the screamer is in fact blocking his or her ears to blot out the shriek coming from an agonized and erupting natural world. In many interpretations the red sunset is believed to be a reflection of real sunsets caused by the eruption of Krakatoa in 1883. *The Scream* was the last in a series of works depicting the sunset over the bridge, a man standing on the bridge gazing at the sunset, and then the screaming figure. Munch called it the last of his studies in love.[7]

Though primarily remembered for *The Scream*, Munch produced a range of powerful and expressionist work now known by morbid titles like *Anxiety*, *Melancholy*, *The Vampire*, *Jealousy*, and *Death in the Sickroom*. In this work he aimed to capture emotions, and in the case of *The Scream* (originally called *Despair*[8]) that emotion was horror. Munch's *Scream* is essential not just for expressionism in art, but also for the period's existentialist philosophy that it so clearly captures. So iconic has the work become that it is instantly recognizable by nearly everyone, and as a result the painting became a desired commodity. Versions of it were stolen twice, in February 1994 and August 2004, but recovered later, in May 1994 and May 2006, respectively. The painting also lent its face to a number of knickknacks, posters, prints, t-shirts, and key chains. The late Victorian figure's face also influenced the mask worn by the serial killer in Wes Craven's *Scream* movie franchise a century later.

Horror for the Holidays

While in Britain the telling of scary stories was a Christmas tradition, in the United States horror earned its own holiday as Halloween became an increasingly popular celebration in the later nineteenth century and into the twentieth. Halloween is often said to have its origins in ancient Celtic religious practices, especially the festival of *Samhain*, and these became incorporated into Christian ritual. Catholics celebrated All Saints Day on the first of November, known in earlier times as "All Hallows," as hallow was an archaic word for honored or sacred, as in "hallowed halls." In Ireland, the night before, or All Hallows Eve, was a time when it was once thought, following Celtic/Druid practice, that demons, fairies, and the souls of the dead could rise up and walk the earth for a single night. The name became contracted to Halloween. The Irish used to carve turnips into faces for the holiday to scare away the dead. By the nineteenth century, a blend of pagan and modern traditions gave rise to gangs of boys who would roam the Irish countryside playing pranks that could be blamed on the wandering dead. Costumed performers would demand food in exchange for performances to drive away the spirits, and the traditions blended into what became known as trick-or-treating, first called by that name in 1939.

When the Potato Famine hit Ireland in 1846, great numbers of Irish fled to the United States, and they brought their Halloween traditions with them. In America, the Puritans had frowned on Halloween, but a mild version of a harvest celebration occurred in the more lenient Southern states. After the Irish arrived, Halloween developed into its modern form. The Irish turnip-carving turned into pumpkin-carving, since the American gourd was much easier to fashion into shapes than the turnip. The holiday began to be celebrated with parties and spiritualist trappings, so much so that some Victorians tried to have authorities ban the more ghoulish aspects of the celebrations for the moral improvement of the young. It seems likely that absent the spiritualist influence, a holiday celebrating ghosts would not have taken root as easily as it did. By the 1920s, Halloween had become a major American celebration, and its influence traveled back to Europe where the American version of costumes and pumpkins became widespread by the twenty-first century. In America, Halloween celebrations came to rival those of Christmas, and in the early twenty-first century Halloween spending was second only to its December rival.

Spiritualism on the Stage

Ghosts were popular subjects on the Victorian stage, with many plays featuring ghostly characters, some of which were holdovers from the eighteenth century Gothic plays. The eighteenth century "phantasmagoria," a pre-cinema form of image projection related to the magic lantern, was often and publicly used to create the illusion of translucent ghosts or skeletons and to heighten the dramatic effect in nineteenth century productions. It involved drawing ghostly images on slides that a lens and light would project over the heads of the audience, sometimes on a smoke screen, to produce its specters. So effective were these projections that viewers were said to swat at the illusory ghosts or even to flee the room in terror, though less effective shows occurred when the drawings were of inferior quality or contained mistakes or flaws. Etienne-Gaspard Robertson used the phantasmagoria to great effect around 1800, calling up ghosts from the plays of Shakespeare, Gothic novels, and the specters of the French Revolution's villains. Such a show, by a partner of Madame Tussaud, became a hit in Britain, and they continued under various showmen into the 1830s.[9] Authors used the phantasmagoria in their fiction, and Poe referenced the machine in his stories, especially "The Fall of the House of Usher." By the mid- and late–nineteenth century, middle class families purchased their own magic lanterns to hold their own ghost shows.[10]

Another impressive way to create a stage ghost, and one still in use today, is the "Pepper's ghost" technique. It was named for John Henry Pepper, a professor who modified a phantasmagoria invented by Henry Dircks in 1862 to work in British theaters. In this illusion, a large piece of glass or a mirror is positioned on a forty-five–degree angle so that the viewer cannot tell that it is there at all. When special lights are turned on or off, the mirror reflects an offstage actor portraying the ghost or some other character, making it appear that the entity has materialized out of nothing, and vanishing can be achieved by reversing the process. In addition, if the mirror is painted black, only light colored objects will be partially visible, giving the ghost a translucent and spectral air. It was used to great effect in an 1862 adaptation of Charles Dickens's ghostly 1848 novella *The Haunted Man*, which told of a professor haunted by a ghostly twin until he learned the true meaning of forgiveness and Christmas. One viewer thought the ghosts had the air of "unmistakable reality."[11] Pepper's ghost was also used in the French cabaret under the name Cabaret du Néant, or Cabaret of Death.

Professor John Henry Pepper, though, was not merely famous for inventing his ghost illusion. Pepper also gave dazzling lectures on science, in the tradition of Michael Faraday and William Brande. These eminent British scientists demonstrated their discoveries for the public and developed a repertoire of astounding visual effects for the amusement of those who paid to see them on stage. Pepper in particular took pains to explain how his "ghost" was done so the crowds would learn the rational and scientific principles behind it. This was meant to be an effective counter-measure to the spiritualists Pepper also wrote a series of popular science-is-fun books for boys, the *Playbooks*, that were continuously published until the twentieth century, because Pepper believed that everyone (well, at least every *male*) needed strong training in science and reason to navigate the modern world. Thus his stage shows were meant to morally uplift boys and men, and some of his theatrical science show lingered into the twentieth century in the guise of Don Herbert's *Mr. Wizard*.[12]

However, science educators like Professor Pepper had to compete with the equally entertaining and exceedingly popular stage shows of the psychic mediums. Mediums traveled across the United States and around the world giving performance lectures and sitting for private readings in the homes of wealthy patrons. On stage they typically performed in a trance, claiming that they spoke not on their own but in the voice of their spirit guides who would deliver truths from the spirit world. In a typical trance lecture, the medium asked the audience to elect a jury who would decide upon a topic on which the medium would consult the spirits. The male-dominated juries often selected scientific topics that the (usually) female medium would be presumed not to know about. After the jury announced the topic, the medium would enter a trance. Thereupon the "spirit" would hold forth on the stated topic for an hour or more. By the end of the performance, the best mediums, like Emma Hardinge or Cora Richmond, could leave the audience cheering or reduce them to tears.[13] The mediums attracted large crowds and much attention, and adoring admirers were a dime a dozen. Hardinge was dismayed when a young man became obsessed with her and claimed he used his "astral body" to stalk her. He ended up in an insane asylum.[14]

Unfortunately, the great age of medium-performers ended when local governments in the United States began enforcing laws against fortune telling and faith healing at the end of the nineteenth century. Wills made under the influence of Spiritualism were declared invalid, and spiritualists could be committed to asylums since they were obviously insane.[15] This lasted until the middle of the twentieth century, when in Britain spiritualists pressured the government to repeal the Witchcraft Act of 1735, legalizing fortune telling and psychic readings. In the United States, anti-fortune telling laws remained on the books but were enforced with increasing rareness.

Also on the late Victorian stage was the reemergence of Faust, this time as an opera by the Frenchman Charles Gounod. Premiering in Paris in 1859, the opera loosely followed a part of Goethe's epic poem. In this version, the action centers on Faust and Marguerite, a village girl Faust loves and with whose love Mephistopheles tempts Faust to resign his quest for faith and science in favor of the black arts. Faust realizes that although he has lived in pursuit of learning he lacks true knowledge, but when Mephistopheles grants Faust's wishes, Faust wishes only for youth. Faust impregnates Marguerite but does not marry her. The shame of her sin nearly condemns her to Hell and does send her to prison, and there is a weird ballet set on Walpurgis Night, filled with ghosts, witches, and demons. In her prison cell Marguerite's prayers call down angelic saviors who lift her to Heaven even as her lover's unanswered prayers leave him condemned to eternal hellfire. The opera was a smashing success on both sides of the Atlantic. It played at the Paris Opera alone 1,500 times before 1917,[16] and it opened the New York opera season each year through the nineteenth century. The opera made cameo appearances in Edith Wharton's *Age of Innocence* (1920), where it frames the beginning of Books I and II; and it is the same opera performed at the Paris Opera House during the reign of Gaston Leroux's Phantom of the Opera, lending some of its tragic import to that doomed figure.

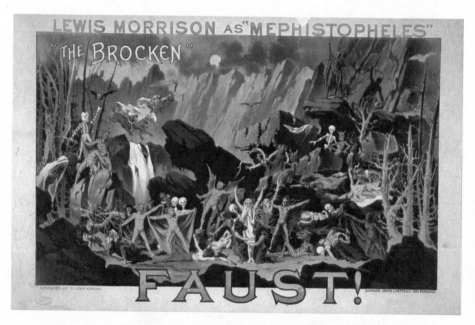

Poster for *Faust*. The opera *Faust* was one of the most popular on the Victorian stage, opening most seasons of the New York Opera and delighting legions of fans. This poster shows Mephistopheles (top right) commanding the legions of the damned on the Brocken, a German mountain known for the spectral effect caused by climbers' shadows playing off the mist that enshrouds the peak. This gave rise to the legend of the Brocken specter and the peak's association with evil (Library of Congress, LC-USZ6-437).

Horror on the Screen

With the coming of cinema, we find the horrors of mind and soul making the same transition the horror of the body made when Edison filmed the first *Frankenstein*, and *Jekyll and Hyde* started its run of multiple remakes. Only this time the horror emerged from post–World War I Germany rather than Britain or the United States. The first and greatest of the early horror movies (then called "photoplays") dealing with the broad themes I have lumped under the rubric of spiritualist horror was Robert Wiene's Expressionist film *Das Kabinett des Doktor Caligari* (*The Cabinet of Dr. Caligari*) (1919), an immortal classic widely credited with launching the horror genre in cinema.

In the German town of Holstenwall, Francis and his friend Alan attend a carnival where a Dr. Caligari (Werner Krauss) displays a sleepwalker named Cesare (Conrad Veidt), a giant of a man who sleeps in a coffin. Cesare tells Alan that he will die the next day. He does, and Francis suspects that Caligari is behind the death. Meanwhile, the father of Francis's girlfriend Jane has also been killed, and Jane too suspects Caligari's involvement in the crime. It turns out that Caligari is using the somnambulant Cesare to commit murders, but the brute falls in love with Jane when he is meant to murder her. He carries her swooning form across the rooftops, but he collapses in his flight and plunges off a mountain to his death, sparing Jane the ignominy of rape. Jane and Francis confront Dr. Caligari, but he escapes and a chase ensues.

Reasoning that Caligari might be an escaped mental patient, our heroes venture to the local asylum where they discover the good doctor is in fact the asylum's director! When he is away at night they pore over his journals and learn that the director fantasized about an ancient mountebank named Caligari who had a murderous somnambulist pet. The asylum director went mad and assumed the guise of Caligari and then wanted to conduct an evil experiment to discover whether a mental patient (Cesare) could be mesmerically provoked to commit murder. As the director wrote, "I must know everything. I must penetrate the heart of the secret. I must become Caligari!" Caligari conducted this experiment in the guise of a circus performer. Armed with this knowledge, the townsfolk bring the body of dead Cesare to the asylum where Dr. Caligari becomes uncontrollably upset upon seeing his life's work lifeless before him. The asylum attendants drag the mad doctor away to his cell, and everyone rejoices.

Unfortunately, the story is not over: A framing device added by producers looking to soften the anti-authoritarian message of the film[17] (Caligari was meant to symbolize Prussian control over the German people) drags us back to the present where we learn that the whole story was actually the ravings of Francis, who is in truth an inmate at the asylum. Jane and Cesare are his fellow patients, and Dr. Caligari (or the director, or whoever he really is) promises to cure Francis of his delusions.

The Cabinet of Doctor Caligari (1919). The mad scientist Dr. Caligari (Werner Krauss) presents his hypnotized accomplice, Cesare (Conrad Veidt), as part of his traveling shoe. Dr. Caligari was one of the first in a long line of evil psychiatrists in horror, culminating seventy years later with Hannibal Lecter, the cannibal psychiatrist. The ability to manipulate others' minds made psychiatrists particularly menacing figures in horror (Kino International).

The most impressive part of *Caligari* is the visually arresting expressionist sets by Hermann Warm. The odd angles and sharply stylized backdrops are instantly recognizable and have influenced horror films down through the years, including James Whale's *Frankenstein* and Tim Burton's many films. Rooftops tilt crazily, trees are twisted into painful contortions, and sharp shadows are indicated with a thick, black paint. *Caligari* probably did more than any other film to use set design to externalize the mental state of the characters in it, the off-kilter backgrounds suggesting a world of madness outside normal reality and in the realm of the mythical, the mystical, and the mental. When *Caligari* premiered in New York in 1921, the Hearst newspaper chain advocated banning it because it challenged American supremacy in film, and anti–German crowds clamored for a wholesome "American" replacement for the "morbid and grotesque" European photoplay.[18]

But despite the controversy, *Caligari* helped launch the horror genre in film, and it did so with a tale of a mad scientist who uses the institutional authority of science to manipulate, control, and kill. Here the psychiatrist is the villain, his mastery over his patients' minds complete and incontrovertible. He is, in effect, in a position of godlike authority and power, and he misuses it in a way that produces only death and terror. Even with the framing device, the story is still one of the horrors of mental illness. The revolution in mental hygiene pioneered by Sigmund Freud manifested itself as the mad psychiatrist whose special knowledge about the workings of the mind left patients vulnerable, their souls open to invasion and manipulation and control.

Caligari was responsible for launching a wave of mad scientist cinema, which as we shall see became the dominant theme of the 1930s golden age of horror film. In Japan, the film's influence helped create an entire genre of "mad scientist murders" in detective fiction (and later film), in which scientists use their mastery of science and privileged position in society to carry out a series of debauched, violent, unsettling murders on a helpless population ignorant of their methods and unable to resist their power. The films, Sari Kawana believes, are meant to imply that fanatical devotion to pure materialist science is incompatible with traditional and humane ethics. This point could carry over equally as well to *Caligari*.[19]

Another film from 1919, *When the Clouds Roll By*, also features a psychiatrist (Herbert Grimwood) who tries to drive a patient (Douglas Fairbanks) to madness and suicide. In the twist ending, the psychiatrist is revealed to be an escaped asylum patient.

The story of the Golem was also brought to film during this era, with Henrik Galeen and Paul Wegener's *Der Golem* (1915). In this version, the old Jewish legendary creature is reanimated in twentieth century Prague and goes on a killing spree for love of his new master's wife. The classic film version of the story, *Der Golem, wie er in die Welt kam* (1920), remains in the sixteenth century, where a rabbi breathes life into a clay figure to protect Prague's Jews from persecution. The rabbi gives the Golem a version of a human soul, imbuing him with human emotions. When the rabbi's assistant uses the creature to commit murder and kidnap the rabbi's daughter, the Golem rebels and the plot unravels. The film is widely considered a masterpiece of German horror, and its plot and *Caligari*–style sets prefigure James Whale's *Frankenstein* films.

Films like these were produced in the wake of the First World War when the public began to develop misgivings about the dogma of Progress and the triumph of science after seeing the horrors science brought to life during the course of that long and deadly conflict. The revolutionary developments in science in the twentieth century's first decades would inspire a new kind of cosmic horror that brought the art of horror to its most developed and philosophical state.

PART IV

Terror from Outside
Cosmic Horror
(c. 1895–c. 1945)

10

SCIENCE AND SOCIETY

In biological and spiritualist horror, we saw the way horror writers attempted to deal with scientific challenges to traditional views of the human body and the human mind. However, in these works the authors tended to focus on the individual. We have seen how Victor Frankenstein and Dr. Moreau were special cases of science crossing boundaries, and we have explored how Professor Guildea and *The Turn of the Screw*'s unnamed governess came to terms with ghostly entities that invaded their normal, rational lives. But in all these cases, the focus was on the individual and the way he or she reacted to a very specific set of circumstances revolving around that individual's personal world. Even the entities at play in biological and spiritualist horror — Dracula, the Frankenstein monster, Guildea's idiot ghost — were individuals possessed of personalized wants and desires, and (for many) the ability to reason on human terms and engage humanity at its own level. Dracula may have been nearly the embodiment of evil, but he was human once, too. Guildea's ghost may have been mindless, but it had human emotions and needs.

By the turn of the twentieth century, however, a new type of horror emerged, drawing on larger themes that sought to understand the individual's place in society at large and even in the cosmos itself. This breed of horror, which I am calling cosmic horror after H. P. Lovecraft's usage, typically deals with entities and experiences that transcend individuals, societies, whole cultures, or even humanity itself. Sometimes this takes the form of alien life forms, and other times it manifests only as an individual's encounter with the truly weird in a way that shatters his understanding of the way the world works. Ghosts and biological monsters do not quite reach this level because even for non-believers they are familiar creatures, while the truly weird presents situations that humans only barely understand and removes humans from the center of creation toward a peripheral place in the universal order. Cosmic horror represents the individual's fear of losing himself in the face of larger forces beyond his control.

This particular school of horror writing represents the genre at its apex, subsuming within it all that came before and influencing all that would come after. However, it did not emerge *ex nihilo*, and its development was intimately tied to the revolution in the scientific understanding of the universe that emerged in the run-up to the First World War, and the chaotic and traumatic aftermath of that first war of industrial killing.

Bound by Blood

Prior to the Victorian age, individuals viewed themselves as residents of their village, practitioners of a certain faith, and subject to a local lord or more distant monarch or regime. There was little understanding of ethnic groups as we conceive them today, and few would have considered themselves genetically related to distant peoples on the basis of shared cultural traits like language and dress. That changed in the wake of the French Revolution and Napoleonic Wars as medieval empires and kingdoms gave way to nation-states over the course of the nineteenth century.[1] A state's people became the foundation on which the state wielded power, "We the People of the United States" being the most famous example. In Revolutionary France, the government acted in the name of the French people, while its enemies still followed the old dictum of "God, king, and country." Napoleon, too, reorganized Europe into new kingdoms based partly on ethnic identities rather than dynastic ownership. Though the Congress of Vienna tried to undo these changes, in the aftermath of Napoleon and the revolutions of 1848 even the most autocratic governments, like Czarist Russia, claimed to act on behalf of the peoples residing within their borders and on behalf of their ethnic cousins in other lands. The change was most obvious in the Habsburg domains when in 1867 the Austrian Empire gave way to the hybrid Dual Monarchy of Austria-Hungary to recognize the national claims of the Hungarian Magyars.

Therefore, the individual at the end of the nineteenth century came to be viewed as a member of a specific group, a nation, bound by blood to others of his ethnicity and his race. Most importantly, the nation was distinct from the Other, the outsiders who are necessarily an oppositional force. With its verities apparently justified by Darwinian survival of the fittest, the Victorian individual could also rest assured that his nation and his state were superior to all others by biology and science, a belief that became known as nationalism: "Nationalism is an ideology which imagines the community in a particular way (as national), asserts the primacy of this collective identity over others, and seeks political power in its name, ideally (if not exclusively or everywhere) in the form of a state for the nation (or nation-state)."[2] It was an outgrowth of the Romantic Movement, when an irrational appeal to emotion, bonds, and blood was not just persuasive but also seemingly natural and self-evident.[3] So effective was nationalist ideology that the very idea of state and nation merged so that today they are interchangeable. Nationalism has become the *sine qua non* of political legitimacy; a modern state absent a nation must inevitably fail.

It has been said that nationalism justified total war, for any nation worthy of the name believes itself superior to its enemy who therefore deserves to be completely destroyed.[4] The emerging nationalist feelings of the nineteenth century contributed to the liberation of Greece in 1831, and the unification of Italy in 1861 (completed in 1870) and Germany in 1871. It also led individuals across Europe and the Americas to conceive of themselves as part of larger biological-cultural entities that were both immutable and natural into which the individual vanished as just one of "the American people," "pan–Slavs," or the German *Volk*. This was symbolized in the advent of military camouflage, in which the armies in which nation-states symbolized themselves became undifferentiated masses of khaki, beige, and gray.[5] On the other hand, nationalism's call for an independent homeland for each nation led to the breakup of ancient multi-national empires like Austria-Hungary in 1918, and its emphasis on the biological reality of nationhood implied that certain nations were biologically superior, yielding a racism that culminated in Hitler's Holocaust.

Vanishing into History

As a direct result of nationalist ideology, the history of each glorious nation became the living proof whereby modern peoples could find their collective identity. Therefore, archaeology became a passion in the late Victorian and Edwardian periods. Nations needed a past on which to draw, and it became necessary to exhume ancient cultures to find the "authentic" traditions of the nation. Where these were absent, nations were not above making them up out of pseudoscience and whole cloth, or appropriating those of other cultures or mythology.

In the United States, there was a problem of history. The descendants of Europeans could not claim European history as their own (they had, after all, left Europe for a reason), but in the New World there were only Native Americans, who were racially distinct and viewed as culturally inferior. Unlike ancient Europeans, the Indians of North America had not built great stone cities or left impressive monuments. However, Americans made extreme efforts to craft an ancient past for the emerging American nation. Building on claims by Spanish missionaries, some began to call Native Americans one of the ten Lost Tribes of Israel, and American abolitionists prayed for their conversion to Christianity as a sign of the coming Millennium. It was claimed that certain native tribes had customs that were similar to those of the ancient Hebrews.[6] Further, the Mormon Church adopted this idea and claimed that Christ had visited North America to preach his gospel to them. Others argued that "lost tribes" of Caucasians wandered America, remnants of earlier European voyages. In making these claims, Americans appropriated Native America as a surrogate history which they could append to the emerging narrative of the American nation.

This also explains the rage for claiming Cherokee princesses as ancestors during the late nineteenth century.

But Americans did more than appropriate Native American history (even as they sought to restrict Native Americans to reservations until they would "die out"). They also assigned Native American works to ancient European cultures in an effort to show that anything noble in native culture was "really" European and therefore white. In the United States this took the form of the pernicious "myth of the Moundbuilders," a mysterious race alleged to have built the great earthen mounds scattered across the North American landscape, and which once served as temple mounts, tombs, and astronomical observatories over the course of more than two millennia of construction. Though Thomas Jefferson excavated a mound in 1782 and demonstrated that it was Native American, scholars and antiquarians insisted that the mounds were "really" the work of Phoenicians, wandering Irish monks, or a "lost race," since it was self-evident that Native Americans were too intellectually stunted to have piled dirt into great earthen works, a skill only sophisticated Europeans could master. The belief in the lost race theory lingered on into the late nineteenth century, when the Smithsonian's John Wesley Powell appointed Cyrus Thomas, himself a believer in the lost race, to investigate the mounds. In 1894 Thomas reported back that his investigation had changed his mind; the mounds were entirely the work of Native Americans. His report became the last and definitive answer on the subject.[7]

But mounds were hardly the end of the imaginative archaeology of the period. Many writers claimed that the similarity of the pyramids of the Maya and pre–Inca peoples to those of ancient Egypt demonstrated that they were actually built by Egyptians. More imaginative writers, like Ignatius Donnelly, a former United States Congressman from Minnesota, thought that the similarities between the ancient cultures of the Americas and those of the Old World indicated a common source for both, which was the lost continent of Atlantis. He was inspired in part by Heinrich Schliemann's 1878 discovery of the previously mythical city of Troy. Since Troy was real, it became just possible that mythological realms like Atlantis might be, too. In *Atlantis: The Antediluvian World* (1882) Donnelly traced the history of the continent, freely embellishing on Plato's brief references to the continent, widely viewed until then as allegorical. Donnelly's Atlantis was a technological marvel in which men wielded the power of gods, and in fact were confused for them by later generations who had but distorted memories of the lost continent after a volcano sent it to the bottom of the ocean. These memories they fashioned into the historic religions and cultures of the Old and New Worlds, and the traces of Atlantis can still be seen today in global myths of a flood and similar religious practices in a variety of primitive societies.[8] The lost continent became a cultural icon, and psychics like the "sleeping prophet" Edgar Cayce began to claim contact with lost Atlantis, holding forth on its technical wonders. Though scientifically sloppy,

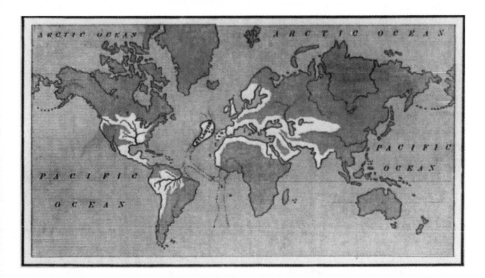

"The Empire of Atlantis." This illustration from Ignatius Donnelly's *Atlantis: The Antediluvian World* shows in white the territory Donnelly thought Atlantis once controlled, which encompasses every ancient civilization then known except China. Such speculations meshed well with some Social Darwinian interpretations of human evolution, which imagined a master (white) race ruling over less evolved peoples (Library of Congress, LC-USZ62-90566).

Atlantis became the most influential book ever written on the subject of lost civilizations, and its intellectual descendents in the guise of Erich von Däniken and Graham Hancock are still being published today.

Other lost continents began to pop up in the wake of Atlantis, notably Lemuria and Mu. Lemuria was an imaginary continent connecting Africa and India, which was first proposed by English zoologist Philip L. Sclater to scientifically explain the presence of lemurs on both sides of the Indian Ocean in a time before the theory of plate tectonics was widely accepted. The German scientist Ernst Haeckel later proposed that Lemuria was actually the place where humans evolved. Lemuria was then adopted by Madame Helena Blavatsky, a spiritualist medium and charlatan who created Theosophy, an influential practice that combined Spiritualism with bizarre cult archaeology to give grandeur and historical depth to the spiritualists' claims. In her (often plagiarized) works *Isis Unveiled* (1877) and *The Secret Doctrine* (1888) Blavatsky railed against "materialist" science and posited a universe of mystery and magic. She claimed that humanity was one of seven root races that had and would rule the earth in succession (we're fifth; the Atlanteans were fourth, and sixth is coming soon), thus making evolution a tool of spiritual advancement.[9] Though the Society for Psychical Research declared her a fraud (she burned her house down to destroy the evidence), Blavatsky had a large following, headed a widespread cult, and influenced a number of later writers of both fact and fiction, including the Satanist Aleister Crowley.

Blavatsky's followers, like W. Scott-Elliot, expanded on her vision, claiming that the Theosophical masters, from their citadel in Tibet and in the planes beyond earth, used "astral clairvoyance" to flesh out Blavatsky's doctrine and reveal that peoples from Venus had visited Earth and that the seven races represented only decay as the pure spirit of the first race became encased in flesh and degraded through time. Different human races descended from different sub-races of the Lemurians under Venusian tutelage, culminating in the appearance of Aryan man, the most perfect human form.[10] In 1926, the self-titled "Colonel" James Churchward invented another new continent, Mu, in the Pacific Ocean, revealed to him on self-translating magic tablets in the Naacal language in Tibet. Of course, Mu was a multiracial empire dominated by perfect white Aryans whose superiority all acknowledged. Unlike Theosophical notions, Muvians were not subject to evolution, but their island vanished in a volcanic explosion, the standard method of disposal for unwanted continents.[11]

The racist implications of Atlantean, Lemurian, and Muvian speculation dovetailed nicely with the chauvinistic assumptions of nationalism, and it was no coincidence that the Nazi party adopted a similar line in their recreation of a glorious, German, and completely Aryan past. Heinrich Himmler, the head of the SS, sent archaeological expeditions around the world to find proof of Blavatsky's claims, the lost continent of Atlantis, and the origins of the Aryan race somewhere in Tibet, home to Theosophy's ascended masters. The swastika, as an ancient Tibetan symbol, was studied by German Theosophy in 1896 and became the Nazi symbol of Aryan purity in the 1920s under this influence.[12]

In the United States, Charles Fort busied himself collecting newspaper and scientific journal accounts of the weird and unexplained, such as incidents of frogs falling like rain, poltergeists, and extraterrestrials, which he published in *The Book of the Damned* (1919) and its three sequels, *New Lands* (1923), *Lo!* (1931), and *Wild Talents* (1932). He hoped his collections would embarrass scientists, whom he likened to arrogant and dogmatic priests of secular faith, into admitting that they could not explain everything. In this, Fort considered himself a true skeptic, accepting neither science nor faith, but others considered him a crank who could not distinguish truth from fiction. His work begat a Fortean Society and their magazine, *Fortean Times*, which carries the torch today.

Purifying the Stock

Because individuals were now viewed as secondary to larger populations, whether national or racial, some scientists began to apply the concepts of

Darwinian evolution to human populations. These scientists believed that whole populations were subject to the same Darwinian forces as animals in the wild. Therefore, each nation or race required the strongest population possible to increase the likelihood of producing the best possible children to further the nation or race into the future. Society, in other words, was biology by other means. Ernst Haeckel, of Lemurian fame, advocated a hierarchy of races leading up to white Aryans at the top of the heap, and he argued that Darwinian evolution was a universal explanation of the world and a justification of Germanic supremacy therein. Since the fittest survive, and the German Aryans were fittest, they therefore had the evolutionary imperative to preserve their breeding stock by eliminating "contamination" from non–Germans, deviants, the "genetically inferior," and the mentally or physically disabled. The individual was to be sacrificed for the good of the race.[13] This led directly to the Nazi policies of sterilization, euthanasia, and the Holocaust.

In pre-war England and the United States, scientists differed slightly in that they considered the English and white Americans, the Anglo-Saxons, to be the highest breed of human stock. British and American scientists worried that the white race was degenerating because the poor, the criminal, and the inferior were out-breeding the best elements of society, producing a degraded and mongrel population. Sir Francis Galton, a cousin of Darwin's, advocated for government-controlled selective breeding to increase the intelligence and fitness of the population. He called his system "eugenics," and by the outbreak of the First World War both Britain and America had official eugenics policies and university departments devoted to the scheme's promotion.[14]

Alfred Binet, the French scholar who classified "subnormal" human intelligences, had developed a scale meant to diagnose whether a child had mental retardation. He proposed that the retarded could be classified into three groups (in descending order of intelligence): morons, idiots, and imbeciles. Henry Goddard and Lewis Terman immediately saw how to apply this scale as a test of intelligence. The Stanford-Binet test was to measure a person's "intelligence quotient" to demonstrate scientifically the superiority of the white race and to weed out morons, idiots, and imbeciles from the population. The test was applied to immigrants, more than three and a half million of which entered the United States between 1890 and 1900; the country then had a population of only seventy-seven million. Immigrant groups were banned because their nation or race rated poorly on IQ tests, and between 1921 and 1924 Congress instituted a series of discriminatory immigration policies meant to restrict immigration to desirable races.

The Eugenics Records Office, supported by John D. Rockefeller, Alexander Graham Bell, and others, sought to promote

> the study of America's most effective blood lines; and the methods of securing the preponderance and relative increase of the best blood strains; the study of the origins of and the best methods of restricting the strains that produce the defective and delinquent classes of the community....[15]

Under the influence of eugenics, nearly seventy thousand American citizens suspected of harboring faulty genes were forcibly sterilized under a patchwork of state laws. Other laws restricted morons, imbeciles, and idiots from marrying to avoid passing on the "taint" of inferiority. The U.S. Supreme Court upheld these laws in the 1927 *Buck v. Bell* decision, which held that Virginia had the right to forcibly sterilize its citizens; and eugenic claims were used to justify prohibitions on racially mixed marriages. These policies continued into the 1960s, when many eugenics laws were finally repealed. In other countries sterilizations continued for several more decades, and indeed may continue even today. In every case, the individual's rights were set aside in favor of the alleged benefits to larger groups.

Moving Heaven and Earth

Since this is a book on the horror genre, I have necessarily explored the negative side of science; but science and its applied form, technology, had also worked wonders in the early twentieth century, changing eons-old world-views and shaking humanity's very conception of its role in the cosmos at large. This was best exemplified at the 1939 World's Fair in New York, where the World of Tomorrow presented a vision of the future that became standard for much of the twentieth century: Television, robots, crisp modern architecture of spheres and spires, push-button convenience, and a model of "Democracity," a utopian community of the future. Technology, the Fair argued, would usher in a virtual Millennium of peace and progress. The Jetsons would have recognized it as home.

In the preceding decades, the invention of the automobile and the airplane revolutionized transportation and consequently made the world seem much smaller. Journeys that used to take days or weeks to cover could now be made in much less time. Crossing the Atlantic by ship took two weeks in 1850, but by the time *Titanic* went down in 1912, the ship was set to break the Atlantic crossing record by taking less than nine days. Airships cut the travel time still further, and when Charles Lindbergh crossed the Atlantic in 1927 in under thirty-four hours, the ocean was no longer a vast barrier between Europe and the United States. Automobiles connected people as never before, moving them quickly across town and between cities and freeing them from the set routes and schedules of the train system. Henry Ford's Model-T was priced for the average man, and he sold more than a million by 1920, creating a nation of peripatetic car drivers. As a result the automobile went from oddity to essential, and in the process it allowed people to escape the cities and live virtually anywhere, though this contributed to the slow breakdown of social relationships and family life.

However, this was also the era of "mass" production, when consumer

Flying car. No single image has summed up society's hopes for a technologically utopian future like the flying car, seen here in a 1905 illustration. In the twentieth century, some of the greatest thinkers and visionaries imagined that scientific and technological advances would lead to an unprecedented era of peace, prosperity, and freedom. Instead, within ten years of this charming illustration, technology and science were employed in the service of destruction and war.

products were targeted to presumably homogenous demographic groups. Unlike today's world of niche production, the early twentieth century industrial world created products meant to appeal to the largest possible audience, and consumers had to fit their lives into what the large trusts and conglomerates provided rather than find products and services tailored to their needs. Henry Ford, maker of only one color of car, said it best: a man could have any color Model-T he wanted so long as it was black. There was no choice; conform or do without. Newspapers, and the emerging film and radio industries, became "mass media," aiming at large general audiences. Once again, the individual became one more faceless entity in a large crowd defined by others. The individual was an advertiser's demographic, a newspaper's readership, or a film's audience.

This view of the individual's insignificance found an uncanny echo in developments in the natural sciences. The first development touched on questions of human uniqueness and humanity's relationship to the cosmos. In 1895 Percival Lowell, the famed astronomer, discovered life on Mars. Gazing up at the Red Planet from his telescope, Lowell thought he saw lines across the surface of Mars, and he deduced that the regularity of the lines implied that they were the work of an extraterrestrial intelligence: "Their very aspect is such as

Mars. When the astronomer Percival Lowell looked at Mars, he thought he saw canals (actually an optical illusion). From this he concluded there was intelligent life on the Red Planet, sparking a wave of Martian-themed alien invasion horror stories ranging from H.G. Wells's *The War of the Worlds* to the movie *Invaders from Mars* to the Looney Tunes' Marvin the Martian (NASA, ESA, and the Hubble Heritage Team [STScI/AURA]).

to defy natural explanation, and to hint that in them we are regarding something other than the outcome of purely natural causes."[16] Lowell ignored his own maxim, "A very slight hint in the eye goes a long way in the brain,"[17] and took an artifact of his telescope and some wishful thinking for Martian-hewed canals whose visibility followed the agricultural cycle of the Martian seasons! Though we recognize today Lowell's error, in his time his discovery forced many to confront the possibility that humanity was but one species among many cosmic intelligences, and that the especial place humans held in the traditional cosmos, already challenged by Darwin, was now permanently broken.

The situation did not improve with Albert Einstein's publication of the special theory of relativity in 1905 and general relativity in 1915. Einstein's work revolutionized physics and appeared to overturn the mechanical cosmos advocated by Newton and virtually canonized for three centuries. Einstein believed that time and space were not universal absolutes, as previously assumed, but were functions of the observer's velocity. The viewer's speed determined such former givens as length, width, height, and time. Further, mass and energy were interchangeable at a ratio of $e = mc^2$ (energy = mass time the speed of light squared), soon to be the most famous equation in all physics. This shocked physicists who thought they were discrete phenomena, and many refused to accept the new theory, even after its truth was demonstrated with an experiment during an eclipse in 1919. Even more bizarre was Max Planck's quantum mechanics, which described a micro-world in which the normal laws of physics seemed suspended or inverted. In the popular mind, relativity and quantum mechanics came to stand for a cosmos unhinged from traditional absolutes and subject to individual interpretation.

Einstein's theories completed a sea-change in human thought, supplementing Darwin's rewriting of biology and Freud's revelations about the human mind. In this new world of science triumphant, the old verities had fallen away in a remarkably short time, replaced with a coherent and comprehensive set of theories that laid out a relative, materialist, and accidental universe. Taken together, evolution, psychoanalysis, and relativity insisted that humans were nothing more than irrational objects of pure chance, evolving by accident from a mindless and changing cosmos, subject only to what natural laws relativity left intact, and progressing toward no fixed goal.

In 1910, when Haley's Comet appeared in the sky, the pope reassured Catholics that the event was wholly natural and astronomical, and did not portend any judgment of God toward a wicked world. Perhaps in 1914 he reconsidered his claim.

Wars and Rumors of War

The futility of existence never seemed clearer than in the aftermath of the First World War, when Europe collectively committed suicide, empires were left broken and in ruins, nine million soldiers were dead, and countless civilians perished with them. Coming at the end of a series of political assassinations that included three American presidents, the czar of Russia, the king of Italy, and the empress of Austria, the June 1914 assassination of Austrian Archduke Franz Ferdinand, heir to the empire's throne, by a Serbian nationalist hardly seemed the sort of event that would trigger total war. But the international situation was tense, and the series of rivalries that developed among the Great Powers of Europe moved haltingly toward war when the Austrian response to the assassination drew Germany, Russia, France, and Britain into the widening war.

The resulting conflict lasted from 1914 to 1918, and the images from it are still potent: gas masks, trenches, aerial dogfights, and everywhere the stench of death. Over the course of the conflict, the very tools science had hailed as miracles had been transmuted into horrific weapons of war. New forms of guns and gunpowder only made them more lethal. Advances in chemistry gave rise to chemical weapons, like mustard gas, whose poisonous effects were so ghastly that they defy description. The war would use 128,208 tons of poison gas, closing off lungs, causing enormous pain and bleeding and killing perhaps half a million. Advances in flight gave rise to airplanes that brought bombs, dogfights, and death. Even the invention of the automobile only served as a basis for an early version of the tank. Telephones and telegraphs gave commanders better control over their troops, but this only made attacks more effective.[18] However, the Allied Powers and the Central Powers were about evenly matched, and despite the best efforts of German and British science, neither side gained a solid advantage. Only with American intervention in 1917 did the war turn decisively for the Allies.

The poet William Owen captured something of the abject horror of a wartime gas attack in his poem "Dulce et Decorum Est" (1917, published 1921):

> Men marched asleep. Many had lost their boots
> But limped on, blood-shod. All went lame; all blind;
> Drunk with fatigue; deaf even to the hoots
> Of disappointed shells that dropped behind...
> If you could hear, at every jolt, the blood
> Come gargling from the froth-corrupted lungs,
> Obscene as cancer, bitter as the cud....[19]

It is impossible to underestimate the effects of World War I and the flawed Peace of Versailles that followed. As H. G. Wells put it in his epic history of the world, *The Outline of History*, just a few years after the war:

> The world in the year after the great war was like a man who has some vital surgical operation very roughly performed and who is not yet sure whether he can now go on living or whether he has not been so profoundly shocked and injured that he will presently fall down and die. It was a world dazed and stunned.... Everything went on, now that the strain of the conflict had ceased, rather laxly, rather weakly, and with a gusty and uncertain temper.[20]

The war introduced the concept of shell shock, and it applied metaphorically to the psyches of the home front as much as to the soldiers who experienced war first hand. Another shock to the system happened at the end of the war with the outbreak of the great influenza, known as the Spanish Flu. It spread rapidly around the world, sickening millions and killing more than the entirety of the Great War itself. By the time it was over, somewhere between twenty and forty million had died agonizing deaths, and it must have seemed like God was visiting a great plague upon a war-torn and benighted world. The unusual flu killed people in their prime, rather than the elderly and children, and its reach and morbidity made it deadlier than the Black Death that ravaged fourteenth century Europe. Governments turned to scientists to stop the illness, and heroic public health measures helped contain its spread through isolation, quarantine, and hygiene. Perhaps more than any other set of events, the World War and the influenza pandemic cemented the relationship between science and government that would last into the twenty-first century.

But with so many dying from war, from disease, and from God-knew-what-else, it was no wonder that many came to believe the world was coming to an end. During World War I, millennialist beliefs rose dramatically, and the coming of the Russian Revolution in 1917 seemed to signal that the forces of the Antichrist were on the march as the atheist communists seized control of formerly Orthodox Russia and spoke in self-conscious ways about destroying the old world and everything in it in preparation for a glorious Millennium of the proletariat. The Soviets themselves viewed the establishment of the Soviet Union as the dawn of a new age, and in Germany Adolf Hitler began to develop the idea that the old Teutonic belief in *Gotterdammerung*, the fiery end of the old world, must come to pass before a new world of Aryan glory could be born.[21]

Even for those less dramatically inclined, the great trauma of war and plague symbolized the decline and decadence of Western civilization, a culture contaminated by racial, cultural, and genetic impurities. Oswald Spengler, the German historian-philosopher, captured the mood in his *Decline of the West* (1918), in which he held that Western civilization was in terminal decline. He thought that the West was like Faust, reaching for the unattainable and forbidden, and like Faust descending into nothingness when the quest is exposed as folly. He likened civilizations to the seasons, viewing the Middle Ages as the springtime of the West, the Renaissance as its summer, the Enlightenment as its fall harvest of riches, and the modern world as the long, cold winter of civilization. Democracy served only as a mask for plutocracy, and dictatorship was the inevitable result of corruption and decay. Worse, there were no eternal verities or truths, only relative truths that shift with the sands of time.

The glamorous American revival of the 1920s seemed to rebut Spengler's thesis, but the frivolity of the Jazz Age was itself only a mask over deeper problems that emerged in 1929 when the New York Stock Exchange crashed, and the world was plunged into a long, deep economic crisis, the Great Depression.

Americans lost billions as banks went bust; the gross national product fell to half its 1929 level in just four years. Manufacturing declined by anywhere from thirty to eighty percent, by industry. Farms virtually ceased to function, as prices plummeted (one Oklahoma county's wheat harvest fell from $1.2 million in 1931 to just $7,000 in 1933) as collapsing markets and a plague of locusts turned agricultural land into the Dust Bowl. Unemployment reached record levels; one in four Americans was out of work.[22] It was the worst economic crisis in the history of the Western world, and the situation lasted with varying severity for a decade. It seemed as though capitalism, science, and industry had failed. Governments around the world sought to alleviate the Depression's harshest aspects through programs as diverse as Franklin Roosevelt's New Deal in the United States and Hitler's military preparations in Germany. Despite Roosevelt's efforts, and because of Hitler's, the international situation deteriorated and the world crisis of the Depression slid into global catastrophe as a renewed World War seemed not just possible but likely.[23] Amidst the chaos and the confusion of the interwar years, the individual had become a cog in the great machinery of business, government, and war.

The period paradoxically saw an efflorescence of horror fiction and film as those hit hardest by the Depression — the unemployed with time to kill — turned toward horror to deal imaginatively with the mounting horrors of the world around them. Franklin Roosevelt may have proclaimed that "the only thing we have to fear is fear itself," but for millions in the war and Depression years, confronting the horror of fiction was a useful tonic to exorcise fear itself.

11

LITERARY DEVELOPMENTS

The great changes that marked the era between the end of Victoria's reign and the Second World War altered forever the way individuals thought of their place in the world and in the cosmos at large. In the fifty years between 1895 and 1945 the world had changed completely, so much so that later generations, even as early as the 1920s, could only look back at the Victorian era as a strange and distant memory of an alien world. The new universe unfolding in this era was an age of relativity, of a cosmos in which humanity was a recent and passing phenomenon, just one small species among an infinity of planets, stars, and space. On Earth, the world was racked by continuing crisis, and the nations of the world seemed in an endless Darwinian competition in which only the fittest would survive and all else would perish before the inevitabilities of biological reality.

In horror fiction these tensions were transmuted into "cosmic" fiction, which told terrifying tales of individuals who come into contact with vast forces beyond their abilities to comprehend or control. In cosmic horror, the protagonist comes to realize that he (it is almost always a "he") is a small and puny member of a transient and fragile species poised perilously before natural, supernatural, or extraterrestrial forces that at any time could overwhelm him and all humanity. But in this, the protagonist and the reader find a sense of wonder and awe at the grandeur of the universe and the great secrets still left for mankind to discover. It is the paradox of horror: The unknown forces that threaten are also the forces that amaze and awe. This is also the paradox of science, where the discovery of new natural laws lays out an ever grander view of reality but also reduces humanity's place in it.

Though the weird tale is not synonymous with the horror story, the two overlap like circles in a Venn diagram, so that one bleeds seamlessly into the other. The weird tale, in its most perfect form, explores these issues in ways that help readers to process and explore the double-sided coin that is the divide between the known and the unknown. The weird tale primarily utilizes the Discovery Plot wherein the protagonist discovers a great secret about the cosmos and is forced to come to terms with an intrusion of vast, cosmic forces into his everyday reality, often with mind- and soul-shaking results. The form's greatest practitioner, H. P. Lovecraft, wrote that in an age when belief in ghosts and vampires was no longer tenable, there were two factors that still made for a truly great weird tale:

> [F]irst, a sense of impatient rebellion against the rigid & ineluctable tyranny of time, space, & natural law—a sense which drives our imaginations to devise all sorts of plausible hypothetical defeats of that tyranny—& second, a burning curiosity concerning the vast reaches of unplumbed and unplumbable cosmic space which press down tantalizingly on all sides of our pitifully tiny sphere of the known. Between these two surviving factors I believe that the field of the weird must necessarily still seek occasional expression....[1]

Cosmic horror is more than just weird tales, but in the weird tales of cosmic horror, as in no horror before or since, the tension between science and superstition, between the known and unknown, between the quotidian and the infinite, are laid bare. The ambiguity of human knowledge becomes the major subject of this breed of horror, and in the cosmic we find horror art in its finest form, facing terrors that shake the soul of character and reader alike with a stark confrontation of the vast changes science had wrought.

An Intrusion from Beyond

Cosmic horror was the literary force that most clearly reflected the changing role of the individual against a backdrop of nationalism, racism, and relativity. The former two concepts greatly interested the American humorist Mark Twain (1835–1910) ever since he explored racism in *The Adventures of Huckleberry Finn* (1884). After the Spanish-American War, he turned increasingly dark, and some of his last writings impinge on the territory of horror. The incomplete "The Great Dark" (1898, but unpublished until the 1960s) told a, well, *dark* tale of a family exploring the microbial world with a microscope. They are transported into the microscope's miniature universe, forced to confront the monsters of the tiny kingdom and experience the cosmic pessimism that pervades a world filled with forces larger than the individual and which threaten to overwhelm him at every turn. As the water in which the ship sails dries, the passengers come ever closer to death at the hands of the (scientific) light beam from the microscope. "The Mysterious Stranger" (c. 1910) exists in several variant versions, but the final version features a stranger (Satan's nephew in earlier versions) who arrives in an Austrian village around 1590 and uses magical powers to demonstrate to the villagers that God and heaven are frauds, religion is a hoax, and that reality is itself nothing but a dream whose dreamer floats in empty cosmic nothingness.

When Percival Lowell thought he found life on Mars, H. G. Wells turned his discovery into a tale of terror with *The War of the Worlds* (1896), which takes the form of science fiction but is imbued with the spirit of horror. In the novel, Mars is a dying planet whose inhabitants decide to invade the Earth to find a new place to live. They arrive in cylinders and mount an invasion on large robotic tripods. They bring with them distinctive red foliage that overtakes the Earth and threatens to turn the planet into a reddened duplicate of Mars itself. Humanity is helpless before the alien onslaught (Wells self-consciously likens the situation to the fate of natives before European colonizers), and the survivors of the Martian invasion hide in pockets across a battered landscape. Their best efforts are fruitless, and it seems that the invaders are to be triumphant. A mad curate raves that the Martians have destroyed his church and his Sunday school, by which he means their extra-biblical existence defies his faith, and he comes to believe the aliens are God's punishment at the End of Days.

Wells takes pains to point out that the Martians are subject to the laws of evolution, and as such they have developed large brains and shriveled bodies, having evolved into creatures of mind rather than body. Though human opposition failed to stop the cosmic invaders, the Martians are eventually defeated, but by biology — "slain by the putrefactive and disease bacteria against which their systems were unprepared ... slain after man's devises had failed, by the humblest things that God, in his wisdom, has put on this earth."[2] The Martians died in their tripods, squishy masses of putrefaction. Thus it is only by a flaw in the Martians that humanity is saved, for otherwise the human race would have expired before the unstoppable outside forces that had descended on it.

A more subtle intrusion of outside forces occurs in Robert W. Chambers's (1865–1933) *The King in Yellow* (1895). An artist by training, Chambers produced a number of historical novels about the American Revolution, the Civil War, and the Franco-Prussian War. He wrote specifically for the middle-class market, and he produced more than six million words of fiction, most of which are now forgotten. *The King in Yellow*, however, lives on. It is a loosely connected series of stories centering on a mysterious two-act play of the same title, which drives its readers to madness. The play apparently takes place in the mythological world invented by Ambrose Bierce, including the city of Carcosa, whose inhabitant we have previously met. It references mysterious names and figures: The King in Yellow, the Pallid Mask, the Phantom of Truth, and, most chilling of all, the Yellow Sign, which makes its bearer susceptible to mind control from another world. (Yellow, as in Gillman's "Yellow Wallpaper," was the color of madness.) Chambers never fully describes any of these suggestive titles and objects, instead letting the reader fill in the ambiguity of their interrelationship with whatever horrors his or her imagination can conjure. Similarly, the second act of the play is never revealed, giving the reader pause to consider what horrors must lay in the redacted text.

In "The Yellow Sign," an artist has a dream about a hearse driven by a rotting hulk of putrid flesh, a dream shared by the model he loves, Tessie. In it, the corpse-driver gargles in an unearthly squeal, "Have you found the Yel-low Sign?"[3] The artist discovers an onyx tablet engraved with the Yellow Sign, and he is frightened by a hideous church watchman. In her quest for answers, the artist's beloved reads from the forbidden *The King in Yellow* after finding it in the road. The artist himself had been afraid to touch the volume: "I had always refused to listen to any description of it, and indeed, nobody ever ven-tured to discuss the second part aloud, so I had absolutely no knowledge of what those leaves might reveal."[4] The dreams started at the same time the book arrived, and it appears there is a connection. The artist reads the book all the way through, and the result is tragic. He and Tessie come to understand the power of the onyx tablet, and they become obsessed by the revelations of *The King in Yellow*. One night the church watchman comes to retrieve the Yellow Sign, and when it is over, the artist lies dying, Tessie is dead, and the watch-man a heap of putrescence, his reanimated corpse having rotted away with the passing of whatever force vitalized it.

"The Repairer of Reputations" is set in the future world of 1920, replete with science fiction devices, including on-demand suicide chambers. The story tells of a young man, Hildred Castaigne, who is confined to an asylum after being thrown from a horse. Upon his release he goes into business with a disfigured recluse named Mr. Wilde, who is believed to be insane, though the narrator knows better. Together they concoct revenge fantasies to repair the rep-utations of their clients. Castaigne possesses a copy of *The King in Yellow* and upon merely glancing at the first words of the second act becomes obsessed with a book he meant to consign to the flames for fear of his sanity:

> If I had not caught a glimpse of the opening words in the second act I should never have finished it, but as I stooped to pick it up, my eyes became riveted to the open page, and with a cry of terror, or perhaps it was of joy so poignant that I suffered in every nerve, I snatched the thing out of the coals and crept shaking to my bed-room, where I read it and reread it, and wept and laughed and trembled with a horror which at times assails me yet.[5]

So cunning and compelling is this forbidden book that Castaigne feels that his very reason and soul suffered at the hands of its infernal genius. By the end of the story, Wilde has convinced Castaigne that he and his military-hero cousin are the last descendents of the dynasty that ruled Carcosa, and that by murdering his cousin Castaigne will wear the crown of the King in Yellow. After some ghastly doings, Castaigne dies in an asylum for the criminally insane.

"In the Court of the Dragon" is the story of an encounter in church with otherworldly music and the creature that plays it. The narrator's body sits safe in the church, but his soul is transported to Carcosa, where he falls prey to the fearsome King in Yellow.

The stories in *The King in Yellow* are a bit too light and sentimental to frighten effectively, but their suggestion of worlds beyond our own and forbid-den knowledge that can connect us to them only at the price of sanity was highly influential in the development of horror. Chambers was the first to create an artificial mythology to add depth to his stories and an intimation of greater forces at work, a hallmark of the cosmic. In his stories we see that the price of knowledge is the loss of the sanity and reason that make a person an individual, and all who come across the forbidden secrets of the universe eventually lose themselves in the great tide of time and space.

Chambers wrote a number of other horror stories, among them "The Maker of Moons" (1896) about an evil Chinese sorcerer who can control the psychically linked offspring of a crab-reptile monster called Xin; "The Key to Grief" (1897) which follows the plot of Bierce's "Occurrence at Owl Creek Bridge"; and even some humorous horror tales about a zoologist who searches out legendary animals. His later work did not match *The King in Yellow*, however, though many stories are entertaining in their way.

In Austria-Hungary, Franz Kafka's "The Metamorphosis" (1915) presented a view in many ways the opposite of Chambers. Here a man, Gregor, turns into a giant bug for no discernable reason. His family eventually shuns him; he is confined to his room, grows physically smaller, and mentally deteriorates. Eventually he dies, forgotten and unmourned. Here it is the act of rejecting and forgetting, rather than of accepting and knowing, that destroys Gregor.

Encounters with the Outside

Around the turn of the twentieth century, Algernon Blackwood and Arthur Machen both explored cosmic horror in their writings, the former concentrating on the mysterious unknown forces that threaten to break through the veil of reality and the latter exploring ancient survivals whose very existence threatens the rational order of science, history, and reason. In the works of both, humanity appears as an arrogant and ignorant interloper pretending to the thrones of entities and forces beyond its comprehension.

Arthur Machen (1863–1947), a Welsh Decadent writer, Anglo-Catholic and (temporarily) member of the Hermetic Order of the Golden Dawn, an occult group drawing on freemasonry, theosophy, and Enochian magic, strongly opposed the scientific and materialist views of the late Victorian world, favoring instead a romantic and spiritualist view. To that end, his fiction tended to depict a world where civilization is a mere veneer covering over ancient survivals of older worlds, drawn primarily from Celtic mythology. Too, he saw civilization as a guardian against the untamed forces of an evil Nature waiting to reclaim its dominance of the Earth. In "The Great God Pan" (1890, revised 1894), Machen told of a scientific experiment gone horribly wrong. Dr. Raymond believes that with "a trifling rearrangement of certain cells" he can open up the mind to experience another reality wherein dwell powerful and supernatural creatures, among them the Great God Pan from Greek mythology.[6] He analogizes this to the power of telegraph wires to carry thoughts across the world; and so too can human thoughts contact the powers that lay beyond our vision. Dr. Raymond performs his experiment upon Mary, a girl he rescued from homelessness and whose life he feels therefore belongs to him. Mary experiences at first wonder in the face of her new vision, but this turns to terror and convulsions, leaving her a mindless idiot. "It could not be helped," Dr. Raymond comments objectively and blithely.[7] She gave her mind for science.

Years later Clarke, who observed the strange experiment, pieces together the story of Helen Vaughan, a woman who seems to have a supernatural power to destroy the men she comes into contact with, driving them to suicide. A doctor who attends Helen's death records the horrible, cosmic, and evolutionary demise:

> Here too was all the work by which man had been made repeated before my eyes. I saw the form waver from sex to sex, dividing itself from itself, and then again reunited. Then I saw the body descend to the beasts whence it ascended, and that which was on the heights go down to the depths, even to the abyss of all being. The principle of life, which makes organism, always remained, while the outward form changed.[8]

It transpires that the deceased was the daughter of Mary, who did not just see the Great God Pan but experienced his amorous attentions, which presumably were the convulsions referenced earlier. She was a half-breed, partly an earthbound human and partly a cosmic entity from the spheres beyond human. As she dies, the flesh that bound her disintegrates into the elements from which it came.

Because of the sexual nature of the god's transgression with mortal flesh, and the implications that her convulsions were orgasmic, some early reviewers found righteous outrage in Machen's story. One particularly virulent commentator, art critic Harry Quilter, used "Pan" as an example of "intense" literature that threatened civilization:

> "The Great God Pan" is, I have no hesitation in saying, a perfectly abominable story, in which the author has spared no endeavor to suggest loathsomeness and horror which he describes as beyond the reach of words.... There is but one point of view from which such writing can be tolerated, and that is the point of view of those who deny that there is any obligation, any responsibility laid upon a writer not to produce unwholesome work.... Why should he be allowed, for the sake of a few miserable pounds, to cast into our midst these monstrous creations of his diseased brain?[9]

Quilter, who also worried that the "intense" vogue for interior decorating would lead to effeminate men and hysterical women (cf. "The Yellow Wallpaper," Chapter 8), argued that only by banning such stories could the masses be lured back to the warm embrace of traditional religion instead of the morbid unbelief of twisted literature — a theme that would echo in horror criticism into the twenty-first century. Of course, as a result of such comments, "Pan" went on to become a best-seller.

Machen's work made frequent use of the themes of rationalism and the veil it throws over true reality. "The Inmost Light" (1894) told of a scientist who seeks after forbidden and occult knowledge, which he attains and feels compelled to use to imprison his wife's soul in an opal. She agrees to his experiment, and an unnamable entity takes her place. *The Three Imposters* (1895) was a loosely constructed frame holding together a number of otherwise unrelated short stories. Two of them are worth discussing.

"The Novel of the Black Seal" relates the tragic history of Professor Gregg, "whose one thought was for knowledge" and who is researching the history of "little people," the pre-human inhabitants of Celtic lands.[10] He has traced bits of legendry, inscriptions, and a mysterious black seal, which range in age from four thousand years to a few months, and all of which hint at the survival of these ancient creatures when taken together. His secretary, Miss Lally, is a skeptic who gives some credence to other scientists' belief that Gregg is mad. In an ancient book they discover that the black seal is the fabulous Ixaxar, the stone of sixty characters, the possession of the inhuman creatures. As the ancient horror Gregg unleashes begins to mount, Miss Lally finds her skepticism and rational view of the world unraveling. Professor Gregg goes off one day and does not return. In his papers Miss Lally finds an explanation: that he has gone in search of the little people, the Celtic fairies, in reality a pre-human race whose true horror legend has cloaked in lies. Once again, the pursuit of forbidden knowledge drove a scientist to his doom, and it is notable the way Celtic lore and a sense of place define the horror the scientist experiences.

"The Novel of the White Powder" also relates the story of a scholar brought low. This one is a lawyer-in-training shut up with his books, who develops a digestive complaint. For this he takes medicine, but an unfortunate substitution exchanges his sulphate of quinine for the tincture used by witches to commune with Satan. This causes his body to dissolve into a diabolical mess, the fruits of "an evil science which existed long before Aryan man entered Europe."[11]

Characters from *The Three Imposters* return in "The Red Hand" (1895) in which they use the tools of scientific investigation and logic to uncover the anti-rational supernaturalism at the heart of reality. "The White People" (1904) is often considered one of the true masterpieces of weird literature. It begins with a skeptic and believer arguing the merits of materialism and the way such beliefs suppress the true supernatural aspect of real sin. To make his case, the believer brings out an old book, the diary of a girl. The diary tells of her gradual indoctrination into a witch-cult, though the girl herself does not really understand what is happening to her. So subtle is the narrative that many readers miss the climax of horror when the girl becomes pregnant by an unknown entity and faces the existential terror of having to give birth to a monstrous creature. She kills herself instead, and her parents conspire to cover up the event with naturalistic explanations. As in "Pan," once again aberrant sexuality is a gateway to cosmic horror, inviting in things that should not be.

Nevertheless, in both stories, it is the cosmic element rather than the sexual that provides the most memorable elements of horror.

In 1914 Machen wrote "The Bowmen," a tale (told in the style of a newspaper account) of the return of the ghost of St. George and the bowmen of Agincourt to help the English during a particularly desperate battle in World War I. The British public believed the story true, and it gave rise to the legend of the Angels of Mons who supposedly were seen guarding British soldiers in that place. Machen spoke out against the delusion.[12] Arthur Machen, Christian and mystic, had to deny the validity of the most popular supernatural occurrence of his career.

Algernon Blackwood (1869–1951) was a world traveler, mystic, occultist, and devotee of Theosophy; and his interest in the spiritual influenced his horror fiction, the best of which he produced in the decade following the 1906 publication of his first collection of stories. In "Smith: An Episode in a Lodging House" (1906) a doctor comes into contact with "entities" he believes, but cannot prove, "were from some other scheme of evolution altogether, and had nothing to do with the ordinary human life, either incarnate or discarnate."[13] Only an occult adept named Smith, replete with secret knowledge, can banish them before they can kill with their unnatural "vibrations." In "The Man Who Found Out" (1909) a professor who is both scientist and mystic translates the ancient Tablets of the Gods, which reveal humanity's true purpose, a revelation unrecorded in the story but which drives the learned man to suicide. In "The Man Whom the Trees Loved" (1912), Mr. Bittacy, an austere Englishman, is possessed of a singular love of nature, attributed in the story to a taint in his pure English stock by a Eurasian ancestor who produced in Bittacy a love of the beautiful. This he manifests as a dedication to trees. His marriage gradually decays as Bittacy comes to love the trees more than his long-suffering wife and cannot bear to be separated from them. He comes to think, as the occultists and theosophists might, that the trees have a collective consciousness and he becomes an animist and mystic. Bittacy's wife, a committed and conventional Christian, cannot understand his cosmic faith, and she tries to talk her husband out of it, fearing what lies in the primitive forest primeval. After a great storm her husband vanishes into the trees he loved, his voice one among the many howling winds. Blackwood also wrote a number of horror tales featuring John Silence, a medical doctor turned psychic investigator. Inevitably, he discovered the truth of some theosophical or spiritualist claim.

Blackwood's two masterpieces, "The Wendigo" (1910) and "The Willows" (1907), both began as real-life incidents that the author used as springboards for horror. "The Wendigo" found its origins in a wendigo panic which apparently occurred during one of Blackwood's trips to Canada. The wendigo is a mythical creature that Algonquin Indians are said to believe was once a human that developed cannibal tastes. Now it is a supernatural entity, sometimes made entirely of ice, that walks the forests searching for human prey. Humans are believed to sometimes develop wendigo psychosis, whereby they become convinced they are turning into wendigoes and develop an appetite for human flesh. In the story, Joseph Défago, a French-Canadian who by virtue of his defective Latin race suffered from fits of depression, asserts that the wilderness holds no wild things which he fears. He is guiding a Scotsman through the Canadian wilderness with the occasional assistance of an Indian. As a wilderness guide and a French-Canadian he represents the middle ground between the "civilized" British man, Simpson, and the "wild" Indian, Punk, making him a liminal figure uniquely susceptible to the "Outer Horror"[14] about to barrel down on the group.

They are pursued by a strange *smell* which is completely unknown but somehow disturbing. Simpson let the feelings pass, but Défago does not. He vanishes in the night, and Simpson, left alone, tries to track him down to escape the claustrophobia of the tree-dense woods. He follows Défago's tracks in the mud and leaves, lightly dusted with new snow, but these soon pale before giant tracks of an unknown creature, which horrify Simpson in an indescribable way with the suggestion of to what they may belong. Gradually, Défago's tracks transformed into duplicates of those of the unknown creature. Fortunately, the Scot was "grounded in common sense and established in logic," so he could preserve his sanity and manhood.[15] Simpson's psychologist uncle attempted to convince him that loneliness and terror led him to delusions: "Like many another materialist, that is, he lied cleverly on the basis of insufficient knowledge *because* the knowledge supplied seemed to his own particular intelligence inadmissible."[16] Simpson rejects his uncle's attempts to provide flimsy scientific cover for the events he witnessed, understanding the difference between his uncle's "truth" and the absolute truth of the world outside of man's theories and laws. A new expedition fails to find a trace of Défago, but an encounter with the unexplained left Dr. Cathcart shattered, his materialist theories void before the unknown—for Défago returned to them, but in a broken and distorted form, wrong in proportion and barely like a living thing. Défago declares that he has met the Wendigo. Simpson comes to understand what happened:

> Out there, in the heart of unreclaimed wilderness, they had surely witnessed something crudely and essentially primitive. Something that had survived somehow the advance of humanity had emerged terrifically, betraying a scale of life still monstrous and immature. He envisaged it rather as a glimpse into prehistoric ages, when superstitions, gigantic and uncouth, still oppressed the hearts of men; when the forces of nature were still untamed, the Powers that may have haunted a primeval universe not yet withdrawn.[17]

Défago eventually returned mad and mindless. He lasted but a few weeks before dying. Punk declares that Défago had about him a most unusual odor. The stark and spare narrative clearly illuminates both the tensions between skeptic and believer and the awe and terror experienced when humanity comes into contact with the great cosmic forces that defy human reason, and human faith.

"The Willows" is perhaps the greatest tale of cosmic fear in the horror canon. Where "The Wendigo" was blunt in its attack on materialism, "The Willows" was subtle, and more effective. Taking its setting from two trips Blackwood made down the Danube in 1900 and 1901, the story opens with a traveler leaving Vienna for the marshy wilds of Austria-Hungary's riparian artery — the same Austria-Hungary home to the vampires Carmilla and Dracula. As did Jonathan Harker in *Dracula*, the traveler leaves civilization behind in Vienna and travels into the dark unknown of the east, where the wild things live. But here the danger is no longer in human form but something that exceeds the traveler's ability to understand. The traveler and his companion, the Swede, travel down the river in a Canadian canoe, marveling at the clumps of willows, whose swaying makes them appear almost alive, representing some unknown power which triggered "awe touched somewhere by a vague terror" that cold reason could not disperse.[18]

A passing Hungarian boatman crosses himself and shouts an unintelligible warning. This the Swede and the traveler ignore, setting up camp on an island "almost unknown to man ... remote from human influence, on the frontier of another world, an alien world, a world tenanted by willows only and the souls of willows. And we, in our rashness, had dared to invade it, even make use of it!"[19] Imagining the willows as aliens from "another evolution altogether," the traveler comes to believe the willows were actively against the interlopers on their island.[20] The traveler begins to see creatures moving in the willows, or perhaps as part of the willows, inhuman and awesome in their grandeur, moving him to a Burkean state of animistic worship. He wonders seriously if the horror was but a hallucination, but further strange noises that defied naturalistic explanation disturbed him even though no physical evidence indicated any occurrence. He begins to feel as though the bushes are moving nearer when he is not looking, closing in on him and the Swede — deliberately and with malicious intent. He laughs nervously, "for the knowledge that my mind was so respective to such dangerous imaginings brought the additional terror that it was through our minds and not through our physical bodies that the attack would come, and was coming."[21]

The outside forces wreck the canoe, forcing the traveler and the Swede to stay on the island, a place the Swede believes is inhabited by beings beyond comprehension that accidentally touch earth in this place. The traveler tries to dismiss the events with feeble naturalistic explanations, but the Swede will have none of it, calling it self-deception. Nevertheless, the traveler tries to reason that the Swede has gone mad, that his companion is responsible for the damaged canoe. The figures in the willows, he holds, were nothing more than wind-blown leaves. Funnel-shaped holes in the sand were the result of whirlwinds, the strange sounds but wind blowing through branches. But then the food begins to disappear, and despite the traveler's attempt to rationalize this as his own forgetfulness, it becomes obvious that something else is responsible. They had strayed, the Swede said, into "a spot held by the dwellers in some outer space, a sort of peep-hole where the veil between had worn a little thin."[22] He thinks they are to be sacrifices to these strange outer powers. "The whole experience," the traveler said, "whose verge we touched was unknown to humanity at all. It was a new order of experience, and in the true sense of the word *unearthly*."[23] The two men frighten themselves terribly discussing the coming horror and the characteristics of the unseen entities barreling down on them, surrounding them, leaving no escape. They attack through the mind, utilizing their fear, and it is only distraction—fainting or pain—that breaks conscious thought enough to save them. The attack only ends when the entities find a substitute sacrifice, and the traveler and the Swede discover the man's corpse floating in the river the next morning, marked with the same funnel-shaped holes left in the sand.

In "The Willows" Blackwood encapsulated the twin notions of awe and terror that accompany a true glimpse of the cosmic, and the horrible feeling of insignificance mankind experiences when confronted with a universe both greater and more powerful than he could imagine. The individual is reduced to a mere speck before unseen powers.

Gods from Outer Space

Such ideas fascinated Howard Phillips Lovecraft (1890–1937), the Providence, Rhode Island, author of cosmic fiction straddling the boundaries between horror, science fiction, and fantasy. Lovecraft drew on the works of Poe, Machen, Blackwood, and the Irish fantasist Lord Dunsany in developing his fictional technique. Though many of his mature tales were superficially similar to those of Machen and Blackwood, Lovecraft's was a unique vision, for he did not share the occult and spiritualist beliefs of his predecessors but instead pursued his cosmic fear from the position of an atheist, under a philosophy he referred to as "scientific materialism," which essentially held that the visible world was synonymous with reality and the scientific method was the only logical way to understand it. Further, while until now we have been able to consider works individually as self-contained episodes, Lovecraft's fiction coalesces around a dark mythology that attains its true cosmic import and grandeur only when considered as a whole. This vision, which we shall explore in detail, was highly influential and shaded the work of many, if not most, of the horror authors who followed. In this, Lovecraft's writings are the cynosure into which previous horror pours and out of which subsequent horror emerges.

Lovecraft was born to a father who went mad from uncured syphilis and a mother who followed him into madness decades later. A nervous child prone to what he called "breakdowns," Lovecraft spent a good deal of his life downwardly mobile, falling from the wealthy upper-crust to poverty at the end of his life. Aside from an unhappy period in New York, where he was briefly married and confirmed his racist and xenophobic prejudices against immigrants, he lived his whole life in Providence, whose ancient buildings he held to be synonymous with his happiness. Lovecraft was an autodidact and greatly interested in science. He wrote weird fiction as a hobby and for his own artistic fulfillment, though he revised others' stories for profit. An ardent letter-writer with a wide circle of correspondents, Lovecraft produced perhaps a hundred thousand letters to supplement his poetry and short fiction, which amounted to nearly one hundred short stories, novels, fragments, and revisions. He died of intestinal cancer, aged only forty-six.

In his early fiction, Lovecraft made use of Poe-inspired situations and motifs. The prose-poem "Nyarlathotep" (1920) described a foreign entertainer who put on a science show, using his devices to destroy the world. "The Unnamable" (1923) told of a horrible creature living inside a deserted old house abutting a cemetery. The more famous "Pickman's Model" (1926, published 1927), described an artist whose horrible canvases were drawn from life, while "The Outsider" (1921, published 1926) used a panoply of Gothic imagery to tell a dark little fable. The unnamed narrator lives alone in a dark castle, ignorant of who he is or where he lives. He dwells in perpetual night amidst corpses and the trappings of the tomb. One day he climbs the highest tower in the castle only to discover that it reached up to a level surface, a new ground. Above, there was light, and he encounters a fetid, monstrous corpse-creature that shocks him horribly, more so in the instant when he realizes the creature is his own reflection. "The Music of Erich Zann" (1921, published 1922) suggested vast realms of cosmic space as a musician's strange music opens a gateway to the unplumbed depths of space, killing him with its awesome revelation. In addition, Lovecraft wrote a number of fantasies, which we will not consider here, and dark science-fiction, like "Cool Air" (1926, published 1928), about a scientist keeping his dead self alive via air conditioning, and the exquisite "The Colour Out of Space" (1927) in which a meteor brings a horrible wasting death to a remote farm, turning living tissue into brittleness of a color not seen in the human spectrum.

Lovecraft's greatest contribution to our theme of knowledge-horror began in 1926 with "The Call of Cthulhu" (published 1928), the first in a series of short stories and novellas that took for their background an interrelated but fragmentary set of dark legends, myths, and allusions that were later known as "The Cthulhu Mythos." The Mythos was first and foremost concerned with the role of knowledge in human affairs and the unrelenting horror that knowledge yields when too much or the wrong kind of knowledge pierces humanity's comforting illusions. This is best expressed in the famous first paragraph of "Cthulhu":

> The most merciful thing in the world, I think, is the inability of the human mind to correlate all its contents. We live on a placid island of ignorance in the midst of black seas of infinity, and it was not meant that we should voyage far. The sciences,

each straining in its own direction, have hitherto harmed us little; but some day the piecing together of dissociated knowledge will open up such terrifying vistas of reality, and of our frightful position therein, that we shall either go mad from the revelation or flee from the light into the peace and safety of a new dark age.[24]

In the story, Francis Wayland Thurston is the possessor of such horrible knowledge, which he and he alone has pieced together from unrelated events and documents, and it threatens his very sanity and soul.

Thurston has a file belonging to his grand-uncle, a distinguished professor who suffered assassination at the hands of the Cthulhu Cult, of which Thurston is initially ignorant. There are suggestive quotations from theosophy and from anthropological works. In the documents, Thurston discovers that in 1925 his grand-uncle, a professor of archaeology, was asked to decipher some hieroglyphs on a bas relief made by an artist, based on horrible dreams. The clay sculpture depicted a monster with a squid's head and rudimentary wings, posed before Cyclopean and oddly angled architecture. He heard in his dreams strange words: *Cthulhu fhtagn*. During the period in which the artist suffered his dreams, other sensitive persons—artists, poets—around the world experienced the same nightmare visions, though businessmen and the unimaginative were unaffected.

Another document, relating an earlier (1908) experience, found the professor and other academics listening to the tale of an Inspector Legrasse from Louisiana, who had in his possession a stone idol depicting the same tentacled monster. This sculpture, however, was older than any known culture and of an art style and stone unique in the world. The only remote similarity was a bas relief found among Eskimo devil-worshippers. Both the Eskimo and the degenerate cult from which Legrasse confiscated the idol chanted the same inhuman liturgy:

> Ph'nglui mglw'nafh Cthulhu R'lyeh wgah'nagl fhtagn ("In his house at R'lyeh dead Cthulhu waits dreaming").[25]

Legrasse tells the assembled academics what he was told by the members of the cult, themselves racial hybrids and mentally ill, symbolically lower down on evolution's ladder and thus closer to the primal past. They worshipped the Great Old Ones, titanic god-like creatures that came to earth from the sky long before humanity arose. They were hidden in the deep places of the earth, waiting for the time of their glorious resurrection, when Great Cthulhu, their high priest, would call and they would rise again. The cult waited in secret for this time so they could liberate the gods, trapped by the spells that preserved them in their secret crypts, dead but dreaming. The idol was Cthulhu.

Only an old man named Castro was willing to tell more of the cult's beliefs "that paled the speculations of the theosophists and made man and the world seem recent and transient indeed."[26] Castro explained that the Great Old Ones were omniscient beings who could fly between worlds "when the stars were right," but who went into a type of suspended animation "when the stars were wrong," meaning at different points in the great churning cycle of the universe.*[27] The secret cult dedicated to the Old Ones had always existed, in every culture and every age, and the Old Ones talked to men in their dreams. But Cthulhu's city of R'lyeh had sunk beneath the waves deep in the past, and the waters cut off communication. Nevertheless, the resurrection of the Old Ones was sure to occur:

> The time would be easy to know, for then mankind would have become as the Great Old Ones; free and wild and beyond good and evil, with laws and morals thrown aside and all men shouting and killing and reveling in joy. Then the liberated Old Ones would teach them new ways to shout and kill and revel and enjoy themselves, and all the earth would flame with a holocaust of ecstasy and freedom. Meanwhile the cult, by appropriate rites, must keep alive the memory of those ancient ways and shadow forth the prophecy of their return.[28]

Thurston travels to New Orleans and interviews those left alive, confirming what his uncle had written. At this point he is still committed to materialism, but a further piece of evidence destroys his faith in that philosophy. A copy of the *Sydney Bulletin* for April 18, 1925, featured a story about a derelict ship carrying only one survivor possessed of an idol not unlike the Louisiana cult sculpture. Thurston investigates this anomaly and discovers the Norwegian survivor is now dead, but that he left a narrative of his terror. In the South Pacific, the ship encountered an uncharted island — the merest citadel of the Old Ones' R'lyeh — which had risen from the waves. The ruins on this citadel were all *wrong*, non–Euclidean, irrational, from another reality altogether. The ship's crew unwisely explored the island and accidentally set the monstrous green bulk of Great Cthulhu free. He chased them into the water, and the sailors crashed their boat into the monster, but the plastic creature re-formed itself. Madness and death ensued, but after a great storm R'lyeh vanished again beneath the waves. Thurston concludes his discussion by praying that his manuscript is lost forever so mankind might be safe from the horrible truth buried in that vast underwater necropolis.

"Cthulhu" defined the outlines of Lovecraft's self-constructed mythology, and subsequent tales built upon it. "The Dunwich Horror" (1928, published 1929) told of a supernatural birth in the backwoods of Massachusetts, where a certain Wilbur Whateley was born to an inbred, unmarried woman in an old house filled with occult tomes and secret knowledge from the ancient past. The child grows rapidly into manhood — too fast to be entirely human — and he seeks out the fabled book of dark wisdom, the *Necronomicon* of the Mad Arab Abdul Alhazred, to find a spell whereby he might let in Yog-Sothoth, his father,

---

*This refers to the so-called "precession of the equinoxes," famous in occult lore. This is the apparent change in the house of the zodiac against which the sun rises on the vernal equinox. The slow cycling of the stars is actually caused by Earth's wobbling axis, which completes a cycle every 26,000 years.

a cosmic being who is one of the Old Ones and who is the key to and guardian of the gate between realities. Wilbur is killed trying to steal the *Necronomicon* from the Miskatonic University library, and it is revealed that below the waist he was an inhuman monster of tentacles and whitish ooze. The university professors learn from Wilbur's diary what he planned to do and, armed with the spells, they aim to seal the gate. They encounter an indescribable and gigantic creature of mouths, tentacles, and a half-human face — Wilbur's brother, who looked more like his father. A lightning bolt zaps the creature out of existence in a mockery of Christ's crucifixion. The librarian, Richard Armitage, explained what the monster was:

> It was — well, it was mostly a kind of force that doesn't belong in our part of space; a kind of force that acts and grows and shapes itself by other laws than those of our sort of Nature. We have no business calling in such things from outside, and only very wicked people and very wicked cults ever try to.[29]

After "Dunwich," Lovecraft began to modify his mythology, gradually replacing the supernatural Old Ones with extraterrestrials and aberrant evolutionary creatures whom early humans mistook for gods. The change allowed for an ambiguity that enriched the mythology and provided enough variation of interpretation — like real myths — to give it a superficial plausibility. "The Whisperer in Darkness" (1930, published 1931) introduces the Mi-Go, a race of aliens whose outpost is on Yuggoth — the newly discovered planet Pluto — who have invaded rural Vermont. They worship Nyarlathotep, the messenger of the Old Ones, and they use their technological expertise to steal human brains and seal them up in containers to take back with them to space. "The Shadow Over Innsmouth" (1931, published 1936) told of a man who discovers an ancient taint in his bloodline, one that condemns him to transform into a horrible fish-creature, a Deep One, as a result of a forbidden mating between a sea captain and an immortal amphibian. Though fearful, the narrator comes to accept his fate and his glorious future beneath the sea off the Innsmouth coast.

Lovecraft's longest and most sustained work, *At the Mountains of Madness* (1931, published 1936) recast the Cthulhu Mythos in materialist terms. This time, a 1935 Miskatonic University scientific expedition to the Antarctic discovers an ancient horror buried beneath the ice. It is told in the form of a plea from one of the expedition members, Prof. William Dyer, to the scientific community to abandon Antarctica to the snows. Dyer has discovered a vast range of mountains, higher than the Himalayas, but even though he is familiar with the revelations of the *Necronomicon* and Poe's *Narrative of A. Gordon Pym*, he is unprepared for the horror that lies within. The expedition uncovers the frozen and preserved remains of several unclassifiable creatures, beings millions of years old and occupying the middle ground between plant and animal, a revelation that would recast biology, they believe, as profoundly as Einstein rewrote physics. Since Dyer has read the *Necronomicon*, he names these creatures Elder Things after their similarity to the occult monsters therein, and he notices that the specimens bear traces of regressive evolution, as though higher forms decayed into the specimens they found. When Dyer and his companions return to base camp, he finds the camp destroyed and those left behind dead.

Dyer and his student, Danforth, fly toward the mountains, where they discover a great Cyclopean city of unearthly architecture: "The effect of the monstrous sight was indescribable, for some fiendish violation of known natural law seemed certain at the outset."[30] The city stretched for miles and was composed of every geometric possibility, and it all was weathered with the proof of its age of millions of years. The effect is shocking, but the researchers keep their poise: "In my case, ingrained scientific habit may have helped; for above my bewilderment and sense of menace there burned a dominant curiosity to fathom more of this age old-secret" before which Atlantis and Lemuria are but recent trifles.[31]

They enter one of the city's buildings, and they discover that the Elder Things left a record of their civilization in murals along the structure's walls,

Egyptian ruins. Inspired by images of ruins like these at Karnak and drawing from Theosophical ideas about the origins of civilization, H. P. Lovecraft's fiction posited a world in which ancient ruins were the remnants of an extraterrestrial civilization that once ruled the Earth and predated the human race (Library of Congress, LC-DIG-ppmsca-04530).

done in a style nearly photorealistic but completely alien to human art. The murals depicted maps, scientific information, and of course history. The Elder Things were the Great Old Ones of the *Necronomicon* and the Cthulhu Cult, and they came to earth in the distant past and created life on the infant planet, a product of an "alien evolution."[32] Other aliens, too, came to the young earth, and they were all possessed of advanced science. They created earth life for food, and later for slaves—the plastic, formless shoggoths they could mold into desired shapes. Evolution acted on these early creations, giving rise to earthly forms, including, eventually, humanity. The Old Ones warred with the spawn of Cthulhu, another alien, and they divided the earth among them. Vast changes in geology buried the Cthulhu creatures beneath the waves, and the Old Ones reigned supreme until the coming of the Mi-Go from Pluto pushed them out of the northern hemisphere.

Poorly done late murals show that, decadent and in decay, the Old Ones succumbed to a revolt of the shoggoths, who tried to imitate and carry on the old ways but produced instead a bizarre parody of Old One art. Danforth and Dyer recognize that the Old Ones were, by virtue of education, learning, and culture in some sense men like them, but the shoggoths were a cosmic fear unlike any other, mocking parodies of the Old Ones, condemned to imitating their fallen masters for all eternity. The two are chased out of city by a shoggoth shouting Poe's phrase, "Tekeli-li," which is presumably the lost language of the dead Old Ones as mumbled by the "nightmare plastic column of foetid black iridescence."[33] Danforth, glancing back as they fly away, sees something unnamed that sends him into madness.

Lovecraft's last major work was "The Shadow Out of Time" (1935, published 1936), which told of the Great Race of aliens who could swap minds with other creatures across time and space, thus giving themselves immortality. They use this power to drag minds back in time to their base in prehistoric Australia where they are compiling a library of universal knowledge. A human dragged back in time thinks it a period of mental illness until he finds evidence in his own handwriting in the million-year-old ruins of the Great Race's rediscovered library.

These and Lovecraft's dozens of other stories tended to revolve around a bookish protagonist who only gradually assembles literary, archaeological, or scientific evidence that hints of horrible truths that tend to drive him to madness or death. In Lovecraft, as in no author before or since, the price of knowledge is the loss of one's sanity and reason in the face of a cosmos both grander than any in human imagination and colder and more indifferent than can be conceived. This "cosmic indifference," the idea that the universe (and the Old Ones) cared nothing for humanity was best expressed in the thoughts of the dream-traveler Randolph Carter from "Through the Gates of the Silver Key" (1933, published 1934), a collaborative fantasy Lovecraft wrote with E. Hoffman Price:

He wondered at the vast conceit of those who had babbled of the *malignant* Ancient Ones, as if They could pause from their everlasting dreams to wreak a wrath upon mankind. As well, he thought, might a mammoth pause to visit frantic vengeance on any angleworm.[34]

As Nietzsche might have put it, the cosmos is so utterly alien to human reason that it appears beyond good and evil, paying no mind to the small moral creatures on a tiny fleck of dirt orbiting a third-rate star. This, ultimately, is the horror from beyond.

Unfortunately, critics disapproved. Ten years after Lovecraft's death, the influential Edmund Wilson appraised him in *The New Yorker*, dismissing his fiction as "hackwork" whose "only real horror ... is the horror of bad art and bad taste" on account of Lovecraft's fondness for adjectives and the juvenile flavor he saw in the "omniscient conical snails," the Old Ones. Lovecraft's admirers were, in Wilson's words, "infantile."[35] It would be several more decades before a critical reappraisal rightly placed Lovecraft among the masters of horror.

The Lovecraft Circle

Lovecraft gave his creations verisimilitude by mentioning them in the same breath as real works of occult or anthropological lore. Lovecraft also playfully inserted his fictional creations, like Cthulhu or the *Necronomicon* into works he revised or ghostwrote for others. Thus some two dozen stories appearing under the bylines of Hazel Heald, Zealia Bishop, Adolphe de Castro and others featured the same set of monsters and blasphemous secrets, often under variant names. Cthulhu, for example, appeared as "Clulu" in Heald's "Winged Death" (1933, published 1934) and "Tulu" in Bishop's "The Mound" (1930, published 1940). This sort of variation compared favorably with real mythological figures known by many names, like Parsifal/Percival or Quetzalcoatl/Kukulkan, giving a spurious credibility to the Lovecraft myth-cycle. It was thus that William Lumley's "The Diary of Alonzo Typer" (1935, published 1938) came to feature one of Lovecraft's best summations of his mythology:

> Truly, there are terrible primal arcana of earth which had better be left unknown and unevoked; dread secrets which have nothing to do with man, and which man may learn only in exchange for peace and sanity; cryptic truths which make the knower evermore an alien among his kind, and cause him to walk alone on earth.[36]

Another revision, "The Loved Dead" (1923, published 1924), was a graphic tale of necrophilia that caused a storm of outrage upon its publication in *Weird Tales* and was said to have caused the magazine to be banned in Indiana.

Lovecraft also encouraged his friends to incorporate his creations into their fiction, and he used some of theirs in his. Clark Ashton Smith, Robert E. Howard, Robert Bloch, August Derleth, and many others utilized Lovecraft creations and contributed their own to the growing body of Cthulhu-themed fiction. In addition, the emerging "Lovecraft Circle," as they became known, made use of earlier horror props, like Chambers' Yellow Sign and Arthur Machen's references to Aklo letters and Voorish signs, indirectly appending those works to the emerging Cthulhu Mythos, which could now be read back into earlier horror. In this, the Mythos prefigured the intertextuality of the postmodern movement.

Clark Ashton Smith (1893–1961) invented the toad-god Tsathoggua and contributed *The Book of Eibon* as a counterpart to Lovecraft's *Necronomicon*. Many of his stories utilizing Mythos themes were fantasies, fables, or science fiction set primarily in the lost continent of Hyperboria, the medieval French province of Averoigne, or Earth's last continent, Zothique; but a distinct minority were horror. Among these, "The Return of the Sorcerer" (1931) stands out as a creepy revenge tale in which the *Necronomicon* reveals to a sorcerer the cause of mysterious visitations. The brother he killed has the power to reanimate his disarticulated body and send the parts after his murderer. "Ubbo-Sathla" (1933) tells of a man who uses a mysterious gem and the *Necronomicon* to plumb Earth's history but experiences a "monstrous devolution" back through a million lifetimes to the primal ooze that was Ubbo-Sathla, who lived amidst the ruins left by Earth's alien gods.[37] Robert E. Howard (1906–1936), best remembered for his Conan the Cimmerian sword-and-sorcery fantasies, wrote several horror tales utilizing Cthulhu themes, inventing Friedrich von Junzt's *Nameless Cults* as a companion to the *Necronomicon*. "The Black Stone" (1931) concerned a mysterious old monolith in Hungary that appears older than mankind. It has already driven mad the poet Justin Geoffrey, and the narrator too goes mad upon discovering the hidden truth only hinted at in *Nameless Cults*, that the monolith is merely a spire atop an ancient citadel not wholly abandoned by the *things* that lived within. Frank Belknap Long and Robert Bloch each contributed a number of worthy stories, taking the Cthulhu Mythos into new territories.

With so many authors writing of the same mythology, it was no wonder that readers were sometimes fooled into thinking the Cthulhu Mythos was a real myth cycle or true occult revelation. Robert E. Howard asked for clarification early on, and readers often sent letters to Lovecraft's publishers asking about the mythological entities and forbidden books in the stories. Lovecraft tried to dissuade readers from belief, noting that "[w]e never, however, try to put it across as an actual hoax; but always carefully explain to enquirers that it is 100% fiction."[38] Nevertheless, some refused to accept his denials, and even today some Satanists and occultists believe in the *Necronomicon* and Cthulhu as legitimate antiquities or unholy revelations of eternal truths.

August Derleth (1909–1971) became Lovecraft's posthumous publisher and carried Lovecraft's legacy forward, saving him from obscurity with Arkham House, a firm dedicated to keeping Lovecraft and the Cthulhu Mythos in print.

Derleth also contributed new works, both during Lovecraft's lifetime and, especially, afterward. He built on fragments from Lovecraft's notebooks to produce
"collaborations" published as the novel *The Lurker at the Threshold* (1945) and
stories collected later as *The Watchers Out of Time* (1974). *Lurker*, which contains 1,200 words of Lovecraft to 47,800 of Derleth's, uses multiple narrators
to relate a story of an ancient evil, madness, and trans-dimensional gods. "The
Thing that Walked on the Wind" (1933) made use of the wendigo, and "The
Return of Hastur" (1939) added Ambrose Bierce's creation to the Mythos, with
the added complication that in the story H. P. Lovecraft's "The Call of Cthulhu"
is held by the characters *within Derleth's story* to be truth: "the ghastly things
half hinted in this revealing story purporting to be only *fiction* [open] up a vista
of undreamed horror, of age-old evil."[39] It was all quite dizzying.

But Derleth had his own view of how the Mythos ought to work, one
derived from his staunchly Catholic faith. He recast the Lovecraftian Old Ones
as gods of nature, assigning each to one of the Aristotelian elements. Thus
Cthulhu, for example, became a water god, which was strange since in "The
Call of Cthulhu" water blocks Cthulhu's telepathic powers; and the wendigo,
now called Ithaqua, became an air god. To these creatures, which Derleth
viewed as evil, he added a new race, the Elder Gods, who were forces of cosmic good and who helped humans oppose the Old Ones. Cthulhu was now
imprisoned in R'lyeh not as the result of mindless geologic changes but by the
active punishment of the Elder Gods for Cthulhu's (read: Satan's) sins. Therefore, in Derleth's words, the Mythos had become "basically similar to the Christian Mythos, particularly in regard to the expulsion of Satan from Eden, and
the power of evil to survive."[40] Thus Lovecraft's unique knowledge-horror was
rendered conventional. Derleth continued to write his brand of Cthulhu-
themed fiction until his death. Much of it was collected in *The Mask of Cthulhu*
(1958) and *The Trail of Cthulhu* (1962).

As we shall see, the Cthulhu Mythos and its knowledge theme only grew
over time, influencing generations of horror writers. Cthulhu fiction is produced today in greater amounts than during Lovecraft's lifetime.

Mass-Produced Horror

The horror literature of the age reflected the new, more uncertain world
not just in the cosmic stories we've discussed but also in the quantity of horror produced. While literary horror, as represented by *Dracula*, *The Turn of the
Screw*, and other masterpieces of the Victorian imagination, declined after the
turn of the century, horror migrated "down market" to an increasingly less
elite audience. Between 1920 and 1945, the *Publisher's Weekly* best-seller lists
featured plenty of melodrama, crime, and even some science fiction, but little
by way of horror. Isak Dinesen's (Karen Blixen's) *Seven Gothic Tales* cracked

the top ten in 1934. Its stories used Gothic trappings but were designed to instruct rather than frighten. Alexander Laing's *The Cadaver of Gideon Wick* was a best-seller in late 1934, telling a cautionary tale about a scientist who blackmails and impregnates women to obtain fetuses on which he can conduct experiments in altering evolution. The novel, however, takes the form of a murder mystery when the scientist is found dead. Laing's medical thriller *The Motives of Nicholas Holtz* (1936) told of a company that created a deadly virus and then tested it on a Pennsylvania town in the hope of selling it as a biotoxin on the international market. It was mad science for money.

Under the literary vogue for realism, the culture mavens and critics increasingly relegated horror to one of many genres unfit for "serious" literature, which in this era was defined as "realism" tinged with "moral uplift." Horror, as kin to fantasy, was not "real," and horror, as sensation, was not uplifting or particularly moral in the traditional sense. While Machen and Blackwood had written "literature" published in well-read magazines and collected in hard-bound books, Lovecraft and his followers were forced into the literary ghetto.

The audience for Victorian biological and spiritualist horror was self-consciously the middle and upper classes, who were literate, could afford hard-bound books, and subscribed to the literary magazines; but in the new era horror moved from the elite to the newly literate masses, beginning in 1896 when Frank Munsey's *Argosy* magazine inaugurated the age of the pulps. These cheap magazines were printed on inexpensive wood pulp instead of glossy paper (hence the name) and offered thrills, chills, and the pleasures of reading to all who could afford their low prices. This is where horror thrived when serious literature moved on toward Jazz Age exuberance.

However, the pulps were widely derided as inferior literature, fit only for the menial classes and children, and even then were dangerous and possibly corrupting to good literature and good minds. In 1936 a high school teacher named Anita Forbes addressed the National Council of Teachers of Education to condemn the pulps, their lurid covers of half-naked women, and the hackwork quality of the writing therein: "'Pulp' magazines, by their emphasis on the sensational, their failure to individualize characters, their eternal sameness of plot, and their simplification of human motives, cater to the false views of life to which adolescents still cling."[41] By her estimate, ninety percent of high school boys read the pulps, and she worried that they would prevent them from understanding a world "more highly complex and more utterly unpredictable than ever."[42] Nor was she alone; educators across the country worried their students would be lost to the "pulps," and working-men who found their thrills in the pages of magazines like *Weird Tales, Unknown, Horror Stories,* or *Astounding Stories* risked the opprobrium of the elite. Edmund Wilson found the era's revival of supernatural horror deeply disturbing, viewing it as a regression away from his idea of great horror, which revolved around exploring abnormal psy-

Pulp magazines. With their colorful and lurid covers, pulp magzines drew in a wide audience of readers who bought the inexpensive publications at newsstands like this one in California. On sale this day were publications that ran the gamut from western to detective to science fiction titles (Library of Congress, Prints and Photographs Division, FSA/OWI Collection, LC-DIG-fsa-8c32317).

chology.[43] The only saving grace was that pulp horror had precious little effect on the literature of good taste.

Let us stipulate, though, that much of what was published in the pulps was not of the highest quality. We should also stipulate that, always excepting the Lovecraft Circle, many of the tales were simply variations or derivatives of earlier biological or spiritualist horror. These were sometimes clever but rarely original. The stories were written for a specific audience and at a specific level.

They were full of sensation and meant to entertain, and on that merit ought they to be judged. Nevertheless, among the thousands of stories published in the pulps there were some true gems, and there was a growing body of literature devoted to the cosmic. We have already encountered "The Night Wire" in our discussion of spiritualist horror, and it was first published in the September 1926 issue of *Weird Tales*. To give a flavor of the pulp cosmic, a few examples should suffice.

G. G. Pendarves's "The Eighth Green Man" (1928) talks of the terror that waits beyond the material world of everyday life:

> Not for nothing have I learnt in pain and terror that the walls of this visible world are frail and thin — too frail, too thin, alas! For there are times — there are places when the barrier is broken ... when monstrous unspeakable Evil enters and dwells familiarly amongst us![44]

The speaker here is a famous explorer, Raoul Suliman d'Abre, who is trying to convince an avowed materialist, Nicholas Birkett, that neither should pass down a road where Raoul believes unspeakable danger resides. Along the road they encounter the Seven Green Men, which appear to be large topiary creations in the shape of armored warriors. Raoul and Birkett stop at an inn where the innkeeper suggests that Birkett join an ancient order called the Sons of Enoch. Back in town the father of the sixth green man tells the pair that the inn is accursed and the green men steal the souls of those who pledge themselves to the Sons of Enoch. Birkett tries to back out of his pledge too late, and the innkeeper is revealed as a powerful master of forces beyond human comprehension. Birkett ends up the eighth green man, despite Raoul's best efforts.

Other stories discussed outside forces impinging on individuals. Hugh B. Cave's "The Brotherhood of Blood" (1932) introduces us to Paul Munn, an authority on the supernatural who has plumbed the depths of forbidden knowledge, producing learned volumes on the occult and spiritualism. Munn says that to become a vampire, one must study the forbidden arts until one becomes possessed of infernal powers, and he never thought he would need that knowledge. But his mind is changed by a young woman from a family plagued by vampire deaths comes seeking Munn's help to stop the same fate from befalling her. When she becomes a vampire he gives himself to her to be together forever. The effort fails when an evil scientist, Dr. Threng, devises a trap for Munn's beloved, leaving her dead. Munn resurrects as a vampire to seek revenge. In Loretta Borough's "What Waits in Darkness" (1935), a woman seeks psychiatric help for a repeated dream of blood and violence, only to suffer a real nervous breakdown when, despite reassurances from professionals and family — skeptics all — finally her dream comes to pass with horrible consequences.

In "Escape" (1938) by Paul Ernst, a mathematician-inventor confined to a mental asylum harnesses invisible forces to create an invention by which he can escape. He accomplishes this task to the amazement of the staff, who can see nothing of what he works on, grounded as they are in quotidian reality.

Edmund Hamilton's "The Seeds from Outside" (1937) is an under-cooked tale about a meteor that crashes in an artist's backyard. Since the artist confesses he is no scientist, he declines to report the discovery of an alien pod inside the meteor and instead opens it to discover two small seeds. These he plants, only to see the seeds turn into human-shaped plant people. Before the tale is over, the plant man and the plant woman are dead, and the artist flees to Arizona to escape the horror of green things.

In "Mimic" (1942) Donald A. Wollheim describes a horrible race of creatures hiding beneath humanity's nose. The story begins by listing some of the great achievements of human knowledge — the discovery of America, aviation, physics — and how recent they are in the grand scheme of things: "We know little or nothing. Some of the most startling things are unknown to us."[45] The narrator then tells us of a man in a black cloak who never spoke and seemed to avoid human society. One day this stranger dies, and by chance the narrator has the opportunity to examine the body. He discovers that the stranger has no eyebrows and no nose, only suggestive splotches of color that give the illusion of features when poorly lit. Worse, "The suit — was not a suit. It was part of him. It was his body."[46] The knowledge that the man was actually a giant insect cleverly camouflaged by evolution to blend in to human society was too much: "The mind rejects it, and it is only in afterthought that one can feel the dim shudder of horror."[47] The bug's eggs hatch and fly out the window as little winged men. The narrator is even more horrified to discover evolution has helpfully provided a predator in the form of a bat-like creature camouflaged as a chimney. The difference between "Mimic" and the nineteenth century's biological horror is striking: Like the earlier creatures, "Mimic's" is a beast-man, but here human agency played no role in its creation and the sense of the "Other" is heightened because this creature only assumes the form of man without any of the humanity within.

John W. Campbell, Jr.'s "Who Goes There?" (1938) was first published in August in *Astounding Science Fiction*, which the author edited. The magazine had published Lovecraft's *At the Mountains of Madness* just a few months earlier, and the later story shares many details in common with Lovecraft. Scientists in the Antarctic discover an alien spacecraft buried in the ice, twenty million years old. Inside they find a tentacled creature, which they thaw out in their research station and discover is not quite dead. The alien turns out to be a shape-shifter who uses this power to assume the identities of the researchers and kill them off, leaving the dwindling crew to wonder which of them is the alien. After learning how to kill the creature, the remaining scientists discover that it was busy building alien technology, including an anti-gravity device with which it might have taken over the world.

As we will see in Chapter 14, a later breed of "shudder pulp" would take horror to new extremes. The pulps provided a useful service, preserving the tradition of horror when highbrow literature abandoned it. The "realistic" fiction of the era failed largely to address the important developments in science and society that contributed to the "unpredictable" quality of the new era; horror did this, and it did it for those most affected by the startling changes in society, the lower and middle classes who felt the wars and the Depression most gravely. It was not just an "escape" from the problems of the world; it was a way of exploring them in a symbolic way. This process began at the end of the Victorian era and continued through the Second World War, turning horror into a twisted mirror in which the disasters of war and science could find their literary reflection.

12

HORROR IN THE ARTS

Though cosmic horror had brought the genre to its apex of creativity, vision, and scope, horror literature had slipped from the realm of serious literature to a disposable commodity printed in cheap magazines. Therefore, the influence and reach of printed horror was consequently that much narrower. Mainstream pulp fiction like *Argosy* or *All-Story* had half a million and a quarter million readers respectively when they merged in 1920. *Weird Tales*, however, had a circulation of less than fifty thousand in the 1920s, while the pulp magazine industry as a whole sold around twenty million copies a month. Pulps devoted to westerns, science fiction, mystery and detection, and even railroad stories readily outsold horror by large margins into the '30s. Even in the economically troubled times of the Depression, action magazines like *Doc Savage* attracted three hundred thousand or more readers. Old-fashioned printed horror was losing out.

The driving edge of horror from this point forward transferred from the realm of the printed word to that of the celluloid image, though in this era horror made up just one percent of movies released — but what a percent! Movies took up the reins of horror-as-art and reignited the public appetite for the macabre and the bizarre. But as cosmic horror translated to movies and radio, there was a significant difference compared with its literary counterpart. While printed horror had the ability to explore the psychological states of its characters in great detail and paint complex and subjective portraits of horror across time and space, movie and radio horror had to deal with a different vocabulary. To that end, the cosmic had to be presented in the language of film and radio, which meant simplifying and condensing the horror, symbolizing it in a character, usually a scientist, who could represent knowledge-horror in his or her actions. Thus was born the mad scientist stock character, whose long reign at the box office brought big profits, as did the supernatural creatures with which he was often paired. A study of American and British horror films from 1931 to 1984 found that nearly one in three had a scientist or his creation as villain, and nearly forty percent of horror threats came from scientific or psychological research.[1]

The Golden Age of horror cinema began with the release of the Universal production of *Dracula*, which was the studio's most profitable film for 1931.[2] As the story is commonly told, this was due in large measure to the effects of the Great Depression, which began following the crash of the New York Stock Exchange in October of 1929. The years of misery which followed produced a great deal of tension and stress, and critics have noted that it was hardly coincidence that the popularity of cinematic monsters coincided with the waxing and waning of the Depression, and then World War II.[3] Americans, and people around the world, turned to film as an escape from everyday life; and in horror films they found a particular type of release. However, this correlation is only partially true; after all, horror achieved a remarkable reemergence in the 1990s, during a period of unprecedented economic prosperity.

Critics have historically discussed horror films in terms of sex, and specifically Freudian psychoanalytic views of sex, whereby horror's primary concern is a fear of sex, usually female sexuality.[4] Thus vampires are phallic symbols or fanged vaginas; Frankenstein's Monster a parody of birth; the wolf man anxiety over puberty; and any mutilation a playing-out of castration anxieties.* But part of this is because many horror filmmakers, even as far back as the 1930s, purposely used Freudian ideas in their scripts during a wave of Freud-mania in that time. "Why should we take psychoanalysis seriously in thinking about Hollywood movies?" asked William Paul, "because Hollywood took psychoanalysis seriously."[5] However, 1930s horror emerged at a time defined by multiple crisis points, including the damaging effects of the Great War's industrial and scientific forms of mass death, widespread anxieties about cultural decadence, and the changes in world-view wrought by science. These factors contributed to the horror cinema of the era, even beneath the knee-jerk Freudianism, but before we explore how film dealt with these themes, we should first mention how horror carried on in the more traditional arts.

Horror on Canvas

The surrealists believed that the unconscious mind, especially as manifested in dreams, was the gateway to higher truths. Some of these gateways led down the path to nightmares, which surrealist art occasionally captured on canvas. Like the Romantics, surrealists opposed an over-reliance on pure reason, which they blamed for World War I and its mechanical horrors, retreating

---

Beginning in the 1980s, scholars slowly moved to deemphasize strictly Freudian readings of cinema. Steven Shaviro, for example, agreed that psychoanalysis was the best tool for understanding "sexuality under advanced capitalism," but failed to provide "satisfactory" explanations. Shaviro advocated a "radical rethinking of sexuality" that would move beyond Freud to "oppose the dominant male-heterosexual order" symbolized by Freud while preserving the centrality of sexuality in interpreting cinema and art (Steven Shaviro, The Cinematic Body [Minneapolis: University of Minnesota Press, 1993], 67–68).

to an irrational dream world of unconscious fancy. In the visual arts, this tended to manifest as a combination and juxtaposition of the abstract elements of Dada and Cubism with the psychological — and psychosexual — insights of Sigmund Freud. Salvador Dalí's *The Persistence of Memory* (1931) is one of the most famous of surrealist paintings, and its sparse landscape populated by melting watches spoke eloquently about rifts in time and space, and the uncertain confusion of the human unconscious. Dalí's other works tended to recast everyday objects into bizarre, outlandish, and often highly sexualized landscapes. *The Metamorphosis of Narcissus* (1937) depicts body parts disarticulated and reconfigured into a nightmare vision reminiscent of some of the tortures in Hieronymus Bosch's *Garden of Earthly Delights*.

Perhaps lower down on the hierarchy of cultural products, the artists employed by the pulp magazines churned out an enormous amount of horror art to illustrate the covers and interiors of *Weird Tales*, *Horror Stories*, *Terror Tales*, and other publications. Covers by artists like John Newton Howitt, Margaret Brundage, and Virgil Finlay were usually painted on canvas, though few originals survive. Most were done in a colorful style that straddled the border between the realism of a photograph and the wackiness of a cartoon, producing an instantly recognizable "pulp" look. The cover of *Weird Tales* for October 1930 shows a knife-wielding ghost about to attack a damsel tied to a tree. In February 1933, the cover showed a man fighting a giant scorpion while a woman screams helplessly from the spider's web in which she is bound. January 1938 featured a nearly naked woman and an old crone sitting before a sky of bats, in a witch-scene reminiscent of Goya by way of *Playboy*. *Terror Tales* featured a woman being pulled into a sea of blood, a bound woman attacked with a knife, and a bound woman menaced by crawling zombies just in 1935's first three months. Covers for *Horror Stories* featured comely young women boiled alive by a mad scientist, coated in molten wax by a mad doctor, attacked by elderly vampires, and so on. The pulp horror cover themes were monotonous, but always effective, if misogynistic.

Horror on Stage

As in previous eras, horror was still prevalent on the stage. In 1923 Hamilton Deane dramatized *Dracula* for the first time since Bram Stoker's own *pro forma* adaptation at publication. He was able to do so because Stoker's widow wanted an "official" adaptation to counter a pirated version playing in German cinemas (see below). The new play was first performed in Derby in June of 1924, at the Grant Theatre, where it succeeded spectacularly. Deane brought his play to London in February of 1927, where it premiered on Valentine's Day, complete with hired actors to "faint" during the show for added effect. The actor Raymond Huntley played Dracula, and Deane himself took the part of

Van Helsing. Deane would also produce a new, Peggy Webling–scripted stage version of *Frankenstein*, bloodier and more dramatic than earlier adaptations, entitled *Frankenstein: An Adventure in the Macabre* (1927).

The American producer Horace Liveright brought *Dracula* to the United States, where he hired John Balderston to punch it up: tightening the action, cutting extraneous characters, and rewriting most of the dialogue. Huntley declined to reprise his role for the American version, and when the play opened at the Fulton Theatre in October 1927, the part of the vampire count went to an actor born in a part of Hungary now in Romania, who possessed a distinctive and uncertain grasp on the English language. Learning his lines phonetically, Bela Lugosi gave a career-making performance as the undead. His halting pronunciation seemed like a voice from the grave while his dark good looks and suave Continental bearing made him something of a sex symbol, despite a face painted a sepulchral green. In his cape and tuxedo, the Lugosi Dracula would become the defining version of the vampire count, canonized by the movie version filmed in 1930 with Lugosi in the title role. Every Dracula thereafter would work within or against this one. Critics, however, panned his performance as stiff and unnatural, as though vampires should be natural and lithe.

The Deane-Balderston production ran on Broadway for a year and two more on tour. It was the most successful play in America up to that day, earning two million dollars; and this was *before* the stock market crash that supposedly kick-started horror.[6] Other popular horror plays in those years included *The Bat* (1920), a crime drama with a serial killer dressed as a bat (precursor of Batman, perhaps?), and *The Monster* (1922) by Crane Wilbur, the latter dealing with a patient in a sanitarium, a former scientist named Dr. Ziska, who has taken over the place with the intent of conducting bizarre medical experiments on a beautiful young woman. Both *The Bat* and *The Monster* were later filmed, the latter with Lon Chaney starring.

In Germany, the composer Carl Orff set twenty-four medieval poems from the *Carmina Burana* to music between 1935 and 1936. When the composition was first performed in 1937 at the Frankfurt Opera, Orff's *Carmina Burana* became hugely popular in Nazi Germany, and after its use in Oliver Stone's bloody *Natural Born Killers* (1994) its distinctive and dramatic section "O Fortuna" became associated with horror films, even though the composition is most frequently heard in comedies and commercials.

German Screen Horror

Following *The Cabinet of Dr. Caligari*, Weimar Germany was on the cutting edge of silent horror cinema, where the genre's next major work was produced. The filmmaker F. W. Murnau, who had already filmed *Jekyll and Hyde* without permission, produced an unauthorized adaptation of *Dracula*, which he shot under the title *Nosferatu* and released in 1922. Bram Stoker's widow, Florence, was outraged, and she sued successfully to have the film pulled. Fortunately, a few copies survived, giving us a glimpse at horror's first truly chilling masterpiece.

Nosferatu opens with an estate agent named Renfield,* who possesses mystical and alchemical treatises from Dracula, sending his employee, Jonathan Harker, to Dracula's castle to finalize the count's purchase of a house in the German city of Bremen. On the way, peasants warn Harker about the dread count, and he finds an old book that relates the habits of the vampire. Nevertheless, he goes to Dracula's castle and encounters the count, a tall, gaunt beast-man, bald and with a hooked nose and dark eyes (memorably played by Max Schreck). At the castle, Dracula sees a photograph of Mina, Harker's fiancée, and develops an unnatural desire for her. Dracula attacks Harker, and while he is in a swoon loads coffins onto a barge for transport to Bremen. Dracula travels there aboard a ship, and he kills the whole of the ship's crew, famously rising stiffly from an opened coffin in perhaps the film's most effective single shot.

In Bremen, Dracula occupies his new house, conveniently located across from Mina's, and in the wake of the vampire's attacks it seems that the bubonic plague has descended on the city. In a new ending devised by Murnau, Jonathan returns from Dracula's castle with the old book, from which Mina learns that the only way to save Bremen from the vampire plague is to sacrifice herself to the vampire. This she does, and the audience feels the dread of anticipation as *nosferatu*'s shadow creeps up the stairs and enters Mina's bedroom. She invites the vampire in, but while he feeds upon her, dawn approaches. The rising sun kills Dracula, and he vanishes into thin air. Jonathan tries to rescue Mina, but she dies of her wounds.

It is impossible to describe in a plot summary the visual aspects of *Nosferatu* that made the film so effective. The stylized sets, the creepy monster, and the use of early special effects (like printing a ghostly forest in negative) contribute to an atmosphere of the uncanny that is, in a way literature cannot quite produce, itself a sort of cosmic horror. *Seeing* a possible world where unnatural creatures could, and in fact do, exist is itself cosmic horror. The changes Murnau made to the themes of *Dracula* only added to this sense. Here Dracula is allied with pestilence — plague — which is a force akin to the recent war and influenza that was both a part of the natural world and larger than any one individual. The vampire is seen less as an anomaly or freak than as a dark part of our own cosmos, subject not to occult forces but to natural law (the sun). But, as in literary cosmic horror, the price for mastery over the dark forces is annihilation.

---

*Following American convention, the names are those of the novel. The German original used different names in hopes of avoiding Florence Stoker's lawsuit, renaming Dracula, for example, Count Orlock.

Nosferatu (1922). The gaunt and pestilent visage of Max Schreck's count provided one of the most horrifying versions of the vampire on screen. This was decidedly unattractive, animalistic, and repulsive. Though *Nosferatu* is often called one of the scariest movies of all time, most screen Draculas would follow Bela Lugosi's more romantic take on the creature (Kino International).

One could be forgiven, however, for feeling that *Nosferatu* was exclusively about sex, especially after reading the academic literature. Richard McCormick imagined the vampire as a "feminized" character possessed of woman's erotic power, which overcomes the ineffectual and impotent Jonathan, in line with Freud's "phallic woman" and "castration anxiety" hypotheses.[7] Janet Bergstrom, also following Freudian theory, complained that Mina was "lacking a sexual dimension" which the vampire instead possessed, for the count was sex personified.[8] Instead, it is probably more accurate to view *Nosferatu* as a composite in which sexual themes ran alongside a number of others, importantly the larger cosmic themes we have been exploring.

Among his other works, Murnau also produced a version of *Faust* (1927), though this film was more fantasy than horror. Its most important relationship to horror is the appearance of Mephistopheles, who sports the same black cape, pale visage, and widow's peak Bela Lugosi used as Dracula. Fritz Lang produced the science fiction tale *Metropolis* (1925), in which a mad scientist creates a dystopia of oppression, and *M* (1931), the first film depiction of a serial killer (Peter Lorre), who claims that his evil was biological, not a product of his will.

The Vampire on American Screens

In the United States, horror had a rocky start. Some promising work was done in *The Man Who Laughs* (1928) and the Lon Chaney vehicles *The Hunchback of Notre Dame* (1923) and *The Phantom of the Opera* (1925), in which the "man of a thousand faces" used his unmatched makeup skills to create memorable monsters that seemed like evolutionary freaks from some unnatural selection, but such films were more melodrama than horror. (Horror scholar David Skal would later call Chaney's Erik from *Phantom* a "ruined penis" engaged in "visual rape" of the audience.[9]) A number of films produced by Tod Browning used themes of mutilation and vengeance. For example, *The Unknown* (1927) featured Chaney as a criminal pretending to be an armless circus freak. He later has a doctor remove his arms to win the love of a woman who is pathologically afraid of arms. She overcomes this fear too late for Chaney, who enacts a revenge fantasy against the man the woman now loves. The now-lost *London After Midnight* (1927) found Chaney playing a vampire with a mouth full of sharp teeth (Skal, monotonously, thinks them a Freudian *vagina dentata*). It transpires, however, that the vampire is not real but instead a character created to help tease out a mystery. The film was later remade as *Mark of the Vampire*.

The real landmark for American horror came in 1931, with the release of the two defining classics of the genre: Tod Browning's *Dracula* and James Whale's *Frankenstein*. Both were based on classic biological horror, but both

The Phantom of the Opera (1925). David J. Skal thinks that Lon Chaney's portrayal of Erik in *The Phantom of the Opera* suggests a "ruined penis," but the combination of skull and vampire in Erik's face provide a deathly terror that requires no Freudian reading. Chaney's makeup for this role influenced horror monster makeup for decades (www.doctormacro.com).

films made significant alterations to the source works that transformed the horrors into a powerful new vision in line with the cosmic trends of the era.

Dracula opens with Renfield (Dwight Frye)—crucially, not Harker—arriving in Transylvania to meet with Count Dracula so the latter can sign a lease for the London property of Carfax Abbey. The peasants in the small village where he stops are frightened and warn him to stay away from the vampire. Thinking them superstitious, he travels on to Dracula's castle where he is greeted by the aristocratic count in the cobwebbed ruins of his Gothic home, one of the cinema's greatest examples of creepy set design. The vampire (Bela Lugosi, reprising his stage role) stands on the ruined stairs in the Great Hall and intones coldly, "I am ... Dracula. I bid you ... welcome." Unnerved, Renfield follows Dracula upstairs to his chamber, where they conduct business. Left alone, Renfield is about to be attacked by Dracula's three wives when the count returns and banishes them.

When next we meet Renfield he is on board the ship carrying Dracula to England. Renfield is now a blithering madman who has lost his reason and sanity in service to the vampire. He is transferred to Dr. Seward's sanitarium near London. Dracula takes up residence nearby and later chances upon Seward, his daughter Mina, and her fiancé John Harker at a theater where he has come to feed. There is no real connection between Dracula and Mina other than the encounter of random chance, but he has chosen her as a victim and begins coming to her in the night. Concerned about his daughter's declining health, Seward calls in a specialist, Prof. Van Helsing (Edward Van Sloan). Unlike the novel's Van Helsing, this one is not an occult theorist on the fringe of acceptable science. Instead he symbolizes the newfound authority of institutional science, proclaiming plainly, "Gentlemen, we are dealing with the undead ... Nosferatu, the vampire." Despite Harker and Seward's initial scoffing, Van Helsing quickly demonstrates the vampire's reality by tricking Dracula into revealing that he casts no reflection. There is no longer doubt, and the other men immediately submit to Van Helsing's unquestioned expertise and authority. Even Dracula must compliment the scientist: "Your will is strong, Van Helsing."

Mina is now in the grip of the vampire and slave to his hypnotic commands. Van Helsing orders Dracula's destruction, by stake, during the daylight hours when he is powerless. Before this plan can be put into effect, Dracula steals Mina and carries her away to Carfax Abbey. Van Helsing follows, and when the vampire settles into his coffin to rest, he kills Dracula by driving a stake into his heart. Mina is freed from the taint of the vampire, and order is restored.

Because *Dracula* placed Renfield rather than Harker in the Transylvanian scenes, the later events in London are no longer the direct result of Harker's actions. The Seward family encounters the vampire simply by chance and coincidence. The horror is no longer personal, as it was in the novel, but the result of impersonal forces of nature—the vampire—acting wholly according to their essential natures. This Dracula is no longer the evil scientist plotting eternal world domination; he is instead an unquestioned part of the natural landscape, a force rather than an individual, and one who works as a nightmare nature might, through fixed patterns and set natural law. Encountering Dracula expands the worldview of those who meet him to encompass aspects not found in their philosophy, but like Lovecraft's alien gods, he is ultimately part of the natural order, albeit a natural order far more complex than human science previously admitted.

Lugosi, however, added a stark sensuality to Dracula that masked the cosmic implications of the film behind a veil of lightly suppressed eroticism. When out of her right mind, Mina prefers the handsome stranger to her passive lover, though I am not sure I would go so far as David Skal, who says, tiresomely, that Dracula "is a 'castrated' seducer who cannot penetrate in the conventional way; all sex energy is

Bela Lugosi as Dracula. Bela Lugosi gave Count Dracula sex appeal and a snappy wardrobe, two aspects missing from Max Shreck's portrayal. As a result of Lugosi's powerful performance, most subsequent Draculas would follow in his footsteps, and the black cape and tuxedo became standard issue for vampires in the popular imagination (www.doctormacro.com).

displaced to his mouth."[10] I think that analysis is a bit simplistic; instead, Dracula represents the unexplored forces of nature — sex among them — that Mina, as a woman and (presumably) a virgin — has never experienced. She succumbs to the wild and primitive which stand opposed to civilization and science. In the end, only Prof. Van Helsing, man of science, can restore the dominance of civilization and put nature back in its repressed place.

Before discussing 1931's other horror masterpiece, we should briefly trace the remainder of the era's vampire productions. A Spanish-language version of *Dracula* was shot simultaneously with the English-language version utilizing the same sets in the hours when the Americans weren't using them. The plot is the same, though many believe the atmosphere of the Spanish version is superior. *Dracula's Daughter* (1936) attempted to continue the *Dracula* story, but since the original count was dead, the story follows his daughter, Countess Maria Zaleska (Gloria Holden). She travels to London, where Prof. Von Helsing (Van Sloan again) faces trial for Dracula's murder. Zaleska seeks the aid of a psychiatrist to help her overcome her urge to drink blood, which in this film takes on the quality of a mental illness or an addiction. With shades of *Carmilla*, Zaleska seduces a street girl, and the horror eventually comes to a climax when the male characters chase the deranged lesbian vampire back to Transylvania to destroy her. *Mark of the Vampire* (1935), the remake of Chaney's *London After Midnight*, saw Bela Lugosi don a cape again to play Count Mora, a vampire whom villagers believe stalks their town. Professor Zelen (Lionel Barrymore), a vampire expert, is on hand to uncover the truth when it seems Mora has murdered Sir Karol Borotyn. In the end it is revealed that the horror is fake, and the vampire an actor hired to help uncover the truth about Sir Karol's demise.

Son of Dracula (1943) featured Lon Chaney, Jr., in the role of Dracula, masquerading in an atmospheric New Orleans as Count Alucard (Dracula backward). He has come to seek the "virile soil" of the New World to continue his hideous life. He gradually takes over the old Greek revival mansion of a morbid heiress, who breaks her engagement to Frank to marry him to gain vampiric power herself. Especially effective is a scene showing Dracula floating across a swamp, like an unholy Christ walking on water. Here Dr. Brewster (Frank Craven) and Prof. Lazlo (J. Edward Bromberg), as men of science, are charged with piecing together the truth about the vampire and helping Frank stop his supernatural menace. The Hungarian Prof. Lazlo is the Van Helsing figure.

The Return of the Vampire (1944), the last of these early vampire films, found Bela Lugosi playing a vampire once again. In 1918, an English family is tormented by a vampire, who holds sway over a servant he has turned into a werewolf. The vampire is Armand Tesla, who was once an eighteenth century scientist but whose mastery of science led him to become an undead vampire. Dr. Tesla is dispatched at the end of the Great War, but Nazi bombings during the blitz uncover his grave, which cemetery workers discover, removing the iron stake that killed him and restoring him to life. Tesla re-enslaves his werewolf and uses his powers to stalk the family of Lady Jane Ainsley (Frieda Inescort), who along with her now-dead mentor put him down last time. Lady Jane is a scientist of the highest caliber, but even her reputation fails to convince a skeptical Scotland Yard that Tesla is a vampire; and the police want to charge Ainsley with Tesla's 1918 murder, if they can find the body.

The vampire intends to destroy Lady Jane's family and then take over the world. In an evocative scene, Tesla stands behind Lady Jane, who is playing an organ. He is framed in the doorway, shot so he appears between Lady Jane and the organ. She knows he is there but does not look at him. He speaks: "What a fool you are. With all your scientific knowledge you have achieved nothing. You are too late to stop what I have set out to do." Indeed, it seems that this might be the case; but Lady Jane uses psychology to reason with the werewolf, whom she rescued from lycanthropy once before. When a Nazi bomb knocks out Tesla, the werewolf drags the body into the sunlight, where the vampire melts away, freeing him from Tesla's control. In the end it is suggested that Tesla was not the vampire's real name, implying he was actually the hideous Dracula. After all this, the Scotland Yard inspector still refuses to believe in the supernatural since no evidence remains: "You don't believe in this vampire business, do you?" Then, turning to the camera, asks the audience, "And — do you people?" This undercuts the horror by breaking the fourth wall.

As Rick Worland explained, the film related in many ways to World War II anxieties, with the vampire as the German menace and the female scientist as a Rosie-the-Riveter stepping in for the absent male authority figures.[11] The rarity of a female vampire hunter makes this film special, though the effect is undercut by the need for a male to destroy the vampire instead of Lady Jane.

In all these vampire films, we see an essential narrative: A scientist serves as the sole authority figure capable of studying a new phenomenon, understanding its position in the natural world, and bringing it under human control. The human view of the cosmos is expanded, but the triumph of science over nature is assured. This plays out the essential narrative of society's conception of science at its best.

Dead Men and Wolf Men

A different view of science animates *Frankenstein*. In James Whale's version of the tale, based on Webling's play, Dr. Henry Frankenstein (not Victor, the medical student) is the scientist set on making life out of dead tissue. To that end, Frankenstein (Colin Clive) and his hunchbacked assistant Fritz (Dwight Frye) prowl graveyards and gallows stealing corpses to sew into an artificial man. When work is nearly done, Frankenstein sends Fritz to the local medical college to obtain a brain for his creature. Fritz sees two bottles on display, labeled normal and abnormal. He takes the healthy brain but drops it. Afraid to upset his master, Fritz brings the abnormal brain without telling him, and by this subterfuge the brain of a homicidal maniac is implanted into the Monster (Boris Karloff), causing the creature to be born biologically evil, unlike the literary Creature who does evil in response to society's rejection.

Frankenstein is working in a medieval watchtower, but in a laboratory of futuristic scientific equipment from the coming space age, a bizarre cacophony of instruments that reinforce the irrational, Gothic horror in their mysterious and almost magical power.[12] As electricity dances across the machines and imbues the creature with unnatural life, Frankenstein shouts the immortal words "It's *alive*...! Oh, in the name of God! Now I know what it feels like to be God!" With those blasphemous words, the creature comes to life. And thus is Shelley's naïve medical student turned into an arrogant mad scientist, drunk on his own hubris.

The film's look takes its inspiration from *Dr. Caligari*, which Whale's direction transformed into an Art Deco-Gothic hybrid of medieval futurism, filled with stone staircases, deep shadows, and an otherworldly look that set it, and subsequent horror films from Universal Studios, in a world of their own, outside conventional time and space. This was reinforced through an anachronistic pastiche of medieval peasantry, Victorian furnishings, and futurist scientific instruments placed in a vaguely European location that was both everywhere and nowhere. Whale created his own cosmos of fear. The Monster, as played by Boris Karloff with iconic makeup, a flattened head, and bolts sticking out of the sides of his neck, was not the articulate, reasoning being of Shelley's novel. This monster was primal, child-like, aggressive, and largely wordless. He stumbles about like a force of nature, acting like a caged animal. Henry is upset by the failure of his creation to live up to his high ideals, especially when the monster kills Fritz. The Monster escapes and begins to wander through the hills and forests.

He comes across a peasant girl by a lake, and at first it seems that the Monster and the child will strike up a friendship. But in a chilling moment of incomprehension, the Monster tosses the girl into the lake, hoping to float her like the flowers they had tossed in. She drowns, and when her father carries the girl back into town during the festivities for Frankenstein's wedding, the villagers decide to end the Monster's reign of terror. They chase the Monster to an old windmill, where he has holed up, having taken Henry hostage. The Monster hurls Henry down to the ground, but he lives. The villagers set fire to the windmill, and the Monster appears to burn up.

As Henry Frankenstein put it, the scientific endeavor was worth the cost in human lives and psychic harm:

> Have you never wanted to do anything that was dangerous? Where should we be if no one tried to find out what lies beyond? Have you never wanted to look beyond the clouds and the stars, or to know what causes the trees to bud? And what changes the darkness into light? But if you talk like that, people call you crazy. Well, if I could discover just one of these things, what eternity is, for example, I wouldn't care if they did think I was crazy.

The film was an even bigger success than *Dracula*, taking in twelve million dollars against costs of less than three hundred thousand. With an average ticket price of a quarter, this meant around forty-eight million tickets were sold, though obviously some were repeat viewers. However, censorship boards demanded that blasphemous and violent content be censored, and after the film's initial run the uncensored version remained unseen until 1985. Whale followed up *Frankenstein* with an even more impressive film, *Bride of Frankenstein* (1935).

In *Bride*, Henry Frankenstein is recovering from the events of the previous film and preparing for marriage to Elizabeth when his former mentor, Dr.

Boris Karloff as Frankenstein's Monster. With makeup by Jack P. Pierce, Boris Karloff provided the iconic Frankenstein's Monster with its flat-topped head, neck bolts, and undead appearance. Like Bela Lugosi's Dracula, Karloff's Monster virtually defined the creature in the popular imagination and is instantly recognizable. No later interpretation of Shelley's monster matched the cultural resonance of Karloff's portrayal (www.doctormacro.com).

Septimus Pretorius (Ernest Thesiger), arrives to convince Frankenstein to join with him to create life from dead tissue. He has been experimenting with techniques that produced homunculi, miniature people he keeps in bottles. He wants to combine his research with Frankenstein's to create a perfect artificial human. Henry initially refuses, but sees the appeal of producing a successful experiment.

Meanwhile, the Monster has escaped the flames of the windmill to find himself in the woods, where he meets with an old blind man and learns from him to speak. He is now a more sympathetic figure than before; the audience is meant to feel for him when angry villagers pursue him through the woods and nearly crucify him in a parody of Christ. The Monster meets with Dr. Pretorius by chance, and Pretorius seizes the opportunity to use the Monster to force Henry into the monster-making business by promising a bride to the lonely, angry Monster. This they make, and the stunning, startling Bride of Frankenstein (Elsa Lanchester) is animated in another climax of lightning and electricity, her cone of black hair streaked with white, an icon of feminine horror. However, she hates her betrothed, shrieking at the sight. Upset at the rejection, the monster resolves to die, bringing the laboratory crashing down around him and his Bride, but letting Henry Frankenstein and his betrothed, Elizabeth, escape. "We belong dead," the Monster says of himself, Pretorius and the corpse-bride.

The film was followed by *Son of Frankenstein* (1939), which did not have the benefit of Whale, but nevertheless was effective and creepy. Wolf von Frankenstein (Basil Rathbone), Henry's son, brings his family to the old castle to restore his dead father's honor. He finds the body of the Monster and reanimates it with the help of a bestial assistant named Ygor (Bela Lugosi). He is opposed by Inspector Krogh (Lionell Atwill), a one-armed lawman maimed as a child by the Monster's first rampage. The two men's opposition provides a suspenseful tension that only resolves after the Monster is again loosed.

The Ghost of Frankenstein (1942) found Ygor blackmailing another Frankenstein son, Ludwig, into patching up his best friend, the Monster, yet again, this time replacing its diseased criminal brain with the scheming Ygor's own, so the two friends can be together forever. This Ludwig does because he wants to save the life of his father's creation. The new and improved Monster rampages, and a mob of torch-wielding villagers reappears.

Naturally, despite the *prima facie* evidence that the Frankenstein movies, like the book, deal primarily with the effect of science on individual and society, most analyses tend to view the films through the lens of sexuality and gender. Thus for Kay Picart, the films represent "male parthenogenesis" for the Monster and his maker and "the specter of the eruption of uncontrolled female reproductive and sexual power" for the Bride.[13] For Elizabeth Young, *Bride* is a discussion of "anxieties involving gender, sexuality, and race" culminating in homoeroticism and a "psychoanalytic paradigm of male rivalry and female erasure."[14] The Monster, in her view, represents both blacks and homosexuals.

The Frankenstein films invert the message of the vampire movies, for in these films the scientist is the agent of evil, and even the most well-meaning of researchers become drunk with hubris and loose new horrors on the world. While the scientist in the vampire movies restores civilization and human dominance, this scientist is a destabilizing entity who tears asunder the order and tradition of settled life. He is the other side of the scientific coin — the power for change, which is seen as bad.

Universal Studios, responsible for *Dracula* and *Frankenstein*, continued their horror franchise with *The Mummy* (1932) with Boris Karloff as the title corpse. *The Mummy* was essentially *Dracula* in rags, this time with an archaeologist as the scientist whose expertise helps put down the monster. More original was *The Wolf Man* (1941), in which Lon Chaney, Jr., plays Larry Talbot, the prodigal American-raised son of John Talbot (Claude Rains), a Welsh aristocrat. Larry returns to the ancestral home after the death of his older brother, and while there meets shop clerk Gwen (Evelyn Ankers). For a fun date they learn about werewolf lore at a gypsy camp ("Even a man who is pure in heart and says his prayers by night may become a wolf when the wolfbane blooms and the autumn moon is bright"), where Larry is bitten by (you guessed it) a werewolf while trying to save Gwen's friend Jenny from attack. When the police investigate, they find a man's body, not a wolf's, beside Jenny's corpse, and they believe Larry's mind has snapped, in his shock substituting a wolf for the human. Larry changes into a werewolf and realizes that he is a danger to others, especially Gwen, when a gypsy woman explains what has happened.

When wolf attacks multiply, he tries to convince his father of his lycanthropy, but the man of science will hear of no such thing: "Gypsy woman? Now we're getting down to it. She's been filling your mind with this gibberish. This talk of werewolves and pentagrams. You're not a child, Larry, you're a grown man and you believe in the superstitions of a gypsy woman!" Sir John organizes a hunting party to catch the marauding wolf to prove that his son is not one. On this hunt, Sir John, the skeptic, kills the wolf when it is attacking Gwen, but finds his faith in material explanations shattered when the animal's corpse changes back into his son. The most compelling conflict in the film is that between the skeptical scientist father and the sympathetic believer, his son.

The werewolf had more than a dozen outings in various studios' films of the period. Following *The Wolf Man*, the werewolf took over in the popular imagination the role of shape-shifter from Dr. Jekyll, whose own transformations were splashed on the big screen again in 1920, 1931, and 1941, each time with a renewed emphasis on Freudian sex theory. The films tended to view Victorian sexual repression as evil, thus excusing Jekyll's transformation as a way to free his libido, incidentally erasing much of the moral opposition between Jekyll and Hyde.[15]

Monster Mashes

With the success of *The Wolf Man*, Universal began to combine their horror film stars into collaborative films. It was a way of garnering excitement for fading franchises, which, through too many sequels and copycats, had been run down from big-budget films to smaller B-movies appealing increasingly to younger crowds. *Frankenstein Meets the Wolf Man* (1943) found Larry Talbot resurrected, but his doctor thinks the reborn man has a mental affliction which causes him to *believe* that he is the late Larry. Larry wants to return to the dead to stop his killing spree, but instead he resurrects the Frankenstein Monster to find Henry Frankenstein's notes, in which he hopes to learn of a cure (don't ask me why there should be one there). Larry's doctor becomes a mad scientist seeking to transplant Larry's "life essence" into the Monster to cure it. Monster battles monster until villagers blow up the dam and wash the monsters away. *House of Frankenstein* (1944) finds Boris Karloff playing a mad scientist trying to build his hunchbacked assistant a new body. The two take over a traveling carnival holding Dracula's skeleton, which comes back to life. Mayhem ensues; the mad scientist resurrects the Monster and the Wolf Man. Angry villagers etc., arrive, and everyone ends up dead. *House of Dracula* (1945) had a scientist, Dr. Edlemann (Onslow Stevens), looking for a cure for Dracula's (John Carradine) vampirism. The doctor is also treating Larry Talbot for lycanthropy and a female hunchback for her spinal deformity. Next the doctor stumbles on the Frankenstein Monster. Dracula uses the doctor's science against him, turning the doctor into a semi-vampire during a botched transfusion. Crazy with vampire blood, Dr. Edlemann succeeds in reviving the Monster just as the villagers, etc., arrive. The doctor did, however, manage to cure Larry, so there is a happy ending.

The monsters next appeared together again in a comedy, *Abbott and Costello Meet Frankenstein* (1948), where Dracula (Bela Lugosi) is posing as a scientist and is intent on resurrecting the Frankenstein Monster, while Larry Talbot (Lon Chaney, Jr.) teams up with the title comedians to stop him. The film was one of the rare breed that was equally effective as both a comedy and a horror film — and in a good way. The final scene where the Monster is destroyed on a burning dock was reused in *Freddy vs. Jason* (2003), another monster mash that was equal parts comedy and horror, but not in a good way.

The Universal cross-over films had the effect of placing the horror monsters—Dracula, the Frankenstein Monster, and the Wolf Man — in the same mythic universe, creating a distinctive Universal Horror cosmos that in its effect was to film what H. P. Lovecraft's Cthulhu Mythos was to literature. After this, horror movie monsters would come to be seen as inhabiting a single horror universe. Previous films, and each new monster could now be "read back" into the new inter-textual horror cosmos.

Other Big Screen Horrors

The era was the high-point of the mad scientist movie. As Christopher Toumey has shown, science-horror can be distinguished from science fiction in the way science and knowledge are depicted. Science fiction assumes knowledge and technology are equivalent to progress and provides elaborate explanations for how its equipment is meant to work. By contrast, science-horror presents technology as an irrational, inexplicable tool of scientists and knowledge as evil. These scientists are presented as mad because knowledge in these films corrupts both the scientist and the innocent bystanders his studies affect. "Ultimately," Toumey says, "the evil of science is depicted and condemned principally in terms of the character of people who are scientists."[16] The depiction of these scientists, however, has changed over time, becoming increasingly depraved and sadistic, a function of both the simplification of narratives inherent in film and the "debasement" that occurs when making sequels and remakes, in which the mad scientist devolves into a stock character, defined by nothing more than his madness.[17] This coarsening is not intentional, Toumey argues, but a function of the economics and politics of movie-making. The depiction of such scientists does, however, inform our understanding of the mad scientist and the critique of science he offers.

By 1945, Hollywood had released more than one hundred twenty horror films, most of them B-pictures of middling quality. It is impossible to summarize the whole output in a few paragraphs, but a good number of the films followed the same pattern as the monster movies we've discussed, either with a mad scientist loosing a monster on the world or a good scientist struggling to put down a monster, or both. *Murders in the Rue Morgue* (1932) had Bela Lugosi as a mad scientist with a talking ape; he wants the beast to sire a child by a virgin to prove the theory of evolution. *The Black Cat* (1934) has Lugosi as a mad doctor seeking revenge on Boris Karloff, playing a high priest of Satan. When bad science and bad religion meet, annihilation is the only outcome. On the lower end of the production spectrum, *The Devil Bat* (1940) had Lugosi as (another) mad scientist, this one seeking revenge on a cosmetics company by siccing his giant bats on its executives.

The character of the mad scientist was given a darker tint in an adaptation of H. G. Wells's *The Island of Dr. Moreau*, the frightening *Island of Lost Souls* (1933), which follows the novel's outline with the addition of an alluring panther-girl for the hero to befriend. Moreau (Charles Laughton) has made himself explicitly a god of the beast-men, and Bela Lugosi plays the strange creature that serves as his prophet. In this version, Moreau, who wears the white suit of a traveling gentleman, hopes the shipwrecked Edward will consent to father a child with the panther-girl so Moreau can see what result such an "experiment" will produce, whether he has truly turned animals into humans. This Moreau is the apex of the mad scientist, coldly rational, lacking any ethical or moral qualms, and devoted wholly to his experiments. In place of Wells's drawn-out decline of Moreau's island, the island of lost souls collapses in a climax of violence and revenge. Wells hated the movie for vulgarizing his meditation on science, notably for changing Moreau into a sadist, but in many ways this film distills the horror of science divorced from any moral compass into a purer tincture.

The moody *White Zombie* (1932) essentially recasts *Dracula* as zombie feature with Bela Lugosi (again) as "Murder" Legendre, a mill owner who uses a semi-scientific potion to turn people into zombies. Murder, though human, possesses a Haitian fortress not too far removed from Dracula's castle. He has turned a young man's fiancée into a zombie, and tries to do the same to him when he arrives to rescue her. Legendre thinks he succeeds, but when he orders the zombie man to destroy his enemy, a missionary, he instead kills Legendre. The title of the film reflects the fact that Legendre's undoing comes when he attempts to convert Caucasians into zombies; the white elite didn't care when he stuck to native blacks. Several more zombie movies were made in the 1930s and '40s, with varying success: *Revolt of the Zombies* (1936); *King of the Zombies* (1941); *I Walked with a Zombie* (1943); and *Revenge of the Zombies* (1943), in which the evil Nazi scientist making his zombie army for Hitler claims, "It is my hypothesis that metabolism, although vital to prenatal and adolescent development, is not essential in later life." However, the cannibal corpse of later years would have to wait for George Romero; these zombies were the creation of mad scientists for their unique aims. The zombie itself was of secondary concern to the villain's role.

Freaks (1932), from *Dracula* director Tod Browning, is widely considered one of the scariest movies filmed, but it does not live up to its reputation. The movie is a bland eugenicist's nightmare about circus freaks who seek vengeance on a scheming acrobat, making her "one of us" in a rather literal way. The movie is praised today for its use of real circus freaks with a wide range of physical challenges, disabilities, and deformities to play the movie's characters; but the film itself is only scary if you find such physical differences frightening. Most Americans of the 1930s apparently did, however, rejecting the film and running out of the theaters when it played.[18]

Horror trappings could also be found in adventure and science fiction films like *The Lost World* (1925), about finding dinosaurs; and *King Kong* (1933), in which a giant ape from a lost world falls in love with Fay Wray and wreaks havoc on New York City. The early *Kong* sequences on his home of Skull Island, especially those that hint that the island was once home to an advanced, lost civilization, rival the straight horror films in their creepiness.

Serials were exciting short films aimed at children and teenagers and shown at Saturday matinees, often as part of an afternoon of entertainment. Each episode ended in a cliffhanger to keep kids coming back for the whole of a serial's usually fifteen-week run. Of the two hundred thirty-one serials produced between 1929 and 1956, about half were westerns, and most of the rest science fiction or gangster serials. By my count just seven could be thought of as primarily horror, and six more as using significant horror elements. However, villains in many serials adopted horror guises, often dressing in costumes reflecting horror characters, such as ghosts, skeletons, or monsters—like the skull-faced title villain from *The Crimson Ghost* (1946). In horror, crime, sci-fi, and adventure serials the scientist is always there, putting the plot into motion with an amazing discovery or a villainous scheme. *The Phantom Creeps* (1939) stars Bela Lugosi (yet again) as a mad scientist, this time Dr. Alex Zorka, who uses a radioactive meteorite to create a prototype robot to use in fashioning a robot army to make himself world dictator. Across the range of serials, we find the character of the scientist appearing time and again. In my unscientific survey, I found twenty-eight good scientist characters (including archaeologists, doctors, chemists, inventors, and so on), most of whom were kidnapped, tortured, or killed by the villain of the piece to steal their knowledge. I also found twenty-eight mad scientists using their scientific know-how to commit crimes or take over the world. Here was a juvenile version of knowledge-horror for impressionable kids.

From 1930 to 1968, the restrictive Production Code (a.k.a. Hays Code) of censorship regulated how violent screen horror could be, so the era's movies rarely showed blood or gore, nor were they allowed to present overtly sexual material or denigrate religion. Instead, horror films focused on atmosphere and creating a universe of terror that was equal parts mental and cosmic. The end result of these screen horrors was that by the end of the Golden Age of screen horror in 1945, audiences had been exposed to an alternate cosmos in which knowledge was threatening; science was evil, and the natural world a mysterious realm outside the purview of institutional science.

Horror Over the Air

Though horror had colonized the screen, it was not entirely absent from its rival medium: the radio. During the 1920s, the radio industry expanded rapidly, and by the mid–1930s, most United States homes were equipped with a radio set, providing access to a range of programming, including soap operas, drama, comedy, and a not-insignificant amount of horror. The best known example of radio horror was Orson Welles' 1938 adaptation of H. G. Wells's *The War of the Worlds* for *Mercury Theater on the Air* on New York's WABC and nationwide on CBS. On October 30 Welles staged the adaptation in the form of a news report, presenting the alien invasion as a breaking news event with the air of truth about it. The show begins as though a musical performance, but the show is quickly interrupted:

> Ladies and gentlemen, we interrupt our program of dance music to bring you a special bulletin from the Intercontinental Radio News. At twenty minutes before eight, central time, Professor Farrell of the Mount Jennings Observatory, Chicago, Illinois, reports observing several explosions of incandescent gas, occurring at regular intervals on the planet Mars....

Over the course of the hour-long broadcast, new interruptions, and then sustained news coverage featuring interviews with "scientists" and "witnesses" tell the story of the Martian invasion, as canisters containing the creatures fall down to New Jersey, where this version was set. Skeptical scientists turn to believers when faced with the Martian menace. Says the announcer:

> Ladies and gentlemen, this is the most terrifying thing I have ever witnessed.... Wait a minute! Someone's crawling out of the hollow top. Someone or ... something. I can see peering out of that black hole two luminous disks ... are they eyes? It might be a face. It might be....

The Martians eventually unleash poisoned gas, cutting off the announcer, but before the hour is up Earth's bacteria kill them, as related by the only person still able to speak over the air, one of the professors from earlier in the show.

Even though Welles explained both during and at the end of the broadcast that the program was only a radio play, about one in three listeners believed it was real and a national panic ensued.[19] News accounts indicated that dozens sought treatment for shock and hysteria, roads were clogged with traffic jams, some New Jersey residents rushed out of their homes with wet handkerchiefs over their mouths to block the effects of the Martian "gas," and Princeton University sent a team to find the "meteorite." The *New York Times* chided people for failing to consult its radio listings, which clearly stated that *War of the Worlds* would be on. "I heard the broadcast and almost had a heart attack," Bronx resident Louis Winkler told the *Times*. "It was a pretty crummy thing to do."[20] Editorials demanded radio self-censor for the good of the nation, and the FCC sought to define its ability to regulate such dangerous programming.

Elsewhere in radio-land, horror found a less dramatic, but more regular role on the schedules of the major radio networks. Orson Welles played the title *Shadow*, "student of science, and a master of other people's minds," a superhero vigilante who knows "what evil lurks in the hearts of men."

WOR's *The Witch's Tale* (1931–1938) had a 113-year-old crone named Nancy telling horror stories about ancient curses, severed hands, restless spirits, and so on. The witch served as a frame to link each story, the ancestor of Rod Serling's *Twilight Zone* persona and the Crypt-keeper from *Tales from the Crypt*. NBC's *Lights Out* (1936–1939, 1942–1947) presented original suspense and horror tales, including a number voiced by Boris Karloff: "Lights out, everybody! This is the witching hour, the hour when dogs howl and evil is let loose on the sleeping world!" Under the auspices of writer Arch Oboler, *Lights Out* produced some of the most memorable horror on radio, including the episode "Cat Wife" (June 17, 1936) in which Karloff's wife turns into a giant cat, which a psychologist wants to publicize in the name of science ("Who cares about science?!" Karloff says in killing him), and "Chicken Heart" (March 10, 1937), in which the title organ, Dr. Albert's failed experiment at "an eastern scientific institution," doubles in size each hour and destroys the world ("a joke of the cosmos," the scientist says). Obler would use innovative sound effects to make his horrors sound real, such as chopping a cabbage in half to represent severing a head, or chewing on Life Savers to represent snapping bones. "I write about the terrors and monsters within each of us," Oboler said.[21]

Inner Sanctum Mysteries (1941–1952), which was named after a popular line of mystery novels it promoted, aired on NBC Blue (later known as ABC) and then CBS. The show offered more extreme horror fare, with such intentionally outré titles as "The Corpse Who Came to Dinner" (November 16, 1941). Many episodes featured the word "death" in the title, and celebrities like Boris Karloff and Orson Welles lent their voices. The show opened with a creaking door, and a slightly nutty narrator introduced each outlandish and improbable murder story with bad puns, a tactic the Crypt Keeper would adopt for television in the 1980s. The creaking door became so famous that it, along with NBC's distinctive chimes, is the only sound on radio to have its own trademark.[22] Stories ranged from classics, like Poe's "House of Usher" and Maupassant's "The Horla," to original compositions. In a standard episode, a scientist who develops an elixir of immortality ends up sentenced to life in prison for murder.

The Mutual Network's *Weird Circle* (1943–1947) featured a number of classic horrors including Poe stories, *Jekyll and Hyde*, and *Frankenstein*. Mutual's *Mysterious Traveler* (1943–1956) was another anthology in which a nameless traveler aboard a speeding train introduced tales "of the strange and terrifying." CBS's *Escape* (1947–1954) broadcast a number of adaptations of classic horror, including Algernon Blackwood's "Ancient Sorceries," Richard Connell's "The Most Dangerous Game," Poe's "House of Usher," and Robert Hichens's "How Love Came to Professor Guildea."

CBS's *Suspense* (1942–1962) was a long-running anthology of dark stories, some horror and some mystery. Celebrities like Jack Benny and Cary Grant appeared. In its most famous tale "Sorry, Wrong Number" (May 25, 1943), an invalid (Agnes Moorehead) overhears a murder being plotted when telephone wires get crossed. *Suspense* would also dramatize H. P. Lovecraft's "The Dunwich Horror" (November 1, 1945) with mixed results. In the United Kingdom, *Appointment with Fear* (1943–1949, 1955) on the BBC presented a number of radio plays of horror and suspense, some original and some adapted from horror classics. Many were duplicates of plays produced for CBS's *Suspense*, as the show's main writer, John Dickson Carr, worked on both series. *The Man in Black* (1949) continued the franchise with similar stories.

Inner Sanctum at its height in 1946 clocked an impressive 14.6 in the Hooper ratings (representing five million of America's thirty-four million radio homes), a far cry from the 30.2 the number one program, *Fibber McGee & Molly*, racked up, but still high for a horror program. With numbers like that, horror radio had introduced the genre to more people than currently read horror in the pulps by a factor of forty. Combined with the tens of millions who saw *Frankenstein* and other horror films, audio and visual horror had penetrated into everyday life in a way high-brow novels and literary ghost stories never did. Horace Walpole's *The Castle of Otranto* had just a few thousand readers in 1764, but now horror had *millions* of viewers and listeners. For the first time since the inception of the genre, horror was not just popular, it was nearly universal; and it was art, too.

Cosmic horror was the genre's crossroads, summing up all that had come before it in a terrifying culmination and birthing all future visions of horror, beginning with the materialist horrors of the Atomic Age. The horror genre would never again surrender its popular status, nor would it again match the nearly uniform heights it reached across the media during its golden age; literature, art, stage, cinema, and radio all saw masterpieces. As the world sank once more into the darkness of world war, horror stood triumphant, but when the atomic bomb fell on Hiroshima on August 6, 1945, something significant had changed, and horror would never be the same.

PART V

The Age of Alienation
Psycho-Atomic Horror
(c. 1940–c. 1975)

13

SCIENCE AND SOCIETY

Cosmic horror had proposed a world-view defined by anxiety and the lurking fear that unseen and unknown terrors awaited just beyond the pale of the visible, normal world. But with the coming of the Second World War, true horrors beyond human imagining had stripped away the veil cosmic horror used as its signature devise. The horror stood naked for all to see, in the mass slaughter of war, in the death camps of the twentieth century dictators, and above all in the atomic menace that at any moment threatened to destroy the world and everyone in it. The old monsters and the old trappings of Gothic horror, which had served the genre so well for two centuries, now seemed old and stale. What use was Dracula in the face of Hitler? How could Frankenstein's Monster compare to the Red Army? Why wait for Cthulhu to rise again when a single nuclear bomb could do instantly what the Old Ones had not accomplished in millions of years?

So, as the 1930s gave way to the '40s and the '50s, horror retrenched, and the former creatures of the darkness faded away. In their place there arose two new schools of horror, each drawing its strength from the same cultural forces that worked to define science at mid-century. One school of horror, predominant in literature, focused on psychology, probing the inner workings of the mind to produce its shocks and horrors, largely in absence of the supernatural. The second school, predominant in film, wedded the outline of the monster narrative to science fiction, using the era's scientific advances, especially nuclear science, as an instrument of terror. As we shall see in this section, both types of horror attempted to rationalize fear, providing elaborate and pseudo-scientific justifications to bring horror's irrational impulses squarely under the purview and control of human science.

I have chosen to call this species of horror psycho-atomic in honor of its two component parts, but it could equally well be called "modernist" horror after the dominant philosophy of the era. Modernism, or in its scientific form, "positivism," had emerged in the nineteenth century with the philosophy of Auguste Comte and dominated thought in the early and mid-century. It was a philosophy that held that science was the only way to understand the world, and that scientific knowledge was an objective description of reality. Positivists held that scientific knowledge would continue to accumulate, improving our understanding of the world and leading to progress. These beliefs filtered down from the academy to the creators of horror, and by mid-century, the new horror tended to reflect distorted visions of positivism's materialism and worship of science in an attempt to reconcile the positive aspects of science with the increasingly obvious capacity of science to destroy the world.

A World of War

The Nazi dictatorship provided the most prominent example of the dangers of science in the service of evil. When Hitler came to power in 1933, he set about mobilizing Germany's scientists and inventors to implement Nazi ideology. There were some initial triumphs, including the Nazi government's campaign to ban smoking after discovering a link between tobacco use and cancer, and the modernization of Germany's infrastructure, notably the construction of the *autobahn* roads. However, Hitler's government tended to view science as an extension of ideology. If the state could fight cancer, why could it not fight a genetic "cancer" that threatened the body of German health? From such reasoning came compulsory sterilization and euthanasia.[1] Physicists were compelled to reject "Jewish" physics, which included Einstein's theory of relativity and most theoretical physics. Similarly, higher mathematics were sacrificed to practical applications, since theory was, here too, seen as "Jewish" and therefore un–German. Darwin's theory of evolution was twisted to justify Aryan superiority. But this was only the public face of a dictatorship that presented itself as the model state. Beneath the surface, darker tinges stirred, though most in America would not know the full extent of Nazi brutality until after Germany surrendered.

With the outbreak of a war on September 1, 1939, the world had a glimpse of Hitler's technological prowess, which employed to devastating effect with his *blitzkrieg*, or lightning war, against Poland. This new type of war-craft utilized tanks, aircraft, motorcycles, and automobiles, tied together with power of radio, through which German commanders could control military maneuvers in a way no previous military machine had been able to do. Germany could survive Allied oil embargoes through the scientific development of synthetic fuels, and Hitler's scientists worked endlessly to create bigger and more powerful missiles to launch rocket attacks against Great Britain to compliment the bombs the Luftwaffe dropped by plane during the Blitz.[2]

The Allies also recruited science to the war effort, developing a host of new technologies to help defeat the Axis powers. Radio detection and ranging, known later as radar, was developed to defend against the Blitz, and the British and Americans built the first true computer, Colossus, to break Nazi Germany's most complex system for encoding messages, Enigma. The Colossus was the first computer to use the system of Boolean logic — ones and zeros in sequence — to produce its calculations, making it the ancestor of all modern computing technology.[3] The result of this massive effort was the eventually technological superiority of the Allied side, but also the completion of the coupling of government and science begun in World War I. Science was now an institution, akin to Congress, Parliament, or the courts; and from this point on, the pronouncements of science had an institutional authority.

The war that was now ending was the deadliest in human history, taking more than sixty million lives from the direct effects of combat, famine and disease caused by war, or deliberate policies of extermination. The scale of the carnage was unprecedented; for the first time in history a war had claimed more than 1.2 percent of the *entire population of the Earth*, and that represented only battlefield deaths.[4] Taking civilian deaths into account, two and half percent of all people — 25 in every 1,000 humans — were dead. Such killing had never been seen before, not even in the First World War. The volume of deaths would eventually serve as justification for President Harry Truman's decision to use the most advanced technology of war to bring the conflict to a close in the hopes of saving the lives of U.S. and Allied soldiers.

The United States, the United Kingdom, Germany, and the Soviet Union all employed scientists with the aim of producing the one weapon that could stop the war in its tracks: the atomic bomb. Nuclear physics advanced rapidly in the 1930s, and by 1939 scientists had overcome most of the challenges involved in inducing uranium to explode in a massive nuclear chain reaction. Concerned that Germany was locking up the available supply of uranium, Albert Einstein wrote to President Roosevelt urging him to secure uranium supplies for a future American bomb effort. This effort would take the form of the Manhattan Project, in which American and British scientists worked to create a bomb so powerful it could destroy an entire city in an instant. The German nuclear project failed for many reasons, but the Anglo-American project succeeded. By the time the first atomic bombs were ready for use, Germany had surrendered, but its Axis partner, Japan, had not. President Truman ordered a pair of atomic bombs dropped on Hiroshima and Nagasaki. In Hiroshima, 140,000 died in an instant; 74,000 in Nagasaki.[5] Truman called the dawning atomic age a "new era in the history of civilization," adding that

> Never in history has society been confronted with a power so full of potential danger and at the same time so full of promise for the future of man and for the peace of the world. I think I express the faith of the American people when I say that we can use the knowledge we have won not for the devastation of war but for the future welfare of humanity.[6]

J. Robert Oppenheimer, the scientist responsible for creating the atomic bomb by virtue of his position at the head of the Manhattan Project, later worried that despite Truman's high-minded rhetoric, the bomb was a mistake, and one for which science was responsible: "the physicists have known sin, and this was a knowledge they cannot lose."[7] The morality of science was further compromised by the involvement of former Nazi scientists in the American and Soviet weapons programs after the war. The Soviet Union would create its own atom bomb in 1949, attributed in part to Communist spies stealing America's

Nuclear explosion. The bombing of Nagasaki, seen here, and Hiroshima in 1945 showed how devastating nuclear war could be. The atomic bomb gave humans the destructive power to do in an instant what previous wars took years to accomplish, and the budding Cold War soon made it possible to annihilate the entire world's population with the press of a button (National Archives).

secrets, thus inaugurating the Cold War and its attendant paranoia, suspicion, and the specter of world-wide destruction. At any moment it was conceivable that America and the Soviet Union would blow themselves to bits in "mutually assured destruction" (MAD), and it was this threat of global annihilation that prevented the outbreak of a disastrous third world war. In the United States and in Europe, many turned to religion to make sense of science's horrors. Reports of apparitions of the Virgin Mary hit record levels, and preachers like Billy Graham argued that nuclear weapons portended the end of the world and the return of Christ.[8] It was the beginning of a religious revival that would in the next decades challenge the legitimacy of science.

A Science of Cruelty

When Allied forces entered the concentration camps scattered across the ruins of Hitler's Europe, they encountered a sight unparalleled to that point in human history. The Allies found camp after camp filled with the walking dead, skeletons wearing coats of flesh, moving like zombies amidst piles of corpses and the machinery of death. It was like Bruegel's *Triumph of Death* come to some sickening un-life.

These were the survivors of the Holocaust, Hitler's systematic massacre of Jews, Gypsies, homosexuals, the mentally and physically disabled, and anyone else deemed inferior. At least seven million died in the Holocaust, six million of them Jews, victims of Nazi Germany's obsession with purifying the Aryan race.[9] In some places, the Nazis used the most advanced technologies for killing, pumping showers full of Zyklon B, a poisoned gas, and cremating the bodies. At Auschwitz, nearly two thousand corpses a day could be cremated; but as the war dragged on, the trappings of sterile and scientific extermination fell away. Jews were shot and dumped into mass graves, or simply thrown into open pits and buried alive as the Nazi brutality outstripped their engineers' ability to hide it beneath a veneer of scientific efficiency. For years many would wonder how such a tragedy could have occurred, and how ordinary men and women became part of a campaign of killing.

Almost as bad was the discovery of what Nazi Germany's doctors had done to the condemned in the name of science. It began with the euthanasia policies, providing "mercy killings" for the terminally ill, the retarded, and those "unfit" to live. During the war, the concentration camps became sadistic playgrounds for a phalanx of Drs. Moreau, some three hundred fifty doctors in all.[10] Prof. Heinrich Berning coldly recorded the symptoms of starving Soviet prisoners until they dropped dead. Other doctors froze their prisoners, or infected them with rare diseases to see how they would suffer and die. Still more experiments involved transplanting organs or deliberately infecting wounds the doctors had induced. Dr. Sigmund Rascher used a mobile pressure chamber to

Bodies at Gusen Camp. The Holocaust took the lives of eight million people, mostly Jews, and showed how an industrial society could revert to shocking barbarism. Victims were starved, forced to work, and experimented on in an escalating cycle of cruelty overseen by the German government and medical authorities. In time, the stark images of the Holocaust would be reflected in the depiction of zombies and victims in horror literature and horror arts (National Archives).

simulate the effects of falling out of an airplane. He repeated his experiments on one victim three times until he succeeded in simulating a fatal fall. Dr. Josef Mengele, the most notorious of the Nazi doctors, injected dye into victims' eyes to see if he could change their color. He conducted notorious studies on Jewish twins involving infections, mutilations, and, almost inevitably, death.[11]

When the Red Army marched into German-occupied Eastern Europe, Stalin appropriated the German concentration camps and added them to his system of camps, the Gulag, in which more than one million political prisoners died of malnutrition and poor conditions between 1934 and 1953 and almost a million more were executed.[12] The best that could be said for Stalin's concentration camps was that he was ecumenical about his killing; race and religion did not matter—political concerns sent you to the Gulag.

The Soviet dictatorship provided a perfect example of the horrors unleashed when all-powerful politicians tried to remake society along "scientific" principles. Under Josef Stalin, the Soviet Union attempted to implement policies and programs to bring to fruition Karl Marx's promise that communism would provide a materialist and scientific path toward perfecting humanity. Stalin's scientists differed from Hitler's; they believed that criminal tendencies and social deviance were not inborn, genetic failures but were instead the products of social conditions, the remnants of bourgeois mentality. Stalin ordered his psychologists to reject Freudian theory, and he favored Lamarckian evolution over that of Darwin. Stalin outlawed the study of genetics, favoring Lysenko's idea that plants, and people, could be retrained by the environment. To that end, Stalin enforced policies meant to eliminate the "backward" nature of folk-culture among the populations under Soviet rule, molding them into the Soviet "new people" by cutting them off from their cultures and divorcing them from nature's instincts and impulses, replacing them with "the rational desire to master and control those urges."[13]

Communism and Nazism were ideologies that sought to use science to recreate humanity in service of ideology. The Nazi experiment was horrific. The Soviet Union was meant to be a utopia of equality and prosperity, and for a time intellectuals in the West bought into the fiction. But the cruelty of the Soviet dictatorship, the failure of its socialist science, and political imperialism of communism soon dispelled that myth. When the Iron Curtain divided Europe into democratic and communist halves, in the eyes of the West the Soviet world had become a nightmare land of oppression and horror. The horror only escalated as more countries—China, Korea, Cuba, etc.—turned communist. The world was now divided into three camps: Those allied with the United States, those allied with the Soviet Union, and those who played the two "superpowers" off one another. And over all hung the shadow of nuclear annihilation that could come at any time, as it almost did during the Cuban Missile Crisis of 1961, when for twelve days in October it was perfectly possible to believe that humanity might not survive until November.

To that end, countless Americans constructed backyard bomb shelters and planned for the end of the world. Schools taught children to hide under their desks, to "duck and cover," when the bombs came, as though that would protect them from the awesome power of the atomic bomb and its deadlier cousin, the hydrogen bomb, developed during the 1950s. By the 1960s, intercontinental ballistic missiles could shoot nuclear weapons anywhere on Earth without notice.

The Free World

In the United States, Congress acted to define America against the "god-less" communists (they were officially atheist) and "pagan" fascists (Hitler promoted a German occultism) by reinforcing America's Christian values. To this end, "In God We Trust" was added to paper money in 1954, and "under God" inserted into the Pledge of Allegiance. In the House of Representatives, the House Committee on Un-American Activities (1938–1975) grew out of an earlier committee investigating Nazi propaganda within the United States. During the Cold War the committee turned its attention to Hollywood, looking for communist infiltration in the entertainment industry and eventually forcing the blacklisting of three hundred actors, artists, and industry workers accused of being communists and communists sympathizers. During one hearing, an oblivious Rep. Joe Starns of Alabama famously demanded to know whether the Elizabethan playwright Christopher Marlowe, author of *Dr. Faustus*, was a communist.[14]

On the Senate side, Sen. Joseph McCarthy charged that the United States government harbored a number of communists and communist sympathizers. He called hearings in the Senate to ferret out the communists and expel them from government. McCarthy claimed, without proof, that the State Department was rife with Soviet spies and communists who were undermining America's foreign policy. The atmosphere of intimidation and fear rising from McCarthy's bullying tactics led the *Washington Post* to coin the term "McCarthyism," and President Eisenhower publicly criticized the senator for his actions. On March 9, 1954, CBS's Edward R. Murrow, the respected newsman, delivered a devastating report on *See It Now,* using his own words to paint McCarthy as demagogue and buffoon who had "terrorized" and intimidated. Murrow closed his broadcast with a peroration summarizing all that was wrong with McCarthyism:

> His primary achievement has been in confusing the public mind, as between the internal and the external threats of Communism. We must not confuse dissent with disloyalty. We must remember always that accusation is not proof and that conviction depends upon evidence and due process of law. We will not walk in fear, one of another. We will not be driven by fear into an age of unreason....[15]

After McCarthy's ill-fated attack on the army, which he claimed was overrun with communist spies, and attacks on Murrow, public backlash led the Senate to censure him. He died two and half years later, still railing against communists.

By then the threat from communism in the public mind was no longer spies and infiltrators, but the Soviets' perceived superiority in science. The Russians launched the first satellite, *Sputnik*, in 1957, and America mobilized its scientists and students to duplicate the achievement and pull ahead in what became known as "the space race." Science and math received renewed emphasis in American schools, NASA became the symbol of American ingenuity, and the effort culminated in the greatest achievement of Western science: landing a man on the moon in July 1969. For the first time in human history, a creature of this earth walked on another cosmic body.

The era also saw the rapid development of technology and science in other areas: Television largely superseded radio; automobiles became nearly universal; ENIAC, the first reprogrammable electronic digital computer (Colossus could do only one program), ushered in the era of the computer; antibiotics promised to eliminate disease; the identification of DNA provided an explanation for how evolution could work. All of this (and more) refashioned the way the Free World viewed the world. Everywhere there was progress, and this progress was thanks to science. But increasingly advances in science were no longer the province of dedicated amateurs but, instead, of the government, the military, major universities, and large-scale corporations—what President Eisenhower would call "the military-industrial complex" when referring to the symbiosis of the army and the corporations that supplied it with weapons and materiel. Though it brought new wonders, science was never more remote, more mysterious, or more a part of the structure of authority than in the postwar years.

But despite the institutionalization of science, the effect of Einstein's relativity began to filter down from the elite to the general public: If time and space were defined in part by the observer, then absolutes no longer applied. Worse, with each new advance in science, it emerged that the benighted masses were laboring under falsehoods and delusions. Yesterday's truths were superseded by "truer" truths; only the pronouncements of science could sort truth from lies because information was now so complex, and coming so fast, that only trained specialists could make sense of it. Unfortunately, those experts disagreed.[16] As a result, the public stood between warring experts: some saying processed foods were the ultimate in nutrition, others preaching a back-to-nature approach; some saying the earth was warming, others that it was cooling; some arguing communism was the wave of the future, others that it was doomed to failure. Truth had become another commodity.

At the same time, psychoanalysis, psychiatry, and psychology—in their various forms—became the preferred way of understanding the human mind; that is, viewing the mind as something to be understood through science and its methods. In 1938 electroshock therapy was first used to treat mental problems. By the 1950s the figure of the psychiatrist ("shrink") listening to a patient reclining on a couch was nearly universal, and increasing numbers of individuals sought therapy. In 1952 the American Psychological Association classified mental illnesses for the first time in the *Diagnostic and Statistical Manual of Mental Disorders*. In this era, Freudian theory was rejected by most psychologists in favor of behavioralist models focusing on actions rather than mental states. However, the science fiction writer L. Ron Hubbard created an ersatz psychoanalysis called *Dianetics: The New Science of Mental Health* (1950), which returned to Freud's idea that childhood trauma caused adult neuroses, expanding his theory to imagine that words uttered by parents caused cancers and other diseases later in life. The repressed memories of these words he later called "engrams." Hubbard first described Dianetics in the pulp sci-fi magazine *Astounding Science Fiction*, and then in book form. Psychologists called it quackery.

The Horror Within

Questions lingered, though, about the trauma of World War II and how it was that so many Germans had come to participate in the mass murder of the Jews. Could it happen anywhere? Beginning in July 1961, Stanley Milgram conducted a series of experiments to answer this question. He paid volunteers four dollars apiece to sit in his Yale laboratory and take part in a study he pretended involved learning and punishment. The subject, designated the "teacher," was to turn a knob to deliver an electric shock to the "learner" whenever that individual incorrectly answered the teacher's questions. Milgram found that so long as an authority figure, in this case a scientist in a lab coat, provided direction and reassurance, nearly two-thirds of "teachers" willingly delivered fatal electric shocks, unaware that the "learner" was an actor and the setup a hoax.[17]

Milgram was delighted to learn of a later experiment that seemed to confirm his results about the "dark side of human nature," the Stanford Prison Experiment, conducted by his high school friend, Philip Zimbardo.[18] In the summer of 1971, researchers at Stanford assigned student volunteers to the role of "prisoner" or "guard" in a mock prison built on campus and superintended by Zimbardo. They were paid fifteen dollars and screened for psychological health and stability. Once inside the mock prison, the young men degenerated into all manner of sadism and torture, the uniformed guards acting out violent and sexually humiliating scenarios on the prisoners. The prisoners were made to clean toilets with their hands and to perform homosexual acts on one another. The experiment ended after only six of a planned fourteen days when one researcher finally objected to conditions in the prison. Fifty others saw nothing wrong with sadism and torture.

Both experiments underscored the susceptibility of individuals to authority. The prisoners in the Stanford experiment accepted their own degradation rather than walking out; the guards performed as aggressively as they felt Zimbardo's authority allowed, and Milgram's recruits did whatever the researcher asked of them. These experiments provided a partial answer to the question of Nazi Germany: The horror wasn't unique to fascism, it was within each one of us. Each experiment was also criticized for ethical violations and the trauma it produced in its participants. Nevertheless, in 2001 the BBC tried to recreate the Stanford experiment for television, but had to halt the experiment early when an ethics committee objected to conditions in the prison. In January 2007, ABC News in the United States recreated the Milgram experiment, supposedly for science but actually to torture individuals for entertainment.

The atomic era's fascination with the horror within the individual led to a number of psychological, psychoanalytic, and psycho-sexual theories to explain one of the century's most bizarre killers, Ed Gein, who would become the inspiration for the horror genre's depictions of serial killers for the rest of the century and into the next, influencing everyone from *Psycho*'s Norman Bates to *The Texas Chain Saw Massacre*'s Leatherface, to the villains in Sci-Fi Channel movies of the week.

In November 1957, police investigating the disappearance of Bernice Worden, the owner of a hardware store, traced her to the farm of Gein, an eccentric loner. There they found her naked, headless, and strung up like meat. That was only part of the horror. Police discovered that Gein had furnished his home with objects made from the bodies of more than forty dead women he had dug out of a local graveyard. His soup bowl was a skull cap, his lampshades made from human skin. He stuffed and mounted women's faces like trophies, heavily rouged, and kept their vaginas in boxes. Gein even sewed together dead women's skins to make himself a bodysuit complete with breasts and a vagina so he could play the part of a woman — one special woman. The refrigerator was well stocked with human organs, and a human heart waited to be cooked in the smokehouse kitchen. Gein claimed he "didn't have anything to do with it," but changed his story and said he wanted to take women apart to see "how things work."[19]

Though Gein murdered only two women (the other was Mary Hogan, in 1954), his case would "stun the nation," as *Life* magazine put it. Confined to the Central State Hospital for the Criminally Insane, he would become the subject of intense psychological interest. Doctors would conclude that Gein's mother had poisoned his mind, impressing on him the evils of sex and her own exalted place in the female pantheon. After her death in 1945, Gein apparently sought to "replace" his mother with corpses, victims, and a suit that would allow him to "become" her.

Another violent crime, this one in Kansas, also spawned a type of literary horror. Truman Capote traveled to Holcomb, Kansas to document the 1959 murder of a farmer and his family by a pair of parolees. Capote said he was creating a new form of literature, the non-fiction novel, and he called his detailed study of the murder, its causes, and its aftermath *In Cold Blood* (1965).

The Milgram and Stanford experiments, Ed Gein, and *In Cold Blood* all offered stark testimony that beneath the shining surface of mid-century America there lived a darkness and a horror that civilization had not entirely eradicated, an irrationalism science needed to explain.

Projecting the Horror Skyward

We have seen that earlier generations were plagued with imaginary monsters: vampires, witches, ghosts, and snake men from lost civilizations. Such creatures were quaint by the modernist standards of the post-war years. With modern architecture stripping away ornamentation and leaving behind massive canyons of glass-walled boxes and modern design streamlining everything from automobiles to sofas, there were fewer dark corners and Gothic crannies in which such demons of the imagination could hide. Instead the post-war generation would find its monsters had taken to the sky, where it was thought that visitors from other worlds were making frequent and dramatic forays into earthly terrain. The new monsters came dressed in the trappings of science and technology. It was the birth of the UFO. The *War of the Worlds* panic, and to a lesser extent the confusion about the reality of Lovecraft's alien gods, had demonstrated that the American public was ready to believe that extraterrestrials were real and were visiting the Earth. It only took a spark move aliens from the realm of fiction to accepted fact.

On June 24, 1947, businessman Kenneth Arnold was flying his small plane near Washington State's Mt. Ranier when he saw nine objects gliding across the sky. He estimated the arc-shaped craft darted away from him at 1,200 miles per hour, traveling "like a saucer would if you skipped it across water." A journalist reporting the story confused Arnold's description of the craft with his claims for their flight, christening the unexplained objects (likely birds) "flying saucers."[20] Within days, the story had spread around the world and people as far afield as Canada, New Zealand, and Australia reported their own sightings of flying discs that month. In July 1947, a secret government weather balloon crashed in Roswell, New Mexico. A legend sprang up, thanks in part to sensational news reports and an inept government attempt to hide its anti–Soviet spy balloon, that an alien spacecraft had crashed in Roswell and was spirited away to a government facility. Because Roswell was home to the Air Force base housing the *Enola Gay*, the plane that dropped the atomic bomb on Hiroshima, later UFO investigators would claim the aliens were drawn by this nuclear connection.

Fears of alien invasion neatly paralleled fears of Soviet invasion, and sightings of what the Air Force called "unidentified flying objects" continued through the 1950s, with photographs and occasionally filmed pictures. The Air Force launched a series of investigations into UFOs to see what they were and whether they posed a security risk: Project Sign in 1947, Project Grudge in 1948, and Project Blue Book from 1952 to 1970. The projects concluded that UFOs posed no threat, and most were the result of hysteria, fabrication, or the misidentifications of natural phenomena or human artifacts. The scientific researcher behind Blue Book, the skeptical Dr. J. Allen Hynek, became less sure of his skepticism when he could not explain some of the sightings, later attributing UFOs to advanced aliens with well-developed spiritualist mental powers.

The government rightly concluded, however, that there was no evidence that UFOs were alien spacecraft.[21]

At the height of the UFO craze, some began to insist they had met with the occupants of the flying saucers. In November 1952, George Adamski claimed that tall, blonde Venusians in glittering flight suits took him on a tour of the universe and explained their compulsion to help the Earth overcome its political, economic, and social problems. Adamski provided "proof" of his claims in the form of photographs of flying saucers, which he fabricated from bottle coolers and chicken feeders.[22] Samuel Thompson claimed in 1950 that the Venusians came to him in the shape of leprechauns. Howard Menger's Venusians were beautiful, vegetarian women who had been coming to him in his sleep at his New Jersey home since the age of ten. Taxi driver George King, in the United Kingdom, founded the Aetherius Society in 1954 after meeting with seven-foot-tall Venusians who subsisted entirely on air. The Venusians had named him Earth's ambassador to the Interplanetary Parliament they held on Saturn.[23] All these aliens were human-like, only more perfect, and they wanted "to serve man," in the words of Damon Knight, who would skewer them mercilessly in a short story of that name.

Founded by Ernest and Ruth Norman in 1954, the Unarius (Universal Articulate Interdimensional Understanding of Science) Academy of Science went one step further, all but worshipping science itself. They claimed that fourth-dimensional physics revealed by the "space brothers" from Venus revealed that the material world is an illusion, reality is merely energy, and each human soul — as energy — is immortal and lived innumerable lives. The group channeled the ascended spirit of scientist Nikola Tesla as a prophet, and they constructed a large replica UFO to welcome the aliens. The organization famously predicted that UFOs would land in the United States in 2001, and when that failed to happen, the group predicted future landings.

In 1952, L. Ron Hubbard, who once wrote for some of the same magazines as H. P. Lovecraft, expanded his Dianetics into a new religion which drew on science fiction and alien encounters. Dubbed Scientology, a Latin-Greek hybrid word meaning something like "the study of knowledge," Hubbard's religion is said to hold that seventy-five million years ago Xenu, head of a galactic federation, brought billions of aliens to the Earth, locked them inside volcanoes and detonated hydrogen bombs to scatter their souls, or thetans, across the globe. These souls cling to human souls and cause trauma and pain. However, this knowledge is said to be so secret that only the highest ranking Scientologists are allowed to know the truth about Earth's early history. The Church of Scientology, which charges believers to take "courses" to rid themselves of engrams and thetans, currently claims ten million members worldwide and is popular with celebrities.

In the hard sciences, Immanuel Velikovsky tried to fire-bomb geology by claiming that the planet Venus was once a comet that had passed near Earth during Biblical times, giving rise to the narratives of the Old Testament. Science therefore had Earth's whole history wrong. Scientists scoffed at his idea that the destruction of Jericho, the appearance of the Lord, and the plagues of Egypt were the result of the comet's effects, but members of the public found it fascinating and thousands became devoted followers.

An age of aliens and atom bombs saw the possibility of invasion and annihilation lurking behind the shining veneer of progress, and it was no coincidence that the era of fallout shelters, duck-and-cover, and backyard bunkers produced a horror literature and horror media that reflected the new realities of the Cold War. Themes of paranoia, psychology, aliens, and the evils of science found their expression in the novels, stories, cinema, and television of the age. If glittering science fiction stories about the conquest of space and the glories of progress reflected the official view of life, horror provided a dark mirror in which the undercurrents of fear could find eloquent expression.

14

LITERARY DEVELOPMENTS

In a famous essay in the May 27, 1944, edition of *The New Yorker*, Edmund Wilson disparaged the revival of horror that had occurred over the preceding two decades, as exemplified in a number of anthologies of ghost stories popular in the 1940s, like Boris Karloff's *Tales of Terror* (1943), and the era's horror movies. He supposed that the electric light had banished ghost stories and monsters, which he viewed as "antiquated" and decidedly un-modern. He said that the horror of the nineteenth century and the cosmic period could not possibly "scare anyone over ten." Instead, Wilson proposed that modern society required modern horrors "not merely by attempting to transpose into terms of contemporary life the old fairy tales of goblins and phantoms but by probing psychological caverns where the constraints of that life itself have engendered disquieting obsessions."[1] For Wilson, the *psychological* manifestations of horror were the most important aspects of the literature of fear. Terror was to be found within the human mind rather than in the outside world.

For better or for worse, the horror literature of the postwar years followed Wilson's dictum, turning to the psychology of the human mind to find the source of terror. The era's modernist literature rejected Victorian romanticism and instead focused on exploring alienation and everyday reality. Modern horror stories did not always completely abandon the supernatural, but they transformed the situations, trappings, and monsters of older horror traditions, transmuting them into a refined horror in which character and psychology took pride of place as first among equals in the pantheon of fear. Where monsters were employed, they took new forms. The traditional monsters of horror — vampires, ghosts, and so on — became tools to examine characters' psychology and alienation from society, and new monsters reinforced the scientific point of view. Earthly monsters were often created by human action, not by an all-powerful natural world, the product of science gone bad, not nature primeval. Other monsters came from beyond our world, aliens subject to different evolutionary imperatives.

The two sides of the scientific coin are still present, as they were in earlier forms of horror, but now the assumptions underlying the good and the evil science does have changed. The trend toward psychologizing and materializing horror was not new; Poe had written stories of diseased minds, and Ann Radcliffe's Gothic horrors provided materialist explanations. But in the psycho-atomic horror of mid-century, science is treated as a given, a body of knowledge that has objective truth and which exists to explain away the horrors of the visible world, even as it causes new horrors to be born. There is little of the fight between skeptics and believers, not the way spiritualist or cosmic horror saw it, but instead the scientific world-view is now the assumed default position; and whatever monsters stumble into the light eventually find themselves subsumed into the scientific understanding of the material world.

Transitioning Toward a New Horror

The great period of psychological horror was prefigured in the works of Conrad Aiken, who counted Freud among those whose ideas he inserted into his horror stories. "Silent Snow, Secret Snow" (1934) tells of a young boy who imagines a fantasy world filled with snow, which he believes is better than his quotidian life; and he retreats into that world, having gone mad. William Faulkner's "A Rose for Emily" (1930) is perhaps the greatest of the early psychological horrors. The story tells of Miss Emily Grierson, who lived in an old Victorian house in the Deep South until the day she died, attended only by an old black servant. In earlier times, her domineering father ran her life, and after his death she took up with a Yankee construction foreman named Homer. He vanished one day, and the townsfolk presumed he returned north, imagining their presumed marriage went sour. She shut up the house and spent the rest of her life —forty years— a recluse. When she died, they found in her house a secret bedroom in which lay the body of a man, curled up in the pose of an embrace, "but now that long sleep that outlasts love, that conquers even the grimace of love, had cuckolded him."[2] An indentation in the neighboring pillow and some strands of gray hair indicate that Homer did not lie in that bed alone most nights.

This was how respectable literature did horror. Of course, academics tended to focus on the sexual aspects of the story, rather than the horrific ones, arguing, as Judith Fetterley did, that the story is really about a "violation of the expectations generated by the conventions of sexual politics."[3] In other words, it is Emily's gender more than her necrophilia that frightens us, for a *man* sleeping beside a corpse would be some species of normal. Gregory S. Jay, despite his obvious obsession with "patriarchy" and "subjects of race, class, and gender," perhaps had it right when he said that the story was instead a complex portrait of a society whose structure in its entirety serves to force Emily into her grotesque actions.[4]

The less respectable forms of writing transitioned toward the new horror too. During the run-up to World War II, "shudder pulp" magazines like *Horror*

Stories and *Terror Tales* specialized in the "weird menace" variety of horror (as opposed to the largely straightforward supernatural horror of *Weird Tales*) in which shapely young women were placed in sexually provocative situations by sadistic torturers. This particular category of horror took violence and gruesomeness to new extremes, but in so doing it also reinforced a materialist-psychological view of horror. In typical "shudder" stories, the hero must rescue a girl, defeat a human menace posing as a supernatural creature, and uncover the truth behind the extreme violence. It almost always transpires that the sadistic violence was perpetrated at the hands of a madman, frequently a crazed scientist, who is seeking revenge for a world that denies him the freedom to pursue his horrible research wherever it may lead. Often, he uses science fiction devises to commit his crimes. During and after the war, the "weird menace" stories achieved the apex of their popularity, eventually giving rise to the horror comics of the 1950s.

Perhaps the best example of this was "The Molemen Want Your Eyes" (1938), from *Horror Stories*. Larded with exclamation points, the story related the escape of sexual offenders from the county asylum, who later (presumably) died in a mine. Years later, while Phil and Jane are out looking for a missing Dr. Lockwood, they discover the shivering and naked Lydia, a friend of Jane. She is a bleeding mess, her eyes surgically cut from her head. Many graphic complications ensue, and the mysterious Porter Larkin thinks the sex fiends are not dead but have atrophied through a type of twisted devolution into mole people, blind and mad. Someone is stealing eyes to transplant into these fiends to restore their sight: "'Impossible!' I blurted. 'Is it?' Larkin returned quietly. 'Every day modern medical science is doing things that were thought impossible just a short time ago....'"[5]

They worry the criminal may be Dr. Lockwood, who possibly inherited the same taint of madness as his brother, a disgraced doctor from the county asylum who was convicted of an indescribable sex crime, and who is even now being executed for his sin. Another theory is proposed: Lockwood is trying to clear his brother by proving a twisted theory that retinas retain the last image they see even after death. For this, he would need fresh eyes. Attacked by molemen, Phil discovers that they bear the eyes of missing people. Unfortunately, the molemen have carried off Jane's sister Cathy, violating both her eyes and other parts of her body. Phil is also shocked to learn that Larkin is actually a federal agent investigating the crimes. While Phil plans to send Jane to Washington with Larkin to keep her safe, she is kidnapped.

Phil follows the molemen back to their cave where they have strapped Jane to an operating table where Dr. Lockwood comes to operate: "She lay nude and helpless, her lovely body quivering with terror, under the hands of the demon in white."[6] Lockwood raises his scalpel to cut out the girl's eyes, but at the last moment Phil manages to stop him. Only when the police and the federal agent arrive is the truth revealed: Lockwood was already dead, his place taken by Sam Eustace, a criminologist trying to restore his reputation after failing to vindicate Lockwood's brother. He had been working with the molemen, fooling them into thinking he could restore their sight. Eustace committed his heinous crimes in the hopes of "solving" them himself for the glory.

Weird Tales also ran a number of stories that trended toward psychological forms of horror, spiced occasionally with atomic fears. Fritz Leiber's "Mr. Bauer and the Atoms" (1946) was about a man dying of cancer who tells his doctor that he is obsessed with the idea that the atoms inside his body are possessed of the same energy as the atoms that make nuclear bombs explode. He worries that his cancer is attacking his atoms, splitting them, making him radioactive. Dr. Jacobson tries to tell Mr. Bauer politely enough that he is nuts, but Mr. Bauer begins to glow green. He kills himself, and his corpse becomes increasingly radioactive. It is implied that an explosion is imminent.

"Thinker" by Malcolm Kenneth Murchie (1949) is set in an insane asylum where the famous psychiatrist Dr. Larabie Warren has learned to hide his feelings of superiority over the mentally ill. A nameless old man is one of his patients; he had made a nuisance of himself by issuing dire predictions, accosting people on the street, and casting spells. He also has an uncanny ability to predict the future. Warren has granted him a rare interview, during which the skeptical Warren tries to uncover the secret behind the old man's apparent psychic abilities. The old man explains that since he created the world and everything in it, he naturally knows everything: "You see, my dear Doctor Warren, one creates in the mind. Not in the biology laboratory. Not the science of the genes, the atom, but of the mental."[7] The old man tells Warren, who thinks the geezer has a god complex, that he is dying and that when he dies the material world will vanish with him. It was, Warren thought, a psychiatric case for the textbooks. But when the old man passes on, Warren realizes only too late the horrible truth.

Similarly, Robert A. Heinlein's "They" (1941) from *Unknown Worlds* was a case study in paranoia, in which a man begins to think himself an outsider and the normal world corrupt. Other people confused him: "'They went to work to earn the money to buy the food to get the strength to go to work to get the money to buy the food to earn the money to go to'—until they fell over dead."[8] The man believes that the rest of humanity are automatons designed to distract him from the knowledge that he is the center of the world—"arranged to appear crazy in order to deceive him as to the truth."[9] His psychiatrist tries to explain the illogic of the situation, but when he discovers one day that it is raining only on one side of his house, he realizes the truth. The reader, but not the man, observe a scene in which creatures of an unknown provenance discuss the experiment they conducted, creating a whole world to test the man.

Societies That Failed

Nazi Germany and the Soviet Union promised to remake society along the dictates of science. To a lesser extent, the Western world too tried to use science to create a better civilization, but such attempts must have seemed hollow when World War II revealed how tenuous civilization was and how inherently amoral scientific "progress" could be. In literature, Yevgeny Zamyatin's *We* (1921), Aldous Huxley's *Brave New World* (1932), and George Orwell's *1984* (1948) explored the consequences of societies gone mad, positing future worlds in which all-powerful governments control society and everyone in it. Zamyatin's Great Benefactor, Huxley's World Controller, and Orwell's Big Brother all employed rationalism and science to enslave humanity in service of ideology, the individual reduced to a cog in the great machine of the State. Orwell's totalitarian government attempts to reduce language to a simplified New Speak to control the way its citizens think, and therefore what they can communicate and know. Huxley's World Controller, Mustapha Mond, explains that

> truth's a menace, science is a public danger ... [Earlier generations] seemed to have imagined that [scientific progress] could be allowed to go on indefinitely, regardless of everything else. Knowledge was the highest good, truth the supreme value; all the rest was secondary and subordinate.... What's the point of truth or beauty or knowledge when the anthrax bombs are popping all around you? That was when science first began to be controlled—after the Nine Years' War. People were ready to have their appetites controlled then. Anything for a quiet life.[10]

Horror literature pursued the idea of dystopia, of a failed society of nightmare and suffering, across the decades of the mid-twentieth century. Damon Knight's "To Serve Man" (1950) told of an alien race that came to Earth promising a utopia of peace, prosperity, and happiness. Unfortunately the extraterrestrial rulers who promised such boons were not the altruists they claimed to be. They have left behind a book, which dedicated researchers begin to translate. The title was *To Serve Man*. The world foolishly assumes the aliens mean only to improve life for Earthlings, and they willingly enter the aliens' spacecraft. Only too late do they learn that *To Serve Man* is a cookbook. Here the aliens are not unlike the communists and Nazis who seduced nations with promises of better lives only to sacrifice them in the inferno of oppression and war.

Jerome Bixby's "It's a *Good* Life" (1953) is a disturbing story of a telekinetic child who has taken a town hostage. His mental powers give him control over everyone and everything. Little Anthony is too young to understand exactly what he is doing, and his attempts to "help" are as horrific as his rages. He makes animals commit bizarre acts of self-mutilation, and he breaks people as easily as objects. But through it all everyone needed to keep smiling and tell Anthony how good he was. "They'd always say 'Good,' because if they didn't try to cover up how they really felt, Anthony might overhear with his mind, and then nobody knew what might happen."[11] Anthony hated singing, and on the one night when he made television—that is, when he used his mind to create pictures, for there was no real television, no electricity, and perhaps no outside world—one townsperson dared to sing. Anthony turned him into a something so monstrous it could not be described. He sent it, along with all the other things he'd killed, out into the corn field. Everyone agreed that Anthony had done a *good* thing.

In its way, the story is perhaps one of the most powerful tales of the way individuals are forced to acquiesce to the mad ravings of those in power, for which we could as easily read Eisenhower's "military-industrial complex" as Hitler, Stalin, or Mao. The innocent smile of a child does little to hide the irrational primitivism hiding within the minds of those who reject traditional civilization and community.

Another atomic age dystopia could be found in William Golding's *Lord of the Flies* (1954). Golding began his training at Oxford in the sciences but switched to English after two years. Drawing on this and his experiences in World War II, he set out to "trace the defects of society back to the defects of human nature."[12] The resulting book tells of a group of British schoolchildren stranded on a desert island after their plane crashes, killing the adults on board.

An isolated island. In horror literature, islands (like Gothic castles) function as self-contained worlds where the rules of civilization do not apply. Stories as diverse as *The Island of Dr. Moreau, Lord of the Flies,* and *Jurassic Park* all make use of island settings to isolate their horrors from the larger world and to create a microcosm to highlight larger trends that apply to the largest island of all: the Earth. This particular island once belonged to Alexander Selkirk, the real-life Robinson Crusoe, and was later turned into a penal colony (Library of Congress, Prints and Photographs Division, LC-USZ62-119656).

The boys try to organize a society of their own based on the principles of liberty, equality, and brotherhood. Ralph, the leader, and Piggy, his friend, go so far as to establish a parliament to make decisions. For a while, this seems to work, but another boy, Jack, leads a breakaway faction. Appealing to the wild and the violent urges in the boys, he creates a tribe based on hierarchy and dominance. The boys believe the island is haunted by a "beastie" of some sort, and a line is crossed when Jack kills a pig. Death has come to the island, and the pig's head is stuck on a pike as an offering for the beast, which Ralph believes is imaginary. Flies congregate on the rotting hulk, and another boy, Simon, comes to believe the head is Beelzebub, the Lord of the Flies. When he runs down to the encampment to tell the boys what the Lord of the Flies said to him, the boys mistake him for the beast, and they kill him. More boys defect to Jack's wild and uncivilized society, and during a raid on Ralph's camp, Piggy is killed. Ralph flees:

> He argued unconvincingly that they would let him alone, perhaps even make an outlaw of him. But then the fatal unreasoning knowledge came to him again ... These painted savages would go further and further.... He knelt among the shadows and felt his isolation bitterly. They were savages, it was true; but they were human, and the ambushing fears of the deep night were coming on.[13]

Jack's tribe tries to hunt down Ralph and sets a fire to kill him, singing the same chant they used to kill the pig. A passing ship sees the fire and comes to the rescue, just in the nick of time. The island is ruined, many are dead, and Ralph "wept for the end of innocence [and] the darkness of man's heart."[14] But ironically the ship is a cruiser engaged in a great war, in which the darkness of the island is writ large.

The story is self-consciously Freudian and draws on Freud's ideas about the unconscious and the primitive beneath the surface of reason and civilization. It is a dark and disturbing tale about what happens when civilization (read: reason) gives way to the violent emotions of primitive instinct within an individual's, and a society's, psychology.

In a similarly dystopic vein, Anthony Burgess's *A Clockwork Orange* (1962) imagines a future society in which the myth of progress has gone terribly wrong. Set in a future England after a communist takeover (both of government and English slang, now infused with Russian), the book tells of Alex, a moody teenager given to fits of ultra-violence, his term for extreme recreational mayhem. He considers ultra-violence truly "horrorshow," his slang term for good, since bloody horror films are equated with enjoyment and pleasure. Alex is the leader of a gang of adolescents who terrorize their community by committing assaults until one leaves an old woman dead and Alex is arrested. Even after his sentence of fourteen years in prison, Alex continues his violence, fatally beating a cellmate. To leave prison years early, Alex agrees to subject himself to "The Ludovico Technique," which uses a nausea-inducing drug and total sensory immersion in violent imagery to induce in the subject a repulsion for violence, the same making the subject sick whenever he sees or attempts violent acts. Alex's eyes are propped open, and an unaware Alex naively comments that the film he's about to see must be quite horrorshow if they take such measures to insure he sees it. "Horrorshow is right friend," said one of the attendants. "A real show of horrors."[15]

After his treatment, Alex cannot even think of violence without becoming violently ill. Dr. Brodsky, who administered the treatment, declares it a success: "What is happening to you now is what should happen to any normal healthy human organism contemplating the actions of the forces of evil, the workings of the principle of destruction."[16] The doctor understands that Alex knows what is right but chooses to do wrong, "the heresy of an age of reason,"[17] and this must be controlled. Only by removing the ability to do evil can the state enforce the doing of good. Alex is now devoid of the ability to make moral choices, but neither can he do wrong. He has become, in his words, a clockwork orange, a term he learned from a man he assaulted, who was writing a book on humanity's attempt to impose the strict rules of industry and machines onto the soft fruit of the human soul. Hereafter, Alex is subject to recriminations from those he had wronged, who now exact revenge on the helpless boy. In a final chapter left out of the first American editions, Alex renounces violence but holds it to be a normal part of life.

A Clockwork Orange spoke about the fate of free will in an age of science, and whether psychological manipulation deprives of us of our humanity every bit as much as totalitarianism in government. The book also made use of graphically violent scenes of horror, described in ways that anticipated "splatterpunk" and other forms of extreme horror at century's end. The use of a made-up patois of English, Cockney rhyming slang, and Russian did little to mask the graphic content.

Horrors of the Mind

Dystopias presented worlds where society itself has gone mad, but the madness inside the individual was another hallmark of mid-century horror. In the guise of science fiction, "female Gothic," or crime novels, horror continued to probe our anxieties about the role of the individual and his or her fate in a world slightly askew.

Davis Grubb's Night of the Hunter (1953) was a best-selling thriller in which a convicted criminal, Harry Powell, masquerades as a preacher and convinces his dead cellmate's wife to marry him. He does so to persuade her to reveal the location of the dead man's hidden loot from his last crime. The woman's children realize that he is evil, and after he murders their mother, he comes after them. The terror of the novel derives from the fear the children experience as the Preacher, as Powell is known, methodically stalks the children, who now are the only ones who know where the money is hidden. The story self-consciously dramatizes the struggle between good and evil, with the Preacher personifying evil incarnate — a human version of the supernatural monster.

Richard Matheson (b. 1926) also attempted to render the supernatural material in *I Am Legend* (1954), a masterful novel which combined material-ized elements of the supernatural with a portrait of the psychological fragility of a man who believes he is the lone survivor of a plague that turned the rest of humanity into inhuman monsters. In the future world of the late 1970s, a virus mutated by atomic radiation has infected most of humanity with the characteristics of the legendary vampire: "And before science caught up with the legend, the legend had swallowed science and everything."[18] Only Robert Neville was left, and Neville, immune from the virus, spends each day killing the vampires that infest his neighborhood and securing his home against attack. Vampire men barrage his house at night, and vampire women pose salaciously to lure the sexually frustrated man outside. Lonely, depressed, and embittered Neville occupies his free time researching the virus, trying to understand sci-entifically exactly how the disease transforms normal humans into creatures that feed on blood and have an aversion to sunlight and a hatred of garlic. These traits, he discovers, have biological bases in the vampires' new constitu-tion. Other vampiric traits, he decides, may not be biological after all:

> Before he had stubbornly persisted in attributing all vampire phenomena to the germ.... There was no reason, he knew, why some of the phenomena could not be physically caused, the rest psychological. And, now that he accepted it, it seemed one of those patent answers that only a blind man would miss. Well, I always was the blind-man type, he thought in quiet amusement.[19]

Neville realizes that the undead remembered the plague-related pseudo-science in the newspapers, which rattled off the traditions of vampirism; and he wonders if they did not internalize the superstitions, reflecting them now in their new state. Traumatized by their unholy resurrection, their minds "snapped," and, insane, they play out the ingrained stereotypes of how vam-pires should behave. He reasons that they are possessed of a profound self-loathing that makes them hysterically blind to their own reflection.

Neville comes to learn that some of the infected have discovered a way to suppress the virus, so they can live as normal humans, though only at night because the virus has made them sensitive to the sun. They reveal to Neville that he has been killing them along with the fully transformed vampires dur-ing his diurnal forays, becoming to them what Count Dracula was to an ear-lier generation: a legend, a villain, a force of evil that kills indiscriminately when the good are asleep.

First marketed as science fiction (it was a tale of the future), *I Am Legend* was perhaps the most effective de-supernaturalization of a classic horror mon-ster, turning the Gothic-tinged beasts of earlier eras into medicalized horrors fully in line with the materialist ethos of its time. Versions of the story were filmed three times, in 1964, 1971, and 2007, and in three different eras of horror, each of which put its own unique spin on the story.

Five years after *Legend*, two masterpieces of modern horror were published: Shirley Jackson's *The Haunting of Hill House* (1959) and Robert Bloch's *Psycho* (1959). Each novel explored the psychology of the characters caught in it. Jackson did this through charting the mental breakdown of a character in the face of the unknown, while Bloch stuck to a purely material view of horror, one that had no place for the supernatural. Both of these themes could be found in *Legend* and were developed separately into new heights of horror.

Shirley Jackson (1916–1965) was already (in)famous for her short story "The Lottery" (1948), which imagined a modern New England town where each year a resident is selected by lottery to be stoned to death to preserve the town's prosperity and appease God. When the story was published in *The New Yorker*, readers canceled their subscriptions and sent hate mail, outraged by the barbarity of the story and its perversion of small-town values. The story remains one of the most banned in American schools. A decade later, Jackson set out to write a ghost novel after concluding that the misguided motives of the Victorians traipsing about haunted houses on behalf of the Society for Psychical Research were far more interesting than the less-than-convincing hauntings they investigated. The result was *The Haunting of Hill House*, roundly considered one of the finest horror novels ever written. Its opening passage is justly famous for its invocation of terror and dread, connected intimately with scientific inquiry, reason, and the insanity that springs from them:

> No live organism can continue for long to exist sanely under conditions of absolute reality; even larks and katydids are supposed, by some, to dream. Hill House, not sane, stood by itself against its hills, holding darkness within; it had stood so for eighty years and might stand for eighty more ... and whatever walked there, walked alone.[20]

Dr. John Montague, an anthropologist and "man of science"[21] inspired by Victorian ghost hunters, undertakes to conduct a study of the old Gothic pile to determine scientifically whether Hill House is truly haunted. But Dr. Montague notes that in the modern age of the 1950s, those willing to investigate the paranormal are few and far between. Dr. Montague has to search out a team, which is to include psychics and other sensitive persons. He manages to attract Eleanor, a dreamy, middle-aged spinster (she was 32, which then was considered old) who was once the victim of a poltergeist and Theodora, a bold and vivacious woman of pronounced psychic power. The owner of Hill House insists that her nephew Luke accompany the crew during its summer stay at the abandoned mansion. These were the people who arrive at Hill House. Some of them will live to leave it.

The bulk of the novel follows Eleanor's perspective as the sheltered woman initially feels excitement at the first big thing to happen in her small life. As

Victorian interior. Both *Psycho* and *The Haunting of Hill House* feature old Victorian mansions and find in their overstuffed décor a source of horror. In the mid–twentieth century the elaborate and cluttered style favored by the Victorians, as seen in this 1901 interior of the White House East Room, seemed to be the antithesis of the sleek, clean, minimal style synonymous with science and progress (Library of Congress, Prints and Photographs Division, LC-USZ62-46830).

she arrives she thinks how romantic old Hill House is, with its Victorian neo–Gothic encrustations, towers and turrets jutting about in opposition to all the sane laws of twentieth century design. As she gets closer, she changes her mind. The house is diseased; its ornate Gothicism almost makes it seem alive, and it seems to be watching and waiting. Its interior is a maze of rooms, all dark and dreary in the style of the 1870s or '80s. The layout is disorienting, making the new arrivals feels lost both in space and time. Worse, "every angle is slightly wrong"[22] — stairs that aren't level, corners that aren't square, floors that dip toward a center, and stories that fail to align. The whole of the house is askew, mad like a mind that has lost its reason; and Dr. Montague believes many of the so-called supernatural occurrences at Hill House are a result of the anti-rational construction: "We have grown to blindly trust our senses of balance and reason, and I can see where the mind might fight wildly to preserve its own familiar stable patterns against all evidence that it is leaning sideways."[23]

Dr. Montague explains his experimental purpose, to test the house to find out whether it is haunted by a ghost or just a place where evil and darkness congregate. It has a bad reputation for the number of deaths and the misery attached to those who have lived in it, since the wife of its builder, Hugh Crain, died minutes before seeing her husband's construction. After the death of the last of the Crain family, the house turned evil. Dr. Montague denigrates the skeptics who propose ridiculous naturalistic explanations for the unknown, for people "are always so anxious to get things out into the open where they can put a name to them, even a meaningless name, so long as it has something of a scientific ring."[24] Dr. Montague, however, rejects spurious claims that Hill House's irrationally evil atmosphere is the result of classic ghosts, the survival of an individual personality, as much as he rejects theories blaming earthquakes or sunspots. Instead his is "pure" science seeking to derive theories from observations.

Eleanor and Theodora become good friends, and it is strongly hinted in some scenes that Theodora is a lesbian, while others hint at heterosexual leanings. The ambiguity contrasts with Eleanor's pronounced chastity, which leaves Eleanor vulnerable to Hill House's malign influence. This influence begins to manifest as feelings of unease and an odd smell in the library where a servant had once killed herself. Eleanor comes to think that objects in the house move when she isn't looking, and she feels a malevolent cold in the nursery, where the last Crain had spent her miserable life. At night, Eleanor and Theodora hear loud banging on the wall and the door that frighten them terribly.

As the frights escalate, it becomes increasingly uncertain where individual and collective delusions leave off and supernatural horror begins. Dr. Montague has not ruled out natural explanations, and he warns that the so-called ghost is harmless since the modern, rational mind in invulnerable to ghosts' irrationality; it is only the doubting unconscious that is subject to their primitive pull. His diatribe on the ways of the ghost is interrupted by the discovery of chalk writing on a hall wall which asks Eleanor to come "home." It is never clear who or what wrote the message — was it Eleanor herself? — but it becomes increasingly clear that Eleanor is slowly going mad, which may be the result of possession by the spirit of the house. The message is repeated in red paint, or perhaps blood, on a bedroom wall.

Dr. Montague's wife and a schoolmaster named Arthur arrive for a weekend, and they engage in some spiritualist party tricks, the trappings of old-fashioned ghost hunting: automatic writing and séances, worthless and superstitious frauds in the mind of Dr. Montague, for they are unscientific. The planchette, however, reveals Eleanor's deep desire to find a home in Hill House, especially since she harbors guilt about her mother's death, which left her without ties to what she could call "home." When Theodora rejects Eleanor's request to come join her after leaving Hill House, the stage is set for the final crisis. Eleanor, now half-mad and believing herself to be one with Hill House, nearly tumbles to her death on the library stairs (the library, of course, being the seat of knowledge); and Dr. Montague and the others agree she must go home. Eleanor rejects this, but they insist. As they send her away, she reflects on the way Hill House was the only meaningful event in her wasted life, and her car crashes into a great tree, killing her. It is purposely unclear whether it was her own will or that of the house that did her in.

Dr. Montague leaves teaching when the results of his study fail to impress his scientific peers, and Hill House stands as it always has.

Jackson's novel cleverly left the supernatural manifestations ambiguous enough that either an otherworldly or a naturalistic explanation could plausibly explain the events. Framing the tale as a scientific expedition further linked the story to a naturalistic view, though it is not without irony that the scientist — an anthropologist — fails to understand what is happening to Eleanor until it is too late. So caught up is he in his study (even measuring a cold spot with a tape measure) that he is blind to the human cost of his research. By grounding the horror in the psychology of a sad and lonely woman, Jackson wove together "The Yellow Wallpaper" and *The Turn of the Screw* in a way that reflected the modernism of the period. The horror was mental, rather than physical; and the old, ornate world of the Victorians symbolized the antithesis of the clean, sleek, and rational world of modern architecture and modern thought. Supernaturalism could be seen now as another modern pathology, akin to schizophrenia or neurosis.

Academics, however, preferred to emphasize the psychosexual elements of the novel. Roberta Rubenstein, for example, read the novel as the story of a woman trapped in a house that "functions figuratively as the externalized maternal body, simultaneously seductive and threatening."[25] Eleanor thus sacrifices herself to the "house/mother." Angela Hague rightly sees in Eleanor, and all Jackson's writing, a reflection of the empty lives of 1950s housewives, and the repression and paranoia of the era.[26]

Jackson followed up *Haunting* with *We Have Always Lived in the Castle* (1962), a psychological study of the remaining members of a family largely killed by a poisoning. The surviving children, now grown, are shunned by their village, and it is assumed one of them was the murderer. By the end of the tale, the villagers have destroyed their house, the murderer is revealed, and the agoraphobic family members live happily amidst the ruins, alone and unmolested.

Robert Bloch (1917–1994), whom we last met as a member of the Lovecraft Circle, graduated to the new field of psychological horror with *Psycho* (1959), a horror novel whose main attraction was the insanity of the villain. At the beginning of the book we are introduced to a pudgy, balding, pasty alcoholic named Norman Bates, who is reading a book on the Incas and their grotesque preservation of dead bodies for use as musical instruments and totems. In the early chapters the reader is meant to understand that Norman is the very acme of Freudian neurosis, a complete mamma's boy, totally devoted to his mother, even now at age forty. Mother castigates Norman for shying away from the world, "[h]iding away under the covers of a book."[27] Norman protests that he is improving his mind with books of history and civilization. "And I'll bet," his mother says, "it's just crammed full with nasty bits about those dirty savages," even worse than the book of psychology he had been reading.[28] Norman is stuck in an arrested development, and he suffers from an extreme case of Freud's Oedipus complex, which he tried to discuss with Mother without success.

Meanwhile a certain Mary Crane has embezzled money and is fleeing town when she stops at Norman's motel. There she makes his acquaintance, and he tells her how his mother doesn't like the two of them spending time together. Norman explains that his mother didn't handle it well when his father died, or when her new boyfriend died. Mother kills Mary while she showers, and Norman covers it up to protect her. An insurance detective looking for the embezzled money also meets his fate at the hands of Mother, and Norman conceals this as well. Eventually Mary's boyfriend Sam Loomis and her sister Lila get suspicious and find their way to the motel. On the way, they learn from the local sheriff that Norman's mother committed suicide with her lover, and this so broke Norman that he was institutionalized. At the motel, Lila sneaks into the Bates house and discovers a home moldering in the ghosts of decrepit Victoriana, the very antithesis of modernism. Norman's library is stuffed with Lovecraftian tomes on "abnormal psychology, occultism, theosophy"—subjects above the station of a "rural motel proprietor."[29] It is evident that Norman must be mentally ill, for he is pursuing forbidden knowledge, the kind that is unhealthy for mind and soul.

In the basement Lila finds the shrunken, leathery corpse of Mrs. Norma Bates. As she examines the body, Norman, dressed as his mother, attacks, but Sam stops him before he can kill again. Afterward, Sam reports on psychiatrist Dr. Nicholas Steiner's lengthy treatise on the psychological reasons for Norman's bizarre behavior. He was, Steiner said, a transvestite who so identified with his mother that he wanted to become her. In a fit of jealousy he killed his mother and her boyfriend, stole Mother's corpse, and preserved it. He then made himself into his mother, dividing his mind between Norman and Norma.

Thus, Norman's body was killing without Norman's knowledge. The frightening part of the story is his own ignorance of his actions. The moral of the story comes from Lila's lips: "Then the horror wasn't in the house ... It was in his head."[30] In the final chapter, we learn that Norma has now taken over completely and there is no more Norman Bates. Finally, we have a novel that provides its own psychosexual analysis, no additional work required!

Psycho was first published as part of the Inner Sanctum Mysteries, tied in to the radio show of the same name. Bloch later wrote two sequels. *Psycho II* (1982) told of an escaped Norman Bates killing his way through Hollywood where filming began on a movie based on his life. In *Psycho House* (1990) the Bates Motel is again the scene of murders when it is reopened as tourist attraction ten years after Norman's death. Bloch would go on to write a number of horror and suspense novels and screenplays, including *Strange Eons* (1978), in which the book's characters only gradually discover that H. P. Lovecraft's Cthulhu stories were in fact truth masquerading as fiction.

As Lila noted, the horror of *Psycho* is almost entirely the horror of Norman's twisted psyche, one likely based on serial killer Ed Gein, whom we met in the last chapter. Bloch lived just fifty miles from Gein when the killer was discovered decorating his house in body parts and crafting a "woman suit" of human flesh to become his dead mother, and Bloch recalled how he used the few facts about Gein available in news reports and combined them with Freudian theory (though he preferred Jung himself) to create his tale.[31] From this true-life inspiration, *Psycho* succeeded in completing the pattern of psychologizing horror's frights, turning away from the supernatural and toward more earthly forms of terror. It also returned crime fiction to the horror fold, from which it had largely been divorced since Poe concluded C. Auguste Dupin's morbid ratiocinations. As a result of *Psycho*, an entire genre of "crazed killers" emerged, including Thomas Harris's creation, Hannibal Lecter, and Leatherface from *The Texas Chain Saw Massacre*. Killers like these were not traditional horror figures in that they did not draw upon supernatural powers (though Norman believed in them) but instead committed inhuman acts because of the horror in their minds.

Modern Horror

The themes of paranoia, psychology, and the failure of modern society found expression in areas outside traditional horror venues. Science fiction publications, men's magazines, and even some mainstream literary publications carried stories and novellas tinged with a certain darkness that closely approximated horror. True, it was not the same horror as the monsters-and-blood style popular in earlier years, and in this era it went under other names: sci-fi, fantasy, mystery, or crime. But within these genres there were a number of tales that crossed over into the territory of horror.

Frederik Pohl's satirical "The Tunnel Under the World" (1955) from the *Galaxy* science fiction magazine was another paranoid vision of the normal world gone mad. Guy Burckhardt wakes up each morning from a horrible dream of explosions and death, which he puts down to fears about nuclear war. It is June 15, but so is the next day and the day after that. Guy thinks himself mad, but he begins to see that he is living through the same day again and again, though no one else remembers. He sees a subtle difference, however: Each day the advertisements surrounding him change, pleading for him to buy new products. Guy finds just one other person in town who recognizes what is going on, and together they try to discover whether Martians or Russians are responsible for the horror perpetrated upon them. When they stumble upon the control room, they understand that *advertisers* have taken over their town, using it as a bizarre psychological experiment to perfect their pitches—wiping out each day's work, resetting the town, and starting fresh with a new June 15 and new advertising. But the horror does not stop there.

Guy discovers that the townspeople are robots, in which a transplanted mind has been given human form. "Could it know that it was a robot?"[32] he wonders, trying to absorb the knowledge that he too is one of the machines. He learns that the advertisers resurrected a town of 21,000 killed in an explosion, mapping their minds onto robots that forever live out the same day. The worst of it comes when the advertiser in charge of the project lets Guy see the full range of the horror: He allows Guy to try to escape, and when he does, Guy sees there is nowhere to go. The town is a scale model, built on a table top. Guy Burckhardt is trapped in an endless June 15 of "terror beyond words."[33]

The story was dramatized for the sci-fi radio program *X-Minus One* (March 14, 1956) and the British science fiction television anthology *Out of the Unknown* (December 1, 1966). It was made into an Italian movie as well.

Kurt Vonnegut's "Harrison Bergeron" (1961), from *The Magazine of Fantasy and Science Fiction*, offered yet another dystopia where the state mandates conformity. In this case, the United States in 2081, under the jurisdiction of the Handicapper General, enforces mediocrity by dragging down every individual to the group average. Ballerinas have weights tied to their feet, the beautiful wear clown noses, and the intelligent have electronic devices to rattle their thoughts. No one should be better than anyone else, and everyone is by these measures "equal every which way" and incapable of unfairly abusing any talent that might set him apart.[34] Harrison Bergeron, age fourteen, genius and athlete, tries to change this, appearing on television without his handicaps, evoking freedom and release. He is shot to death by the Handicapper General, and those watching it all unfold barely remember anything at all. It was merely "something real sad on television," but nothing to think too hard about.[35] Vonnegut's satire *Cat's Cradle* (1963) concerned a deceased atomic scientist who cared nothing for morality and ethics, only research. He made a substance called "ice nine," which freezes water at any temperature. It destroys the Earth when a chunk ends up in the ocean.

Charles Beaumont's "The Howling Man" (1960) told of a distant European monastery, St. Wulfran's, where a man is kept locked in a cell. A traveler discovers this man, who tells him that the monastery's monks are mad and believe him to be the Devil. The traveler finds this quite strange and confronts the abbot, who explains that despite his education and understanding of Freudian psychology, he knows the Devil is real and that by imprisoning him they have ended war and the greater evils. The traveler frees the prisoner because he is convinced that religious superstition is madness. Wars break out, and it is implied that the prisoner may well have been Hitler, devil incarnate. Order is restored when the monks recapture the Devil. Beaumont's hymn to cultural relativism, "The Jungle" (1956), is a dark revenge fantasy in which a Bantu medicine man curses Richard Austin, who had helped build a city in the jungle. The shaman condemns this cultural imperialism and wishes the jungle to come to Austin's city. Austin believes he has done right, reasoning that you do not let people live in backwardness and disease "because their culture had failed to absorb scientific progress." No, you bring them enlightenment: "That is logic."[36] But despite Austin's faith in science, it is not the only way of knowing and the shaman's magic can peel back the veneer of material civilization to reveal the wild and the untamed undergrowth. The shaman conjures up the jungle's legions to force Austin into admitting the Bantus' right to exist and the equality of their culture and way of knowing. When Austin thinks he has escaped, he discovers a horrible truth. Both stories became episodes of television's *The Twilight Zone*, as did "To Serve Man" and "It's a *Good* Life," discussed earlier.

The film director and television presenter Alfred Hitchcock was the high priest of mystery and crime horror. We will explore his filmed horrors in the next chapter, but one of his lesser known contributions to the horror genre was a series of anthologies in which he collected dark tales of horror, the supernatural, and unspeakable crimes, providing his readers with what he called "a shudderingly good time."[37] Under titles like *12 Stories They Wouldn't Let Me Do on TV* (1957), *A Hangman's Dozen* (1962), and *Stories Not for the Nervous* (1963), Hitchcock rode to the top of the best-seller lists, bringing a little bit of murder and horror into America's parlors. More than one hundred anthologies have appeared under the Hitchcock banner, many produced after his death.

In *A Hangman's Dozen* we find Richard Matheson's "The Children of Noah" (1957), a story about halfway between "The Lottery" and "To Serve Man." Mr. Ketchum is pulled over for speeding in the small town of Zachry, Maine, population 67. The police lock him up and tell him he will have to remain in jail until he can see the judge and pay for his "crime." They feed him a sumptuous breakfast, and only later does he realize that the small town is not what it seems. There is a barbecue scheduled for that evening, but unfortunately, after a meeting with the town's fanged matriarch, it seems the town will have Mr. Ketchum for dinner. Robert Arthur's "An Attractive Family" (1957) told of a homicidal clan trying to get rid of an unwanted relative who isn't quite as gullible as they think. In Richard Stark's "The Curious Facts Preceding My Execution" (1960), a man who murders his wife is undone by the mundane details of suburban life — salespeople, telephone calls, nosy neighbors — that prevent him from leaving the scene of the crime. Ray Bradbury's "The October Game" (1948) is a gruesome fable about a deranged man who uses the occasion of Halloween to get back at his wife by murdering their daughter during a party for the neighborhood children. The kids are gathered in the pitch-dark basement for a Halloween house of horrors game, and they eagerly pass around what the man says are eyeballs, guts, and bones, but they know are really marbles, chicken innards, and soup bones. "Then ... some idiot turned on the light."[38]

Stephen King remarked that the horror of the 1950s masqueraded as science fiction, mystery, and crime stories because society wanted to pretend that horror had been tamed. This impulse, King said, led to Richard Matheson's placement among the authors of science fiction rather than those of horror. The same could be said for the horror genre as a whole, whose literary output in this era wore the mask of other genres, hiding within them like some corrupting disease, producing new outgrowths of horror and consuming some of the life from these host genres, rather like the science fiction disease that returned vampires to the modern world in *I Am Legend*. Soon enough full-blown horror would emerge again in literature. But before we can tell that story we must first examine the way horror infected science fiction cinema and television, producing some of the weirdest and most bizarre tales yet filmed — and not always in a good way.

15

HORROR IN THE ARTS

During World War II, horror entertainment risked the ire of government and cultural leaders, who worried that morbid films in particular would damage the war effort. The British Board of Film Censors banned the exhibition of horror movies during the war for fear they would undermine the nation's morale. In the United States, the Office of War Information used its control of export licenses to mold horror films into agents of propaganda, and even those not directly altered by OWI fell under its influence, such as *The Return of the Vampire*, which we have seen had anti–Nazi themes, and *Black Dragons* (1942), with Bela Lugosi as an evil Nazi doctor. Culture mavens, too, criticized horror's appropriateness in wartime. *Variety* said that *The Wolf Man*, released just days after Pearl Harbor, was "dubious entertainment at this particular time," though later films in the series earned their approval. As *Time* magazine put it in 1944, the era's horror films, with rare exception, "explain away all supernatural antics as the deliberate hocus-pocus of a mad scientist, estate-grabber or Axis agent."[1] Add "mental illness" and "atomic radiation" to the mix, and the description holds true into the 1960s as well.

After the war, the old horror monster franchises faded into campy silliness, epitomized by the *Abbott and Costello Meet ...* series in which the comedians encountered, in succession, *Frankenstein* (1948); *The Killer, Boris Karloff* (1949); *The Invisible Man* (1951); *Dr. Jekyll and Mr. Hyde* (1953); and *The Mummy* (1955). Cartoons, too, mocked the monsters, albeit lovingly. Warner Bros.' Looney Tunes found Porky Pig meeting ghosts, Daffy Duck trying to deliver a telegram to Jekyll and Hyde, Tweety turning into a Hyde-like monster, and Bugs Bunny battling Jekyll and Hyde, a Frankenstein-inspired hair-monster (twice), vampires, witches (three times), and evil scientists (twice). In "Water, Water Every Hare" (1952) the Karloff-like scientist has a blinking neon sign on his gloomy castle which reads "Evil Scientist / Boo!" The evil scientist wants Bugs Bunny's brain to power his robot, and to get it he looses Rudolph (later renamed Gossamer), the large red-hair monster first seen in "Hair-Raising Hare" (1946), in which Bugs was also trapped in an evil scientist's castle. In both films, Bugs triumphs over both monster and evil scientist alike.

While the traditional horror creations languished undead in their tombs, new forms of horror emerged to replace them and terrorize audiences in a way that seemed in tune with the anxieties of the mid–twentieth century, and in a range of media uniquely suited to this particular moment in history.

Horror in the Comics

The comic book was born in the 1930s out of bound collections of daily newspaper comic strips, and it soon took on a life of its own. With the introduction of the first superhero, the extraterrestrial Superman, and his arch-nemesis, Luthor, a mad scientist, comic books became a staple of children's (and many adults') reading diets. In May 1939, *Detective Comics* introduced Bat-Man (later Batman), a dark and brooding superhero in cowl and cape who, like a vampire, adopted the form of a bat and lived in a world drawn from horror conventions and Gothic trappings. Bob Kane admitted that Batman was modeled in part on Bela Lugosi's Dracula, and it is often said that Spring-Heeled Jack and radio's *The Shadow* were influences as well.[2] As millionaire playboy Bruce Wayne by day and the Batman by night, the hero shares aspects with horror monsters like Jekyll and Hyde as well as the vampire, splitting his life into "day" and "night" activities. In early adventures, Batman was a violent vigilante preying on Gotham City's criminals. Batman's image lightened considerably during the 1940s, especially after the addition of his teen sidekick, Robin, in *Detective Comics* #38 (April 1940). Academics studying his later incarnations would pounce on the "homoerotic" aspects of the Batman-Robin dynamic, or, as Matthew Joseph Wolf-Meyer would have it, Batman's support for "hegemonic capitalism" and his relationship to "the class system."[3] Magazine Enterprises' Ghost Rider dressed as a specter and had horror-themed adventures in the Old West in the pages of *Tom Holt* from 1949 until 1958, when the Comics Code (see below) forced his retirement.

However, comic books had a more gruesome outlet for horror, whose art is lurid even by today's standards. The Entertaining Comics Group (EC Comics, formerly Educational Comics), publishers of *Mad* magazine, published a number of comic books with horror themes: *Tales from the Crypt*, *The Vault of Horror*, *Weird Science-Fantasy*, *Crime SuspenStories*, and *Shock SuspenStories*, the picture-book descendants of the shudder pulps. For just ten cents, any boy (and more than a few girls) could experience the worlds of terror and fear in four-color format.

The horror comic era started in 1950, when *Tales* and *Vault* made their debut, replacing EC Comics' earlier line of soft and cuddly kiddie comics and Bible stories. The new horror comics featured richly detailed art that carefully displayed every ounce of putrescent flesh and every bloody gash in the corpses splattered across their covers. *Crime SuspenStories* #22 (May 1954), for example, showed on its cover a man holding the severed head of a murdered woman by her blonde hair, the woman's eyes rolling back in her head and saliva or blood pouring from her mouth. In his other hand, the man holds a bloody axe over the corpse, whose legs alone are visible. The story to which it is attached tells of a man who murders his wife, only to find himself on a television program where his friends and neighbors fete him, discovering by accident that no one has seen his wife. In the end, they put the pieces together and he is arrested for murder. Other EC stories were adapted works from Poe, Lovecraft, and other classic horror authors, or told original tales of revenge and murder. Most were introduced by recurring characters, such as the Crypt-keeper, who framed the tales.

Imitators abounded: *Weird Worlds* (Atlas Comics), *Terror Tales* (Fawcett), *Black Cat Mystery* (Harvey Publications), and so on, numbering in the dozens. *Black Cat* #50 (June 1954) graphically depicted on its cover the disintegration of a man's hands and face in the presence of radium, bones emerging from melting flesh. *Terror Tales* #6 (March 1953) has a screaming man face to face with a skeleton, the word "BEWARE!" printed above the title. The stories, usually, were simple, direct and morbid. Guts and gore were the rule, and plot development was usually curtailed to allow the comics to maximize the visual aspect of their horror.

Kids loved the comics, and EC started a "Fan-Addict Club," complete with membership card and club pin. Horror was now the province of teenagers, a position it would largely retain into the twenty-first century. Adults, however, thought the comics were objectionable. Robert Warshow, whose own son was obsessed with horror comics, tried to convince him that the comics would rot his mind and destroy his taste for real literature — even reading Poe was preferable to this—but he was forced to concede that if the alternative was "boring" and "stultifying" comics like *Donald Duck* or *The Lone Ranger*, at least horror comics were interesting, inventive, and stimulating.[4]

Not so, argued Dr. Frederic Wertham, a psychiatrist and author of *Seduction of the Innocent* (1954), a book arguing that comics systematically presented vulnerable children with adult content, including sex, violence, and morbidity. Wertham famously claimed that Batman and Robin were homosexual lovers and Wonder Woman a lesbian with a bondage fetish, and that their examples pushed children toward these behaviors, thus corrupting the youth. He saved his harshest attacks for horror comics, which he thought celebrated criminality and encouraged kids to commit crimes. Though *Seduction* was largely anecdotal and would not stand up to scientific scrutiny, Wertham's scientific credentials bolstered his case in the public mind. The U.S. Senate held hearings, calling William Gaines, the publisher of EC Comics, to defend his horrors, especially the cover of *Crime SuspenStories* #22, described above, and which Sen. Estes Kefauver thought in bad taste. "A cover in bad taste," Gaines responded, "might be defined as holding the head a little higher so that blood

Cover of *Crime SuspenStories*. The United States Senate held hearings to determine whether EC's horror comics were too explicit for children. At the hearing, Sen. Estes Kefauver singled out *Crime SuspenStories* #22 (1954) as being in particularly bad taste. The comic's publisher, William Gaines, responded that it would only be in bad taste if the woman's severed head was held so high that blood could be seen dripping from it. As a result of the hearings, the comic industry voluntarily banned horror comics (Benjamin Samuels).

could be seen dripping from it, and moving the body over a little further so that the neck of the body could be seen to be bloody."[5]

Citizens groups and newspapers rallied to Wertham's cause, pressuring the comics industry to clean up its act. They did so in September 1954, enacting a Comics Code of self-censorship. It banned graphic violence and all sex, along with the very concepts of "terror" and "horror," and some supernatural creatures, like zombies. Thirteen U.S. states restricted the sale of comic books, and the United Kingdom passed a law in 1955 to prevent the sale of horror comics.[6] They vanished virtually overnight, and of course the children of the postwar Baby Boom never did anything wicked again.

Higher up the cultural ladder, Charles Addams (1912–1988) produced a series of morbid psychological sight-gag cartoons for *The New Yorker* beginning in 1935 and lasting through his death in 1988. His most famous creation was his "family," a group of ghouls who lived in a crumbling old Victorian mansion and were decidedly anti-modern, celebrating death, morbidity, and other Victorian pursuits. A 1946 cartoon depicts a rotting bedroom, with a father (later named Gomez) making shadow puppets in the shape of a bat to put his daughter to sleep while her ghoulish and gaunt mother (later Morticia) looks on.

Similarly, the illustrations of Edward Gorey offered a macabre, Edwardian world of gaunt and pale humans inhabiting a nightmare landscape. His *Gashleycrumb Tinies* (1963) presented a disturbing alphabet of death ("A is for Amy who fell down the stairs...") with waif-like children experiencing shocking ends. Gorey illustrated a version of *Dracula*, designed the sets for a 1977 Broadway version of the same, and created in 1980 the title sequence for PBS's *Mystery!* By his death in 2000, Gorey had written or illustrated more than one hundred books.

At mid-century the work of Addams and Gorey was decidedly bizarre and an affront to the clean, rational, scientific world — appearing as morbid psychology in action, a highbrow version of the horror comics.

Screen Horrors

If the pure horror story was in retreat with the fall of the horror comics, a species of horror was alive and well on the big screen. During the 1950s, horror films began to gain in prominence, rising from the middling one percent of new releases that had characterized the genre since its inception to 6.9 percent in 1957.[7] In terms of pure profit, the genre racked up more money than the entire hardcover book industry, all genres included, which *Playboy* said in 1959 made horror one of America's staple commodities, "like breakfast cereal or soap."[8] However, science had become the "organizing principle" for horror films in the 1930s (and remains so to this day),[9] so it is unsurprising that in

1950s horror took the form of science fiction and crime films, within which we find distorted reflections of the scientific advances of the psycho-atomic years: psychological terrors and atomic horrors.

The Uninvited (1944) was possibly the only great ghost movie before Shirley Jackson's *Haunting of Hill House* came to the screen in 1963. *The Uninvited* told of Roderick and Pamela Fitzgerald (Ray Milland and Ruth Hussey), a pair of siblings who purchase an abandoned sea-side mansion. Unfortunately, the house has been haunted since the death of its last occupant, Mary, whose daughter Stella is still living in the area. Her grandfather sells the Fitzgeralds the house in the hope of keeping Stella away from the ghosts, which he thinks want to harm her. Though Roderick doesn't believe in ghosts or spiritualism, he agrees to hold a séance in the house in the hopes of keeping Stella away. During the fake séance, a real ghost message comes through, and we learn that the house is haunted by Stella's mother *and* the ghost of a woman who was Mary's husband's mistress. The two women are battling over poor Mary, who comes close to death by the time she learns that the mistress was her real mother. With the revelation, the spirits depart, and Mary is freed from the hauntings. Throughout the movie, supernatural manifestations increase with each revelation about the central mystery, and the film effectively delivers a sophisticated tale of spiritualist horror, one grounded in the psychology of the characters—human and ghostly.

Cat People (1942) was another species entirely, and a more clearly psychological horror. A Serbian émigré, Irena Dubrova (Simone Simon), falls in love with a newspaper editor, Oliver Reed (Kent Smith), who asks her to marry him. This she fears to do because in her village the elders say that she is the last of a race of cat people, descendants of witches, who have been cursed, turning into large black panthers at the merest hint of sexual union, even so little as a kiss. Inevitably, they kill the men who love them. How they reproduce is anyone's guess—paternal lines only, I suppose. Oliver doesn't buy into the old superstitions, and Irena eventually goes into therapy with Dr. Louis Judd (Tom Conway), who tells her that her soul is disturbed.

> IRENA: When you speak of the soul, you mean the mind, and it is not my mind that is troubled.
> JUDD: What a clever girl! All the psychologists, all the theologians have tried for centuries to find that subtle shade of difference between mind and soul ... and you have found it!

Judd makes a move on Irena, who rebuffs him. She becomes jealous of Oliver's friend, Alice, with whom he has been spending more time while Irena works out her mental issues. One night she steals a zookeeper's key and frees a black panther from its cage. It is purposely left ambiguous whether the subsequent events stem from attacks from this panther, or whether the jealous Irena really is cursed, until the truth is revealed in the movie's climax. Stylish and creepy, *Cat People* was the first of the great psychological horror films.

The movie's producer, Val Lewton — who once wrote for *Weird Tales*—followed it with more than a half-dozen psychological horror films, including an adaptation of Robert Louis Stevenson's story "The Body Snatcher" and *Isle of the Dead* (1945), which preceded Richard Matheson's *I Am Legend* in attempting to explain away vampires as the products of disease. The film took its inspiration from Arnold Böcklin's painting of the same name, and the island in the film is modeled on it. The year is 1912, and Greek Gen. Nikolas Pherides (Boris Karloff) is traveling to a small island to visit his wife's grave during an outbreak of septicemic plague. The plague has arrived on the island, forcing the general to stay in the island's one house with its handful of tourists and residents. Gen. Pherides, an ardent materialist, puts no stock in the superstitious Greek who interprets plague deaths as vampire attacks and a cataleptic resident as a vampire, but as the story wears on, the general's attitude changes: "Cooped up here waiting for death — naturally his mind goes back to the things he believed when he was an ignorant lad in some mountain village." *Isle of the Dead* is the story of claustrophobia and the horrors it can unleash on tortured minds.

Together, these films pointed toward a new, more psychological horror; however, as the 1940s gave way to the 1950s, a different type of horror emerged. This one drew its inspiration less from Freudian psychology and more from the twin terrors of nuclear war and communism. By 1951, science fiction had become a hotbed of horror.

Horror from Space

In that year, *The Day the Earth Stood Still* dramatized the arrival of extraterrestrials on earth, in the characteristic flying saucer of mid-century sightings. This alien comes in peace, to warn the Earth that its war-like ways and nuclear technology has made it a threat to the universe's other planets, and unless Earth gives up its militarism, the planet will be destroyed. *The Man from Planet X* (1951) featured an alien invasion via a planet hurtling through space. Another hurtling planet threatened the Earth in *When Worlds Collide* (1951). In both films, a scientist discovers the coming horror and struggles to imagine a way out of it; the latter film involved building a fleet of spaceships to colonize the new planet, over the objections of U.N. bureaucrats who refuse to believe the Earth is in danger.

The Thing from Another World (1951) adapted John W. Campbell's "Who Goes There?" improving significantly on the original. This time the horror takes place at the North Pole, rather than Antarctica, where the Air Force has uncovered a flying saucer, frozen in the ice millions of years before. They try to open the saucer, but succeed only in making it explode, obliterating it from existence. The military men also find a frozen alien beside the ship, and they take it back to their research station, where Dr. Arthur Carrington (Robert Corn-thwaite) examines it. In his amoral pursuit of knowledge, Carrington unleashes the Thing on the men (and woman) of the research station, but he wants to preserve the creature for study rather than kill it, even when it starts offing the others: "It doesn't matter what happens to us; the only thing that matters is our thinking." He wants to reason with it, to turn it from enemy to ally, for knowledge is a universal desire and goal. Dr. Carrington discovers that the creature is not only vastly intelligent, it is also biologically a plant — a virtually immortal vegetable vampire that feeds on mammalian blood, what one character calls "an intellectual carrot." It also lacks anything resembling human morality or emotion.

Bullets won't kill the creature, and in exasperation the station's only woman recommends boiling the creature, since that's what a 1950s woman does with a vegetable. The military men reject that suggestion, and instead they try to electrocute the monster. Dr. Carrington tries to stop them from destroying the extraterrestrial, pleading with the monster: "I'm not your enemy; I'm a scientist!" The creature hits him and rampages on, stumbling into the electric trap, which kills it. The moral of the story was to "Keep looking; keep watching the skies!"

The next year saw *Red Planet Mars* (1952), one of the most propagandistic of the alien invasion films. A scientist, Chris Cronyn (Peter Graves), creates a device that appears to receive signals from Mars. When this is revealed, the public is shocked, the stock market collapses, and Western Civilization seems on the brink of complete devastation. Worse, the Soviets want to use the opportunity to launch a world war. A new signal from Mars relates part of Christ's Sermon on the Mount. In a meeting with the president, Chris argues against releasing the message, but his wife Linda (Andrea King) disagrees:

CHRIS: This can't go out — it isn't scientific.
LINDA: Maybe it is the one scientific truth we've forgotten.

The president agrees to broadcast the message, and soon the international mood changes. Jubilation reigns when it seems that the Martians are God-fearing Christians, too. The Soviet Union falls in a wave of Orthodox Christian religious revival. Peace appears to break out across the globe.

A former Nazi arrives at Chris's laboratory to reveal that he has been feeding Chris the messages, not Mars, to destroy the West and the Soviets for what they did to his beloved Germany. Linda disputes this, citing key differences between the Nazi's transmissions and real ones from Mars. A new transmission comes through, refuting the Nazi's claims; unable to accept it, he fires his gun at the machine, destroying it and the scientists. Chris and Linda are hailed as God's prophets by the U.S. government. Take that, godless communists!

In 1953, *It Came from Outer Space* found aliens crash-landing on Earth and impersonating townsfolk to get the supplies they need to take off again.

Invaders from Mars (1953) found the Martians again meddling with humans, this time seeming to steal their minds, leaving a mark on the back of their victims' necks. The story is told from the point of view of a small boy, who turns to psychologists and scientists to help end the alien invasion. In a bizarre conclusion, we discover the whole movie was the boy's dream, but as he wakes up we see the Martians landing again, perhaps indicating the story was a premonition of things yet to come. *The War of the Worlds* (1953), a film noted for its special effects, transferred H. G. Wells's novel to modern-day Los Angeles but otherwise followed the outline of the book's plot. It added a twist right out of *Red Planet Mars*, though, indicating at the end that God had created the bacteria that kill the Martians specifically for that purpose. Take that, godless commie Martians! *Earth vs. the Flying Saucers* (1956) was exactly that, and the saucers manage to take out a fair number of familiar monuments before the alien menace is subdued. *It! The Terror from Beyond Space* (1958) found a spaceship crew menaced by an alien hiding on board, a plot reused in *Alien* two decades later.

It didn't take one of the era's ubiquitous rocket scientists to realize that there was a crude dynamic generally at work in the alien invasion films: aliens = communists, Red Planet = Red Army. But the best of the alien invasion films was probably *Invasion of the Body Snatchers* (1956), which muddied the simple allegory with depth and complexity. Dr. Miles Bennell (Kevin McCarthy) returns to his hometown of Santa Mira to attend to urgent calls from his patients, who inexplicably fail to appear for their appointments. So instead he begins to spend time with an old girlfriend who has just arrived back in town, Becky Driscoll (Dana Wynter), rekindling their romance. But Becky's cousin Wilma has become convinced that her uncle Ira is not really her uncle Ira, despite looking like him and possessing all his memories. A small boy says that his father is not really his father. In both cases, it seems, the only difference between the originals and the replacements is the complete lack of emotion the new versions exhibit. Miles learns from the local psychiatrist that the town is brimming with paranoid delusions, with many people claiming their friends and relatives are impostors. However, the delusions are anything but.

Miles' friend Jack calls with an urgent plea. There is a dead body in his house, but one that is unformed and incomplete, resembling Jack in general but not in detail. For example, it lacks fingerprints. The body later transforms into an exact duplicate of Jack, scaring everyone even more. In Becky's house, Jack finds a duplicate of *her* lying in wait in her basement. He calls the psychiatrist for help, but the psychiatrist explains that it is all a hysterical delusion. Miles isn't buying that when he discovers large seed pods in a greenhouse, busy hatching plant-based copies of him, of Becky, and their friends. It transpires that the "pod people" have replaced most of the town's residents, changing the warm and friendly faces of familiarity with the cold, emotionless stare of vegetable life. The psychiatrist explains that the pod people hatched from seeds that drifted to Earth from the uncharted depths of space, growing in secret and absorbing the look and the memories of those it grows near, turning into "perfect" duplicates—duplicates that are better than the originals for they lack emotions or individuality. The film ends with Miles, half-mad, trying desperately to escape the pod people and Santa Mira, screaming "You're next!" to passing motorists. The studio forced an epilogue suggesting that the FBI, warned of the pod invasion, was on the case and would stop the alien menace.

The film is often read as an allegory about communists, or, alternately an allegory about McCarthyism, with each villain read into the aliens attacking humanity. What made *Invasion of the Body Snatchers* great was the ambiguity of the alien menace. They aren't clearly-defined stand-ins for communists, McCarthyites, or any other particular breed of villain but can represent any threat. Even more impressive, the aliens are a cosmic accident, blown to Earth by chance, and reproducing by Darwinian forces rather than a sustained and intelligent invasion. In this, the film has shades of H. P. Lovecraft, whose *At the Mountains of Madness* and especially "The Shadow Over Innsmouth" explored the same themes. *Invasion* was filmed again in 1978, 1993, and 2007.

From Britain, *The Quatermass Xperiment* (1955), known as *The Creeping Unknown* in the United States and based on a BBC-TV miniseries, finds three astronauts returned to Earth, but only one is alive. This astronaut appears to be developing a bizarre alien infection, and Dr. Quatermass (Brian Donlevy) spends a great deal of time studying the poor man as he transforms into a vegetable creature that destroys animal life with a touch. The mad scientist has refused to transfer the astronaut to a hospital, keeping him in his private lab for experiments, and from which he escapes. The TV miniseries found the good Dr. Quatermass, paragon of reason, appealing to the astronaut's vestigial consciousness to help stop the monster, but the cinema version finds an amoral and obsessive Dr. Quatermass narrowly saving humanity from the creature, which is attempting to spore and thus invade the Earth. The British government found the film so terrifying they slapped it with an X certification, restricting it to adults-only viewing.

Other evil alien horrors included an evil giant eye that moves on its own (actually an alien from a radioactive cloud) in 1958's *The Crawling Eye,* and a giant floating brain in *The Brain from Planet Arous* (1958), also an alien, who steals a scientist's body. These pointed toward the strange body horrors of the 1960s while sticking to 1950s atomic horror conventions.

Director Ed Wood's sublimely ridiculous *Plan 9 from Outer Space* (1958) was perhaps the worst alien menace movie. The film concerned "grave robbers from outer space." We are introduced to an old man (Bela Lugosi, in his last role) and his wife (Maila Nurmi, TV's Vampira), both of whom have risen from their graves during a wave of UFO hysteria in Los Angeles and have begun killing. It seems the UFOs are causing the dead to rise from their graves, and Washington becomes concerned when the spaceships begin appearing there as well. We meet the aliens, who explain that they have failed in their efforts to contact Earth's governments because Earth people refuse to believe aliens exist. Therefore, they have launched Plan 9, the resurrection of the dead, to prove their existence through undeniable actions. The aliens are duly concerned about nuclear weapons, fearing they place us just one step closer to the ultimate explosive weapon: a solarmanite reaction, which splits photons the way nuclear bombs split atoms and which would destroy the whole universe. The aliens think that humans are dumb enough to use it "because all you of Earth are *idiots!*" The humans attack and destroy the aliens' flying saucer to prevent them from destroying the Earth. The weird dialogue and cheap production values made this film a cult classic. Lugosi died during filming and was buried in full Dracula regalia.

And so it went on, one alien invasion after the next. We will take leave of them and turn instead to a far more exciting field of '50s horror: the monster movie.

Return of the Son of the Atomic Beast from Beyond the Stars

Older monster films tended to follow a pattern: A monster is discovered, its properties deduced, and the duration of the film is spent trying to put it down. From the 1920s to the 1940s, the monster was usually some folkloric creature lurking in the natural world, just beyond the realm of scientific knowledge — a vampire, a werewolf, and so on. That changed with the advent of the nuclear bomb, and horror responded by dressing itself up in a sci-fi costume. If anything justifies my classification of 1950s horror as "atomic" it is the wave of monster movies from the 1950s into the 1960s which featured nuclear radiation or atom bombs creating some horrible creature that in turn sets its sights on destroying humanity. In each case, it is humankind — especially science — that causes the horror, like a race of nuclear-armed Frankensteins. Horrific violence and chaos inevitably ensue.

A 1952 re-release of *King Kong* (who was natural, not atomic) had done well at the box office and inspired a rash of giant monster films. The first was *The Beast from 20,000 Fathoms* (1953). In the Arctic a U.S.–Canadian military team detonates a hydrogen bomb as part of an experiment. The bomb appears to defrost a dinosaur flash-frozen in the Arctic ice, and several scientists spend a great deal of time arguing over whether it is possible for a hundred-million-year-old reptile to survive in the ice. While they bicker, the creature begins to rampage, taking out broad swaths of the Eastern seaboard on its way to its former nesting grounds. One scientist wants to keep it alive to study it, so he follows it in a diving bell. It eats him. As the creature approaches New York, we learn that it is not only destructive but also toxic, making it doubly dangerous.

In the end, only a radioactive isotope shot into the creature's wounded neck can stop it. This highlights the ambiguity of nuclear power: It stopped the creature, but it also brought it to life.

Creature from the Black Lagoon (1954) found another prehistoric beast menacing a scientific expedition, but this time no nuclear power was required. The creature was a species of fish-man; the lead scientist bizarrely decides that in the name of science he must bring it back alive, so under no circumstance should it be killed. The creature carries off a beautiful woman, and only when things look really bad does the crew kill the monster. *Godzilla: King of the Monsters!* (1956) brought us back to the nuclear creature theme. Substantially reworked from a Japanese original, the American re-edit spliced Raymond Burr into a shortened Japanese film. The atomic bomb has created Godzilla, a sort of dinosaur, who is radioactive and on a rampage, destroying Tokyo. Since Japan was the site of the first nuclear bombs used in war, the film has a powerful resonance, making the monster into a symbol of the death-dealing power of nuclear weapons and the inhuman corruption they represent.

Creature from the Black Lagoon (1954). In the 1950s, inhuman monsters symbolized the unruly power unleashed by humanity's mastery of the atom. Some, like Godzilla, were literally born of nuclear power, while others, like the fishy creature from the Black Lagoon seen here, merely represented the unreasoning, irrational forces lurking behind the veneer of science. Here we see the creature (Ben Chapman) menacing a woman (Julie Adams) in an archetypical scene of monster-on-girl violence.

Them! (1954) found the fallout from atomic testing during the Manhattan Project creating a mutant strain of giant ants in the Southwestern desert. These begin to reproduce, and the military — under the direction of scientists, of course — is forced to battle the bugs with flame throwers in their cavernous nests to stop them. The allegory was obvious: Harnessing natural forces for nuclear weapons is bad and threatens to destroy the world. In the giant bug vein, *Tarantula* (1955) found scientists experimenting with radioactive chemicals, which create a giant spider that terrorizes the surrounding area. *The Deadly Mantis* (1957) imagined a giant praying mantis rampaging, but never really explained where it came from. *Earth vs the Spider* (1958) dispensed with even the pretense of explanation. The spider just is. Once incapacitated by the authorities, high school officials store the spider in the gym, where an unfortunate musical set by a teen rock band restores it to life to rampage some more. The German film *It's Hot in Paradise* (1960, dubbed 1962, reissued in 1963 as *Horrors of Spider Island* absent nudity) stranded nubile young dancing girls when their plane crashes on a desert island. A giant radioactive spider bites the girls' manager (it already killed and strung up a scientist), and he turns into a ravenous wolf-like creature who, inevitably, lusts after the women and sublimates that by strangling them instead. *The Fly* (1958) found a scientist turning himself into the title bug when his teleportation experiment goes horribly wrong. Though *The Fly* is a film about science gone bad when a scientist over-reaches, scholars like Cyndy Hendershot chose to read it as a sexual metaphor whereby forbidden scientific experimentation stands in for forbidden coupling, which I suppose made the mutation a symbol for venereal disease.[10] *Mothra* (1961) had a giant moth.

Creature with the Atom Brain (1955) found an ex–Nazi mad scientist creating radio-controlled zombies with the aid of nuclear radiation. *Day the World Ended* (1955) begins with nuclear war destroying Earth life, and a mutant monster terrorizes the few survivors. The monster is vanquished when clean rain kills it, since it can only survive amidst nuclear radiation.

X the Unknown (1956) found radioactive mud terrorizing Britain, and *The Blob* (1958) had a meteor crash to Earth and unleash an ever-expanding mass of sticky goo. The creature terrorizes a town until a quick-witted teenager (Steve McQueen) discovers that the creature hates the cold. The military carries the Blob off to the North Pole to keep it good and docile, at least until global warming sets in. In a nice change of pace, a mad scientist in the British film *Konga* (1961) works to turn plants into carnivores and hypnotizes a chimpanzee to commit murders, including killing the boyfriend of a student on whom he has a crush. When his assistant injects a chemical into Konga, the chimp, to re-hypnotize him, he grows to enormous size and starts rampaging. King Kong returned in Japan in 1962 (dubbed, 1963) in *King Kong vs. Godzilla*, which pretty much summed up the giant monster genre.

You get the idea. Literally- or metaphorically-nuclear monsters wreak havoc and only the flip side of the same science that created them can put them down again. The movies were plagued by poor special effects (the shrews in *The Killer Shrews* [1959] were dogs wearing carpet) and wooden plots; later generations would find them humorous and hokey, gleefully pointing out the visible zippers on the actors' monster suits. Yet they still kept on coming: *The Giant Gila Monster* (1960), *Attack of the Giant Leeches* (1960), both self-explanatory, and perhaps the worst monster movie of the era: *The Horror of Party Beach* (1964), the self-proclaimed first "horror-monster musical."

The Horror of Party Beach begins with some teen-angst beach drama, followed by the dumping of radioactive waste into the ocean, where the toxic sludge escapes its canisters and begins to attach itself to a human skull lying on a sunken ship. This skull becomes the frame for a radioactive sea monster, complete with bug eyes, gills and fins, and what seems to be hot dogs stuffed into its mouth. Meanwhile, on Party Beach, a bunch of rock 'n' roll teenagers are having a beach party, along with perhaps the world's geekiest rock band, the Del-Aires.* Much dancing and gyrating ensue. A sunbathing girl becomes the creature's first victim; soon more monsters are on the loose. Teenagers beware! More creatures form from the radioactive waste, and they attack and kill more than twenty nubile young women at a slumber party pillow fight. Panic ensues, but the beach parties continue, albeit with less "action around here" than before the deaths started.

Scientist Dr. Gavin (Allen Laurel) at first thinks the sunbather's death is the result of human action: "I have no doubt we'll find a totally reasonable explanation for the girl's death." Later, he tries to combat the creatures to save his daughter and her boyfriend from their clutches. Working with one of the creature's severed arms, Dr. Gavin deduces some of the monsters' properties:

> Of course! This creature needs the ordinary necessities of human life! Protiants, fats, sugars, and so forth. But since its organs are so decomposed that they can neither produce nor retain the oxygen necessary for its survival, it needs the only food which can keep it alive [human blood].... It's a giant protozoa!

Worse, it's radioactive! His superstitious black housekeeper, Eulabelle (Eulabelle Moore), a walking stereotype spouting off about ghosts and voodoo, makes the accidental discovery that sodium dissolves the monsters like slugs. Thus our heroes race to obtain enough salt to stop the monsters before they kill again. But the town is low on sodium, so they have to drive an hour to Manhattan to buy some. Using Geiger counters to track the radioactive creatures, Dr. Gavin's daughter manages to get herself cornered by the monsters. Only Dr. Gavin's timely arrival with bags of sodium saves the day.

---

*The Del-Aires were a real band from Patterson, New Jersey, with a number of singles to their name; sample song: "Zombie Stomp" (written for the movie). When asked if there were any good stories from the Horror of Party Beach shoot, the Del-Aires' Bobby Osbourne told the website Bad Movie Planet, "Nah, not really."

Mercilessly mocked by *Mystery Science Theater 3000*, and listed as one of the fifty worst movies of all time in Harry Medved's 1978 book of that name, *The Horror of Party Beach* ranks beside *Plan 9 from Outer Space* in that rare pantheon of sublimely awful horror cinema, disastrous but deliriously entertaining.

Unfortunately, more monster movies followed, including *The Beach Girls and the Monster* (1965), which was more or less the same thing, but with more sex. This time surfers are being murdered, and there is suspicion that the creature is really a rival surfer's jealous parent. *Die, Monster, Die!* (1965) was allegedly based on H. P. Lovecraft's "The Colour Out of Space," but is set in England and tells the story of how Boris Karloff used a radioactive meteorite to grow giant vegetables. He's some species of Satanist who saw the meteorite as a gift from the "Outer Ones." The radioactive rock starts mutating things wildly, forcing his daughter's boyfriend to come rescue her when all hell breaks loose. *The Giant Spider Invasion* (1975) was a late entry in the genre, based on a miniature black hole crashing into the Earth and releasing the title creatures, which a NASA scientist must suppress. Fortunately, while the monster movie rolled on into ridiculousness, a purer horror returned to the big screen.

Other Horrors

In the mid–1950s a few producers and directors figured that there was an audience for horror that did not feature large creatures in rubber suits. Murder was a good place to start. *House of Wax* (1953) found the soon-to-be horror legend Vincent Price encasing people in molten wax to make lifelike sculptures, remaking a 1933 film. This version boasted 3-D effects to complement the evil-genius plot. *The Night of the Hunter* (1955) stuck close to the book, but added set design inspired by *The Cabinet of Dr. Caligari* to increase the creepiness. Mad scientists, particularly doctors, were also popular.

The Brain That Wouldn't Die (1959) finds a sexually frustrated mad surgeon (Jason Evers) preserving, over her objections, the head of his girlfriend (Virginia Leith), whom he accidentally killed. He procures a model to use as an unwitting body donor for his girlfriend's brain, and he also keeps a monster in his closet. As his colleague tells the severed head: "There is a horror beyond yours, and it's in there, locked behind that door! Paths of experimentation twist and turn through mountains of miscalculation, and often lose themselves in error and darkness." The severed head and the monster in the closet come to an understanding that they both hate the mad scientist, and they team up to dispatch him. The French film *Eyes Without a Face* (1959, dubbed into English in 1962) finds another mad doctor with feelings of guilt. This time the doctor kills young women to graft their faces onto his disfigured daughter, who eventually recoils from the horror perpetrated in her name and seeks to end it. The Italian *Atom Age Vampire* (1960, dubbed into English in 1963) finds yet another mad doctor restoring the face of a disfigured stripper with a radioactive chemical, but his treatment only works if she had constant access to the glands of young women. The crazy doctor has fallen in love — well, has become sexually obsessed — with the stripper, so he uses another radioactive chemical to turn into a monster to obtain these precious glands, and a radiation machine to change himself back. The stripper and her boyfriend figure out what's going on and help put a stop to it. As Patrick Gonder pointed out, such films (and many atomic creature films) reflected a realization that the body could no longer be viewed as a unified whole, but as a collection of separate parts (like DNA and genes), parts that science could put together and take apart at will. He then stretches the analogy to imagine these medical horrors as racist fears of African genes in Caucasian stock, but the earlier point is valid.[11]

The supernatural made a comeback, too. In our next section we'll discuss the return of traditional horror monsters at Britain's Hammer Films, but for now let's talk ghosts. *13 Ghosts* (1960) dealt with the fallout from the death of a parapsychologist who scientifically investigated ghosts throughout his life, imprisoning them in the house his nephew and family eventually inherit. Mayhem ensues. One of the best of the 1960s ghost films was *The Haunting* (1963), a moody and atmospheric adaptation of Shirley Jackson's *The Haunting of Hill House*. With only a few minor changes the movie follows the novel's plot, and the black-and-white photography (utilizing odd angles to mirror Hill House's unorthodox geometries), combined with High Victorian sets that stopped just short of going over the top, gave the film a cool elegance that beautifully translated Jackson's work to celluloid. It was a triumph of atmosphere, and rightly hailed as one of horror's greatest films.

Jackson's book is said to have inspired another movie, *House on Haunted Hill* (1959), which starred the suave and aristocratic Vincent Price as Frederick Loren, a millionaire who has rented a haunted mansion and invited his wife and a number of guests to stay the night for a payment of $10,000 — if they survive. The guests include a psychiatrist interested in studying the effects of a "haunted" house on its inhabitants; the drunken owner of the mansion, who entered it but once before with near-deadly results; a test pilot; a secretary; and a gossip columnist. Each needs the money for a number of reasons, and so they agree to be locked into the house with their horrible host. The supernatural occurrences begin soon after, and the characters panic. Loren's wife, Annabelle, tells the other guests that he is insane and is planning murder. As the guests struggle to separate the natural from the supernatural and truth from fiction, a number of twists and turns reveal that nothing is what it seems. At one point, a character is trapped in the basement where a skeleton comes walking toward her. In the original theatrical run, a glowing plastic skeleton flew over the audience's heads to heighten the experience. As the story winds down, we see that the supernatural had nothing to do with the house on Haunted Hill, and Loren is more evil than he seems. At least until the final twist. *House on Haunted Hill* is in every way a true horror classic, but one that mere words can barely describe without destroying the thin film of screen magic that makes it work. Price could also be seen in *The Last Man on Earth* (1964), based on Richard Matheson's *I Am Legend*. The film sticks fairly close to the book, since Matheson wrote a draft of the script before expressing his disappointment with changes the Italian producers made. In the film the vampires are simply accepted for what they are, and the final revelation of the legendary status of Robert Morgan (Neville in the book) never develops. He is cut down in a church in a bleak ending, staked like a vampire while crying out that he is the last true man.

Alfred Hitchcock, the famed director of suspense and mystery films, was duly impressed by *House on Haunted Hill*, as well as its high box office grosses. He wanted to make his own low-budget horror movie, and the end result was *Psycho*, a generally faithful adaptation of Robert Bloch's novel. Much has been said about the genius of Hitchcock's production, and there is little I can add to it. The images from the film — Marion's (Mary in the book) death in the shower, the Bates mansion*, Mother's corpse — are iconic. The music is legendary. In terms of plot, the film follows the novel almost exactly, down to the lengthy disquisition on Freudian psychology that explains away Norman's little problem. Hitchcock, however, improved upon Bloch by casting Anthony Perkins as Norman. This Norman, young, polite, and good-looking, was a far cry from the pudgy weirdo from the novel. Since he seemed likable, the viewer is made to sympathize with him, rendering the coming horror that much more emotionally devastating based on Daphne de Maurier's short story.

Hitchcock followed with another horror film, *The Birds* (1963), based on Daphne du Maurier's short story, in which birds attack a seaside town for no reason. They come in massive numbers, and they take over. Pecking ensues. A family is trapped in their house while the birds gather outside and try to kill them.

I saved for last a discussion of the best of the era's horror films, one that combined the bleakness of *I Am Legend*, whose adaptation as *The Last Man on Earth* was an inspiration,[12] with the psychological depth of *Psycho*. Director George Romero's *Night of the Living Dead* (1968) straddles the line between the body horrors discussed in our next section and the psychological and nuclear horrors of this section. It is, in many ways, the apex of the horror movie.

Siblings Johnny (Russell Streiner) and Barbara (Judith O'Dea) arrive at a cemetery to visit their father's grave when they are attacked by a slow-moving old man who tries to bite them. Barbara flees after the old man kills Johnny. She runs to a distant farmhouse and lets herself in. She tries to call for help,

---

The look of Bates's crumbling Victorian mansion was inspired by Winslow Homer's paintings and the Addams Family cartoons of Charles Addams and continued the trend of finding horror in neo–Gothic architecture, which the reader will remember arose from the Gothic vogue created by Horace Walpole and The Castle of Otranto.

The *Psycho* house. In bringing Rober Bloch's novel to the screen, Alfred Hitchcock drew on Charles Addams's cartoons to create a crumbling Victorian setting for the movie's horror that could contrast with the uncluttered, modern architecture of the "normal" world outside the space inhabited by Norman Bates, continuing the trend of transforming the Victorian era into a source of horror.

but the phone is dead. She takes a large kitchen knife for protection and explores the farmhouse, discovering a half-eaten corpse on the stairs. She tries to flee the house, but instead runs in to Ben (Duane Jones), who is also seeking shelter from a lethal attacker. As Ben explains how he escaped a violent mob and came here searching for gas, more of the slow-moving creatures arrive. They begin to surround the house. From the radio, the two learn that mob violence has broken out across the United States, with lurching killers eating the flesh of their victims. As Barbara and Ben try to fortify the house, they stumble across several people in the basement, a family of three and a man and his girlfriend. The family's daughter has been bitten by one of the killers and is gravely ill.

Ben and the girl's father, Harry Cooper (Karl Hardman), clash over the best way to protect themselves from the mob. Stoic Ben wants to fortify the whole house; the panicky, angry Cooper wants to hide in the basement and barricade its door. The characters spend the duration of the film playing out their own private psychodramas as they attempt to figure out what is going on, and try to make sense of the situation they have unwittingly found themselves playing out. From the television in the house, they learn that the dead are returning to life to feast on the flesh of the living, who then become zombies too. It is thought that a space probe returning from Venus may have brought back some strange radiation that has caused this inexplicable phenomenon. The federal government has mobilized its resources and is combating the plague, killing the zombies by burning them or shooting them in the head. This may be good for the country, but it does nothing for the isolated people in the small farmhouse.

Night falls. An expedition out of the farmhouse to find gas for a stalled truck turns deadly for the expendable man and his girlfriend, whom the zombie mob eat in a protracted and graphic scene of carnage. The zombie mob attacks the house. In poetic justice of a sort, Johnny returns from the dead to drag Barbara to her death. The small girl becomes a zombie and consumes her parents. Only Ben is left to defend against the onslaught of the undead. He waits out the night in the basement. As morning comes, he hears the sounds of the guns and dogs of police and deputized hunters hunting down the zombies. Relieved, he prepares to rush out of the house to safety, only to have the police mistake him for a zombie and shoot him dead, on orders of the police chief. "That's one more for the bonfire," the chief says. Under the closing credits we see Ben's corpse burning in a mass cremation.

Variety called the film the "pornography of violence."[13] Film critic Roger Ebert described a viewing he attended in Chicago in January 1969. The film played on a Saturday afternoon, during a matinee attended mostly by little children, who were by and large the intended audience for most horror movies:

> The kids in the audience were stunned. There was almost complete silence. The movie had stopped being delightfully scary about half way through, and had become unexpectedly terrifying. There was a little girl across the aisle from me, maybe nine years old, who was sitting very still in her seat and crying.... I felt real terror in that neighborhood theater last Saturday afternoon. I saw kids who had no resources they could draw upon to protect themselves from the dread and fear they felt.[14]

Ebert wondered what parents were thinking sending kids to see such a movie, and he expressed hope that the new motion picture ratings system replacing the Hays code would stop scenes like this from happening again. That didn't exactly work out as planned.

Though *Night* follows the outlines of the standard monster movie and shares plot elements with several earlier films, it ultimately transgresses or inverts the previous conventions of the genre, establishing new conventions for future horror films. The characters make serious mistakes, listening to the heroic Ben when they ought to have followed the cowardly Cooper. The child is not sacred but is in fact an agent of evil. Worst of all, the authorities, who in most other films stand for truth, justice, reason, and order, fail here. Knowledge does little good; death happens despite science and logic and reason. In fact, the more the characters learn from television and radio, the more they think they can win, and the closer they come to death. Scientists and the army bicker over the cause of the outbreak and what to do. Though the government makes the right moves, they are protecting the public as a whole, doing nothing for the individual. The police kill Ben without a second thought or even stopping to check whether he is living or undead. The police are, in effect, a zombie army of a different order. The military-industrial complex frays at the seams.

Night of the Living Dead was Invasion of the Body Snatchers with the guts (literal and figurative) to follow the darkness and the bleakness to its true conclusion. This willingness to be existentially dark in plot, tone, and message made this the harbinger of the horror of the future.

Horror on Radio and Television

It would be a long time before television presented anything as stark as Night of the Living Dead, but it and the older medium of radio contributed some memorable horror. The radio drama Quiet, Please! (1947–1949) was perhaps the last new entry in the radio horror genre, but one often judged among the best. Its episodes combined fantasy, horror, and suspense into a heady, surreal mixture in which good is (usually) victorious and evil vanquished at the end of each half-hour episode. In "If I Should Wake Before I Die" (February 27, 1949) a scientist obsessed with pure knowledge is oblivious to the negative consequences of his work. He cares nothing for application, only acquisition of knowledge, even at the cost of millions of lives: "Knowledge is the goal! All else is unimportant! Never forget that."

"The Thing on the Fourbleboard" (August 9, 1948) is the show's most famous broadcast, often called the best radio horror play of all time. An oil field worker, Porky, is drilling the deepest hole in the world, which uncovers anomalies. In a core drilled out of rocks millions of years old, they find a gold ring—and a petrified finger still attached. But when they clean the finger, they discover that it is invisible beneath the mud and dirt. After a drinking bout, Porky's friend Billy is found dead, and Porky is suspected of the murder. After another suspicious death, the site is shut down for twenty years. The invisible creature had snapped a rope, and a man was squashed by falling metal. Porky finds the gold ring at the site, and he hears the crying of some invisible child. Throwing a can of red paint at the invisible creature, he discovers that the creature has the face of a little girl, the body of a spider, and a missing finger. She was made entirely of living stone. Porky takes the creature home with him and covers it up with greasepaint and a long dress, making it his wife. A final twist explains to us what the weird creature likes to eat. The play drew elements from Fitz James O'Brien's "What Was It?" and Lovecraft's ancient horrors. The story, however, veers into morbid psychology in its dramatic and surreal climax, showing us that the real monster is not the innocent creature.

Quiet, Please! never made it to television, but radio's other horror programs had brief TV runs. The success of the mystery play "Sorry, Wrong Number" on radio's *Suspense* turned the program toward psychological horror, and other thriller radio series followed suit, ushering in a wave of psycho-horror that would lead smoothly into the television era, where *Suspense* would air on CBS from 1949 to 1954.[15] *Suspense* offered in both its radio and television incarnations murder mysteries, crime stories, and spine-tingling creepiness that usually stopped just short of traditional horror. The show tended to focus on horrors within the American home because its audience was largely female. Thus academics like Allison McCracken argue that *Suspense* served to "overturn postwar structures and reveal the repressions and social controls" faced by Americans, especially women.[16] *Lights Out!* aired on NBC from 1949 to 1952, and *Inner Sanctum* aired in television syndication for ten months in 1954. Though individually the shows did not fare very well, they paved the way for a number of classic series that inserted horror into TV land once and for all.

Alfred Hitchcock Presents (CBS, 1955–1962) featured the affable film director sardonically introducing a new short play each week, rather like the Cryptkeeper and his ilk did in the EC horror comics. The stories were by turns dark, morbid, or weird and reflected Hitchcock's taste for suspense and horror tales. The series' best-known episode was "Lamb to the Slaughter" (April 13, 1958), based on Roald Dahl's 1953 short story, in which a housewife kills her husband, the chief of police, with a frozen leg of lamb. When the cops come to investigate, they question the woman and comment on the delicious smell of lamb coming from the oven. She offers them a meal, and they unwittingly eat the evidence. The very first episode, "Revenge" (October 2, 1955), found a man trying to avenge his wife's rape. When the traumatized woman points to her rapist, he kills the man. However, minutes later the woman sees men she says are the rapist again, and again, and again. Only then does the man realize that his wife never knew who the rapist was. "Breakdown" (November 13, 1955) offered a terrifying portrait of a paralyzed man mistaken for dead. Only 1950s sensibilities prevented the autopsy from going through to its intended conclusion. "The Perfect Crime" (October 20, 1957) featured Vincent Price as a famous detective who has solved every case he encountered and keeps mementos of them on his shelves. A lawyer for one of the men executed on Price's evidence shows up and explains that Price sent the wrong man to his death. To keep his reputation intact, Price murders the lawyer and cremates him in his kiln, turning the ashes into clay to make a vase, which he displays as an artifact of "the perfect crime."

However, for my money, the most frightening single line in the Hitchcock canon comes at the end of "The Case of Mr. Pelham" (December 4, 1955), based on a 1940 short story by Anthony Armstrong. Albert Pelham is a successful businessman who discovers that his friends and associates remember meeting him at times when he wasn't there. He discovers someone has been eating his food, wearing his clothes, and even signing his checks—all in perfect imitation of his own actions. Fearing for his own sanity, he eventually crosses paths with his double, who is an exact duplicate of him in every way. The double has Mr. Pelham hauled away to an insane asylum, but before he goes Mr. Pelham asks the doppelganger a question, with a chilling answer:

PELHAM: Why? Why did this have to happen to me? Why?
THE DOUBLE: No reason. It just did, you see.

I can still remember how effective that cold illogic was the first time I saw the program as a kid on a weekend *Alfred Hitchcock Presents* marathon. It sums up the horror of it all: Bad things happen without logic or reason, and no knowledge can protect against them. "The Case of Mr. Pelham" was made into a feature film, *The Man Who Haunted Himself*, in 1970 with Roger Moore in the title role.

Though Hitchcock's stories were frequently dark and appeared to end in horror, the network made Hitchcock give the stories happy, or at least just, endings. Therefore, after the horror, Hitchcock reappeared to offer unconvincing explanations of how the criminal was "really" caught. The woman with the lamb tried the same trick on husband number two, but forgot to plug in the freezer, so the lamb was too soft. The detective from "The Perfect Crime" was caught when the maid knocked over the vase and found the lawyer's gold fillings embedded in the shards. And so on. Boris Karloff hosted a similar program, *Thriller* (NBC, 1960–1962), that in its brief run presented stories of suspense and horror, with contributions from Robert Bloch.

Rod Serling's *The Twilight Zone* (CBS, 1959–1964) was primarily a science fiction and fantasy program, but one that flavored its sci-fi with heavy doses of horror. Episodes typically featured an alien menace serving to highlight a moral lesson or allegory, often with a shocking twist ending. Many of the episodes dealt with our themes of science, knowledge, and the unforeseen consequences of their use and abuse. Serling, who penned many of the episodes, appeared onscreen as an omniscient narrator who wanders into the action to set the stage. The first *Twilight Zone* opened with this narration:

There is a fifth dimension, beyond that which is known to man. It is a dimension as vast as space and as timeless as infinity. It is the middle ground between light and shadow, between science and superstition; and it lies between the pit of man's fears and the summit of his knowledge. This is the dimension of imagination. It is an area which we call *The Twilight Zone*.

The program's many episodes have become so iconic that there is little left to say. "Time Enough at Last" (November 20, 1959), from a 1953 Lyn Venable short story, found Henry Bemis (Burgess Meredith) longing to be alone with his books, getting his wish when a nuclear war leaves him the lone survivor, with a sad twist. "To Serve Man" and "It's a *Good* Life" were both adapted into *Zone* episodes now better known than the source material. Coming after *The Day the Earth Stood Still*'s alien savior, "To Serve Man" must have made a strong impression with its subversion of a 1950s horror staple.

In the realm of purer horror, Richard Matheson, who was a writer for *Zone*, adapted his own "Nightmare at 20,000 Feet" (1961) for an episode of the same name (October 11, 1963). William Shatner plays Bob Wilson, a salesman who suffered a nervous breakdown and is now flying home from a stay in a sanitarium. He thinks he sees a gremlin on the wing of the airplane, but whenever he calls for help, the gremlin disappears. Wilson becomes worried that the beast means to down the plane by sabotaging the wing, and he steals a gun to kill it. He breaks open the plane window and shoots wildly at the creature, which is tearing at the wing. When the plane makes an emergency landing, Wilson is hauled off-in a straitjacket, but the camera pulls back to reveal the mangled wing, indicating that Wilson was in his right mind all along. "The Hitch-Hiker" (January 22, 1960) found a woman being stalked by a mysterious hitch-hiker who eventually helps her realize she is dead.

"Will the Real Martian Please Stand Up" (May 26, 1961) was a claustrophobic tale of humans trying to figure out which of them is not human in a snowbound diner. The second-to-last episode, "The Fear" (May 29, 1964), found a police trooper and a woman trapped one night in an isolated house where they think they are being attacked by a giant alien. Large fingerprints and footprints indicate this, and when morning comes they see the monstrously large space creature. The officer shoots, it deflates, and they realize that miniature aliens were attempting to scare them. Until the rather silly ending the episode was a stark portrait of terror. However, the single best *Twilight Zone* tale of terror is "The Invaders" (January 27, 1961), which also featured miniature aliens.

Agnes Moorehead, whom we last met on radio's *Suspense*, here plays an unnamed old woman in an isolated farmhouse "untouched by progress" in the middle of a dark moor. She hears a noise on her roof and goes up to investigate. There she discovers a small flying saucer, and from it emerge tiny robot-like creatures. Frightened, she returns inside and tries to defend herself against the invaders. The creatures proceed to break into her house and attack her repeatedly over the course of several terrifying hours. The woman does her best to fight back, eventually taking her axe and smashing the flying saucer and dispatching most of its occupants. The last dying creature radios for help, and in the final shot we see that the flying saucer is stamped "U.S. Air Force." "These are the invaders," Rod Serling closed by saying, "the tiny beings from a tiny place called Earth, who would take the giant step across the sky to the question marks that sparkle and beckon from the vastness of the universe only to be imagined." The episode was shot almost entirely without words, amplifying the terror.

The Twilight Zone ran for 156 episodes, with modest ratings. It inspired a movie version in 1983, two revival series (*The New Twilight Zone* from 1985 to 1989 and UPN's *The Twilight Zone* in the 2002–2003 season), a ride at Disney World, and countless cultural references, adaptations, and knockoffs. The original show perpetually aired in reruns, and New York's WPIX-TV would run all-day New Year's marathons, a tradition the Sci-Fi Channel continues today.

ABC offered a similar program, *The Outer Limits*, from 1963 to 1965. Like *Zone*, *The Outer Limits* told science fiction stories in an anthology style. The disembodied voice (Vic Perrin) introducing the show claimed to be "controlling transmission" in the name of an unspecified "we" who ordered viewers to "sit quietly." The episodes tended to be darker than the *Twilight Zone*, and to feature more vicious aliens—on orders from the network, who wanted new monsters each week. In "Demon with a Glass Hand" (October 17, 1964), a man discovers he is a time traveler from an era when aliens rule the world. The horror comes when the man learns the truth about himself, that he is in fact a robot, and so his life and his feelings are simply the false face of mechanical actions. Here knowledge again destroys happiness. Pointedly for our theme, "The Architects of Fear" (September 30, 1963) depicts a group of scientists who decide to try a desperate experiment to end the nuclear arms race and unite the world by providing a common enemy. They choose one of their own to undergo extensive chemical treatments and surgery to become a "Thetan," a fake extraterrestrial, against whom Earth's people can rally as one. He is supposed to land at the U.N. and announce an invasion, but his ship crashes in the woods, where hunters shoot him. He staggers back to the lab where he has a final meeting with his wife before dying.

The Outer Limits probed the depths of our humanity and the uneven relationship between science, knowledge, and happiness, often with decidedly discomfiting results. The program was canceled when it failed to outdraw *Mr. Magoo* on NBC.[17] *The Outer Limits* would be revived in 1995 in a rare remake that equaled or exceeded the original.

The British series *Tales of Mystery* (ITV, 1961–1963) dramatized Algernon Blackwood's horror tales, including "The Man Who Found Out," and a number of his lesser stories, which made up the whole of the series' content. The show was notable for its dark and moody atmosphere and its pioneering use of special effects. John Laurie played Blackwood, introducing each new tale.

By the mid–1960s, horror was a staple of the television diet, albeit in the science fiction and crime forms characteristic of the era. As we shall see, television paved the way, though, for the full-scale revival of horror in its traditional forms that occurred shortly after and did not abate again. This breed of horror would have more in common with *Night of the Living Dead* than *The Day the Earth Stood Still*, a bloody mess focusing its horrors on the human body and the horrible things that could be done to it.

PART VI

The Human Machine

Body Horror
(c. 1965–c. 2000)

16

SCIENCE AND SOCIETY

Scholar and horror fan Jonathan Lake Crane argued in 1994 that the monsters of the golden age of horror cinema — Dracula, the Wolf Man, Frankenstein's Monster, and the Mummy — ceased to be frightening when horror moved on to new and more explicit terrors. Only small children, he said, felt any fascination or fear at the tottering monsters of the 1930s horror films.[1] However, little children were exactly the audience for the old horrors when they debuted on the infant medium of television in 1957, when Screen Gems licensed them to American TV. Fifty-two Universal films, mostly horror and mystery, were sold into syndication under the "Shock Theater" banner, including *Dracula*, *Frankenstein*, and other well-known classics. Indeed, they became classics in large part due to this television exposure. The local programs featured campy hosts dressed as ghouls, such as KABC's Vampira (Maila Nurmi), who began her reign in 1954 showing independent horror films from the golden age; WISH's Selwin (Ray Sparenberg), and WABC's Zacherley (John Zacherle). Elena M. Watson interviewed an astonishing sixty-eight such hosts, and there were dozens more at stations across the United States, some of whom continue to introduce horror films today.[2]

Kids loved the old monster movies, and a plethora of tie-ins sprang up to take advantage of it. Hagiographic magazines like *Famous Monsters of Filmland* (debuted 1958) relived the glories of 1930s and '40s horror films. Novelty songs like "The Monster Mash" (1962), sung by Bobby Pickett doing an impression of Boris Karloff, turned the monsters into cuddly icons, and even plastic monster model kits (debuted 1962, which we saw described in Freudian terms in the introduction) helped turn kids into horror connoisseurs. Count Chocula and Franken Berry cereals arrived in 1971 for kids who wanted to breakfast with their favorite monsters. But as these kids grew up, they wanted more explicit and more frightening horrors. Along with horror comics, horror television and its offshoots made horror a genre increasingly dominated by teenagers and pre-teens, to whom horror media would increasingly cater.

But the new horrors for a new era necessarily explored different concerns than films made for different moments in history. The 1970s, give or take five years, were the "gloomiest" in America's modern history, when the Western world seemed to be "teetering on the edge of an abyss" and America in steep decline.[3] President Jimmy Carter addressed the perceived "malaise" of 1970s America in an infamous speech:

> It is a crisis of confidence. It is a crisis that strikes at the very heart and soul and spirit of our national will. We can see this crisis in the growing doubt about the meaning of our own lives and in the loss of a unity of purpose for our Nation. The erosion of our confidence in the future is threatening to destroy the social and the political fabric of America.[4]

It was no surprise then that the horrors of the 1950s — giant insects, flying saucers, and omnipotent scientists — were replaced by angry animals, psycho slashers, and the failure of institutional authority. The culture had changed, and so did the horrors that it produced. This section deals with body horror, a heady mixture of themes surrounding the profound advances in medical science, including reproductive technologies, genetic manipulation, and cloning, which left the body a foreign and vulnerable commodity ripe for horror's exploitation. It also deals heavily in the postmodern rejection of science and objective knowledge, which denied the power of reason in favor of Romantic notions about the supremacy of emotion and physical experience.

A World of Horror

It has become something of a cliché to say that America lost its innocence when John F. Kennedy was assassinated in Dallas on November 22, 1963. It was the first time such an event had been reported on live television — though the famed Zapruder film of the assassination would not be seen publicly for years after — and in the days that followed, America was convulsed with a shared grief. When the president's assassin, Lee Harvey Oswald, was gunned down live on NBC's air, millions of Americans witnessed their first real-life murder. Before the decade was out, Robert F. Kennedy and Martin Luther King, Jr., would both die from assassins' bullets, and many began to wonder what had become of the civil and stable society they had imagined America to be.

Part of the newfound instability came from internal changes in American political culture — the Civil Rights movement, the anti-war movement — and part of it came from an international change in social mores. On the political front, the established authorities no longer commanded the same respect they once did, brought low by mismanagement, corruption, and scandal. The American presidents Lyndon Johnson and Richard Nixon exhibited megalomaniacal tendencies that alienated them from the public and eventually cost both men their jobs. Nixon's involvement in the Watergate scandal, directly ordering the cover-up of a break-in he ordered against his rivals, is often said to have shattered the implicit faith Americans had in their government. Never before had an American president resigned office, or faced prosecution for criminal actions conducted while in office. The British government of Harold Macmillan tottered in 1963 under the Profumo scandal, in which John Profumo, the secretary of state for war, admitted to lying about an affair with a prostitute who was also involved with a Soviet attaché.

At the same time, the world was becoming more complicated. Britain and France were quickly dissolving their century-old colonial empires, creating a large number of newly independent states, which were racked by civil war, poverty, and eventual tyranny. These new states, along with other non-aligned countries, used their freedom to play America and the Soviet Union off each other, letting the superpowers compete for the privilege of propping up their tyrannies. By the end of the 1970s, the world had more dictators than ever before, including Augusto Pinochet in Chile, Francisco Franco in Spain, Kim Il Sung in North Korea, and dozens of others. In Iran, the secular shah, himself a dictator, was overthrown in 1979 in favor of the Ayatollah Khomeini and the Islamic Revolution, portending the aggressive revival of radical Islam.

Worse, these dictators were committing atrocities on a scale seen only in the Nazi death camps of World War II or the Soviet Gulag. Uganda's Idi Amin killed three hundred thousand countrymen. In Chairman Mao's China, up to thirty million people had died of famines, and the dictator launched a Cultural Revolution in 1966 to purge the state of intellectuals who disagreed with Mao's positions. The intellectuals were sent to "re-education" camps; and other so-called "intellectuals," as young as middle school students, were forcibly deported to the countryside to be indoctrinated into Maoist thought. They would not return home until the late 1970s. In Cambodia, the dictator Pol Pot emulated Mao and sent the intellectuals and the educated — that is, those who could oppose him — into the countryside for their "re-education." In what became known as the "killing fields," Pol Pot and the Khmer Rouge killed more than a million people, out of a population of just over seven million. It was, proportionally, the most extreme killing of the twentieth century.[5] The Khmer Rouge targeted any sign of intelligence, including those who wore glasses and thus appeared smart.

In neighboring Vietnam, the United States sustained a long and bloody war against the communist Viet Cong in North Vietnam in defense of the non-communist but corrupt government of South Vietnam. Nearly sixty thousand American soldiers died, and more than two million Vietnamese. As the war dragged on without victory, and repeated escalations failed to unseat the communists, the American public turned on its government. An emboldened Congress responded after Nixon's resignation, refusing President Ford's requests to continue the war. Saigon, the South Vietnamese capital, fell to the communists April 29, 1975, and the war ended.[6] It was the first war the United States had lost (the earlier Korean War ended in stalemate). For the next twenty-five years, the so-called Vietnam syndrome left Americans unwilling to enter into future wars unless they were sure of swift and decisive victory.

During the 1970s the Cold War dragged on, and in the 1980s the new American president, Ronald Reagan, confronted what he called "The Evil Empire." A combination of American defense spending—forcing the Soviets to keep up—and Soviet premier Mikhail Gorbachev's policies in Moscow led to a cracking of the Soviet bloc. The liberation of the eastern European states from Iron Curtain in 1989, followed by the dissolution of the Soviet Union in 1991, was a glorious and largely bloodless end to a Cold War that repeatedly threatened to end the world in a massive volley of nuclear death. The euphoria surrounding the new, democratic world emerging in the 1990s led historian Francis Fukuyama to proclaim the "end of history" in which the whole world would live peacefully in universal, Western-style democracy.[7] By the turn of the millennium, most of the world's people lived under some form of democracy for the first time in history. The great story of human evolution had ended in the triumph of America and its values. Or so it seemed.

Real-Life Horrors

One troubling trend was the increase in terrorism. Rod Serling, of *Twilight Zone* fame, penned a TV-movie called *Doomsday Flight* (1966), based on an unpublicized real-life incident, in which a bomb was placed on an airplane. The film was the first media depiction of a threat to airliners. The first copycat called in a terrorist threat based on the scenario while the film was still airing, and more followed over the next several days. No bombs were found. Serling told reporters, "I wish to God I had written a stagecoach drama starring John Wayne instead."[8] When the film was rerun in 1971, the Federal Aviation Administration saw a link between it and threats to aviation. The agency asked TV stations not to show the movie,[9] but they did and more bomb threats poured in. Haunted for the rest of his life by the incident, Serling vowed never again to publicize a new crime for entertainment. But from that time on, planes were fair game for terrorists. In the 1970s the Palestinian Liberation Organization staged several high-profile takeovers and bombings of airliners. It was the first step toward a world in which Western technology and science would be turned against its creators.

Another real-life horror was the increase in crime plaguing America's decaying inner cities, and spreading to more affluent suburbs. In the United States, postwar affluence, the automobile, and the Interstate Highway System allowed the rich and the middle class to abandon city centers for the suburbs and smaller towns, and as a result city neighborhoods became hotbeds of violence and penury. In a vicious cycle, poverty and crime reduced the willingness and ability of city governments and businesses to invest in city infrastructure, promoting more decay that only reinforced the cycle of poverty and crime. In Europe, large low-income housing projects constructed in rings

Riot damage in Washington D.C. 1968. Riots and unrest plagued America's cities in the 1960s, and many neighborhoods like this one in Washington, D.C., were reduced to rubble. Scenes of mob violence and the breakdown of the social order found a clear reflection in horror movies and horror literature, which increasingly depicted individuals alienated from a society gone mad (Library of Congress, LC-U9-18949-12).

around city centers created cordons of decay, poverty, and crime. In each case, the result was the same: Large sections of the urban world became vast tracts of violence, vice, and desperation. In 1965, the Watts section of Los Angeles erupted in five days of looting and violence, in which six died and the area suffered $35 million worth of damage. It was but one of a wave of riots with various causes in at least eight major cities across the United States in the second half of the 1960s. Fifty-five died when rioters again took to the streets of Los Angeles in 1992, following the verdict in the Rodney King trial. In New York, a 1977 blackout led to widespread riots, looting, and arson, costing an estimated $300 million in damage. *Time* magazine noted that the bad behavior compared poorly to the restrained politeness of the great blackout of 1965, which featured no violence, "illuminating in a perverse way twelve years of change in the character of the city, and perhaps of the country."[10] But all was not right in the old days either; infamously, in 1964 New York City resident Kitty Genovese was attacked twice and murdered in the sight of dozens of her neighbors, who did nothing because they "didn't want to get involved." Only a half-hour after the attacks began did someone finally call the police.[11]

New York City was the most famous example of urban decay, and Times

Square became its poster child. Once a glimmering icon of urban might, by the 1960s, it was home to prostitutes, drug dealers, and violence. In the 1970s, the area recorded more crime than any other in New York. It had become an extravaganza of gambling, pornography, hustling, larceny, and every other type of vice. Times Square had become "synonymous in the minds of a worldwide public with violence and crime."[12] On one day in 1986, in the filthy movie theaters lining the square, films comprising the "XXX Best Porn in Town" played next to the horror film *Friday the 13th Part VI: Jason Lives*. The area would finally be cleaned up when economic prosperity returned in the 1990s. During the 1970s and 1980s, "urban renewal" efforts across America tore down Victorian-era city centers and replaced older neighborhoods with what future generations called the "soulless container architecture" of blank, block buildings and alienating cities built for automobiles rather than humans.[13]

Many saw in the decay of America's urban centers the failure of the technocratic utopia science and government had been expected to usher in. At the World's Fair of 1939, science had promised by 1960 a glorious future world of shining cities, push-button convenience, and rapid transit. Instead, twenty years after the deadline, America's poor lived in the ruins of that imaginary future. Serial killers— the Zodiac Killer, Ted Bundy, John Wayne Gacy, and the cannibal Jeffrey Dahmer — became household names. In the crime-ridden New York of 1976, the serial killer David Berkowitz, known as the "Son of Sam," began killing teenagers, turning the city into a hotbed of fear. The shootings continued into 1977, leaving six dead and several more injured. Berkowitz claimed to be a Satanist, and blamed his killing spree on pornography and the occult.

The counter-culture movement of the late 1960s— its hippies and tie-dyed idealists— had explored the occult as a legitimate path toward knowledge. Satanism was a way of negating traditional values, opposing the tyranny of imperialism, government, and whatever else one disliked. In the 1970s, New York was the hub of the occult, where a man pretending to be a Greek Orthodox priest published what he said was the genuine *Necronomicon*, H. P. Lovecraft's fictional tome, made up of bits and pieces of Sumerian mythology sprinkled with the names of Cthulhu and Mythos creatures. Though a hoax, some followers of Anton LaVey's Church of Satan began to use the mass-market paperback as an occult text to conjure demons and probe the mysteries of existence. The book was the brainchild of Peter Levenda and followers of the early twentieth century Satanist Aleister Crowley.[14] The Church of Satan later had to explain to its members that the *Necronomicon* was not real.[15]

Occultism was the flavor of the day. LaVey, of the Church of Satan, had founded his cult in San Francisco, the epicenter of the counter-culture, in 1966. He parodied Christian faith with a derivative *Satanic Bible* (1969) that reversed traditional teachings and cast Satan as the hero of the human story. Charles Manson, inspired by Satanism and San Francisco's hippie culture, attracted a group of twenty-five mostly female followers, his "family," who held him to be the reincarnated Christ. Manson predicted the coming of the apocalypse based on his idiosyncratic combination of Satanism, Beatles music, Nazi occult beliefs, and science fiction. He also foresaw a coming race war in which blacks would defeat whites and Manson would rule them all. To bring about this glorious millennium, violence was necessary — termed "helter-skelter" after a Beatles song. In August 1969, Manson and his family murdered eight people, including actress Sharon Tate, in Los Angeles in a bloody and macabre orgy of killing that a fascinated American media broadcast into living rooms each night.[16]

Another cult leader, the Rev. Jim Jones, managed to outdo Manson in every conceivable horror. Jones ran a church called the People's Temple, which he founded in Indiana in 1956 before eventually relocating to San Francisco. He amassed more than three thousand followers. After the media began to look into Jones's control over his followers, including their sex lives, he moved the People's Temple to Guyana. He called the new settlement Jonestown, and one thousand of his followers lived there with him, under his complete control. In 1978 a U.S. Congressman and an NBC camera crew came to investigate the cult. Jones had them murdered, and then he and his followers committed "revolutionary suicide," an act they had rehearsed many times, by drinking poison-laced Flav-R-Aid, a British version of Kool-Aid. When investigators found the bloated bodies rotting in the tropical sun, they were stunned: 637 adults and 276 children were dead, most willingly killing themselves to leave a corrupt world.[17] The carnage was broadcast on television for the entire world to see.

Manson and Jones were merely the most extreme of a wave of occultism, millennialism, and cults flooding America in the 1960s and 1970s. In 1966, *Time* asked, is God dead? With empty churches, even some Christians answered yes. Uri Geller, an Israeli spoon-bender, claimed he had psychic powers and became a media sensation, convincing some scientists of his power, though not magicians like James "The Amazing" Randi, who reproduced his feats with simple parlor tricks. The sociologist Edward A. Tiryakian reported in 1972 that college-aged students had become obsessed with the occult. Occult bookstores ringed America's college campuses, witchcraft (newly rechristened Wicca) was becoming a popular alternative faith, and the ivory tower bowed before the rage for all things occult, teaching courses and seminars in it. America's — and indeed the Western world's — youth willfully rejected not just the political and social aspects of the so-called Establishment, but in seeking out the supernatural and the Satanic as alternative paths to knowledge, they effectively rejected science, or at least reduced it to one path among many for seeking out truth. Tiryakian said this was due to a "loss of confidence" in the dominant scientific view of reality,[18] and it portended the coming of a new culture, a New Age.

In this, New Age believers found welcome allies in the academy where a new philosophy, post-modernism, was coming to the fore, displacing the older positivist modern philosophy that had served science well in the postwar years.

Postmodernism was, and is, an unwieldy collection of ideas that defy a single description; but in general postmodernism rejected the institutional authority of science, denied that there was any one path toward knowledge, and privileged the subjective experience of reality over claims that there was an objective reality to experience and understand. It was a version of Romanticism dressed up in ten dollar words. Postmodern thinkers tended to dwell heavily on ideas imported from feminism and Marxism, especially the role of sex and gender in every aspect of life, and the traits of what they called "late capitalism," a catch-all for the current state of the political and economic spheres. "Late capitalism" was meant to imply that capitalism's replacement was imminent, though logically any period of capitalism is "late capitalism" to the individuals living under it. Hallmarks of postmodernism included a promotion of multiculturalism, a devaluation of tradition and authority, and a promotion of relativism. All things being equal, it therefore stood to reason that there was no objective truth, only ways to view the world based on the individual's race, class, and gender. Science, therefore, was but one belief among many, and not necessarily a very good one at that.

On the other side of the debate, traditionalist Christians and their allies in government tried to restrict the teaching of evolution in favor of what they called "creation science," the belief that God created the world and science can demonstrate evidence of the truth of Biblical narratives. In 1968 the United States Supreme Court ruled that Biblical literalism could not be taught as science, and in 1987 it ruled that "creation science" was not science at all and also could not be taught. Nevertheless, conservative Christians spent the better part of four decades fighting to push Darwin out of the nation's schools and restore prayer, Genesis, and God. In a perversely postmodern twist, the creationists argued that science was simply one way of knowing, as was faith, and both ought to be taught in schools, a position most Americans accepted, since most Americans disbelieved evolution in favor of creationist teachings.

Sex and the Single Alien

Of special interest, one particular New Age belief, the ancient astronaut theory, followed post-modernism's line of thought and directly challenged the authority of science. In 1968 a Swiss hotelier named Erich von Däniken published a book called *Chariots of the Gods?*, which made a shocking and startling statement:

> I claim that our forefathers received visits from the universe in the remote past, even though I do not yet know who these extraterrestrial intelligences were or from which planet they came. I nevertheless proclaim that these "strangers" annihilated part of mankind existing at the time and produced a new, perhaps the first, *homo sapiens*.[19]

This "ancient astronaut theory" postulated that ancient monuments and artifacts around the world bore testament to the arrival of spaceships, whose occupants were worshipped as gods by primitive humans who were too inexperienced and naïve to realize the truth. By extension, sacred texts like the Bible encode records of the aliens' visitations, their scientific experiments, and their actions on Earth. The aliens Däniken said, created humanity using advanced genetic technology. His theory made use of Ignatius Donnelly's and Helena Blavatsky's old theories and dressed them up in biotechnological clothes, with an attack on mainstream science thrown in for good measure. In his two dozen books, many best-sellers, Däniken argued that arrogant scientists were willfully overlooking compelling evidence that Earth was colonized in the distant past by aliens who genetically engineered mankind. Scientists were so wedded to their dogma that they were blind to the self-evident truth of these theories, and to his mind their opposition to his ideas only confirmed his beliefs. Däniken's idea was not exactly new, but he was the first to make a fortune peddling it. He had borrowed many of the central concepts of the ancient astronaut theory from Louis Pauwels's and Jacques Bergier's 1961 book *Morning of the Magicians*, which in turn was influenced by H. P. Lovecraft's fictional accounts of aliens who served as ancient gods.[20] Horror fiction had accidentally begotten its own Frankenstein's Monster of a theory.

Rod Serling was duly impressed with the ancient astronaut theory, and narrated an NBC documentary on the subject in 1973, *In Search of Ancient Astronauts*, which led to a series, *In Search of*, narrated by Leonard Nimoy, which argued across its many episodes that there were mysteries that defied science, a discipline that did not have all the answers. Däniken himself became a celebrity, appearing on *The Tonight Show* and interviewed in *Playboy*. His theory was read, watched, and debated by millions in the 1970s, despite the objections of scientists that the ancient astronaut theory was hogwash. By 1975, professors reported that their students were arriving in class already believing in ancient astronauts and alternative histories of the past. In 1984, one student in four believed in prehistoric alien visitation; in 1994 belief reached one in three. Perhaps as a result of such beliefs, in 1984, three out of four students rejected the idea that humans evolved from earlier species, though only one in two did so in 1994.[21]

Chariots spawned a number of imitators and extrapolators, with paperback volumes numbering in the hundreds of titles. Robert Dione's *God Drives a Flying Saucer* (1973) was perhaps the most direct. Hal Lindsey's *The Late Great Planet Earth* (1970) took a more traditional stance, predicting the imminent end of the world with the added twist that a returning Jesus Christ would lift his followers to Heaven (the Rapture) before Satan and the Antichrist would battle Christ for the remaining sinners. Lindsey took the founding of the state of Israel in 1948 as the beginning of the countdown to destruction.

Meanwhile, the aliens themselves were keeping quite busy. In the 1950s the UFO craze was largely confined to sightings of flying saucers and chance meetings with Venusians. In the 1960s, something changed. Twelve days after

ABC's *The Outer Limits* broadcast the first depiction of an alien with the now-famous wrap-around bug eyes, Betty and Barney Hill, a New Hampshire couple, claimed a similar creature kidnapped them and subjected them to medical tortures exactly like those in *Invaders from Mars*. They made these claims under hypnosis, in "regression therapy" that sought to retrieve suppressed memories, a technique since discredited. The same technique caused a nationwide Satanism scare in the 1980s when therapists unwittingly created in small children false memories of abuse at the hands of satanic cults that never existed. After the Hill case was turned into a 1975 NBC TV-movie, *The UFO Incident*, alien abduction reports multiplied considerably, all drawing on the same narrative the Hills and their therapists had unknowingly concocted out of the spare parts of movies and television shows.[22] The first major abduction after the Hills, that of Arizona logger Travis Watson, happened only days after the NBC movie aired. Hundreds more followed in the next ten years, and indeed continue to this day. In the 1980s men and women alike claimed that the aliens sexually abused them — including the famous "anal probes" — and some women claimed the aliens had made them artificially pregnant.

An interesting facet of alien abductions, and the ancient astronaut theory, was their obsession with projecting science onto the extraterrestrials. The ancient astronauts were presumed to be masters of genetic engineering, and the aliens of modern UFOs were thought to perform medical experiments on their helpless victims. In both cases, popular culture imagined godlike beings in control of science — medical and biological science — which they wanted to use and abuse on human beings.

Sex and the Single Scientist

It was not likely coincidental that the aliens of the 1970s and the 1980s were interested in biotechnology, while their earlier counterparts spent their time discussing nuclear weapons and world peace. The cutting edge of science had changed; nuclear power was no longer the wave of the future. The disasters at Three Mile Island in 1979 and Chernobyl in 1986 demonstrated the dangers of even civilian uses of nuclear power, and they spawned enormous fears that nuclear waste or a plant meltdown would contaminate large sections of the planet and produce dangerous cancers and other mutations. Space travel had also ceased to be cutting edge technology. After reaching the moon in 1969, NASA ended the lunar program in 1972. No one at the dawn of the space program would have predicted that after achieving the greatest technical feat in human history, America would reduce space exploration to a small orbiter that barely reached outer space, the space shuttle.

No, the science of mid-century had disappointed and failed to live up to its potential. Instead, the most active area of science occurred in the fields of

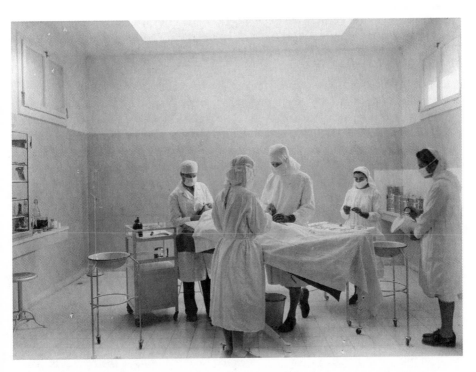

Operating room. Hospitals were temples of science and progress, but doctors' increasing ability to manipulate the human body provoked anxieties about the body that found their expression in horror. Organ transplants, plastic surgery, and reproductive technology all becam fodder for horror (Library of Congress, Prints and Photographs Division, LC-DIG-matpc-00583).

biotechnology and medicine. The first successful kidney transplant took place in 1953, and the first successful heart transplant occurred in December 1967. With the discovery in 1970 of a powerful immunosuppressant drug that could prevent rejection, organ transplants became viable, and doctors could now combine pieces of different individuals, much the way Victor Frankenstein had done with the dead. By the 1980s, most transplant recipients lived for several years after their surgeries. By the 1990s, it was not unheard of for one individual to receive an almost complete set of new organs. In 1982 Robert Jarvik developed the first artificial heart, raising the specter of cyborgs, humans that were part machine. Artificial hips, pacemakers, and other implants made cyborgs everyday occurrences.

Science had also provided new discoveries in the realm of sex and reproduction. The introduction of the birth control pill in the late 1950s had decoupled sex from reproduction, and this event is often cited as a contributing factor to the sexual revolution that swept the Western world in the 1960s. By 1965 the pill was America's most popular form of birth control.[23] Conservative lawmakers, the clergy, and especially the pope would condemn birth control as unnatural and an affront both to nature and to God, and it took years to overturn legislation banning birth control. Implicit in this was the idea that science had trespassed on territory to which it had no right. Science, in this view, had created a world of hedonism divorced from divine sanction.

In 1961 a sedative given to pregnant women, Thalidomide, was discovered to produce monstrous birth defects. Here was fuel for the opinion that science did not have all the answers and was in fact dangerous. Religious and political conservatives again complained that secularism, liberalism, and science were undermining nature and God when the United States Supreme Court ruled in 1973 that women had a constitutional right to abortion. In time, the debate over abortion would become a defining issue in American politics and a proxy for the confrontation between religious conservatives and secular liberals. It was the first step toward the politicization of science.

In 1978 scientists created the first "test tube baby" through in-vitro fertilization. The act of reproduction was now a medical process that could be wholly separate from the sex act. Advances in fertility treatments would soon allow the infertile to have children and for single parents to shop for anonymous sperm donors to father children they might never meet. By the turn of the millennium, parents could choose their children's genders, and some could select embryos pre-screened to avoid genetically inherited diseases, or more troublingly, to be born with the same medical conditions as their parents, like deafness, blindness, or dwarfism. In 1997 scientists created the first cloned animals, and many feared the technology would soon be applied to humans. Though many claimed to have done this—including a UFO–worshipping cult called the Raëlians—human cloning has not yet happened, though scientists warn it is only a matter of time. The U.S. government sought to ban cloning for any purpose, but European governments favored "therapeutic cloning" to cure disease.

In the 1980s and 1990s, medical technology made it possible to keep the dead alive almost indefinitely after their brains had ceased to think, and human life spans reached record levels. Cardiac defibrillators jump-started stalled hearts and made resurrection a common occurrence. Every day the dead awoke through electric shocks, just like the movie version of Frankenstein's Monster, and the number of people who were "technically" dead of heart attacks or cardiac arrest but lived again rose steadily. Plastic surgery allowed bodies to be reshaped, and limb and face transplants turned individuals into patchworks people. The unraveling of the human genetic code promised to reveal the secrets of evolution and was seen as one of the triumphs of modern science. Genetic technology also created "chimeras"—animals that combined traits from multiple species—and so-called "Frankenfoods" that changed the genetic makeup of plants ostensibly to make them more nutritious, but with unknown consequences for the future. Environmental activists worried that untested Frankenfoods would harm the environment and human beings.[24] There was some precedent for this: DDT and other pesticides were introduces as wonder chemicals to improve crop yields, but they destroyed the environment and brought some species to the brink of extinction. Rachel Carson's *Silent Spring* (1962) had exposed chemical companies' disinformation and disregard, and it was not inconceivable that the biotech companies were repeating their mistakes. Nature, Carson and later activists argued, should not be slave to unguided and unguarded scientific manipulation and control.

Beginning in the 1980s, epidemic diseases outstripped science's ability to combat them. Antibiotics and vaccines had been "wonder drugs" that many thought would end disease as we knew it. It seemed that way when small pox, a disease that claimed fifteen million lives a year, was eradicated in 1979. Polio, too, had been virtually eliminated. Then, in 1981 a new disease struck homosexuals in the United States and spread around the world. Eventually known as Acquired Immune Deficiency Syndrome, AIDS acted like a vampire: Transmitted by bodily fluids, it destroyed the body from within, and caused its victims to waste away before a raft of infections it could not fight. By 2000, AIDS was the single largest killer in much of sub–Saharan Africa and Southeast Asia. Some conservatives saw the disease as God's punishment for sexual transgressions. In Britain, mad cow disease destroyed the brains of those who had eaten beef three decades earlier, and flesh-eating bacteria inflicted grisly damage on their victims' bodies. Other antibiotic- and vaccine-resistant forms of diseases like staph infections and tuberculosis emerged.[25] Science, it seemed, could no longer provide answers.

17

LITERARY DEVELOPMENTS

The children who grew up in the 1950s and 1960s watching *House of Dracula* and its kin on their black-and-white televisions grew into the teenagers and young adults who debated the ancient astronaut theory and alien abductions. As they grew up, they demanded a horror literature that matched their expectations for ever-increasing explicitness and savagery. By and large, they found this at the movies rather than in literature, where visual gore could more effectively trigger the excitement and visceral fear that is the pleasure of experiencing horror. In response, literature became more cinematic, aping the movies' style, pacing, and tone. It is not too much of a stretch to posit that in this period, horror ceased to be a literary style or theme but instead became a genre, subject to the lowered expectations and restrictions implicit in the idea, even as horror continued its now-traditional role of reflecting darkly the negative consequences of science and new forms of knowledge. The overriding theme might best be expressed by Stephen King, who wrote in one novel of the terrible fear that "one's body might not be a friend at all but an enemy implacably dedicated to destroying the superior force that had used and abused it since the disease of reason set in."[1] A better epitaph for this period of horror could not be written.

It is undeniable, however, that literature of any stripe — let alone horror — had lost its position at the leading edge of culture and instead served its most important function as the source material for movies and television. In the 1970s and 1980s, surveys and studies found that reading for pleasure declined among children and adults, taking up as little as five percent of leisure time for children, seventy percent of whom rarely read for pleasure. Educators called the phenomenon "aliteracy," meaning that people knew how to read but chose not to.[2] Television was blamed for much of this, and research in the 1980s and 1990s tended to find a link between TV viewing and a loss of interest in the written word.[3] This only sought to reinforce the changes in novels and short stories that had turned them into treatments for future cinematic adaptations or substitutes for film when visual stimulation was unavailable. Horror stories therefore became increasingly graphic and explicit to appeal to movie audiences.

Blood and guts were described with an exactness once reserved for detailing character or setting. Plots and writing, too, tended to become more direct, more movie-like, and simpler. Stories also tended to refer to or reference earlier horror as self-aware shorthand, creating a postmodern meta-horror where an understanding of earlier works became necessary to fully appreciate new tales.

If there was a positive aspect for horror, it was this: More horror literature was produced in the 1980s and 1990s than in any period before, and the amount of horror literature grew almost exponentially through the 1990s and into the new millennium. There were just fewer readers to devour this cornucopia of horror. In 1971, none of the top twenty-four titles read by adolescents were horror; however, eleven of the top twenty-four were horror in 1994, mostly "teen horror" by authors like R. L. Stine, whose "brand" was the *Goosebumps* series.[4] The trouble was convincing these kids to keep reading as they reached adulthood, rather than retreat into movies, television, and video games.

Toward a New Horror

There were only a few ways to make horror explicit: obscene language, descriptions of extreme violence against the body, and sexual frankness. Not coincidentally, such coarseness matched the changing scientific and cultural views on the body and on sex in which the body was laid bare and raw. The new, more explicit horror could be seen clearly in Richard Matheson's *Hell House* (1971), which reproduced much of Shirley Jackson's *The Haunting of Hill House*, but retooled it for a different era, with different mores and different expectations, more firmly grounding the horror in the corporeal and the physical. The psychological ambiguities of the earlier story here give way to horrors based on body and flesh. In *Hell House*, as in *Hill House*, four people arrive at an abandoned mansion to investigate its alleged haunting. They are a scientist, here the physicist Dr. Lionel Barrett in place of the anthropologist Dr. Montague; a sexually voracious woman with psychic powers, here Florence Tanner in place of Theodora; the Eleanor role is filled by the scientist's wife Edith, a latent lesbian; and the role of the young man goes this time to another psychic who has a connection to the old house. Whereas Luke from *Hill House* was merely heir to the old place, Benjamin Fischer in *Hell House* is the only survivor of a previous expedition to Hell House.

They have come to the old Belasco mansion in the Christmas week of 1970 because a dying millionaire has asked Dr. Barrett to prove scientifically the existence of life after death so that he might die confident about where his eternal soul will reside. Barrett is to conduct scientific investigations, while the two mediums are to employ their spiritualist art to reach their conclusions. The millionaire sent them to the Belasco house because it is said to be the most haunted house in the world, possessed of the spirits of decadent Jazz Age ghosts whose debauchery and sexual excess corrupted them into evil, chief among them Emeric Belasco, the house's builder and leader of the debauchery. Belasco, it transpires, was a genius who studied deeply of the sciences and the dark arts, including the occult, and used his powers to mentally dominate his guests and turn them toward sensuality and destruction as part of his experiments and almost anthropological studies in evil. Under his auspices men and women became like animals, "a group of drug-addicted doctors started to experiment on animals and humans, testing pain thresholds, exchanging organs, creating monstrosities," and the "guests" killed and ate one another as they reveled in freedom and joy.[5] The house has been shut up now for thirty years, and a previous expedition — the one Fischer attended as a child — ended in insanity and death.

Dr. Barrett is a skeptic about spiritualism, but he has a scientific theory about energy that he believes can explain so-called "super-normal" events, reasoning logically that even if spiritualist manifestations are real they do not prove the existence of ghosts but may instead represent unconscious human powers; "This is the alternative I offer: *the extended faculties of the human system not as yet established.* The faculties by which, I am convinced, all psychic phenomena are produced."[6] This he intends to prove with electronic equipment at the Belasco house, a house that has a swamp in the front yard called "Bastard Bog" because it was there that Belasco disposed of his guests' unwanted pregnancies. The interior is done up in antique Gothic style, broken only by a few incursions of Jazz Age furniture. Like the library in Hill House, Belasco's chapel is contaminated by an atmosphere that repulses the psychics, perhaps due to the crucifix sporting an enormous erection. Unlike Hill House, Belasco's home reflects a strong personality — his — and an old recording of his voice instructs his "guests" that in his house Aleister Crowley's law prevails, for guests shall do as they will.

Florence, who becomes the focus of the house's attentions, come to feel that she can sense the presence of personalities in the house, not just that of Emeric Belasco but that of his sad and vulnerable son, Daniel, and she begins to manifest ectoplasm and other physical symptoms during her psychic trances, something unprecedented for a "mental" medium. The spirit of Daniel appears to take a sexual interest in Florence, which escalates from caresses to her eventual rape by the spirit at the hands of the ghost and murder via the obscene chapel crucifix. Other manifestations occur, with escalating violence, and one by one the occupants of Hell House are tempted, cajoled, or assaulted into various sundry fates, usually sexual in nature and resulting in profound physical and mental injuries. Dr. Barrett blames these occurrences on the unconscious minds of the psychics, convinced that material explanations underpin each telekinetic attack, while the psychics believe Belasco's shade is controlling a number of ghosts who commit the assaults.

Dr. Barrett's ideas take a hit when Florence uncovers what she believes is Daniel's corpse, still wearing the ring he had in her visions. He cautions her not to assume that this discovery will make him reconsider his deeply held "scientific convictions of a lifetime": "That I cannot see; and never will."[7] He has become obsessed with proving his theory that psychic phenomena are extensions of biology via electromagnetic radiation emitted from the body. His great invention, the Reversor, a gigantic machine that uses electricity to cleanse a space of the electromagnetic radiation, will in theory end the house's psychic terrors and help propel parapsychology to "its rightful place beside the other natural sciences," too often overlooked by unscientific practitioners of what goes by the name of science.[8]

The Reversor appears to do its job, and Hell House's evil energy dissipates. But at the moment of Dr. Barrett's triumph, the spirit of Hell House possesses the Reversor, and it — and Barrett's dreams of science triumphant — explode in his face, killing him when he thinks he is completely wrong and his theories destroyed. Fischer and Edith discover the truth, that the entities in the house were in fact but one — Emeric Belasco himself, who survived death to continue his experiments in evil. However, though Dr. Barrett's theories were wrong, and personality does survive death, the Reversor did its job, and Belasco's power fades away. They find his corpse behind the chapel's altar, where he went to die, encasing the room in lead, apparently aware in his scientific and occult knowledge about the electromagnetic basis of ghosts. Dissipated, Belasco and Hell House are finally dead.

The carnality of *Hell House* masks the conflict between science and (spiritualist) faith the book describes. As in *I Am Legend*, Matheson seems to argue that the faith-based world of the mediums' beliefs must bow before science, and in the end even the most horrible of supernatural nightmares is reducible to natural law. Symbolically, therefore, we are meant to understand that no area of human endeavor is entirely free from scientific probing, even if we do not yet understand why or how it will occur. In dispensing with the psychological ambiguity of *The Haunting of Hill House*, Matheson has created a different relationship between knowledge and horror, one where the horror resides only in our imperfect mastery of science rather than in our imperfect understandings of our own souls. Though the characters on *Hell House* are as flawed as those in *Hill House*, their inner demons make them vulnerable only when external forces operate and science fails them. In its way *Hell House* is more frightening than *The Haunting of Hill House*, but it is the horror of the body rather than the terror of the soul that governs this book.

Children of Horror

Anxieties surrounding reproduction, contraception, abortion, and Thalidomide found their expression in a number of horror novels that explicitly dealt with these topics with only a thin layer of supernaturalism overspreading the reproductive horror. Ira Levin's *Rosemary's Baby* (1967) turned pregnancy into its own horror story. The novel tells of Rosemary Woodhouse, a housewife who is married to Guy, an unsuccessful actor. She is a lapsed Catholic, from a large Irish family in Omaha, though they no longer speak to her because

Gothic townhouse. *Rosemary's Baby* continued horror's tradition of locating horror's nightmares within Victorian mansions, the lineal descendants of the Gothic castle. Like the ornate façade of the Vanderbilts' Manhattan mansion (above), *Rosemary's Baby*'s Branford was Gothic in its architecture, both old and ornate, which was an aesthetic affront to twentieth century modernism (Library of Congress, Prints and Photographs Division, LC-USZ62-55956).

her husband is a Protestant. Together they take an apartment in the Bramford, a massive old pile of an apartment house, fitted out in ornate and outdated Victorian detail. The Victorians, as pre-moderns, are taken to symbolize the atavistic evil of the past. The Bramford is notorious for its shady past — cannibals and witches formed its Victorian tenancy, and an abandoned baby was found dead in the basement as recently as 1959. An unusual number of suicides plagued the building. An older, educated British writer, Hutch, serves as the novel's Van Helsing character, warning Rosemary about these problems and telling her to be careful.

Rosemary ignores his advice and settles in to the old apartment, but the stories bother her, mentally: "To know the spot where the baby had lain, to have perhaps to walk past it on the way to the laundry room and again on the way back to the elevator, would have been unbearable. Partial ignorance, she decided, was partial bliss."[9] Rosemary befriends another young woman in the building, who soon dies under circumstances the old couple she lived with called suicide. Over time Rosemary and Guy befriend this pair, Minnie and Roman Castavet, who take an unusual interest in the young couple. Shortly thereafter Guy decides he is willing to have a baby with Rosemary. One drunken night Rosemary becomes pregnant, but her only memories of the event are a strange dream that a creature like the Devil or Pan had violently raped her while Guy and the Castavets watched. As her pregnancy progresses, Rosemary becomes sickly and loses weight. Her doctor tells her this is normal, and Minnie Castavet feeds her strange herbal remedies on the advice of the doctor. Hutch is concerned, but he is murdered before he can tell Rosemary what he has learned from an old book, *All of Them Witches*, which he wills to her.

Meanwhile, Guy's career has taken off, and it looks as though the Woodhouses are heading toward prosperity at last. Rosemary feels some relief when she starts gaining weight. Only slowly does she put the pieces together. Roman and Minnie are Satanists, living under false names; Rosemary's doctor is in league with them, and her husband has made a deal with the Devil, surrendering his wife's body to Satan in exchange for material prosperity. When the baby is finally born, Rosemary is told that it died. She figures out the truth and breaks into the Castavets' apartment, where the child is worshipped as the Antichrist. Rosemary knows that she should kill the child and save the world, but her maternal instincts get the better of her and she joins the Satanists to raise the boy, imagining she can influence his future for the good.

Rosemary's Baby launched a cycle of "demon child" books and films that lasted for more than a decade after the book's release. The most notable of its successors in print was *The Exorcist* (1971), William Peter Blatty's novel of a little girl possessed by a demon and the fight to remove the satanic burden from her innocent soul. Blatty's career began as a humor novelist and comedy screenwriter, but when work ran short he turned to horror. He based *The Exorcist* on a supposedly true demonic possession of a teenaged boy in 1949, changing the age and gender to find a more sympathetic victim. The book begins with Father Merrin, who is a paleontologist and Jesuit priest. He finds a small statue of an Assyrian god in the sands of Iraq, and he feels the evil emanating from it, instinctively understanding that something bad had begun anew.

In another an old rental property — not unlike *Rosemary's Baby*'s Bramford, but colonial and in Georgetown — another performer, the atheist actress Chris MacNeil, finds her adorable eight-year-old daughter Regan is starting to act different. She has begun communicating with an invisible friend, Captain Howdy, via a Ouija board; she claims her bed shakes in the night and furniture moves on its own; and she has become inexplicably temperamental, with angry fits, and a refusal to eat. Chris has a medical doctor examine her, but the tests are inconclusive. Ritalin does no good. During a party, Regan leaves her bed to urinate in front of the guests and predict one guest's imminent death.

Further tests, the best science have to offer, fail to solve the case. During one appointment, Regan begins to shout wildly: "She pulled up her nightgown, exposing her genitals. '*Fuck* me! *Fuck* me!' she screamed at the doctors, and with both her hands began masturbating frantically."[10] Neurologists and psychiatrists are puzzled; and all the while, the symptoms keep growing worse. It becomes clear that Regan thinks she is possessed by a demon. One of the doctors suggests that Regan might benefit from a religious exorcism, not because demonic possession is real but because Regan thinks it is. When Chris finds Regan shouting obscenities and masturbating with a crucifix, her head spinning beyond the natural range of the neck, she decides to seek out a priest. It is interesting to note that the signs of possession — obscenities, violence, and sexual awareness — are all accepted adult behaviors. The horror comes when a child displays precocious knowledge of adulthood years before her time.

Meanwhile, another priest, Father Damien Karras, who is also a psychiatrist, is struggling with his faith. He finds God lacking amidst the evidence of his indifference to the world: murder, decay, Thalidomide babies, and doubt itself. Materialism simply had more evidence behind it, since God seemed to stay silent. When Chris comes to him for help, he is skeptical; but moved by her exasperation, he agrees to investigate her daughter's case. He wants to ascribe Regan's behavior to material causes, a psychiatric condition. She has the traits of possession, "*but the problem is how do you* interpret *the phenomena?*"[11] After going through all the evidence, Father Karras and Father Merrin perform an exorcism on the girl, Karras believing the ritual might do good even if the possession is only in her mind. The duration of the novel is concerned with Karras's battle between faith and doubt as the exorcism gradually convinces him that evil is real. If the Devil is real, then God must be, too. As Merrin says of possession:

> I think the point is to make us despair; to reject our own humanity, Damien: to see ourselves as ultimately bestial; as ultimately vile and putrescent; without dignity; ugly; unworthy. And there lies the heart of it, perhaps: in unworthiness. For I

think belief in God is not a matter of reason at all; I think it is finally a matter of love; of accepting the possibility that God could love *us*....[12]

After the demon kills Merrin, Karras comes to accept God's love. He gives himself to the demon so it will leave Regan, and in the final act of sacrifice kills himself with his remaining will to end the demon's reign. Karras overcame the limitations of science and reason to accept the supernatural, and died a hero's death.

The Exorcist differed from its predecessors in its relationship to science. Older works like *Dracula, Frankenstein,* and *Psycho* had all located their horrors within the matrix of science, and so supported at some level positivist and scientific world-views. Whether the horror was supernatural, psychological, or the result of overreaching science, science itself could be brought in to explain and understand what happened. Even *Dracula,* one of the most purely supernatural tales, makes use of a scientist, Van Helsing, to incorporate the newly confirmed supernatural menace into the world-view of science. *The Exorcist* does not. Father Merrin is pointedly an archaeologist — a scientist — but he and Father Karras, as priests, understand that there are supernatural events that defy science, stand outside its ability to analyze and assimilate, and ultimately form an alternative way of knowing and of comprehending the world. In returning to the idea that religious horrors are fundamentally *outside* of and *opposed* to scientific scrutiny, *The Exorcist* marks itself as the first great postmodern horror story.

As a sign of its influence, and its appeal to a religiously inclined, postmodern America, in the wake of the book and the movie version, Americans flocked in record numbers to seek exorcisms for themselves and loved ones.[13] Pentecostal churches made a special show of "deliverance ministries" that provided a Protestant version of the Catholic rite of exorcism for the thousands they saw as spiritually possessed.

Kingdom Come: The Stephen King Brand

The saga of the demon child continued past puberty with *Carrie* (1974), a novel about a telekinetic teenager, by the up-and-coming horror writer Stephen King (b. 1947). Every exploration of the horror genre must sooner or later deal with King, a one-time English teacher whose work is horror's most popular and most read. King's horror, as many have noted, is written by a horror fan (King was a reader of EC's horror comics at an early age) for other horror fans, whose primary exposure to the genre was from film. As a result it has a certain derivative or familiar quality that both propelled it to mainstream success but somewhat weakened its literary effectiveness.

Framed by a series of transcripts, articles, and book excerpts, *Carrie* told of a teenager, Carrie White, who is abused by her mother and her classmates.

In an infamous scene, when she has her first period during a gym class shower, the girls humiliate her. With the onset of puberty, Carrie discovers her teleki-netic powers— described in the novel as a recessive genetic condition confirmed by science — along with some telepathy. Her mother considers this witchcraft, and she finds Carrie's budding sexuality sinful, forbidding her from attending the prom. When Carrie goes anyway, her classmates humiliate her again by drenching her in pig blood. Incensed, the girl uses her powers to burn down her high school, killing everyone inside, and then destroys much of her home town. Carrie returns home, where her mother tries to kill her to keep her from Satan's clutches; mortally wounded, Carrie kills her, too, with telekinesis before succumbing herself.

Though the hardcover sold just thirteen thousand copies, paperback sales topped one million in the first year. *Carrie* was even banned in some school districts for obscenity. King followed up *Carrie* with *'Salem's Lot* (1975), a novel he described concisely as "vampires overrunning a small Maine town." It repeated the pattern of modest hardcover sales but extraordinary paperback sales, reaching number one on the *New York Times* best-seller list. Stephen King was now a brand name, identified with horror in a way no previous author — certainly none with such sales figures— had been before. Movie versions of the two books, *Carrie* (1976) on the big screen and *'Salem's Lot* (1979) on televi-sion, drove more readers to King. Horror, it seemed, had gone mainstream.

King had written a short story called "Jerusalem's Lot" (1978) that served as an homage to all things H. P. Lovecraft — ancient evils, scholarly protago-nists, steadfast skeptics in the face of otherworldly powers, etc. The title town reappears, in abbreviation, as 'salem's Lot, a town in Maine to which novelist Ben Mears returns after many years to write a book about the Marsten House, a dilapidated, gabled old pile perched high above the town. It is introduced with Shirley Jackson's description of Hill House and, like its predecessor, the Marsten House is possessed of great secrets of ancient sins. Ben thinks it is cursed by Hubert Marsten, an evil man who murdered and killed in the name of an unknown evil, and continues to radiate his unclean madness, like a "supernat-ural beacon":

> I think it's relatively easy for people to accept something like telepathy, or precog-nition, or teleplasm because their willingness to believe doesn't cost them any-thing. It doesn't keep them awake nights. But the idea that the evil that men do lives after them is more unsettling.[14]

It seems the old place was finally sold to a Mr. Straker and a Mr. Barlow, antique dealers from Europe. Though the town is unaware of it, Barlow is a vampire, and he slowly turns the residents of Jerusalem's Lot into the undead in a series of scenes involving dozens of townspeople, a King trademark. Mark Petrie, a young boy, is a fan of Universal's horror monsters and builds Aurora models of Frankenstein's Monster, Dracula, Mr. Hyde, and the Mad Scientist, happy that the Frankenstein's Monster model glows green "just like the plastic

Jesus" he got at church.[15] Both, after all, had risen from the dead, as did vampires. When his dead friend Danny rises and hovers outside Mark's window, he is prepared, knowing the traits of vampires and how to oppose them, using a little cross from his monster model kits to ward off the fiend. Horror movies are good for something after all, transmitting occult knowledge across the years; a knowledge adults can't fathom after the "ossification of the imaginary faculties" that turns dreamy kids in to dull, conformist adults.[16]

Ben slowly wakes to the realization that the town is under assault by vampires, but not before making heroic efforts to dismiss the creatures as the products of madness, of disease, or of some unknown medical condition. This becomes impossible when confronted with evidence in the form of corpses that rise again. Materialism, of course, can no longer play a role here, and there are obviously horrors that stand outside a fragile and ineffective science's ability to explain them. Soon enough, Jerusalem's Lot is a virtual ghost town, inhabited by the undead alone. The survivors, Ben and Mark, a drunk Catholic priest named Callahan, and a few others, track the evil back to its source: Barlow in the old Marsten House. In the face of the vampire, Callahan's faith falters, leaving him open to Barlow, who corrupts him. God may not be present, but evil was. Ben and Mark confront Barlow in his grave, and they kill him in something of an anticlimax. Later, they set fire to the Marsten House, and presumably the dead town, though the completeness of their victory over the remaining vampires is left ambiguous.

The book is grounded in the (often boring) details of daily life, and earthy in a crudely quotidian way. More significantly, *'Salem's Lot* was a postmodern horror story. Traditional to the point of virtually replicating much of *Dracula*, *'Salem's Lot* is nevertheless meta-textual, existing in a world of interlocking references. Unlike *I Am Legend*, King's book could not stand alone. Without *Dracula*, a book it explicitly references (as did *Legend*) and with which the characters are conversant, it does not exist. Without the audience's presumed foreknowledge of vampires and their traits, culled from Hollywood films, it makes no sense. Because the audience already knows the horrors, there is no intellectual engagement about the unknown, as the science fiction writer Fritz Leiber said in complaining about modern horror's explicitness and lack of rigor.[17] There were no real explanations—no attempt to probe the nature of the supernatural, the nature of the horror, as Lovecraft or Poe had done. It was all effects without *cause*. The horror is simply a given, a realm outside of science and knowledge — irrational.

This was true of much of King's fiction. His third novel, *The Shining* (1977), drew heavily on *The Haunting of Hill House* to craft an unhealthy hotel housing spirits that drive its inhabitants to the brink of madness, exploiting weaknesses in their personalities, just as Hill House had done for poor Eleanor. (He'd be even more explicit about this in the 2002 TV miniseries *Rose Red*, which was closer to *Hill House* than even *Hell House* had been.) *The Shining* told the story of Jack Torrance, his wife, and their son, Danny. They are spending the winter snowed in at the Overlook Hotel, where Jack has taken a job as the caretaker during the months when the place is abandoned. Though a beautiful old Victorian pile (aren't all haunted houses?), the Overlook has a shady past, full of death, violence, and shadowy connections to the Mafia. This fascinates Jack, a would-be playwright and recovering alcoholic, who intends to write a book about the place during the long months in the cold. His son is telepathic, a gift called "the shine" or "the shining," and he senses immediately that all is not well. He sees rather graphic ghosts in the Overlook's rooms, and Jack begins manifesting the signs of alcoholic rage, even in the absence of alcohol, degenerating into the abusive drunk his father once was. Jack's mind deteriorates as the winter drags on, and he threatens and attacks his family. Eventually the evil force that dwells in the Overlook possesses him completely. But before he can finish off his wife and son, Jack forgets the one duty he needed to undertake above all others— to tend to the hotel's aging boiler. Left alone, the boiler overheats, the hotel burns to the ground, and the entity inside — the one wearing Jack's mangled corpse as a suit, the "single group intelligence"—"losing thought and will," died with the home that was the monster itself.[18]

And so it went on, novel after novel, story after story. In thirty years, King had written more than three dozen novels and nearly seven dozen short stories and novellas. Most of his novels became best-sellers, many also movies. Their titles are so familiar, so much a part of popular culture that no explanation is needed: *Pet Sematary*, *It*, *Christine*, *The Stand*, *Misery*, and so on, and so on. His books were sold in every bookstore, gas station, and supermarket check-out aisle, millions upon millions of copies, the best-read author of the late twentieth century. In the 1980s, Ben P. Indick summed up King's appeal best: "King has put [fear] into the shopping basket, next to the tomato sauce, the Sanka and the Tab. Fear has become a commonplace, no longer the evil dispensation of noble or supernatural villains. No one can be trusted...."[19] It is testament to King's talents that he outlasted Sanka and Tab. However, I think the author Don Herron appraised King most insightfully when he argued that King popularized horror but did not contribute to the genre's development, reworking but not expanding on earlier horror themes. However, Herron said, he did add vulgarity, excrement, and obscenities, so that was something.[20]

King has also written frequently in the related genres of dark fantasy (the *Dark Tower* series, for example) and science fiction (*The Stand*, *The Langoliers*), always with heavy doses of darkness. In *The Tommyknockers* (1987), King makes use of the ancient astronaut theory, imagining the discovery of a flying saucer (millions of years old) buried under a small town in Maine. As in *'Salem's Lot*, the gradual uncovering of the ancient evil leads the whole town to destruction through carefully staged scenes involving the townsfolk individually and in groups. The ship was uncovered by Bobbie, a novelist, who explains to her philosopher friend Gard that even though the spacecraft is somehow changing

Early twentieth century hotel. Stephen King's Overlook Hotel shares many architectural details with this hotel, built in Panama at the same time as the Overlook's fictional construction. As many have noted, *The Shining*'s hotel is nothing more than a haunted house blown up to a colossal scale, returning it in some respects to the dimensions and the functions of the Gothic castle of two centuries past (Library of Congress, LC-USZ62-121900).

the townsfolk into amoral copies of the aliens, possessed of only one will and one intelligence, uncovering the ship was never a question:

> Man, the idea that whether or not to dig something like that up could ever *be* a function of free will ... you might be able to stick that to a kid in a high-school debate, but we out on de po'ch, Gard. You don't really think a person *chooses* something like that, do you? Do you think people can choose to put away *any* knowledge once they've seen the edge of it?[21]

And so they follow the knowledge to the inevitable edge of the abyss, saved at the last minute by a forest fire that clears the town of its alien occupants and Gard's efforts to fly the evil ship out into space and away from the Earth. As we've seen, King tended to favor explosive, cinematic endings where flames strike the sets and smoke draws a curtain over the performance and cuts short the darker implications of his horrors. What would it be like to pursue knowledge to the point of destruction? What would it feel like to lose one's humanity to an alien consciousness? We'll never know. Humanity, in King's works, almost inevitably triumphs over what they perceive is evil, often without a detailed grappling with the nature of the evil, or of the knowledge they've gained.

After being struck by a van in 1999, King decided to cut back on his writing, and in 2002 announced his retirement. However, he continued writing new books anyway, including the first horror novel by a major author to be released electronically, *Riding the Bullet* (2000), about a young man who gets a ride from a dead man. When Amazon.com made it available for free download, its servers crashed from the demand.

Cthulhu Rises Again: The Lovecraft Brand

Stephen King claims H. P. Lovecraft as an influence, and his short story "Crouch End" (1980) found tourists in London encountering an alien from Lovecraft's mythos. However, typical of postmodern horror, the story's characters are themselves familiar with Lovecraft, undercutting the verisimilitude of the best Cthulhu Mythos fiction. By the time King wrote "Crouch End," and the earlier Lovecraftian "Jerusalem's Lot," the Cthulhu Mythos was making a triumphant resurrection, like that of Cthulhu when the stars were right. During the 1950s, Lovecraft's popularity was at low ebb, kept alive mainly among horror aficionados and August Derleth's Christianized pastiches and derivations. But beginning in the 1960s and '70s a new generation of horror writers began to use Lovecraftian trappings in their stories, finding in the Cthulhu Mythos a set of symbols for horrors that advances in science and knowledge had only made more potent with the passing of time. The revival came, in part, thanks to Hollywood's discovery of Lovecraft in the mid–1960s and exceptional sales for paperback reissues of Lovecraft in the 1970s.

Writers like Ramsey Campbell, Brian Lumley, Lin Carter, Stuart David Schiff, Edward P. Berglund, and others produced notable works of Lovecraftian horror in the 1960s and '70s, and with each passing year more Cthulhu-oriented fiction entered the horror market, both in specialty publications like *The Arkham Collector* or *Crypt of Cthulhu* devoted to Lovecraft, and in more mainstream venues like *Alfred Hitchcock's Mystery Magazine*. The turning point probably came when L. Sprague de Camp released *H. P. Lovecraft: A Biography* (1976), which was the first from a major American publisher (Doubleday; Ballantine for the paperback) to seriously explore Lovecraft's life, though from a Freudian perspective, and introduced the writer to many who had never heard of him before. Critics followed suit, and a number of critical studies appeared.

Karl Edward Wagner's "Sticks" (1974) was one of the best of the new breed of Mythos horrors, telling of an illustrator of horror stories who finds little, intricate lattice bundles of sticks decorating a ruined house, made by an unknown hand. He submits these designs as illustrations for a story, unaware until the end that they are occult symbols that will return the Old Ones to earth. It was a postmodern story, as most of the new breed were, purposely referencing *Weird Tales* and other horror works as part of the story's universe. Wagner, a disillusioned psychiatrist, made such meta-textual references a recurring part of his horror fiction. T. E. D. Klein's "Events at Poroth Farm" (1972) finds a college professor reading horror for an upcoming course, only to find himself in the center of real supernatural events. Klein's "Black Man with a Horn" (1980), another gem of the genre, told of an old man who becomes intrigued by a museum specimen, a cloth depicting what seems to be a black man blowing a horn. The more he learns about what it *really* shows, the more he realizes the cosmic horror unfolding around him. The story is, however, postmodern: The characters reference H. P. Lovecraft and Robert W. Chambers, and the narrative itself "degenerates into an unsifted collection of items which may or may not be related," as it admits.[22] Klein's few other forays into horror fiction were similarly powerful. Gahan Wilson's "H. P. L." (1990) takes Lovecraft himself for a character, imagining and alternate history where he does not die in 1937, but lives on as one of the few to know the truth about the Old Ones.

The quality of these stories was high, though many Lovecraftian tales were not so good; but they all shared a trait: They worked best when the reader already knew the Lovecraftian background material and was familiar with Cthulhu and his ilk. In the 1980s and 1990s, Cthulhu-themed fiction became one of horror's staples, rivaling vampires as a subject in the sheer volume of stories and novels produced. By the turn of the twenty-first century, dedicated publishers like Necronomicon Press and Chaosium were churning out Mythos-related fiction at a steady clip, and mainstream horror publishers followed suit. Titles like *The Nyarlathotep Cycle* (1997) collected fiction related to just one of Lovecraft's entities, while the anthologies *Shadows over Baker Street* (2003) and *Hardboiled Cthulhu* (2007) placed Lovecraftian creatures into other genres, in this case Sherlock Holmes and 1930s gangster fiction, respectively. It was horror as both mash-up and pastiche. In general, the more focused a story was on the superficial aspects of Lovecraftian fiction, the less successful it was. But it was what the fans wanted.

In the Mythos vein, the writer Brian Lumley produced a series of novels from 1975 to 1989 featuring a character called Titus Crow, who differed from Lovecraft's overawed protagonists in that Crow actively fought against the Old Ones and their minions, engaging in violent and explicit confrontations. Lumley followed Derleth's, rather than Lovecraft's, version of the Mythos, however, referring to the alien monsters by the fan-boy moniker "Cthulhu Cycle Deities," abbreviated "CCD" in some tales. A later series of novels, *Necroscope* and its successors, between 1986 and today dealt with more traditional horrors, including communication with the dead via a biologically based telepathy, and vampires, which Lumley imagined as leech-like creatures from an alternative universe that invade the host's body and confer immortality.

It would be impossible to select just one of Ramsey Campbell's almost uniformly excellent tales to stand for his entire body of work — which, like Stephen King's, is best considered as a body — comprising more than two dozen novels, more than a dozen collections of short fiction, and uncollected stories. His early work, like "Cold Print" (1969), was heavily influenced by Lovecraft, though his later tales take on a distinctive tone and color that mark them as Campbell's own. He continues to write in the Cthulhu vein from time to time, but in later years he produced a remarkable amount of horror fiction that ranged from psychological to supernatural horror, often in the distinctive quiet tone of the British writers of the early twentieth century, but with a modern touch. In *The Nameless* (1981), Campbell describes a cult whose members surrender their names, symbolically surrendering their individuality and their humanity, their ability to make decisions. *The Face That Must Die* (1979, revised 1983) explored the inner life of a serial killer from the killer's point of view. The novel is closely grounded in daily life, drawing details from the underbelly of decay in the urban world of 1970s England. Horridge, the killer, is insane and unaware of his actions, and his strained efforts to apply logic and reason to his circumstances create a sort of paranoid, surreal madness of their own. The story revolves around Horridge's efforts to flush out the killer of gay men in the area, with the expected results. *Midnight Sun* (1990) told of a children's book author who returns to his ancestral home only to surrender his reason and his humanity to an ancient snow monster which uses him to obtain human victims in its quest to overrun the earth. The author falls for the creature's promise of immortality and, like Jack Torrance in *The Shining*, his mind deteriorates as the forces around him (a haunted woods rather than hotel, but snowy all the same) push on to their horrific conclusion.

The Loved Dead: Brand Anne Rice

We have seen that the works of Stephen King tended to assume the quotidian nature of supernatural horror. Anne Rice's *Interview with the Vampire* (1976) continued the trend toward normalizing the supernatural and dealing directly with the biological and psychological implications of horror creatures. While Dracula may have been a blood-sucking immortal, he was never as introspective as Louis, the "hero" of *Interview*. Louis spends the novel telling his life story to an enraptured young man with a tape recorder. Louis was once a human, a twenty-five-year-old man in the New Orleans of 1791, when he was attacked by a vampire and turned into a creature of the night. The change was indescribable, but in Louis's mind clearly related to sex, as shown by his pregnant metaphor: "I can tell you about it, enclose it with words that will make the value of it to me evident to you. But I can't tell you exactly, any more than I could tell you exactly what is the experience of sex if you have never had it."[23]

Louis's attacker is the vampire Lestat, who wished to possess Louis's plantation. As their relationship develops there is obvious homoeroticism, and the linkage between vampirism and sex is made explicit when Louis and Lestat feed on prostitutes they were in the process of copulating with. Unlike the literary Dracula, but much like his filmed counterpart, the vampires are eternally youthful, smooth of skin, and snappy dressers. They are cultured and elegant and possessed of a full slate of human emotions, though over time these drain away as the tolls of immortality grind against them.

Louis spends the better part of the novel contemplating the philosophical implications of vampirism, the great boredom of immortality, the sadness at watching the familiar world pass away around him, the psychic pain of living an eternal life in an unchanging body. After a ten-year-old girl is turned into a vampire and appears to kill Lestat out of hatred for what he did to her, the girl and Louis depart for Paris where they discover vampires playing out a Victor-Victoria scenario in a theater where they pretend to be humans playing vampires. Adventures ensue, and Louis ends up destroying the theater of vampires when they attempt to kill him for violating the vampiric code. However, the leader of the theater formed another homoerotic bond with Louis, and together they return to the New Orleans of the present where Lestat still unlives, weak but longing for Louis, whom he has not forgotten.

The summation of the novel is a meditation on the nature of good and evil and the biological impulses that compel humans and vampires to act against the moral codes they know to be right but which nature in its myriad forms forces each creature to act against:

> I wanted love and goodness in this which is living death.... It was impossible from the beginning because you cannot have love and goodness when you do what you know to be evil, what you know to be wrong. You can only have the desperate confusion and longing and chasing of phantom goodness in its human form. I was damned in my own mind and soul. [There was a] degree of coldness I would have to attain to end my pain. And I accepted that.[24]

To survive in the Darwinian world, everything human had to die. Only the animal self could carry on and live against the degradations of a pathological society and a seditious biology. The body itself turned on its master, becoming an instrument by which the soul is corrupted and destroyed.

Rice continued Lestat's story in a number of sequels, together comprising *The Vampire Chronicles*, all exploring the psychosexual aspects of the human personality through the prism of vampirism. She wrote additional horror novels about vampires, witches, and mummies, turning in 2005 to another supernatural being who rose from the dead, Jesus, as the subject for a non-horror series.

Short Cuts

But we should not overlook developments in the field of short fiction in the 1970s and 1980s. After all, it is often noted that horror is primarily a genre expressed in short fiction, rather than in novels, even if it is the novels that are best remembered. The number of horror magazines, horror anthologies, and other venues for short horror fiction exploded during this time, before a culling period reduced them to more manageable levels in the first half of the 1990s. *Weird Tales* was revived, and every publication from the highbrow *New Yorker* to the middle range *Playboy* to semi-professional horror fanzines published scary stories — so many that it is impossible to list them all, let alone take them together. It is probably not an exaggeration to suggest that the annual output of short horror stories numbered in the thousands, with a total in this period of perhaps more than one hundred thousand stories, depending on where one draws the lines of what counts as horror and what venues count as publication.

A few were brilliant, more were clever, many were acceptably entertaining, and the majority of them were schlock or derivative pastiches. Notable in the period is Dennis Etchinson's "The Dead Line" (1979), a story often said to have the most frightening opening paragraph in all horror literature: "This morning I put ground glass in my wife's eyes. She didn't mind. She didn't make a sound. She never does."[25] The man's brain-dead wife is being kept artificially alive in a hospital for the medical community to use for blood transfusions, antibody production, organ transplants, "in the name of science ... in the name of their beloved research," until there is nothing left, not even skin and bone.[26] He tries to ruin her body to save her from that fate, a fate that in real life has come to pass under the names of "life support" and "organ donation." Beverly Evans's "In the Land of the Giving" (1981) told a similar story from the victims' perspective, brainwashed into imagining their limb and organ donations — their own bodily mutilation — is an altruistic act. They remain conscious through the years-long process of removal and amputation, all the while experiencing the joy of giving.

Harlan Ellison fictionalized the Kitty Genovese murder to explore the dark underbelly of urban life in "The Whimper of Whipped Dogs" (1973), where he compared New York City to an insane asylum and acts of violence to a black mass at which the city's residents paid homage to the dark gods of their little lives.

David Morrell, best known for writing *First Blood*, the book that inspired the *Rambo* movie series, wrote "Black Evening" (1981), a gruesome tale that bears some resemblance to "A Rose for Emily," but with a bloodier, more explicit development. Investigators think old Agnes has been abducting children, but realize too late that she was protecting her husband Andrew, who everyone thought was gone but had really gone insane decades earlier. In their crumbling mansion, he uses the kidnapped girls as living dolls, until he breaks them. Alan Rodger's "The Boy Who Came Back from the Dead" (1987) tells of an eight-year-old boy who rose from his grave a year after burial. Family life continues as though it were never interrupted, the only hitch being that no one would believe his resurrection. Told from Walt's perspective, it seems that aliens came and woke him from his grave and they want him back. School kids make fun of him, and Walt's mother beats him and tries to send him away with the aliens.

A wave of vampire-themed stories in the late 1980s and early 1990s, like Peter M. Spizzirri's "Angels, Strange Angels" (1995), found the undead either fearing the AIDS virus or serving as a symbol for its transmission.

Horror Thrillers

Michael Crichton brought horror themes into the realm of the thriller, combining science, horror, and action into potboiler novels that were best-sellers and frequently turned into movies. *The Andromeda Strain* (1969) related the tale of an extraterrestrial disease that caused fatal blood clotting, killing a town. The scientists sent to investigate are powerless to stop it, and the disease abates only when it spontaneously mutates into a benign form. The ending of the novel implies that *something* from outside sent the disease to Earth as a warning against space exploration. *Eaters of the Dead* (1976), which playfully lists the *Necronomicon* in its bibliography, related the narrative of a medieval Arab ambassador who falls in with a band of Vikings and uncovers a surviving colony of Neanderthals somewhere in Russia. The novel uses the framework of an editor-scientist examining the manuscript to provide pseudo-scientific footnotes and analyses to lend spurious credibility to the text. *Congo* (1980) told the story of a scientific expedition to the lost city of Zinj, located in the rain forests of central Africa. There the expedition hoped to uncover Zinj's vast diamond mines and to examine a new species of ape, which they think may have been a hybrid of gorilla and human or chimpanzee. They bring along Amy, a gorilla who learned sign language. In scenes reminiscent of *At the Mountains of Madness*, bas reliefs in an abandoned temple tell of how the people of Zinj trained the strange white gorillas to guard their diamond mines with single-minded ferocity. But the Zinjians are gone now, centuries dead. Instead the true horror of the situation becomes evident when the scientists realize a strange truth: The temple was actually a deadly school.

"Who teaches them now?"
"They do," Elliot said. "They teach each other."[27]

The apes were as bright as humans, and even more deadly. The border between man and beast, written in DNA, had been breached: "[W]ith modern DNA hybridization techniques and embryonic implantation, ape-ape crosses were certain, and man-ape crosses were possible."[28] The Zinjians had somehow done this in the remote past, whether by technology or a fortuitous mutation it was impossible to say. In the way of lost cities and horror films, the characters only escape a gruesome fate at the hands of the killer apes when a volcano erupts and buries Zinj forever.

Sphere (1987), a story similar to Stephen King's *Tommyknockers* of that same year, involves the discovery of an ancient spaceship and its ability to unlock hidden horrors in the human unconscious. Crichton's science-horror masterpiece, however, was *Jurassic Park* (1990). The story concerns "the most stunning ethical event in the history of science," the commercialization of genetic engineering and its broad power to outpace humanity's efforts to understand their implications.[29] A corporate titan, John Hammond, has invested in a company, InGen, that has developed a technique to recreate the DNA of extinct species. He has used this power, derived from DNA in blood that mosquitoes trapped inside amber had sucked from their victims, to grow dinosaurs. These he has installed on Isla Nublar, a small rock off the coast of Costa Rica henceforth to be known as Jurassic Park, the most exciting amusement park in human history.

However, the park's investors are worried that something is wrong, and Hammond brings in a team to assuage their fears, including a botanist, a paleontologist, and a chaos mathematician. The staff explains to them that every safeguard has been taken: The animals are all female, so there is no breeding. Each species is secured behind electric fences to prevent predation. They lack an enzyme that must be artificially supplied: "These animals are genetically engineered to be unable to survive in the real world. They can only live here in Jurassic Park. They are not free at all. They are our prisoners."[30] Of course, they had to breed predators for show: *Tyrannosaurus rex* and vicious, man-sized velociraptors. They are no danger, of course. They've been "secured."

The mathematician uses chaos theory to predict that the park is inherently unstable and that it will collapse into chaos predictably and inevitably. Biology, he says, will find a way. And so it comes to pass, for the island's computer programmer has made a deal to steal InGen's dinosaur technology, and to do so he shuts down the island's electricity during a storm. A dinosaur kills him before he can turn it on again. The island's human inhabitants soon become aware that something is wrong. One by one the park's systems fail, and the animals escape their cages and attack. Order breaks down, and nature goes on a rampage. The humans discover that the park was never in order, even when the systems were running, for amphibian DNA spliced into the dinosaurs' genetic code to patch gaps gave them the ability to change sex, and the animals were breeding. By the time the electricity is restored, the park is in ruins and a number of the humans, including Hammond, are dead. The fences are down, and the ordered system has fallen back into a state-of-nature "equilibrium," wherein the creatures found their balance killing and eating one another.[31] The Costa Rican military destroys the island to end the dinosaurs' unnatural existence, but some have escaped to the mainland, reminders from another time of the hubris of a humanity that believed itself the greatest member of creation. In this, the dinosaurs function much like Lovecraft's Old Ones, earlier rulers of a vanished earth, who are indifferent to human dreams, agents of chaos and the wild, and best left alone unless those who summon them have the strength to put them down.

Crichton would continue writing variations on the *Frankenstein* theme, including *Prey* (2002), about nanotechnology, and *State of Fear* (2005), about global warming.

Thomas Harris's *Red Dragon* (1981) continued the trend evidenced in *Psycho* of bringing crime fiction into the realm of horror with a heavy dose of psychological abnormality and a heavier dose of graphic and extreme violence. The story concerns Will Graham, an FBI agent called back from retirement to investigate graphic murders committed by a serial killed known as the "Tooth Fairy." In order to track down the killer, Graham enlists the aid of another serial killer, Dr. Hannibal Lecter, who was once a brilliant psychiatrist but was also a cannibal and murderer. Lecter is a genius, but he used his mental powers for evil, leading to his eventual capture at the hands of Graham. Graham tries to convince Lecter to help, asking the good doctor to test his brilliance against the new killer on the block:

> "I thought you might be curious to find out if you're smarter than the person I'm looking for."
> "Then, by implication, you think you are smarter than I am, since you caught me."
> "No, I know I'm not smarter than you are."
> "Then how did you catch me, Will?"
> "You had disadvantages."
> "What disadvantages?"
> "Passion. And you're insane."[32]

However, the new killer is even more insane, and as the body count rises, Graham comes to realize that Lecter is manipulating both him and the Tooth Fairy, Francis Dolarhyde, in a convoluted master plan. Dolarhyde has a split personality, the baser of which is obsessed with William Blake's painting of a red dragon, which the more normal personality believes must be eaten to stop his homicidal urges. Dolarhyde is torn by his past abuse (*à la* Norman Bates), his current love for a woman, and his need to murder. He contrives to kill the woman and himself while burning down the house in which his grandmother abused him, but the plan goes wrong when Graham arrives to stop him. Graham believes he has killed Dolarhyde, but he has not, and the killer returns to stalk Graham until a climactic showdown. Hannibal Lecter, apparently amused by the situation, sends a letter to a convalescing Graham:

> I am without my books—the learned Dr. Chilton [his keeper] has seen to that. We live in a primitive time—don't we, Will?—neither savage nor wise. Half measures are the curse of it. Any rational society would either kill me or give me my books.[33]

Though the gruesomeness of the Tooth Fairy's crimes is vividly described, the darkest passages reflect Will Graham's own mind, which is capable of understanding the insanity of serial killers in a superhuman way. Graham must channel his killer instincts into fruitful endeavors, catching those who are unable or unwilling to do the same. Lecter, intellectual and cultured, is also sadistic and inhuman, a psychiatrist who misuses his mastery of the mind to manipulate and destroy. He is the evil scientist to Graham's good researcher. Dolarhyde, mystical and mad, is vulnerable to Lecter's manipulations and Graham's dogged efforts to catch him. However, this picture of intellectual prowess is muddied by Graham's vulnerability to Lecter's efforts, which in the end leave him permanently disfigured. Here bodily disfigurement and the physical descriptions of murder (and, in later works, Lecter's cannibalism) make corporeal the psychological wounds a more refined strain of horror might have been content to leave entirely mental. Harris followed up Lecter's stories with increasingly explicit sequels and prequels: *Silence of the Lambs* (1988), *Hannibal* (1999), and *Hannibal Rising* (2006).

Teen Horror

By the mid–1990s, one out of every three books published in the horror genre was aimed at young adults, part of a new breed of literary terrors aimed at the kids and teenagers.[34] Virtually unknown two decades earlier (though anticipated in the young adult suspense novels of the 1970s and 1980s by writers like Lois Duncan), "teen horror" presented watered-down versions of adult horror stories, just scary enough to be fun without tipping into the disturbing horror of the splatterpunks and their ilk. In the U.S., R. L. Stine's sixty-two volume series *Goosebumps* (1992–1997) and multi-volume *Fear Street* offered young adult takes on classic horror stories, along with some new twists. In Britain, the *Point Horror* series brought out editions of Stine along with other teen-oriented authors of dark deeds. Titles included Stine's *The Babysitter* (1989), J. B. Stamper's *House of Horrors* (1991), and Carol Ellis's *Camp Fear* (1994). Teen horror tales focused on typical aspects of young life (high school, babysitting, first jobs, sleep-away camp), and invested them with the same dark dignity as their adult counterparts. Significantly, though, teen horror implied a familiarity with the conventions of the horror genre and its monsters among young readers, a symbol of how deep knowledge of horror had seeped into the culture.

The novels had their heyday in the early 1990s—when horror was adolescents' most-read genre—and faded from view thereafter, replaced in children's hearts by Harry Potter and fantasy novels; horror's children grew up and graduated to Stephen King and harder horrors, a trend evident even as early as 1995.[35] Teen horror would return in the new millennium, though, with another resurgence of horror.

For slightly younger readers, there was Bunnicula, the vampire rabbit. James Howe's adorable series about a bunny who sucks the juices out of vegetables debuted in 1979 with *Bunnicula: A Rabbit-Tale of Mystery* and was followed by sequels such as *Howliday Inn* (1982) and (with the best title) *The*

Celery Stalks at Midnight (1983), in which Chester the cat tries to save his human family, the Monroes, from the evil rabbit. The stories are told from the point of view of the family's dog, Harold, and revolve around Chester's inability to understand that his detailed knowledge of vampires' dangers doesn't exactly apply to vegetarian critters. Published at regular intervals, the series is still going strong today with almost two dozen titles under the Bunnicula banner.

Extreme Horror

The mainstreaming of literary horror (even to children's books!) had led many younger writers to feel the genre had lost its edge, achieving a bourgeois respectability at a time when horror movies were increasingly transgressive. A new, more extreme horror sought to remedy this problem. S. P. Somtow's *Vampire Junction* (1984) told the story of a vampire trapped in a prepubescent body who is also a rock star. Mixing horror with the forbidden erotic and heavy doses of Jungian psychology, the book is usually cited as the first of the so-called "splatterpunk" horrors for its lyrical description of extreme and graphic violence derived from the blood-soaked movies of the late 1970s (discussed in Chapter 18). Timmy Valentine, the vampire and a castrato, reflects on his two millennia of violence and horror in therapy sessions with Carla, his analyst. It was followed by two sequels, *Valentine* (1993) and *Vanitas* (1995), which continued Timmy's story.

"Splatterpunk" works self-consciously sought extreme violence and gore, often mixing sexuality with bodily mutilation, taking their inspiration from EC comics and slasher films rather than from literary classics. For example, Edward Bryant's "A Sad Last Love at the Diner of the Damned" (1989) is set in George Romero's zombie world from *Night of the Living Dead*. The best known of splatterpunk's authors was Clive Barker, whose *Books of Blood* collected short stories of disturbingly explicit content. "Dread" (1984), for example, described the graphic torture of college students, ostensibly out of the torturer's intellectual interest. It told of pain and the way the victim lived on "long after the mind had begged the body to cease."[36] Barker's novella *The Hellbound Heart* (1986) began with a Lovecraftian setup: A seeker after dark knowledge, in this case ultimate pleasure, encounters forces from outside that have *different* definitions of "pleasure." But the gist of the novel revolves around Frank's efforts to rebuild his ravaged and ruined body by convincing his sister-in-law, who lusts after him, even in ruins, to procure victims whose bodies he can use as raw material. No mere summary can convey the "unrepentant lewdness"[37] of the characters nor the meatiness of the violence and gore. This was the nature of splatterpunk; it was body horror carried "to the limits of its endurance and beyond," in Barker's words.[38] It was sex and guts, lust and blood, mixed together in a self-referencing world of rock 'n' roll, slasher films, and a limits-free enthrallment with explicitness.

Though it was ultimately an offshoot of horror cinema, Ramsey Campbell, Stephen King and literary critics of the 1980s predicted that splatterpunk would be "the wave of the future" on which all subsequent horror would build.[39] It was not to be; the stars were not right. Extreme horror passed away by the early 1990s, lingering on as a remote influence on more mainstream works like Bret Easton Ellis's *American Psycho* (1991) and Chuck Palahniuk's *Fight Club* (1996), both violent tales of disaffected and disillusioned males in a corrupt and decayed America. Splatterpunk, however, did set the stage for the extreme horror to come with the dawning of the new millennium.

18

HORROR IN THE ARTS

In this phase of horror, literature had largely followed developments in cinema, where the cutting edge (if you'll forgive the pun) of horror found its violent expression. In the 1950s and early 1960s, pure horror films—the kind with dark lighting, fits of screaming, and Gothic horrors or monstrous killers—were few and far between, tucked beneath a range of science-fiction alien and creature films reflecting the era's preoccupations. As we move into the late 1960s and especially the 1970s, this changed. For the first time since the early 1940s, horror was again a genre largely, but not completely, distinct from science fiction and fantasy, and increasingly marketed as such to a generation that grew up labeling themselves as "horror fans." What the fans wanted, the fans got; and the young fans of the new era wanted more sex, more violence, and more explicit gore.

By 1960, mad scientists—and scientists in general—were disappearing from horror movies, to be replaced by what the British writer on popular culture Christopher Frayling called "sex and psychos," in which the body became the playground for madmen and misfits.[1] Concurrent with this change in villain was a change in hero, no longer the authority figure of military man or scientist trying to restore order but the unskilled, unknowing everyman who, as often as not, fails before the irrational horror. And that was the point: The irrational nature of the horror threw into question the very essence of reason, questioning our knowledge of the world's workings. As Isabel Cristina Pinedo explained, classical horror had followed set narratives where the forces of science and reason served to restore the rational order and suppress or classify the irrational horrors it uncovers. Instead, postmodern horror forced an acceptance of the irrational and the failure of the rational world-view; as often as not, the monster wins.[2]

It was dark stuff for dark times. This new school of horror was evidently quite successful, since more and more horror films were made. In 1957, horror made up just 6.9 percent of new releases, but in 1973 the number had risen to 9.1 percent, reaching 12 percent in 1983. By 1984, three out of every four horror films *ever made* were less than twenty-five years old.[3] Because the horror of the 1970s and '80s was saturated with sex, academics and critics, who began considering horror as a genre seriously only in those decades, assumed that since contemporary horror reflected preoccupations with sex, all horror always had. They began to "read back" '70s and '80s sexual obsessions into earlier horror works, with the result that pseudo–Freudian readings of horror became universal, to the exclusion of nearly all others.

In this period, horror in its more traditional form also invaded television, replacing early science fiction tinged–horrors and network-neutered endings with darker tones and more satisfying and natural conclusions. Horror could also be found in comics and cartoons, on stage, in music, and in role-playing games. In a very real sense, horror overtook and assimilated into virtually every aspect of culture.

All of this horror, though, imbued the outward forms of Gothic or Victorian horrors with a new sense of purpose, one drawn and derived from developments in society, including changing views of the human body derived from scientific advances that had rendered bodies into machines—machines that can, would, and do break down with terrible frequency. Even though the stories horror told were often quite simple, they were still relevant—perhaps more so in that their direct, bloody storylines reduced the complexity of modern life to an easy-to-understand storyline: The world is dangerous. Transgress boundaries, and you die. Even if you do everything right, you still might die. And it's going to be a horrible death.

A Bloody Good Time

In 1971 Dennis L. White surveyed horror films and found that they represented an extension of everyday fears taken to their extreme. Older horror films were good, in their way, but modern horror films, realistic in their depictions of horror and contemporary in their settings, were better because they helped viewers understand that society was the root of horror, and horror films illuminated the nature of society.[4] Society, we have seen, was largely the story of science; and so, it was not much of a stretch to see horror cinema's cultural critique as saying something about the scientific theories that underlay the societal structures that White saw horror critiquing. In this period, horror was concerned—almost obsessed—with explicit violence coupled to sexuality, a reflection of the changes brought about by the sexual revolution, the reproductive choices science offered that decoupled sex from reproduction, and a medical view of the body that left it subject to new, bloody horrors.

An early example of this new breed was the output of Britain's Hammer Films, the company that made *The Quatermass Xperiment*. In 1957 the company revived old-fashioned horrors with a more violent version of the Frankenstein story, *The Curse of Frankenstein*, which focused on Baron Frankenstein's pursuit of knowledge and its complications, much as earlier screen versions had done, but with more blood. In fact, it was the first major horror film to show explicit, red blood. From then on, horror would depict violence in a realistic way, eventually freeing the genre from the restraints of plot, logic, and storytelling.

In Hammer's version of *Dracula* under the title *Horror of Dracula* (1958) in the U.S., Jonathan Harker already knows of Dracula's (Christopher Lee) vampire heritage upon his arrival, in Germany (not Transylvania); in fact, Harker is there (as a librarian and cataloger of Dracula's books, no less) to destroy the unholy beast. The focus is not on whether such things can be, as it was in the 1931 *Dracula*, but how to overturn and destroy an unnatural order. The hero of the story, more so than in the novel or previous film version, is Abraham Van Helsing (Peter Cushing), the man whose knowledge of the occult gives him the power to combat the horror. In this *Dracula*, Dr. Van Helsing travels to Castle Dracula to rescue Jonathan, fully armed with knowledge about Dracula's powers and his weaknesses. Van Helsing, and thus the knowledge he represents, is a much more active hero than before, returning to the home of Jonathan's fiancée to try to save Lucy and destroy Dracula. In 1931, the horror derived from ignorance of the vampire's existence, but now the horror derives from (the viewer, if not the characters) having knowledge of the vampire but succumbing to his now blatantly sexual appeal anyway. Lucy first, then Mina actively conspire with Dracula to provide him with blood. It is a voluntary oblivion.

The success of *Curse of Frankenstein* and *Dracula* led Hammer to produce new versions of classic horror stories over the next two decades: the werewolf, Jekyll and Hyde, the mummy, the Phantom of the Opera, and so on. However, the company is best known for the half-dozen entries in their Frankenstein series (1957–1974) and the seven sequels to the Dracula film (1958–1974). Each sequel in both series was more outrageous and bloody than the one before it, and with each passing film the sexual aspects of the stories grew more prominent. The later films placed the traditional horror monsters in contemporary society, bringing them cape, fangs, and all into the twentieth century. In *The Satanic Rites of Dracula* (1974), a satanic cult engages in sexually explicit occult practices in honor of Dracula (Christopher Lee), who is masquerading as a property developer. He is plotting to use the bubonic plague to wipe out life on earth, and a descendant of Abraham Van Helsing (Peter Cushing) has to infiltrate the sex cult and stop him. Nudity and explicit violence ensue, and Dracula dies, impaled on a bush.

In the United States, American International Pictures had revived some of the old monsters with titles like *I Was a Teenage Werewolf* and *I Was a Teenage Frankenstein* (both 1957), which retold classic horrors from a youthful perspective, with heavy doses of medical-biological and atomic horror. They then moved on to a series starring Vincent Price based on Edgar Allan Poe's stories,

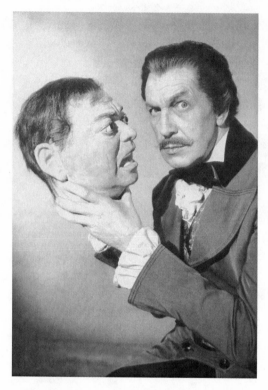

Vincent Price. Vincent Price became a horror icon for his elegant delivery of often campy material, like **House on Haunted Hill**. Here we see Price holding the severed head of Peter Lorre for an interpretation of Edgar Allan Poe's "The Black Cat" in the film **Tales of Terror** (1962), one of a number of Poe interpretations Price filmed in the 1960s (www. doctormacro.com).

beginning with *The Fall of the House of Usher* (1960) and continuing through *The Tomb of Ligeia* (1965), in imitation of Hammer's bloody horrors. However, the splatter genre began in earnest with Herschell Gordon Lewis's independent, low-budget film *Blood Feast* (1963), a notoriously bloody film about a demented Egyptian caterer who kills in order to obtain body parts for cannibal feasts in honor of his goddess, Ishtar, whom he hopes to resurrect by his offerings. The film graphically depicted the killer pulling out the tongue of a young woman. Its poster promised that the full-color spectacle was more grisly than anything "in the annals of horror." Lewis also helmed a number of slash-and-gore follow-ups, including *Two Thousand Maniacs!* (1964), about a crazed town slicing-and-dicing innocent tourists, and *The Gore Gore Girls* (1972), in which a killer is slicing-and-dicing strippers. Nudity and violence ensue.

Between 1963 and the end of the major slasher franchises around 1990, there were dozens upon dozens of variations on the theme, some good, most bad, a few unwatchable in their awfulness. Thus was born the blood-and-guts film, in all its full-color glory, carried to new extremes in the Italian and German exploitation studios, whose output was bloody, violent, and often badly dubbed for English-speaking countries. The Europeans had seen American and British horror and tried to top it with ever more explicit versions. *Operazione Paura* (1966), released as *Kill, Baby ... Kill!* in 1968, involved a ghostly girl who causes anyone who sees her to bleed to death, usually by cutting their own throats. The German horror film *Die Schlangengrube und das Pendel* (1967) became *The Torture Chamber of Dr. Sadism*, which told of a count (Christopher Lee) who murders virgins in his dungeon before being executed. He returns from the dead to seek vengeance on the descendants of his intended thirteenth victim. All these films featured Gothic trappings— grim castles, moody atmospherics, endangered maidens— and enough gore to keep an undertaker in business for years. Such films whetted the appetite of Anglo-American audiences for similarly brutal outputs from their own studios.

This they got with independent "sexploitation" films like *The Touch of Her Flesh* (1967), which told of a man who gets run over by a car after finding out his wife is having an affair. Permanently embittered by womankind, he commits increasingly violent rampages against hookers, strippers, and women in general, many of whom are nearly nude. *Touch*'s producers, Michael and Roberta Findlay, followed the film with ever more explicit sequels and new productions, like *The Curse of Her Flesh* (1968), which continued *Touch*'s killing spree, and *Shriek of the Mutilated* (1974), in which a professor and his students trekking through the Himalayas become food for a cannibal cult and the Yeti.

More mainstream horror films nevertheless began to incorporate bloody motifs into their more standard revenge fantasies. In *The Abominable Dr. Phibes* (1971), the title character (Vincent Price), a Ph.D. in theology, uses his Biblical knowledge to seek revenge on the nine medical professionals, doctors and a nurse, who failed to save his wife during an operation. Phibes bases his murders on the plagues of Egypt preceding the Exodus, and in the final torture, he forces one of the doctors to operate on his own son, who is locked to an operating table beneath a vat of acid. Phibes has implanted a key beside the boy's heart, and the doctor has just six minutes to cut it out and unlock his son before the acid kills him. At the end we learn that Phibes was himself horribly mutilated in the accident that took his wife's life, and we get a final glimpse of his disfigured, skull-like face. In its punishment of the medical profession, *Phibes* has a modern flavor that belies its 1930s setting; and the elaborate tortures the mad doctor devises anticipate the later torture schemes of early twenty-first century horror, like the *Saw* series. The character returned in *Dr. Phibes Rises Again* (1972), in which he tries to use the ancient knowledge contained in a pre–Dynastic Egyptian scroll to resurrect his wife. This time Phibes's rage is directed against archaeologists who might prevent him from completing his mission.

With their stories pitting theology against science, the *Phibes* films also dramatized the religious-scientific tension coming to the fore in modern society. However, scholar Harry Benshoff read the *Phibes* films as homosexual allegories, as gay "camp," because of the films' humor, and Price's performance and rumored sexual orientation. Rick Worlan, however, correctly places the *Phibes* films as an important transition toward the graphic violence of 1970s horror.[5]

African-American cinema, the so-called "blaxploitation" films, made their own version of classic horrors. *Blacula* (1972) features a black vampire sired by the original Dracula, while *Blackenstein* (1973) has a mad doctor performing strange genetic "DNA" and "RNA" experiments that trigger evolutionary regression. The result of the doctor's experiments is something like a Frankenstein's Monster, only African-American, who rampages as in the original.

Birthing Occult Horrors

In contrast to the emerging blood-and-guts brand of horror, the occult also found its cinematic expression. *Rosemary's Baby* came to the screen in 1968, under Roman Polanski's direction. A generally faithful adaptation of the book with Mia Farrow as Rosemary, the film version was moody, atmospheric and aimed squarely at a mainstream audience primed by the pill and Thalidomide to watch a story about a demonic baby. Under its influence, a number of evil baby movies were produced, with increasingly vile children. *It's Alive* (1974) and its two sequels dealt with a monstrous infant born with a penchant for violent killing. *Embryo* (1976) finds a scientist developing a technique to rapidly age embryos into adults, but the first such creature becomes a murderous psycho. In *The Brood* (1979) a psychiatrist uses a controversial technique to cause his patients to physically manifest their emotions. One woman does this by birthing her negative emotions as weird, mutant killer children. In the final scene, censored in some countries, the woman gives birth to yet another mutant and licks it clean, in a primitive, primal scene. Rhona Bernstein saw *Rosemary's Baby* as a symbol of the patriarchy's attack on motherhood, while Lucy Fischer saw these films as "skewed" documentaries of "the societal and personal turmoil that has regularly attended female reproduction."[6] However, the films likely reflect a discomfort with the scientific decoupling of sex and birth, and the newborn monsters chemicals had created.

The Omen (1976) took place at a later stage in the life of the metaphorical demon child. At a hospital, two women give birth. The first woman's baby dies. The second woman's baby lives, but *she* dies. Robert Thorn (Gregory Peck) agrees to a priest's proposal that he exchange his wife's dead baby for the live one. As the baby, little Damien, grows older, his new mother, Katherine, notices strange things about him. Animals fear him; he throws fits at the sight of a church. His first governess shouts his name when she commits suicide. Thorn gradually comes to accept another priest's claim that Damien is the son of Satan when the priest's prophecy that Damien will claim Katherine's unborn child as his first victim. This happens when Damien knocks Katherine off a balcony, causing her to miscarry. After discovering a 666 birthmark (the mark of the Beast) on Damien's head, Robert is finally convinced of the horrible truth. He uses special knives obtained from an archaeologist in Israel to try to murder Damien and stop the coming Apocalypse, but the police kill Robert just before the fatal blow. Little Damien smiles at the funeral, hand in hand with the president of the United States, Robert's old friend. The movie featured one of

Hollywood's first graphic decapitation scenes. A rousing success at the box office, *The Omen* gave birth to a number of sequels, including *Damien: The Omen II* (1978), a third *Omen* film in 1981, and a 1991 TV-movie sequel, *Omen IV*. The original film was remade in 2006.

Combined, *Rosemary's Baby* and *The Omen* formed a sort of popular counterpart to Arthur Machen's story "The Great God Pan." Rosemary's rape is reminiscent of Pan's sexual assault in the story, and the antics of young Damien compare favorably with those of Pan's death-dealing offspring. The difference, however, was that Machen's story was cosmic, with Pan representing vast forces humanity could barely comprehend, while these new versions place the horror squarely in the Judeo-Christian tradition, replacing the awe of the cosmos with a retreat into the superstition of traditional faith.

In this vein, William Peter Blatty's *The Exorcist* came to theaters in 1973, following the novel's plot closely. Scenes in which Regan (Linda Blair) is possessed by the demon were so frightening, intense, and effective that some audi-

The Exorcist (1973). No movie did more the legitimize the supernatural than *The Exorcist*, which sociologist Michael Cuneo has said led to a revival of the rite of exorcism in the Catholic Church and a flourishing of deliverance ministries in evangelical churches to drive out demons from the possessed. The film's high production values and powerful imagery helped make it a horror classic.

ence members fainted, and others became violently ill. It also brought cinematic profanity to new heights. "Your mother sucks cock in Hell!" must have been shocking for some in the audience back then. Critics often regard the film one of horror cinema's best; sociologist Andrew Cuneo cited it as contributing to the widespread introduction of exorcism rites and deliverance ministries into evangelical churches in the United States, where casting out demons became a religious alternative to psychotherapy, and for a record demand for Catholic exorcisms in the 1970s.[7] Catholics were of two minds on the film. Some, like the Archdiocese of New York, found it spiritual and authentic, while others, like the Jesuits, worried about its effects on the impressionable people calling to request exorcisms.[8] The film also served Christian fundamentalists in their developing battle with the secular world, citing it as an example of the strength of faith in the face of a flawed secular science that refuses to accept God's transcendence. *The Exorcist* spawned a couple of awful sequels and a raft of imitators, including the title characters in *Poltergeist* (1982), who kidnap a young girl, and *The Amityville Horror* (1979), whose ghosts drove a young couple out of a house once home to a murderer. Based on a "true" story later exposed as a hoax, *Amityville* inspired a number of sequels.

Brian De Palma's screen version of Stephen King's *Carrie* (1976) gave the world a moving image of a demonic teenager, following the menstruation and telekinesis outlines of its book source, but flattening the story by removing the journalistic framework and telling the tale as a straightforward narrative. De Palma also dropped King's overwrought destruction of Carrie's hometown in favor of a more limited disaster, emphasizing the horrors of high school over those of the supernatural. *Carrie* sparked a wave of King adaptations, including Stanley Kubrick's *The Shining* (1983), which shifted the story's focus away from Danny and toward Jack (Jack Nicholson), and cut out the explosive finale in favor of a more restrained conclusion. *Christine* (1983) was about an evil car, and *Children of the Corn* (1984), based on the short story of the same name, had demented children enthralled by a pint-sized preacher kill all Gaitlin, Nebraska's adults and set up a fundamentalist community of their own. A doctor and his girlfriend stumble on the kids' blood cult and almost end up sacrifices to a Lovecraftian monster who blows up in a "Dunwich Horror"–style orgy of explosions and lightning — a departure from the story, where the alien god got his doctor dinner. More than a half-dozen sequels followed.

Speaking of "The Dunwich Horror," it too was part of the occult revival and strange birth frenzy of the 1970s, coming to the screen in 1970 under its original title, but without much of the original story. Wilbur Whateley (Dean Stockwell) is once again in search of the *Necronomicon*, a book also sought by Prof. Henry Armitage (Ed Begley) and his shapely young assistants, Nancy (Sandra Dee) and Elizabeth (Donna Baccala). Armitage refuses to lend Whateley the book, so Wilbur seduces Nancy and brings her back to his old mansion, where his unseen brother rattles around in the attic and an old Stonehenge-like stone formation glares down at the house. The professor and Elizabeth come looking for Nancy, and they realize that Whateley is the spawn of eldritch powers and is trying to call down the Old Ones to impregnate Nancy. Elizabeth lets the unseen brother loose, and special effects resembling an acid trip ensue until the monster is defeated.

A more sober look at the occult took place in *The Wicker Man* (1973), a film in which a conservative Christian British policeman, Sgt. Howie, goes in search of a missing girl on the island of Summerisle, where a tip suggested she could be found. Instead, Sgt. Howie finds a neo-pagan cult practicing sexual fertility rites, and some nudity, too. The cultists disclaim knowledge of the girl's whereabouts, but then say she is dead. The policeman stays to investigate the cult, disguising himself to infiltrate their May Day celebration. He has come to believe the girl may have been the victim of human sacrifice. The cultists, however, are aware of what he is doing. It transpires that the girl is alive and well, used as bait to lure Sgt. Howie to the island. *He* is to be the human sacrifice. He is forced into a large wicker statue, it is set alight and he is burned to death. With his dying breaths, Howie calls on God to avenge him against these pagan unbelievers. It is interesting to note that the intellectual tension is between Christians and occultists, while earlier horror stories would almost invariably have set occultists against secular rationalists, as in *Isle of the Dead*. Times were changing, and it was clear that in popular culture, science was losing out.

The Legend of Hell House (1973) more or less faithfully transcribed Richard Matheson's *Hell House*, returning ghosts to the big screen, providing a materialist counterpoint to the occult horrors. *The Island of Dr. Moreau* (1977) told the H. G. Wells story with a few changes: Now the animals are made into men via a gene-altering serum, and Moreau (Burt Lancaster) intends to use it to turn his visitor (Michael York) into an animal. Thus the misguided, amoral inquiry of Wells's doctor is transformed into sadistic evil. Better human-animal hybrids could be found in *Planet of the Apes* (1968) which found astronauts stranded on a future Earth where evolved apes use religion to suppress science to prevent the public from learning that humans once ruled the planet, a truth that might upset the faith and the society it governs.

Dracula (1979) had Frank Langella playing an erotically charged Count, who manages to slay Van Helsing and escape triumphant. Director Werner Herzog adapted Dracula, too, with *Nosferatu: Phantom der Nacht* (1979), which recreated the classic 1922 *Nosferatu* in a style both colder and more emotional. This Dracula is an isolated, lonely monster, and the plague he brings devastates minds as much as bodies. Van Helsing fails to stop the vampire, and Jonathan Harker's wife, Lucy, must give herself to the creature to end his reign of terror. However, the vampire has already claimed Jonathan, and though Dracula is dead, Jonathan can carry on, spreading the plague, unburdened by human emotion. This *Nosferatu* imagines no triumph over death, disease, and madness.

Slash and Dash

As horror moved into the 1970s, blood and gore became the rule rather than the exception. The old staples of the discovery and overreacher plots still existed, but they were supplemented by what we could call the "accident plot": One or more innocent characters accidentally transgress a boundary and encounter a monster they did not know existed — or could exist — which then hunts the protagonists until it is either vanquished or succeeds in eliminating the transgressors. The difference from the discovery or overreacher plot was one of intention: these innocents do not seek forbidden knowledge, nor do they welcome it when it is thrust upon them.

In 1972, *Deliverance*, based on James Dickey's 1970 novel of the same name, sent a bunch of city slickers into the country to commune with nature and get in touch with their inner primitive before a dam floods the area for good. They are Bobby (Ned Beatty), Drew (Ronny Cox), Lewis (Burt Reynolds), and Ed (Jon Voight). During their ill-starred trip, the men encounter some unsavory hillbilly men bearing firearms. The hicks make Bobby strip, force him to squeal like a pig, and viciously sodomize him. They try to force Ed to perform oral sex. Lewis kills the raping redneck with an arrow, but the other escapes. As the men flee down the river, consumed with fear and shame, they worry that the escaped hillbilly is stalking them. Amidst injuries and a fatal clash with the redneck, Drew ends up dead. The remaining men dispose of the bodies of the hillbilly and Drew, and they lie to the local sheriff about what happened. Though not strictly speaking a horror film, *Deliverance* dealt effectively with questions of civilization and barbarism, urbanity versus the state of nature, and the regression of the human to the animal state in the face of the primitive and the absence of civilization. These themes carried over into horror's versions of *Deliverance*'s story of the dark doings in America's underbelly, which replaced sodomy with slashing, and added screaming young women to the mix.

Director Wes Craven's *The Last House on the Left* (1972) follows the outlines of Ingmar Berman's *The Virgin Spring* (1960), an art film about parents who take revenge on the men who rape and murder their daughter. Craven's gory, explicit, and raw treatment of the story finds two teenage girls traveling into New York City to see a band called Bloodlust in honor of one girl's seventeenth birthday, over the objections of that girl's worried parents. Meanwhile, a pair of rapist-murderers escapes from prison with the help of two accomplices. The girls run into the offenders while trying to score some pot, and the thugs take them hostage. They stuff the girls into the trunk of their car, which breaks down — conveniently enough — in front of the worried parents' house. They take the girls into the woods, brutalize and kill them, and then ask to stay the night at the parents' house. The tortures the captors think up are meant to be horrifying — including forcing the girls to perform homosexual acts on one another. The parents piece together what really happened and descend to the offenders' level to seek a bloody and grotesque revenge.

The Forgotten (1973), also known as *Don't Look in the Basement*, tells of a nurse (Rosie Holitik, a former *Playboy* model) who takes a job at a secluded sanitarium. At the asylum, she learns that the doctor running the place had been murdered by a patient. In his stead, Dr. Geraldine Masters (Annabelle Weenick) has taken over with a strict, disciplinarian philosophy. The nurse is deeply unsettled by the free rein the inmates seem to have over the sanitarium, and order appears to gradually be breaking down. When all hell seems to be breaking loose, the nurse discovers the horrible truth: Dr. Masters was the patient who killed the old doctor. The inmates are running the asylum.

Another insane asylum figured in *Silent Night, Bloody Night* (1974), a film that set the stage for the mad slashers to come. The old Butler mansion is finally being sold, decades after it served as an insane asylum, and years after the current owner's grandfather, William, burned to death in the old pile. The lawyer conducting the sale is murdered by an axe-wielding killer while having sex. The killer then begins calling townsfolk. Speaking in a quiet, menacing whisper, the man uses these calls to lure the sheriff and the telephone operator up to the Butler house, where he kills them in scenes of startling and graphic violence. Meanwhile, on Christmas Eve the last of the Butlers, Jeffrey (James Patterson), decides to pay a last visit to the Butler house before selling it off. He learns from old newspapers that his grandfather was actually his father, since William raped and impregnated Jeffrey's mother, his own daughter. But it gets worse.

According to the grandfather's diaries, the rape sent Jeffrey's mother into madness, which caused the old man to turn the house into an asylum. Unfortunately, the doctor he hired to run the place was greedy and corrupt, living the high life while ignoring the patients. One night, William sought revenge by releasing the inmates. In flashback we see how they killed the doctor and the staff in an orgy of on-screen violence that mere words cannot describe. The scene is truly chilling, especially when we view one inmate trying to gouge out the doctor's eyes with a broken bottle. The rampage took the life of William's daughter, prompting him to seek revenge. Since then, William faked his own death and lived a shadow existence preparing for his bloody vengeance, which took the form of the killings from earlier in the film.

Jeffrey, however, has learned additional forbidden knowledge that seals his fate. He discovers that the mayor and the other townsfolk are in fact the insane asylum inmates, who spent the last four decades covering up their unstable pasts. The mayor kills Jeffrey to protect the secret, and we catch only a glimpse of the killer before Jeffrey's girlfriend shoots him dead. The house is then demolished.

The Canadian film *Black Christmas* (1974), released in the U.S. as *Silent Night, Evil Night*, used much the same setup. A sorority house is the setting for anonymous threatening phone calls from a maniac, but this time the calls are sexual and obscene, leading the girls to nickname him "the Moaner." The psycho killer is hiding in the house's attic and picks off the girls one by one, though with more restrained violence than other films in the genre. Jessica (Olivia Hussey) thinks the killer is her boyfriend Peter (Keir Dullea), who is upset about her plans to abort his child. When Jessica is attacked by the killer, she flees, only to run into Peter. Assuming he is the killer, she kills Peter. The police agree that Peter is the killer, and close the case. Jessica thinks she's safe. In the last shot, we see two dead bodies in the attic and hear a voice say, "Agnes, it's me, Billy." Then the phone rings downstairs.

But the most famous of these early slasher films is probably director Tobe Hooper's *The Texas Chain Saw Massacre* (1974), loosely based on the life of serial killer Ed Gein — just enough, in fact, for the film to claim it was inspired by true events. The story opens with news reports that corpses in Muerto County, Texas (*muerto* being Spanish for dead), have been disinterred and turned into some kind of bizarre art. College students Sally, Pam, Jerry, Kirk, and wheelchair-bound Franklin travel to Muerto County to check on Sally's grandfather's grave. He's fine, but they aren't. On the way back home, they stop to pick up a hitchhiker, who goes crazy and slashes Franklin with a razor before the kids can remove him from the vehicle. It gets worse from there.

The kids stop at a run-down gas station, where the attendant tells them there is no gas, but offers some "homemade" venison. With their remaining gas, they decide to go up to the dead grandfather's old house to spend the night. Kirk and Pam wander off and, attracted by the sound of a generator, stumble across an old farmhouse. On the porch, they find a human tooth. Nevertheless, they hope the residents have some gas to spare, and they knock on the door. The door falls open, and Kirk enters, only to encounter a large man wearing a mask of some kind of leather — later seen to be human skin. The man kills Kirk and drags him back to the kitchen. Pam tires of waiting on the porch and enters the house. She wanders into the dining room and stumbles on a scene of unremitting horror: The furniture is crafted from human body parts, and bones litter the floor. Screaming, she is captured by the masked man (retroactively named Leatherface), who hangs her alive on a meat hook, forcing her to watch him butcher Kirk's corpse with a chainsaw.

Jerry goes to investigate his missing friends and stumbles across the farmhouse. Inside, he finds Pam inside the freezer, alive but dying. Pam tries to flee, but Leatherface returns, kills Jerry, and locks Pam back in the freezer. Back at the car, Sally and Franklin are fighting about what to do when the masked man emerges from the woods and kills Franklin with his chainsaw. Sally (Marilyn Burns) runs into the woods, Leatherface chasing after her with his revving chainsaw. Sally stumbles into the farmhouse, only to find a terribly old man sitting next to a desiccated corpse. Leatherface is right behind her, so she jumps out a window and continues to run, reaching the gas station. There she learns

Old cabin. America's backwoods were littered with the crumbling remains of old cabins and farmhouses. During the 1970s, the backwoods became associated with horror because they lay outside the boundaries of urban and suburban "civilization." As a result, rural houses like this one photographed by Marion Post Wolcott in 1940 became loci of horror in works ranging from *The Texas Chain Saw Massacre* to *The Blair Witch Project* (Library of Congress, Prints and Photographs Division, FSA-OWI Collection, LC-DIG-fsac-1a34336).

too late that the attendant and the hitchhiker from earlier in the film are Leatherface's brothers, and the men bring Sally back to the farmhouse.

Inside the house, the men keep Sally tied to a chair, and they bring Grandpa, the withered old man, down to partake in the feast they've made from the previous victims' meat. They cut Sally's finger and let Grandpa suck the blood, and then they give him a mallet to deliver the *coup de grâce*. In a morbidly funny and horrific tableau, the old man tries repeatedly to bludgeon Sally while his grandsons cheer on, but he is too frail to complete the act. The hitchhiker takes the mallet to finish her off, but Sally seizes the momentary confusion to escape. She runs to the road, where a passing tractor-trailer runs down the pursuing hitchhiker. Leatherface returns to harass her some more with his saw, until she jumps into the back of a passing pickup and escapes. Leatherface is left to twirl madly with his chainsaw against the sunrise. By the time the film is over, Marilyn Burns, as Sally, has spent nearly half the movie screaming at the top of her lungs. In this, she was perhaps the first "scream queen," as horror movie victims are sometimes called.

Texas Chain Saw Massacre dealt with the failure of rational civilization, the animalistic nature of humanity, and the horror of learning the truth about the human condition, when comforting illusions about "good" and "right" are stripped away. Critics hated the movie, calling it a "vile piece of sick crap," in the words of *Harper's*, and Britain banned the film until 1999. Nevertheless, it grossed between thirty and one hundred million dollars in its first seven years against a budget of $125,000, making it one of horror's most profitable.[9] The film yielded three sequels which traded the suspenseful intensity and irrational violence of the original for increasingly graphic gore. The first film was remade in 2003 for no discernible reason.

Combining aspects of the *Massacre* with *Deliverance*, Wes Craven's *The Hills Have Eyes* (1977) placed a family in the middle of a hostile desert where a family of deformed cannibals preys upon them, forcing the survivors to descend to the cannibals' bestial level to survive.

Return of the Creature Feature

Slasher movies would dominate horror in the 1980s, but before we discuss the most prolific horror form, we should survey the bizarre horrors that grew out of the 1950s and '60s "creature feature," those radiation-induced monsters who stalked the fringes of mid-century science. In the 1970s they gave way to darker monsters who owed more to fears of nuclear meltdown and mutation and the devastation poisons had wrought on the environment than the wonders of atomic science. *Night of the Lepus* (1972) finds a scientific serum made from hormones and mutated blood, designed to control the rabbit population, inadvertently creating a race of giant carnivorous rabbits. In *Sssssss* (1973), a scientist is worried that nuclear weapons and ecological destruction will leave only cobras to inherit the earth, so he tries to create a process to transform humans into snake creatures. Nuclear waste enlarged ants to enormous size in *Empire of the Ants* (1977), and the bugs turn humans into their chemically subordinated slaves. More prosaic attacks occurred in *Jaws* (1975), where a shark menaces a beach community, and the horrendous *Squirm* (1976), which featured a town overrun with evil worms.

The disaster films of the 1970s were horror films in their way. *The Towering Inferno* (1974), *Airport* (1970), and *The Poseidon Adventure* (1972) were all monster movies, only the monster was the modern technology in which the victims were trapped. *Inferno's* burning skyscraper, *Airport's* threatened jetliner, and *Poseidon's* tipped-over cruise ship all began their films as triumphs of modern technology over the limits nature imposed. But when these technologies go wrong — as invariably they must in horror films — they became monsters every bit as awful as the vampires or aliens of earlier film cycles. In a way they were worse, because when the monster is a technical wonder like a tower, a plane, or a ship, the victims are trapped *inside*; the monster has already consumed them before the horror even begins.

A wave of dark science fiction straddled the horror boundaries. *The Omega Man* (1971) found Charlton Heston — who once played Moses — as the last man on earth in a new adaptation of *I Am Legend*. He is the only survivor of a bacteriological war between the Soviet Union and China, which turned those who survived into strange albino zombie-vampires. Heston's Robert Neville alone was unaffected because he was a military scientist with access to an experimental vaccine. In a drastic departure from Matheson's secular views, Neville becomes a Christ figure because his blood has manufactured antibodies that can cure the afflicted. But not all the zombies want to be cured, for they follow a crazed cultist who believes that the afflicted are the chosen ones and to be human is to be damned.

Soylent Green (1973) imagined the year 2022, when humanity is living in a broken-down, failed society plagued by global warming, overpopulation, and pollution. There is no food, little education, and the government uses scientifically engineered alternatives, the newest being "Soylent Green." Detective Robert Thorn (Charlton Heston) discovers that the bodies of those who attend government-run euthanasia clinics are turned into food: "Soylent Green is people!" *Logan's Run* (1976) imagined a future where everyone over thirty was killed to control the population. *Blade Runner* (1982) imagined a dystopian future, but with robots.

The Thing with Two Heads (1972) was a new entry in the medical-horror corpus, this time featuring a dying doctor grafting his head onto a man about to be executed. The Caucasian doctor is horrified to realize his "donor" body is black. *The Clonus Horror* (1979) was a prescient horror film that told of clones specifically grown to provide replacement parts for wealthy government politicians, including the American president. The operators of the clone farm tell their charges that they are "going to America" when they are sent to cold storage for their organs to be ripped out. Our hero is a clone who uncovers the plot and tries to escape, only to realize that there is nowhere to run. He is recaptured, and his parts harvested. The film is marred by the limitations of its budget, but it effectively explores the problems of bioethics in an era of rapid medical advances. Michael Bay's sci-fi film *The Island* (2005) and Kazuo Ishiguro's literary novel *Never Let Me Go* (2005) both reused this premise without credit.

The darkest, and best, of horror-science fiction was Ridley Scott's suspenseful *Alien* (1979). Sometime in the future the onboard computer of the spaceship *Nostromo* rouses the crew from cold storage to investigate a non-human signal emanating from a small moon. While some of the crew are out exploring the moon's harsh terrain, Ripley (Sigourney Weaver) uses the computer to decipher the signal. It turns out the signal is not a distress call as they had assumed but a warning. The crew on the moon discovers a large, alien spaceship; its dead pilot bears evidence that his chest burst from the inside out. Below the ship, they find a cave filled with alien eggs, one of which breaks open; a little alien attaches itself to a crew member's helmet. Then it eats through the helmet and attaches itself to the crewman. Efforts to remove it only prove that its blood is acidic enough to eat through metal. However, all seems well when the creature lets go and drops dead. The *Nostromo* takes off.

In space, the crew prepares to return to their cryogenic sleep when the crewman's chest bursts open and an alien creature emerges. The remaining crew members try to hunt the thing down to dispose of it, but it soon grows into a large, vaguely anthropoid monster. As designed by H. R. Giger, who later produced an illustrated *Necronomicon*, the creature intentionally resembles Lovecraft's alien monsters, a strange fusion of the biological and the mechanical. The creature, like Lovecraft's aliens, simply exists to fulfill its Darwinian ends. As the *Nostromo*'s science officer put it, "I admire its purity, its sense of survival; unclouded by conscience, remorse, or delusions of morality." As the creature picks off the crew, the survivors conclude that destroying the *Nostromo* is the only way to stop the alien, though this doesn't quite work as planned. Three sequels followed over the next twenty years, with diminishing returns.

A similar claustrophobia and alien panic infested John Carpenter's *The Thing* (1982), a re-imagining of John W. Campbells's "Who Goes There?" in which an ancient alien critter is thawed out at an Antarctic research station. This darker version intentionally depicts the alien menace as a sort of disease, retaining the novella's shape-shifting creature that reproduces prodigiously. This leaves the men trapped in the ice station wondering who among them may be an alien, providing grist for a film about suspicion, paranoia, and madness. As in *Alien*, the survivors decide to destroy their research station to stop the creature, which they fear wants to infect the rest of the world. In a bleak, hopeless ending, death is the only comfort remaining to the men.

Predator (1987) used an invisible alien hiding in the jungle to attack a team of U.S. commandoes. It was a sort of extraterrestrial version of Ambrose Bierce's "The Damned Thing," but with Arnold Schwarzenegger and a lot of machine guns. As in *The Thing* and *Alien*, the encounter with the scientific anomaly yields only death. Clive Barker's *Hell Raiser* (1987) adapted his *The Hellbound Heart*, but with less metaphysical development and a more menacing look for the lead Cenobite, known now as "Pinhead." Seven sequels followed. It turns out that the Cenobites can be bribed with promises of knowledge, or outwitted.

Mimic (1997) took the central idea of the old pulp story of the same name but gave the giant insects camouflaged as humans a less cosmic, biotechnological twist: A team of scientists genetically engineered the creatures to eradicate disease-carrying cockroaches, but the bugs began to evolve into something monstrous.

Horror and Humor

Ever since parodies of Mary Shelley's *Frankenstein* graced the nineteenth century stage, horror and humor have been tied together. As Noël Carroll pointed out, horror situations are often *prima facie* silly ("giant rabbits!") absent the emotional fear felt by the audience, which is the defining difference.[10] The 1970s and 1980s saw a wave of films that used both emotions simultaneously.

Mel Brooks's *Young Frankenstein* (1974) spoofed James Whale's *Frankenstein* films with a loving recreation of the Universal horror look and feel. *An American Werewolf in London* (1981) found a Yankee tourist attacked by a werewolf that locals pretend doesn't exist. He has to figure out how to kill himself to stop the rotting ghosts of his victims from haunting him. *Ghostbusters!* (1984) and *Ghostbusters II* (1989) were comedies that used advanced technology to combat ghosts, who were said, like those in *Hell House*, to have a materialist explanation.

The Evil Dead (1980) and its two sequels, *The Evil Dead II* (1987) and *Army of Darkness* (1992), combined horror with humor, and buckets of blood, so much so that *Evil Dead* was banned in many countries. In the first two (both being essentially the same story), a group of young people in an isolated cabin use an ancient spell book (the *Necronomicon* in the sequels) to call up Lovecraftian deities, who kill them off. In the third film, the last survivor, Ash (Bruce Campbell), is propelled back in time where he must battle the undead to retrieve the *Necronomicon* and return home. It is perhaps the single best battle with the legions of the undead in cinema. Lovecraftian themes permeated *Re-Animator* (1985), *From Beyond* (1986), and *Bride of Re-Animator* (1991), which succeeded on their humor-horror merits but lost something of Lovecraft's cosmic atmosphere in pursuit of gore. *Killer Klowns from Outer Space* (1988) and *Attack of the Killer Tomatoes* (1978) were pretty much as their titles advertised.

Comedies using superficial aspects of horror included *The Rocky Horror Picture Show* (1975), *Beetlejuice* (1988), and the two *Addams Family* movies (1991 and 1993). The 1976 French adult film *Spermula* featured sex-hating aliens who take the form of beautiful women to conquer our planet by exhausting Earthmen, only to succumb to the pleasures of the flesh themselves.

Slice and Dice: Reign of the Slasher

For scholar Carol J. Clover, the difference between pornography and horror is that the former is obsessed with sex, the latter with gender. She describes the way slasher films make sexuality and violence two sides of the same coin, with killing equating to rape. The victims, usually, are those who transgress sexual boundaries—who, like teens of the 1960s and '70s, reject 1950s values and pursue sex outside of marriage and reproduction. Clover sees gender confusion in these stories—with killers who are confused about their sexuality attacking those who have normal sex lives, while the girl who survives the killing does so because she is "boyish," displaying male virtues.[11] Given the cultural climate at the time these films were made, there is little to dispute here. The filmmakers intentionally larded their films with sex and Freud, and the psychosexual interpretation of horror is therefore justified. The academy, in general, hated the fact that most victims of horror's killers were female, and so ignored or denigrated the films because of their perceived hostility to feminism.[12] Some argued that female victims are "homoerotic stand-in[s]" for teen males, and slasher films a discussion of "male-on-male sex" and "phallocentrism."[13] Clover took a less extreme position, arguing instead that both killer and victim are androgynous creatures trying to navigate life in a society where sexual boundaries were breaking down and old categories no longer fit.

The slasher film, in its classic 1980s form, was a story of forbidden knowledge, in this case carnal knowledge. The films were aimed squarely at teenagers, for whom society still expected sex to remain a mystery. Therefore, in the slasher films, teenagers—especially young girls—who obtain forbidden knowledge of sex are mercilessly punished by the psycho killers for their transgressions.

Director John Carpenter's *Halloween* (1978) was the best of these sex-and-slash films. The story begins in Haddonfield, Illinois, in 1963, when six-year-old Michael Myers, donning a discarded Halloween mask, stabs his sister after she has sex with her boyfriend. Fourteen years later, Dr. Sam Loomis* (Donald Pleasence) arrives at the state mental hospital for Michael Myers's legally mandated hearing. Instead, he finds the patients are wandering the grounds and Myers (Nick Castle) has escaped. Loomis knows that Myers is "purely and simply evil," in his words, and he pursues the escaped lunatic, convinced that the fellow is somehow supernaturally evil. The scientist blinks from reason in the face of irrational madness.

Meanwhile in Haddonfield, Myers has started stalking Laurie (Jamie Lee Curtis), a shy, single girl, after she stops by the old Myers house to drop off a key for her real-estate agent father. Myers is hiding inside and follows Laurie, hovering just out of her sight, giving only the occasional glimpse as she goes about her routine. On Halloween night, Laurie and her friend Annie are both baby-sitting kids in the same neighborhood. Annie pawns her charge off on Laurie so she can get some alone time with her boyfriend.

Before she can do so, Myers, who now wears a stolen white-painted William Shatner mask, kills her. Another of Laurie's friends, and *her* boyfriend, both get the Myers treatment for presuming to have sex. This friend manages to call Laurie and scream into the phone while Myers strangles her.†

Worried, Laurie goes across the street to see what has happened. There

---

*A name, the careful reader will note, also shared by the rescuing male in Psycho.
†Note, however, that though the promiscuous teens die, Myers does not discriminate; the slasher genre itself does. This is a fine enough distinction, but Myers couldn't have known which of the teens were having sex, and the last of his targets, Laurie, isn't having sex at all. Therefore, the film itself rather than its psycho killer is punishing teens who transgress sexual boundaries.

Michael Myers. Wearing his distinctive white Halloween mask and clutching a large knife, Michael Myers set the standard for 1970s and '80s psycho killers like Freddy Krueger, Jason Vorhees, and their ilk. The figure of the menacing killer stalking teenagers (usually girls) across darkened neighborhoods became so clichéd that the 1990s saw a number of tongue-in-cheek satires like the *Scream* series.

she finds the dead bodies of her friends, and Myers attacks her. Screaming ensues. Laurie does her sensible best to ward off the killer, stabbing him with whatever sharp objects are handy. The terror ends only when Dr. Loomis makes an appearance and shoots the madman several times. However, at the end we see that Myers's fallen body has disappeared.

Halloween was delightfully simple and straightforward, and film critics liked it almost as much as the viewing public, which made the movie a success. The film's score was especially effective. *Halloween* was followed by a number of inferior sequels that turned Laurie into Michael Myers's lost sister and made him into a superhuman killer of supernatural proportions, a sort of Druid science experiment to embody absolute evil.

The slasher films that followed *Halloween* lost something of the magic and replaced the almost restrained violence of the film with increasingly explicit gore and an almost single-minded focus on killing sexually promiscuous teens. *Friday the 13th* pulled a reverse *Psycho* and had the mother of drowned boy Jason Vorhees pick off the sexually active counselors at Camp Crystal Lake, where the drowning had occurred years earlier when a previous generation of counselors were also busy having sex. In the last shot, an undead young Jason appears to attack the last survivor. The sequel (1981) brought Jason Vorhees out to avenge his mother's death, apparently never having drowned but having lived some weird feral existence. Over the course of eight increasingly silly sequels, Jason gained a hockey mask, superhuman powers, and ended up in outer space.

Wes Craven's *A Nightmare on Elm Street* (1984) found the spirit of a murdered child molester, Freddy Krueger (Robert Englund), attacking teenagers in their dreams, which produce physical manifestations on their real bodies. These teens are the kids of the parents who burned him alive a decade earlier. Over the course of a half dozen sequels, *Nightmare* explored the boundaries between reality and dreams with diminishing but gorier results, and then went postmodern with *Wes Craven's New Nightmare* (1994) in which Freddy stalks an actress from the first movie. In the *Nightmare* sequels, the characters who survive do so only because they study Krueger, learn his methods, and apply their knowledge to escape. They must reject the scientific model of dreams and accept Krueger's irrational abilities.

Many, many more slashers of various flavors followed: *Child's Play* (1988) had a demon doll. *The Hitcher* (1986) had an evil and violent hitchhiker stalking a young man who had the misfortune to pick him up. And so on, and so on. But by the end of the 1980s, the slasher was largely played out, at least until the mid–1990s.

Television and Music

Elsewhere in culture, rock 'n' roll acts self-consciously cultivated an anti–Establishment image by incorporating horror motifs and satanic overtones, as if to live up to 1950s worries that rock was the devil's music.* Black Sabbath, Alice Cooper, and

Marilyn Manson was perhaps the most prominent, and in their wake sprang up a "Goth" culture which opposed and inverted social norms by emphasizing the outward trappings of horror movies: black clothing, pale skin, morbid outlooks. Metallica recorded an instrumental piece they named "Call of Ktulu" after H. P. Lovecraft's story. A band calling itself H. P. Lovecraft produced psychedelic rock in the late 1960s, making use of the harpsichord among other archaic sounds. Michael Jackson's *Thriller* was perhaps the most ambitious, with its lengthy and elaborate zombie-and-werewolf music video done in the style of a horror film, with narration by Vincent Price.

On television, the seeds of Goth culture could be found in *The Munsters* (CBS, 1964–1966) and *The Addams Family* (ABC, 1964–1966). Both families lived in old Victorian mansions and frightened neighbors with their unconventional, anti-modern outlooks. Both shows celebrated the warmth of superficially ghoulish families in the modern world. *The Munsters* used characters based on the Universal Horror monsters, including Herman (Fred Gwynne), a Frankenstein's Monster; Lily (Yvonne DeCarlo), a Dracula's daughter; and Grandpa Dracula (Al Lewis), the Lugosi-style vampire. *The Addams Family* took its inspiration from Charles Addams's morbid cartoons. Gomez (John Astin), the Latin lover, and Morticia (Carolyn Jones), in her slinky black dress, enjoyed a healthy sex life, one of television's first. Notably, the Addamses supported a number of "odd" and "frightening" positions—home schooling, alternative medicine (witch doctors), gourmet food (yak), wetland (swamp) preservation, and Victorian interior design—that are now "normal," while the bland modernism of their "normal" neighbors strikes today's viewers as outlandish and bizarre. Both programs were cancelled within days of each other despite respectable ratings. *Scooby-Doo* (CBS, 1969–1974; ABC, 1976–1986) is the most successful children's cartoon of all time. A team of young people and their dog, Scooby-Doo, investigate supernatural mysteries like ghosts from outer space, Dracula, zombies, and so on. They inevitably discover, with the help of celebrity guest stars like the Harlem Globetrotters, Phyllis Diller, and Sonny and Cher, that the horror is in fact a human being in disguise who "would have gotten away with it if it weren't for you meddling kids." Unfortunately, later incarnations traded the show's uniquely skeptical point of view for a credulous one, replacing the human monsters with "real" supernatural creatures.

The horror-themed soap opera *Dark Shadows* (ABC, 1966–1971) ran more than twelve hundred episodes and utilized the whole panoply of Gothic horrors in its stories: vampires, werewolves, zombies, ghosts, Frankenstein-style monsters, witches, and of course dark and stormy nights. The program dealt with

---

An honorific once bestowed on jazz and the blues, but applied by worried parties to each new development in music that challenged conventional musical taste.

the tensions between the family resident in Collinwood Mansion and the towns-folk of Collinsport. In its second year, the soap opera introduced Barnabas Collins, a two-century-old vampire, who becomes the love interest for Dr. Julia Hoffman, who wants to cure him from his curse. The introduction of the Leviathan and its cult gave a Lovecraftian flavor to the Gothic soap. It was cancelled in favor of the game show *Password*. The nighttime soap opera *Beauty and the Beast* (CBS, 1987–1990) used Gothic themes in the epic love story of Catherine, a normal woman, and Vincent, a sort of Phantom of the Operatic cat-man who lives in the sewer. NBC's *Passions* (1999–2007) flavored its daytime suds with witches, warlocks, zombies, a living doll, and other Gothic ingredients.

More serious television horror tended to focus on the psychological rather than the brutal, on account of network standards and practices. As a result, TV horror was a bit tepid compared to cinema offerings, which may have discouraged the genre's fuller development on TV. Television had some success with a number of made-for-TV movies that utilized horror themes. *The UFO Incident* (NBC, 1975) had dramatized the Betty and Barney Hill alien abduction and framed it as a frightening tale of extraterrestrial horror. *Duel* (ABC, 1971) from a young Steven Spielberg, and based on a Richard Matheson story, found David Mann (Dennis Weaver) pursued by a psycho driving a large truck. The unseen truck driver tries to kill the motorist repeatedly as he chases him across the desert. Mann decides to turn the tables, cast off his civilized veneer, and go on the attack. He uses his briefcase to jam the accelerator, jumps out of his car, and lets the vehicle crash into the truck. The truck explodes and falls off a cliff.

Satan's School for Girls (ABC, 1973) featured a young woman's quest to discover the cause of her sister's suicide at an elite boarding school. She unwittingly discovers that the school is home to satanic cultists who believe she has potential in the dark arts. *'Salem's Lot* (CBS, 1979) was televised as a two-part, four-hour miniseries that followed the outlines of Stephen King's novel, though necessarily condensing some of the book's expansive array of characters for time and clarity. *The Night Stalker* (ABC, 1972) and *The Night Strangler* (ABC, 1973) — scripted by the ubiquitous Richard Matheson — found reporter Carl Kolchak (Darren McGavin) tracking down supernatural menaces. In the first film, Kolchak stalks a Las Vegas serial killer who is really a vampire, over the derision and objections of his editor and the police, who refuse to believe in such things. The second film finds Kolchak in Seattle, where every twenty-one years women are murdered and drained of blood. He discovers that a century-old alchemist has been using their spinal fluid to keep himself alive, two decades per dose. With their mix of horror and humor, the films were ratings winners.

After the movies, the comedy-horror television series *The Night Stalker* (ABC, 1974) followed Independent News Service reporter Carl Kolchak's investigations into the supernatural, the paranormal, and the bizarre. Each episode featured a "monster of the week" (as ABC had done with *The Outer Limits*), and Kolchak was the only one who could stop the vampire, witch, werewolf, alien, or evil Spanish moss monster. The program was cancelled just twenty episodes into its first and only season. Another ABC series, *The Sixth Sense* (1972) featured Gary Collins as Dr. Michael Rhodes, a college professor with an interest in the paranormal. Each episode featured the parapsychologist investigating cases of alleged extra-sensory perception, hauntings, or other spiritualist phenomena, and of course concluding that they were real. The show was cancelled after twenty-four episodes.

Over on NBC, Rod Serling tried out a new anthology series, one skewing away from *Twilight Zone*–style fantasy and toward horror. Named *Night Gallery*, the program ran for three seasons (1970–1973) after impressive ratings for a 1969 TV-movie of the same name. The TV movie version featured three short tales. The first told of an ungrateful heir who murdered his uncle to inherit the old man's house. However, a painting on the wall seems to subtly change each day, showing the old man emerging from his grave and making a slow march to the house. This scares the heir literally to death. The second story, directed by Steven Spielberg, featured a blind woman who paid a man to give her his eyes, which she has implanted into her own head for just a glimpse of light, knowing full well that they will last only minutes. The third tale revolves around a Nazi living in South America and his fixation with a museum painting. Each of the movie's characters ends up dead, punished for their sins.

The series picks up where the movie left off, with Serling introducing a number of stories per hour-long episode from his "museum of the outré," where a series of bizarre painting illustrate key concepts or themes from the upcoming tale: "Each captures on a canvas, suspends in time and space, a frozen moment of a nightmare." Many were based on well-known horror tales like Conrad Aiken's "Silent Snow, Secret Snow" (October 20, 1971), H. P. Lovecraft's "Pickman's Model" (December 1, 1971), and Clark Ashton Smith's "The Return of the Sorcerer" (September 24, 1972), here transformed into a psychedelic acid trip with Vincent Price as the sorcerer and Bill Bixby as the ill-fated translator of the *Necronomicon*. Nice touches include the goat who shares the dinner table with the men and Price's shapely assistant, and the rather well done crawling body parts of the original story's severed sorcerer.

The tale "The Dead Man" (December 16, 1970) told of a doctor who uses hypnosis to induce the symptoms of disease in a susceptible patient and what happens when the experiment continued after the point of death. "A Death in the Family" (September 22, 1971) depicted an undertaker's gruesome hobby, turning his charges into a tableau of the family he never had, a conceit reused more than once by other horrors.* But the stories that stand out for me are "Green Fingers" (January 5, 1972) and "A Miracle at Camafeo" (January 19, 1972). The former tells a creepy tale of an old lady with a preternatural talent for gardening. When she refuses to sell her land to a business developer, he has

The 2004 slasher movie Shallow Ground, *for example, had a villain crafting a family tableau of rotten corpses, and the 2001 Fox-TV mystery-themed reality show* Murder in Small Town X *climaxed with the discovery of the same.*

her killed, but not before she buries her severed thumb in her garden. "Everything I plant grows," she says, and she returns to take revenge. The latter tells of a swindler who is faking a back injury for the insurance money. He travels to Camafeo, a Mexican shrine, to stage a fake miracle to justify abandoning his crutches. At the shrine, a blind boy also comes to pray for sight. The swindler leaves the shrine, confident he pulled a fast one, only to discover that whatever powers inhabit the shrine have taken his sight and given it to the boy.

The program won an Emmy for "They're Tearing Down Tim Riley's Bar" (January 20, 1970), a psychological study of a broken man whose life is reduced to a few ghosts in an abandoned bar. However, *Night Gallery* also featured a number of sub-par tales, and a few outright groaners. John Astin and Phyllis Diller in "Pamela's Voice" (January 13, 1971) comes to mind, the story of a man who can't escape his wife's annoying voice, even after her death. "Professor Peabody's Last Lecture" (November 10, 1971) managed to turn a lecture on the Cthulhu Mythos into a "humorous" story of the Old Ones' revenge on the lecturer, transforming Prof. Peabody into a tentacled thing without him noticing the transition. Worse, the producers filled time with brief, "humorous" vignettes like Dracula at a blood bank to make a "withdrawal." Such jokes were old when Dracula was young.

In Britain, *Thriller* (ITV, 1973–1976) was something of a cross between *Night Gallery* and *Alfred Hitchcock Presents*. "A Killer in Every Corner" (February 1, 1975) had unsuspecting psychology students spending the night at the home of a professor who stocked his house with serial killers dressed as servants as an "experiment" to see whether his "cure" for killer instincts really works. "Death in Small Doses" (February 23, 1974) found an evil butler poisoning his mistress and driving her to the edge of insanity in hopes of seizing her fortune.

In the 1980s, anthology shows abounded. The syndicated *Tales from the Darkside* (1983–1988) offered some Reagan-era horrors. Stephen King contributed "Word Processor of the Gods" (November 25, 1984), in which the title writing device has the power to make whatever is typed on it come true. Disasters ensue, and as the device threatens to self-destruct, its owner types a final story to fix the damage he wrought and make a better reality than he began with. In the episode "A New Lease on Life" (January 26, 1986), a man discovers that the hi-tech apartment building he lives in is more than it seems to be. The "technological" devices are in fact a façade masking a living monster within the building's walls, one that feeds on the tenants' garbage. When the apartment renter tries to kill the monster, he ends up inside the garbage disposal, a meal for the creature.

CBS trotted out a new version of *The Twilight Zone* (1985–1989), which remade old episodes and added some new ones, and HBO launched *Tales from the Crypt* (1989–1996), based on the old EC comics and hosted by a decaying corpse, the Crypt Keeper. The stories were horror, but with humor, and always with twist endings. "Top Billing" (June 26, 1991), based on a story from *Vault of Horror* #39 (October–November 1954), was my favorite. Barry Blye (Jon Lovitz) is a frustrated actor having a really bad day. He strangles a rival in order to take his place in a production of *Hamlet*. When he arrives at the theater, the overbearing director (John Astin) is thrilled with his new hire. Unfortunately, Barry soon discovers that his part in *Hamlet* is Yorick, who is dead. Oh, and the "theater" is really an insane asylum and the rest of the crew inmates who murdered the staff. The Crypt Keeper closed with these groaners: "Barry axed for the part and he got it. But typical Barry; they still couldn't have used his face. It's just as well. The critics would have cut him to pieces. Ha, ha, ha!" Reviewing the episode, a critic for *The New York Times* complained that the Crypt Keeper's desiccated corpse looked too much like then-current Persian Gulf War images of starving and dying Iraqi children for his comfort, calling it "disorienting."[14]

Perhaps the best of the new anthologies was Showtime's revival of *The Outer Limits* (1995–2001; Sci-Fi Channel, 2002). The series dealt predominantly with science fiction themes in a sci-fi context — extraterrestrials, cutting edge technology, and bioengineering — but its stories were often quite dark and often strayed into the realm of horror. At its best, *The Outer Limits* used its sci-fi and horror trappings to explore the human condition, and the role of science and faith in a changing society. The episode "If These Walls Could Talk" (July 30, 1995) was one of the best with horror themes, and the most original materialist take on ghosts since *Hell House*. The narrator begins the story:

> Ghosts. Haunted houses. Many maintain that such concepts have no place in our computerized twentieth-century reality. But until man conquers death, one inevitable question will always linger within the recesses of the human mind. What lies beyond?

The tale proper tells of a woman who seeks out a physicist who is famous for debunking the supernatural, a skepticism born of a fake medium's bungled séance to contact his dead wife. The woman offers the skeptic money to investigate the disappearance of her son, whose ghost she believes she heard in an old, haunted Victorian house. While in the house, the skeptic debunks the woman's hopes, explaining away the sounds and groans as a faulty heater. What he cannot explain away is the face of the missing son emerging from a wall. Breaking through, he finds a hidden laboratory belonging to the scientist who once owned the house, and a meteorite that later analysis shows contains an extraterrestrial enzyme that absorbs into any material it touches. The old house, therefore, is itself alive in a literal way, more than Hill House or Hell House had been — and the ghosts within it are nothing more than the absorbed remnants of its earlier meals. Fortunately, the alien essence is allergic to alcohol, and a generous provision of liquor causes the old pile to collapse, dissipating the horror within. Therefore, the supernatural is relegated to a branch of science, and the survival of the soul after death has no place in this materialist cosmos.

Under the influence of *The X-Files* (see Chapter 21), later seasons of *The Outer Limits* played up conspiracy angles and tended to portray government forces suppressing or corrupting scientific research for evil purposes. To the last, however, the show never lost the sense that the human body and the human mind were as alien as any extraterrestrial.

Gaming

Horror fans came to want horror to be interactive, and gaming provided a way to do this safely. Similar in play to *Dungeons and Dragons*, the role-playing game *Call of Cthulhu* (1981) from Chaosium put players in the position of characters in the world of the Cthulhu Mythos. One player is the "Keeper of Arcane Lore," who acts as a master of ceremonies while the other characters "investigate" mysteries surrounding the Old Ones and their minions. Each new revelation reduces the players' sanity levels, and though they may "solve" the mystery, they cannot truly win against the invincible Old Ones. Unlike *Dungeons*, *Cthulhu*'s challenges are largely intellectual rather than based on combat and battle.

The introduction of the video game in the 1970s created the potential for new vistas for horror, but most early games were about killing things and watching them bleed. Termed "survival horror" in later years, the thrust of the games was to shoot, maim, slice, or kill as many monsters and other assorted villains as possible without getting oneself killed — thus "surviving" the game. The primitive graphics of the early years of video games made many of them seem vaguely cartoonish, but as the years wore on, the capacity for gore grew, and in the 1990s, and especially the new millennium, video games rivaled cinema in their bloodthirsty extremes. Along the way they also picked up some storytelling skills.

Texas Chainsaw Massacre (1983) for the Atari system let players take the role of Leatherface in order to kill as many victims as possible without running out of gasoline for the chainsaw. If that happened, the victims fought back. *Halloween* (1983) and *Friday the 13th* (1985) got the video game treatment shortly thereafter. *Castlevania* (1986) for Nintendo was the first game with classic horror characters. It let players battle Dracula and his minions. In Japan, *Sweet Home* (1989) for Nintendo trapped five people in a mansion with a ghost and other monsters and challenged the player to get them out. It was the inspiration for *Resident Evil* (1996), which placed four members of a law enforcement squad inside a deserted mansion to discover clues to grisly cannibal murders. The team discover through old documents, CDs, and other evidence that Umbrella Corporation has been conducting unethical experiments on humans and animals, exposing them to the T-virus, which turns living creatures into horrible monsters. The team blows up the worst monster and goes home. *Alone in the Dark* (1992) presented a murder-mystery in a monster-infested mansion. *Clock Tower* (1995) had a mad slasher named Bobby stalking a girl named Jennifer in an old mansion with a pair of giant scissors. Under a satanic altar, Jennifer learns that Bobby's forgotten brother is a giant mutant baby, and Jennifer accidentally burns him and the house down.

These early games essentially recapitulated the plots of slasher films and science-run-amok movies. It would be for a new breed of extreme horror to give video games their own unique take on horror and science, and to bring graphic violence of a verisimilitude unprecedented in entertainment.

PART VII

A Failure of Free Will

*The Horror of Helplessness
(c. 1990–present)*

19

SCIENCE AND SOCIETY

Surveying the horror scene at the end of the 1990s, Laura Wyrick asked where all the slashers had gone. Done in by excessive special effects and a raft of middling sequels, they had all but vanished with the end of the 1980s. She noted that since the great age of the slasher film had passed by, the release of movies like *Bram Stoker's Dracula* (1992) and *Mary Shelley's Frankenstein* (1994) meant that horror seemed poised for a return to its origins in the Gothic and the intellectual.[1] She was wrong. A decade earlier, Stephen King and others had predicted that splatterpunk would be horror's dominant mode. They, too, were wrong. Keeping this in mind, we encounter the most problematic of the seven themes I have outlined in this book, what I have labeled the "horror of helplessness," but which might better be described as the failure of free will. Of course, all horror is at some level about the loss of control, but it is my contention that scientific conceptions about the mind — and the religious reaction to them — produced a sense of fatalism that found its expression in contemporary horror, primarily in two forms.

The first, and most prominent form, is the sort of "extreme" horror that only grew more gruesome and more explicit as the 1990s gave way to the 2000s. This brand of horror focused its gaze on the sufferings of the victims rather than the predations of the monster. In films like *Saw* (2004), the purpose of the movie was to display the physical and mental torturing of the innocent victims, in as drawn-out a way as possible. There is no real reason for the suffering (or at best a shallow and superficial one), and it is obvious that the reason for the torture is less important than the suffering itself. The second form dealt with destiny and the idea that the hero or heroine had no choice but to suffer at the hands of the monster, that the horror was inevitable and the best that could be hoped for is bare survival, never real triumph. Both posited that horror was no longer the aberrant doing of rare monsters but an accepted part of everyday reality.

However, since this trend is so recent, I am not sure it has yet to fully define itself. Imagine, for example, the view from 1925, when cosmic horror was coming to the fore but H. P. Lovecraft had not yet given it its defining form. From this perspective, the works of Algernon Blackwood might have looked like variants on the ghost story (as indeed they were seen at the time), and Arthur Machen's work as variants on biological horror, rather than as part of a new type of horror. I don't believe that the horror of helplessness has yet seen the defining work that crystallizes the trend. It may not happen, in which case what I outline in this section may come to be seen as simply a variation on the body horror of the preceding era. Or it might have already happened with the "extreme" horror films, but if so, we are still too close to the event to see clearly the shape of horror's future.

Therefore, this section will be conjectural, to a point, outlining what looks like an emerging theme, though only time will tell whether it has staying power.

A Holiday from History

On the surface, the 1990s should have been a low ebb for horror. The great bull market that began in 1987 signaled an age of prosperity unprecedented in human history. During the 1990s, nearly every economic and social indicator showed marked adjustments for the good. People were living longer lifespans than at any time before, with better health and more material possessions. Household income rose with the stock market, and more millionaires were coined in the dot-com boom than at any time before or since. Crime fell to record low levels. With the death of communism in Europe, democracy seemed to be triumphant; and Europe had put aside its conflicts to join in an ever-expanding European Union. Scientific advances improved life dramatically: hormones and anti-depressants adjusted moods, little blue pills helped the impotent have sex, new fertility treatments let the infertile conceive. Technology, too, advanced rapidly: computers revolutionized life, the Internet connected the world, and cell phones made communication constant.

It was the "go-go Nineties," or what columnist George F. Will called the "holiday from history,"[2] when the gloom and doom of much of the twentieth century had been abandoned in favor of a new Gilded Age of peace, prosperity, and the pursuit of even more of the same. Politicians could look forward to an American-led world where democracy reigned and Western values were universal. Giddy pundits predicted that the stock market would continue to rise indefinitely, generating a utopia of wealth and progress. The Dow Jones Industrial Average, which had doubled and then doubled again and again in the 1990s, reaching 11,000 by the eve of the new millennium, was said to be capable of reaching 36,000 points in the coming decade.[3] Even war seemed newly fresh: The hi-tech Persian Gulf War, as sanitized by television, made the expulsion of Iraq's Saddam Hussein from occupied Kuwait seem bloodless. Better, it was a truly international war, with the United States and the dying Soviet Union fighting on the same side for the first time since the Second World War.

Even the impeachment of the American president in 1998, and his trial in 1999, was largely a goofy distraction — a sex scandal turned into Constitutional crisis that left Bill Clinton more popular than before and his religious and conservative opponents looking foolish and out of touch.

As though to mirror the frivolity of the 1990s, New Age pseudoscience saw renewed interest. UFO sightings continued apace, and many claimed world governments were suppressing evidence of alien landings and alien abductions. Crop circle enthusiasts thought shapes in grain fields were alien signals, though they were almost all hoaxes. Ancient astronauts were back, this time as a "lost civilization" that proponents like the British author Graham Hancock claimed lived 12,500 years ago and influenced Earth's early cultures and religions. Evidence, he said, could be had in geological estimates of the age of Egypt's Sphinx or the astronomical alignment of ancient monuments. Ghosts saw a resurgence in popularity, as self-described ghost hunters tried to track down elusive spirits with a range of scientific-sounding devices, like electromagnetic frequency (EMF) readers that allegedly monitored ghosts' frequencies. In 1999 there was even a *Complete Idiot's Guide to Ghosts and Hauntings*, and cable television presented a stream of documentaries on all manner of pseudoscience. Skeptics and scientists protested the new supernaturalism, but for many believers it was merely "great fun," as one "ufologist" described one of his investigations.[4] Alleged psychic mediums found a new vogue, reusing spiritualist frauds and tricks to "talk" to the dead. This time "psychics" like Sylvia Browne and John Edward performed on television, rather than on stage, for audiences in the millions — more than ever consulted psychics during the heyday of mediumship in the nineteenth century.

The façade of the long 1990s — approximately 1989 to 2001 — was glittering. To be an American, or a Westerner in general, was to live in what was probably the happiest and most prosperous era in human history. So what on earth was left to be afraid of?

Barbarians at the Gate

The ending of the Cold War seemed to release a wave of anxieties that had been suppressed and subsumed under the all-pervasive imperative of fighting godless communism. The end of the uneasy stability the two superpowers provided, combined with continued decolonization, created troubles and faults around the world. At first they seemed like isolated incidents, but in retrospect they portended worse things to come.

In Rwanda and in the disintegrating remains of Yugoslavia, ethnic hatreds led to genocide, with millions dead. The international community largely stayed out of the conflicts and let Hutus liquidate Tutsis in Rwanda and Serbs massacre Muslims in Bosnia. It was assumed that the Rwandan and Bosnian conflicts were ancient, eternal, and based on age-old blood feuds. As such, there was really nothing that could be done. There was too much history to undo; to some extent, without colonial or communist overlords, it was *inevitable* that the ethnic groups would fight. This view of the intractable nature of ethnic strife belied the actual history of the regions, but it was widespread nonetheless. In the Middle East, the Israeli-Palestinian conflict also took on the tone of intractable, inevitable hatred. In all cases, political opinion makers argued that there might be no solutions because ethnic difference automatically equated to ethnic conflict.

The Israeli-Palestinian conflict in particular was a source of a number of fears. Palestinians began a wave of suicide bombings, and the Israelis retaliated in a cycle of vengeance that periodically threatened to escalate into a larger, regional war. In the United States, conservative evangelical Christian leaders cheered on the Israelis, seeing in the Jewish state the fulfillment of Biblical prophesies heralding the coming of Armageddon and the Millennium of Christ's return. Religious leaders Pat Robertson and Jerry Falwell preached that nuclear war over Israel would be God's judgment on mankind, but there was no reason to fear because good Christians would be raptured to Heaven before the final battle.[5] Presidents Ronald Reagan and George W. Bush both subscribed to versions of the idea that Israel was the key to Christ's second coming, and the latter was sometimes reported to have acted on those beliefs. In South Korea, the Rev. Sun Myung Moon proclaimed *himself* the second coming of Christ, and he had close ties to politicians in the United States, including President George H. W. Bush and other prominent Republicans, some of whom attended his "coronation" as world savior in a U.S. Senate office building in 2004.[6]*

In Waco, Texas, the religious cult leader David Koresh of the Branch Davidians predicted the end of the world for 1995, thought he would save the chosen — his cult members — and believed the U.S. federal government was the force of the Antichrist. This resulted in a fifty-one-day standoff in 1993 with the Bureau of Alcohol, Tobacco, and Firearms and the FBI, culminating in a fiery apocalypse limited to the members of the cult. White supremacists, acting in the name of Waco and the race war they predicted, opposed the federal government as evil. Timothy McVeigh bombed the Alfred P. Murrah Federal Building in Oklahoma City on April 19, 1995, killing 168 people. It was the worst act of terrorism on American soil in the twentieth century.

The strange UFO cult Heaven's Gate committed mass suicide in 1997, and thirty-nine cult members died. They had believed reports on Art Bell's supernatural radio program that a flying saucer was trailing behind the Hale-Bopp

---

*At least a dozen sitting members of Congress attended, including both Democrats and Republicans, but most denied knowing that Moon would be crowning himself. However, a Democratic Congressman, Danny Davis of Illinois, carried Moon's crown and bowed to the new Messiah and Prince of Peace, who announced that he had saved both Hitler's and Stalin's souls with his magic powers.

comet, the brightest to approach the Earth in years. The cult's leaders, who drew their philosophy from New Age occultism, *Star Trek*, *Star Wars*, and Christian millennialism, preached that their followers must shed their "containers" (bodies) to join the UFO and fly to Heaven. Some group members, including their leader, Marshall Applewhite, a former professor, had been castrated to free themselves from the burden of sex.[7] It was the largest mass suicide on United States soil. (Jonestown was in Guyana.)

A secular terrorist known as the Unabomber (Theodore Kaczynski) sent mail bombs to universities and airlines from 1978 through 1995 to protest the destructive nature of science and technology. Kaczynski, a Ph.D. in mathematics, believed that science and technology had taken on a life of their own and were driving "industrial society" toward anarchy, unhappiness, and destruction. In 1995, *The New York Times* and *The Washington Post* published the bomber's manifesto, *Industrial Society and Its Future*, in which Kaczynski wrote that science was not a genuine pursuit of knowledge but instead a meaningless activity that fails to satisfy biological imperatives while working to enrich the powerful and make scientists feel superior to mere mortals:

> Thus science marches on blindly, without regard to the real welfare of the human race or to any other standard, obedient only to the psychological needs of the scientists and of the government officials and corporation executives who provide the funds for research.[8]

Kaczynski was arrested in 1996 in a primitive Montana cabin after his brother recognized his writing style from the manifesto. A brief technology scare in 1999 made many believe that the world's computer systems would crash on January 1, 2000, termed the Y2K (or Millennium) bug. Doomsayers thought planes would fall from the sky, electric grids crash, and global trade grind to a halt. However, nothing happened.

If the Unabomber offered a secular critique of American society, religious groups had their own problems with what many conservatives called "liberals," "leftists," or "secularists," by which they meant both their political opponents and those who did not believe in traditional religion, including atheists and materialists, in which group they classified scientists. Under the guise of promoting traditional values, religious conservatives pressed the American government, at the local, state, and national levels, to reject the well-established principle of evolution in favor of "creation science," or later "intelligent design," which postulated that a supernatural creator — obviously a reference to God — had created the world and its species. Evolution, they said, must be wrong because species are just too complex to be the product of random chance. In 2005, President George W. Bush declared his support for intelligent design: "You're asking me whether or not people ought to be exposed to different ideas, and the answer is yes."[9] A federal court later ruled that it was not science and therefore could not be taught.[10]

America's religious conservatives gained influence and power during the period between 1994 and 2007 when Republicans largely controlled Congress and owed much of their electoral success to evangelical leaders, who turned out Christian conservatives to vote for the party. While some on the political left worried about the potential for theocracy when born-again evangelical George W. Bush became president in 2001, few realized that the new administration's domestic policies amounted to a "war on science" by "the anti-science president," in the words of journalist Chris Mooney. The administration placed severe limits on stem cell research using cells from human embryos, repudiated the scientific consensus on global warming, and pressured scientists to skew their findings to support political ideas, many drawn from religious ideology.[11] Truth, free inquiry, and objective reality — in short, the Enlightenment — was out of style.

The Fate of Free Will

But what was so bad about science that religious groups felt so strongly that it needed to be opposed at all costs? The short answer was that science supported a materialist understanding of the universe at odds with religion's transcendent claims. However, that was only part of the story. The bigger part of the story was the gradual diminution of the human position in the cosmic scheme at the hands of advances in scientific knowledge and the anxieties this provoked in society at large. The 1990s and the new century saw the culmination of this centuries-old process.

We have already seen the first acts of the story. Copernicus had removed the Earth from the center of the cosmos, which disturbed the Church. Newton showed that the universe was governed by fixed laws, reducing the room for divine intervention. Geology demonstrated that Earth was older than the Bible said it was. Evolution reduced humans to just another animal, governed not by special creation but by natural law. Science's investigation of spiritualism cast doubt on the survival of the soul after death. Psychology reduced human behavior to primitive, evolutionary drives. Medical advances gave doctors the power to rebuild the body, just like any other machine. The scientific model of humanity was now what H. P. Lovecraft had said it was: an inconsequential species on a third-rate planet, subject to no higher power than the blind workings of evolution and accident. It was a terrifying notion.

So what was left for the human race, a species that for thousands of years had considered itself special and imbued with soul and spirit? In the 1990s, only two areas were still left open for human exceptionalism: The mystery of consciousness and the possibility of free will. Science — or more accurately, scientism — then proceeded to destroy both.

René Descartes said, "I think, therefore I am," and for centuries this was proof enough that each human body had a consciousness in it, an "I" in control of the machine. Sometimes thought of as the soul, it could still be imagined as the executive agency that represented the "essential" human. It is what makes you "you" and me "me." But, as psychologist Steven Pinker explained in a 2007 *Time* magazine cover story, even this small comfort was a lie science had exposed for the fraud it was. MRI machines learned to read people's minds, electrical stimulation of brain areas could induce hallucinations every bit as real as reality, and even out-of-body experiences could be explained as tricks of brain function. The near-death experience of white lights and long tunnels turned out to perfectly describe the oxygen deprivation of the dying brain, rather than a trip to Heaven. There was no soul, and not even a real "you":

> Scientists have exorcised the ghost from the machine not because they are mechanistic killjoys but because they have amassed evidence that every aspect of consciousness can be tied to the brain.... Another startling conclusion from the science of consciousness is that the intuitive feeling we have that there's an executive "I" that sits in a control room of our brain, scanning the screens of the senses and pushing the buttons of the muscles, is an illusion.[12]

Experiments showed that the sense of self was merely the brain's way of making sense of a number of independent circuits firing at once. Science and philosophy now agreed that the soul is an illusion, and that the brain is all that is. A few philosophers still held out hope for consciousness, but scientists believe it too is an illusion. We are, they held, nothing but meat machines playing out preprogrammed roles.

These preprogrammed roles, in turn, were governed by the theory of evolution. In the 1990s, genetic determinism became widespread as the unraveling of the human genome led to hopes that genes could explain human behavior as thoroughly as human biology. Science had learned that a range of conditions, from cancer to obesity to depression, had genetic roots, so why not human behavior, too? A whole new branch of evolutionary theory, evolutionary psychology, emerged to explain human behavior in terms of genes, biology, and adaptive advantage. The germ of the theory was simple: Early humans engaged in certain behaviors. These made them more fit to reproduce. Therefore contemporary human behavior can be explained in terms of these early adaptations. This led to many bizarre and controversial claims, many of which were opposed by other scientists but widely embraced in popular culture.

Richard J. Herrnstein and Charles Murray argued in 1994 in *The Bell Curve* that racial and ethnic groups were genetically predisposed to higher or lower intelligence levels. Consequently, they said, poverty and crime were the inevitable result of the genetic inferiority of certain groups.[13] Randy Thornhill and Craig Palmer argued in 2000 that men were genetically programmed to rape and have extramarital affairs; they could not help it, for it was a biological inevitability born of the evolutionary imperative for men to fertilize as many women as possible.[14] Criminals were said to have a genetic predisposition for crime and therefore could not seriously be expected to reform. The economic historian Niall Ferguson argued in 2006 that "optimal outbreeding" pressures, meaning finding a mate that was not a close relative but not a complete stranger, led to the development of human races, and thus to racial hatred. In his view, derived from the work of evolutionary psychology, war was a genetic imperative, an inevitable product of tribes competing with "the Other" for reproductive advantage and scarce resources.[15] The sociologist Barbara Ehrenreich argued in 2007 that the human desire to dance and have parties derives from ancient tribes that gathered together to pound sticks and rocks, stomp, and make noise to scare off predators.[16] *The New York Times* reported that the belief in signs and superstitions — magical thinking — was a widespread evolutionary adaptation hard-wired into the brain and thus could not be helped. It was "the polar opposite of helplessness," the newspaper said, designed to give the illusion of control.[17] Scientists also suggested that belief in God was merely a product of the brain, an evolutionary development that helped some groups succeed by providing a reason to band together in communities, or perhaps was simply an accidental byproduct of a more useful adaptation. Geneticists tried to isolate a "God gene" that coded for belief.[18]

Under the influence of evolutionary psychology, it became fashionable to believe that the individual was the helpless victim of biology, society, and the cosmos at large. The individual was powerless to fight back, since his or her faults were inevitable, inborn, and unchangeable. The upshot was that free will was taken out of the equation. In the words of evolutionary biologist Richard Dawkins, humans were "robot vehicles blindly programmed to preserve the selfish molecules known as genes."[19] Or as James Watson, the co-discoverer of DNA, put it, those interested in human destiny turned their thoughts to "genetics or to God."[20] The double-helix was now the thread of fate.

From this understanding, proponents of science, like Richard Dawkins and the Committee for Skeptical Inquiry, opposed religious claims and promoted a materialist, scientific worldview. Philosopher Paul Kurtz, of the Center for Inquiry, proposed that religious morals and ethics were dangerous and should be replaced with an ethical theory derived from the scientific understanding of the material world. Since there was no God to whom moralists could appeal, Kurtz reasoned that science could provide the objective knowledge needed to resolve moral problems without recourse to the supernatural or the transcendent. In his view, ethics and morals were natural and empirical phenomena, defined in terms of their usefulness to humanity.[21] However, Kurtz's ideas papered over a larger problem — in the absence of God, morality is therefore *subjective*, and science could at best provide utilitarian analyses of ethical decisions, but could not speak toward an absolute good. Twentieth century dictators may have slaughtered millions, but who was to say this was wrong? Most agree that it is, but this is not a logical proof from scientific postulates; it is an emotional reaction based on a value for human life, one that science's own investigation of the universe showed that the cosmos did not share. Others, like

Eye-shaped nebula. The debate between science and religion heated up in the 1990s and 2000s, as religious believers and materialists argued whether the universe was the product of intelligent design or random chance that merely resembled design, like this nebula that resembles a human eye. Horror found material on both sides of the debate (NASA, ESA, C.R. O'Dell [Vanderbilt University], M. Meixner and P. McCullough [STScI]).

Steven J. Gould, had proposed that science and religion were "non-overlapping magisteria" working in different spheres, and so posed no threat to one another since the former explained the "how" of creation and the latter that "why."

Mainstream religious groups, like the Episcopal Church and (to some extent) the Catholic Church, supported science and even the theory of evolution, reasoning that science could be used to understand God's creation. However, when *Time* asked in 1964 if God was dead, it was pointing to the death of mainstream religious belief, which was in steep decline, siphoned off by science on the one hand and more extreme forms of faith on the other. The percentage of Americans claiming no religious belief rose to a record fourteen percent in 2001, nearly doubling in a decade,[22] but those who identified as believers were increasingly extreme in their beliefs. Fundamentalist groups grew at a rapid pace through the twentieth century, largely in response to the perceived "godlessness" of science. Mark A. Shibley found in the mid–1990s that evangelical churches attracted disaffected individuals who came to the faith out of discomfort with society in general or a personal crisis, often related to health, which contributed to anti-science (specifically anti-medical science) feelings.[23] This was one cause among many for the evangelical revival, the greatest surge of religious feeling since the fires subsided on the Burned Over District.

Evangelical conservatives tended to support restrictions on abortion and embryonic stem cell research, and for keeping alive Terri Schiavo, a brain-dead woman whom evangelicals believed should not be removed from life support. In an extraordinary action, at the behest of his religious supporters, President George W. Bush flew from his vacation home back to Washington on March 21, 2005, to sign emergency legislation aimed at keeping Schiavo alive. Even some Republicans began to wonder whether the party was sliding toward theocracy.[24] Evangelicals believed America was a "Christian nation" that needed to return to God's commandments and repudiate "liberalism" and "secularism" to regain divine favor. It was a classic revitalization movement, the kind that anthropologist Alfred F. C. Wallace once defined as "a deliberate, organized, conscious effort by members of a society to create a more satisfying culture" in response to cultural stress, often by one or more of these methods: reemphasizing traditional values, appealing to a "purer" version of an ideal culture (usually located in a more perfect past), opposing outsiders or non-believers, and imagining a coming apocalypse.[25] All these were present in the evangelical movement.

Evangelical fervor was only one type of religious revival sparked by anxieties over secularism, materialism, and science. Around the world a radical form of Islam arose in the last decades of the twentieth century, preaching hatred for the popular culture of the United States, anger at the influence of Western secularism, and the need to return to traditional religious values to revitalize the Islamic community, or *umma*. A full accounting for the rise of radical Islam is beyond the scope of this book, but Osama bin Laden and the leaders of Al Qaeda specifically used the threat of science, of sex, and of secularism to justify terrorism in the name of Allah. It would be a *jihad*, or holy war, in defense of faith against infidels and the godless.

The Terror

The Dow Jones average peaked at 11,792.98 on January 15, 2000, and then lost 33 percent in the next two years. It would not surpass the old record high for seven years. It was an early indication that the "holiday from history" was nearing its end. In July 2000 the technological triumph that was the supersonic jetliner Concorde crashed in France. Jonathan Freedland of Britain's

Guardian newspaper explained that the crash was an act of God, and the response to it a symbol of humanity's blindness in the face of a powerlessness our species could not understand:

> We'll run around, talking about new safety procedures, tighter rules and improved designs. We'll act as if there is much we can do to make sure this never happens again. We won't admit for a moment our sheer helplessness. For that would fill us with absolute terror.[26]

The human condition, he said, was one of helplessness and fear on which we impose only a fiction of control. Americans would for years attempt to impose the illusion of control on a chaotic world after terrorism came to the United States.

In 1993, Islamic terrorists bombed Manhattan's World Trade Center. In 1998, the terror network Al Qaeda bombed American embassies in Kenya and Tanzania. In 2000, Al Qaeda bombed the American warship *USS Cole*. Then on the eleventh of September, 2001, Al Qaeda–trained terrorists hijacked four jetliners, crashing two into the World Trade Center, one into the Pentagon, and another (intended for Washington, D.C.) into a field in Pennsylvania. The attacks were broadcast live on global television screens, and when the World Trade Center towers collapsed into thundering clouds of debris and nearly three thousand lay dead, observers struggled to find language to describe the horror. Many turned to the language of film, comparing the attacks to a movie, one of the most common metaphors employed. Jane McGonigal watched the attacks on television: "The on-screen spectacle is not a cinematic fiction of terror; it is terrorism, real and immediate. So why am I watching as if it were just another Hitchcock or John Carpenter production?" She was profoundly disturbed by the fact that she reacted to the attacks like she reacted to horror movies, repulsed yet fascinated by "visuals that frighten me."[27]

The columnist George Will employed the iconography of horror to his distillation of the attacks the day after. He argued that the terrorists had used the media to create what was in essence the world's most awful horror movie:

> Terrorism acquires its power from the special horror of its randomness and from the magnification of it by modern media, which make the perpetrators seem the one thing they are not — powerful. Terrorism is the tactic of the weak.[28]

The randomness of terror meant that ordinary Americans (and, after the Madrid bombing of 2004 and the London bombings of 2005, Westerners in general) had to confront the idea that any one of them could at any time become the victim of terrorism. It was a remote possibility, statistically, but a visceral reality emotionally. Unable to cope with the sense of powerlessness and loss of control, many tried to scapegoat and affix blame. The Rev. Jerry Falwell told a television audience:

> I really believe that the pagans, and the abortionists, and the feminists, and the gays and the lesbians who are actively trying to make that an alternative lifestyle, the

September 11, 2001. A man covered in ashes helps a woman walk following the collapse of the World Trade Center. The terrorist attacks of September 11, 2001, were the deadliest on American soil. As Americans struggled to understand events in the days and weeks that followed, many reached for the language of cinema, and horror movies, to make sense of what happened (Library of Congress, Prints and Photgraphs Division, photograph by Don Halasy, LC-DIG-ppmsca-01813).

ACLU, People for the American Way, all of them who have tried to secularize America. I point the finger in their face and say "You helped this happen."[29]

Falwell had to apologize for the comments, but the idea had its attractions for some conservatives who believed materialism was damaging American life. In 2007, the conservative intellectual Dinesh D'Souza argued much the same point, claiming that "liberals," meaning those who supported science and materialism, were responsible for provoking the September 11th attacks by giving Muslim extremists reason to complain about America's corrupt and decadent culture. Only, he argued, by joining America's religious conservatives with Islam's can religion effectively destroy the secular left; i.e., scientific materialism.[30]

After September 11, 2001, the Bush administration began the controversial preparations for the Iraq War, identifying an "Axis of Evil" (Iraq, Iran, and North Korea) opposed to Western values, and eliding the identities of the Al Qaeda terrorists and Iraqi government, a connection that objective investigation failed to substantiate. The American and British governments argued that Iraqi president Saddam Hussein had weapons of mass destruction and intended to use them against the United States and its allies. War, President Bush argued, was the only way to stop this grave threat. Skeptics questioned the two governments' assertions, but a Bush aide told reporters that truth was now a relative concept: "That's not the way the world really works any more. We're an empire now, and when we act we create our own reality."[31] However, there were no weapons of mass destruction in Iraq, and as the war dragged on into its second, third, and fourth years, public opposition grew to the raging violence in occupied Iraq. But despite a change of power in Congress and blue ribbon commissions calling for withdrawal from a war that the American government's own generals thought unwinnable, the president would not change course. The unwanted war was just another thing for the average person to feel powerless about.

In 2000 the eminent historian Jacques Barzun declared that Western civilization was decadent, that apart from science and technology, it was moribund.[32] In 2006, the newly eminent historian Niall Ferguson declared that Western power was in great decline and facing eclipse.[33] Newspapers spoke about "changing baselines," the idea that the foundations of society were shifting — Westerners now accepted that governments had the right to vacate age-old freedoms, that tap water was undrinkable, air often unfit for breathing, and manners coarsening. One environmentalist said that with public apathy and acceptance — that is the abdication of responsibility or control — "you could be accepting the demise of civilization" without knowing it.[34]

Against this widespread attitude of helplessness, decadence, and decline, horror began its own revitalization movement.

20

LITERARY DEVELOPMENTS

As the 1990s gave way to the new millennium, the field of written horror underwent a profound change. The onslaught of horror novels in the 1970s and 1980s had made horror into a genre publishers could profitably market to a niche, but the development of that niche meant that horror increasingly left the mainstream for an insular community of self-conscious horror fans. The old mass market magazines that used to carry horror fiction, and the popular anthologies of the same, had faded away. In their place, an alternative world of horror fandom created its own publishing apparatus parallel to but outside of mainstream literature, which was itself shifting toward the deathly-dull "literary novel" as the exemplar of good taste. Small press publishers, print-on-demand technology, and especially the Internet took up the slack.

But this meant that much of modern horror was produced without traditional safeguards provided by the literary establishment: editors, publishers, and critics who in times past possessed great power to define was "good" or "worthy." The critic Paula Guran complained loudly in 2002 that too much of the new horror was simply imitations of imitations, derivative of derivatives, rewritten movies turned into stories. The horror community, she declared, simply spoke to itself about itself, turning the genre into a "brackish inland swamp of literary incest" that neither engaged with real literature nor even attempted to uphold traditional standards of literary merit.[1] The online horror community banded together to protest Guran's assessment. And they kept cranking it out.

Beginning in 2004, Stephen Jones, the editor of the respected *Best New Horror* series of anthologies, began complaining that there was simply too much horror. Each year he compiled an overview of all the new horror publications from the previous year. The task once took seven pages but in 2004 took ninety. In 2006, Jones argued persuasively that the output of horror was disproportionate to the number of available readers. For all books in every genre, the United States and Great Britain each published two hundred thousand new titles in 2005, an increase of more than fifty percent in ten years.[2] Horror, to be sure, was only a small fraction of that massive number, but even so it represented thousands of new titles each and every year.

No one could seriously attempt to survey all that fiction, and fewer still actually read any of it. A modestly successful book could expect a readership of a few thousand individuals out of a combined Anglo-American population of 360 million and the sixty or so million more in Canada, Australia, and other Anglophone countries. Any one title, even best sellers, might be read by at best three or four percent of the population, while movies and television programs could easily command that audience for even poor performers. Jones said that the decline of reading in favor of movies, television, and the Internet left the horror story and the horror novel imperiled. There were simply too many books and too few readers:

> So then, who is actually reading all these books we're currently producing? Somebody must be ... or there may not be a mass-market horror field around in a decade's time. But then again, there might not be such a thing as books either....[3]

In 2004, the National Endowment for the Arts announced that the number of American adults reading literature hit an all-time low, with less than half admitting to having read fiction in the year (2002) surveyed, and just over half saying they read any book at all.[4] Divide that by the number of titles published and the results were dismal. Yet movies like *Saw III* (2006), for example, grossed $80 million in two months, which translated to a viewing audience of around three percent of the American population (assuming some repeat viewers) for that film alone. DVD sales would expand this audience. By contrast, in a full year Elizabeth Kostova's best-selling* novel *The Historian* (2005) sold fewer than half a million copies, which even if borrowed and shared still meant a readership of less than one quarter of one percent of the American population. The children of the 1970s and '80s, who grew up hating to read, became adults who didn't like it either. The audience for *Goosebumps* graduated to DVD and dot-com rather than hardcover.

Literary Trends

It is impossible to summarize the body of horror produced since 1990, but it would not be unfair to suggest that the vast majority of it was to some degree homage, pastiche, sequel, or reworking of earlier horror themes—postmodernism taken to its logical extreme. Robert Bloch and Andre Norton's *The Jekyll Legacy* (1990) was an unnecessary sequel to Robert Louis Stevenson's masterpiece. Caítlin R. Kiernan continued the *Dracula* story with "Love Spoke Eloquent" (1997). Kim Newman produced a series of *Anno Dracula* novels and stories (1992–) in which the Count conquers Britain, marries Queen Victoria,

---

*A bestseller is usually defined in the United States as a book selling 100,000 or more copies. In the United Kingdom, best sellers move around 25,000 copies; and in Canada, 5,000. There are no set benchmarks, though, and bestsellers can vary in sales.

and births a race of vampires, with which humanity — in the form of famous figures of history, literature, and television — must learn to live. She also resurrected Edgar Allan Poe's ghost to torment a writer in "Just Like Eddy" (1999). Joe Hill's short story "Best New Horror" (2005) capped off the trend, imagining the editor of a *Best New Horror* anthology running across a killer cannibal family modeled on the one from *The Texas Chain Saw Massacre* and then calling on his horror genre knowledge to attempt an escape. He finds the meeting strangely invigorating, but the result was a rather blasé reheating of leftover clichés. All of these types of stories were horror fiction meant for the horror fiction fan, self-referential, self-conscious, and perhaps self-defeating.

We have already mentioned *Shadows Over Baker Street*'s melding of the Cthulhu Mythos with Sherlock Holmes, and Mythos-themed fiction reached a crescendo in this period, with new Lovecraftian works emerging with clockwork regularity but rarely with anything approaching ingenuity.

Brian Lumley's novella *The Taint* (2005) reworked Lovecraft's "The Shadow Over Innsmouth" without substantially improving on the original. It told of a woman who only gradually came to discover that her father, and therefore she too, is one of the Deep Ones, doomed to a fishy future. In the story's climax, we learn that a kindly old doctor is in fact a Deep One who has developed a new genetic technology to suppress the Deep Ones' taint long enough for them to take over the world.

But it is possible, I think, to see in this body of derivative work a subtly new theme pulsing underneath an otherwise-familiar surface. The stories tended to end with the triumph of the monster, and they suggested that to some extent encounters with horror were inevitable, natural, and destined. Lumley's *The Taint*, for example, made it quite clear that the genetic legacy of the Deep Ones is inborn, like the genetic determinism of the evolutionary psychologists, and their triumph is unstoppable. Those with "the taint" must inevitably yield to the Deep Ones' ideology; those who fight it succumb in the end. This isn't new, of course; Lovecraft's original had much the same story, but there the emphasis was on the cosmic destiny of the hero and his gradual awakening to unseen worlds and the horror within. Here the emphasis is clearly on the horror of succumbing body and soul to an alien world beyond one's control.

In 1994, Stephen Jones edited an entire collection of Innsmouth-themed Cthulhu fiction, called *Shadows Over Innsmouth*, including contributions from some of the biggest names in British horror fiction: Ramsey Cambell, Brian Lumley, Neil Gaiman, and so on. Something about the idea of bad genes and flawed destinies certainly had resonance. Gaiman's contribution, the satirical "Only the End of the World Again" (1994), begins when the narrator receives a note from his landlady saying that the rent is late and that "when the Elder Gods rose up from the ocean, all the scum of the earth, all the non-believers, all the human garbage and the wastrels and deadbeats would be swept away, and the world would be cleansed by ice and deep water."[5] Would Jerry Falwell have spoken differently of the Second Coming? The narrator, by the way, was Lawrence Talbot, the Universal werewolf, trapped in a Wolf Man vs. Deep One monster mash-up.

John Brunner's postmodern "Concerning the Forthcoming Inexpensive Paperback Translation of the *Necronomicon* of Abdul Alhazred" (1992) broke apart and reassembled the pieces of Lovecraft's "The Dunwich Horror," this time set in England and at the conclusion of which the servants of the Old Ones plan to disseminate the *Necronomicon* far and wide, blanketing the earth in forbidden knowledge, so evil might triumph.

Studying Dark Arts

H. P. Lovecraft was something of a prophet for modern horror. In 1996, the scholar S. T. Joshi published a new biography of Lovecraft, and in 2005 Lovecraft entered the Library of America, steadily growing in stature and in academic respectability. His bleak vision of amoral cosmic indifference fit perfectly with the tenor of the times. The events of the years surrounding the millennium had brought Lovecraft's vision to fruition; Cthulhu pointed the way toward the godless cosmos of science. Authors Neil Gaiman, China Miéville, and Poppy Z. Brite embraced a form of Lovecraft's ideas, one less concerned with the cosmic implications of a vast and unplumbed universe but more focused on the helplessness and insignificance of humanity in the face of powers greater than it imagined possible.

Thomas Ligotti (b. 1953) produced clever and subtle horror whose carefully chosen words reflect a philosophical and profoundly weird vision. "The Last Feast of Harlequin" (1990), an explicit homage to Lovecraft, told a creepy tale of an anthropologist who travels to the town of Mirocaw to attend a clown performance at an annual festival. There he notes the strange departures from traditional Christmas celebrations, like the fact that all the holiday lights are green — none are red. Beneath the façade of small town virtue, there lies a darker and more horrible truth that threatens to consume anyone who probes too deeply.

Noctuary (1994) brought together a number of Ligotti's evocations of the weird, which perhaps can be best summed up an early line from the collection's first story, "The Medusa" (1991): "We can hide from horror only in the heart of horror."[6] In the story, a collector of press clippings on the mythological snake-haired Medusa begins to piece together random shreds of information into a picture that is increasingly frightening, not unlike the developments of "The Call of Cthulhu." The bits of information come to him haphazardly, through fate or chance: "This was normal. But although these 'finds' proved nothing, rationally, they did always suggest more to Dregler's imagination than to his reason...."[7] After being subjected to a hoax involving a book that was said to *be* the Medusa, Dregler was "left to suffer the effects of a true state of unknowing."[8] Dregler is soon moderately famous as a philosopher and writer on the Medusa, who has become for him a captivating focus for meditations on annihilation and death. At the end he finds the Gorgon he seeks and the stony ending his heart desired like a lost love.

In "The Prodigy of Dreams" (1986), scholar Arthur Emerson spends his days reading of lost worlds and imaginary continents, searching for hints of a world beyond this, of the infinite of which human experience forms only the smallest part. In Lovecraftian fashion, his interests in the occult lead only to a negative revelation whereby he is destroyed in mind and body, dead and one with Cynothoglys, mortician of the gods. "The Tsalal" (1994) tells of a great blackness that existed before the world of gods and men, and still lurks beyond the fragile veil of reality. In "A Mad Night of Atonement" (1989), a scientist receives a revelation from the divine, transforming him into a believer compelled to build a Sacred Ray that will use the methods of science to reveal the presence of God. For this the scientist had been prepared by his research, even before his revelation, "in the accidental manner of great scientific discoveries."[9] And that discovery is that humanity, and indeed all creation, is headed toward disintegration — that corruption, decay, and death are the very *purpose* of God's creation and that "it is modern science itself which will enable us to realize the Creator's dream."[10] The ending of the story bizarrely hints that the narrator is himself the Creator whose magnificently ruined creation still eludes him in its broken perfection.

The volume concludes with many very brief horrors. In "Salvation by Doom" (1994), a tortured prisoner protests his innocence and that they have the wrong man until his torturer asks a simple question: "Are you certain of that?"[11] Unable to answer affirmatively, he dies. In "Death Without End" (1994), a man fools his friends into thinking he lives in better conditions than he does, and in his rotten home he wishes to have "true knowledge" of death.[12] When it is granted, his friends find his desiccated corpse in his crumbling home, though their memories retained the false image he had projected. "The Order of Illusion" (1984) tells of a man jaded by the mockery and irony of the (presumably) modern world, in which the old rites were dead and impotent. He seeks out ancient forms of worship, and even as he achieves a high priesthood, the emptiness of his achievement in its way fills him with wonder.

Ligotti's fiction is carefully written and beautiful to read. Each story dramatizes Ligotti's essentially Lovecraftian view that knowledge of the true world outside our comforting illusions yields only madness and void. But unlike Lovecraft, for Ligotti there is no reason to struggle against the darkness, no culture or accomplishment worth pursuing in the face of the nothingness of the purposeless universe. Instead, it is only the stories themselves — as positive acts of creation — that defy the bleak view contained within their crystalline prose. It was Lovecraftian horror for a fatalistic age.

Short Horrors

Short stories in the horror vein tended to break down into three main types. The first was the pastiche, those derivative tales that recycled or reworked older material, usually without discernibly improving upon the original. The stories reworked or re-invented popular culture products, but counted on familiarity with the original works for much of their effect.

We have already seen a number of derivatives, like *Anno Dracula* or Cthulhu fiction. David J. Schow's "The Absolute Last of the Hallowe'en Horror Nights" (2002) found the monsters of classic horror films infiltrating a Halloween monster-themed party, slipping in among the partiers to do their dirty work. Brian Keene's "'The King,' in: *Yellow*" (2002) mashed together Robert W. Chambers's *The King in Yellow* with dead celebrities like Elvis Presley and Janis Joplin for an unforgettable performance. Steve Nagy's "The Hanged Man of Oz" (2003) found a man obsessed with *The Wizard of Oz* trapped in a horror version of the urban legend about a Munchkin who killed himself on-set. Steven Laws's "The Crawl" (1997) was a tense and suspenseful translation of a slasher movie into prose. A young couple's car has trouble on an isolated stretch of highway. They are attacked by a supernatural scarecrow wielding a scythe. They move through the slasher film's stations of the cross—the tow truck that offers no help, the would-be rescuer who fails, the inescapable killer pursuing at a laconic pace. The story improves on the slasher film in one respect: At the end, the survivors are guilt-stricken because they stood by and let the scarecrow take the man who came to rescue them. They felt *glad* that the creature took him instead, and they now feel shame about that primitive joy.

The second type continued the traditional types of horror tales—weird tales, *contes cruelles*, supernatural horror—but presented a disturbing and fatalistic assessment of the human condition. These stories generally told stories that reflected horror's timeless themes or utilized traditional narrative styles, though with distinctly modern settings or flavors. Nina Kiriki Hoffman's "Broken Things" (1990) found a woman, Ginger, imposing a sense of control on her out-of-control world by finding simple happiness in the death of her rebellious daughter, Anna. Now her daughter could be tamed: "Ginger would do exactly what Anna wanted her to do." New hair, new makeup, some homemade modifications to her figure; she would be the "perfect child."[13] Richard T. Chizmar's "Heroes" (1993) was the heartbreaking story of a son who could not cope with his father's Alzheimer's disease—the dissolution of his father's knowledge and memory, the essence of his person—and so seeks out the aid of what the story implies is perhaps Dracula to give his father a kind of immortality.

David Gerrold's "Satan Claus" (later renamed "... And Eight Rabid Pigs") (1995) begins with Steven Dhor lecturing on the horrors of Christmas. Santa Claus, he said, is merely a kid's version of God. Since Santa is a hoax, so too must be God. Worse, since secular society kicked Christ out of Christmas, for most people Santa is "now their *only* experience of God."[14] He holds, in ironic fashion, that there must also be a Satan Claus to punish the wicked. He describes Satan Claus's vile appearance and how his clothes are made from the skins of those whose souls he takes, dyed black with their sins. Steven and his friends add to the ersatz legend, fleshing it out; and Steven writes a story about it. Others take it up, and soon children's widespread belief in the power of evil brings the creature to life. We learn in the end that the idea has taken flesh and is in fact the narrator.

Joel Lane's "Wave Scars" (1994) found a gay man mourning the loss of the optimism the end of the Cold War had engendered. He is taken by Steven, a friend with whom he once shared an intimate night, but Steven is haunted. He is trapped in the ghosts of his childhood horror, and he must make an annual pilgrimage to relive the great shipwreck that cost the lives of so many:

> And it happens all the time. Boats go down, cars crash, houses burn; and damaged people spill out into the road. The only way to go on is to realise that it *is* always the same. You have to hold on to the few who mean enough to you to bring out the healer. And sometimes the healer is very difficult to find.[15]

The acclaimed author Joyce Carol Oates made a number of forays into quiet horror. Her story "Blind" (1994) presents a case-study for the terror inherent when deprived of information. The narrator is completely in the dark, for there was no light on a night when she needed to get help upon finding her professor husband dead. Though a housewife without interest in "his science magazines," she is terrified now when the science of electricity has failed her.[16] In the darkness she secures her provisions. Worried that the predicted cosmic doom of the science magazines—the asteroid attack that would end earth life—has come to pass, she seals herself into her house, alone and insane, oblivious to the fact that it is she and not the world that has gone blind, hysterical at her husband's death, a death it is implied she may have caused. Oates's "The Haunting" (2003) told of abused children, their possibly murderous mother, and a basement haunted by caged rabbits. It was a meditation on the impact of sin across time and generations.

Ramsey Campbell, whom we met in Chapter 17, was a master of quiet horror, and not a year went by without new contributions from him. His novella *The Word* (1997) revolved around bitter horror and fantasy critic Jeremy Bates, who hates conventions and fanzines and their low quality, and resents the success of Jess Kray, a sci-fi hack. Kray wrote *The Word*, and Bates can't get a review copy because the publisher says it's "literature," not "genre." The book takes the world by storm, a revelation regarded as blasphemy by the authorities; but its author has become like a Messiah. (Like *The King in Yellow*, *The Word*'s content is only hinted at, never described.) Bates goes nearly mad opposing the book, which he believes is intended to turn its author into a new Christ. Bates denies Kray's claim that the book's wisdom bestows eternal life, and in the end, ravening and crazed, he kills Kray on a TV talk show. "Breaking Up" (2004) used cell phones as a prop for a story about ghostly stalking from beyond the grave. "The Decorations" (2005) was a quietly horrible tale of an old woman's fears, a grandson's nightmares, and the Christmas that brought horror to all.

In the paranoid *X-Files* vein, Terry Lamsley's "Sickhouse Hospitality" (2005) told of a secret hospital, infested by rats, in which scientists perform unnamed experiments on human subjects for undisclosed purposes. When a patient finally escapes, he realizes why no one ever did anything about the rats. Uniformed private security forces lock down the hospital, trapping the sick and dying in the rat-infested structure. The patients thought the men had come to rescue them, but they were there to free the rats.

The Cutting Edge

An increasing percentage of modern short horror featured a renewed passion for extreme horror, even more bloodthirsty in its way than splatterpunk had been a decade earlier. Inspired by the blood and guts of cinema, this breed of horror featured ultra-violence, graphic sex, and attempts to outpace any sense of restriction or taboo. While splatterpunk had largely dealt with extreme violence, the new extreme horror had a fetish for sex.

Sex and violence mixed it up in anthologies like *I Shudder at Your Touch: 22 Tales of Sex and Horror* (1991) and in magazines like *Cthulhu Sex*, which is pretty much what it sounds like, only kinkier. Vampires, after Anne Rice, had become sex objects, too, in the horror stories of writers like Tanith Lee, or in supernatural romances like Katie Macalister's *Sex, Lies, and Vampires* (2005) or erotica like Evangeline Anderson's *Secret Thirst* (2005). In *Secret Thirst*, a female research scientist invented a blood substitute vampires could use to enter normal society. A vampire steals her laptop to pilfer the formula, only to discover her secret desire for erotic submission. The two become trapped in a bondage and domination nightclub where the scientist must act out her secret sex fantasies to survive. Harlequin, the leading publisher of romance novels, created the Nocturne line for its Silhouette imprint to produce "paranormal romance" novels at the rate of one or two per month. Titles included Michele Hauf's *From the Dark* (2006) about vampires and witches and their forbidden love, and Karren Widdon's *Cry of the Wolf* (2007) about a werewolf in love.

John Shirley's "Six Kinds of Darkness" (1988) imagined the New York of the near future, where immigrants have overrun the city and environmental degradation left the atmosphere in ruins. Acid rain had re-carved the ornate façade of a Victorian townhouse into "dainty gargoyles." The house is a sort of hi-tech opium den-cum-brothel. Inside, electromagnetic fields in one room directly stimulate the brain's pleasure centers—sex without touching. Another room provides hallucinogenic images of sexual activity, so that "semen tickl[es] down his legs inside his pants" while the machines make him a helpless, dancing, orgasming marionette.[17] The final room injects the essence of a dead person — thoughts, feelings, pleasures, and pains — letting the user feel the inside of another. Made from the essence of those who overdosed on the pleasure rooms, it was Soylent Green as crack cocaine.

Leslie What's "The Mutable Borders of Love" (2004) told of a woman whose relationships dissolve into ghosts that haunt her forevermore. Christina Faust's "Tighter" (2004) was another tale of unresolved erotic longing, this time the longing of a female escape artist for the type of sadomasochistic bondage that will completely satisfy her. She finds it in the arms of a supernatural man named Kevin who can tie her tighter than she ever dared imagine. But, like love, this S&M is too good to last.

Elizabeth Mackey's "Pinkie" (2005) was a variation on the Ed Gein–*Psycho* story, complete with Robert Bloch–style Freudian castration anxiety made literal. Rennie owns a miracle pig that not only does tricks but also talks and, in fits of anger, murders people. Rennie covers this up, but eventually the cops come looking for some missing people. They find them buried in the garden, and they find Rennie's parents murdered in the basement. In the end, we learn that the pig is just a pig and Rennie is a madman, driven to act out his sexual frustration as murder because his parents had cut off his penis (they feared sex and wanted him to stay pure). Like Norman Bates, he did not know what he was doing when he killed. He shoved his mother's decapitated head up between her legs.

Perhaps the most disturbing mixture of sex and horror could be found in Gemma Files's "Kissing Carrion" (2003). H. P. Lovecraft's "The Loved Dead" had shocked the 1920s with even the hint of sex with corpses, but this tale, inspired by a Toronto sex shop called Lovecraft, took necrophilia to nauseating new levels. Narrated by a ghost, the story describes "carrionettes," which are corpses that Pat Calavera hooks up to a contraption she calls the Bone Machine. This allows her to turn the (dead) human body into a kind of puppet that she can manipulate via remote control. She uses her puppets to perform sex acts to please fetishists. She does this "because she can.... Because she's an extremist, and there's nothing more extreme."[18] Pat likes to control things, and the ghost of one of the unwitting subjects of her puppetry doesn't like it one little bit. Raymond likes to "fuck dead bodies," but only *male* dead bodies — "anyone can fuck the dead ... but the dead, by their very nature, can never fuck *back*."[19] That's where the Bone Machine comes in. Wires and electrodes create an erection, remote controls manipulate the body into Ray's anus, giving him his pleasure. Pat is jealous of her creation, jealous that Ray enjoys the mechanical pleasuring of the rotting dead to her own. As Ray slips from sex fetish to cannibalizing his beloved corpse, Pat lets the body kill Ray. The ghost knows that the flesh is just a container, a useless joke of creation, "Big Bang detritus bought with Jesus' blood," but he still feels some attachment to it nonetheless.[20]

How could anyone top that? Clive Barker's "Haeckel's Tale" (2005) imagined the eminent nineteenth century German evolutionist Ernst Haeckel stumbling across an old man whose wife employed a necromancer so she could enjoy orgies with the dead in a variety of graphically described positions. The corpses rose from their tombs, vigorously pleasuring her one after the next while the woman "was kneading her full tits, directing arcs of milk into the air so that it rained down on the vile menagerie cavorting before her."[21] She conceived an undead baby from an earlier coupling.

In these stories, the powers that raised the dead, the methods by which the dead might function, and in general the "science" and "philosophy" aspects of the horror, are wholly subsumed in the sex. In Barker's story, the scientist is outdone by the magician; in Fines's story, the mechanics of the Bone Machine are less important than the penetration. Compared with *Frankenstein* or *The Island of Dr. Moreau*, these stories were shocking without the profundity of their predecessors.

Horror Across Genres

Paula Guran was not wrong to suggest that straight-up horror had backed itself into an isolated corner, speaking largely to itself. However, there was hope from beyond the limits of horror. Cross-genre hybrids tried to export horror themes out of the publisher- and fan-defined genre into more mainstream fare. Science fiction took up much of the slack, injecting some welcome darkness. Following Thomas Harris's success with *Red Dragon* and *Silence of the Lambs*, crime fiction became darker, too. Crossing horror with crime and detective fiction, F. Paul Wilson's "The Wringer" (1996) followed the adventures of Repairman Jack, a character introduced in 1989. Jack works outside the law to correct "problems," often through the application of violence. "The Wringer" featured Jack trying to stop the torture of a woman and her child, a torture described in loving detail. Jack's adventures continued in a number of novels into the twenty-first century. Elsewhere, violent and bloody psychos were all the rage, as in Bret Easton Ellis's *American Psycho* (1991). Set in the late 1980s, the novel narrated the thoughts of Patrick Bateman, a successful Wall Street banker and psychotic serial killer. He describes the brutal torture and murder of his victims amidst discussions of his everyday life and the pathological way he maintains his veneer of respectability. Bateman hates the unemployed and the homeless, whom he considers genetically inferior and therefore doomed to their destiny. However, he plays the part of the rich, successful playboy so well that not even his own lawyer can accept his confession. In the end, he fails as a serial killer because no one will believe in him; and the futility of his actions depresses him.

Dean Koontz blended horror with science fiction and mystery across many best-sellers. His *Phantoms* (1983) told a sci-fi–horror story about a town under siege from a giant shape-shifting amoeba, *à la* Lovecraft's shoggoths. It consumes people, integrates their memories, and proceeds from this new knowledge base. Thus the creature becomes a cruel, sadistic monster because it has learned that from the people it ate. It is destroyed by genetically modified bacteria trained to eat oil, a substance the creature seems to be made from. *Odd Thomas* (2003) and its two sequels revolved around Thomas, a young man who could talk to the dead and his encounters with increasingly dark forces intent on destroying him. Koontz's later works tended toward thrillers and suspense rather than outright horror.

Thanks to the success of Koontz and Michael Crichton, the thriller genre made use of horror imagery and situations. Arguably, John Grisham's thriller *The Firm* (1991), about a lawyer trapped in a law firm that is actually a front for the Mafia, was a monster story with the firm taking the role of the monster. In its way it was psychologically horrifying in the way of *Psycho*.

Joseph R. Garber's *Vertical Run* (1995) told the story of a former Green Beret named Dave Elliot, now an advertising executive in a forty-five–story office tower. One day his boss tries to kill him in the office, and one by one everyone in the tower turns on him. Utilizing his military training, Elliot manages to make his way out of the homicidal skyscraper. You see, he must die over some biological weapons research the United States apparently acquired from the Axis after World War II: "Rumor was lots of enemy scientists were a-workin' on it then. Rumor is that some folks still are."[22] It turns out that our hero has been infected by a monkey at an illicit biological weapons research facility masquerading as an ultramodern biotech company. The disease is apparently some sort of superbug that lies dormant until it "mutates" into a virulent form that can be contracted by anyone who comes into contact with biological fluids, not unlike a nightmare version of the AIDS virus, but one that kills in seventy-two hours. The government would rather kill Elliot and everyone he came into contact with than reveal the secret weapons program, but Elliot manages to escape to die his preferred way, at the lake he loves.

In A. R. Morlan's short story "Bringing It Along" (1996), Carey and her boyfriend Gary go camping in the Hawaiian jungle. Carey knows Gary intends to scare her by hiding outside the tent and shouting her name in the night. But when he tries, he gets tangled in a vine, falls, and impales his head on the tent-spike. Carey spent the whole night beside the mangled corpse, touching it with her foot but mistaking it for the cat.

A much more elaborate version of that story could be found in Scott Smith's fatalistic thriller *The Ruins* (2006), the story of American tourists who suffer at the hands of an inexplicable natural enemy. It begins with Jeff, Stacy, Eric, and Amy, four young Americans on vacation on the beaches of Cancun, engaging in a last happy vacation before the onset of adult responsibility. Jeff is a practical medical student, exemplar of reason, science and order. His girlfriend Amy is a selfish complainer. Eric is immature and confused about his direction in life. Stacy is Amy's best friend, a wild-child who cheats on her boyfriend whenever she thinks she can get away with, and even when she thinks she can't. The four befriend Mathias, a German tourist whose brother went off with a woman working at an archaeological dig somewhere inland. Mathias asks if they would accompany him while he goes looking for his missing sibling. They agree, after some hesitation, and a Greek tourist who speaks no English, whom they know only under the assumed name of "Pablo," comes with them out of an excess of zeal. His two friends, "Don Quixote" and "Juan," are supposed to follow some time later.

Following a map Mathias's brother left behind, the group travels by bus and then by foot into the Mexican jungle, arriving eventually at the remains of the archaeological encampment. This is where things begin to go sour. They find the encampment in the middle of a clearing, a beautiful glade of rich, green vegetation and blood-red flowers. Climbing the little flower-covered hill they start to examine the scene. They discover dead bodies, including the desiccated corpse of Mathias's brother, and the camp in ruins. Thinking to get help, they try to leave the hill, but Mayan tribesman encircle them and aim their arrows at the tourists if they so much as step in the direction of escape. They are trapped on the hill.

Their American cell phones don't work in rural Mexico, but they hear a phone ringing down an old mineshaft. Lowering Pablo into the shaft to find the phone, Pablo ends up falling, paralyzing him from the waist down. The others try to rescue him, and in the process Eric injures his leg. They don't find the phone. Jeff and Mathias try to make Pablo comfortable, and the group waits for the other Greeks to arrive, an arrival they aren't sure will ever come. Jeff, thinking ahead, wants to post a sign to warn the Greeks, or any other would-be rescuers, about the Mayans and the danger. Only gradually do the kids realize that the pretty little vines decorating the hill are carnivorous and have sucked dry the corpses littering the hill.

When Jeff sees that the vines have destroyed the warning signs he made, he understands. The plants, it turns out, are not just passive leeches but active killers. They can move, and fight, and kill: "Yet even now, having glimpsed this, Jeff still couldn't stop himself from clinging to the old logic, the ways of the world beyond this vine-covered hill...." He sees movement in the brush. "Jeff knew what it was now—knew what had pulled down his sign, too—and felt almost sickened by the knowledge."[23] This was why the Maya guarded the hill and refused to let them leave. They were trying to prevent the killer vine from spreading.

The others only gradually come to accept the reality of the situation, especially when they discover that the vines can imitate sounds—like that "cell phone" in the mine shaft, or even their voices. Amy has seen what the plant can do:

Yet all this was so far beyond what she took to be the immutable laws of nature, so far beyond what she knew a plant ought to be capable of, that she couldn't quite bring herself to accept it. Strange things had happened — dreadful things— and she'd witnessed them with her own eyes, but even so, she continued to doubt them.[24]

To find a language or a framework to cope with the irrational, Eric and Stacy imagine themselves in an action-movie version of their situation, speculating on how the writers would tidy up the story and turn them into stereotypes. Eric would be the comic relief; Jeff the hero; Amy the prissy good girl; Stacy the slut. "Mathias is the villain — definitely. Those scary Germans. They'll

Vine. Even the most innocent and beautiful aspects of nature can be fuel for horror. A ficitional vine not unlike this one attracts American tourists in *The Ruins*, but unlike this vine the book's plant is a much more formidable opponent. Stories involving vengeful aspects of the natural world — from animals to killer plants — became prominent in the polluted 1970s and continued into the era of global warming (Library of Congress, Prints and Photographs Division, LC-DIG-matpc-00391).

have him lure us here on purpose. The vine'll be some sort of Nazi experiment gone awry. His father was a scientist, maybe, and he's brought us here to feed daddy's plants."[25] It's the only way they can make sense of the world, reaching back to movie plot lines and conjectures about mad scientists.

It doesn't matter, of course. The vines kill Pablo and Amy. Eric becomes convinced that the vine is growing inside his wounded leg, and he takes to stabbing himself with a dirty knife to cut out the taint. Stacy panics. Mathias and Jeff try to be reasonable. Jeff does the logical, scientific things: He rations their food, makes preparations to capture rain water to drink, and even considers whether to cannibalize Amy's body to keep them alive. But reason has no place here. The Mayans kill Jeff when he tries to escape the hill to get help, and the vine eats his corpse. Mathias, too, succumbs to the vine. Eric goes mad, and flays himself into a bloody mess trying to cut the vine out of him. The vine laps up the blood as he cuts and cuts. As her last act of compassion, Stacy kills what's left of Eric. Then, believing there is nothing to live for, Stacy commits suicide rather than face isolation and a slow death. The Greeks arrive a few days later, and they wander up the hill, thinking how lovely the flowers are.

The Ruins does not explain its horrors. Characters speculate about the vine and how it gained its powers, but there are no real reasons given. Jeff and Mathias act rationally and try to impose a semblance of order and control; the others are immature or selfish and give in to their dependency and helplessness. It doesn't matter either way, for their fates are the same. The horror approached irrationally; it existed on its own terms, and there was nothing anyone could do about it. The only release is death, and even that was a cold, miserable experience.

Literary Horror

Since the 1970s, "literary fiction" has been the holy grail of writing, the greatest achievement of the author's art, the universal ideal of what a novel "should" be: Long, subjective, intellectually inclined, full of meditation and reflection, and stripped of "commercial" influences like an emphasis on plot or a satisfying ending. The book industry considers literary fiction to be its prestige product, and literary fiction nearly monopolizes awards and honors, and critical adulation. Though critics maintained that literary fiction was a pretentious bore that "places style before content, puts prose before plot and subordinates character and narrative to nebulous aesthetic concerns,"[26] it was still the brass ring for which all authors—including those in horror with pretensions toward literary immortality—strove.

Stephen King tried for much of the 1990s and the 2000s to write a literary novel that would earn the respect of academic critics. *Dreamcatcher* (2001), about aliens that grow in people's rectums, manifesting as extreme flatulence followed by worm-like alien excretions, was not that novel, nor was it meant to be. However, King's intermittent attempts at literary respectability bore little fruit; critics derided his work as hackery or worse, even as the public continued to buy it in record numbers.

In recognition of his influence on the book-buying public and the culture at large, the National Book Foundation awarded King a National Book Award for a lifetime of distinguished contributions to American letters in 2003 — though notably not an award for a particular novel. When King won, Yale professor Harold Bloom blasted the award: "That they could believe that there is any literary value there or any aesthetic accomplishment or signs of inventive human intelligence is simply a testimony to their own idiocy."[27] King took the occasion of his acceptance speech to hope that the academic and critical elite could reconsider the great divide between popular and literary fiction: "I salute the National Book Foundation Board, who took a huge risk in giving this award to a man many people see as a rich hack ... Bridges can be built between the so-called popular fiction and the so-called literary fiction."[28]

King's *Lisey's Story* (2006), however, was meant to be a literary novel, dispensing with many of King's horror clichés in favor of a more realistic portrayal of a woman who spent years married to a famous (and now dead) author, and the fantasy world called Boo'ya Moon inside the author's head that the two shared. It has a pool from which the author drew on the collective creativity of humanity — sort of a Jungian collective unconscious made literal. Reception was mixed: *The New York Times* loved its raw energy and understated pathos; Britain's *The Observer* felt nauseated by its sloppy writing, calling it a "reverse masterclass" in the art.[29]

Critical reception was much more favorable for Cormac McCarthy's *The Road* (2006). McCarthy had an established literary reputation as author of a series of well-received explorations of the darker side of Appalachia and the American Southwest, as well as the romantic *All the Pretty Horses* (1992), all of which dealt at some level with disillusionment and the failure of American, and Western, civilization. *The Road* took this to its logical extreme, narrating a horrific road trip undertaken by a father and his small child through a world completely destroyed by an unnamed apocalypse — which makes this book horror rather than science fiction, in its emphasis on psychology and cruelty.

Civilization is gone; the few survivors are essentially animalistic beasts, preying on one another and consuming each other for food. They tend to keep their victims chained up, amputating limbs one at a time to keep the meat fresh. The father, an educated and literate man driven to desperation, and his son, too young to remember any other life, must avoid these killers and the other terrors they encounter on their way to the South to find warmth for the winter. He carries a gun with two bullets so they might commit suicide if it looks like they will fall victim to the feral people hunting them. The father is sick, though, dying of some unknown illness. He pretends, for the boy's sake,

Post-nuclear landscape. Cormac McCarthy's *The Road* imagines a future world where civilization has been devastated by an unnamed disaster. The ruined, ash-strewn landscape of the novel resembles what happened to Hiroshima after the atomic bomb devastated the area in 1945 (Library of Congress, Prints and Photographs Division, NYWT&S Collection, LCUSZ62-134192).

that salvation awaits them in the South, that there are other good people left in the world. He dies without finding that salvation, but his son is rescued by a man who adopts him into his own family, providing a glimmer of hope that goodness might continue even when civilization, science, reason, and morality all fail.

The boy, it seems, was born good, noble, and moral, uncorrupted by civilization and thus striving toward the good. The *deus ex machina* ending implies a sort of divine salvation for those who believe in goodness. In its apocalyptic bleakness, *The Road* was *I Am Legend* for the postmodern age.

The most literary of all recent horror was Elizabeth Kostova's ponderous opus *The Historian* (2005), a critically acclaimed exploration of the Dracula legend that earned its first-time author a record two million dollar advance. The story is constructed like a set of Russian nesting dolls, with layers built upon layers, flashing back and forth through time in a kaleidoscope of scenes that add up to a whole less than the sum of its parts. The story concerns a historian in 2008 looking back on events that occurred when she was sixteen, in 1972.

In that year she learned that her father Paul was the recipient of a strange book bearing the crest of Vlad Tepes, known as Dracula, Prince of Wallachia, from whom Bram Stoker took his vampire's name. In a complex web of flashbacks, we learn that Paul, a graduate student in the 1950s, his mentor, a Professor Rossi, and Rossi's daughter Helen (also Paul's girlfriend and a grad student) all spent years researching and tracking Dracula, who they believe still lives.

Dracula, it seems, is pulling the strings, depositing the books and enticing these and other scholars onward in a series of tests that will determine who is intellectually fit for the revelation of his existence. Paul was eventually forced to stake Rossi to prevent his transformation into a vampire. Helen, it transpires, is the narrator's mother and a lineal descendant of Dracula, whose followers form an Order of the Dragon and are opposed by a Turkish group founded by Dracula's ancient enemy, the Sultan Mehmed II, who fought Vlad back in the fifteenth century. This has given the vampire an eternal hatred of Islam, which he wishes to destroy.

Rather than the familiar movie vampire of pure evil, Kostova's Dracula returns to a neglected theme in Bram Stoker's novel, that the man who became the beast was once a seeker after forbidden knowledge. Her Dracula possesses a library of old and rare books as well as all the modern works in his field of interest (tyranny), and his tests for the scholars are to determine who is worthy to become — you guessed it — his *librarian*. Better: Dracula prints his own books when he cannot get hold of them! It seems the vampire "became a historian in order to preserve my own history forever."[30] Dracula intends to use his library to give him the knowledge he needs to take over the world, and in the 1950s he wanted Rossi to become one of the undead and go forth to add new volumes to his collection, which already held sections on torture (early, medieval, and modern), heresies, alchemy, witchcraft, "philosophy of the most disturbing sort," and history.[31] Dracula explains that history teaches important lessons:

> History has taught us that the nature of man is evil, sublimely so. Good is not perfectible, but evil is…. Together we will advance the historian's work beyond anything the world has ever seen. There is no purity like the purity of the sufferings of history. You will have what every historian wants: history will be reality to you. We will wash our minds clean with blood.[32]

Dracula claims the bloody twentieth century as his own work, as his knowledge put into action. Rossi refused to aid the vampire, and vampirism was his fate. Helen stood against the monster, and she vanished. In the 1970s, the narrator and her father have tracked Dracula to a French monastery where they confront him. Dracula tries to tempt Paul with Faustian promises of untold knowledge, but he is destroyed when Helen miraculously reappears to fire a silver bullet through the vampire's heart. The story might have ended there, but in 2008, the narrator — now a grown woman and a historian in her own right — stumbles across another of the mysterious old books with Dracula's dragon crest. Someone, or something, might just have survived.

Many, but certainly not all, critics gushed over *The Historian*, finding in it the horror novel of their dreams: safe, without gore, lacking in chills, and completely enraptured by academia. But Kostova intellectualized her horror so much that her scholars—heroes and villains alike—are more wedded to the world of literature and knowledge than even those of M. R. James or H. P. Lovecraft, to the point that any trace of outright horror vanishes before the aesthetics of literary fiction. The "banality of evil" had never been more realistically portrayed. Dracula's view of knowledge, though, is typical of the modern age—it brings only terror and death, and its use is only for true, human evil, unlike, say, Lovecraft's amoral alien knowledge which only appeared evil to humanity. Dracula-as-historian serves as an ethereal metaphor for the power of history to shape the present. Knowledge, it seems, is power; but this power is inherently corrupting and therefore evil.

Is this what horror literature has become, a choice between the gross and gory explicitness of genre horror and an ethereal literary horror intellectualized out of its adventure, wonder and thrills? The best horror literature historically strode the line between intellectual engagement and transgressive shocks, using both against each other to sustain tension and excitement. Too much of one or the other throws off horror's delicate balance, and a tale degenerates into ersatz philosophy or a gross-out freak show. It is only when true, visceral horror is used to illuminate intellectual problems that horror achieves that rare combination of reason and emotion that gives the best of it such power and pull.

21

HORROR IN THE ARTS

In 1994, Jonathan Lake Crane noted that the earlier forms of horror, those that dealt with the supernatural or even abnormal psychology, had largely vanished from the box office, to be replaced by a new breed of horror that focused nearly exclusively on the pain and torture of its victims. Horror films about ideas—the role of science, the strength of community—were gone and "in their place, we have films that reject the stories and stylistic devices of older horror tales in preference for inordinately simple narratives that seem to exist solely to showcase the latest leap forward in stomach-churning special effects." It was, he said, a transformation from stories about villains and their motives to stories about *specific acts*, whose depravity assaulted the audience.[1] He was speaking of the slasher films of the 1980s, but his criticism applies even more to the extreme horror of the 1990s and 2000s.

The new slasher films differed from their older counterparts in a significant way: The older films, as much as they focused on acts of violence rather than character, still played by the old rules. Freddy Krueger and Michael Myers had recognizable origin stories: They were villains drawn from the traditions of horror and served as symbols for anxieties about child molestation and neglect. They killed according to a pattern through a set of clearly defined rules, just like vampires or werewolves. This changed as the legion of sequels drew on, and the new slashers took their impetus from the 1980s horror sequels, which did not need to explain villains introduced years earlier. The rationale for the new psycho killers, therefore, was almost irrelevant to the film, a mere excuse for slashing and killing and maiming. Largely anonymous, the new killers were faceless creatures of the plot, born and bred killers without conscience, or thought, or reason. Because they had no mythic origin and often no set pattern or rules for killing, they symbolized only randomness, the chaos of modern existence that could strike at any time. This is best noted in the *Scream* series where over the course of three films there were at least five people behind the faceless killer's mask, with no noticeable differences.

Recent horror cinema has become increasingly bloodthirsty, increasingly simplistic, and increasingly popular. Video games followed suit. It would be left to the more regulated and restricted realm of television, prevented by law or by advertisers from becoming too explicit, to take up the banner of traditional horror, albeit with a postmodern sensibility.

Revival of the Classics

The 1990s saw what at first blush looked like a sea-change in horror. The 1980s slasher films had played themselves out, and jaded audiences grew tired of the spectacle of endless recycled sequels and knock-offs. Instead, the "classic" horror monsters—those committed to film in the era of Universal Studios' dominance of the horror genre in the 1930s—seemed to be the flavor of the week. New versions of *Dracula, Frankenstein, The Mummy, Jekyll and Hyde, The Island of Dr. Moreau,* and others all graced the screen. But they did not portend the revival of older horror forms they seemed to augur.

The acclaimed director Francis Ford Coppola spent lavishly on *Bram Stoker's Dracula* (1992), a film which followed the plot of Stoker's novel more closely than earlier interpretations, but largely replaced the horror of the vampire with a (new) epic love story. The movie adds a new prologue in which Dracula is seen fighting the Turks, only to have his wife commit suicide when she thinks he died in battle. Angry at what Dracula interprets as God's capriciousness, he rejects religion, thus consigning him to the legions of the undead. This completely reverses Stoker's intellectual scientist-vampire in favor of a faith-based monster fueled by an emotion: love. When Jonathan Harker (Keanu Reeves) arrives at Castle Dracula, the fiend (Gary Oldman) sees in a portrait of Harker's fiancée, Mina (Winona Ryder), the reincarnation of his beloved. He then undertakes the mechanics of the plot of Stoker's novel in order to win Mina, who falls for the vampire. Unlike the novel, or even earlier films, it is not science that saves the day but religious faith; and the suppressed sexuality of the original is here laid bare in sometimes graphic detail, as when Dracula's brides sexually service Jonathan Harker before attacking him. *Dracula 2000* (2001) brought the legend into the new millennium, with the vampire attacking teenagers. The movie reveals that Dracula is actually Judas Iscariot, made into a vampire by his betrayal of Christ, thus completely subsuming the vampire's forbidden knowledge origins into a new religious paradigm. The direct-to-DVD *Dracula II: Ascension* (2003) and *Dracula III: Legacy* continued Judas Dracula's story.

Kenneth Branagh produced *Mary Shelley's Frankenstein* (1994), a largely faithful adaptation of the original novel, with himself as Victor and Robert De Niro as the monster. Though overwrought, the film successfully dramatized the tragedy of a man who thought he could play God—with the emphasis shifted toward a contemplation of the monster and its place in God's creation: "Yes, I speak, and read, and think, and know the ways of man," the Monster says. But, he also asks "What of my soul? Do I have one? What of these people of which I am composed?" It is impossible not to see in these questions an echo of the crisis of free will and the fate of the soul swirling in the worlds of science and faith.

Director John Frankenheimer produced a new version of *The Island of Dr. Moreau* (1996), with Marlon Brando in the title role. In the year 2010, this Dr. Moreau travels around his petty kingdom garbed in white, with his face smeared with white cream (he's allergic to the sun), and riding in a knock-off Popemobile. Moreau has developed a technique to combine human and animal DNA, transforming animals into humans. However, the technique is imperfect, and daily injections are needed to prevent any return of animal traits. The film breaks down much the way Moreau's island does once the animal-men figure out how to disable the electroshock chips implanted to keep them in line. Moreau's visitor, Edward, thinks the experiments are "satanic," and there is an abundance of theological speculation on the nature of evil and whether Moreau is evil or is suppressing evil through his work. In short, the film substituted for Wells's meditation on the amorality of science a treatise on theology, science be damned.

Mary Reilly (1996), based on a novel by Valerie Martin, retold the story of *Jekyll and Hyde* from the perspective of a lonely Irish maid (Julia Roberts) working in Dr. Jekyll's (John Malkovich) house. She's in love with the good doctor, and also finds herself attracted to Mr. Hyde. The tragedy then unfolds from her perspective, to its inevitable conclusion. *The Mummy* (1999) and *The Mummy Returns* (2001) transposed the old Universal horror film into an action-adventure yarn, minus the horror. Though not strictly speaking classic horrors, ghosts made a return call. *The Haunting* (1999) and *The House on Haunted Hill* (1999) both got big-budget but brainless remakes. *The Sixth Sense* (1999) featured a little boy (Haley Joel Osmont) who "can see dead people," the psychologist (Bruce Willis) trying to help him, and the rather obvious twist ending that for all his scientific wisdom the psychologist couldn't process emotionally the fact that he was himself dead. *The Others* (2001) was more of the same crossed with an inverted *Turn of the Screw*. A woman (Nicole Kidman) and her two kids live in a creepy old mansion that she comes to believe is haunted. When she hires some new servants, a chain of events makes her realize the awful truth: She and the kids are the ghosts, and they are doing the haunting. A 2004 version of *Phantom of the Opera* was based on Andrew Lloyd Weber's legendary musical, which has been performed constantly since 1986.

With so many remakes of classic horrors, it was inevitable that someone would want to slap them all together, as Universal had done in films like *House of Frankenstein*. *The League of Extraordinary Gentlemen* (2003), based on a graphic novel of that name, teamed a vampire-infected Mina Harker with Dorian Gray, the Invisible Man, and some non-horror Victorian heroes to battle Mr. Hyde and the non-horror Sherlock Holmes villain Moriarty. The wretched *Van Helsing* (2004) was a mash-up of old Universal horror monsters forced into battle with one another in a plot not unlike that of *Abbott and Costello Meet Frankenstein*, though less successful.

Gabriel Van Helsing (Hugh Jackman), of uncertain relationship to Abraham, is employed by the Vatican to set out for Transylvania to stop Count Dracula (Richard Roxburgh) from carrying out a dread evil with the aid of the Frankenstein Monster, the Wolf Man, and Igor, last seen as the late Dr. Frankenstein's helper. There is a tedious subplot about a Romanian family of vampire hunters who need to stop Dracula to save their souls, but the heart of the movie concerns Dracula's quest to "prove God is not the only one to create life" and give life to a horde of small bat-things that are the stillborn children of the vampire and his brides. To do this, he needs to wire the Frankenstein Monster to a bunch of electrodes and galvanize the bat-kids into un-life. Despite some loving recreations of Universal horror scenes in the opening reel and sly references throughout, the film fails as horror because all of the characters (and the audience) are fully apprised of the supernatural, the powers and limits of the various creatures, and how to kill them. The heroes—Van Helsing, his assistant, and the Romanian huntress—move through their paces, but they never *react* to the horror or appear to feel any terror, for they know exactly what to do. The film devolves into an action picture that employs horror tropes without the atmosphere of horror.

Similarly, *Freddy vs. Jason* (2003) found Freddy Krueger playing the Dracula role, reviving another '80s staple, Jason Vorhees, playing the Frankenstein Monster's part, so Jason's killing spree would help revive forgotten memories of Krueger, allowing him to attack children again in their dreams. Silly and gory, the film dispensed with a number of teenage victims before the two leads battled one another, culminating in a burning dock scene that recreated much of the climax of *Abbott and Costello Meet Frankenstein*. In the end, when the monsters seem vanquished, both return to life, negating any point for the film. The mindless *Alien vs. Predator* (2004) combined those two franchises and posited that the creatures were the ancient astronauts of Erich von Däniken's 1970s pseudoscience by way of H. P. Lovecraft's Antarctic *At the Mountains of Madness*.

Remakes of *Halloween* (2007), *House of Wax* (2005), *Invasion of the Body Snatchers* (as *Invasion*, 2007), *I Am Legend* (2007), *The Omen* (2006), and *The Hills Have Eyes* (2006) proved that Hollywood had run out of ideas, returning to older films to recycle them, amp up the sex and the violence, and capitalize on earlier successes. The Japanese made original films that found horror in ultra-modern life and technology, such as *Ringu* (1998), which imagined a haunted videotape that drove watchers to suicide. Japanese horror (known to fans as j-horror) dealt with psychological terror and the survival of ghosts and spirits in the modern, scientific world—memories of a past we cannot escape, no matter how many computers or light bulbs we have. Americans remade many j-horror films for domestic audiences, with mixed results. Most were not as good at the originals.

Other Adaptations

In addition to the revival of the classics, more recent horror literature got the screen treatment. Versions of Michael Crichton's *Jurassic Park* (1993), *Sphere* (1998), *Congo* (1995), and *Eaters of the Dead* (2001, under the title *The 13th Warrior*) all came to the screen, in decreasing order of effectiveness. *Jurassic Park* jettisoned much of Crichton's science-based book in favor of fantasy, but effective sequences with nasty velociraptors stalking children were truly frightening. The sequel *The Lost World: Jurassic Park* (1997) was a muddled mess, with dinosaurs running amok in San Diego. *Jurassic Park III* (2001) was narrower in focus and thus tenser and more effective. Several characters land at an abandoned test site where scientists had engineered dinosaurs to rescue a couple's son. They have to outwit the dinosaurs through the ruins of corporate science's hubris. The movie cuts to the action quickly and wastes little time with extraneous exposition. Anne Rice's *Interview with the Vampire* (1994) and *Queen of the Damned* (2002) found success in theaters telling the story of Rice's sexually charged vampires and their troubled existence.

Based on Thomas Harris's novel, *The Silence of the Lambs* (1991) won an Oscar for Best Picture. *Silence* finds FBI trainee Clarice Starling (Jodie Foster) traveling to a mental institution to interview Hannibal Lecter (Anthony Hopkins) in the hope that he can provide information about "Buffalo Bill," a serial killer (modeled on Ed Gein) who skins his victims. Lecter, the cultured serial killer cannibal, was once Buffalo Bill's psychiatrist before all that unpleasantness. He agrees to help Clarice, but only on the condition that she offer a *quid pro quo*: information about her dark childhood. Knowledge is the currency of their exchange, and Clarice describes her inner secrets in exchange for Lecter's professional insights into Buffalo Bill. Lecter explains, gradually, that Buffalo Bill believes himself to be a transsexual and likely tried to have gender reassignment surgery but would have been rejected. He suggests checking the records. He knows who Bill is, but won't say. It's much more fun to play with Clarice's mind instead.

Clarice comes to realize that Buffalo Bill is trying to fashion a suit of skin to turn himself into a woman. The identity of the killer is eventually found in the Johns Hopkins records of rejected reassignment patients. Clarice tracks him to the home of the former employer of one of his victims, and she realizes the man who answers the door is the killer himself. Buffalo Bill tries to get the drop on Clarice, but she shoots him dead. Meanwhile, Lecter has escaped custody and killed a number of people. He calls Clarice during her graduation from the FBI academy, congratulates her, and says that as a sign of respect he will not hunt her down. He would appreciate a reciprocal courtesy.

Hopkins's menacing yet restrained performance made *Silence of the Lambs* a great film, and propelled Hannibal Lecter into the role of a Dracula for the modern age. At just seventeen minutes of screen time, it was the shortest leading male performance to win the Oscar for Best Actor; but every minute plunged the viewer into a thick atmosphere of terror and dread. *Hannibal* (2001) and *Hannibal Rising* (2007) both adapted the Harris novels of the same names but lacked the power and the horror of the earlier work. They were disgusting and vile, but not scary.

Red Dragon (2002) filmed the original Lecter novel, remaking the superior *Manhunter* (1986). In 2000, *American Psycho* was filmed, adapting the novel. *Fight Club*, its violent twin, came to screens in 1999.

The Teen Slasher

The main event in 1990s and 2000s horror was not the classic monster, or even the literary adaptation. Instead the most profitable and fertile field of horror was the return of the slasher in ever more outrageous and explicit forms. A fresh wave of slice-and-dice horror began with *Scream* (1996) and was only gaining ground a decade later, by which time horror movies had become not just a Hollywood staple, but the most consistent performers in the major studios' arsenals. By the middle of the first decade of this century, horror movies were being released at the rate of one or two each week, and with rare exception, they all managed to make back their costs. Most were made on a budget of ten million dollars or so, and many returned one hundred million or more.

Scream came from director Wes Craven and a script by Kevin Williamson. It continued the self-conscious, self-referential strain from Craven's *New Nightmare* two years before. The story concerned young Sidney (Neve Campbell), a high school girl who finds herself targeted by a serial killer who already murdered two of Sidney's classmates. The killer dresses in a black robe with a ghostly white mask modeled on Edvard Munch's *The Scream*. He calls his victims on the phone and taunts them with questions about horror movie trivia. He begins by asking "What's your favorite scary movie?" Sidney at first accuses her boyfriend, Billy Loomis* (Skeet Ulrich), of being the killer. He is arrested but released when threatening phone calls continue, proving Billy wasn't the caller. Meanwhile a tabloid reporter (Courteney Cox) shows up to cover the serial killing story, further complicating Sidney's already harried life.

Sidney attends a party with her best friend and the friend's boyfriend Stu (Mathew Lillard). There another teen, horror fan Randy (Jamie Kennedy), explains that the killer is following the classic rules of horror movies, drawn

Loomis is the surname of the boyfriend Sam in Psycho *and the doctor Sam in* Halloween. *It is one of many in-joke allusions throughout the* Scream *series.*

from repeated viewings of *Halloween* and *Friday the 13th*: You don't survive if you drink, do drugs, or say "I'll be right back." And above all, never, ever have sex. This doesn't bode well for Sidney, who lost her virginity to Billy not long before. Of course the killer starts slicing-and-dicing the teens, in gruesome and explicit ways, which makes up most of the remainder of the film, as Sidney tries to stay alive while it seems that all her friends are being killed. Only when Billy comes out quoting Norman Bates ("We all go a little mad sometimes") and Stu emerges with the voice synthesizer used to make the threatening phone calls does

Sidney realize the awful truth: There are two killers, working together. Sidney kills Stu; the reporter shows up and kills Billy. But like all good horror films, the killer isn't really dead. Billy pops back up a few more times before Sidney shoots him in the head, ending his reign of terror. The film earned one hundred million dollars and became a cultural sensation.

The genius of *Scream* was the way it played with horror conventions and offered characters who had seen and loved earlier horror films. They try (though they usually fail) to avoid the mistakes of their filmic predecessors, and they wittily allude to such staples as *Psycho*, *Halloween*, *Carrie*, *A Nightmare on Elm Street*, and at least a dozen others. The horror was postmodern, of course, with enjoyment of the film increasing exponentially with each "classic" the audience had previously seen. But at a deeper level, it also depicted an American society of superficial affluence and happiness cursed with an underside of irrational madness waiting to break out at any time. The first of two sequels, *Scream 2* (1997) was even more self-referential, featuring a copy-cat killer (actually, killers) recreating the crimes of the first movie after the release of a film, *Stab*, about the events of *Scream*. The hall-of-mirrors effect was clever, but the film was not as fun as the first outing. *Scream 3* (2000) found Sidney being stalked on the set of *Stab 3*, which was dressed to duplicate her original house from *Scream*. As in the previous films, the identity of the killer is virtually irrelevant to the movie, which found the killer knocking off actors in the order of their deaths in the script for *Stab 3*.

Most 1990s "teen horror" films had the same flaw: The purpose of the film was to showcase witty dialogue, attractive casts of young adult stars, and gruesome killing scenes, so the killer's identity is often an afterthought, spliced in at the last minute to give some sort of resolution to the film. However, the revelation of the killer has little to do with what came before and *any* character could appear under the killer's mask without changing the impact of the movie, or its effectiveness, in the least. The implied message was that *anyone* could potentially be the killer; *everyone* has the capability for insanity and irrational violence and is therefore suspect.

I Know What You Did Last Summer (1997), also from writer Kevin Williamson (based on Lois Duncan's much less bloodthirsty 1973 young adult novel), found a group of attractive teenagers running someone over while drunk

I Know What You Did Last Summer (1997). In the 1990s, horror movies aimed at teenagers featured attractive casts of often well-known young actors who were picked off one by one by the mysterious (and largely anonymous) killer. Here Ryan Phillippe, Jennifer Love Hewitt, and Sarah Michelle Gellar contemplate their next move.

driving. They dump the body into the ocean but find that the next year some-one dressed as a hook-wielding fisherman is stalking them and picking them off one by one. The killer turns out to be the man they ran over, who was busy murdering someone else that night; but none of this really matters since it is revealed only at the end while the "meat" of the movie is the killing. *I Still Know What You Did Last Summer* (1998) made little sense at all. The sequel found the son of the original villain, and the villain himself, staging a fake radio contest to lure some of the original cast to a Bahaman island during hurricane season for bloody revenge. The direct-to-video *I'll Always Know What You Did Last Summer* (2006) found new teenagers doing what the old ones did ten sum-mers before, this time stalked for no good reason by what seems to be the undead corpse of the first movie's villain.

Urban Legend (1998) was a modestly clever slasher film in which the killer staged the murders of college students to resemble urban legends, which are popular folkloric stories—often of the horror variety—that claim to be factual and impart moral lessons. They are frequently performed—that is, told aloud—like campfire ghost stories, and until the 1970s academics assumed that "hard-headed, rational Americans" were immune to the sort of semi-supernatural folklore represented by the tales, which were only studied widely in the 1980s and 1990s.[2] Each legend claims to be a true story that happened recently, often to someone known to an acquaintance of the teller, and thus just far enough removed to remain plausible without being directly known to the listeners. The tales almost always aim to drive home a point about contemporary morality or ethics. In the horror vein, this usually amounts to asking men to avoid sexually adventurous women and for women to avoid positions of vulnerability or threats to their chastity. The legends are, in their way, a knowledge source in the form of horror, not unlike the moral lessons of ancient mythology.

Famous urban legends include the female driver worried about the creepy gas station attendant's odd behavior only to realize too late that he is trying to warn her of the psycho killer in the back seat of her vehicle. Another is the woman who hears her college roommate having what she thinks is sex, so she goes to bed without turning on the light. She goes to sleep but wakes up to find her roommate mutilated and blood scrawled on the wall: "Aren't you glad you didn't turn on the lights?" Both of these appeared in the film, which followed the teen-slasher genre to the inevitable reveal of the mad killer. This time the killer is a woman who holds the film's heroine responsible for her fiancé's death. *Urban Legend* was followed by two middling sequels.

The Blair Witch Project (1999) was the Lovecraftian tale of three documentary filmmakers who get lost while searching for the Blair Witch, a legendary old crone who haunts the woods near Burkittsville, Maryland. After finding occult bundles of sticks (much like those in Karl Edward Wagner's story "Sticks"), they get picked off one by one, recording their fright. The film's innovation was to give the actors cameras to film their own story, improvised without scripted dialogue, which gave the film a documentary verisimilitude. The filmmakers used the nascent World Wide Web to promote the film, claiming it was real footage of murdered young people. Many bought into the hoax, prepared to believe that a supernatural witch haunted America's backwoods. With grosses of more than two hundred million dollars worldwide, it was the most profitable independent film of the twentieth century. A more traditional sequel was a disaster.

Idle Hands (1999) was a gory horror-comedy about a young man (Devon Sawa) whose right hand becomes possessed by evil and commits murder when he isn't looking. He chops it off, as Ash did with *his* possessed hand in *Evil Dead II*, and teams up with his rotting, undead friends to stop the evil hand from ruining his love life. Sawa gave a much stronger performance in *Final Destination* (2000), where he played a teenager on a class trip to France. On board the plane, he has a premonition of doom just before the plane takes off. His panicked reaction gets him and several other teens kicked off the plane. In the film's most effective scene, as the teens argue, in the background we see through an airport window the plane take off and explode. The teens have "cheated death," and death wants them back, preferably in the order in which they would have died had they stayed on the plane. Fated to die, they try to avoid the inevitable, with poor results. The fatalistic film was followed by two painful sequels, which reinforced the idea that humans are pawns in the power of a fate they cannot control or alter.

Torture Porn

If teen slashers were self-conscious and sometimes funny horror films, they had a dark message that horror could and would happen randomly to innocent people. In recent years, horror films took this idea to new extremes, creating ultra-violent, ultra-gory movies that reveled in the sheer unpleasantness of the situations they concocted. Teen slashers of the 1990s were celebrity-filled fun; but many of the new films were torture for profit, simulated snuff films. None of this is to say that they were all bad. A few were quite good; but the overall tone was so dark and so violent that they bore little resemblance to what had come before. Bleak and nihilistic barely begin to describe them.

The trend began innocently enough. High-velocity splatter came first. *From Dusk Till Dawn* (1996), for example, was a vampire picture from director Robert Rodriguez featuring some criminals trapped in a roadside bar filled with bloodsuckers. Violent, bloody, and sexually explicit, it was at least better than its two sequels. The bleakness also began around this time, an existential dread that filled the screen with darkness, leaving only the thinnest veil of hope. *Se7en* (1995) found two police officers investigating a sickening series of grisly murders based on the seven deadly sins described in the Bible. Only the killer left the nihilistic, dark, and disturbing film unscathed.

Dark City (1998) was a brilliantly bleak examination of identity, social control, and horror that was something like "The Tunnel Under the World" crossed with Dante's *Inferno*. John Murdoch (Rufus Sewell) awakes with no memory, but a doctor (Kiefer Sutherland) calls to warn him that a group of "Strangers" are coming for him. John also learns that he is wanted for a string of murders, but he doesn't feel that he is capable of murder. Slowly, John begins to notice anomalies: It is always night. At midnight, everyone falls into a deep sleep. No one can manage to leave the city in which they live. Chased by the Strangers, John is awake during one such midnight coma when he sees what the Strangers do to the city: They remake the cityscape each night, erecting or collapsing buildings, assigning new identities to the inhabitants, and injecting them with new memories. John learns from the doctor that the Strangers are aliens who are using the humans in experiments to learn about the essential human nature — whether our memories and knowledge make us who we are or if it is inborn: Are our memories real? Did the past ever happen? What is true? John also learns that he has psychokinetic powers, as the Strangers do, and he uses these to defeat the aliens. He discovers that the city is a floating space station, and he turns the city toward the light, giving a glimmer of hope for the future, but a future defined by the humans' uncertain relationship to their own past, or the truth. The idea of a human with near-magical powers transcending the limits of (artificial) reality was also used in *The Matrix* (1999), where computers, rather than aliens, enslaved humans in a fake world.

The new horror combined ultra-violence with such existential bleakness. *28 Days Later* (2002) was probably the best of the new breed of horror. The story was essentially the same as *I Am Legend*, but darker since the heroes were essentially powerless to fight back. Animal rights activists break into a lab and free some chimpanzees they think are being tortured. The scientists in charge object, claiming the chimps are infected with a genetically altered disease, "The Rage," that turns anyone infected into a rabid, homicidal zombie. Twenty-eight days later the world is in ruins. Most are dead, and those that live are largely infected zombie monsters. Jim (Cillian Murphy) awakens in his hospital bed, where he had been comatose. He wanders through the abandoned center of London, where he stumbles across a few uninfected survivors. They explain that the government tried to stop the outbreak, but failed. Civilization is at an end. The survivors and a few soldiers take cover in a fortified mansion and wait for the attacking zombies to die of starvation. Twenty-eight days later Jim and few others are rescued by a helicopter, indicating that somewhere someone has survived. A sequel, *28 Weeks Later* (2007), tells what happens when the Rage virus gets loose during an effort to repopulate Britain.

Saw (2004) was the first of the torture movies. It begins with two men chained on opposite sides of a grimy bathroom, a corpse sprawled between them. An audio tape explains that one man must kill the other in order for either to leave the room. In flashbacks we learn that one of the men is a doctor whose wife and child are being held hostage by the Jigsaw killer, a serial nutjob who devises elaborate torture schemes in order to show his erstwhile victims that they are wasting their precious lives. One such previous torture involves a sort of inverted bear trap that will rip apart the victim's jaws if he does not complete the killer's puzzle before time runs out. Time, alas, is never on the victims' sides, and the situation becomes more grotesque since the hidden killer chooses to manifest himself as a small, clown-like puppet on a tricycle. As for the men in the room, they weren't going anywhere. The key to their chains was washed down the drain back at the beginning of the film. Oops. After an hour and a half of torture and pain, a nihilistic ending makes the viewer wonder why anyone would sit through such unpleasantness.

Saw II (2005) begins with a torture reminiscent of *The Abominable Dr. Phibes*, when Phibes made a doctor operate on his own son: Here a man is locked into a vice that threatens to crush his head if he does not remove a key implanted behind his eye in time to unlock the device. Whereas Dr. Phibes's torture was emotional and centered on the doctor's pain and panic at having to operate on his own son, Jigsaw's torture focuses exclusively on the physical

Saw (2004). Recent torture horror films have featured graphic scenes of human suffering. In this relatively tame scene from *Saw,* a man (Cary Elwes) chained to the floor of a dirty bathroom struggles to reach a cell phone in order to avoid a more horrible fate of bodily mutilation and murder.

terror and pain experienced by the solitary victim who is not master of his own destiny. The emphasis has shifted, and the audience is meant to enjoy the sickening torture inflicted on the helpless victim. The plot of the second film involves several people experiencing grotesque and deadly tortures in pursuit of a missing boy. *Saw III* (2006) had an unfortunate soul forced to tear implanted chains out of his raw flesh to escape a bomb. He doesn't. Another man is being tortured to show him just how wrong it is to hold a grudge about the car accident that killed his son. This process involves several nauseating and gruesome tortures, all graphically displayed.

It turns out that the Jigsaw killer is dying of cancer, and it really made him *appreciate* the value of life. He wants to share this sweetness and light by torturing innocent people to make them, you know, really *feel* how great it is to live. One man in *Saw III* eventually tracks down the dying Jigsaw and kills him, only to learn too late that Jigsaw had kidnapped his daughter, and by killing the killer, he lost his only chance to save her. Oh, and he has triggered a bizarre torture device that killed Jigsaw's doctor, too. *Saw IV* came to theaters in 2007 with more of the same.

Though the killer claims to have a reason for his tortures, this is superficial coloring. He kills because he can kill. He is dying, so he does not care what happens to him. But even this is just a superficial reason grafted onto a film series that the Motion Picture Association of America worried was too dark for an R-rating (restricting viewers under seventeen). "This movie is too dark? That's what I set out to do! It's a horror movie," the film's director, Darren Lynn Bousman, said.[3]

Hostel (2006) was, if possible, even more brutal. American college students looking for easy sex are lured to a youth hostel in Slovakia where rich businessmen pay large sums of money for the privilege of torturing people for fun. One patron enjoys delving into human bodies with a power drill and cutting Achilles tendons. Another likes to melt eyeballs with a blowtorch. One victim manages to escape and takes bloody revenge on one of the torturers. The director, Eli Roth, justified the film as a discourse on Americans' attitudes to the rest of the world, but its sadistic brutality distracted from any political point it tried to make. Roth claimed that the actions of the Bush administration drove Americans to seek out cinematic tortures to deal with the world situation.[4] A sequel followed in 2007. The derivative *Turistas* (2006) found another group of young Americans stranded outside the United States. They are visiting Brazil, and their bus crashes. They fall into the clutches of a mad doctor named Zamora who vivisects them (in one case piling extracted organs next to a girl's naked breast) and donates their organs to poor, needy countrymen disenfranchised by America's cultural, economic, and medical domination.

Rob Zombie's *House of a Thousand Corpses* (2003) was a visually assaulting tale of teens in backwoods Texas who encounter a cannibal family who outdo the *Texas Chain Saw Massacre* family at every level of grotesquerie. *The Devil's Rejects* (2005) continued their story and leavened its vicious, violent heart with a sugaring of satire, but in the end horror and death reign. The Australian film *Wolf Creek* (2005) graphically mutilated and tortured young women, prompting critic Roger Ebert, himself a horror fan, to complain:

> There is a line and this movie crosses it. I don't know where the line is, but it's way north of "Wolf Creek." There is a role for violence in film, but what the hell is the purpose of this sadistic celebration of pain and cruelty?[5]

At least Zombie's films had tried to be entertaining; most of the torture horror films—and dozens were produced in just a few years—had exchanged any semblance of purpose or philosophy for the "fun" of watching other people suffer. To that end, Christian conservatives like L. Brent Bozell III might have had a point when they protested the release of a remake of *Black Christmas* on Christmas Day 2006, claiming it was an affront to Jesus.[6] They had not, however, protested *Wolf Creek*'s Christmas release the year before, nor did they seem particularly troubled by graphic horror at any other time.

Horror movies had come a long way from *Nosferatu* and *Frankenstein*, but in postmodern times, who was to say whether the abandonment of ideas in favor of ever more graphic violence through the century of film was a good or bad thing? It certainly made more money.

"Fastened to a Wheel." In the background we see a Christian martyr tied to a wheel and left to die, while in the foreground another is tied to a wheel and rolled over iron spikes. The creators of torture horror movies read up on historical tortures, like those inflicted on the Christian martyrs, to develop their own sadistic set pieces. However, modern torture horror had no redeeming religious message or promise of eternal salvation.

Horror Video Games

There was now a certain type of horror fan for whom the enjoyment of horror was purely the excitement of violence and gore rather than the emotions and intellectual engagement of earlier horror. They wanted to be *in* the horror films. Therefore, video games largely followed the lead of horror movies, only with (if possible) even more blood and gore. Most horror games involved some variation on the player running about shooting and killing a range of supernatural creatures, watching them bleed and die. *Doom* (1993) and its sequels involved a Marine battling demon spawn and zombies on Mars after a teleportation device unwittingly opens the gates to Hell. A film version came out in 2005 but failed to improve on the game experience. *Half-Life* (1998) found a physicist forced to battle alien creatures accidentally unleashed when nuclear experiments tear a rift in the fabric of space. *Half-Life 2* (2004) continued the physicist's fight to use science to combat the aliens, who have now overrun Earth.

Less overtly violent video games included *Silent Hill* (1999), which was set in a decaying small town that fluctuated between our reality and another world populated by violent supernatural entities. Moody and atmospheric, the game and its many sequels involved questions about the nature of reality, epistemology, and sexual frustration. A film version came out in 2006. John Carpenter's movie *The Thing* became a video game in 2002, largely following the movie's plot. *The Call of Cthulhu: Dark Corners of the Earth* (2005) brought Lovecraft to video games. The story involved a man who is released from a mental asylum and is traveling to Innsmouth to investigate a missing person. The man struggles to keep his fragile sanity in the face of alien gods, crazed cultists, and the revelations familiar from Lovecraft's bleak but awesome cosmos. Similarly, *Eternal Darkness* (2002) told of a young woman, an old mansion, and the fight to stay sane against the power of dark gods and ancient secrets.

However, video games served largely to create interactive versions or derivatives of horror movies; their most important contribution was to encourage movies to emulate their pacing and graphic violence. We are nearing the day when video games will tell unique horror stories tailored to the medium's strengths, but we aren't there yet.

Horror Television

In the 1990s and 2000s, television carried on horror's best traditions, not because television was inherently superior but because of two factors that separated the small screen from other media. First, television had the freedom to tell stories in the way novels did — over long periods of time and in many chapters. With the introduction of horror series with recurring characters and continuing plots, rather than variety-style anthologies, the new programs of the 1990s and 2000s were able to harness television's unique format to tell more involved narratives. Second, broadcast and basic cable television could not be as graphic as movies and this restriction forced horror television to remain more intellectual and thoughtful than a ninety-minute film needed to be, both to meet government or corporate decency guidelines and to sustain viewers through multiple episodes and seasons.

Opposite Extremes

Cable tried to reproduce the success of movie and video game horror. The Sci-Fi Channel produced a number of low-budget horror films for their weekly "Scinema Saturday," "the most dangerous night on television." Some were original productions, and others were independent films or direct-to-video releases. Most were derivative copies of better horrors (including a number of video games), and a fair number were action pictures devoted to killing. The best shown on Sci-Fi was the direct-to-video *Dog Soldiers* (2002), which had a British army unit and a zoologist trapped in a house surrounded by werewolves. The direct-to-video *Dracula 3000* (2004) aimed to retell the Dracula story by way of *Alien* and ended up both laughably bad and nihilistic as the remaining astronauts plunge their ship into the sun to kill the count and themselves. Sci-Fi's original films like *The Fallen Ones* (2005), about an archaeologist (Casper Van Dien) who uncovers a giant son of a fallen angel at a dig, or *Dead and Deader* (2006), about a zombie Marine (Dean Cain) fighting other zombie Marines, made use of old horror clichés. *Boo* (2006) was about a haunted hospital. A ridiculously large number of the films starred Casper Van Dien, who was best known for *Starship Troopers* (1997), an action movie about a future fascist society whose young soldiers must battle giant insects intent on invading Earth. What Sci-Fi lacked in quality it more than made up in quantity.

Showtime produced a series of anthology programs under the banner *Masters of Horror* (2005–) that gave free rein to horror directors to produce the most vile and gruesome stories possible since the pay network did not need to abide by federal decency guidelines. Clive Barker's "Haeckel's Tale" (January 27, 2006) was one of the episodes, as was "The Screwfly Solution" (December 8, 2006), based on a James Triptree short story about a manufactured virus that turns men into psycho killers whenever they become sexually aroused. Tobe Hooper of *The Texas Chain Saw Massacre* gave Ambrose Bierce's "The Damned Thing" (October 27, 2006) a bloody makeover. It was cinematic graphicness come to the small screen.

Children's TV, on the other hand, continued what *Scooby-Doo* had started, and the popular dog still encountered the supernatural through the 1990s and 2000s. Cartoon Network's *The Grim Adventures of Billy and Mandy* (2001–), formerly *Grim and Evil*, found two kids befriending the Grim Reaper. The best of the horror cartoons was *Count Duckula* (ITV, 1988–1993), the story of a vegetarian vampire duck. The program opened with a pompous invocation of horror mythology, introducing the Duckula family seat:

> Castle Duckula, home for many centuries to a dreadful dynasty of vicious vampire ducks—the counts of Duckula! Legend has it that these foul beings can be destroyed by a stake through the heart or exposure to sunlight. But this does not suffice, however, for they may be brought back to life by means of a secret rite that can be performed once a century when the moon is in the eighth house of Aquarius....

A mix-up in the secret resurrection formula, substituting ketchup for blood, makes the latest Count Duckula a bit different from his predecessors. The humor of this often brilliant series revolves around the count's attempt to be true to his vegetarian nature and his self-proclaimed destiny to be a celebrity while the townsfolk, vampire hunters, and his own butler insist on viewing him as the product of his heritage, a creature of evil, fated to blood-sucking badness by his genetic destiny. Adventures included run-ins with other vampires, a Frankenstein Monster, mummies, mad scientists, the Phantom of the Opera, and other horror staples. The worst of all horrors Duckula encountered was the noxious "Planet Cute," of whose sugar-coated niceness the less said, the better.

Investigating the Unexplained

Twin Peaks (ABC, 1990–1991) brought something of a Gothic freakiness to network television with its story of an investigation into the murder of a young beauty queen in an eccentric small town, including a moody atmosphere and supernatural events drawn from horror films. However, *The X-Files* (Fox, 1993–2002) was the first successful series to focus largely on horror and fear. The story involved FBI agents Fox Mulder (David Duchovny), a believer in the paranormal, and medical doctor Dana Scully (Gillian Anderson), a skeptic, who are charged with investigating seemingly paranormal events for the bureau. This setup neatly recalled some of the better ghost stories of the nineteenth century, but this time the supernatural entities were not from the otherworld but from another world.

Mulder believes that "the truth is out there," that UFOs are alien spacecraft, and that the U.S. federal government is engineering a cover-up to prevent the public from learning the truth about the ongoing visitations. Scully, on the other hand, sees no evidence for Mulder's beliefs. In fact, the bureau sent her specifically to debunk and refute Mulder's work on the so-called "x-files," inexplicable or unclassifiable reports that seem to defy science.

In the early years, the program was dominated by stand-alone episodes in which the agents investigated such odd or inexplicable cases. Usually Mulder would conclude that something supernatural had happened while Scully insisted on a (sometimes implausible) rational explanation. "The Jersey Devil" (October 8, 1993) found the agents seeking a legendary monster in the woods near Atlantic City. The disturbing "Home" (October 11, 1996) found the agents investigating a clan of inbred, deformed, and murderous backwoods freaks who want to kidnap a woman to breed. As Scully explained in the episode "Daemonicus" (December 21, 2001):

> An X-File is a case that has been deemed unsolvable by the Bureau; because such a case cannot be solved it may beg other explanations ... a vampire, perhaps. Science, however, tells us that evil comes not from monsters, but from men. It offers us the methodology to catch these men, and only after we have exhausted these methods should we leave science behind to consider more ... extreme possibilities.

As the show progressed, Scully's skepticism gradually broke down before the sheer number of odd, supernatural, or extraterrestrial encounters she experienced. Finally she became more of a believer than she was willing to admit, though her belief was grounded in evidence. As a good scientist, she assembled the data, understood the pattern, and drew a conclusion. There is nothing *prima facie* anti-science about the existence of aliens, or vampires, or the supernatural, if science can investigate and understand it. Like a latter-day Van Helsing, she admits the supernatural when science can digest it and bring it into the real world of evidence and reason. Mulder, however, was always a man of faith for whom evidence was confirmation of belief rather than a prerequisite for acceptance.

The heart of *The X-Files* was the relationship between Scully and Mulder, but the best-remembered part of the show was the conspiracy the agents gradually exposed. By the end of the show, the conspiracy had come to dominate the program. As embodied in such shadowy characters as the Cigarette Smoking Man (William B. Davis), the conspiracy involved a dark cabal in league with extraterrestrials. They are preparing the way for an invasion that has already begun, and they use the power of the federal government to enforce silence and ignorance of their true purposes.

With its themes of faith and doubt, science and belief, and paranoia about the government, big science, and large corporations, *The X-Files* captured the undercurrents of 1990s America and became a cultural phenomenon. It inspired a number of lesser series, including *Millennium* (Fox, 1996–1999), about end-of-the-world prophesies; the similar *Revelations* (NBC, 2005); *Dark Skies* (NBC, 1996–1997), which was an *X-Files* set in the 1960s; and *FreakyLinks* (Fox, 2000–2001), about a website whose webmaster investigates the supernatural. *Invasion* (ABC, 2005–2006) sustained an atmosphere of fear and dread better than any other. It dealt with the aftermath of a hurricane, during which aliens replaced several people in the Florida town of Homestead with genetic clones imbued with an extraterrestrial essence. The rub was that the clones didn't know they weren't human, and only gradually is the extent of the aliens' plan for world domination revealed. The show was essentially *Invasion of the Body Snatchers*, but with an emotional depth and intensity that blurred the distinction between human and alien and asked whether we can ever know exactly who we are, or if our actions and beliefs are truly our own.

When Joss Whedon created *Buffy the Vampire Slayer* (WB, 1997–2001; UPN, 2001–2003) from a failed 1992 comedic movie of the same name, he described the show as a cross between *The X-Files* and the teen angst drama *My So-Called Life*,[7] in which the female victim of the slasher movies would become empowered as the female hero of a TV series. The series opened with the arrival in the idyllic California town of Sunnydale of Buffy Summers (Sarah Michelle Gellar), a girl condemned by fate to stand against the forces of darkness as humanity's one weapon against a plague of vampires and other classic horror monsters, which included a Frankenstein's Monster, Count Dracula, a mummy, werewolves, witches, pagan cults, giant insects, etc. The series deftly blended horror with comedy, contrasting the darkness of the paranormal world with the sunny, affluent brightness of 1990s America; and the show ably integrated classic horror with the traumas of adolescence, using the vampires and other monsters to symbolize the terrors of high school, college, and beyond. For example, in one episode a girl ignored by her peers literally becomes invisible. In another, a teacher engaging in sexually inappropriate relationships is actually a giant praying mantis, a bug often said (erroneously) to eat the heads of its mates. Buffy's college roommate is, literally, a demon from hell.

In the series' first episode, "Welcome to the Hellmouth" (March 10, 1997), Buffy does not appreciate fate's forcing her into a life she did not choose, and she reacts angrily when she realizes that the librarian in her new school, Rupert Giles (Anthony Stewart Head), is actually a Watcher assigned to oversee her development into a superhero and vampire-killing machine:

> BUFFY: Oh, why can't you people just leave me alone?
> GILES: Because you are the Slayer. Into each generation a Slayer is born, one girl in all the world, a Chosen One, one born with the strength and skill to hunt the vampires...
> BUFFY: "With the strength and skill to hunt the vampires, to stop the spread of their evil," blah, blah, blah... I've heard it, okay?
> GILES: I really don't understand this attitude. You, you've accepted your duty, you, you've slain vampires before...
> BUFFY: Yeah, and I've both been there and done that, and I'm moving on.

Throughout the series' seven seasons, Buffy repeatedly has to make choices between the duty destiny seems to have assigned her and the life she imagines she could lead if she weren't condemned to be the hero she only slowly grows to become. This is perhaps best demonstrated in her tortured relationship with Angel (David Boreanaz), a centuries-old vampire who, unlike the other undead, has a human soul and human feelings. He and Buffy fall in love, but Buffy must sacrifice Angel, condemning him to Hell, in order to save the world from evil. Several times in the series, Buffy runs away from home to escape her fate, but she is always dragged back to fight anew. By the time Buffy and her friends* defeated the series' last villain, a primeval evil known as The First, the battle had called up legions of girls who shared Buffy's superhuman powers, a phalanx of slayers. At the end of the last episode ("Chosen," May 20, 2003), after the destruction of that ancient evil, one of Buffy's friends asks: "You're not the one and only Chosen any more. Just gotta live like a person. How's that feel?" Buffy smiles. It seems she was able to alter destiny, after all, though not by surrendering her birthright but by empowering a generation of others.

Buffy the Vampire Slayer attracted a small but loyal audience of around three million viewers, but it is safe to say that few series have ever had as large an impact on academics as *Buffy*. A nascent "Buffy Studies" movement attempted to ensconce *Buffy* alongside the masterpieces of American literature and film, and academics endlessly dissected *Buffy*'s feminism, gender relations, philosophy, mythology, imagery, and so on, in dozens of books and hundreds of published articles. In 2006, there was a "Slayage" conference to bring together academic researchers in Buffy Studies. Rhonda Wilcox, billed as the world's foremost *Buffy* expert, argued in *Why Buffy Matters* (2005) that the program proves "that television can be art and deserves to be so studied ... *Buffy* matters for the reason all art matters—because it shows us the best of what it means to be human."[8] By contrast, Lorna Jowett's *Sex and the Slayer: A Gender Studies Primer for the Buffy Fan* (2005) focused exclusively on sex and gender issues, discussing the contrary academic positions on *Buffy*: that she is a post-feminist icon empowering women, that she is a "heteronormative, unself-consciously white, commodified text," as one quoted academic explained it, or that she "challenges gender constructions," as the author would have it.[9] (You see, Buffy is strong and rescues men so she challenges stereotypes of passive females, etc.)

More intriguing was the discussion of *Buffy* and science in a volume examining the show through the lens of philosophy. One scholar commented on the way *Buffy* approached the supernatural from an ambiguous perspective, half way between materialism (science, reason) and occult belief (magic, emotion), both of which are seen as valid and thus enriching one another, which "allows us to enjoy the fruits of science without impoverishing our engagement with the world."[10] Another praised the show for taking a middle-ground approach between postmodern rejections of objectivity and modernist celebrations of science. A third examined the show's presentation of human irrationality. The lesson learned is that in *Buffy*, the monsters are real, but they follow natural law of a sort, thus making them knowable, if not exactly scientific.

Buffy's friends call themselves the "Scooby Gang" after the cartoon Scooby-Doo, *since both investigate supernatural mysteries. In a meta-postmodern twist, Sarah Michelle Gellar, who plays Buffy, went on to star as the ditzy Daphne in the live action* Scooby-Doo *movies.*

Buffy spawned a spin-off, *Angel* (WB, 1999–2004), which followed Buffy's vampire lover (who, I should note, escaped the hell she sent him to and wasn't too upset about the trip) after he broke up with her and moved to Los Angeles. A darker program than *Buffy*, it dwelled heavily on the themes of fate and destiny. Angel was cursed by gypsies to live with a dual nature, a vampire body inhabited by both a demon and a human soul. He is also destined, through an ambiguous ancient prophecy, to take part in the events leading up to a major battle between good and evil, on which the fate of the world hinges. Angel struggles to overcome his curse, and to end up on the right side of destiny's plan, as he and a small band of followers fight against the powerful forces of darkness (embodied in the law firm of Wolfram & Hart). Unlike *Buffy*, *Angel* does not end in triumph, and the last time we see our heroes, they are preparing to fight the good fight for a final time against a sea of enemies larger and more powerful than they. Angel knows he will likely not live through the battle, yet he joins anyway, because it is fate and because it is right.

The British series *Hex* (Sky One, 2004–2005) was *Buffy* in a boarding school but with religious undertones instead of humor. The fallen angel Azazeal impregnated a student, and a ghost and the immortal daughter of the Elizabethan astrologer John Dee must work together to defeat the newborn antichrist and avert the end of days. The antichrist is tutored by Mephistopheles, while the young Dee has the Archangel Raphael on her side.

A new TV movie of *Dracula* (BBC, 2006) found a nobleman calling the count to London to cure his syphilis. The program self-consciously played up the sex angle, relating vampirism to the sexually transmitted disease. Both Drs. Seward and Van Helsing quickly abandoned any pretense of science in an unhesitating acceptance of religious orthodoxy as the only way to battle the (sexual) scourge.

Return of the Supernatural

Television had been kind to latter-day spiritualists claiming the ability to communicate with the dead. "Psychics" like John Edward, James van Praagh, Sylvia Browne, and Allison Dubois all either had their own nonfiction programs or appeared frequently on news and documentary programs to promote their "gifts." It was inevitable that fictional versions would emerge. *Medium* (NBC, 2005–) was based on the life of Allison Dubois. In the show, Allison (Patricia Arquette) is a housewife possessed of a special talent to communicate with the dead and thus solve crimes. Her gifts strain her relationships and occasionally frighten or endanger her. *Ghost Whisperer* (CBS, 2005–) came from the mind of James van Praagh but featured a female psychic who could talk to the dead and help them heal rifts and bond with the still-living.

Afterlife (ITV, 2005–) is a dark and dour variation on *Medium* by way of

Ghost Whisperer. As in *Medium*, a lower-middle-class housewife with stringy blonde hair, Allison (Lesley Sharp)—this time Mundy rather than Dubois—uses her psychic powers to contact the dead and solve crimes. Again, the police and the bereaved come to her for aid despite strong institutional skepticism, and in the end her psychic revelations prove true. The added complication in *Afterlife* is a psychologist named Robert Bridges (Andrew Lincoln) who is academically skeptical of Allison's power and is studying her for a book as a case of abnormal psychology. He has a dead son of his own, and the emotional center of the program revolves around Allison's attempts to convince the skeptic of her abilities and give him hope of contacting his child. The dour and dull *Sea of Souls* (BBC, 2004–) followed a parapsychologist who investigates the paranormal using the tools of science.

Supernatural (WB, 2005–2006; CW, 2006–) was a cross between *Buffy the Vampire Slayer* and *The X-Files*, borrowing the youthful angst of the former and the dark tone of the latter in what was the first horror drama to play terror straight, without tempering by science fiction, crime drama, or comedy. Each episode was designed to play like a miniature horror movie, reproducing the style and tone of contemporary horror: shadows, gloom, and washed-out colors meant to reflect night and death. It followed the adventures of two young men on a cross-country road trip to kill monsters.

After Dean Winchester's (Jensen Ackles) father disappears, Dean recruits his estranged collegiate brother Sam (Jared Padalecki) to help track him down. Sam agrees to join after a demon burns his girlfriend alive, just like it did to the boys' mother twenty years earlier. The Winchester family, we learn, are in the demon-hunting business, traveling around the country to save people from wendigos, ghosts, shape-shifters, and anything else that goes bump in the night. The boys' father had them learning the art of slaying the supernatural from the time they were in diapers. Dean followed his father's lead, but Sam rebelled and turned his back on fighting horror until horror came for him.

Sam and Dean share the secret knowledge that there are supernatural occurrences happening just beyond the surface of modern life, but they work to suppress the horror and preserve the veneer of rational society. As Sam said in "Nightshifter" (January 25, 2007), it's "better to stay in the dark and stay alive." But Sam still believes in the transcendent power of good, while Dean explained in "Houses of the Holy" (February 1, 2007) that "there's no higher power ... just chaos and random, unpredictable violence that comes out of nowhere." For him, the supernatural isn't a cosmic force but an extension of the material world, subject to the (sometimes undiscovered) laws of nature and the efficacy of exorcisms, silver bullets, and ghost-busting rock salt. Science may not recognize the creatures of the night, but the brothers have proof in the form of their own experience, a pure and practical type of science.

The brothers battle a new monster most weeks, but the heart of the story is the heavy hand of destiny that shadows their "hunting" trips. Sam has psychic powers, and a demon is planning to use him in a cosmic battle to take over the world. "In *Supernatural*," show creator Eric Kripke said, "we don't play it as the elation and joy of having this power ... [We]'re talking about the grand issues of faith and hope and evil and destiny."[11] This terrifies Sam, who worries whether he is doomed to surrender his good nature to an evil he cannot control, so much so that he makes Dean promise to kill him if the time should ever come. Dean, too, is haunted by reminders that his path in life was not his choice. In "No Exit" (November 2, 2006), Dean tried to talk a girl, Jo, out of becoming a "hunter":

> DEAN: You got options. No one in their right mind chooses this life. My dad started me in this when I was so young. I *wish* I could do something else.
> JO: You *love* the job!
> DEAN: Yeah, but I'm a little twisted.

Supernatural, *Buffy the Vampire Slayer*, and *Angel* were something unique in horror, series defined by the struggles and triumphs of the heroes, not the evil of the villains. Like Buffy and Angel before them, Sam and Dean must surrender a normal life in pursuit of a destiny thrust upon them, a fate they did not choose. In this, they share a sense of predestination with the victims of contemporary horror films, who are thrust into deadly situations through no fault of their own. But unlike most of those sorry victims, television's characters battle back against the horror, challenge their fates, and fight the good fight. Even if that struggle fails, they will have stood against the forces of horror and chaos and crafted from the hand destiny dealt the life of a hero. In this way, television's horror provided a sense of hope against the gathering storm. The heroes may be condemned to know the true nature of the world around them, but that knowledge does not lead to paralysis or death but to a vitality that can, as Hamlet put it, "take arms against a sea of troubles, and by opposing end them."

These programs, more than two and half centuries after the beginning of the horror genre, are still haunted by the dark and irrational fears that tear at the logical and rational daylight world. But here, no matter how hard the fight, or how great the cost, humanity will not surrender to the tyranny of unreason. We will struggle to learn, to know, and to fight. The monsters of the dark may pose to us Hamlet's famous question: "To be or not to be?" But the hero knows only one answer: To be.

CONCLUSION

> Modern horror is too easily explained; indeed, the real world has
> outrun horror, and the headlines are now worse than anything
> Stephen King can imagine. In the 19th century, there was belief in
> evil, because there was belief in good. That makes [older horrors]
> sort of optimistic, in a way.
>
> — Roger Ebert[1]

The optimism of older horror still lives on in the television series that
imagine that there are still heroes who stand against the darkness. But they are
few and far between. Contemporary horror too often forgets that true horror
need not be a bleak tale of dissolution, destruction, and annihilation. As we
have seen, there are other ways to tell stories, where the end need not prophesy endless doom. A story can still end well and be horrifying. Even stories that
do end in death need not be nihilistic. Two and half millennia ago, Aristotle
analyzed tragedy in his *Poetics* and identified catharsis as the cleansing rain that
makes the bloody spectacle worthwhile. The death of Hamlet exalts us because
it closes out the story and ties up loose ends. The blinding of Oedipus similarly produces a burning feeling of closure, for the horror underlines the tragedy
and brings the tragedy to its preordained end. Through catharsis, the blood and
the gore of horror can be transfigured into a sacred offering, and the story
transformed into a thing of beauty.*

We see this in much of the best horror, which is essentially ancient tragedy
in modern clothes. What are the fiery destruction of Dr. Moreau's dream, the
icy death of Victor Frankenstein, or the execution of Dracula but reflections of
the tragic hero's ancient doom? Horror traditionally held on to the idea that

---

*Psychologists like Dolf Zillmann conducted experiments to disprove catharsis and demonstrate
that viewing violent content does not purge the mind but instead makes viewers more violent.
While this may be a case for the negative effects of media, it says nothing about the artistic mer-
its of a clear, if tragic, resolution against the nihilism of modern horror (Jennings Bryant and
Dolf Zillmann, Media Effects: Advances in Theory and Research [Mahwah, New Jersey:
Lawrence Erlbaum, 2002], 553).

the good man can withstand horror and survive or even triumph, or that by staying clear of forbidden dangers, one might stay safe. The best of horror is in this way optimistic.

This is what modern horror and many in its audience have forgotten in their rush to produce more sensational, more violent, and more extreme tales of suffering without the hope for redemption offered in tragedy. Thus today, optimism and hope wither before random, chaotic, and inevitable violence. Horror in the twenty-first century no longer bears much resemblance to its source material, but each permutation from the Gothic onwards seemed logical enough at the time, until at last the anguish of Shelley's monster and the cosmic vistas of Lovecraft's alien gods gave way to bashing bodies until they bled a lot. And all the while, audiences demanded more.

This, then, is the tragedy of horror. The genre began auspiciously in the Gothic period and through the Victorian age as a vehicle for ideas and even philosophy. But after the 1930s, horror increasingly came to be dominated by sensation, and the grand ideas and deeper insights gave way to spectacle, and spectacle to violence and gore, until in the end little was left but the gore, which became the definition of the genre. It would be easy enough to blame this trend on popularization and read the history of horror as a story of an elite art form gradually debased as it moved from salons and drawing rooms to magazines, movie theaters, and the Internet. But horror has always worn two faces: Gothic horrors were sold to the wealthy in leather-bound editions and to the masses as redacted chapbooks and, later, penny dreadfuls. There has always been high art and popular entertainment in horror. Instead, I am inclined to suggest that movies helped drive ideas out of horror. There are some things that movies do better than literature: conveying emotion, producing visual spectacle, and creating a sense of experiencing what occurs on screen. But there are other things movies do less well than printed words, and among these is the transmission of complex ideas. It can't be any other way: Even an epic movie has much less time and many fewer words to explore its ideas than any novel, or even many short stories. Simplification was inevitable, and the thoughtful ambiguity of earlier horror generally gave way to crude tales of good and evil. As cinema became the dominant art form, literature began to appropriate its methods, and a sort of feedback loop made each generation of horror more bloodthirsty, and less philosophical, than what came before. There were always exceptions and always will be, but they became fewer as the process dragged on.

But it was not always so. Even in its current state, horror preserves the memory of a genre intimately involved with the most important project of Western civilization: science. From *The Castle of Otranto* to *The Haunting of Hill House*, from *Psycho* to *Saw*, the story of horror is the story of the ambiguous and often contradictory feelings Western civilization has for the knowledge, science, and philosophy that underpins that civilization. Early horror dealt with these themes directly, criticizing, as *Frankenstein* did, the hubris of those who would seek out new knowledge without contemplating its dangers. Later horror, like that of H. P. Lovecraft, wondered whether knowledge and science had done anything more than bring us to the edge of the abyss, and whether the price of that knowledge was too high. Recent horror reflected discomfort with institutional science and the mechanistic, amoral worldview it engendered.

This was unique in the canon of Western literature, and no other body of texts—not even science fiction—so clearly deals with the double-faced nature of our relationship with our civilization's defining institution. Horror, and horror alone, dared to take on the Western world's highest ideals, its very image of itself as a rational arbiter of nature's secrets, and to challenge us to explore and reconsider our relationship with science.

But horror was not uniformly anti-science, nor was it uniformly pro-science. Instead, horror as a genre was of two minds, just like society itself. Some horror portrayed science positively, as the only method for understanding and combating the supernatural and the irrational. Works like *Dracula*, *Hell House*, and even *Psycho* put their faith and trust in the ability of science to study vampires, ghosts, and madmen and place them confidently in new categories of the natural world. Another strain, perhaps more common, told stories of encounters with the supernatural that defied science, cast doubt on the utility of human knowledge, and held out hope that science was wrong and that there were other things and other ways of knowing of equal or greater validity. It was the *cri de coeur* of traditional belief, the animistic shamanism of the earliest hunter gatherers, who, ten thousand years ago, regularly engaged the spirit world and sought the protection of the gods against vengeful spirits. By contrast, science was a recent development, and materialism a passing fad before the unbroken succession of supernaturalism making up the bulk of human existence.

What Does It All Mean?

It might almost seem that scientists and academics take a special interest in horror because horror has taken a special interest in *them*. Horror has flourished by feeding off anxieties about science, knowledge, and philosophy, anxieties that cast doubt on the rational world the Enlightenment sought to call into being. At the risk of anthropomorphizing abstractions, science and the academy responded by trying to suppress horror through explaining away its attractions and exposing its methods to the rigors of analysis and rational thought, as though to lay bare the horror would rob it of its power. Psychoanalysis began the process by imagining the attraction of horror as a meeting with repressed feelings stored in the unconscious, especially sex and gender issues. Psychologists chimed in to say that violent media make for violent people, and horror is a symptom of a vicious society.

After them, a number of explanations have been proposed for what horror "really means." We have seen that David J. Skal is committed to often-absurd Freudian readings of horror, but he believes that the larger purpose of the genre is to use its psycho-sexual symbolism to explore a different trauma, war, which is "reflected and transformed in the shared anxiety rituals we call monster movies."[2] Thus, for him, horror is attractive because it draws in audiences to process the trauma of war. However, this theory failed to account for horror that had nothing to do with war, or for the attraction of its primary audience — teenagers — who were too young to have experienced war. (See Appendix.)

Joseph Maddrey saw the essential nature of horror films as a commentary on the changing face of American culture, reading each new development as a reflection of anxieties about cultural change. Horror movies were for him "the signature works of a changing country."[3] But every film captures information about the time and place in which it was made, and there is no more a reflection of America in horror than there is in *Gone with the Wind* (1939) or *American Beauty* (1999). Besides, a good number of films were made outside America, after all.

E. Michael Jones concluded that horror was an anti–Enlightenment reaction born of the sexual immorality of the French Revolution. He views horror's monsters and themes as subconscious attempts to reestablish the moral order by repudiating sexual excess.[4] Superficially, this accords well with psychoanalytic theories about repression, phallic symbols, and the like, but it does not account (without straining credulity) for many ghosts or for Lovecraft's alien gods, both horrors of the mind or soul rather than the body. Jones skips over horrors that fail to fit his theory, focusing instead on sexual metaphors, leaving only a limited theory applicable to special cases. His argument about sex and politics, however, elides nicely into political readings of horror.

Roger Horrocks similarly argued that horror is a "conservative genre" in which transgressions against conventional morality (not just sexuality) are punished. The villain is dispatched, and a conservative, repressed society is restored. A few films, he says, offer "radical" political views, like *Night of the Living Dead*, but these only serve to remind us how much better our normal society is.[5] Horrocks reports that in Britain horror movies are attended largely by young men of the lower classes in a "bourgeois-bashing exercise in defiance" who can attend films and enjoy them without the "shame" attached to them by the upper classes, who as upholders of the conservative order cannot bring themselves to derive pleasure from transgressing the boundaries that define their social world.[6] Stephen King largely agrees with this conservative reading of horror, holding in *Danse Macabre* that the writer of horror fiction "is neither more nor less than an agent of the status quo."[7] Others argued that certain horror films were "really" leftist political statements, and some went so far as to argue, against facts, that zombie-themed films were made during Republican administrations and vampire films during Democratic ones, implying that the monsters symbolized traits associated with those parties (see Appendix). How, one could ask, do we square this conservatism with academics' claims that horror is "transgressive" and critics' assertions that it dwells on the fringes of acceptable taste? To argue that it uses liberal means to conservative ends is no answer.

So where does this leave us? Horror is "really" about:

A. War
B. Culture
C. Sex
D. Politics
E. All of the above
F. None of the above

These are partial answers, but not complete ones. All of these ideas had some truth in limited application, but they failed to capture the range of horror, from *Udolpho* to Cthulhu to *Halloween*. In addition, there was one more explanation, proposed by Noël Carroll, that attempted a universal theory of horror based on an understanding that most, if not all, horror stories dealt at some level with science, knowledge, and philosophy.

Why Horror?

This understanding, that horror traditionally offered a method to explore the existence of things that challenged the paradigms and predictions of contemporary science, offers an explanation for why anyone would want to spend time immersed in a world of blood, gore, and fear, things we typically avoid in everyday life. As Carroll noted in his answer to the question of why horror fiction exists, the pleasures of horror are a paradox, but he proposed that

> to a large extent, the horror story is driven explicitly by curiosity. It engages its audience by being involved in processes of disclosure, discovery, proof, explanation, hypothesis, and confirmation. Doubt, skepticism, and the fear that belief in the existence of the monster is a form of insanity are predictable foils to the revelation (to the audience, to the characters, or both) of the existence of the monster.[8]

Thus, for Carroll, the pleasure of horror is the gradual revelation of the monster's properties, traits, and aspects and watching the protagonists try to wrap their heads around impossible creatures that defy the categories of science (to be both living *and* dead, for example) and to struggle to assert control over phenomena that defy our knowledge and our understanding. For him, the pleasure of horror is essentially "cognitive," satisfying our desire for "knowing the putatively unknowable."[9] This explanation is seductive, and it clearly delineates a major theme of the present study. But while his theory tells us much about the *construction* of horror and its underpinnings, it says less about *why* those underpinnings take the form they do. For example, we might legitimately ask why knowing the unknowable should take place in the context of horror rather than the context of science fiction or fantasy, two closely related genres.

Carroll believes this is because things which challenge our assumptions and knowledge are inherently disturbing, thus producing horror. He does, however, note that horror movies are not interchangeable with movies with monsters in them (like *Star Wars*), and another element must be present: the emotion of fear.[10] But this undercuts the earlier argument that the pleasure of horror is cognitive, based on curiosity and the desire for knowledge. We are back to square one, knowing *how* horror works, but not *why*.

I agree with Carroll to the extent that his explanation is true for me, and it is the interplay of science and faith, of skepticism and belief that provides my own enjoyment of horror. This also likely explains my distaste for contemporary torture horror, which does not follow Carroll's patterns and is far less concerned with science and knowledge than it is with body horror. I could enjoy horror completely free of violence, but there are legions of horror fans who are disappointed if a horror story lacks the requisite requirement for gore. It would not be too far from the truth to suggest that their enjoyment of horror is not entirely cognitive, and this is far from an illegitimate reaction.

Carroll simply dismisses stories without monsters as not really horror because the mentally ill, serial killers, and torturers—even animal antagonists like the shark from *Jaws*—are fully understood by science, even if they commit awful acts.* Thus stories about them or featuring them are not horror movies but some other, unspecified drama and their audiences therefore not really horror fans. This neatly solves the problem by arbitrarily eliminating that which does not fit, but it is precisely this type of popular horror that virtually defines the genre for the millions who troop to the theaters to see *The Texas Chain Saw Massacre* or *Saw*, or buy novels by Stephen King or Clive Barker. So, if we yield to Carroll stories about monsters, where does that leave the fan of "scary movies" that seek only to shock and frighten rather than to engage intellectually? Outside formal theory, these are "horror," too.

Joanne Cantor studied college students' experience with horror, and she found that nearly all the students she surveyed had intense and emotional reactions to horror. One student, for example, reported that after watching *Scream* there were still times

> when I am walking alone to my apartment that I get visions in my head of the
> mask they wore and I get completely freaked out and will basically sprint to my

---

*As noted in the introduction to this book, Carroll later held that his theory could be expanded to include serial killers or wild animals by concluding that their actions or traits were outside the range of behavior admitted by science. He personally did not consider this the case. However, under this more expansive reading, his theory could legitimately include anything *simply* by shifting our concepts of "normal" or "science," rendering it so broad that it would cease to have any explanatory utility or value.

apartment. I *now* check under the bed, inside the closet and shower when I get home to make sure no one is there.[11]

This, clearly, is not someone who went to the movies for a science lesson; however, Cantor believes evolutionary psychology could explain what happened. She views reactions to horror as neurological rather than aesthetic, claiming that we fear on-screen or literary horror because we identify with the characters in the film and feel fear when they are in danger. As a response we become conditioned, like Pavlov's dogs, to viewing the story's monsters or scary situations as frightening stimuli. Therefore, empty rooms and Halloween masks can trigger fear responses in the brain's amygdala even after the movie has ended or we put down the book. Evolution, she says, favored early humans who could best process potentially harmful stimuli and thus avoid predation, a skill carried over to the experience of horror tales.[12]

Thus horror is subsumed in science. MRIs and evolutionary psychology reduce even horror art to just another mental state, and art becomes biology writ large. But neither Carroll's view nor Cantor's investigation really points us toward the *why* of horror. I doubt the answer will be found on an EEG or in the realms of philosophy. Perhaps audiences enjoy horror for the same simple reasons people jump out of airplanes or play the lottery: because there is pleasure in risk and excitement in fear. However, I think that uses and gratifications theory — drawn from communication theory, psychology, and sociology rather than the psychoanalysis, evolutionary psychology, or philosophy usually used to think about horror — offers the most reasonable answer currently available. This body of theories holds that the audience actively chooses the media they consume, and that they do so in order to satisfy psychological, social, or environmental needs. These vary by individual, and any one medium (like, say, a horror movie) can serve "a multiplicity of needs and audience functions," including satisfaction of curiosity, diversion, empathy, or social utility.[13]

Uses and gratifications research into the enjoyment of horror films has found that audiences have a number of different reasons for watching the films. Some go for the excitement, others because they identify with the characters, and still others because the communal relationship of watching with a group fills deeper needs. Patricia A. Lawrence and Philip C. Palmgreen discovered that horror movie viewers typically had a strong desire for excitement and psychological stimulation.[14] But one viewer might seek out a horror movie for escape and diversion, and another might come to the film for the social utility of being able to talk about it with others. Still other viewers might be interested in the film's message or moral, while a few might be motivated by nothing more than sating a deep desire to witness carnage and bloodshed. (Disturbingly, some research finds that those who view horror for the gore are more likely to be violent or aggressive than those who seek it out for other reasons.[15])

Therefore, we need not try to push all horror fans into a single box, or probe their heads with MRIs to generalize about audiences. We can understand that everyone approaches horror for an individual reason, and that all of these reasons are legitimate. It is a bit of a cop-out, of course, to argue that people enjoy horror because it meets some unspecified individual need, but I believe the answer to "why horror" lies within each individual rather than in the mists of time or behind the veils of philosophy. Horror is what we want it to be.

Continuity and Change

It is precisely its malleable nature that makes horror so powerful and able to last through the three centuries of the printed word and the century of cinema, retaining its popularity and visceral impact. Through these centuries, each new innovation in horror tended to follow a pattern. Upon publication or release, reviewers denounce the horror as scandalous and an affront to public morals (cf. *The Castle Spectre*, "The Great God Pan," or *Texas Chain Saw Massacre*, for example). The public embraces it, and popular success forces a critical reexamination. Academics then deduce that the horror was in fact a brilliant new way to think about sex and gender issues, and they rhapsodize about its "transgressive" aspects. Finally, after age mellows its terrors and more extreme horrors incite indignation anew, the older horror is accepted into the canon, sometimes decades after initial publication or release. This was, in part, due to academia's traditional prejudice against horror and anything popular. Witness, for example, the hysterics that attended the inclusion of Lovecraft in the prestigious Library of America: Many literary critics, such as Steven Schwartz, fumed over the admission of a "popular" writer, wondering whether Zane Grey, Mickey Spillane, and other "hacks" should enter "the American pantheon."[16]

It wasn't always the case, of course. Earlier generations accepted eventually *Frankenstein*, *Dracula*, or *The Haunting of Hill House* into the realms of classic literature without serious complaint, and Lovecraft gradually followed the *cursus honorum* of horror and entered the canon. There is nothing inherently unliterary about horror; there is, however, a perception carried over from schlock films and mass market novels that horror is less than literature and an inferior species of film. But a glance at the Western canon will find an extraordinary number of horror novels and films, testament to their enduring relevance and quality.

More so than any other genre (barring perhaps science fiction, with which it shares some territory), horror has become a modern mythology, whose demigods—Dracula, the Frankenstein Monster, the Wolf Man, etc.—are instantly recognizable and yet ambiguous enough to take the shape of whatever container we pour them into. This has allowed horror to stay relevant through the decades and centuries, remaking its nightmares to reflect current anxieties and fears.

To take just one example among many, the figure of the vampire has persisted from the early nineteenth century through today. Though the vampire's essential characteristics—its blood-drinking and biting—have remained, the creature took on new traits in each period, becoming an embodiment of each new stage of horror, and of science. The early nineteenth century vampires, like Polidori's Lord Ruthven, were Gothic creatures, full of Romantic traits and aristocratic detachment, irrational entrants in a rational, Enlightenment world. Stoker's Count Dracula was a creature of biological horror, a beast-man who blurred distinctions between animal and human, as Charles Darwin had done. The 1931 cinematic Dracula, however, was no beast but a suave aristocrat. He was a cosmic creature whose very existence expanded the vistas of science and promised, like Einstein, worlds beyond imagining. The Hammer vampires of mid-century and those of Stephen King's 'Salem's Lot were creatures of sex and violence, in tune with the biotechnological revolution. The vampires of Bram Stoker's Dracula and Dracula 2000 were remade anew, this time as religious figures lodged in the battle of fate and free will, and the search for God in a material universe.

Similarly, the mad scientist has enjoyed a lifespan of two centuries, and today's crazed researchers preserve many of the Faustian characteristics of their progenitors. Victor Frankenstein sought out forbidden knowledge to seize the power of God and create life itself. Dr. Moreau sought to seize the power of evolution and blur the distinction between beast and man, in the process making himself a demigod. Frankenstein imagined he was doing good, and Moreau too imagined there was honor in his pure research, unmoored from ethics. Cinema's Henry Frankenstein sought to harness the forces of the cosmos and to make men into gods. Later mad scientists became increasingly sadistic, the high ideals and amoral research of their predecessors replaced with a dark inclination toward cruelty and torture. Psychiatrist Hannibal Lecter stands near the end of the line begun with Faust and Frankenstein, a mad scientist wholly consumed by his passions and urges, caring nothing for the well-being of others. He uses his science to persuade victims to mutilate and kill themselves, a far cry from Frankenstein's quest for knowledge. Like Frankenstein, Lecter disdains lesser scientists, viewing himself as the arbiter of truth who dares pursue research to its darkest limits. Symbolically, the brilliant cannibal is the embodiment of scientific rationalism superimposed on the base animal that is the human. Therein lay the contradiction at the heart of horror: How can the quest for scientific knowledge sit comfortably on creatures shaped by evolution merely to survive and reproduce? High ideals and base motives mingle uncomfortably under a veneer of objectivity and rationalism.

As though to bring us full circle, Hannibal Lecter, the mad scientist, shares many traits with Count Dracula—from the Bela Lugosi–inspired appearance,

Hobgoblin hall. Like the vampire and the mad scientist, the place where they are found — the spooky old house or castle — has continued relatively unchanged over two centuries. The haunted castle of 1764 is virtually interchangeable with the haunted house of the nineteenth, twentieth, or twenty-first centuries. This particular haunted house illustrated Longfellow's *Tales from a Wayside Inn* in a 1904 edition.

to their noble heritage (Lecter, like Dracula, is a European count), to their blood lust, to their desire to toy with their victims in elaborate mind games.[17] They also share a façade of culture and learning which masks bestial instincts beneath. Lecter is therefore both scientist and vampire, as was Dracula himself in Stoker's novel. Both, too, are Mephistopheles, the demonic tempter from *Faust*, luring the innocent with promises of preternatural knowledge and power.[18] And so the categories collapse into one, the mad scientist is ultimately a monster like any other; and the monster is therefore a multifaceted symbol for the ambiguous and frightening nature of scientific advances that too quickly outpace our ability to integrate them into the moral and cultural fabric of our lives.

Science and Horror

As I hope this book has demonstrated, the horror genre is intimately tied to Western civilization's contradictory and ambiguous feelings toward the place of science, knowledge, and philosophy. But why should this be? I believe that horror reflects these themes for several reasons. The first concerns the origins of the horror genre. When Horace Walpole invented the horror genre in 1764, he was writing in a specific context, reacting against the classicism, rationalism, and materialism of the Enlightenment. In that context, ghosts and monsters were irrational and a frightening affront to intellectual orthodoxy, in a way they would not have been in a more credulous time. From the early Gothic writers, horror inherited as its legacy a sustained critique of the Enlightenment. (It was a critique, not always an opposition, of course.)

The second factor is the pervasiveness of science in our society. Between Walpole's time and our own, science has come to dominate nearly every aspect of life in ways that the early Gothic writers could barely imagine. Science has set itself up as the only legitimate arbiter of truth; therefore, horror must engage science because it is the dominant ideology whose violation is the essence of horror.

Lastly, horror is a conservative genre — but I do not mean conservative in the political sense.* Instead, I mean that horror repeats and recycles its icons and ideas through the ages. The ghost of the eighteenth century is still active in the twenty-first. The Frankenstein Monster still cries out nearly two centuries after its creation. Count Dracula has yet to die a true death more than a century after Stoker. Cthulhu and his extraterrestrial cohorts still lurk beyond the threshold three-quarters of a century after Lovecraft invented them. Psy-

---

*This appears to contradict what I said earlier about modern horror bearing little resemblance to earlier horror, but the contradiction is only apparent. The outward forms — ghosts, vampires, haunted houses, etc.— were retained with steady but minor accumulations of change, but the soul of horror underwent radical transformations.

cho killers still stalk the night half a century after *Psycho*. Therefore, horror's early exploration of science and knowledge echoes down through the ages, continued by emulators and artists who need not even be aware that in continuing the story of horror they continue horror's exploration of knowledge.

In the nineteenth century, T. H. Huxley, the great scientist, argued that the arts, especially literature, must yield before science as the arbiter of truth and the method by which a person becomes educated. In this he was opposed by the poet Matthew Arnold, who argued that science was but a partial truth, and that beauty and the holistic world needed literature to make sense of science's revelations. Literature, Arnold said, was the "criticism of life."[19] In the twentieth century, C. P. Snow, the scientist and novelist, complained that while it was true that scientists as a whole were specialists with little knowledge of the arts, the producers and consumers of literature (and here we might profitably include film, too) were equally ignorant of science: "So the great edifice of modern physics goes up, and the majority of the cleverest people in the western world have about as much insight into it as their neolithic ancestors would have."[20] As a result, the sciences and the humanities are worlds apart and misunderstand each other, competing sources of knowledge rather than complementary ones. For Snow, literature, as an upholder of tradition, must yield to science, the force of the future. Indeed a great deal of fiction has yielded, retreating into the realm of drama and sexuality and abandoning claims to knowledge and greater truths.

Horror stands opposed to this sublimation of the arts, and its critique of science offers us a glimpse of the wider world beyond the limits of science. It is true that science is the best method we have (and likely ever will) to understand the material world, but scientific understanding necessarily restricts the realm of the possible. Each new discovery disproves a thousand alternatives, and something of the magic of *possibility* vanishes before knowledge of the world's true condition. Horror fiction, in all its myriad forms, strikes back against this reductive tendency and allows us an imaginative space in which to believe — even for a moment — in the existence of the impossible. It is the "criticism of science." The fright we feel at horror is in part the thrill of experiencing a lifting of the constrictions scientific understanding imposes on how we view the world. As H. P. Lovecraft wrote in "The Whisperer in Darkness":

> To shake off the maddening and wearying limitations of time and space and natural law — to be linked with the vast *outside*— to come close to the nighted and abysmal secrets of the infinite and the ultimate — surely such a thing was worth the risk of one's life, soul, and sanity![21]

Horror connects us to the holy terror of the ancient shamans thousands upon thousands of years ago when the entire world was alive with magic and possibility and terror. To know fear is to touch the realm of the spirits and connect with the powers that lie beyond human understanding. This is why we seek out horror, and this is why horror, at its best, might be the closest secular, materialist society can offer to transcendence.

APPENDIX:
DOES WAR MAKE
HORROR MOVIES?

In *The Monster Show*, David J. Skal suggests that horror movies' "life and death issues very often have their roots in war and its aftermath. Caligari, Nosferatu, the Frankenstein Monster, the Wolf Man, and the giant radioactive bugs of the 1950s can all trace their lineage in one way or another to the cultural trauma of war."[1] In some cases this is ostensibly true, as in *Nosferatu*'s reflection of post-war Germany. However, in other cases there is no correlation at all. The chart below outlines the major periods of horror movie production, as identified in his book, and the periods when the United States was at war. If there were the causation Skal suggests, we should expect a pattern whereby the horror movies are produced at a consistent interval during or following a conflict.

Major Horror Movie Cycles	*Periods of U.S. Conflict*
	World War I (1917–1918)
Universal Horror cycle (1931–1946)	
	World War II (1941–1945)
	{Cold War (1945–1991)}
Atomic Monster Movies (1951–1965)	Korean Conflict (1950–1953)
	Vietnam War (1965–1975)
Slasher Films (1973–1985)	
	Persian Gulf War (1990–1991)
Teen Slashers (1996–2000)	
	War on Terror (2001–present)
Torture Films (2002–present)	Iraq War (2003–present)

(Sources: Dates of American involvement in conflict are from standard reference sources. Horror movie cycles are drawn from David J. Skal's *The Monster Show*, except for the most recent cycle which began after the publication of Skal's 2001 revision.)

As the chart indicates, there is no easy correlation between horror films and periods of war, which with the inclusion of the nebulous Cold War and

War on Terror meant that the United States would have been at war of some sort for nearly all of the years covered by horror films. Therefore, a spurious correlation appears simply because there was so much conflict. No matter when a horror movie was made, it would be near enough to *some* war for Skal's purposes. The most notable contraindications are the major horror cycles of the 1930s and the 1990s, during periods when the country was not at war and had not been for years prior.

Skal mitigates his claims about a direct correlation by arguing that 1930s horror were distorted reflections of World War I two decades later, 1950s monster movies reflected World War II ten years after the fact, and horror in the 1990s reflected Vietnam, twenty-five years later. In a limited sense this is true, and Skal cites the 1990 movie *Jacob's Ladder* (about a dead Vietnam veteran) as an example. But so broad is Skal's reading of war imagery that literally *any* violence can be viewed as a reflection of whichever war he imagines is culturally relevant. (He reads *Bram Stoker's Dracula* [1992] as a Vietnam allegory because the count began the movie as an anti–Turkish warrior.) *Individual* films may reflect earlier conflicts, but there is no *collective* sense that horror cycles are based on war.

While it is obvious that some horror films drew from war imagery, it is not clear empirically that there is causation, rather than a superficial correlation. However, there is a stronger correlation between horror film florescence and economic volatility, which means a period of pronounced change in economic conditions—for better or worse. The economic historian Niall Ferguson proposed that warfare is most likely during periods of rapid economic growth or rapid economic decline, conditions which created the conditions necessary for social instability.[2] It should not surprise us to find that horror movie cycles correlate quite well with periods of significant economic expansion or contraction, as shown in the chart below:

Major Horror Movie Cycles	*Economic Volatility*
Universal Horror cycle (1931–1946)	Great Depression (1929–1930s)
Atomic Monster Movies (1951–1965)	Postwar Boom (1947–1968)
Slasher Films (1973–1985)	Stagflation and Recession (1971–1980)
Teen Slashers (1996–2000)	Tech Boom (1994–2000)
Torture Films (2002–present)	Dot-Com Bust and Recession (2000–2003)

(Sources: Economic periods are as defined by the U.S. Department of State's "Outline of the U.S. Economy" (http://usinfo.state.gov/products/pubs/oecon/chap3.htm) and other standard sources. Horror movie cycles are drawn from David J. Skal's *The Monster Show*, except for the most recent cycle which began after the publication of Skal's 2001 revision.)

Though this correlation may be coincidental (no matter when a horror cycle begins, there are always going to be economic conditions, after all), it appears that new cycles in horror tend to emerge at a time when the American economy is experiencing change, and consequently the lives of average Americans are also changing in response. The new cycle of horror typically begins a few years after economic conditions change — about the amount of time you would expect if producers were making films after new conditions become apparent, giving them time to be made and marketed — and the horror craze plays itself out about the same time as the economic cycle. Horror movies, after all, are a business. Notice, too, that "lighter" or "fun" horror films, like the atomic monsters and teen slashers, occur during booms, and "darker" and disturbing horror during more uncertain times.

However, since correlation does not prove causation, future work would need to be undertaken to demonstrate conclusively whether economic trends effect the production and reception of horror films. Until then it is merely an intriguing idea.

Do Zombies Vote Republican?

In 2006, a writer for Amazon.com's blog suggested that zombie films correlated with Republican administrations and vampire films with Democratic administrations.[3] The theory was picked up on *The Huffington Post*[4] and has been circulating on the Internet ever since due to its usefulness in caricaturing one's political opponents. (Paradoxically, *Reason*'s Tom Cavanaugh argued that zombie films, while politically leftist, making the zombies anti–GOP, also embody fears about Marxist classlessness in which the mindless hordes are all equal in death.[5]) While superficially seductive as political analogy, it does not hold up under analysis.

The charts below present selected films in the zombie and vampire cycles. As can be seen, there is no correlation between the films' years of release and the government in power. Further, many were filmed several months or even years before the release date, during which time administrations could change.

Selected Zombie Films

Movie Title	Year	U.S. Administration
White Zombie	1932	Republican
King of the Zombies	1941	Democratic
I Walked with a Zombie	1943	Democratic
The Plague of the Zombies*	1966	Democratic*
Night of the Living Dead	1968	Democratic
Revenge of the Living Dead	1972	Republican
Dawn of the Dead	1978	Democratic
Day of the Dead	1985	Republican
Return of the Living Dead	1985	Republican
Resident Evil	2002	Republican
Land of the Dead	2005	Republican

*British-made film released under a Labour government (the rough equivalent of the Democrats in the United States).

Selected Vampire Films

Movie Title	Year	U.S. Administration
Dracula	1931	Republican
Son of Dracula	1943	Democratic
(Horror of) Dracula*	1958	Republican
The Last Man on Earth†	1964	Democratic
Satanic Rites of Dracula§	1973	Republican
The Lost Boys	1987	Republican
Bram Stoker's Dracula	1992	Republican
Interview with the Vampire	1994	Democratic
From Dusk Till Dawn	1996	Democratic
Shadow of the Vampire	2000	Democratic
Underworld	2003	Republican

*British-made film released under a Labour government (the rough equivalent of the Democrats in the United States).
†Italian-made film released under a liberal Christian Democratic government.
§British-made film released under a Conservative government (the rough equivalent of the U.S. Republicans).

CHAPTER NOTES

Preface

1. Oliver Goldsmith, *The Deserted Village* (Boston: Samuel E. Cassino, 1892), 1, 3.

2. Noël Carroll, "Nightmare and the Horror Film: The Symbolic Biology of Fantastic Beings," *Film Quarterly* 34, no. 3 (Spring 1981): 17.

3. Noël Carroll, *The Philosophy of Horror; or, Paradoxes of the Heart* (New York: Routledge, 1990), 59.

Introduction

1. H. P. Lovecraft, *The Annotated Supernatural Horror in Literature* (New York: Hippocampus, 2000), 21.

2. Walter Evans, "Monster Movies: A Sexual Theory," *Journal of Popular Film* 2, no. 4 (1973): 353–65; Richard K. Sanderson, "Glutting the Maw of Death: Suicide and Procreation in *Frankenstein*," *South Central Review* 9, no. 2 (Summer 1992): 49–64; Joan Copjec, "Vampires, Breast Feeding, and Anxiety," *October*, 58 (Autumn 1991): 24–43.

3. David J. Skal, *The Monster Show*, revised edition (New York: Faber and Faber, 2001), 339.

4. Ibid., 277.

5. Dolf Zillmann and Rhonda Gibson, "Evolution of the Horror Genre," in *Horror Films: Current Research on Audience Preference and Reactions*, eds. James B. Weaver III and Ron Tamborini (Mahwah, N.J.: Lawrence Erlbaum Associates, 1996), 15–16.

6. David Lewis-Williams and David Pearce, *Inside the Neolithic Mind* (London: Thames & Hudson, 2005), 26.

7. Miranda and Stephen Aldhouse-Green, *The Quest for the Shaman* (London: Thames & Hudson, 2005), 12.

8. Adrienne Mayor, *The First Fossil Hunters* (Princeton: Princeton University Press, 2001); Adrienne Mayor, *Fossil Legends of the First Americans* (Princeton: Princeton University Press, 2005).

9. Lewis-Williams and Pearce, *Inside the Neolithic Mind*, 159.

10. Aeschylus, *Prometheus Bound*, trans. George Thomson (New York: Dover, 1995), 45–46.

11. Barry Keith Grant, "Sensuous Elaboration: Reason and the Visible in the Science Fiction Film," in *Alien Zone II: The Spaces of Science Fiction Cinema*, ed. Annette Kuhn (London: Verso, 1999), 17.

12. Noël Carroll, *The Philosophy of Horror; or, Paradoxes of the Heart* (New York: Routledge, 1990), 15.

13. Stephen King, "Some Defining Elements of Horror," *Danse Macabre*, in *Horror*, ed. Michael Stuprich (San Diego: Greenhaven Press, 2001), 34–45.

14. Lovecraft, *Annotated Supernatural Horror in Literature*, 23.

15. Kuno Franke, "The Faust Legend," in *Lectures on the Harvard Classics*, eds. William Allan Neilson et al., vol. 51 of Harvard Classics, ed. Charles W. Eliot (New York: P. F. Collier, 1909–1914), Bartelby.com, 2001, http://www.bartleby.com/60/204.html (15 October 2006).

16. Christopher Marlowe, *Doctor Faustus* (New York: Dover, 1995), 1.

17. Ibid., 4–5.

18. Ibid., 56.

19. Ibid.

Chapter 1

1. Robert D. Mayo, "How Long Was Gothic Fiction in Vogue?" *Modern Language Notes* 58, no. 1 (January 1943): 58–64.

2. J. T. Dobbs, "Newton's Alchemy and His Theory of Matter," *Isis* 73, no. 4 (December 1982): 511–28.

3. Richard F. Jones, "Puritanism, Science, and Christ Church," *Isis* 31, no. 1 (November

1939): 65–67; Lotte Mulligan, "Puritans and English Science: A Critique of Webster," *Isis* 71, no. 3 (September 1980): 456–59.

4. Jacques Barzun, *From Dawn to Decadence: 500 Years of Western Cultural Life* (New York: HarperCollins, 2000), 266.

5. Mulligan, "Puritans and English Science," 461.

6. Barzun, *From Dawn to Decadence*, 263.

7. Cotton Mather, *Magnalia Christi Americana; or, The Ecclesiastical History of New England*, vol. 2 (Hartford, CT: Silas Andrus, 1853), 448.

8. Ibid., 449.

9. Paul Boyer and Stephen Nissenbaum, eds., *The Salem Witchcraft Papers: Verbatim Transcripts of the Court Records in Three Volumes* (New York: De Capo Press, 1977), vol. 1, *Nehemiah Abbott Jr. to Abigail Faulkner, Sr.,* 88.

10. Boyer and Nissenbaum, *The Salem Witchcraft Papers*, 107.

11. Linda R. Caporael, "Ergotism: Satan Loosed in Salem?" *Science* 192 (April 1976): 21–26.

12. John Putnam Demos, *Entertaining Satan: Witchcraft and the Culture of Early New England* (New York: Oxford University Press, 1982).

13. Sally Hickey, "Fatal Feeds?: Plants, Livestock Losses, and Witchcraft Accusations in Tudor and Stuart Britain," *Folklore* 101, no. 2 (1990): 131–42.

14. Katharina M. Wilson, "The History of the Word 'Vampire,'" *Journal of the History of Ideas* 46, no. 4 (October 1985): 577.

15. Raymond T. McNally and Radu Florescu, *In Search of Dracula: A True History of Dracula and Vampire Legends* (New York: Warner Paperback Library, 1974), 138–39.

16. Wilson, "History of the Word 'Vampire,'" 579.

17. Ibid., 580.

18. Montague Summers, *The Vampire* (Dorset Press, 1991), 1–2.

19. Quoted in Summers, *The Vampire*, 27.

20. Dudley Wright, *The Book of Vampires* (Mineola, NY: Dover, 2006), 69; though anything from this unscholarly work should be taken with more than a few grains of salt.

21. Wright, *Book of Vampires*, 7.

22. Wilson, "History of the Word 'Vampire,'" 582.

23. Wright, *Book of Vampires*, 5; McNally and Florescu, *In Search of Dracula*, 140.

24. Summers, *The Vampire*, viii–ix.

25. Paul S. Sledzik and Nicholas Bellantoni, "Brief Communication: Bioarchaeological and Biocultural Evidence for the New England Vampire Folk Belief," *American Journal of Physical Anthropology* 94 (1994): 269–74.

26. McNally and Florescu, *In Search of Dracula*, 139.

27. Abraham C. Keller, "Lucretius and the Idea of Progress," *The Classical Journal* 46, no. 4 (January 1951): 185.

28. Roy S. Porter, *The Enlightenment*, 2nd edition, *Studies in European History* (New York: Palgrave, 2001), 11.

29. James Schmidt, "What Enlightenment Project?" *Political Theory* 28, no. 6 (December 2000): 737.

30. Porter, *The Enlightenment*, 2.

31. Voltaire, *Philosophical Dictionary*, trans. H. I. Woolf (New York: Knopf, 1924), Hanover College, March 2001, http://history.hanover.edu/texts/voltaire/volancie.html (3 November 2006).

32. Quoted in Alice P. Kenney and Leslie J. Workman, "Ruins, Romance, and Reality: Medievalism in Anglo-American Imagination and Taste, 1750–1840," *Winterthur Porfolio* 10 (1975): 132.

33. Fred Kaplan, "'The Mesmeric Mania': Early Victorians and Animal Magnetism," *Journal of the History of Ideas* 35, no. 2 (October-December 1974): 692.

34. Gertrude Himmelfarb, *The Roads to Modernity: The British, French, and American Enlightenments* (New York: Alfred A. Knopf, 2004).

35. Richard W. Lyman and Lewis W. Spitz, eds., *Major Crises in Western Civilization*, vol. 2 (New York: Harcourt, Brace & World, 1965), 71–72.

36. Gordon Wright, *France in Modern Times* (Chicago: Rand McNally, 1960): 70.

37. Ibid.

38. Anthony David Smith, *The Ethnic Origins of Nations* (Malden, MA: Blackwell, 1988): 179–82.

Chapter 2

1. Friedrich Nietzsche, *The Birth of Tragedy*, trans. Clifton P. Fadiman (New York: Dover, 1995).

2. David B. Morris, "Gothic Sublimity," *New Literary History* 16, no. 2 (Winter 1985): 300.

3. Terrence Des Pres, "Terror and the Sublime," *Human Rights Quarterly* 5, no. 2 (1983): 135.

4. Edmund Burke, *The Works of the Right Hon. Edmund Burke*, vol. 1 (London: Holdsworth and Ball, 1834), 38–47.

5. Noël Carroll, "The Nature of Horror," *The Journal of Aesthetics and Art Criticism* 46, no. 1 (Autumn 1987): 57.

6. Noël Carroll, *The Philosophy of Horror; or, Paradoxes of the Heart* (New York: Routledge, 1990), 224 n. 69.

7. Quoted in E. F. Bleiler, Introduction to *The Castle of Otranto*, by Horace Walpole (Mineola, NY: Dover, 2004), xi.

8. Morris, "Gothic Sublimity," 305–06.

9. Toni Wein, *British Identities, Heroic Nationalism, and the Gothic Novel, 1764–1824* (New York: Palgrave Macmillan, 2002), 51.

10. Horace Walpole, *The Castle of Otranto* (Mineola, NY: Dover, 2004), 27.

11. Ibid., 28–29.

12. Ibid., 104.

13. James P. Carson, "Enlightenment, Popular Culture, and Gothic Fiction," in *The Cambridge Companion to the Eighteenth Century Novel*, ed. John J. Richetti (Cambridge: Cambridge University Press, 1996), 262.

14. Morris, "Gothic Sublimity," 300–01.

15. Clara Reeve, preface to *The Old English Baron*, in *The Old English Baron: A Gothic Story by Clara Reeve; also The Castle of Otranto: A Gothic Story by Horace Walpole* by Clara Reeve and Horace Walpole (London: J. C. Nimmo and Bain, 1883), 11.

16. Ibid., 13.

17. Ann Radcliffe, *The Mysteries of Udolpho* (New York: Barnes & Noble, 2005), 263.

18. E. J. Clery, *The Rise of Supernatural Fiction 1762–1800* (Cambridge: Cambridge University Press, 1995), 106–14.

19. Peter Brooks, "Virtue and Terror: The Monk," *English Literary History* 40 (1973): 249–63.

20. Ruth Perry, *Novel Relations: The Transformation of Kinship in English Literature and Culture, 1748–1818* (Cambridge: Cambridge University Press, 2004), 398.

21. Martin Rubio, *Thrillers* (Cambridge: Cambridge University Press, 1999), 41.

22. Carson, "Enlightenment, Popular Culture, and Gothic Fiction," 262.

23. Robert D. Hume, "Gothic versus Romantic: A Reevaluation of the Gothic Novel," *PMLA* 84, no. 2 (March 1969): 282, n. 1.

24. Edgar Allan Poe, *Edgar Allan Poe: Complete Tales and Poems* (Edison, NJ: Castle Books, 2001), 183.

25. Ibid., 53.

26. Ibid., 55.

27. Ibid., 762.

28. Ibid., 770.

29. Adam Frank, "Valdemar's Tongue, Poe's Telegraphy," *ELH* 72, no. 3 (2005): 635.

30. Poe, *Complete Tales and Poems*, 245.

31. Ibid., 251.

32. Ibid., 817.

Chapter 3

1. Alice P. Kenney and Leslie J. Workman, "Ruins, Romance, and Reality: Medievalism in

Anglo-American Imagination and Taste, 1750–1840," *Winterthur Porfolio* 10 (1975): 137.

2. Karen Lang, "The Dialectics of Decay: Rereading the Kantian Subject," *The Art Bulletin* 79, no. 3 (1997), 417.

3. Quoted in Catesby Leigh, "Romantic Rot," review of *The Way of All Flesh* by Midas Dekkers, *National Review* (February 5, 2001), Find Articles.com, http://www.findarticles.com/p/articles/mi_m1282/is_2_53/ai_69388685 (November 18, 2006).

4. Lang, "Dialectics of Decay," 416–17.

5. See discussion in James D. Kornwolf, "High Victorian Gothic; or, The Dilemma of Style in Modern Architecture," *Journal of the Society of Architectural Historians* 34, no. 1 (1975): 37–47; and Alice P. Kenney and Leslie J. Workman, "Ruins, Romance, and Reality."

6. Matthew Sweet, *Inventing the Victorians: What We Think We Know About Them and Why We're Wrong* (New York: St. Martin's, 2001), 76, 79–81.

7. Bertrand Evans, *Gothic Drama from Walpole to Shelley*, University of California Publications in English vol. 18 (Berkeley: University of California Press, 1947), 49.

8. Ibid., 49–50.

9. Michael Gamer, *Romanticism and the Gothic: Genre, Reception, and Canon Formation* (Cambridge: Cambridge University Press, 2000), 150.

10. M. G. Lewis, *The Castle Spectre* (London: J. Bell, 1798), 100, reprinted by the University of Parma, February 16, 2000, http://www2.unipr.it/~dsaglia/Lewis/CastleProsp.html (November 18, 2006).

11. Jeffrey N. Cox, ed., *Seven Gothic Dramas 1789–1825* (Athens: Ohio University Press, 1992).

Chapter 4

1. Jeremy Cohen, "The Bible, Man, and Nature in the History of Western Thought: A Call for Reassessment," *The Journal of Religion* 65, no. 2 (1985): 157–59.

2. Ernst Mayr, "The Nature of the Darwinian Revolution," *Science* 176 (1972): 983.

3. Mayr, 981.

4. Desmond King-Hele, "The 1997 Wilkins Lecture: Erasmus Darwin, the Lunaticks and Evolution," *Notes and Records of the Royal Society of London* 52, no. 1 (1998), 170–77.

5. Charles Darwin, *The Origin of Species* (New York: Signet Classic, 2003), 459.

6. Mayr, "Nature," 988.

7. Keith Ward, "Nature Red in Tooth and Claw," *Science & Theology News Online Edition* (March 1, 2002), http://www.stnews.org/Commentary-1893.htm (accessed November 21, 2006).

8. H. G. Wells, *The Outline of History* (New York: Macmillan, 1921), 53.

9. Alex Boese, *The Museum of Hoaxes* (New York: Dutton, 2002), 98–100.

10. Niall Ferguson, *Empire: The Rise and Demise of the British World Order and the Lessons for Global Power* (New York: Basic Books, 2002), 240.

11. R. Beverly Eggerston, *Four Days at Chicago: Descriptive and Historical* (Richmond, Virginia, 1901), 9, as cited in *World's Columbian Exposition: Idea, Experience, Aftermath* (1997), http://xroads.virginia.edu/~ma96/WCE/title.html (accessed 21 November 2006).

12. Ian Ross and Carol Urquhart Ross, "Body Snatching in Nineteenth Century Britain: From Exhumation to Murder," *British Journal of Law and Society* 6, no. 1. (Summer 1979): 109.

13. Ibid., 112.

14. Ibid., 114.

15. Jas. R. Willamson, "Premature Burial," Letter to the Editor, *Metaphysical Magazine* IX (January-June 1899) (New York: Metaphysical, 1899), 321.

16. Karl P. N. Shuker, *The Unexplained: An Illustrated Guide to the World's Natural and Paranormal Mysteries* (Dubai: JG Press, 1996), 34–36.

17. L. Perry Curtis, *Jack the Ripper and the London Press* (New Haven, CT: Yale University Press, 2001), 66.

18. Mary S. Hartman, *Victorian Murderesses: A True History of Thirteen Respectable French and English Women Accused of Unspeakable Crimes* (New York: Schocken Books, 1976), 270–71.

19. Curtis, *Jack the Ripper*, 19–22.

20. "The Murder of Mary Kelly in Whitechapel," *Penny Illustrated*, November 17, 1888, reprinted in *Casebook: Jack the Ripper*, http://www.casebook.org/press_reports/penny_illustrated_press/18881117.html (accessed November 21, 2006).

21. Thomas S. Duke, *Celebrated Criminal Cases of America* (San Francisco: James H. Barry, 1910), 447–67.

22. Ibid., viii.

23. Review of *The Story of the Congo Free State* by Henry Wellington Welk, *Bulletin of the American Geographic Society* 37, no. 3 (1905), 187.

24. See discussion in Martin Ewans, *European Atrocity, African Catastrophe: Leopold II, the Congo Free State, and Its Aftermath* (London: RoutledgeCurzon, 2002).

25. "Some Things the Report of the King's Commission Says," in *King Leopold's Soliloquy* by Mark Twain (Boston: P. R. Warren, 1905), 48.

Chapter 5

1. Noël Carroll, "The Nature of Horror," *The Journal of Aesthetics and Art Criticism* 46, no. 1 (Autumn 1987), 57.

2. Mary Shelley, "Preface to the Last London Edition," *Frankenstein; or, the Modern Prometheus* (Boston, 1869), 11–12.

3. Mary Shelley, *Frankenstein; or, the Modern Prometheus* (Boston, 1869), 25.

4. Ibid., 31.

5. Ibid., 43.

6. Ibid., 45.

7. Ibid., 95.

8. Ibid., 131.

9. Ibid., 159.

10. "The Monster Made Man; or, The Punishment of Presumption," in *The Monster Made Man: A Compendium of Gothic Adaptations*, ed. Franz J. Potter (Zittaw Press, 2004), 15–17.

11. Bette London, "Mary Shelley, *Frankenstein*, and the Spectacle of Masculinity," *PMLA* 108, no. 2 (March 1993): 253–67; William Veeder, *Mary Shelley & "Frankenstein": The Fate of Androgyny* (Chicago: University of Chicago Press, 1986); Devon Hodges, "*Frankenstein* and the Feminine Subversion of the Novel," *Tulsa Studies in Women's Literature* 2, no. 2 (Autumn 1983): 155–64; H. L. Malchow, "Frankenstein's Monster and Images of Race in Nineteenth Century Britain," *Past and Present* 139 (May 1993): 90–130.

12. Christopher P. Toumey, "The Moral Character of Mad Scientists: A Cultural Critique of Science," *Science, Technology, & Human Values* 17, no. 4 (Autumn 1992): 412.

13. John Polidori, *The Vampyre*, University of Adelaide e-text archive, http://etext.library.adelaide.edu.au/p/polidori/john/vampyre/chapter.html (accessed November 26, 2006).

14. Ibid.

15. Thomas Preskett Prest, *Varney the Vampire; Or, the Feast of Blood*, Electronic Text Center, University of Virginia, http://etext.lib.virginia.edu/toc/modeng/public/PreVar1.html (accessed November 26, 2006).

16. Ibid.

17. J. Sheridan LeFanu, "Carmilla," *Masterpieces of Terror and the Supernatural*, eds. Marvin Kaye and Saralee Kaye (New York: Barnes and Noble, 1993), 179.

18. Ibid., 193.

19. Ibid., 210.

20. Bram Stoker, *Dracula: A Mystery Story* (New York: W. R. Cadwell, 1897), v.

21. Ibid., 2.

22. John Allen Stevenson, "The Vampire in the Mirror: The Sexuality of Dracula," *PMLA* 3, no. 2 (Mar. 1988): 139–49; Stephanie Demetrakopoulos, "Feminism, Sex Role Exchanges,

and Other Subliminal Fantasies in Bram Stoker's *Dracula*," *Frontiers: A Journal of Women Studies* 2, no. 3 (Autumn 1977): 104–13; Talia Schaffer, "'A Wilde Desire Took Me': The Homoerotic History of *Dracula*," *ELH* 61, no. 2 (Summer 1994): 381–425.

23. Stoker, *Dracula*, 136.
24. Ibid., 176.
25. Ibid., 114.
26. Ibid., 302.
27. Charles Godfrey Leland, *Gypsy Sorcery and Fortune Telling* (New York: Scribner's, 1891), 128–29.
28. Stoker, *Dracula*, 279.
29. Ibid., 114.
30. Arthur Conan Doyle, *The Sign of Four*, *The Complete Sherlock Holmes Vol. 1* (New York: Barnes & Noble, 2003), 126.
31. Bram Stoker, "The Squaw," *The Omnibus of Crime*, ed. Dorothy Sayers (New York: Harcourt, Brace, 1929), 1056.
32. Ibid., 1058.
33. Barry Pain, "The End of a Show," *The Omnibus of Crime*, ed. Dorothy Sayers (New York: Harcourt, Brace, 1929), 1137.
34. Fitz-James O'Brien, "What Was It?" *The Dark Descent*, ed. David G. Hartwell (New York: Tor, 1987), 870, 872.
35. James Payne, quoted in *The Strange Case of Dr. Jekyll and Mr. Hyde* by Robert Louis Stevenson (New York: Scribner's, 1886), title page.
36. Robert Louis Stevenson, *The Strange Case of Dr. Jekyll and Mr. Hyde* (New York: Scribner's, 1886), 132.
37. Janice Doane and Devon Hodges, "Demonic Disturbances of Sexual Identity: The Strange Case of Dr. Jekyll and Mr/s Hyde," *Novel: A Forum on Fiction* 23, no. 1 (Autumn 1989): 63–74.
38. Susan J. Wolfson and Barry V. Qualls, "Tensions and Anxieties in *Dr. Jekyll and Mr. Hyde*," *Horror*, ed. Michael Stuprich (San Diego: Greenhaven Press, 2001), 154.
39. Stevenson, *Jekyll and Hyde*, 135.
40. Oscar Wilde, *The Picture of Dorian Gray* (Ware, Hertfordshire, UK: Wadsworth, 1992), 308.
41. Ibid., 312.
42. Joseph Conrad, *Heart of Darkness* (New York: Dover, 1990), 45.
43. Chinua Achebe, "An Image of Africa," *The Massachusetts Review* 18, no. 4 (Winter 1977): 782–94.
44. H. G. Wells, *The Island of Dr. Moreau* (New York: Signet Classic, 1988), 40.
45. Ibid., 59.
46. Ibid., 72.
47. Ibid., 74.
48. Ibid., 74–75.
49. Susan J. Navarette, *The Shape of Fear:*

Horror and the Fin de Siecle Culture of Decadence (Lexington: University of Kentucky Press, 1998), 112.

Chapter 6

1. Yoram S. Carmeli, "Wee Pea: The Total Play of the Dwarf in the Circus," *The Drama Review* 33, no. 4 (Winter 1989): 128.
2. Bluford Adams, "'A Stupendous Mirror of Departed Empires': The Barnum Hippodromes and Circuses, 1874–1891," *American Literary History* 8, no. 1 (Spring 1996): 34–56.
3. Matthew Sweet, *Inventing the Victorians: What We Think We Know About Them and Why We're Wrong* (New York: St. Martin's, 2001), 144.
4. Ibid., 144–45.
5. "Death of Krau," *Time*, April 26, 1926, *Time Archive* http://www.time.com/time/magazine/article/0,9171,721905-1,00.html (accessed February 21, 2007).
6. Sweet, *Inventing the Victorians*, 142–43.
7. Ibid., 144.
8. Alex Boese, *The Museum of Hoaxes* (New York: Dutton, 2002), 78–81.
9. *Grotesque: The Diabolical and Fantastic in Art* (Victoria, Australia: National Gallery of Victoria, 2004), 16.
10. "*A Fool There Was*: No Doubt of That," review of *A Fool There Was* by Porter Emerson Browne, *The New York Times*, March 25, 1909, p. 9.
11. Richard Brinsley Peake, *Presumption; or, the Fate of Frankenstein*, University of Maryland, http://www.rc.umd.edu/editions/peake/toc.html (accessed December 3, 2006).
12. Timothy Morton, ed., *A Routledge Literary Sourcebook on Mary Shelley's Frankenstein* (London: Routledge, 2002), 29.
13. Steven Earl Forry, "Dramatizations of Frankenstein, 1821–1986: A Comprehensive List," *English Language Notes* 25, no. 2 (December 1987): 63–79.
14. Raymond T. McNally and Radu Florescu, *In Search of Dracula: A True History of Dracula and Vampire Legends* (New York: Warner Paperback Library, 1974), 157.
15. Christopher P. Toumey, "The Moral Character of Mad Scientists: A Cultural Critique of Science," *Science, Technology, & Human Values* 17, no. 4 (Autumn 1992): 430.
16. David J. Skal, *The Monster Show: A Cultural History of Horror*, revised edition (New York: Faber and Faber, 2001), 141.
17. Richard J. Hand and Michael Wilson, "The Grand-Guignol: Aspects of Theory and Practice," *Theater Research International* 25, no. 3 (Autumn 2000): 266–75.

Chapter 7

1. A. N. Wilson, *God's Funeral: A Biography of Faith and Doubt in Western Civilization* (New York: Ballantine, 1999), 10.

2. Desmond King-Hele, "The 1997 Wilkins Lecture: Erasmus Darwin, the Lunaticks, and Evolution," *Notes and Records of the Royal Society of London* 52, no. 1 (January 1998): 171.

3. Quoted in A. N. Wilson, *God's Funeral*, 277.

4. Frederic J. Baumgartner, *Longing for the End: A History of Millennialism in Western Civilization* (New York: St. Martin's, 1999), 158–59.

5. Ibid., 163.

6. Ibid., 164–65.

7. R. Laurence Moore, "Spiritualism and Science: Reflections on the First Decade of the Spirit Rappings," *American Quarterly* 24, no. 4 (October 1972): 478; Werner Sollors, "Dr. Benjamin Franklin's Celestial Telegraph, or Indian Blessings to Gas-Lit American Drawing Rooms," *American Quarterly* 35, no. 5 (Winter 1983): 467–68.

8. Joe Nickell, "Magicians Among the Spirits," in *Investigating the Paranormal* (New York: Barnes & Noble, 2001), 18–27.

9. Deborah Blum, *Ghost Hunters: William James and the Search for Scientific Proof of Life after Death* (New York: Penguin, 2006), 13–16.

10. R. Laurence Moore, "The Spiritualist Medium: A Study of Female Professionalism in Victorian America," *American Quarterly* 27, no. 2 (May 1975): 205.

11. Sollors, "Benjamin Franklin's Celestial Telegraph," 459–80.

12. Moore, "Spiritualism and Science," 478; Nickell, "Magicians Among the Spirits," 18–27.

13. Moore, "Spiritualism and Science," 474–75.

14. Moore, "Spiritualism Medium," 205.

15. Sollors, "Benjamin Franklin's Celestial Telegraph," 469.

16. Quoted in Moore, "Spiritualism and Science," 475.

17. George Eliot, letter to Harriet Beecher Stowe, July 11, 1869, *British and Irish Women's Letters and Diaries*, http://www.alexander street4.com/cgi-bin/asp/bwld/documentidx.pl?docid=S7136-D052 (accessed December 6, 2006).

18. Moore, "Spiritualism and Science," 477.

19. Sollors, "Benjamin Franklin's Celestial Telegraph," 470–72.

20. Quoted in Moore, "Spiritualism and Science," 486.

21. Francis X. Roellenger, "Psychical Research and 'The Turn of the Screw,'" *American Literature* 20, no. 3 (November 1948): 405.

22. Alan Grove, "Röntgen's Ghosts: Photography, X-Rays, and the Victorian Imagination," *Literature and Medicine* 16, no. 2 (1997): 144.

23. Ibid., 165.

24. Benjamin Radford, "Soul Scales," *Skeptical Inquirer* 31, no. 1 (January-February 2007): 28.

25. Havelock Ellis, "Freud's Influence on the Changed Attitude toward Sex," *The American Journal of Sociology* 45, no. 3 (November 1939): 309–17.

26. Harold Bloom, *Genius: A Mosaic of One Hundred Exemplary Creative Minds* (New York: Warner Books, 2002), 179.

27. Ellis, "Freud's Influence," 309–17.

28. Blum, *Ghost Hunters*, 210–11.

29. Sigmund Freud, "The 'Uncanny'" [Das Unheimliche] (1919), *Standard Edition*, Vol. XVII, trans. James Strachey (London: Hogarth Press, 1955), 217–56.

Chapter 8

1. Srdjan Smajic, "The Trouble with Ghost-Seeing: Vision, Ideology, and Genre in the Victorian Ghost Story," *ELH* 70, no. 4 (2003): 1107.

2. Quoted in Smajic, "The Trouble with Ghost-Seeing," 1131, n. 1.

3. Ibid., 1109.

4. Sir Walter Scott, "The Tapestried Chamber," *The Garden of Romance: Romantic Tales of All Time*, ed. Ernest Rhys (London: Kegan Paul, Trench, Trubner, 1897), 140.

5. Ibid., 143.

6. Ibid., 144.

7. Mrs. Henry Wood, "Reality or Delusion?" *Classic Ghost Stories*, ed. John Grafton (Mineola, NY: Dover, 1998), 73.

8. J. Sheridan Le Fanu, "An Account of Some Strange Disturbances in Aungier Street," *Classic Ghost Stories*, ed. John Grafton (Mineola, NY: Dover, 1998), 3.

9. Ibid., 4.

10. Ibid.

11. J. Sheridan Le Fanu, "Green Tea," *The Omnibus of Crime*, ed. Dorothy Sayers (New York: Harcourt, Brace, 1929), 890.

12. Ibid., 916–17.

13. Ambrose Bierce, *The Devil's Dictionary* (New York: Dover, 1993), 42.

14. Ibid., 86.

15. Ambrose Bierce, "Moxon's Master," *The Complete Short Stories of Ambrose Bierce* (Lincoln: University of Nebraska Press, 1984), 94.

16. Daniel Canty, "The Meaning of 'Moxon's Master,'" *Science Fiction Studies* 23, no. 70 (November 1996), http://www.depauw.edu/sfs/backissues/70/notes70.htm (accessed December 9, 2006).

17. Ibid.

18. Francis X. Roellinger, "Psychical Research

and 'The Turn of the Screw,'" *American Literature* 20, no. 3 (November 1948): 401–12.

19. Henry James, *The Turn of the Screw*, in *Two Magics* (New York: Macmillan, 1916), 42.

20. Ibid., 49.

21. Ibid., 64.

22. Ibid., 72.

23. Ibid., 74.

24. Quoted in Willie van Peer and Ewout van der Camp, "(In)compatable Interpretations? Contesting Readings of *The Turn of the Screw*," *MLN* 110, no. 4 (September 1995): 692.

25. Van Peer and van der Camp, "(In)Compatable Interpretations," 699–700.

26. Charlotte Perkins Gilman, "The Yellow Wallpaper," *The Dark Descent*, ed. David G. Hartwell (New York: Tor, 1987), 461–62.

27. Ibid., 463.

28. Quoted in Jane F. Thraikill, "Doctoring 'The Yellow Wallpaper,'" *ELH* 69, no. 2 (2002): 555, n. 8.

29. Thraikill, "Doctoring 'The Yellow Wallpaper,'" 525–66.

30. Frederic Taber Cooper, *Some English Story Tellers: A Book of the Younger Novelists* (New York: Henry Holt, 1912), 353.

31. Edmund Wilson, "A Treatise of Tales of Horror," *The New Yorker*, May 27, 1944, 75.

32. Robert Hichens, "How Love Came to Professor Guildea," *The Omnibus of Crime*, ed. Dorothy L. Sayers (New York: Harcourt, Brace, 1929), 672.

33. Ibid., 684.

34. Ibid., 689.

35. Ibid., 693.

36. Ibid., 701.

37. Ibid., 702.

38. Ibid., 703.

39. Ibid., 713.

40. E. and H. Heron, "The Story of Baelbrow," in *Detection by Gaslight: 14 Victorian Detective Stories*, ed. Douglas E. Greene (Mineola, NY: Dover, 1997), 257.

41. M. R. James, *Ghost Stories of an Antiquary* (London: Edward Arnold, 1905), 153.

42. Ibid., 209.

43. Arthur Conan Doyle, *The Best Supernatural Tales of Arthur Conan Doyle* (New York: Dover, 1979), 111.

44. Oliver Onions, "The Beckoning Fair One," in *The Dark Descent*, ed. David G. Hartwell (New York: Tor, 1987), 832–33.

45. Ibid., 843.

Chapter 9

1. Alan Grove, "Röntgen's Ghosts: Photography, X-Rays, and the Victorian Imagination," *Literature and Medicine* 16, no. 2 (1997): 151.

2. Alex Boese, *The Museum of Hoaxes* (New York: Dutton, 2002), 92–93.

3. Quoted in Grove, "Röntgen's Ghosts," 152.

4. Boese, *Museum of Hoaxes*, 93–94.

5. Carla Lathe, "Edvard Munch's Dramatic Images 1892–1909," *Journal of the Warburg and Courtauld Institutes* 46 (1983): 199.

6. Quoted in Arthur Lubow, "Edvard Munch: Beyond 'The Scream.'" *Smithsonian* 36, no. 12 (March 2006): 58–67, Expanded Academic ASAP database, Thomson Gale (December 6, 2006).

7. Lathe, "Edvard Munch's Dramatic Images," 197.

8. Ibid., 194.

9. Terry Castle, "Phantasmagoria: Spectral Technology and the Metaphorics of Modern Reverie," *Critical Inquiry* 15, no. 1 (Autumn 1988): 39.

10. Ibid., 42.

11. Ibid., 39–40.

12. J. A. Secord, "Quick and Magical Shaper of Science," *Science* 297 (September 6, 2002): 1648–49.

13. R. Laurence Moore, "The Spiritualist Medium: A Study of Female Professionalism in Victorian America," *American Quarterly* 27, no. 2 (May 1977): 209.

14. Ibid., 210.

15. Ibid., 219.

16. S. H. Rous, *The Victrola Book of the Opera*, fourth edition (Camden, NJ: Victrola Talking Machine Company, 1917), 125.

17. David J. Skal, *The Monster Show: A Cultural History of Horror*, revised edition (New York: Faber and Faber, 2001), 43.

18. Ibid., 44–48.

19. Sari Kawana, "Mad Scientists and Their Prey: Bioethics, Murder, and Fiction in Interwar Japan," *Journal of Japanese Studies* 31, no. 1 (2005): 89–120.

Chapter 10

1. Philip Bobbitt, *The Shield of Achilles: War, Peace, and the Course of History* (New York: Alfred A. Knopf, 2002), 144–204.

2. Philip Spencer and Howard Wollman, *Nationalism: A Critical Introduction* (London: Sage Publications, 2002), 2–3.

3. Albert Guérard, "Herder's Spiritual Heritage: Nationalism, Romanticism, and Democracy," *Annals of the American Academy of Political and Social Science* 174 (July 1934): 1–8.

4. Bobbitt, *The Shield of Achilles*, 196.

5. Ibid., 204 note.

6. M. W. Stirling, "Some Popular Misconceptions About the American Indian," *The Scientific Monthly* 32, no. 2 (February 1931): 173.

7. Brian Fagan, *Ancient North America*, third edition (New York: Thames & Hudson, 2000), 32–35.

8. For a fuller discussion, see Jason Colavito, *The Cult of Alien Gods: H. P. Lovecraft and Extraterrestrial Pop Culture* (New York: Prometheus, 2005), 37–41.

9. L. Sprague de Camp, *Lost Continents: The Atlantis Theme in History, Science, and Literature* (New York: Dover, 1970), 54–60.

10. Ibid., 60–67.

11. Ibid., 49–50.

12. Christopher Dale, *Himmler's Crusade: The Nazi Expedition to Find the Origins of the Aryan Race* (New York: John Wiley, 2003), 8–31.

13. John Cornwell, *Hitler's Scientists: Science, War, and the Devil's Pact* (New York: Viking, 2003), 74–79.

14. Ibid., 85–90.

15. "The Eugenics Records Office," *Science* 37, no. 954 (April 1913): 554.

16. Percival Lowell, *Mars*, second edition (Boston: Houghton-Mifflin, 1896), 153–54.

17. Ibid., 159.

18. David Stevenson, *Cataclysm: The First World War as Political Tragedy* (New York: Basic Books, 2004), 145–60.

19. Candice Ward, ed., *World War One British Poets* (Mineola, NY: Dover, 1997), 21–22.

20. H.G. Wells, *The Outline of History*, third edition (New York: Macmillan, 1921), 1053–54.

21. Frederic J. Baumgartner, *Longing for the End: A History of Millennialism in Western Civilization* (New York: St. Martin's, 1999), 195–212.

22. David M. Kennedy, *Freedom from Fear: The American People in Depression and War 1929–1945*, The Oxford History of the United States (New York: Oxford University Press, 1999), 163.

23. See Alonzo L. Hamby, *For the Survival of Democracy: Franklin Roosevelt and the World Crisis of the 1930s* (New York: Free Press, 2004).

Chapter 11

1. H. P. Lovecraft, letter to Harold S. Farnese, September 22, 1932, *Selected Letters*, vol. 4 (Sauk City, WI: Arkham House, 1976), 70.

2. H. G. Wells, *The War of the Worlds* (New York: Pocket Books, 1988), 178.

3. Robert W. Chambers, *The King in Yellow and Other Horror Stories* (Mineola, NY: Dover, 1970), 14.

4. Ibid., 17.

5. Ibid., 22–23.

6. Arthur Machen, *The Three Imposters and Other Stories* (Oakland, CA: Chaosium, 2000), 2.

7. Ibid., 7.

8. Ibid., 46.

9. Harry Quilter, "The Gospel of Intensity," *The Contemporary Review* LXVII (January-June 1895), bound edition (London: Ibister, 1895), 772–4.

10. Machen, *Three Imposters*, 142.

11. Ibid., 210.

12. Arthur Machen, *The White People and Other Stories* (Chaosium, 2003), 176–83.

13. Algernon Blackwood, *Ancient Sorceries and Other Weird Stories* (New York: Penguin Books, 2002), 12.

14. Ibid., 167.

15. Ibid., 171.

16. Ibid., 176.

17. Ibid., 189.

18. Ibid., 23.

19. Ibid., 28.

20. Ibid., 29.

21. Ibid., 37.

22. Ibid., 49.

23. Ibid., 50.

24. H. P. Lovecraft, *Tales* (New York: Library of America, 2005), 167.

25. Ibid., 177–8.

26. Ibid., 182.

27. Ibid.

28. Ibid., 183.

29. Ibid., 413.

30. Ibid., 523.

31. Ibid., 526.

32. Ibid., 539.

33. Ibid., 581.

34. H. P. Lovecraft, *The Dream Cycle of H. P. Lovecraft: Dreams of Terror and Death* (New York: Del Rey, 1995), 367.

35. Edmund Wilson, "Tales of the Marvelous and the Ridiculous," *The New Yorker* November 24, 1945: 100, 103–04.

36. H. P. Lovecraft and Others, *The Horror in the Museum and Other Revisions* (New York: Carroll & Graf, 1997), 88.

37. Clark Ashton Smith, "Ubbo-Sathla," *Tales of the Cthulhu Mythos* by H. P. Lovecraft and Others (New York: Ballantine, 1998), 44.

38. H. P. Lovecraft, letter to William Frederick Anger, August 14, 1934, *Selected Letters IV* (Sauk City, WI: Arkham House, 1976), 16.

39. August Derleth, *The Cthulhu Mythos* (New York: Barnes & Noble, 1997), 123.

40. Quoted in Ramsey Campbell, editor's note to *The Cthulhu Mythos* by August Derleth (New York: Barnes & Noble, 1997), xi.

41. Anita P. Forbes, "Combating Cheap Magazines," *The English Journal* 26, no. 6 (June 1937): 476.

42. Ibid., 477.

43. Edmund Wilson, "A Treatise on Tales of Horror," *The New Yorker*, May 27, 1944, 72–82.

44. G. G. Pendarves, "The Eighth Green Man," in *Weird Tales: Seven Decades of Terror*, eds. John Betancourt and Robert Weinberg (New York: Barnes & Noble, 1997), 56.

45. Donald A. Wollheim, "Mimic," in *100 Creepy Little Creature Stories*, eds. Robert Weinberg, Stefan Dziemianowicz, and Martin H. Greenberg (New York: Barnes & Noble, 1994), 305.

46. Ibid., 309.

47. Ibid.

Chapter 12

1. Christopher Frayling, *Mad, Bad, and Dangerous? The Scientist and the Cinema* (London: Reaktion Books, 2005), 41.

2. Raymond T. McNally and Radu Florescu, *In Search of Dracula: A True History of Dracula and Vampire Legends* (New York: Warner Paperback Library, 1974), 160.

3. David J. Skal, *The Monster Show: A Cultural History of Horror*, revised edition (New York: Faber and Faber, 2001), 114–15; Curtis Harrington, "Ghosties and Ghoulies," *The Quarterly of Film, Radio, and Television* 7, no. 2 (Winter 1952): 194; Edmund Wilson, "A Treatise on Tales of Terror," *The New Yorker*, May 27, 1944, 72.

4. For a discussion of the various psychoanalytic film theories of horror and their advocates, see Steven J. Schneider, ed., *Horror Film and Psychoanalysis: Freud's Worst Nightmare* (Cambridge: Cambridge University Press, 2004).

5. William Paul, "What Does Dr. Judd Want? Transformation, Transference, and Divided Selves in *Cat People*," *Horror Film and Psychoanalysis: Freud's Worst Nightmare*, ed. Steven J. Schneider (Cambridge: Cambridge University Press, 2004), 159.

6. McNally and Florescu, *In Search of Dracula*, 160; Skal, *The Monster Show*, 84.

7. Richard W. McCormick, "From *Caligari* to Dietrich: Sexual, Social, and Cinematic Discourses in Weimar Film," *Signs* 18, no. 3 (Spring 1993): 649–50.

8. Janet Bergstrom, "Sexuality at a Loss: The Films of F. W. Murnau," *Poetics Today* 6, no. 1–2 (1985): 189.

9. Skal, *The Monster Show*, 68.

10. Skal, *The Monster Show*, 126.

11. Rick Worland, "OWI Meets the Monsters: Hollywood Horror Films and War Propaganda, 1942–1945," *Cinema Journal* 37, no. 1 (Autumn 1997): 47–65.

12. Christopher P. Toumey, "The Moral Character of Mad Scientists: A Cultural Critique of Science," *Science, Technology, & Human Values* 17, no. 4 (Autumn 1992): 414.

13. Caroline Joan ("Kay") S. Picart, "Visualizing the Monstrous in Frankenstein Films," *Pacific Coast Philology* 35, no. 1 (2000): 23.

14. Elizabeth Young, "Here Comes the Bride: Wedding Gender and Race in *Bride of Frankenstein*," *Feminist Studies* 17, no. 3 (Autumn 1991): 403, 408.

15. Toumey, "The Moral Character of Mad Scientists," 430–33.

16. Toumey, "The Moral Character of Mad Scientists," 415.

17. Ibid., 411–37.

18. Robin Larsen and Beth A. Haller, "The Case of *Freaks*: Public Perception of Real Disability," *Journal of Popular Film and Television* 29, no. 4 (Winter 2002): 164–72.

19. Richard J. Hand, *Terror on the Air!: Horror Radio in America, 1931–1952* (Jefferson, NC: McFarland, 2006), 7.

20. "Radio Listeners in Panic, Taking War Drama as Fact," *The New York Times*, October 31, 1938: 1, 4; "Geologists at Princeton Hunt 'Meteor' in Vain," *The New York Times*, October 31, 1938: 4.

21. Gerald Nachman, *Raised on Radio* (New York: Random House, 1998), 311–15.

22. Ibid., 317.

Chapter 13

1. Richard Overy, *The Dictators: Hitler's Germany, Stalin's Russia* (New York: W. W. Norton, 2004), 250–53.

2. John Cornwell, *Hitler's Scientists: Science, War, and the Devil's Pact* (New York: Viking, 2003), 242–61.

3. Ibid., 260–80, 290–95.

4. Niall Ferguson, *The War of the World: Twentieth Century Conflict and the Descent of the West* (New York: Penguin, 2006), xxxv, chart.

5. Ibid., 574.

6. "Truman's Message to Congress on Atom Bomb," *The New York Times*, October 4, 1945: p. 4.

7. Quoted in Cornwell, *Hitler's Scientists*, 432.

8. Frederic J. Baumgartner, *Longing for the End: A History of Millennialism in Western Culture* (New York: St. Martin's, 1999), 214–16.

9. Overy, *The Dictators*, 197.

10. Cornwell, *Hitler's Scientists*, 357.

11. Ibid., 356–66.

12. Ferguson, *The War of the World*, 578; Overy, *The Dictators*, 194–96.

13. Overy, *The Dictators*, 254–61.

14. J. Michael Sproule, *Propaganda and Democracy: The American Experience of Media and Mass Persuasion* (Cambridge: Cambridge University Press, 1997), 127.

15. Quoted in Carl Jensen, ed., *Stories That Changed America: Muckrakers of the Twentieth Century* (New York: Seven Stories Press, 2002), 144.

16. Jacques Barzun, *From Dawn to Decadence: 500 Years of Western Cultural Life* (New York: HarperCollins, 2000), 750–52.

17. Charles Helm and Mario Morelli, "Stanley Milgram and the Obedience Experiment: Authority, Legitimacy, and Human Action," *Political Theory* 7, no. 3 (August 1979): 321–24.

18. Philip G. Zimbardo, Christina Maslach, and Craig Haney, "Reflections on the Stanford Prison Experiment: Genesis, Transformations, Consequences," *Obedience to Authority: Current Perspectives on the Milgram Paradigm*, ed. Thomas Blass (Mahwah, NJ: Lawrence Erlbaum, 2000), 196.

19. Ronald Gottesman and Richard Maxwell Brown, *Violence in America: An Encyclopedia* (New York: Scribner's, 1999), 20–21; Stephen Rebello, *Alfred Hitchcock and the Making of* Psycho (New York: St. Martin's, 1990), 1–5.

20. Richard Dolan, *UFOs and the National Security State: Chronology of a Coverup, 1941–1973* (Hampton Roads, 2002), p. 18; Karl P.N. Shuker, *The Unexplained* (Dubai: Carlton Books, 1996), p. 135.

21. "Unidentified Flying Objects and Air Force Project Blue Book," *Air Force Link*, October 2005 http://www.af.mil/factsheets/factsheet.asp?fsID=188 (accessed January 6, 2007).

22. Shuker, *The Unexplained*, 137.

23. Ibid., 138.

Chapter 14

1. Edmund Wilson, "A Treatise on Tales of Horror," *The New Yorker*, May 27, 1944: 72–73.

2. William Faulkner, "A Rose for Emily," *The Dark Descent*, ed. David G. Hartwell (New York: Tor, 1987), 479.

3. Judith Fetterley, "A Rose for 'A Rose for Emily,'" *Literary Theories in Praxis*, ed. Shirley F. Staton (Philadelphia: University of Pennsylvania Press, 1987), 270.

4. Gregory S. Jay, "The Subject of Pedagogy: Lessons in Psychoanalysis and Politics," *College English* 49, no. 7 (November 1987): 785–800.

5. Frederic C. Davis, "Molemen Want Your Eyes," reprinted in *The Nostalgia League*, 2002 http://thenostalgialeague.com/olmag/molemen/molemen.pdf (accessed December 30, 2006), 11.

6. Ibid., 22.

7. Malcolm Kenneth Murchie, "Thinker," *100 Wild Little Weird Tales*, ed. Robert Weinberg, Stefan R. Dziemianowicz, and Martin H. Greenberg (New York: Barnes & Noble, 1994), 507.

8. Robert A. Heinlein, "They," *Unknown Worlds: Tales from Beyond*, ed. Stanley Schmidt and Martin H. Greenberg (New York: Bristol Park Books, 1993), 214.

9. Ibid., 217.

10. Aldous Huxley, *Brave New World* (New York: Bantam Classics, 1962), 155.

11. Jerome Bixby, "It's a *Good* Life," *The Twilight Zone: The Original Stories*, eds. Martin Harry Greenberg, Richard Matheson and Charles G. Waugh (New York: MJF, 1985), 129.

12. Quoted in E. L. Epstein, "Notes on *Lord of the Flies*," in *Lord of the Flies* by William Golding (New York: Perigree, 1954), 204.

13. William Golding, *Lord of the Flies* (New York: Perigree, 1954), 184–86.

14. Ibid., 202.

15. Anthony Burgess, *A Clockwork Orange* (New York: Ballantine, 1970), 102.

16. Ibid., 109.

17. Ibid., 116.

18. Richard Matheson, *I Am Legend* (New York: Orb, 1997), 29.

19. Ibid., 114.

20. Shirley Jackson, *The Haunting of Hill House* (New York: Penguin, 1999), 3.

21. Ibid., 5.

22. Ibid., 105.

23. Ibid., 107.

24. Ibid., 71.

25. Roberta Rubenstein, "House Mothers and Haunted Daughters: Shirley Jackson and Female Gothic," *Tulsa Studies in Women's Literature* 15, no. 2 (Autumn 1996): 317.

26. Angela Hague, "A Faithful Anatomy of Our Times: Reassessing Shirley Jackson," *Frontiers: A Journal of Women Studies* 22, no. 2 (2002): 73–96.

27. Robert Bloch, *Psycho* (New York: Tor, 1989), 16.

28. Ibid., 16.

29. Ibid., 201.

30. Ibid., 217.

31. Stephen Rebello, *Alfred Hitchcock and the Making of* Psycho (New York: St. Martin's, 1990), 7–9.

32. Frederik Pohl, "The Tunnel Under the World," *The Oxford Book of Science Fiction Stories*, ed. Tom Shippey (New York: Oxford University Press, 1992), 272.

33. Ibid., 276.

34. Kurt Vonnegut, "Harrison Bergeron," *An ABC of Science Fiction*, ed. Tom Boardman, Jr. (New York: Avon, 1971), 181.

35. Ibid., 186.

36. Charles Beaumont, "The Jungle," *The Twilight Zone: The Original Stories*, eds. Martin Harry Greenberg, Richard Matheson and Charles G. Waugh (New York: MJF, 1985), 172.

37. Alfred Hitchcock, preface to *Alfred Hitchcock's A Hangman's Dozen*, ed. Alfred Hitchcock (New York: Dell, 1966), 8.

38. Ray Bradbury, "October Game," *Alfred Hitchcock's A Hangman's Dozen*, ed. Alfred Hitchcock (New York: Dell, 1966), 147.

Chapter 15

1. "The New Pictures," *Time*, February 21, 1944, *Time Archive* http://www.time.com/time/magazine/article/0,9171,774781,00.html (accessed January 8, 2007).

2. Les Daniels, *Batman: The Complete History* (San Francisco: Chronicle Books, 1999), 144.

3. Matthew Joseph Wolf-Meyer, "Batman and Robin in the Nude, or Class and Its Exceptions," *Extrapolation* 47, no. 2 (Summer 2006): 187–206.

4. Robert Warshow, "Paul, the Horror Comics, and Dr. Wertham," in *Mass Culture: The Popular Arts in America*, ed. Bernard Rosenberg and David Manning White (New York: The Free Press, 1957), 199–217.

5. Quoted in Ronald D. Cohen, "The Delinquents: Censorship and Youth Culture in Recent U.S. History," *History of Education Quarterly* 37, no. 3 (Autumn 1997): 259.

6. Cohen, "The Delinquents," 259–60.

7. Christopher Frayling, *Mad, Bad, and Dangerous? The Scientist and the Cinema* (London: Reaktion Books, 2005), 41.

8. David J. Skal, *The Monster Show: A Cultural History of Horror*, revised edition (New York: Faber and Faber, 2001), 260.

9. Frayling, *Mad, Bad, and Dangerous*, 41.

10. Cyndy Hendershot, "The Cold War Horror Film: Taboo and Transgression in *The Bad Seed, The Fly*, and *Psycho*," *Journal of Popular Film and Television* 29, no. 1 (Spring 2001), *Expanded Academic Index*, Gale Group (accessed January 26, 2007).

11. Patrick Gonder, "Like a Monstrous Jigsaw Puzzle: Genetics and Race in Horror Films of the 1950s," *The Velvet Light Trap* 52 (Fall 2003): 33–44.

12. Kevin Heffernan, "Inner-City Exhibition and the Genre Film: Distributing *Night of the Living Dead* (1968)," *Cinema Journal* 41, no. 3 (Spring 2002): 67.

13. Ibid., 59.

14. Roger Ebert, "*Night of the Living Dead*," *RogerEbert.com*, 2007 http://rogerebert.suntimes.com/apps/pbcs.dll/article?AID=/19670105/REVIEWS/701050301/1023 (accessed January 11, 2007).

15. Allison McCracken, "Scary Women and Scarred Men: *Suspense*, Gender Trouble, and Postwar Change, 1942–1950," *Radio Reader: Essays in the Cultural History of Radio*, ed. Michele Hilmes and Jason Loviglio (New York: Routledge, 2002), 188–89.

16. Ibid., 204.

17. John L. Flynn, "From the Inner Mind to the Outer Limits," *Sci-Fi Universe*, 1995 http://www.towson.edu/~flynn/tol.html (accessed January 11, 2007).

Chapter 16

1. Jonathan Lake Crane, *Terror and Everyday Life: Singular Moments in the History of the Horror Film* (Thousand Oaks, CA: Sage Publications, 1994), 72.

2. See Elena M. Watson, *Television Horror Movie Hosts: 68 Vampires, Mad Scientists and Other Denizens of the Late Night Airwaves Examined and Interviewed*, reprint edition (McFarland, 2000).

3. James T. Patterson, *Restless Giant: The United States from Watergate to Bush v. Gore*, Oxford History of the United States (New York: Oxford University Press, 2005), 15.

4. *Public Papers of the Presidents of the United States: Jimmy Carter 1979, Book II* (Washington, DC: Government Printing Office, 1980), pp. 1235–41.

5. Karl D. Jackson, introduction to *Cambodia, 1975–1978: Rendezvous with Death*, ed. Karl D. Jackson (Princeton: Princeton University Press, 1989), 3.

6. Patterson, *Restless Giant*, 99–101.

7. Francis Fukuyama, *The End of History and the Last Man* (New York: Penguin, 1992).

8. John E. Douglas and Mark Olshaker, *The Anatomy of Motive: The FBI's Legendary Mindhunter Explores the Key to Understanding and Catching Violent Criminals* (New York: Scribner's, 1999), 101–02; Alex P. Schmid, "Terrorism and the Media: Freedom of Information vs. Freedom from Intimidation," in, *Terrorism: Roots, Impact, Response*, ed. Lawrence Howard (Westport, CT: Praeger, 1992), 113–14.

9. *NBC Evening News*, August 10, 1971; *CBS Evening News*, August 10, 1971.

10. "Night of Terror," *Time*, July 25, 1977, *Time Archive* http://www.time.com/time/magazine/article/0,9171,919089,00.html (accessed January 13, 2007).

11. Ronald Gottesman and Richard Maxwell Brown, *Violence in America: An Encyclopedia* (New York: Scribner's, 1999), 28–29; Michael W. Eysenck, *Psychology: An International Perspective* (New York: Psychology Press, 2004), 674.

12. Lynn B. Sagalyn, *Times Square Roulette: Remaking the City Icon* (Cambridge, MA: MIT Press, 2001), 31–32.

13. Jürgen Habermas, "Modern and Postmodern Architecture," *Architecture Theory Since 1968*, ed. K. Michael Hays (Cambridge, MA: MIT Press, 2000), 418.

14. Alan Cabal, "The Doom That Came to Chelsea," *New York Press* 16, issue 23 (2004), http://www.nypress.com/inside.cfm?content_id=8374&return (accessed May 29, 2004).

15. Peter H. Gilmore, "The *Necronomicon*: Some Facts About Fiction," *The Church of*

Satan, http://www.churchofsatan.com/Pages/FAQnecronomicon.html (accessed November 1, 2003).

16. Frederic J. Baumgarten, *Longing for the End: A History of Millennialism in Western Civilization* (New York: St. Martin's, 1999), 230–32.

17. Ibid., 233–38.

18. Edward A. Tiryakian, "Toward the Sociology of Esoteric Culture," *The American Journal of Sociology* 78, no. 3 (November 1972): 510.

19. Erich von Däniken, *Chariots of the Gods?*, trans. Michael Heron (New York: Bantam, 1973), viii.

20. See Jason Colavito, *The Cult of Alien Gods: H. P. Lovecraft and Extraterrestrial Pop Culture* (Amherst, NY: Prometheus, 2005).

21. H. E. Legrand and Wayne E. Bosse, "*Chariots of the Gods?* and All That: Pseudo-History in the Classroom," *The History Teacher* 8, no. 3 (May 1975): 359–60; Kenneth L. Feder, "Ten Years After, Surveying Misconceptions about the Human Past," *Cultural Resource Management* 18, no. 3 (1995): 11–12.

22. See Thomas E. Bullard, "UFO Abduction Reports: The Supernatural Kidnap Narrative Returns in Technological Guise," *Journal of American Folklore* 102, no. 404 (April-June 1989): 147–70.

23. "Timeline: The Pill," *The American Experience*, PBS.org http://www.pbs.org/wgbh/amex/pill/timeline/index.html (accessed January 14, 2007).

24. William Leiss, *In the Chamber of Risks: Understanding Risk Controversies* (McGill-Queens University Press, 2001), 16–40.

25. See Abigail A. Salyers and Dixie D. Whitt, *Revenge of the Microbes: How Bacterial Resistance is Undermining the Antibiotic Miracle* (Washington: ASM Press, 2005).

Chapter 17

1. Stephen King, *'Salem's Lot* (New York: Signet, 1976), 295.

2. Susan B. Neuman, "The Home Environment and Fifth Grade Students' Leisure Reading," *The Elementary School Journal* 86, no. 3 (1986): 335.

3. Johannes W. J. Beentjes and Tom H. A. Van der Voort, "Television's Impact on Children's Reading Skills: A Review of Research," *Reading Research Quarterly* 23, no. 4 (Autumn 1988): 389–413; Peter Benton, "'Recipe Fictions' ... Literary Fast Food? Reading Interests in Year 8," *Oxford Review of Education* 21, no. 1 (March 1995): 99–111.

4. Benton, "'Recipe Fictions,'" 103–04.

5. Richard Matheson, *Hell House* (New York: Tor, 1999), 61.

6. Ibid., 54.

7. Ibid., 125.

8. Ibid., 238.

9. Ira Levin, *Rosemary's Baby* (New York: Dell, 1968), 27.

10. William Peter Blatty, *The Exorcist* (New York: Harper Paperbacks, 1994), 122.

11. Ibid., 253.

12. Ibid., 351–52.

13. Michael Cuneo, *American Exorcism: Expelling Demons in the Land of Plenty* (New York: Broadway Books, 2002), 11–12.

14. King, *'Salem's Lot*, 112.

15. Ibid., 137.

16. Ibid., 243.

17. Fritz Leiber, "Horror Hits a High," *Fear Itself: The Horror Fiction of Stephen King*, eds. Tim Underwood and Chuck Miller (New York: Signet, 1985), 113.

18. Stephen King, *The Shining* (Garden City, NY: Doubleday, 1977), 438, 435.

19. Ben P. Indick, "King and the Literary Tradition of Horror and the Supernatural," in *Fear Itself: The Horror Fiction of Stephen King*, ed. Tim Underwood and Chuck Miller (New York: Signet, 1985), 188.

20. Don Herron, "Horror Springs in the Fiction of Stephen King," in *Fear Itself: The Horror Fiction of Stephen King*, eds. Tim Underwood and Chuck Miller (New York: Signet, 1985), 88–89.

21. Stephen King, *The Tommyknockers* (New York: Putnam's, 1987), 418.

22. T. E. D. Klein, "Black Man with a Horn," in *Cthulhu 2000*, ed. Jim Turner (New York: Del Rey, 1999), 235.

23. Anne Rice, *Interview with the Vampire* (New York: Ballantine, 1977), 15.

24. Ibid., 336–37.

25. Dennis Etchison, "The Dead Line," *Horrors*, ed. Charles L. Grant (New York: Playboy Paperbacks, 1981), 9.

26. Ibid., 17.

27. Michael Crichton, *Congo* (New York: Ballantine, 1993), 249.

28. Ibid., 251.

29. Michael Crichton, *Jurassic Park* (New York: Ballantine, 1993), x.

30. Ibid., 113.

31. Ibid., 370.

32. Thomas Harris, *Red Dragon* (New York: Dell, 2000), 83.

33. Ibid., 448.

34. Stephen Jones, "Horror in 1997," in *The Mammoth Book of Best New Horror*, ed. Stephen Jones (New York: Carroll & Graf, 1998), 1.

35. Benton, "'Recipe Fictions,'" 105.

36. Clive Barker, "Dread," in *The Dark Descent*, ed. David G. Hartwell (New York: Tor, 1987), 367.

37. Clive Barker, *The Hellbound Heart* (New York: Harper Paperbacks, 1991), 160.

38. Ibid., 159.
39. David G. Hartwell, introduction to "Dread" by Clive Barker, in *The Dark Descent*, ed. David G. Hartwell (New York: Tor, 1987), 339.

Chapter 18

1. Christopher Frayling, *Mad, Bad, and Dangerous? The Scientist and the Cinema* (London: Reaktion Books, 2005), 41.
2. Isabel Cristina Pinedo, *Recreational Terror: Women and the Pleasures of Horror Film Viewing* (Albany: State University of New York Press, 1997), 23–26.
3. Frayling, *Mad, Bad, and Dangerous*, 41.
4. Dennis L. White, "The Poetics of Horror: More than Meets the Eye," *Cinema Journal* 10, no. 2 (Spring 1971): 17–18.
5. Rick Worland, "Faces Behind the Mask: Vincent Price, Dr. Phibes, and the Horror Genre in Transition," *Post Script* 22, no. 2 (Winter-Spring 2003): 20–33.
6. Rhona Berenstein, "Mommie Dearest: *Aliens, Rosemary's Baby* and Mothering," *Journal of Popular Culture* 24, no. 2 (Fall 1990): 55; Lucy Fischer, "Birth Traumas: Parturition and Horror in *Rosemary's Baby*," *Cinema Journal* 31, no. 3 (Spring 1992): 4.
7. Andrew Cuneo, *American Exorcism: Casting Out Demons in the Land of Plenty* (New York: Broadway Books, 2002), 49–51.
8. Cuneo, *American Exorcism*, 11.
9. Kendall R. Phillips, *Projected Fears: Horror Films and American Culture* (Westport, CT: Praeger, 2005), 101–02.
10. Noël Carroll, "Horror and Humor," *The Journal of Aesthetics and Art Criticism* 57, no. 2 (Spring 1999): 145–60.
11. Carol J. Clover, "Her Body, Himself: Gender in the Slasher Film," *Representations* 20 (Autumn 1987): 187–228.
12. Sara Trencansky, "Final Girls and Terrible Youth: Transgression in 1980s Slasher Horror," *Journal of Popular Film and Television* 29, no. 2 (Summer 2001), *Expanded Academic Index*, Gale Group (accessed January 26, 2007).
13. Clover, "Her Body," 212–13.
14. John J. O'Connor, "*Tales from the Crypt* Raises Ratings for HBO," *The New York Times*, June 26, 1991, C18.

Chapter 19

1. Laura Wyrick, "Horror at Century's End: Where Have All the Slashers Gone?" *Pacific Coast Philology* 33, no. 2 (1998): 122–26.
2. George F. Will, "The End of Our Holiday from History," *The Washington Post*, September 12, 2001, A31.
3. See, for example, James K. Glassman and Kevin A. Hassett, *Dow 36,000: The New Strategy for Profiting from the Coming Rise in the Stock Market* (New York: Three Rivers Press, 2000).
4. Bob Rickard and John F. Mitchell, *Unexplained Phenomena: A Rough Guide Special* (London: Penguin, 2000), 189.
5. Frederic J. Baumgartner, *Longing for the End: A History of Millennialism in Western Civilization* (New York: St. Martin's, 1999), 240–41.
6. John Gorenfield, "Hail to the Moon King," *Salon*, June 21, 2004 http://dir.salon.com/story/news/feature/2004/06/21/moon/index.html (accessed January 23, 2007).
7. Ibid., 256–60.
8. Theodore Kaczynski, *The Unabomber Manifesto: Industrial Society and Its Future* (Filiquarian Publishing, 2005), 40.
9. Peter Baker and Peter Slevin, "Bush Remarks on 'Intelligent Design' Theory Spark Debate," *The Washington Post*, August 3, 2005, A1.
10. *Tammy Kitzmiller et al. v. Dover Area School District et al.*, 2005.
11. Chris Mooney, *The Republican War on Science*, revised edition (New York: Basic Books, 2005), 237–70.
12. Steven Pinker, "The Mystery of Consciousness," *Time*, January 29, 2007, 62.
13. Steven Fraser, introduction to *The Bell Curve Wars*, ed. Steven Fraser (New York: Basic Books, 1995), 1–10.
14. Elizabeth A. Lloyd, "Violence Against Science: Rape and Evolution," in *Evolution, Gender and Rape* ed. Cheryl Brown Travis (Cambridge, MA: MIT Press, 2003), 235–39.
15. Niall Ferguson, *The War of the World: Twentieth Century Conflict and the Descent of the West* (New York: Penguin, 2006), xliv–xlv.
16. Stephen Amidon, "Ode to Joy," review of *Dancing in the Streets: A History of Collective Joy* by Barbara Ehrenreich, *Salon*, January 22, 2007 http://www.salon.com/books/review/2007/01/22/ehrenreich/ (accessed January 23, 2007).
17. Benedict Carey, "Do You Believe in Magic?," *The New York Times*, January 23, 2007 http://www.nytimes.com/2007/01/23/health/psychology/23magic.html?8dpc (accessed January 23, 2007).
18. Jeffrey Kluger, Jeff Chu, Broward Liston, Maggie Sieger, and Daniel Williams, "Is God in Our Genes?" *Time*, October 25, 2004, *Time Archive* http://www.time.com/time/magazine/article/0,9171,995465,00.html (accessed January 23, 2007).
19. Jonathan Michael Kaplan, *The Limits and Lies of Human Genetic Research: Dangers for Social Policy* (New York: Routledge, 2000), 13.

20. Ibid.

21. Paul Kurtz, "Can the Sciences Help Us to Make Wise Ethical Judgments?," *Skeptical Inquirer* 28, no. 5 (September-October 2004): 18–24.

22. Thomas F. Schaller, *Whistling Past Dixie: How Democrats Can Win Without the South* (New York: Simon and Schuster, 2006), 106.

23. Mark A. Shibley, *Resurgent Evangelicalism in the United States* (Columbia: University of South Carolina Press, 1996), 124–26.

24. Schaller, *Whistling Past Dixie*, 106–08.

25. Alfred F. C. Wallace, "Revitalization Movements," *American Anthropologist* 58, no. 2 (April 1956): 265–67.

26. Jonathan Freedland, "When Death Strikes," *The Guardian*, July 26, 2000, http://www.guardian.co.uk/comment/story/0,,34719 5,00.html (accessed January 22, 2007).

27. Jane McGonigal, "Watching Horror: A Gendered Look at Terrorism, or, Everything I Need to Know I Learned in *Psycho*," *Senses of Cinema* no. 17 (November 2001) http://www.sensesofcinema.com/contents/01/17/sympo sium/mcgonigal.html (accessed January 23, 2007).

28. Will, "The End of Our Holiday from History," A31.

29. "Falwell Apologizes to Gays, Lesbians, Feminists," *CNN*, September 14, 2001 http://archives.cnn.com/2001/US/09/14/Falwell.apol ogy/ (accessed January 22, 2007).

30. Alan Wolfe, "None (But Me) Dare Call It Treason," review of *The Enemy at Home: The Cultural Left and Its Responsibility for 9/11* by Dinesh D'Souza, *The New York Times*, January 21, 2007, http://www.nytimes.com/2007/01/21/books/review/Wolfe.t.html?_r=1&ref=books&oref=slogin (accessed January 22, 2007).

31. Quoted in Mooney, *The Republican War on Science*, 243.

32. Jacques Barzun, *From Dawn to Decadence: 500 Years of Western Cultural Life* (New York: HarperCollins, 2000), 798.

33. Ferguson, *War of the World*, lxvii–lxix.

34. Linton Weeks, "Normal Is a Moving Target: Shifting Baselines Measure How Far We've Come — Or Gone," *The Washington Post*, January 6, 2007, C1.

Chapter 20

1. Paula Guran, "Tribal Stand," *Locus Online*, September 9, 2002 http://www.locus mag.com/2002/Commentary/Guran09_Stan dard.html (accessed January 24, 2007).

2. Stephen Jones, "Horror in 2005," *The Mammoth Book of Best New Horror 17*, ed. Stephen Jones (New York: Carroll & Graf, 2006), 77.

3. Ibid., 78.

4. The National Endowment for the Arts, *Reading at Risk: A Survey of Literary Reading in America*, Research Division report #46 (Washington, DC: National Endowment for the Arts, 2004), ix.

5. Neil Gaiman, "Only the End of the World Again," in *Shadows Over Innsmouth*, ed. Stephen Jones (New York: Del Rey, 2001), 438.

6. Thomas Ligotti, *Noctuary* (New York: Carroll & Graf, 1995), 3.

7. Ibid., 12.

8. Ibid., 18.

9. Ibid., 110.

10. Ibid., 116.

11. Ibid., 149.

12. Ibid., 158.

13. Nina Kiriki Hoffman, "Broken Things," in *100 Twisted Little Tales of Torment*, eds. Stefan R. Dziemianowicz, Robert Weinberg, and Martin H. Greenberg (New York: Barnes & Noble, 1998), 42–43.

14. David Gerrold, "...And Eight Rabid Pigs," in *Night Screams: 22 Stories of Terror*, eds. Ed Gorman and Martin H. Greenberg (New York: Roc, 1996), 197.

15. Joel Lane, "Wave Scars," in *100 Tiny Tales of Terror*, eds. Robert Weinberg, Stefan Dziemianowicz, and Martin H. Greenberg (New York: Barnes & Noble, 1996), 529–30.

16. Joyce Carol Oates, "Blind," *New Masterpieces of Horror*, ed. John Betancourt (New York: Barnes & Noble, 1996), 311.

17. John Shirley, "Six Kinds of Darkness," in *100 Twisted Little Tales of Torment*, eds. Stefan R. Dziemianowicz, Robert Weinberg, and Martin H. Greenberg (New York: Barnes & Noble, 1998), 491, 493.

18. Gemma Files, "Kissing Carrion," in *The Mammoth Book of Best New Horror 15*, ed. Stephen Jones (New York: Carroll & Graf, 2004), 282.

19. Ibid., 286–87.

20. Ibid., 298.

21. Clive Barker, "Haeckel's Tale," in *The Mammoth Book of Best New Horror 17*, ed. Stephen Jones (New York: Carroll & Graf, 2006), 413.

22. Joseph R. Garber, *Vertical Run* (New York: Bantam, 1995), 243.

23. Scott Smith, *The Ruins* (New York: Alfred A. Knopf, 2006), 133–34.

24. Ibid., 154.

25. Ibid., 205.

26. Robert McCrum, "The End of Literary Fiction?" *The Observer*, August 5, 2001 http://books.guardian.co.uk/critics/reviews/0,5917,5 32924,00.html (accessed January 27, 2007).

27. David D. Kirkpatrick, "A Literary Award for Stephen King," *The New York Times*, September 15, 2003, E1, E5.

28. Stephen King, speech to the National Book Awards, *The National Book Foundation*, 2003 http://www.nationalbook.org/nbaccept-speech_sking.html (accessed January 27, 2007).

29. Adam Mars-Jones, "Time for King to Abdicate," review of *Lisey's Story* by Stephen King, *The Observer*, October 22, 2006 http://books.guardian.co.uk/reviews/sciencefiction/0,,1928291,00.html (accessed January 27, 2007).

30. Elizabeth Kostova, *The Historian* (New York: Little, Brown, 2005), 576.

31. Ibid., 584.

32. Ibid., 586.

Chapter 21

1. Jonathan Lake Crane, *Terror and Everyday Life: Singular Moments in the History of the Horror Film* (Thousand Oaks, CA: Sage Publications, 1994), 2–3.

2. Bill Ellis, "Introduction," *Western Folklore* 49, no. 1 (January 1990): 1–7.

3. Rebecca Winters Keegan, "The Splat Pack," *Time*, October 22, 2006, *Time Archive* http://www.time.com/time/magazine/article/0,9171,1549299,00.html (accessed January 29, 2007).

4. Ibid.

5. Roger Ebert, review of *Wolf Creek*, *Chicago Sun-Times*, December 23, 2005 http://rogerebert.suntimes.com/apps/pbcs.dll/article?AID=/20051222/REVIEWS/51220004/1023 (accessed January 30, 2007).

6. L. Brent Bozell III, "Tasteless *Black Christmas*," *Media Research Center*, December 22, 2006 http://www.mediaresearch.org/BozellColumns/entertainmentcolumn/2006/col2006 1222.asp (accessed January 30, 2007).

7. Kathleen Tracy, *The Girl's Got Bite: The Original Unauthorized Guide to Buffy's World*, revised edition (New York: St. Martin's, 2003), 11.

8. Rhonda Wilcox, *Why Buffy Matters: The Art of Buffy the Vampire Slayer* (New York: I. B. Tauris, 2005), 13.

9. Lorna Jowett, *Sex and the Slayer: A Gender Studies Primer for the Buffy Fan* (Middletown, CT: Wesleyan University Press, 2005), 19.

10. Andrew Aberdein, "Balderdash and Chicanery: Science and Beyond," in Buffy the Vampire Slayer *and Philosophy: Fear and Trembling in Sunnydale*, ed. James B. South (Peru, IL: Carus, 2003), 90.

11. Marc D. Allan, "Tough Times Call Out for Superpowers," *The Washington Post*, November 28, 2006 http://metromix.chicago tribune.com/tv/mmx-0611280208nov28,0,669 3283.story?coll=mmx-television_heds (accessed February 2, 2007).

Conclusion

1. Roger Ebert, review of *Mary Reilly*, *The Chicago Sun-Times*, February 23, 1996, *Roger Ebert.com* http://rogerebert.suntimes.com/apps/pbcs.dll/article?AID=/19960223/REVIEW S/602230303/1023 (accessed January 28, 2007).

2. David J. Skal, *The Monster Show: A Cultural History of Horror*, revised edition (New York: Faber and Faber, 2001), 386.

3. Joseph Maddrey, *Nightmares in Red, White and Blue: The Evolution of the American Horror Film* (Jefferson, NC: McFarland, 2004), 1.

4. E. Michael Jones, *Monsters from the Id: The Rise of Horror in Fiction and Film* (Dallas, TX: Spence, 2000).

5. Roger Horrocks, *Male Myths and Icons: Masculinity in Popular Culture* (Houndsmills: Macmillan, 1995): 83–84

6. Ibid., 84–85.

7. Stephen King, "Some Defining Elements of Horror," *Danse Macabre*, in *Horror*, ed. Michael Stuprich (San Diego, CA: Greenhaven Press, 2001), 45.

8. Noël Carroll, *The Philosophy of Horror; or, Paradoxes of the Heart* (New York: Routledge, 1990), 182.

9. Ibid., 184.

10. Noël Carroll, "Humor and Horror," *The Journal of Aesthetics and Art Criticism* 57, no. 2 (Spring 1999): 148–149.

11. Joann Cantor, "'I'll Never Have a Clown in My House'—Why Movie Horror Lingers On," *Poetics Today* 25, no. 2 (Summer 2004): 295.

12. Ibid., 300–01.

13. Elihu Katz, Jay G. Blumler, and Michael Gurevitch, "Uses and Gratification Research," *Public Opinion Quarterly* 37, no. 4 (Winter 1973–1974): 517–518.

14. Patricia A. Lawrence and Philip C. Palmgreen, "A Uses and Gratification Analysis of Horror Film Preference," in *Horror Films: Current Research on Audience Preference and Reactions*, eds. James B. Weaver III and Ron Tamborini (Mahwah, NJ: Lawrence Erlbaum Associates, 1996), 170.

15. Katherine Greene and Marina Krcmar, "Predicting Exposure to and Liking of Media Violence: A Uses and Gratifications Approach," *Communication Studies* 56 (March 2005): 71–93.

16. Steven Schwartz, "Infinitely Abysmal," review of *Tales* by H. P. Lovecraft, *The New Criterion* 23, no. 9 (May 2005): 75–77; Laura Miller, "Master of Disgust," review of *Tales* by H. P. Lovecraft, *Salon*, February 12, 2005 http://dir.salon.com/story/books/feature/2005/02/12/lovecraft/index.html (accessed January 26, 2007).

17. Jonathan Rigby, "Dracula Today," *Hammer Web*, March 2001 http://www.hammer films.com/arts/comment/dracula_today.html (accessed February 4, 2007).

18. Carroll, "Humor and Horror," 148; William Thomas McBride, "Dracula and Mephistopheles: Shyster Vampires," *Literature/Film Quarterly* 18, no. 2 (1990): 116–21.

19. Lionel Trilling, "The Leavis-Snow Controversy," *Beyond Culture: Essays on Literature and Learning* (New York: Viking Press, 1965), 146–47, 159.

20. C. P. Snow, *The Two Cultures* (Cambridge: Cambridge University Press, 1998), 15.

21. H. P. Lovecraft, "The Whisperer in Darkness," *Tales* (New York: Library of America, 2005), 450.

Appendix

1. David J. Skal, *The Monster Show: A Cultural History of Horror*, revised edition (New York: Faber and Faber, 2001), 397.

2. Niall Ferguson, *The War of the World: Twentieth Century Conflict and the Descent of the West* (New York: Penguin, 2006), lix–lxii.

3. Jon, "Happy Halloween and the Year of the Zombie," *Amazon Blog, Amazon.com*, October 31, 2006 http://www.amazon.com/gp/ plog/post.html/ref=cm_blog_pl/104-0831803-5781507?ie=UTF8&pt=personalBlog&aid=Plo gMyCustomersAgent&ot=customer&pd=1162 337177.766&pid=PMCA287JD9GH3ZKFYat11 62331816&iid=A287JD9GH3ZKFY (accessed January 29, 2007).

4. Joshua Bearman, "The Zombie-GOP Connection?" *The Huffington Post*, November 7, 2006 http://www.huffingtonpost.com/josh uah-bearman/the-zombiegop-connection_ b_33489.html (accessed January 29, 2007).

5. Tom Cavanaugh, "We the Living Dead: The Convoluted Politics of Zombie Cinema," *Reason*, February 2007 http://www.reason. com/news/show/118315.html (accessed January 30, 2007).

Selected Bibliography

Horror Texts

A complete bibliography of horror literature would require several volumes of its own. Listed here are texts directly quoted or cited in this book. Those merely mentioned in passing have been omitted.

Aeschylus. *Prometheus Bound.* Trans. George Thomson. New York: Dover, 1995.

Barker, Clive. *The Hellbound Heart.* New York: Harper Paperbacks, 1991.

Betancourt, John, ed. *New Masterpieces of Horror.* New York: Barnes & Noble, 1996.

_____, and Robert Weinberg, eds. *Weird Tales: Seven Decades of Terror.* New York: Barnes & Noble, 1997.

Bierce, Ambrose. *The Complete Short Stories of Ambrose Bierce.* Lincoln: University of Nebraska Press, 1984.

_____. *The Devil's Dictionary.* New York: Dover, 1993.

Blackwood, Algernon. *Ancient Sorceries and Other Weird Stories.* New York: Penguin Books, 2002.

Blatty, William Peter. *The Exorcist.* New York: Harper Paperbacks, 1994.

Bloch, Robert. *Psycho.* New York: Tor, 1989.

Boardman, Tom, Jr., ed. *An ABC of Science Fiction.* New York: Avon, 1971.

Burgess, Anthony. *A Clockwork Orange.* New York: Ballantine, 1970.

Chambers, Robert W. *The King in Yellow and Other Horror Stories.* Mineola, NY: Dover, 1970.

Conan Doyle, Arthur. *The Best Supernatural Tales of Arthur Conan Doyle.* New York: Dover, 1979.

_____. *The Complete Sherlock Holmes.* Volume 1. New York: Barnes & Noble, 2003.

Conrad, Joseph. *Heart of Darkness.* New York: Dover, 1990.

Cox, Jeffrey N., ed. *Seven Gothic Dramas 1789–1825.* Athens: Ohio University Press, 1992.

Crichton, Michael. *Congo.* New York: Ballantine, 1993.

_____. *Jurassic Park.* New York: Ballantine, 1993.

Davis, Frederic C. "Molemen Want Your Eyes." *The Nostalgia League,* 2002 http://thenostalgialeague.com/olmag/molemen/molemen.pdf (accessed December 30, 2006).

Derleth, August. *The Cthulhu Mythos.* New York: Barnes & Noble, 1997.

Dziemianowicz, Stefan, Robert Weinberg, and Martin H. Greenberg, eds. *100 Twisted Little Tales of Torment.* New York: Barnes & Noble, 1998.

Garber, Joseph R. *Vertical Run.* New York: Bantam, 1995.

Golding, William. *Lord of the Flies.* New York: Perigree, 1954.

Gorman, Ed, and Martin H. Greenberg. *Night Screams: 22 Stories of Terror.* New York: Roc, 1996.

Grafton, John, ed. *Classic Ghost Stories.* Mineola, New York: Dover, 1998.

Grant, Charles L., ed. *Horrors.* New York: Playboy Paperbacks, 1981.

Greenberg, Martin Harry, Richard Matheson, and Charles G. Waugh. *The Twilight Zone: The Original Stories*. New York: MJF, 1985.

Greene, Douglas E., ed. *Detection by Gaslight: 14 Victorian Detective Stories*. Mineola, NY: Dover, 1997.

Harris, Thomas. *Red Dragon*. New York: Dell, 2000.

Hartwell, David G., ed. *The Dark Descent*. New York: Tor, 1987.

Hitchcock, Alfred, ed. *Alfred Hitchcock's A Hangman's Dozen*. New York: Dell, 1966.

Huxley, Aldous. *Brave New World*. New York: Bantam Classics, 1962.

Jackson, Shirley. *The Haunting of Hill House*. New York: Penguin, 1999.

James, Henry. *Two Magics*. New York: Macmillan, 1916.

James, M. R. *Ghost Stories of an Antiquary*. London: Edward Arnold, 1905.

Jones, Stephen, ed. *The Mammoth Book of Best New Horror 9*. New York: Carroll & Graf, 1998.

_____, ed. *The Mammoth Book of Best New Horror 15*. New York: Carroll & Graf, 2004.

_____, ed. *The Mammoth Book of Best New Horror 17*. New York: Carroll & Graf, 2006.

_____, ed. *Shadows Over Innsmouth*. New York: Del Rey, 2001.

Kaye, Marvin, and Saralee Kaye, eds. *Masterpieces of Terror and the Supernatural*. New York: Barnes and Noble, 1993.

King, Stephen. *'Salem's Lot*. New York: Signet, 1976.

_____. *The Shining*. Garden City, NY: Doubleday, 1977.

_____. *The Tommyknockers*. New York: G. P. Putnam's, 1987.

Kostova, Elizabeth. *The Historian*. New York: Little, Brown, 2005.

Levin, Ira. *Rosemary's Baby*. New York: Dell, 1968.

Lewis, M. G. *The Castle Spectre*. London: J. Bell, 1798. Reprinted by the University of Parma, February 16, 2000 http://www2.unipr.it/~dsaglia/Lewis/CastleProsp.html (accessed November 18, 2006).

Ligotti, Thomas. *Noctuary*. New York: Carroll & Graf, 1995.

Lovecraft, H. P. *The Dream Cycle of H. P. Lovecraft: Dreams of Terror and Death*. New York: Del Rey, 1995.

_____. *Selected Letters*, Volume 4. Sauk City, WI: Arkham House, 1976.

_____. *Tales*. New York: Library of America, 2005.

_____, and others. *The Horror in the Museum and Other Revisions*. New York: Carroll & Graf, 1997.

_____, and _____. *Tales of the Cthulhu Mythos*. New York: Ballantine, 1998.

Machen, Arthur. *The Three Imposters and Other Stories*. Oakland, CA: Chaosium, 2000.

_____. *The White People and Other Stories*. Chaosium, 2003.

Marlowe, Christopher. *Doctor Faustus*. New York: Dover, 1995.

Matheson, Richard. *Hell House*. New York: Tor, 1999.

_____. *I Am Legend*. New York: Orb, 1997.

Peake, Richard Brinsley. *Presumption; or, the Fate of Frankenstein*. University of Maryland http://www.rc.umd.edu/editions/peake/toc.html (accessed December 3, 2006).

Poe, Edgar Allan. *Edgar Allan Poe: Complete Tales and Poems*. Edison, NJ: Castle Books, 2001.

Polidori, John. *The Vampyre*. University of Adelaide e-text archive http://etext.library.ade laide.edu.au/p/polidori/john/vampyre/chapter.html (accessed November 26, 2006).

Potter, Franz J., ed. *The Monster Made Man: A Compendium of Gothic Adaptations*. Zittaw Press, 2004.

Prest, Thomas Preskett. *Varney the Vampire; Or, the Feast of Blood*. Electronic Text Center, University of Virginia http://etext.lib.virginia.edu/toc/modeng/public/PreVar1.html (accessed November 26, 2006).

Radcliffe, Ann. *The Mysteries of Udolpho*. New York: Barnes & Noble, 2005.

Reeve, Clara, and Horace Walpole. *The Old English Baron: A Gothic Story*, also *The Castle of Otranto: A Gothic Story by Horace Walpole*. London: J. C. Nimmo and Bain, 1883.

Rhys, Ernest, ed. *The Garden of Romance: Romantic Tales of All Time*. London: Kegan Paul, Trench, Trubner, 1897.

Rice, Anne. *Interview with the Vampire*. New York: Ballantine, 1977.

Sayers, Dorothy. *The Omnibus of Crime*. New York: Harcourt, Brace, 1929.

Schmidt, Stanley, and Martin H. Greenberg. *Unknown Worlds: Tales from Beyond*. New York: Bristol Park Books, 1993.

Shelley, Mary. *Frankenstein; or, the Modern Prometheus*. Boston, 1869.

Shippey, Tom. *The Oxford Book of Science Fiction Stories*. New York: Oxford University Press, 1992.

Smith, Scott. *The Ruins*. New York: Alfred A. Knopf, 2006.

Stevenson, Robert Louis. *The Strange Case of Dr. Jekyll and Mr. Hyde*. New York: Scribner's, 1886.

Stoker, Bram. *Dracula: A Mystery Story*. New York: W. R. Cadwell, 1897.

Turner, Jim, ed. *Cthulhu 2000*. New York: Del Rey, 1999.

Walpole, Horace. *The Castle of Otranto*. Mineola, NY: Dover, 2004.

Ward, Candice, ed. *World War One British Poets*. Mineola, NY: Dover, 1997.

Weinberg, Robert, Stefan Dziemianowicz, and Martin H. Greenberg, eds. *100 Creepy Little Creature Stories*. New York: Barnes & Noble, 1994.

_____, _____, and _____, eds. *100 Tiny Tales of Terror*. New York: Barnes & Noble, 1996.

_____, _____, and _____, eds. *100 Wild Little Weird Tales*. New York: Barnes & Noble, 1994.

Wells, H. G. *The Island of Dr. Moreau*. New York: Signet Classic, 1988.

_____. *The War of the Worlds*. New York: Pocket Books, 1988.

Wilde, Oscar. *The Picture of Dorian Gray*. Ware, Hertfordshire, UK: Wadsworth, 1992.

Horror Criticism, Research, and Analysis

Achebe, Chinua. "An Image of Africa." *The Massachusetts Review* 18, no. 4 (Winter 1977): 782–94.

Berenstein, Rhona. "Mommie Dearest: *Aliens, Rosemary's Baby* and Mothering." *Journal of Popular Culture* 24, no. 2 (Fall 1990): 55–74.

Bergstrom, Janet. "Sexuality at a Loss: The Films of F. W. Murnau." *Poetics Today* 6, no. 1–2 (1985): 185–203.

Brooks, Peter. "Virtue and Terror: *The Monk*." *English Literary History* 40 (1973): 249–63.

Burke, Edmund. *The Works of the Right Hon. Edmund Burke*. Volume 1. London: Holdsworth and Ball, 1834.

Cantor, Joann. "'I'll Never Have a Clown in My House'— Why Movie Horror Lingers On." *Poetics Today* 25, no. 2 (Summer 2004): 283–304.

Canty, Daniel. "The Meaning of 'Moxon's Master.'" *Science Fiction Studies* 23, no. 70 (November 1996) http://www.depauw.edu/sfs/backissues/70/notes70.htm (accessed December 9, 2006).

Carroll, Noël. "Horror and Humor." *The Journal of Aesthetics and Art Criticism* 57, no. 2 (Spring 1999): 145–60.

_____. "The Nature of Horror." *The Journal of Aesthetics and Art Criticism* 46, no. 1 (Autumn 1987): 51–59.

_____. "Nightmare and the Horror Film: The Symbolic Biology of Fantastic Beings." *Film Quarterly* 34, no. 3 (Spring 1981): 16–25

_____. *The Philosophy of Horror; or, Paradoxes of the Heart*. New York: Routledge, 1990.

Castle, Terry. "Phantasmagoria: Spectral Technology and the Metaphorics of Modern Reverie." *Critical Inquiry* 15, no. 1 (Autumn 1988): 26–61.

Clery, E. J. *The Rise of Supernatural Fiction 1762–1800*. Cambridge: Cambridge University Press, 1995.

Clover, Carol J. "Her Body, Himself: Gender in the Slasher Film," *Representations* 20 (Autumn 1987): 187–228.

Cooper, Frederic Taber. *Some English Story Tellers: A Book of the Younger Novelists*. New York: Henry Holt, 1912.

Copjec, Joan. "Vampires, Breast Feeding, and Anxiety." *October*, 58 (Autumn 1991): 24–43.

Crane, Jonathan Lake. *Terror and Everyday Life: Singular Moments in the History of the Horror Film*. Thousand Oaks, CA: Sage Publications, 1994.

Daniels, Les. *Batman: The Complete History*. San Francisco: Chronicle Books, 1999.

Demetrakopoulos, Stephanie. "Feminism, Sex Role Exchanges, and Other Subliminal Fantasies in Bram Stoker's *Dracula.*" *Frontiers: A Journal of Women Studies* 2, no. 3 (Autumn 1977):104–13.

Des Pres, Terrence. "Terror and the Sublime." *Human Rights Quarterly* 5, no. 2 (1983): 135–46.

Doane, Janice, and Devon Hodges. "Demonic Disturbances of Sexual Identity: The Strange Case of Dr. Jekyll and Mr/s Hyde." *Novel: A Forum on Fiction* 23, no. 1 (Autumn 1989): 63–74.

Ellis, Bill. "Introduction." *Western Folklore* 49, no. 1 (January 1990): 1–7.

Evans, Bertrand. *Gothic Drama from Walpole to Shelley.* University of California Publications in English Volume 18. Berkeley: University of California Press, 1947.

Evans, Walter. "Monster Movies: A Sexual Theory." *Journal of Popular Film* 2, no. 4 (1973): 353–65.

Fischer, Lucy. "Birth Traumas: Parturition and Horror in *Rosemary's Baby,*" *Cinema Journal* 31, no. 3 (Spring 1992): 3–18.

Flynn, John L. "From the Inner Mind to the Outer Limits." *Sci-Fi Universe.* 1995 http://www.towson.edu/~flynn/tol.html (accessed January 11, 2007).

Forbes, Anita P. "Combating Cheap Magazines." *The English Journal* 26, no. 6 (June 1937): 476–78.

Forry, Steven Earl. "Dramatizations of *Frankenstein*, 1821–1986: A Comprehensive List." *English Language Notes* 25, no. 2 (December 1987): 63–79.

Frank, Adam. "Valdemar's Tongue, Poe's Telegraphy." *ELH* 72, no. 3 (2005): 635–62.

Franke, Kuno. "The Faust Legend." *Lectures on the Harvard Classics.* Ed. William Allan Neilson et al., Volume 51 of Harvard Classics. Ed. Charles W. Eliot. New York: P. F. Collier, 1909–1914. Bartleby.com. 2001 http://www.bartleby.com/60/204.html (accessed October 15, 2006).

Frayling, Christopher. *Mad, Bad, and Dangerous? The Scientist and the Cinema.* London: Reaktion Books, 2005.

Freud, Sigmund. "The 'Uncanny'" [*Das Unheimliche*] (1919). *Standard Edition*, Volume XVII, trans. James Strachey (London: Hogarth Press, 1955), 217–56.

Gamer, Michael. *Romanticism and the Gothic: Genre, Reception, and Canon Formation.* Cambridge, MA: Cambridge University Press, 2000.

Gonder, Patrick. "Like a Monstrous Jigsaw Puzzle: Genetics and Race in Horror Films of the 1950s." *The Velvet Light Trap* 52 (Fall 2003): 33–44.

Greene, Katherine, and Marina Krcmar. "Predicting Exposure to and Liking of Media Violence: A Uses and Gratifications Approach." *Communication Studies* 56 (March 2005): 71–93.

Grotesque: The Diabolical and Fantastic in Art. Victoria, Australia: National Gallery of Victoria, 2004.

Guran, Paula. "Tribal Stand." *Locus Online.* September 9, 2002 http://www.locusmag.com/2002/Commentary/Guran09_Standard.html (accessed January 24, 2007).

Hague, Angela. "A Faithful Anatomy of Our Times: Reassessing Shirley Jackson." *Frontiers: A Journal of Women Studies* 22, no. 2 (2002): 73–96.

Hand, Richard J. *Terror on the Air!: Horror Radio in America, 1931–1952.* Jefferson, NC: McFarland, 2006.

———, and Michael Wilson. "The Grand-Guignol: Aspects of Theory and Practice." *Theater Research International* 25, no. 3 (Autumn 2000): 266–75.

Heffernan, Kevin. "Inner-City Exhibition and the Genre Film: Distributing *Night of the Living Dead* (1968)." *Cinema Journal* 41, no. 3 (Spring 2002): 59–77.

Hendershot, Cyndy. "The Cold War Horror Film: Taboo and Transgression in *The Bad Seed, The Fly,* and *Psycho.*" *Journal of Popular Film and Television* 29, no. 1 (Spring 2001). *Expanded Academic Index.* Gale Group (accessed January 26, 2007).

Hilmes, Michele, and Jason Loviglio, eds. *Radio Reader: Essays in the Cultural History of Radio.* New York: Routledge, 2002.

Hodges, Devon. "*Frankenstein* and the Feminine Subversion of the Novel." *Tulsa Studies in Women's Literature* 2, no. 2 (Autumn 1983): 155–64.

Horrocks, Roger. *Male Myths and Icons: Masculinity in Popular Culture.* Houndsmills: Macmillan, 1995.

Hume, Robert D. "Gothic versus Romantic: A Reevaluation of the Gothic Novel." *PMLA* 84, no. 2 (March 1969): 282–90.

Jay, Gregory S. "The Subject of Pedagogy: Lessons in Psychoanalysis and Politics." *College English* 49, no. 7 (November 1987): 785–800.

Jones, E. Michael. *Monsters from the Id: The Rise of Horror in Fiction and Film.* Dallas, TX: Spence, 2000.

Jowett, Lorna. *Sex and the Slayer: A Gender Studies Primer for the Buffy Fan.* Middletown, CT: Wesleyan University Press, 2005.

Kawana, Sari. "Mad Scientists and Their Prey: Bioethics, Murder, and Fiction in Interwar Japan." *Journal of Japanese Studies* 31, no. 1 (2005): 89–120.

Kuhn, Annette, ed. *Alien Zone II: The Spaces of Science Fiction Cinema.* London: Verso, 1999.

Larsen, Robin, and Beth A. Haller. "The Case of *Freaks*: Public Perception of Real Disability." *Journal of Popular Film and Television* 29, no. 4 (Winter 2002): 164–72.

Lathe, Carla. "Edvard Munch's Dramatic Images 1892–1909." *Journal of the Warburg and Courtauld Institutes* 46 (1983): 191–206.

London, Bette. "Mary Shelley, *Frankenstein*, and the Spectacle of Masculinity." *PMLA* 108, no. 2 (March 1993): 253–67.

Lovecraft, H. P. *The Annotated Supernatural Horror in Literature.* New York: Hippocampus, 2000.

Lubow, Arthur. "Edvard Munch: Beyond the Scream." *Smithsonian* 36, no. 12 (March 2006): 58–67. Expanded Academic ASAP database, Thomson Gale (accessed December 6, 2006).

Maddrey, Joseph. *Nightmares in Red, White and Blue: The Evolution of the American Horror Film.* Jefferson, NC: McFarland, 2004.

Malchow, H. L. "Frankenstein's Monster and Images of Race in Nineteenth Century Britain." *Past and Present* 139 (May 1993): 90–130.

Mayo, Robert D. "How Long Was Gothic Fiction in Vogue?" *Modern Language Notes* 58, no. 1 (January 1943): 58–64.

McBride, William Thomas. "Dracula and Mephistopheles: Shyster Vampires." *Literature/Film Quarterly* 18, no. 2 (1990): 116–21.

McCormick, Richard W. "From *Caligari* to Dietrich: Sexual, Social, and Cinematic Discourses in Weimar Film." *Signs* 18, no. 3 (Spring 1993): 640–68.

McGonigal, Jane. "Watching Horror: A Gendered Look at Terrorism, or, Everything I Need to Know I Learned in *Psycho*." *Senses of Cinema* no. 17 (November 2001) http://www.sensesofcinema.com/contents/01/17/symposium/mcgonigal.html (accessed January 23, 2007).

Morris, David B. "Gothic Sublimity." *New Literary History* 16, no. 2 (Winter 1985): 299–319.

Morton, Timothy, ed. *A Routledge Literary Sourcebook on Mary Shelley's* Frankenstein. London: Routledge, 2002.

Nachman, Gerald. *Raised on Radio.* New York: Random House, 1998.

Navarette, Susan J. *The Shape of Fear: Horror and the Fin de Siecle Culture of Decadence.* Lexington: University of Kentucky Press, 1998.

Nietzsche, Friedrich. *The Birth of Tragedy.* Trans. Clifton P. Fadiman. New York: Dover, 1995.

Peredo, Isabel Cristina. *Recreational Terror: Women and the Pleasures of Horror Film Viewing.* Albany: State University of New York Press, 1997.

Perry, Ruth. *Novel Relations: The Transformation of Kinship in English Literature and Culture, 1748–1818.* Cambridge: Cambridge University Press, 2004.

Phillips, Kendall R. *Projected Fears: Horror Films and American Culture.* Westport, CT: Praeger, 2005.

Picart, Caroline Joan ("Kay") S. "Visualizing the Monstrous in Frankenstein Films." *Pacific Coast Philology* 35, no. 1 (2000): 17–34.

Quilter, Harry. "The Gospel of Intensity." *The Contemporary Review* LXVII (January-June 1895), bound edition. London: Ibister, 1895: 772–74.

Rebello, Stephen. *Alfred Hitchcock and the Making of* Psycho. New York: St. Martin's, 1990.

Richetti, John J., ed. *The Cambridge Companion to the Eighteenth Century Novel.* Cambridge: Cambridge University Press, 1996.

Roellenger, Francis X. "Psychical Research and *The Turn of the Screw*." *American Literature* 20, no. 3 (November 1948): 401–12.

Rosenberg, Bernard, and David Manning White, eds. *Mass Culture: The Popular Arts in America*. New York: The Free Press, 1957.

Rous, S. H. *The Victrola Book of the Opera*, fourth edition. Camden, New Jersey: Victrola Talking Machine Company, 1917.

Rubenstein, Roberta. "House Mothers and Haunted Daughters: Shirley Jackson and Female Gothic." *Tulsa Studies in Women's Literature* 15, no. 2 (Autumn 1996): 309–31.

Rubio, Martin. *Thrillers*. Cambridge: Cambridge University Press, 1999.

Sanderson, Richard K. "Glutting the Maw of Death: Suicide and Procreation in *Frankenstein*." *South Central Review* 9, no. 2 (Summer 1992): 49–64.

Schneider, Steven J., ed. *Horror Film and Psychoanalysis: Freud's Worst Nightmare*. Cambridge, MA: Cambridge University Press, 2004.

Shaffer, Talia. "'A Wilde Desire Took Me': The Homoerotic History of *Dracula*." *ELH* 61, no. 2 (Summer 1994): 381–425.

Shaviro, Steven. *The Cinematic Body*. Minneapolis: University of Minnesota Press, 1993.

Skal, David J. *The Monster Show*, rev. ed. New York: Faber and Faber, 2001.

Smajic, Srdjan. "The Trouble with Ghost-Seeing: Vision, Ideology, and Genre in the Victorian Ghost Story." *ELH* 70, no. 4 (2003): 1107–35.

South, James B., ed. *Buffy the Vampire Slayer and Philosophy: Fear and Trembling in Sunnydale*. Peru, IL: Carus, 2003.

Staton, Shirley F., ed. *Literary Theories in Praxis*. Philadelphia: University of Pennsylvania Press, 1987.

Stevenson, John Allen. "The Vampire in the Mirror: The Sexuality of Dracula." *PMLA* 3, no. 2 (Mar. 1988): 139–49.

Stuprich, Michael, ed. *Horror*. San Diego: Greenhaven Press, 2001.

Thraikill, Jane F. "Doctoring 'The Yellow Wallpaper.'" *ELH* 69, no. 2 (2002): 525–66.

Toumey, Christopher P. "The Moral Character of Mad Scientists: A Cultural Critique of Science." *Science, Technology, & Human Values* 17, no. 4 (Autumn 1992): 411–37.

Tracy, Kathleen. *The Girl's Got Bite: The Original Unauthorized Guide to Buffy's World*, revised edition. New York: St. Martin's, 2003.

Trencansky, Sara. "Final Girls and Terrible Youth: Transgression in 1980s Slasher Horror." *Journal of Popular Film and Television* 29, no. 2 (Summer 2001). *Expanded Academic Index*. Gale Group (accessed January 26, 2007).

Underwood, Tim, and Chuck Miller, eds. *Fear Itself: The Horror Fiction of Stephen King*. New York: Signet, 1985.

Van Peer, Willie. and Ewout van der Camp. "(In)compatable Interpretations? Contesting Readings of *The Turn of the Screw*." *MLN* 110, no. 4 (September 1995): 692–710.

Veeder, William. *Mary Shelley & Frankenstein: The Fate of Androgyny*. Chicago: University of Chicago Press, 1986.

Watson, Elena M. *Television Horror Movie Hosts: 68 Vampires, Mad Scientists and Other Denizens of the Late Night Airwaves Examined and Interviewed*, reprint edition. Jefferson, NC: McFarland, 2000.

Weaver, James B., III, and Ron Tamborini, eds. *Horror Films: Current Research on Audience Preference and Reactions*. Mahwah, NJ: Lawrence Erlbaum Associates, 1996.

Wein, Toni. *British Identities, Heroic Nationalism, and the Gothic Novel, 1764–1824*. New York: Palgrave Macmillan, 2002.

White, Dennis L. "The Poetics of Horror: More Than Meets the Eye." *Cinema Journal* 10, no. 2 (Spring 1971): 1–18.

Wilcox, Rhonda. *Why Buffy Matters: The Art of Buffy the Vampire Slayer*. New York: I. B. Tauris, 2005.

Wilson, Edmund. "Tales of Marvelous and the Ridiculous." *The New Yorker*. November 24, 1945: 100–06.

Wilson, Edmund. "A Treatise of Tales of Horror." *The New Yorker*. May 27, 1944: 72–82.

Wolf-Meyer, Matthew Joseph. "Batman and Robin in the Nude, or Class and Its Exceptions." *Extrapolation* 47, no. 2 (Summer 2006): 187–206.

Worland, Rick. "Faces Behind the Mask: Vincent Price, Dr. Phibes, and the Horror Genre in Transition." *Post Script* 22, no. 2 (Winter-Spring 2003): 20–33.
_____. "OWI Meets the Monsters: Hollywood Horror Films and War Propaganda, 1942–1945." *Cinema Journal* 37, no. 1 (Autumn 1997): 47–65.
Wyrick, Laura. "Horror at Century's End: Where Have All the Slashers Gone?" *Pacific Coast Philology* 33, no. 2 (1998): 122–26.
Young, Elizabeth "Here Comes the Bride: Wedding Gender and Race in *Bride of Frankenstein*." *Feminist Studies* 17, no. 3 (Autumn 1991): 403–37.

Science, Pseudoscience, and Society

Adams, Bluford. "'A Stupendous Mirror of Departed Empires': The Barnum Hippodromes and Circuses, 1874–1891." *American Literary History* 8, no. 1 (Spring 1996): 34–56.
Aldhouse-Green, Miranda and Stephen. *The Quest for the Shaman*. London: Thames & Hudson, 2005.
Barzun, Jacques. *From Dawn to Decadence: 500 Years of Western Cultural Life*. New York: HarperCollins, 2000.
Baumgartner, Frederic J. *Longing for the End: A History of Millennialism in Western Civilization*. New York: St. Martin's, 1999.
Beentjes, Johannes W. J., and Tom H. A. Van der Voort. "Television's Impact on Children's Reading Skills: A Review of Research." *Reading Research Quarterly* 23, no. 4 (Autumn 1988): 389–413.
Benton, Peter. "Recipe Fictions ... Literary Fast Food? Reading Interests in Year 8." *Oxford Review of Education* 21, no. 1 (March 1995): 99–111.
Blass, Thomas, ed. *Obedience to Authority: Current Perspectives on the Milgram Paradigm*. Mahwah, NJ: Lawrence Erlbaum, 2000.
Bloom, Harold. *Genius: A Mosaic of One Hundred Exemplary Creative Minds*. New York: Warner Books, 2002.
Blum, Deborah. *Ghost Hunters: William James and the Search for Scientific Proof of Life After Death*. New York: Penguin, 2006.
Bobbitt, Philip. *The Shield of Achilles: War, Peace, and the Course of History*. New York: Alfred A. Knopf, 2002.
Boese, Alex. *The Museum of Hoaxes*. New York: Dutton, 2002.
Boyer, Paul, and Stephen Nissenbaum, eds. *The Salem Witchcraft Papers: Verbatim Transcripts of the Court Records in Three Volumes*. Volume 1, *Nehemiah Abbott Jr. to Abigail Faulkner Sr.* New York: De Capo Press, 1977.
Bullard, Thomas E. "UFO Abduction Reports: The Supernatural Kidnap Narrative Returns in Technological Guise." *Journal of American Folklore* 102, no. 404 (April-June 1989): 147–70.
Caporael, Linda R. "Ergotism: Satan Loosed in Salem?" *Science* 192 (April 1976): 21–26.
Carmeli, Yoram S. "Wee Pea: The Total Play of the Dwarf in the Circus." *The Drama Review* 33, no. 4 (Winter 1989): 128–45.
Cohen, Jeremy. "The Bible, Man, and Nature in the History of Western Thought: A Call for Reassessment." *The Journal of Religion* 65, no. 2 (1985): 155–72.
Cohen, Ronald D. "The Delinquents: Censorship and Youth Culture in Recent U.S. History." *History of Education Quarterly* 37, no. 3 (Autumn 1997): 251–70.
Colavito, Jason. *The Cult of Alien Gods: H. P. Lovecraft and Extraterrestrial Pop Culture*. New York: Prometheus, 2005.
Cornwell, John. *Hitler's Scientists: Science, War, and the Devil's Pact*. New York: Viking, 2003.
Cuneo, Michael. *American Exorcism: Expelling Demons in the Land of Plenty*. New York: Broadway Books, 2002.
Curtis, L. Perry. *Jack the Ripper and the London Press* (New Haven, Connecticut: Yale University Press, 2001.
Dale, Christopher. *Himmler's Crusade: The Nazi Expedition to Find the Origins of the Aryan Race*. New York: John Wiley, 2003.

Darwin, Charles. *The Origin of Species.* New York: Signet Classic, 2003.

De Camp, L. Sprague. *Lost Continents: The Atlantis Theme in History, Science, and Literature.* New York: Dover, 1970.

Demos, John Putnam. *Entertaining Satan: Witchcraft and the Culture of Early New England.* New York: Oxford University Press, 1982.

Dobbs, J. T. "Newton's Alchemy and His Theory of Matter." *Isis* 73, no. 4 (December 1982): 511–28.

Dolan, Richard. *UFOs and the National Security State: Chronology of a Coverup, 1941–1973.* Hampton Roads, 2002.

Douglas, John E., and Mark Olshaker. *The Anatomy of Motive: The FBI's Legendary Mindhunter Explores the Key to Understanding and Catching Violent Criminals.* New York: Scribner's, 1999.

Duke, Thomas S. *Celebrated Criminal Cases of America.* San Francisco: James H. Barry, 1910.

Ellis, Havelock. "Freud's Influence on the Changed Attitude Toward Sex," *The American Journal of Sociology* 45, no. 3 (November 1939): 309–17.

"The Eugenics Records Office." *Science* 37, no. 954 (April 1913): 553–54.

Ewans, Martin. *European Atrocity, African Catastrophe: Leopold II, the Congo Free State, and Its Aftermath.* London: RoutledgeCurzon, 2002.

Eysenck, Michael W. *Psychology: An International Perspective.* New York: Psychology Press, 2004.

Fagan, Brian. *Ancient North America,* 3rd ed. New York: Thames & Hudson, 2000.

Feder, Kenneth L. "Ten Years After, Surveying Misconceptions about the Human Past." *Cultural Resource Management* 18, no. 3 (1995): 10–14.

Ferguson, Niall. *Empire: The Rise and Demise of the British World Order and the Lessons for Global Power.* New York: Basic Books, 2002.

———. *The War of the World: Twentieth Century Conflict and the Descent of the West.* New York: Penguin, 2006.

Fraser, Steven, ed. *The Bell Curve Wars.* New York: Basic Books, 1995.

Fukuyama, Francis. *The End of History and the Last Man.* New York: Penguin, 1992.

Glassman, James K., and Kevin A. Hassett. *Dow 36,000: The New Strategy for Profiting from the Coming Rise in the Stock Market.* New York: Three Rivers Press, 2000.

Gottesman, Ronald, and Richard Maxwell Brown. *Violence in America: An Encyclopedia.* New York: Scribner's, 1999.

Grove, Alan. "Röntgen's Ghosts: Photography, X-Rays, and the Victorian Imagination," *Literature and Medicine* 16, no. 2 (1997): 141–73.

Guérard, Albert. "Herder's Spiritual Heritage: Nationalism, Romanticism, and Democracy." *Annals of the American Academy of Political and Social Science* 174 (July 1934): 1–8.

Hamby, Alonzo L. *For the Survival of Democracy: Franklin Roosevelt and the World Crisis of the 1930s.* New York: Free Press, 2004.

Hartman, Mary S. *Victorian Murderesses: A True History of Thirteen Respectable French and English Women Accused of Unspeakable Crimes.* New York: Schocken Books, 1976.

Hays, K. Michael, ed. *Architecture Theory Since 1968.* Cambridge, Massachusetts: MIT Press, 2000.

Helm, Charles, and Mario Morelli. "Stanley Milgram and the Obedience Experiment: Authority, Legitimacy, and Human Action." *Political Theory* 7, no. 3 (August 1979): 321–45.

Hickey, Sally. "Fatal Feeds?: Plants, Livestock Losses, and Witchcraft Accusations in Tudor and Stuart Britain." *Folklore* 101, no. 2 (1990): 131–42.

Himmelfarb, Gertrude. *The Roads to Modernity: The British, French, and American Enlightenments.* New York: Alfred A. Knopf, 2004.

Howard, Lawrence, ed. *Terrorism: Roots, Impact, Response.* Westport, CT: Praeger, 1992.

Jackson, Karl D., ed. *Cambodia, 1975–1978: Rendezvous with Death.* Princeton: Princeton University Press, 1989.

Jensen, Carl, ed. *Stories That Changed America: Muckrakers of the Twentieth Century.* New York: Seven Stories Press, 2002.

Jones, Richard F. "Puritanism, Science, and Christ Church." *Isis* 31, no. 1 (November 1939): 65–67.

Kaczynski, Theodore. *The Unabomber Manifesto: Industrial Society and Its Future.* Filiquarian Publishing, 2005.

Kaplan, Fred. "'The Mesmeric Mania': Early Victorians and Animal Magnetism." *Journal of the History of Ideas* 35, no. 2 (October-December 1974): 691–702.

Kaplan, Jonathan Michael. *The Limits and Lies of Human Genetic Research: Dangers for Social Policy.* New York: Routledge, 2000.

Katz, Elihu, Jay G. Blumler, and Michael Gurevitch. "Uses and Gratification Research." *Public Opinion Quarterly* 37, no. 4 (Winter 1973–1974): 509–23.

Keller, Abraham C. "Lucretius and the Idea of Progress." *The Classical Journal* 46, no. 4 (January 1951): 185–88.

Kennedy, David M. *Freedom from Fear: The American People in Depression and War 1929–1945.* The Oxford History of the United States. New York: Oxford University Press, 1999.

Kenney, Alice P., and Leslie J. Workman. "Ruins, Romance, and Reality: Medievalism in Anglo-American Imagination and Taste, 1750–1840." *Winterthur Porfolio* 10 (1975): 131–63.

King-Hele, Desmond. "The 1997 Wilkins Lecture: Erasmus Darwin, the Lunaticks and Evolution." *Notes and Records of the Royal Society of London* 52, no. 1 (1998): 153–80.

Kornwolf, James D. "High Victorian Gothic; or, The Dilemma of Style in Modern Architecture." *Journal of the Society of Architectural Historians* 34, no. 1 (1975): 37–47.

Kurtz, Paul. "Can the Sciences Help Us to Make Wise Ethical Judgments?" *Skeptical Inquirer* 28, no. 5 (September-October 2004): 18–24.

Lang, Karen. "The Dialectics of Decay: Rereading the Kantian Subject." *The Art Bulletin* 79, no. 3 (1997): 413–39.

Legrand, H. E., and Wayne E. Bosse. "*Chariots of the Gods?* and All That: Pseudo-History in the Classroom." *The History Teacher* 8, no. 3 (May 1975): 359–70.

Leiss, William. *In the Chamber of Risks: Understanding Risk Controversies* (McGill-Queens University Press, 2001.

Leland, Charles Godfrey. *Gypsy Sorcery and Fortune Telling.* New York: Scribner's, 1891.

Lewis-Williams, David, and David Pearce. *Inside the Neolithic Mind.* London: Thames & Hudson, 2005.

Locke, John, George Berkeley, and David Hume. *English Philosophers of the Seventeenth and Eighteenth Centuries.* Volume 37. New York: P. F. Collier, 1910.

Lowell, Percival. *Mars*, 2nd ed. Boston: Houghton-Mifflin, 1896.

Lyman, Richard W., and Lewis W. Spitz, eds. *Major Crises in Western Civilization*, Volume 2. New York: Harcourt, Brace & World, 1965.

Mather, Cotton. *Magnalia Christi Americana; or, The Ecclesiastical History of New England*, Volume 2. Hartford, CT: Silas Andrus, 1853.

Mayor, Adrienne. *The First Fossil Hunters.* Princeton: Princeton University Press, 2001.

_____. *Fossil Legends of the First Americans.* Princeton: Princeton University Press, 2005.

Mayr, Ernst. "The Nature of the Darwinian Revolution." *Science* 176 (1972): 981–89.

McNally, Raymond T., and Radu Florescu. *In Search of Dracula: A True History of Dracula and Vampire Legends.* New York: Warner Paperback Library, 1974.

Mooney, Chris. *The Republican War on Science*, revised edition. New York: Basic Books, 2005.

Moore, R. Laurence. "Spiritualism and Science: Reflections on the First Decade of the Spirit Rappings." *American Quarterly* 24, no. 4 (October 1972): 474–500.

_____. "The Spiritualist Medium: A Study of Female Professionalism in Victorian America." *American Quarterly* 27, no. 2 (May 1975): 200–21.

Mulligan, Lotte. "Puritans and English Science: A Critique of Webster," *Isis* 71, no. 3 (September 1980): 456–69.

National Endowment for the Arts. *Reading at Risk: A Survey of Literary Reading in America.* Research Division report #46. Washington, DC: National Endowment for the Arts, 2004.

Neuman, Susan B. "The Home Environment and Fifth Grade Students' Leisure Reading," *The Elementary School Journal* 86, no. 3 (1986): 335–43.

Nickell, Joe. *Investigating the Paranormal.* New York: Barnes & Noble, 2001.

Overy, Richard. *The Dictators: Hitler's Germany, Stalin's Russia.* New York: W. W. Norton, 2004.

Patterson, James T. *Restless Giant: The United States from Watergate to Bush v. Gore*. Oxford History of the United States. New York: Oxford University Press, 2005.

Porter, Roy S. *The Enlightenment*. 2nd ed. *Studies in European History*. New York: Palgrave, 2001.

Radford, Benjamin. "Soul Scales." *Skeptical Inquirer* 31, no. 1 (January-February 2007): 28.

Rickard, Bob, and John F. Mitchell. *Unexplained Phenomena: A Rough Guide Special*. London: Penguin, 2000.

Ross, Ian, and Carol Urquhart Ross. "Body Snatching in Nineteenth Century Britain: From Exhumation to Murder." *British Journal of Law and Society* 6, no. 1. (Summer 1979): 108–18.

Sagalyn, Lynn B. *Times Square Roulette: Remaking the City Icon*. Cambridge, MA: MIT Press, 2001.

Salyers, Abigail A., and Dixie D. Whitt. *Revenge of the Microbes: How Bacterial Resistance Is Undermining the Antibiotic Miracle*. Washington: ASM Press, 2005.

Schaller, Thomas F. *Whistling Past Dixie: How Democrats Can Win Without the South*. New York: Simon and Schuster, 2006.

Schmidt, James. "What Enlightenment Project?" *Political Theory* 28, no. 6 (December 2000): 734–57.

Secord, J. A. "Quick and Magical Shaper of Science." *Science* 297 (September 6, 2002): 1648–49.

Shibley, Mark A. *Resurgent Evangelicalism in the United States*. Columbia: University of South Carolina Press, 1996.

Shuker, Karl P. N. *The Unexplained: An Illustrated Guide to the World's Natural and Paranormal Mysteries*. Dubai: JG Press, 1996.

Sledzik, Paul S., and Nicholas Bellantoni. "Brief Communication: Bioarchaeological and Biocultural Evidence for the New England Vampire Folk Belief." *American Journal of Physical Anthropology* 94 (1994): 269–74.

Smith, Anthony David. *The Ethnic Origins of Nations*. Malden, MA: Blackwell Publishers, 1988.

Snow, C. P. *The Two Cultures*. Cambridge: Cambridge University Press, 1998.

Sollors, Werner. "Dr. Benjamin Franklin's Celestial Telegraph, or Indian Blessings to Gas-Lit American Drawing Rooms." *American Quarterly* 35, no. 5 (Winter 1983): 459–80.

Spencer, Philip, and Howard Wollman. *Nationalism: A Critical Introduction*. London: Sage Publications, 2002.

Sproule, J. Michael. *Propaganda and Democracy: The American Experience of Media and Mass Persuasion*. Cambridge: Cambridge University Press, 1997.

Stevenson, David. *Cataclysm: The First World War as Political Tragedy*. New York: Basic Books, 2004.

Stirling, M. W. "Some Popular Misconceptions about the American Indian." *The Scientific Monthly* 32, no. 2 (February 1931): 172–75.

Summers, Montague. *The Vampire*. Dorset Press, 1991.

Sweet, Matthew. *Inventing the Victorians: What We Think We Know About Them and Why We're Wrong*. New York: St. Martin's, 2001.

Tiryakian, Edward A. "Toward the Sociology of Esoteric Culture." *The American Journal of Sociology* 78, no. 3 (November 1972): 491–512.

Travis, Cheryl Brown, ed. *Evolution, Gender and Rape*. Cambridge, MA: MIT Press, 2003.

Trilling, Lionel. *Beyond Culture: Essays on Literature and Learning*. New York: Viking Press, 1965.

Twain, Mark. *King Leopold's Soliloquy*. Boston: P. R. Warren, 1905.

Voltaire. *Philosophical Dictionary*. Trans. H. I. Woolf. New York: Knopf, 1924. Hanover College. March 2001 http://history.hanover.edu/texts/voltaire/volancie.html (accessed November 3, 2006).

von Däniken, Erich. *Chariots of the Gods?* Trans. Michael Heron. New York: Bantam, 1973.

Wallace, Alfred F. C. "Revitalization Movements." *American Anthropologist* 58, no. 2 (April 1956): 264–81.

Ward, Keith. "Nature Red in Tooth and Claw." *Science & Theology News Online Edition*. March 1, 2002. http://www.stnews.org/Commentary-1893.htm (accessed November 21, 2006).

Wells, H. G. *The Outline of History*. New York: Macmillan, 1921.

Wilson, A. N. *God's Funeral: A Biography of Faith and Doubt in Western Civilization*. New York: Ballantine, 1999.

Wilson, Katharina M. "The History of the Word 'Vampire.'" *Journal of the History of Ideas* 46, no. 4 (October 1985): 577–83.

Wright, Dudley. *The Book of Vampires*. Mineola, NY: Dover, 2006.

Wright, Gordon. *France in Modern Times*. Chicago: Rand McNally, 1960.

INDEX

Numbers in **bold italics** indicate pages with photographs.